MW00711788

MVS COBOL Application Developer's Toolbox

Ranade IBM Series

H. MURPHY • *Assembler for Cobol Programmers: MVS, VM,* 0-07-044129-4

H. BOOKMAN • *Cobol II,* 0-07-006533-0

J. RANADE • *DB2: Concepts, Programming, and Design,* 0-07-051265-5

J. SANCHEZ • *IBM Microcomputers Handbook,* 0-07-054594-4

M. CARATHANASSIS • *Expert MVS/XA JCL: A Complete Guide to Advanced Techniques,* 0-07-009816-6

P. DONOFRIO • *CICS: Debugging, Dump Reading and Problem Determination,* 0-07-017606-X

T. EDDOLLS • *VM Performance Management,* 0-07-018966-8

P. KAVANAGH • *VS Cobol II for Cobol Programmers,* 0-07-033571-0

T. MARTYN • *DB2/SQL: A Professional Programmer's Guide,* 0-07-040666-9

S. PIGGOTT • *CICS: A Practical Guide to System Fine Tuning,* 0-07-050054-1

N. PRASAD • *IBM Mainframes: Architecture and Design,* 0-07-050686-8

J. RANADE • *Introduction to SNA Networking: A Guide to VTAM/NCP,* 0-07-051144-6

J. RANADE • *Advanced SNA Networking: A Professional's Guide for Using VTAM/NCP,* 0-07-051143-8

S. SAMSON • *MVS: Performance Management,* 0-07-054528-6

B. JOHNSON • *MVS Concepts and Facilities,* 0-07-032673-8

A. WIPFLER • *Distributed Processing in the CICS Environment,* 0-07-071136-4

A. WIPFLER • *CICS Application Development Programming,* 0-07-071139-9

J. RANADE • *VSAM: Concepts, Programming, and Design,* Second Edition, 0-07-051244-2

J. RANADE • *VSAM: Performance, Design, and Fine Tuning,* Second Edition, 0-07-051245-0

J. SANCHEZ • *Programming Solutions Handbook for IBM Microcomputers,* 0-07-054597-9

P. DONOFRIO • *CICS Programmer's Reference,* 0-07-017607-8

M. CARATHANASSIS • *Expert MVS/ESA JCL: A Guide to Advanced Techniques* 0-07-009820-4

J. RANADE • *DOS to OS/2: Conversion, Migration, and Application Design,* 0-07-051264-7

K. BRATHWAITE • *Relational Databases: Concepts, Design and Administration* 0-07-007252-3

R.H. JOHNSON, R.D. JOHNSON • *DASD: IBM's Direct Access Storage Devices,* 0-07-032674-6

M. MARX, P. DAVIS • *MVS Power Programming,* 0-07-040763-0

G. HOUTEKAMER, P. ARTIS • *MVS I/O Subsystems: Configuration Management and Performance Analysis,* 0-07-002553-3

A. KAPOOR • *SNA: Architecture, Protocols, and Implementation,* 0-07-033727-6

D. SILVERBERG • *DB2: Performance, Design, and Implementation,* 0-07-057553-3

R. CROWNHART • *IBM's Workstation CICS,* 0-07-014770-1

C. DANEY • *Programming in REXX,* 0-07-015305-1

G. GOLDBERG, P. SMITH • *The REXX Handbook,* 0-07-028682-8

A. WERMAN • *DB2 Handbook for DBAS,* 0-07-069460-5

R. LEFKON, J. KNEILING, P. SOMERS • *Understanding CICS Internals,* 0-07-037040-0

A. FRIEND • *COBOL Application Debugging under MVS: COBOL and COBOL II,* 0-07-022453-6

L. BRUMBAUGH • *VSAM: Architecture, Theory, and Applications,* 0-07-008606-6

MVS COBOL Application Developer's Toolbox

Alex Varsegi

McGraw-Hill, Inc.

New York San Francisco Washington, D.C. Auckland Bogotá
Caracas Lisbon London Madrid Mexico City Milan
Montreal New Delhi San Juan Singapore
Sydney Tokyo Toronto

Library of Congress Cataloging-in-Publication Data

Varsegi, Alex.
MVS COBOL application developer's toolbox / by Alex Varsegi.
p. cm.
Includes index.
ISBN 0-07-067175-3 (H)
1. COBOL (Computer program language) 2. MVS/ESA. 3. MVS/XA.
I. Title.
QA76.73.C25V37 1993
005.4'429—dc20 92-41244
CIP

2 3 4 5 6 7 8 9 0 DOC/DOC 9 9 8 7

ISBN 0-07-067175-3

The editors for this book were Gerald T. Papke and Kellie Hagan, and the director of production was Katherine G. Brown. This book was set in ITC Century Light. It was composed by the McGraw-Hill Publishing Company Professional and Reference Division composition unit.

Printed and bound by R. R. Donnelley & Sons Company.

To my wife, Marie
To my children, Mary and George
To my friend, Dr. Bill Mullner, Chairman, Computer Science Department, Elmhurst College
And to Ron Fordonski and Steve Mansfield of the college of DuPage

Contents

Acknowledgments

I would like to thank my associate, Larry Cheeks, as well as Herman Chin, Maria Reccardi of Computer Associates, and Diane Schroeder of Compuware for providing vital material and assisting in this monumental undertaking.

I would also like to express my gratitude for the tremendous help and support I received from a number of companies, among these IBM, Computer Associates, and Compuware.

Last but not least, a special thanks to Diversified Software, IBM, Innovation Technology, and Syncsort for their valuable contributions in producing this book.

Introduction

This book represents a comprehensive technical review of mainframe productivity tools used primarily in both OS/MVS XA (Extended Architecture) and OS/MVS ESA (Enterprise Systems Architecture) environments. It will highlight some of the more popular software packages on the market currently available for designing and testing application systems, debugging source programs, and capturing real-time transactions for continuous use. In producing this book, I relied primarily on my personal experiences, but I was also fortunate enough to be assisted through a number of consultants made available to me by some of the vendors' staff, as well as my own.

The primary purpose of this book is to make you aware of what a particular productivity tool does and the way it does it, while providing you with some "hot" tips on how to become more efficient in using these packages.

I.1 How This Book Is Organized

In chapter 1, I have focused on a typical MVS environment, including the special topics of IBM's Data in Virtual (DIV) and Innovation Access Method (IAM) by Innovation Technology. The overall tone of this chapter is simplistic because most professionals with strong application experience tend to have a considerably weaker background in systems programming and topics dealing with operating systems.

Chapters 2 and 3 present some of the most advanced concepts in producing command-level CICS source code. Unlike chapter 1, this chapter is very technical and application-oriented. It deals with some interesting ideas in standardizing (and thus performing) high-powered routines, such as those that centrally manage incoming error messages, I/O routines, and Handle Aid and Handle Condition procedures. Chapter 3, on the other hand, continues the technical pace by showing you a number of creative ways to develop user-maintained tutorials. In fact, the source programs I use in this chapter have been physically lifted from a production environment with extensive narratives provided as the mechanics of the code.

Chapter 4 contains two topics. The first one is the CA-ACF2 product, and it represents a security package that provides you with a number of facilities. Among these is the ability to write and maintain rules, restrict access to certain transactions (or files), and so on. The second product has to do with a package produced by the Diversified Corporation, called DOCU/TEXT. One of the major components of DOCU/TEXT is a product called JSCAN, which allows you to scan your JCLs, for example, to resolve consistency-related problems over and above typical syntax errors. In chapter 4, I have also included some samples DOCU/TEXT JSCAN modules that can be triggered through JCL statements.

Chapter 5 focuses on the "new" JCLs, and its primary purpose is to highlight differences that exist between an OS/MVS XA and OS/MVS ESA architecture for conversion purposes.

Chapter 6 undertakes an ambitious plan in an attempt to summarize the IBM ISPF (Interactive System Productivity Facility) / PDS (Program Development Facility) environment. Most of the efforts in this chapter encompass file-development procedures and file manipulation, including some of the frequent and infrequent uses of this text editor. More introductory information about the ISPF package is contained in appendix D.

Chapter 7 deals with the File-AID productivity system. Professionals tend to use the File-AID product as a logical extension to the IBM ISPF environment, which is specifically designed to handle VSAM (Virtual Storage Access Method) clusters and record sized over and above the conventional 80-character record image. File-AID, which is a product of Compuware, saves you a very substantial amount of time using cumbersome IBM utilities, e.g., IDCAMS necessary to build VSAM KSDS (Key-Sequenced Data Set) clusters. What is nice about File-AID is the tremendous structural similarities the software offers with ISPF/PDS, as well as its invokability from ISPF.

Chapter 8 gives you a snapshot of the CA-InterTest productivity tool. CA-InterTest is a powerful tool to perform real-time testing. This system, unlike the IBM EDF (or CEDF) package, tracks not only command-level statements but batch or conventional statements as well. Other added flexibilities of the package include the setting of breakpoints in your program. This allows you to have a close look as the contents of a particular file, data set, or section of your internal memory before and after a potential abnormal termination. Also, to successfully execute a particular program, CA-InterTest will let you modify the contents of such vital areas, even if temporarily until the completion of the test cycle.

The topic of chapter 9 is testing with CICS Playback (a Compuware product). CICS Playback is designed to capture on-line "live" transactions as scripts, for subsequent replay or playback. This is important for two reasons. First, if there is an unreproducable problem during a given production run (in the conventional sense), you can replay the entire system and catch the error on subsequent occasions. Second, CICS Playback also enables you to create a limited test environment out of the captured scripts, so you can use them later in test mode.

The CICS Abend-AID productivity tool, as described in chapter 10, was also developed by the Compuware Corporation, and it serves as an after-the-fact type of control mechanism following a CICS abend. The software is designed to provide the analyst with a very comprehensive snapshot of any real or potential problems in his programs, including files and vital storage areas affected by a crash.

The CA-Verify product, discussed in chapter 11, is another excellent software product, very much like the CICS Playback mechanism, and is designed to capture and later use on-line transactions for testing and verification purposes. CA-Verify, like CICS-Playback, reduces the time and cost associated with testing, and provides the user with more reliable results. The software not only automates testing, but also simulates an array of production conditions, including the capture of terminal inputs from your production environment.

Chapter 12 deals with the CICS dBUG-AID product, the third Compuware software product mentioned in this book. This system is designed to give you on-line, real-time debugging facilities on several levels, as does CA-InterTest. CICS dBUG-AID is a mature product that allows you to set breakpoints and reduce the execution speed of an application transaction to "slow motion," so you can observe the execution of the program in a step-by-step fashion.

Chapter 13 described COBTEST, formerly called TESTCOB, which is available in addition to the previously mentioned CA-InterTest and CICS dBUG-AID line of products. (Incidentally, COBTEST is an IBM-engineered testing tool.) COBTEST is a relatively comprehensive tool that can be triggered in both batch and on-line (real-time) environments. COBTEST, which is a COBOL II debugging tool, is quite flexible for monitoring the execution of VS COBOL II programs. With COBTEST, you can also suspend the execution of a program, continue execution, skip selection of certain codes, correct errors, display output, and so on. As I mentioned previously, you can debug your programs in batch mode, line mode, or full-screen mode. When you are operating in full-screen mode, you must have access to the ISPF productivity tool, as well.

Chapter 14 provides you with an overview of one of the more popular sorting mechanisms on the market (primarily for batch sorts). This software is owned and developed by the Syncsort Corporation. Syncsort will do two things. First, it lets you sort average to high-volume data sets fast and with utmost efficiency. Second, it also offers you a set of report-generator features that lets you perform routines available with programmed (internal) sorts of just about any complexity. This chapter, like all previous ones, contains a great number of practical illustrations.

Chapter 15 provides you with a brief overview of another IBM product, DB2, a relational database. The section dedicated to SQL (Structured Query Language) samples the language as available in both a typical mainframe, but also in an OS/2 microcomputer environment. This chapter also places a great deal of emphasis on certain DB2 key utilities and vendor products, such as SPUFI, ProEdit, DB2/Backup, and more.

Chapter 16 gives you an in-depth review of the CA-Panvalet Library system. CA-Panvalet, formerly owned by the Pansophic Corporation, provides you with the software necessary to maintain your source code and other data sets in a secure environment. The CA-Panvalet system places a great deal of emphasis on protecting your library. For example, a member in production cannot be modified or have its status changed to test for obvious security reasons. Also, a member cannot be deleted from the library with day-to-day general programmer commands because it is considered a management function. Last, the system has a considerable number of safeguards to avoid any possible destruction of its viable library data.

Chapter 17 gives you another view at the library concept with a discussion of CA-

Librarian software. CA-Librarian, very much like the CA-Panvalet product, is a source-code management system. The software's central master file can be used to store data from MVS, VSE, and VM, and it can be simultaneously accessed by users of any of the previously mentioned operating environments.

Chapter 18 deals with the IBM Netview product. The purpose of the chapter is two-fold. First, it tells you about what network is all about and provides you with some basic definitions. Second, it explains how you can have quick access between the ISPF module and any of the CICS partitions without having to log-off one system and sign onto another in an ongoing fashion. While the first topic encompasses a large portion of the system programming area, the second one primarily involves the application analyst.

Last, chapter 19 focuses on some of the coding conventions with regard to CICS-supplied transactions. This chapter gives you an overview on how to use the EDF (Execute Diagnostics Facility) productivity tool to locate real and potential problems in an on-line program. Other control statements deal extensively with CEMT and CECI commands in updating tables, displaying BMS-assembled maps, and locating the contents of a file with insufficient data on hand while using sequential browse techniques.

I.2 Who This Book Is For

This book is geared to a variety of technical people, as follows:

- A project leader or project manager who wants to learn about some of the techni cal aspects of a particular productivity tool prior to acquiring it
- A programmer/analyst who needs some quick reference and especially some "live" examples of using a system
- A director of information systems who is interested in studying some of the idiosyncrasies that exist among the various packages, even if he isn't interested in a lot of detail.
- A student majoring in Computer Science who wants to learn about the realities of the market—topics that are not taught in the classroom but are the bread and butter of the industry
- A systems analyst who needs to be familiar with a number of productivity tools to design proper testing environments, build databases via captured transactions, create and generate meaningful reports, and so on.
- A liaison who interfaces between technical and nontechnical personnel, and needs to be up-to-the-minute on specific nomenclatures used in his environment.
- A security officer responsible for writing extensive rules that define who will and will not have access to a particular file, terminal, and transaction identifier during a specific time and at a specific location.
- Documentation analysts who need a quick and easy automated methodology to generate systems and procedural flow.

- Quality-assurance people who test programs and scan job control for consistency, not merely syntax-related errors.

Last but not least, this book will provide you, the reader, with several state-of-the-art methodologies that need to be considered in general to replace either an aging system in its entirety or part of a not-so-old system with emphasis on internal improvements.

MVS COBOL Application Developer's Toolbox is designed as a multivolumn technical series. Other future volumes will include additional productivity tools as they become available.

Chapter

1

The MVS Environment

1.1 What is MVS?

"Computerese" is loaded with acronyms and abbreviations. MVS is one of them, which simply means *Multiple Virtual Storage*. The words *multiple* and *storage* are fairly easy to explain. *Storage* means core, memory, even direct access facilities such as a disk spindle, and *multiple* means that there are several of these units. The word *virtual*, however, is a bit more difficult to grasp at first. What is it really referring to? Does it mean storage that is real or storage that is imaginary? Let's tackle this concept.

In a system without virtual storage, each storage location has a unique address that is a tangible, "real" location. In order to access data from such an address, MVS simply points to the physical location of the data in main storage and retrieves it. With virtual storage, however, each user has access to virtual rather than to real (physical) storage facilities.

Virtual storage means that each program can assume the storage, that it has an unlimited access to all the main storage that an addressing scheme allows. In fact, the impression is that each user has exclusive control over the entire physical environment to store, and can manipulate it as he pleases. This ability to use a large number of storage locations is important because a program might be too long and too complex, yet both the program and the data must be in main storage so that the processor can access them.

To allow each user to behave as though he has much more real storage than really exists in the computer system, MVS keeps only the active portions of each program in real storage, and stores the rest of the code and data in special data sets usually on high-speed direct-access storage devices, or *DASD*. Virtual storage, then, is the combination of real and auxiliary storage, requiring billions of bytes of storage space. It uses a system of tables to relate the DASD locations to real storage locations and keep track of the identity and authority of each program.

The MVS operating system is no different from any other operating system in that that it is made up of a collection of programs responsible for the internal workings of a computer system. Without an operating system, no matter how sophisticated the hardware, the computer has no intelligence to perform anything. But with an efficient operating system, such as MVS, software can provide the user a means to efficiently handle and schedule expensive resources. What MVS can do is manage storage capacity to make it appear a lot bigger than it is in reality, thereby allowing many users to utilize an enormous amount of storage, which translates into fast execution of jobs and nearly instantaneous response time when processing interactively.

Prior-generation computers and operating systems, the forerunners of OS/MVS, were praised for the great speed with which they could execute thousands of instructions per second. The speed of today's MVS computers is up in the millions. Keep in mind, however, that although the operating system cannot increase the speed of the computer it can certainly maximize its use, thus making the computer seem faster.

1.2 A Review of Multiprogramming

In the era of first-and second-generation computer environments, processing could not handle the demand placed upon it to work and produce more quickly and efficiently. Requests for a specific function such as printing and updating files referred to as jobs were submitted for processing one at a time. The operating system would process each job in a completely sequential fashion—meaning that if you had three requests or jobs in front of you queued up in the system, you had no other choice but to wait until all prior requests were executed.

One of a number of reasons jobs had to wait in this queue was simply that they required information to be accessed and "read in" or to perform other input/output operations (such as printing or punching), which, compared to the electronic speed of the processor, were as slow as a snail. So while a job was temporarily bottlenecked inside the computer waiting for an I/O operation, the processor remained idle. That, unfortunately, was a very inefficient and costly way of processing.

To solve this problem, the concept of *multiprogramming* was developed. When a request or a job cannot use the processor (for whatever reason), the operating system can temporarily stop the job from executing by interrupting it. This allows the CPU, or *central processing unit*, to take up another job that has all of its resources or prerequisites satisfied and ready to roll. Using this technique, the CPU saves all what's relevant about a job before interrupting it so that it can be easily restored.

In a multiprogramming environment, the objective is to keep all major computer resources busy (e.g., input/output devices, CPU, primary storage) because different jobs have different requirements. That is to say that certain jobs rely extensively on the central processor, while others are simply I/O bound. Because each job uses some of the resources available to it in different proportions, it is necessary to switch back and forth between jobs for an optimal sharing.

Multiprogramming is an ingenious concept. It performs complex operations such as the protection of each job, makes instantaneous decisions such as allocating job resources both shareable (disk), and nonshareable (tape), while making sure that there is no contention for nonshareable resources. The methodology used to communicate what particular resource a given job needs to the MVS operating system is done via a *job-control language*. Figure 1.1 highlights the multiprogramming apparatus.

1.3 More on Virtual Storage with Emphasis on the Extended Architecture (XA)

Multiprogramming was undoubtedly a great concept in expediting job execution, but it was far from being a permanent solution to the ever-increasing demand placed upon the environment. First of all, the processing speed of computers had increased so dramatically that, even with the use of multiprogramming, the computer could execute more jobs than it could hold in its own physical storage. Thus, processing again became inefficient because there was not enough storage to utilize all the improvements in the speed of the execution.

Let's, for a moment, talk about the true meaning of *storage*. There are essentially two types of physical storage. The first one is part of the processor, and it has physical attributes, thus the term *real storage*. The other kind of storage is not directly built into the computer; rather, it is available on secondary or auxiliary devices, such as a disk spindle or a solid-state disk device. The operating system accesses data on these secondary devices through an I/O channel. The process of accessing data in this fashion is necessary because the processor can execute programs and data associated with it only if it is all available in real or primary storage.

In the old days, in order to successfully execute a job, the operating system required that the entire program be brought into primary facilities before it would start executing an entire set of instructions. This is, of course, a rather wasteful approach if you stop to think that you need only a small portion of your program in core—the part that's currently being executed. So by bringing only a piece of the program into real storage, the CPU will execute it, moving the "dormant" portion of that very same code back to auxiliary storage. By fetching new instructions, the system can handle a number of application programs simultaneously.

The big question, of course, remains that, with all these bright ideas, just how will

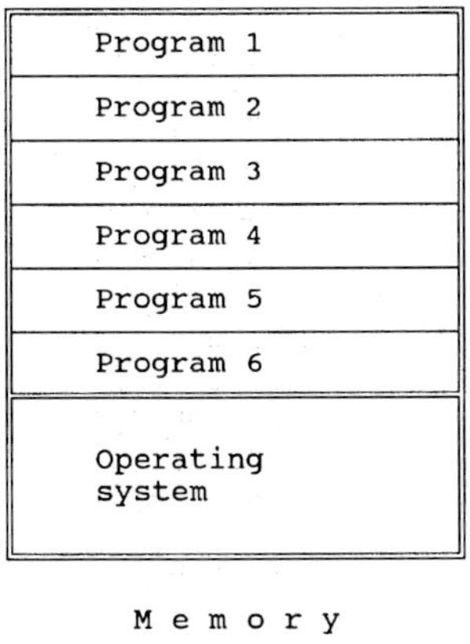

Program 1
Program 2
Program 3
Program 4
Program 5
Program 6
Operating system

Memory

Figure 1.1 The multiprogramming apparatus, where a number of programs share the memory along with the operating system.

the computer monitor each piece of the program—whether in real or in secondary storage repositories.

Virtual Storage in the MVS-XA mechanism (XA is short for *Extended Architecture*) makes it possible for the user to access the maximum amount of storage that can be addressed in 31 bits, even though the system might have much less physical storage available. Virtual storage works because MVS keeps active portions of each address space in real storage and the inactive portions on high-speed DASD (auxiliary storage) devices. It moves them back and forth as necessary to ensure that the program and the data for each user is in real storage when they are needed.

To allow the parts of a program in virtual storage to move between real and auxiliary storage, MVS breaks real storage, virtual storage, and auxiliary storage into blocks. The terminology the system uses is as follows:

- A block of real storage is a *frame*.
- A block of virtual storage is a *page*.
- A block of auxiliary storage is a *slot*.

A page, a frame, and a slot are all the same size: each consists of 4096 (4K) bytes. An active virtual storage page resides in a real storage frame; a virtual storage page that becomes inactive resides in an auxiliary storage slot.

Moving pages between real storage frames and auxiliary storage slots is called *paging*. Figure 1.2 shows how MVS-XA performs paging for a program that has been running in virtual storage. At point 1, parts A, B, and C of a three-page program are in virtual storage. Page A is active and executing in a real storage frame, while pages B and C are inactive because they have been moved to auxiliary storage slots. At point 2, page B is required; the system brings B in from auxiliary storage and puts it in an available real storage frame. At point 3, page C is required; the system brings in C from auxiliary storage and puts it in an available real storage frame. If page A had not been used recently and if the system needed its frame in real storage, page A would have been moved to an auxiliary storage slot, as shown at point 4.

Thus, the entire program resides in virtual storage and the system copies pages of the program between real storage frames and auxiliary storage slots to ensure that the pages that are currently active are in real storage as they are required. Note that neither the frames nor the slots allocated to a program need to be contiguous; thus a page can occupy several different frames and several different slots during the execution of a program. So if page A in this example were to became active again, MVS-XA would move it to any available frame.

1.4 Multiple Virtual Storage and Extended Architecture (XA)

Just as multiprogramming environments became obsolete over the years, with the proliferation of a steadily increasing user community, installations began to outgrow their initial virtual-storage systems. The solution at this time was relatively simple—provide separate virtual-storage tables for each address space in the system. Thus, each address space could have access to a full range of virtual addresses, each con-

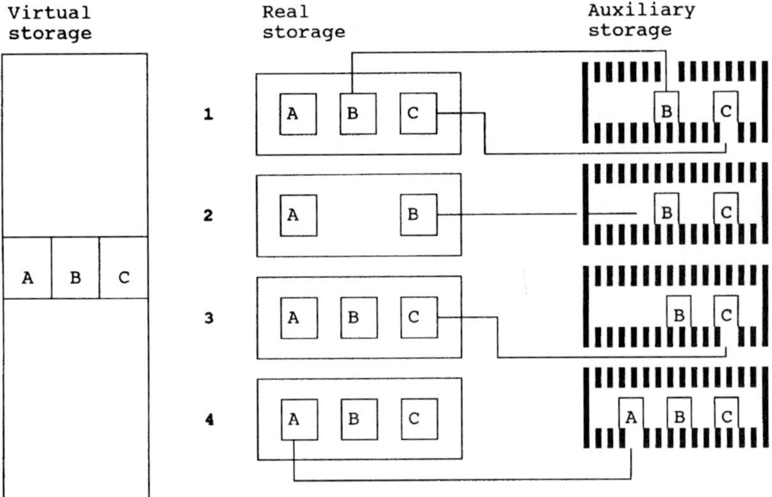

Figure 1.2 Virtual storage page movement.

taining 16 megabytes of virtual storage. Unfortunately, it did not take too long before the Multiple Virtual Storage environment became limited.

First of all, let me explain the method used by MVS to increase the number of virtual storage addresses. Suppose you have a two-column field for addressing and the available numbers range from 00 to 99. This will give you addressability up to 100. If you were to expand the columns by a single digit (000 to 999), you might create an additional 1,000 addresses—ten times that of the previous amount. The philosophy behind the MVS/Extended Architecture, better known as XA, is that it simply increases the number of virtual addresses (this is simply the table size to keep track of the bytes) by increasing the size of the field that holds the addresses.

Computers in the MVS architecture use binaries rather than decimals for tracking addresses. (The binary numbering system recognizes the existence of only a 0 or a 1 digit, and the combination of these numbers provides a valid address of 10010001 or 00100101, up to a maximum of 24 columns or bits.) This, by the way, is also referred to as a 24-bit addressing technique.

XA, on the other hand, expands the field addressability to 31 columns, so you can imagine how much more can be fitted into virtual storage by using this scheme. For example, if you start out at address 0 or 00000000 00000000 00000000 all the way to the maximum binary configuration of 11111111 11111111 11111111, the number of bytes you can address is 16,777,216. But if you were to start with the virtual address of 0000000 00000000 00000000 00000000 all the way up to 1111111 11111111 11111111 11111111, you would have access to 2 billion bytes or, to be precise, 2,147,483,648 bytes (also referred to as 2 gigabytes) of storage location. In contrast, the system has much less real storage. How much less depends on the model of computer and the overall configuration of the system. So, while MVS gives you a mere 16 megabytes of virtual storage, MVS/XA enables you to use an addressing scheme that is some 128 times bigger than its counterpart. Figure 1.3 highlights this concept.

To translate a virtual address into a 31-bit real address, a Dynamic Address Translation scheme (DOT) uses a control register, the Segment Table Origin Register (STOR), a segment table, and 2,048 page tables for each address space. The segment table has one entry for each of the 2,048 segments in the address space; each entry contains, among other things, a pointer to the page table for the particular segment. When address translation occurs, the STOR points to the segment table for the address space and the same virtual address for any others.

The page table for each segment has one entry for each of the 256 pages in the segment. If a page is currently in real storage frame, the entry includes the page-frame real address corresponding to the page. An overview of this is presented in Figure 1.4.

MVS/XA can also manage *multiprocessing,* which is the simultaneous use of two or more processors that share the various system hardware devices. MVS-XA modules normally store the information needed to control a particular unit of work or manage a resource in storage areas called *control blocks*. Generally speaking, there are three types of control blocks within MVS-XA:

System. Each system-related control block represents one MVS-XA system. These contain system-wide information, such as how many processors are functioning.

Resource. Each resource-related control block represents one resource, such as a processor or auxiliary storage device.

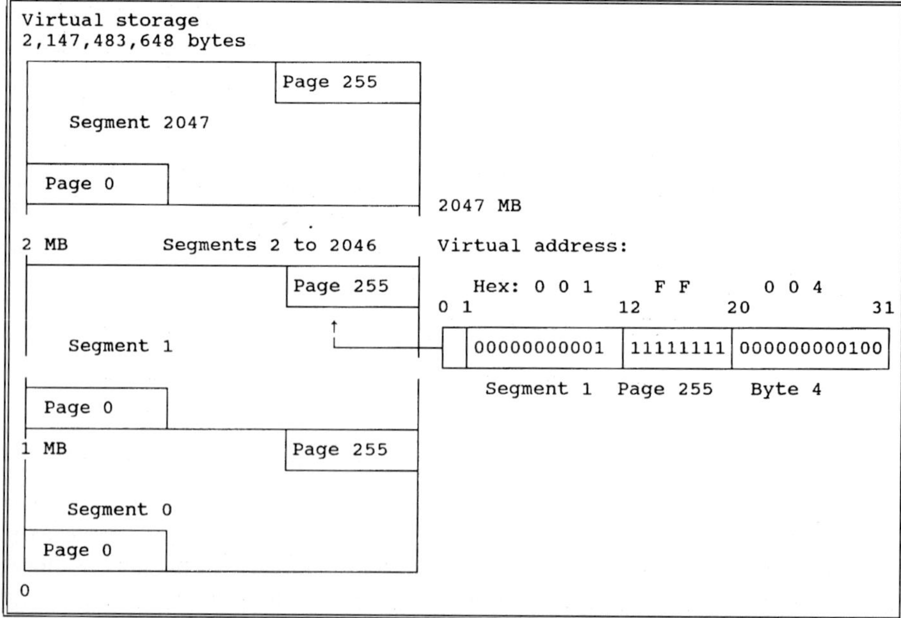

Figure 1.3 Virtual storage address.

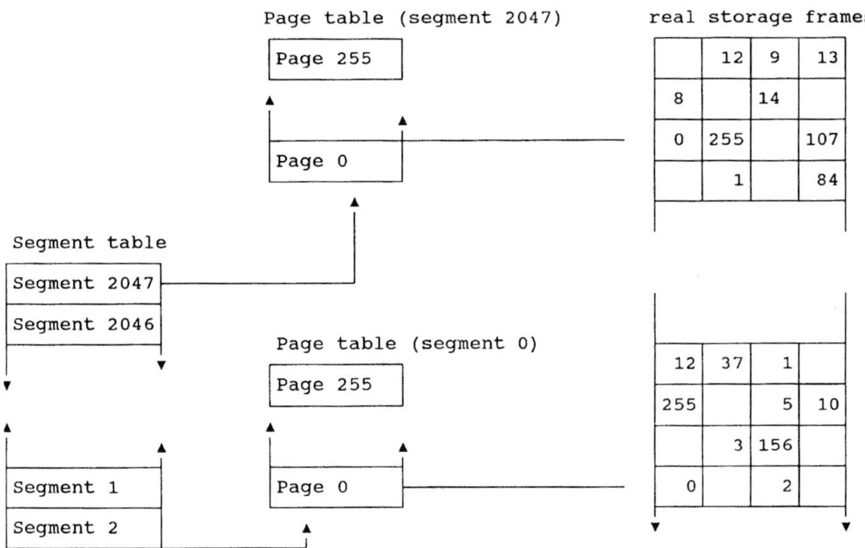

Figure 1.4 Segment table and page tables. (*Courtesy of IBM*)

Task. Each task-related control block represents one unit of work.

Control blocks work as vehicles for communicating throughout MVS. Such communication is possible because the structure of a control block is known to all of its users and, therefore, all can find necessary information about the unit of work or resource.

Control blocks representing many units of the same type can be chained together on queues, with each control block pointing to the next one on the chain. A program can search the queues to find the data for a particular unit of work or resource, which might be an address of a control block or a required unit, or actual data, such as a value, a quantity, or a status flag (for example, where each bit has a specific meaning).

Important things to remember about control blocks are that they are structured, documented, and usually chained together. Figure 1.5 illustrates a queue of task control blocks known as TCBs.

Finally, let me describe to you the *Program Status Word*, or PSW, which is a 64-bit area in the processor that, along with control registers, timing registers, and prefix registers, provides details crucial to both the hardware and the software. The current PSW includes the address of the next program instruction and control information about the program that is running, such as whether it is running in a 24-bit or a 31-bit addressing mode, or whether it is running in the problem program state or supervisor state.

Supervisor state programs are those that supervise and monitor the MVS operating system. *Problem state* programs can be those developed by the IBM Corporation as language translators, compilers, and also application programs written by you, the programmer. Each processor has only one current PSW. Thus, only one of the tasks

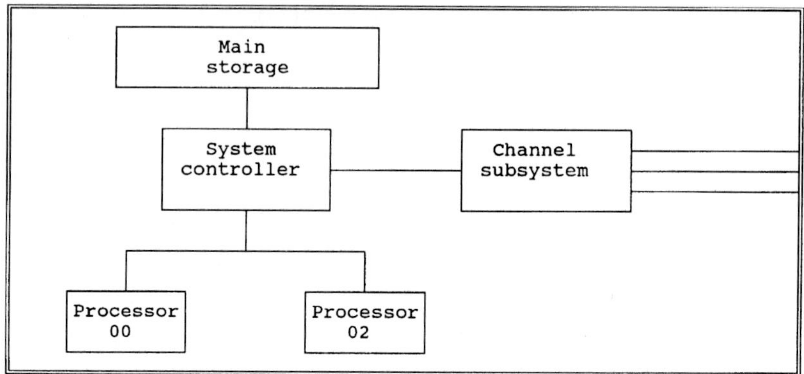

Figure 1.5 The 3081 process complex.

can execute on a processor at any one time. Multiprogramming is possible, however, because an interruption causes the processor to save the contents of the current PSW, while inserting new PSW information in order to process the interruption. Figure 1.6 illustrates the MVS/XA PSW and some of its most important bits.

1.5 Enterprise Systems Architecture/370 (MVS/ESA)

The MVS Extended Architecture (XA) eventually became obsolete for those using super-sized files, so that the concept of address space (as efficient as it seemed at the time of its development) became too small of an area to maintain processing efficiency. To overcome this apparent deficiency, IBM developed a new operating system called the MVS Enterprise Systems Architecture, or MVS/ESA. ESA, unlike the XA machine, allows the application to use multiple two-gigabyte address spaces. The MVS/ESA operating system, in addition to creating these huge address spaces for processing efficiency, also redefines some of the larger applications into a number of functional areas. This concept is especially important when processing CICS applications because the data utilized by each real-time application is segregated into a particular area, thus preventing an application from wiping out a subsequent file—one that, for example, belongs to another application.

What does this all mean in terms of operating efficiency? It means that data spaces are economical for those application programs that continually process the same data. Thus, data can be stored in primary rather than auxiliary storage, where the incredibly slow I/O operations are not required. In addition to the two gigabytes of super storage available for holding the instructions and data of a particular job in an address space, each job can also have access to many data spaces. Thus, you can think of data spaces as expanding virtual storage horizontally rather than vertically, as does MVS/XA.

In a typical MVS/ESA environment, three kinds of spaces are used by the operating system. Among these are:

- Address spaces, referred to as application space, in which only programs can execute and which contains no data.

- Data spaces, meaning that they contain exclusive data for an application. Because a program cannot execute in data spaces, it must be copied into an application space prior to execution. Data spaces are allocated purely to data, so the two gigabytes of storage does not contain any part of the MVS operating system. Data spaces are addressable by the byte and they are virtual-storage-resident during the execution of the job or task.
- Hiperspaces, which enables the storage of temporary data addressable in 4K bytes rather than by individual bytes. The primary function of hiperspaces is to store temporary data sets created through an application program. When such data is required, it is physically moved from hiperspaces into application spaces 4K at a time.

Because data spaces isolate data from programs, data spaces prevent unintentional changes to the data. At the same time, data spaces can permit the sharing of data among selected users.

Along with this technology, IBM developed SMS, which is short for System Management Subsystem. SMS continually migrates data residing on DASD to tape and back to DASD based on priority and usage. SMS allows an installation to set classes of disk data sets with identical attributes. Programmers then create their file in reference to such a class. One of a number of functions of the Storage Management Subsystem is to do away with fragmentation on disk space by setting an efficient balance through usage. In conjunction with this, you don't have to define a block size to SMS any longer—unless you have a specific reason for doing so, SMS will do it for you. And the advantage of letting SMS do the calculation is that it will supply you with the most efficient block-size ratio attained through a set of sophisticated algorithms.

This kind of device independence means that the user does not have to be aware of how a particular device (e.g., disk or tape) is being used by the operating system.

1.6 More on the MVS Operating System

Computer systems and computer resources can be classified into three areas: processors, real storage, and I/O devices. The ultimate goal of the MVS operating system, of course, is to keep all those resources as busy as possible, to use a cliche, "for the maximization of performance." Unfortunately, there is an inherent conflict

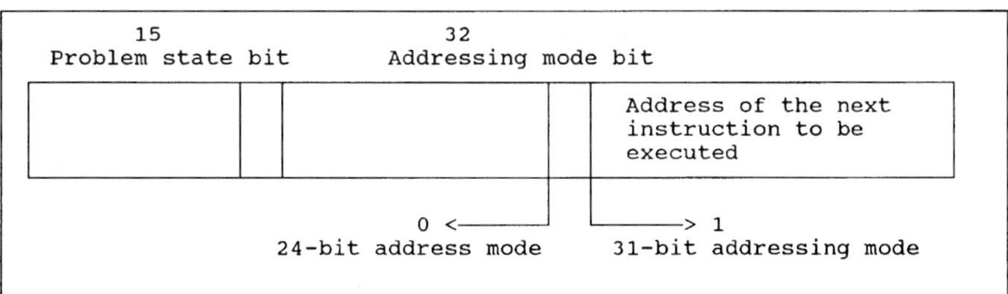

Figure 1.6 The MVS/X program status word.

in this goal. To make sure that all computer resources are kept busy might mean a slow-down in one area—thus not using the system to its fullest potential at some point in time.

One of the tools MVS uses in executing a job is a subsystem within the main operating system called Job Entry Subsystem, or JES. To be more specific, as an MVS user you might rely on one of the Job Entry Subsystems referred to as JES1 or as JES2. Essentially, JES accepts a job and sets it up for execution, while providing temporary storage facilities on disk until the operating system is ready to process it. The relationship between MVS and JES is simply that MVS executes a particular job, while JES is responsible for the more "mundane" details of that job, such as printing an output, purging a job once MVS is through processing it, and so on. To identify a job to JES and consequently to MVS, you need to rely on JCL statements.

JES is actually a very intelligent piece of software. Users can classify jobs, so JES can select them for execution to maximize the efficiency of the operating system in handling expensive resources. For example, JES has the intelligence to select and submit jobs with different requirements so they will not compete with each other for resources, such as those requiring tape volumes or special direct-access devices.

To continually maintain efficiency, the MVS operating system divides each job into separate executable units referred to as *tasks*. MVS selects and sequences work for processing by address space and, within each address space, by task based on the highest priority. While taking action to keep resources as busy as possible, MVS also decides how to process its workload. MVS bases its decision on a priority scheme that is specified by particular shop standards. Normally, a computer installation categorizes jobs into certain groups and each group is denoted by the amount of services or privileges it receives. Thus, as MVS executes the jobs, it repeatedly checks and compares the amount of service each job is getting, as opposed to what is specified for it. It then compensates for either too much or too little of such service.

When MVS processes a workload, it uses a technique that enables the operating system to switch control from one task to another, so that while one task awaits another can execute. In the MVS environment, this is done through *interrupts*. An interrupt is simply an event that changes the specific order in which the CPU executes instructions. Actually, interrupts can be caused by internal or external events. An internal event can be triggered by an application program and an external event can be invoked by a situation unrelated to the currently executing task.

Interrupts are initiated by a system (as opposed to an application) program called an *interrupt handler*. The interrupt handler saves viable information about the application program being interrupted. For example, when an I/O operation is completed, it causes an input/output interrupt. The interrupt handler at this time receives control, saves the status of the interrupted unit of works, and then passes control to handle a function with a higher priority (see Figure 1.7).

1.7 Multiprocessing

Quite frequently, the workload of an installation is held up because many jobs are waiting for execution by a single processing unit. Even with an efficient operating

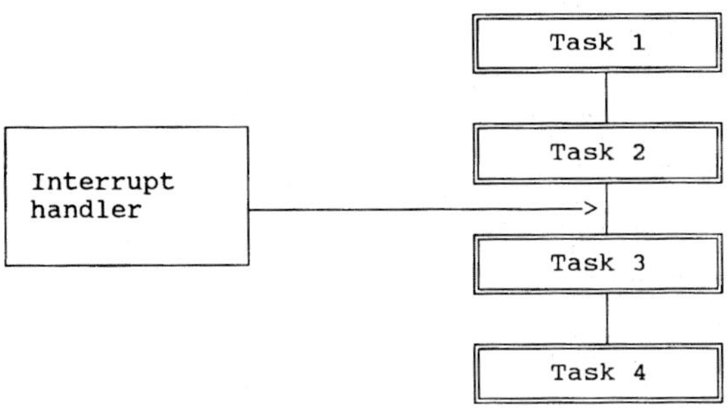

Figure 1.7 Switching control from one task to another through the interrupt handler.

system such as MVS, a single processor can execute only one instruction at a time, which tends to cause bottlenecks—usually in the most crucial moments. To overcome this problem, computer installations use two or a number of processing units. This is referred to as multiprocessing.

To understand just what a multiprocessor does, let's focus on the term *single processor* at first. A single processor, or uniprocessor, contains its own main storage and is controlled by a single operating system in a vacuum. This means that a single processor has no direct communication with other processors in the system. A multiprocessor, on the other hand, can share system resources as well as work. For example, while one of the processors initiates an input/output operation, the other can handle the interrupt that occurs at the end of the operation. This is all possible because MVS breaks up its load into a number of tasks, allowing each task to be handled separately.

Multiprocessing allows more work to be done in the same amount of time and enhances availability; when one processor is unavailable, another can pick up the work and carry on.

There are two types of multiprocessing mechanisms. The first one is called *loosely coupled multiprocessing*, where processors operate under separate operating systems, yet share access to data. The processors are connected by a shared direct-access storage device or channel-to-channel adapters. In this particular situation, each processor has its own operating system and jobs can, if necessary, be routed to a particular processor. An overview of this is highlighted in Figure 1.8.

The second kind of multiprocessing mechanism is referred to as *tightly coupled multiprocessing.* A tightly coupled processor configuration consists of a number of hardware components, such as processors, channel paths, storage and input/output devices. In a multiprocessing environment, it is possible to *reconfigure* the existing system to either add or remove some of the previously mentioned components. The ability to reconfigure the system on the fly is considered an efficient way to maintain operations despite possible malfunctions in the system. You might also need to perform maintenance on some of the components, or a change in the workload might require reconfiguring a single system into two or a number of systems.

Figure 1.9 shows the 3084 processor complex, which usually runs with four processors. The illustration shows sides A and B, which are each composed of two processors. The 3084 processor complex can be reconfigured to become two independent multiprocessing systems, each having two processors.

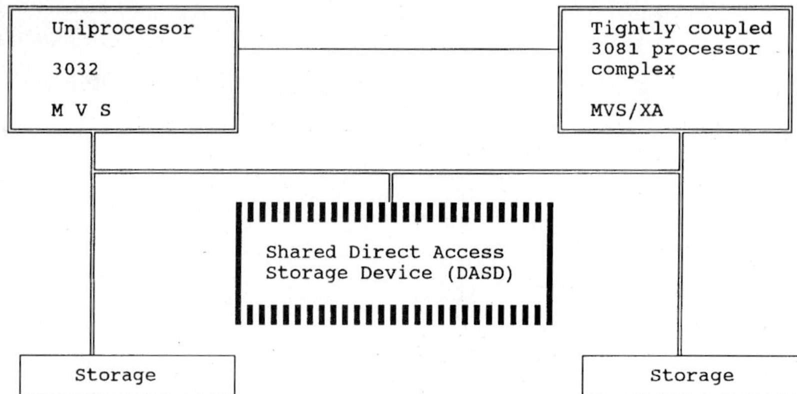

Figure 1.8 Loosely coupled multiprocessing.

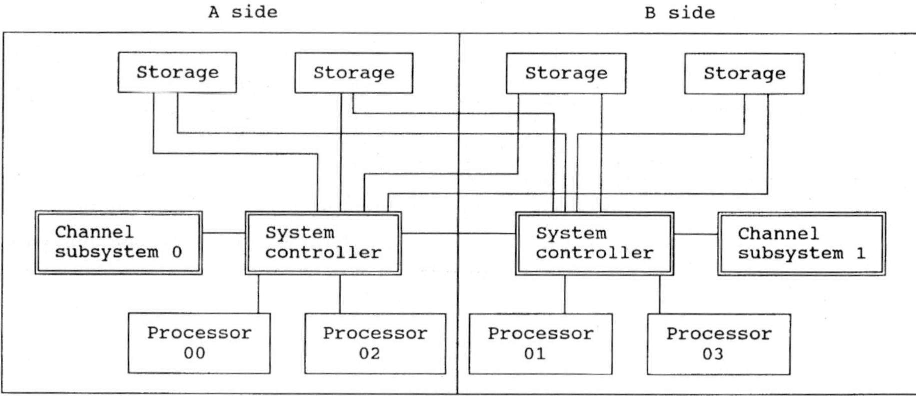

Figure 1.9 Tightly controlled multiprocessing. *(Courtesy of IBM)*

1.8 Data Management Under the MVS Operating System

Managing data simply refers to identifying, organizing, storing, and cataloging information so that it can be easily accessed and retrieved. *DFP*, or Data Facility Product, working in conjunction with the MVS operating system, manages and accesses data stored on disk and tape devices—relieving the users from manual interference.

In order to manage data retrieval from the various auxiliary devices, DFP relies on a retrieval method called *access method*. An access method enables a program to access data in a file that IBM refers to as a *data set*. An access method is determined by the way a particular data set is organized and stored and how such organization is reflected in the code of the source program. To manage the storage and placement of data sets, DFP uses a catalog and a volume table of contents, or VTOC. The catalog contains information about the data set and identifies the volume on which the data set resides. The volume table of contents lists the data sets that reside on a specific volume, as well as information about the location and size of each set.

Historically, users submit requests for processing large volumes of data that rely on the computer's speed. In the early days, requirements contained both scientific and business applications. Both data and source programs were contained on punch cards. Subsequently, jobs and programs were submitted to the computer in a giant batch, which placed little demand on the timely interference by the user-operator.

The ability to store data and programs on magnetic tape and subsequently on disk, and other direct-access devices, allowed more data to be stored. So, for example, instead of storing its order entry, or inventory, a company might store the status of each customer's order. In this way, large *databases* (collections of related data) began to develop. Then users were able to use applications to browse and summarize the data. The result was the development of transaction-oriented systems such as *CICS* (Customer Information Control System) and a hierarchical database called *IMS* (Information Management System) that could query the databases and make the data available for a large user community on a real-time basis.

Transaction-oriented systems provided high performance for a large number of users on a timely basis, which meant an increase in revenue rather than simply a way to cut costs. And businesses that took advantage of computers gained a very decisive competitive edge. As computer processing became faster and less expensive, it was practical to use terminals to connect many users directly to the computer, thus, online applications began to proliferate. At this point, the terminal became the primary I/O device and the users' means to interact with the CPU. In fact, to many users the terminal was synonymous with the computer.

Interactive access to MVS is made possible by Time Sharing Option/Extensions (TSO/E). TSO/E allows a wide variety of users to perform many different kinds of tasks. For example, a systems programmer can use TSO/E to keep MVS and other associated products running smoothly. A business professional can use TSO/E to access data in a corporate database, and an application programmer can use the software to edit, compile, and test application programs. TSO/E can handle short-running applications that use few resources, as well as long-running applications that require large amounts of resources.

Crucial MVS functions are backed up by recovery routines that run only when an error occurs. A recovery routine isolates an error and tries to confine it to a single user or task. At the same time, the recovery routine collects information about the error so that if a system failure does occur, the reason for the failure can be quickly determined and isolated. In addition, MVS enables the computer system to remain available despite hardware failures. For example, if a device fails, MVS isolates the piece of hardware and continues to run with the remaining devices. In a multiprocessing environment, MVS can recover from failure of a processor and continue to work on the remaining (available) processors.

1.9 Data Protection

A rise in the volume of important information stored in computer systems, the ability to access this information through interactive processing, and the growth in the number of computer users all make data more vulnerable to intentional or unintentional misuse. Thus, data protection has become a major concern at most installations today.

Resource Access Control Facility, or RACF, is a product that can provide data security for the resources of an MVS system. RACF protects data from accidentally or deliberately authorized disclosure, modification, or destruction.

RACF allows an installation to define the resources it wants to protect and to control a user's access to those resources. RACF can protect resources such as tape volumes, terminals, direct-access storage devices, data sets, and programs. RACF can log and report attempts to access protected resources. If a user attempts to access a resource but does not have the appropriate authority to do so, RACF can immediately notify security management. This concept is illustrated in Figure 1.10.

1.10 The Innovation Access Method

There are two additional topics that are related to but not closely linked to the MVS operating system. The first is a vendor-designed access method called IAM that is compatible with MVS. The second is an IBM technology also available on MVS that is architecturally similar to the ESA operating system, and is referred to as Data in Virtual, or DIV. Let us start with IAM.

IAM, which stands for Innovation Access Method, was developed by IDP, or Innovation Data Processing, as an alternative to VSAM. IAM does not replace any operating-system access method; rather, it is designed to coexist with them. Thus, you can operate in an environment where some of your data sets rely on VSAM technology, but also utilize IAM with later system developments.

One of the advantages of the IAM solution is that the software can reduce the channel and disk-controller connections that VSAM can cause, thus substantially improving throughput. Normally, IAM file structure takes less space than VSAM simply because of IAM's data-compression technique and thus the auto-release of unused space.

IAM's system-level interface (VIF) enables CICS and other on-line systems, batch programs, and TSO applications to use IAM files in place of indexed VSAM KSDS files without any change made to the programs or JCLs. For an application currently using VSAM cluster(s), find the IDCAMS steps that define the VSAM cluster(s). Simply add the parameter OWNER($IAM) to the DEFINE procedure. The next time the cluster is defined, it will become an IAM file. Consider the JCLs shown in Figure 1.11.

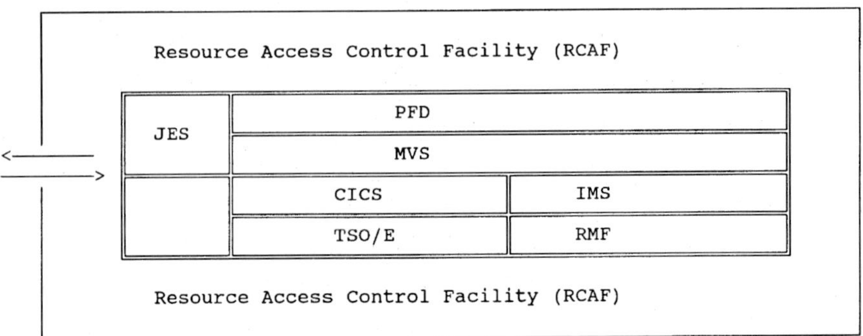

Figure 1.10 A typical RACF environment that provides security.

```
//DEFCLUS   EXEC   PGM=IDCAMS
//SYSPRINT DD      SYSOUT=*
//SYSIN     DD     *
  DEFINE CLUSTER                  -
  (NAME(ACCOUNT.RECEIVE)          -
  RECORDSIZE(408 408)             -
  KEYS(28 0)                      -
  IMBED SPEED REUSE               -
  FREESPACE(10 10)                -
  RECORDS(500000 50000)           -
  VOL(CICS01))
```

Defining a conventional VSAM cluster

```
//DEFCLUS   EXEC   PGM=IDCAMS
//SYSPRINT DD      SYSOUT=*
//SYSIN     DD     *
  DEFINE CLUSTER                  -
  (NAME(ACCOUNT.RECEIVE)          -
  RECORDSIZE(408 408)             -
  KEYS(28 0)                      -
  IMBED SPEED REUSE               -
  FREESPACE(10 10)                -
  RECORDS(500000 50000)           -
  VOL(CICS01))                    -
  OWNER($IAM)
```

Defining an IAM cluster/data set

Figure 1.11 A transparent conversion effort from VSAM.

IAM uses the methodology of learning from experience. It dynamically acquires additional buffers to retain the most often-referenced blocks in memory—the goal being to satisfy as many requests as possible from data that is already in memory, while not just taking ever increasing amounts of storage. To accomplish this, IAM not only acquires but also frees buffers as the demands of the job change.

Also, the system optionally tables records retrieved from the file in virtual storage. On random reads, the software checks to see if the record requested is already in its dynamic table. If it is, it passes it back to the user, eliminating the I/O to the disk. This concept is somewhat similar to what will be discussed in the next section under *Data in Virtual*, with the single exception that IAM does not require programming or file changes.

Actually, the difference between DIV and IAM's dynamic tabling of records is that, unlike DIV, which is geared to work with 4K pages, the IAM method is individual-record oriented. Thus, because it requires less memory for the processing cycle, fewer real pages are required to back up the virtual pages. If the record being requested is not currently in the table, IAM reads the record from the file. If found, the record is passed to the user and tabled for subsequent retrievals. If the record is updated, the system changes the record in the table and on disk. If the table fills up, IAM empties a portion of the table—ensuring that the most recent retrievals are maintained in the table.

Applications that can gain the most from dynamic tabling are those with high file activities where there is a subset of the records in a file and where the files are repeatedly being read with few ever being updated.

An IAM system-level interface (VIF) provides the user with VSAM transparency. VIF allows an unaltered application program executing under MVS, MVS/XA, or

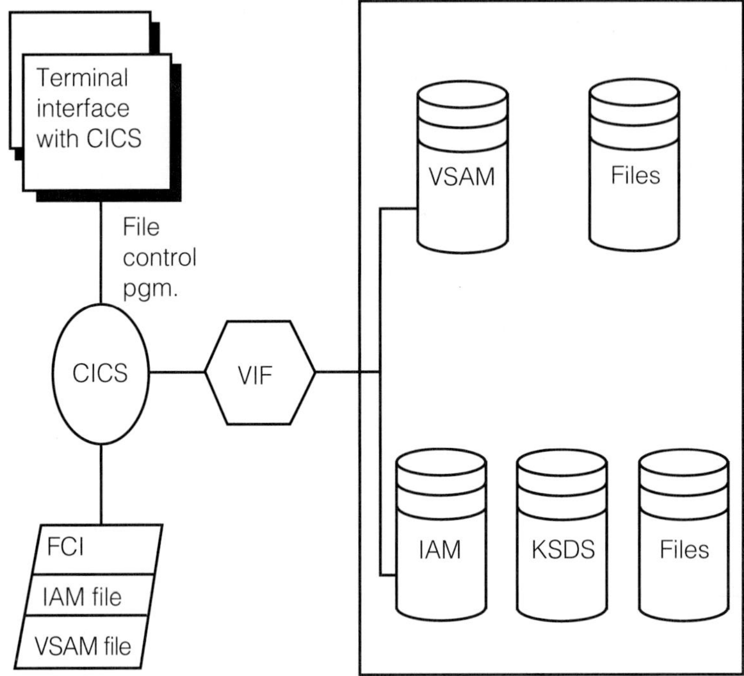

Figure 1.12 Overview of an IAM system-level interface (VIF).

MVS/ESA to access IAM files in place of single-indexed VSAM KSDS files. An overview of this is presented in Figure 1.12.

1.11 Data in Virtual

Note that in one of my earlier publications, *Mainframe Productivity Tools of the '90s*, published by John Wiley & Sons, Inc., I dedicated an entire chapter to the new idea of Data in Virtual (DIV). With DIV, rather than processing through some of the auxiliary storage facilities, such as a direct-access device, you can now load a massive database into main memory and process it there for speed and efficiency. Thus, Data in Virtual provides services that permit application programs to access data on permanent storage as though the data were in virtual storage. As a result, application programmers can create, read, and update data without the time-consuming I/O buffer, block size, or record considerations. Programs that make random accesses to large amounts of data benefit the most from this methodology.

A program views the permanent data as a stream of contiguous information. It specifies permanent data that it will use later by mapping portions of that data into virtual storage. The mapped virtual storage serves as a virtual storage window on the permanent data. Figure 1.13 shows the relationship between permanent data and virtual storage.

Next, the mapped storage is updated using the same programming statements that would be used for any other virtual storage. When the program decides to copy the updates to permanent storage, it requests the Data in Virtual's SAVE service using the DIV macro instruction.

The system processes all of the program's permanent and mapped storage in 4K blocks. These blocks must be on page boundaries in the mapped virtual storage. The I/O processing that occurs for page defaults on the mapped storage and for SAVE requests is quite similar to MVS VIO (virtual I/O) and paging, although in this particular instance a special data set is used for the program's data.

The permanent data accessed via data in virtual must be in a VSAM linear data set. A linear data set contains data only; it has no embedded logical records or other control information. VSAM, however, keeps some control information required during the processing of the data set, such as indicators for whether the data set is open or closed in a separate data set. Your application program does not need to access this data set, although some of the information available in the control data can be used for problem diagnosis, if any.

Permanent data accessed via DIV is called a *data object* from the time your program uses one of the data-in-virtual services called IDENTIFY (see Figure 1.14 for an overview of data in virtual services) to initiate a particular use of the data until the program ends the use by requesting the data-in-virtual UNIDENTIFY command.

A linear data set is simply a new form of VSAM data set. Somehow, the term *data set* invokes visions of complex record-management interfaces. Yet data in virtual allows a program to ignore record-management issues. One of the reasons I am stressing this is that the linear data set is referred to as a *data object* when used by data in virtual.

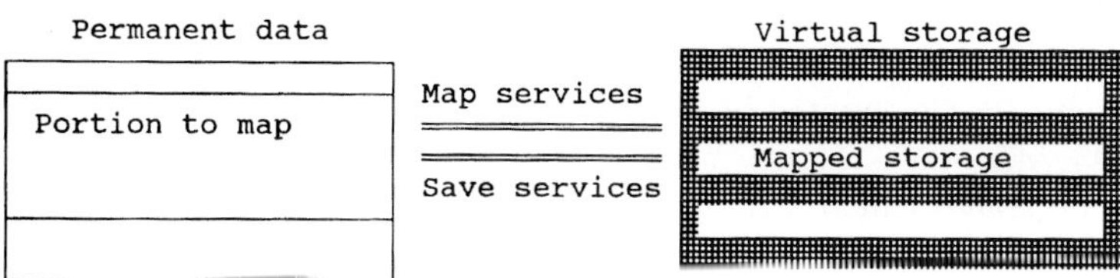

Figure 1.13 Mapped virtual storage.

IDENTIFY	Identifies the permanent data's DDname and obtains an identifier (ID) for the data object to use on later DIV macro requests
ACCESS	Prepares the data object for read or update (causes an open)
MAP	Maps all or part of a data object onto a specified area in virtual storage (causes an eventual read when mapped virtual storage is referenced for the default RETAINS=NO option)
SAVE	Saves all or part of the mapped virtual storage into the data object
RESET	Removes updates that were made to all or part of the mapped virtual storage since the last SAVE request
UNMAP	Removes the mapping of virtual storage
UNACCESS	Terminates the access (causes a close of the data object)
UNIDENTIFY	Terminates the IDENTIFY (ends data in virtual usage of the data object for the specified ID)

Figure 1.14 Data in virtual services commands.

Because the linear data set is a VSAM data set, it is allocated during IDCAMS definition. Note the control statement used to allocate a linear data set (shown in Figure 1.15). The only thing new here is the option LINEAR. In the example, a 10-cylinder data set is allocated on volume DASDID. If this is not enough space, the data set can expand in 10-cylinder increments. While the physical data set is initially 10 cylinders in size, the logical size of the data object is zero. The SHAREOPTIONS (1 3) parameter says that MVS will ensure either of the following:

- That one user can open the data set for updates
- That multiple users can open the data set to read

1.12 The Role of the Solid-State Disk (SSD) and ESTOR MVS-Geared Technologies

The original Solid-State Disk (SSD), often referred to as a drum, was designed to emulate the IBM 2305 Direct-Access Storage Device. It had a fixed head disk, which substantially enhanced the input/output performance by eliminating seek delays. Seek delays or seek time is the amount of time a disk drive spends to find an area such as a cylinder or a track. This involves movement of the access arms between the center of the disk and its circumference.

The purpose of this new architecture was to reduce page delay time, compared to DASD, or simply the time a task spent waiting for a page it needed to transfer from auxiliary storage to real storage in the CPU. The Solid-State Disk improved response time by eliminating rotational delay, which is the time spent by the disk drive awaiting a particular sector that contains the data underneath the read/write head. Unfortunately, this was limited by the capacity constraints of the previously mentioned IBM 2305.

As technology advanced in the first part of the 1980s, the Solid-State Disk was further improved, this time to emulate the IBM 3380 Direct-Access Storage Device. The move increased the capacity of the SSD to the point where it could now be used for a variety of applications, including swapping or transferring the most recently active pages of an address space between virtual storage and auxiliary storage. Swapping is important because you have only so much real memory and you must use that real memory efficiently by moving inactive portions of your application in and out of it.

The advantage of the Solid-State Disk over a conventional Direct-Access Storage Device (DASD) is speed and memory. A Solid-State Disk has a cache, which is a random-access storage area contained in the control unit used to retain frequently used data for faster access by the channel. DASDs have too many moving parts, which

```
//     EXEC   PGM=IDCAMS
       DEFINE CLUSTER         -
       (NAME(DIV.DATA)        -
       VOLUMES(DASDID)        -
       CYL(10 10)             -
       SHAREOPTIONS(1 3)      -
       LINEAR)
```

Figure 1.15 Allocating a linear data set.

slows down the access and consequently the processing of data. One of the major problems with the SSD initially was the lack of protection for data during a power loss or hardware failure, especially in situations when the system had to be reinitiated cold. This problem was corrected in the next generation of SSDs, via batteries. Batteries allowed the user enough time to copy data in a pinch from the highly volatile Dynamic Random-Access Memory (DRAM) to a nonvolatile disk.

While SSDs are extensively used by a typical IBM 390 configuration, they are not the only advanced technology compatible with an ESA environment. Another piece of technology to mention is Expanded Storage (also referred to as ESTOR). ESTOR is part of the central processor, and is also compatible with the IBM 390 configuration. Because it is part of the internal architecture of the system, it has a faster response rate and, thus, better performance.

The MVS operating system writes 40K (in ten 4K pages) to a 47K 3380 track, which means that 15% of the space is wasted. Because the Solid-State Disk emulates an IBM 3380 DASD, a 10-megabyte paging area requires some 12 megabytes of allocated space. This is far from being efficient. ESTOR, on the other hand, is made up of 4K addressable units of memory. Thus, a 10-megabyte paging area requires 10 megabytes of expanded storage.

One other thing—when paging to an expanded storage rather than to a Solid-State Disk, the MVS operating system keeps the current task running. This mode of operation is also referred to as a synchronous mode. When paging to an external device such as a Solid-State Disk, MVS must task switch, meaning that it must temporarily suspend the task that needs a page. At this point, the processor must wait, which creates substantial overhead. This mode of operation, unlike the first kind (ESTOR), takes place in asynchronous mode.

Chapter

2

Advanced Topics for CICS Application Systems

In my recently published book, *Command-Level CICS Programming* (McGraw-Hill, 1991), I provide the reader with a number of techniques in developing application programs ranging in complexity from a simple menu program to advanced tutorials and on-demand reports using an array of selection criteria. Although some of the topics presented in this book are streamlined to an experienced audience, the majority of them are geared to students and technicians with relatively limited background.

In this and the following chapter, I am going to present to you a number of advanced topics in command-level CICS programming, assuming a great deal of technical exposure.

2.1 Introduction to Advanced CICS Programming Techniques

Relative to ongoing technological innovations in the micro industry (with special emphasis placed on the capabilities of micro software), command-level CICS has its work cut out for it in emulating its microcomputer nemesis. Two major accomplishments in mainframe technology make it easy for mainframe systems to compete with and surpass the internal design of microcomputers. These are the enormous memory size and processing speed of mainframe computers, giving the designer all sorts of room for creativity and improvements. In addition to speed and memory size, mainframe computers are also noted for their rapidly increasing reliability. These attributes allow the mainframe programmer to develop user-friendly systems through resourceful innovation, an objective seldom followed in earlier architectures.

2.2 Specifications and Concepts in Developing Advanced Code

Advanced CICS systems and, thus, application programming, essentially entail two types of enhancements. These are external as well as internal enhancements. Let me first focus on what I mean by *external enhancements*.

2.2.1 External CICS design

External enhancements (enhancements modifying a previously aging or marginally performing system) place emphasis on user-friendliness. The purpose of this section is to highlight some of these features.

In an effort to develop state-of-the-art mainframe systems for its line of products, an electronics manufacturer from a midwestern state, Brownly Walters International, began to develop and market a system using the following approach: all CICS maintenance programs were to be driven with browse capabilities. Thus, a change or delete transaction, for example, would be functional in a relatively more flexible browse environment. If a specific record searched were not on file (a browse would immediately display the next available record due to the generic key), the operator could simply press a preassigned function key to clear the panel and start entering the required data.

Browse operations remove a certain amount of harshness from performing day-to-day routine operations, unlike a rudimentary add or inquiry transaction. Suppose that in order to create (or update) a record on file, you need to rely on multiple panels and that each panel encompasses a complex set of edit rules, complex especially for those with little or no prior data entry experience. To overcome such a handicap (and to gain operational fluency in a relatively short period of time), Brownly Walters undertook the development of a company-wide tutorial system.

In developing tutorials, however, this electronics manufacturer required that the users create their own text material for displaying error messages or communicating the nature of the error. The specifications further stated that no such text would be hardcoded into the system, which would result in pages and pages of unmaintainable text. They wanted the ability to independently modify each line of text (without restructuring the rest of the panel on a line-by-line basis), and have each line contain a specific scheme for colorizing and otherwise highlighting words, lines, and full-length messages to emphasize several levels of severity in those messages. (Incidentally, such an environment will be the topic of chapter 3.) To further highlight the latitude and the complexity of this environment, consider the diagram in Figure 2.1.

In order to create an employee record, for example, the operator must complete three panels (Employee Panel & Layout 1 through 3) in succession because each panel contains data fields defined as mandatory for a master record. As a result, Panel 2, for example, will not be accessible to the operator in add mode unless the operator completes the essential requirements. (Changing a record might require a slightly different effort, unless the operator somehow inadvertently removes one or a number of mandatory fields during the update/edit process.)

In change mode, for example, browse provides you with all sorts of "navigational" capabilities. These navigational capabilities can be one of two kinds: horizontal or ver-

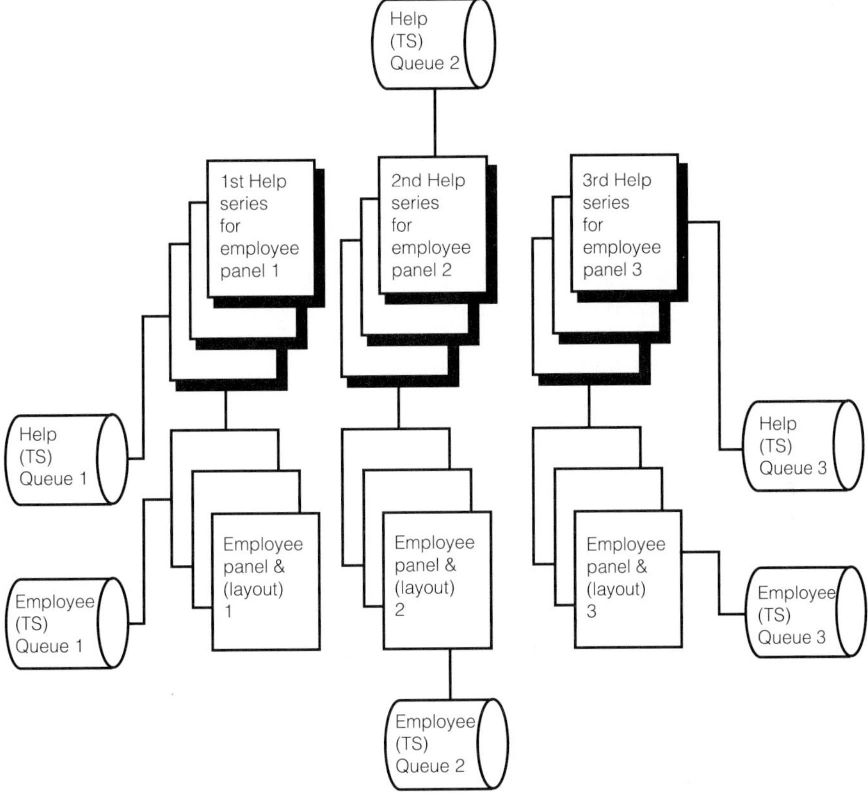

Figure 2.1 Using Browse to create a simple tutorial in a multipanel setting.

tical. Horizontal navigation simply means that you can advance to Panel 2 from Panel 1 via a function key, or advance to Panel 3 from Panel 2, as circumstances dictate.

Vertical navigation provides you with added flexibility so that you can scan or browse all the occurrences pertaining to a single panel type. While continuing the path horizontally means to access the second and consequently the third panel of the same employee, navigating vertically will take you to the first, second, third, fourth, and so on panel each time of a different employee. Note that data pertaining to either horizontal or vertical moves can be loaded into temporary storage by using consecutive item numbers or by creating a new queue for each page and occurrence.

Let's start complicating this multipanel environment by bringing into focus parts of a tutorial subsystem. Suppose the operator on the second panel in the update cycle has no idea of the proper values that can be placed in the skills inventory field. To attain more information on the field, the operator has to press PF1, which will invoke a help screen. Because the panel is not field sensitive, information on a specific data field might not be displayed on the first page of this tutorial. This means that you need to continually browse the pages until the specific reference for a data field is finally located.

The help system, thus, is characterized by the following features at this point:

- There is no limit to the occurrences associated with a particular panel. This means that (theoretically) a transaction-processing panel can contain as many as 100 or even 1,000 pages of explanation, which is of course impractical—yet architecturally possible.
- You can return to the specific employee screen from any one of the help pages by pressing the Enter key or the Clear key, or via a preassigned function key.
- Two pieces of data are also essential if you want to return to the transaction that initially invoked the tutorial panel you now occupy:
  - ~ The proper queue for the suspended data
  - ~ The location of the cursor the last time you exited the transaction while seeking assistance

Completing an ADD transaction, of course, is possible only on the last screen of a multiscreen update cycle, even though this criterion does not hold water in a change environment. If the operator, for example, fails to press the update function key when reaching the last add screen (and having completed all the requirements), he can decide to branch back to a previous submenu prior to pressing a PF key. That means that the record never gets created, and all that was entered into the system will be lost. (This incidentally is not true when the operator needs to scroll back to a previous screen, e.g., to panel 2 from panel 3 or to panel 1 from panel 2, in which case all the data gathered thus far will be safely preserved.)

A second environment involves the same multipanel specifications, but a vastly different tutorial approach. In this model, a tutorial can be invoked through cursor sensitivity. Cursor sensitivity means referencing a particular data field that happens to be where the cursor was last located prior to the branch. Thus, you can place the cursor next to or right on a particular field to be inquired upon and, by pressing the Enter key or a specific PF key, you can reference that field.

Using this technique, only a single element will be invoked and highlighted by the tutorial subsystem, including specific values, edit rules, cross references, and computational requirements—all in reference to the data field alone. In certain CICS systems, text explaining a problem is contained in a boxed-in area on the screen, no more than three or four lines at a time. You can also temporarily overlay parts of an unused area on the screen to display the requested narrative.

2.2.2 Internal CICS design

Internal CICS design is transparent to the user. It is primarily available for the programmer to better communicate potential problems, enforce standards, and develop specialized programs in an application environment that will perform I/Os, such as reading and writing centrally in specialized programs, and Handle Conditions and Handle Aid commands while providing the team with a single error-deciphering scheme. These specialized programs are normally presented in an intermediate to large-scale application environment. This concept is also depicted in Figure 2.2.

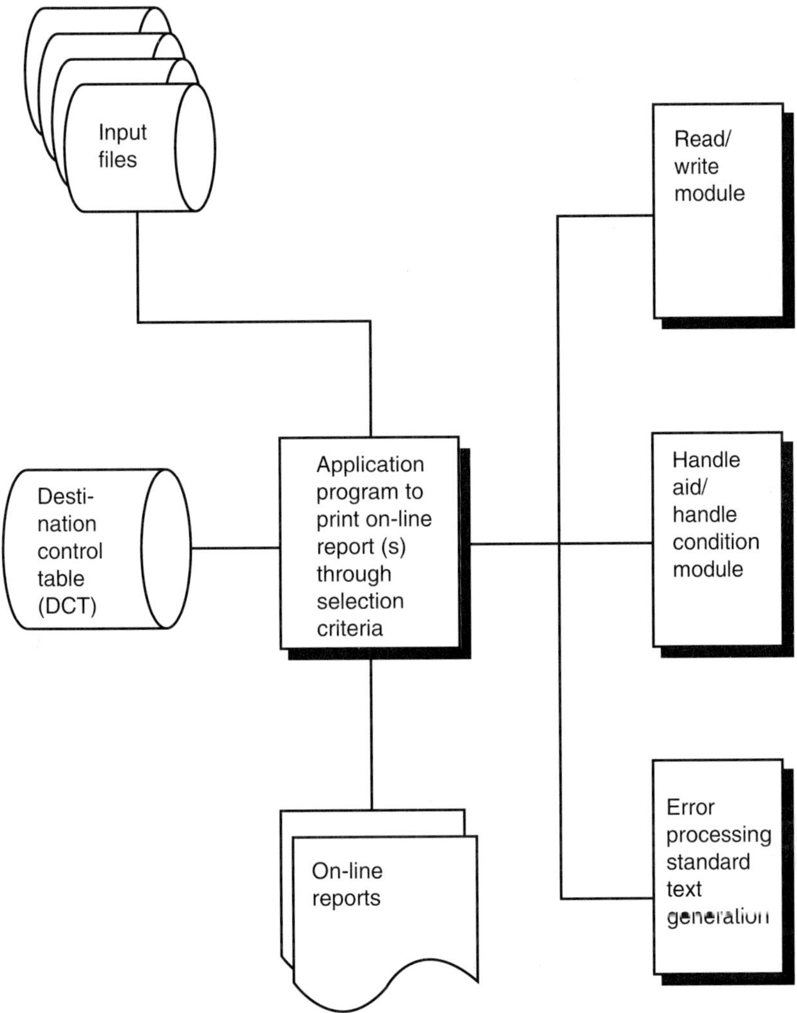

Figure 2.2 An application using "traffic cop" modules.

Note that I used parts of an application program to highlight the mechanics of processing in a centrally managed application system.

When detecting an error condition, this program invokes another processing module by linking to it and then triggering a specific error panel. As I mentioned earlier, the program about to be illustrated uses standardized procedures, those that replace HANDLE AID and HANDLE CONDITIONs with status codes. Many people view Handle Aid and Handle Condition control statements, for example, as error-prone, much too cumbersome for a number of reasons. Both HANDLE AID and HANDLE CONDITION statements are essentially unconditional GO TOs that tend to disrupt the logical flow of the code. As a rule, beginners and less-experienced programmers tend to

```
 BROWSE MODE                  METRA RAIL MATERIAL INVENTORY                  12/13/91   15:49
RMB46M1                       DOCUMENT SEARCH BY DEPARTMENT                  NIRJM       0000

DOCUMENT TYPE: 003   DEPT: ____   DOC #: _______   MATERIAL/RE-STOCKING
----------------------------------------------------------------------------------------------
SEL TYP DEPT   DOC      SITE  PROJCT  USERID    DATE     LINE  DOC   REASON DOC  PICK
              NUMBER          NUMBER                     TOTL  STAT  OPEN   PRNT PRNT
----------------------------------------------------------------------------------------------
P   003 9000 0000717   METRA          NIRGS   09/19/91   001   C                Y    Y
_   003 9000 0000778   METRA          NIRBP   09/26/91   001   O      I         N    N
_   003 9000 0000781   METRA          NIRBP   09/26/91   001   O      I         N    N
_   003 9000 0000792   METRA          NIRGS   09/28/91   001   O      I         N    N
_   003 9000 0000795   METRA          NIRGS   09/28/91   001   C      I         Y    Y
_   003 9000 0000796   METRA          NIRGS   09/28/91   001   C      I         N    Y
_   003 9000 0000829   METRA          NIRGS   10/01/91   001   C                Y    N
_   003 9000 0000830   METRA          NIRGS   10/01/91   001   C                Y    Y
_   003 9000 0000831   METRA          NIRGS   10/01/91   001   C                Y    Y
_   003 9000 0000986   B32            NIRBP   11/01/91   001   C                N    Y
_   003 9000 0000987   B32            NIRBP   11/01/91   001   O      I         N    N
_   003 9000 0001052   S29            NIRGS   11/22/91   004   C                Y    Y

TYPE 'S' OR 'P' INTO A SELECT FIELD, AND PRESS PF9

CLEAR=CANCEL, PF1=HELP, PF3=END, PF7=UP, PF8=DOWN, PF9=INQUIRY/JUMP
```

Figure 2.3 The first menu selection to invoke a main application module.

create a maze of such statements by continuously redefining them and referencing them through various paragraphs.

READ and WRITE statements are also standardized in this environment. As you will soon see, the programmer will set up different keys necessary for a READ or WRITE operation, but then a call routine will invoke another application program that is responsible for performing such an input/output operation.

Large systems tend to use a great deal of standardization and are highly integrated. Smaller systems, on the other hand, tend to shy away from such a high level of integration because of the initial set-up cost. It is far more desirable to develop a sophisticated "traffic cop" system that would manage the environment during its operation from standard read/write I/Os to include a global error-handling scheme for some 150 to 300 application programs.

2.3 Scenario for a Program Prototype

In further illustrating the need to develop such a traffic cop system, I would like to highlight parts of an application program that does rely on such a mechanism to generate one of two "transient" reports triggered through menu selection. The first among a set of multiple menus necessary to invoke this task is a map that is operational in browse mode to allow the user to select a particular number of criteria, such as a department, document number, a destination for the report, record exclusion criteria, etc., by placing the character P in the appropriate spot and then by pressing the Enter key.

For example, I selected document 0000717 to be sent to the METRA building (site) under a user I.D. of NIRGS. The DOC PRNT and the PIC PRNT columns are automatically updated once the transient report is completed. This panel is shown in Figure 2.3. This panel then invokes a secondary menu screen shown in Figure 2.4, where you can also select one of two options. Note that the selection was a 1 (print restock document), exhibited in Figure 2.5. The other report the sample program can also generate is shown in Figure 2.6.

The main aspect of this program is the advanced style in which it is written, providing the system a high level of integration with six or seven additional modules. Because of the enormous size of some of the components involved, let me vary my presentation between PROCEDURE and DATA DIVISIONs because the main body of this command-level program contains several thousand lines of source code, excluding expanded copy and Panvalet statements that are referenced at various times during execution. Consider Figures 2.7 and 2.8.

The first and only HANDLE CONDITION in the program is in place so that, when there is an abnormal termination, this program will branch to a label or paragraph 9270-ABEND-ROUTINE. The response by the system will be contained in a field, CICS-RESP, which is a full-word binary field to be named by the programmer. Full-word binary simply refers to a PIC S9(08) COMP format.

RESP contains the condition that might have been raised during the execution and you will find that it is very much like using VSAM status or return codes. When a transaction executes successfully, the response will be a zero, which is also identical with the key term NORMAL. To put it in programming terms:

```
IF CICS-RESP = DFHRESP(NORMAL)
```

all is well, therefore, else you have an error condition to think about.

The error condition starts on line 596 and it can be triggered, as you can see, a number of ways. (Note that there is a source listing of the error-processing program in appendix B.) All error conditions eventually invoke a standard error routine, high-

```
PRINT/REQUEST          METRA RAIL MATERIAL INVENTORY           12/13/91    15:52
RMP61M1                   MATERIAL RE-STOCK PRINT              NIRJM        0000
================================================================================
REQ/NO.: 0000717       REQ/BY: NIRGS       DEPT: 9000        DOC/STATUS   : C
SITE/ID: METRA         NAME    : SCOTT, GREGORY              REASON/OPEN:
PROJECT:               LAST/UPDATED/BY: NIRGS                DOC/PRINTED: Y
WK/ORDR:               DATE: 12 / 13 / 91                RESTOCK/PRINTED: Y
================================================================================

PRINT/DEST -> 547 W. JACKSON - 3RD/FLOOR/WEST

                       1  -  PRINT  RE-STOCK/DOCUMENT

                       2  -  PRINT  RE-STOCK/TICKET

                       1


PRESS PF12 TO PRINT DOCUMENT(S)

CLEAR=CANCEL, PF1=HELP, PF3=END
```

Figure 2.4 A secondary menu to select one of two transient report options.

```
R-RMP61C-1                                          RAIL MATERIAL INVENTORY SYSTEM        DOCUMENT NUMBER   : 0000717         PAGE: 001
SYSDATE: 12/16/91     SYSTIME:  10:07                      RESTOCK DOCUMENT               DOCUMENT DATE     : 12/13/91
                                                                                          DOCUMENT STATUS   : C  REASON OPEN      :
USER ID:  NIRGS   USER NAME: SCOTT, GREGORY     DOCUMENT      : 9000                      DOCUMENT PRINTED  : Y STOCKLIST PRINTED: Y
SITE ID:  METRA   PROJECT  :                    WORK ORDER NO:                  BELTS &  AIR &                 DRIVE   EMISSION

          METRA
 ITEM     PART     T                                                                                          QUANTITY
 NO       NUMBER   S      DESCRIPTION                 ACCOUNT CODE             DESCRIPTION OF ACCOUNT     UM  RECOV. /
 XXXXXX  999,999                                                                                              SCRAPPED PRICE   VALUE
 001   03-05083-8  N  BONDING AGENT, CONCRETE        00-1801-10503000-A05220  INFORMATION SYSTEMS F.WOOD  GL    15     1.469  22.035
                                                                          MATERIAL IN PROGRESS                 0
                     5 GAL. CONTAINER
 MFG-NO                          COMMENTS: EXCESS MATERIAL ORDERED                   EQUIP. # :
                                                                                              TOTAL RECOVERED VALUE :        0.000
 APPROVED BY : ________________________________________________  DATE  :  ____/____/____
```

Figure 2.5 Transient report number 1.

```
R-RMP61C-1                                          RAIL MATERIAL INVENTORY SYSTEM        DOCUMENT NUMBER   : 0000717         PAGE: 001
SYSDATE: 12/16/91     SYSTIME:  10:07                      RESTOCK DOCUMENT               DOCUMENT DATE     : 12/13/91
                                                                                          DOCUMENT STATUS   : C  REASON OPEN      :
USER ID:  NIRGS   USER NAME : SCOTT, MURPHY     DOCUMENT      : 9000                      DOCUMENT PRINTED  : Y STOCKLIST PRINTED: Y
SITE ID:  METRA   PROJECT   :                   WORK ORDER NO :

 ITEM    BIN       METRA  T                                                  QTY       QTY         NEW
  NO   LOCATION    PART   S        DESCRIPTION                    UM      ON HAND   RECOVERED   QUANTITY     QTY        LINE
                   NUMBER                                                                       ON HAND    SCRAPPED    STATUS
 SHELVED BY  :  ____________________________________________  DATE  :  ____/____/____
```

Figure 2.6 Transient report number 2.

```
PROCEDURE DIVISION.
0000-MAINLINE-CONTROL.
    EXEC CICS HANDLE ABEND LABEL(9270-ABEND-ROUTINE)
                  RESP(CICS-RESP)
                  END-EXEC.
    IF  CICS-RESP = DFHRESP(NORMAL)
        NEXT SENTENCE
    ELSE
        MOVE 'A'                         TO CA-ERR-TYPE
        MOVE 00050                       TO CA-ERR-NUM-PRG
        IF  EIBCALEN LESS THAN +375
            PERFORM 0100-INIT-COMM THRU 0100-EXIT
            PERFORM 9000-ERR-RTNE THRU 9000-ERR-EXIT
        ELSE
            PERFORM 0200-INIT-COMM THRU 0200-EXIT
            PERFORM 9000-ERR-RTNE THRU 9000-ERR-EXIT.
    IF  EIBCALEN LESS THAN +375
        PERFORM 0100-INIT-COMM THRU 0100-EXIT
        MOVE 00012                       TO CA-ERR-NUM-PRG
        MOVE 'A'                         TO CA-ERR-TYPE
        PERFORM 9000-ERR-RTNE            THRU 9000-ERR-EXIT
```

Figure 2.7 Setting up standard error-handling procedures in your program (part 1).

lighted in paragraphs 9000-ERR-RTNE through 9000-ERR-EXIT, and shown in Figure 2.9. Thus, sooner or later every error condition invokes this module, which interfaces with the error-processing program, ISS03C, that does the bulk of the work. Error communication is processed through the COMMAREA. If everything is okay, the following "housekeeping" activities will take place:

- Setting up the required program logic to journalize. Why journalize? Normally, you need to journalize to create a backup file or transaction using before and after images. Typically, when a transaction is okay, you no longer require the before image of a particular record now updated. However, when a transaction bombs out (when your program abends, for whatever reason), you need to recover the before image of the record prior to the file getting corrupted.
- Building an area in temporary storage (queue) for the first time in order to receive the COMMAREA that will now contain the record for processing. A section of this code is shown in Figure 2.10.

Note that the length of the COMMAREA is 602 bytes long and not 375, as dictated by shop standards. This is so because this program uses 227 bytes of additional storage for internal manipulation. However, when the COMMAREA is loaded to be linked to one of the processing programs, it then reformats itself to the 375 standard length. Note that the entire standard communication area is shown in Figures 2.11 through 2.13.

Conceptually, when the first record contained in the communications area is captured, it is placed in a temporary (TS) queue. From there, it will eventually be loaded into transient storage with a trigger level of 1 (printing one line at a time), as described in the destination control table (DCT).

```
     ELSE
        PERFORM 0200-INIT-COMM THRU 0200-EXIT
        MOVE WS-PROG-NAME              TO I-O-JRNL-WORKPGM
        IF  EIBCALEN EQUAL +375
            PERFORM 1000-FIRST-TIME-SEND THRU 1000-EXIT
        ELSE
          MOVE EIBAID              TO  CA-ATTN-KEY
          IF CA-ATTN-KEY EQUAL DFHCLEAR
             MOVE DFHPF3 TO CA-ATTN-KEY, EIBAID
             PERFORM 9030-PF3-RTNE THRU 9030-PF3-EXIT
          ELSE
            IF  CA-ATTN-KEY EQUAL DFHPF9
                PERFORM 9020-PF9-RTNE THRU 9020-PF9-EXIT
           ELSE
             IF CA-ATTN-KEY EQUAL DFHPF12
                   PERFORM 3000-PF12-RTNE THRU 3000-PF12-EXIT
            ELSE
              IF  CA-ATTN-KEY EQUAL DFHPF3
                  PERFORM 9030-PF3-RTNE THRU 9030-PF3-EXIT
              ELSE
                IF  CA-ATTN-KEY EQUAL DFHPF4
                    PERFORM 9025-PF4-RTNE THRU 9025-PF4-EXIT
                ELSE
                  IF  CA-ATTN-KEY EQUAL DFHPF1
                      PERFORM 9040-PF1-RTNE THRU 9040-PF1-EXIT
                  ELSE
                    IF  CA-ATTN-KEY EQUAL DFHENTER
                        PERFORM 2000-ENTER-RTNE THRU 2000-EXIT
                    ELSE
                      MOVE -1        TO SELL
                      MOVE 00001     TO CA-ERR-NUM-PRG
                      MOVE 'P'       TO CA-ERR-TYPE
                      PERFORM 9000-ERR-RTNE
                         THRU 9000-ERR-EXIT
                      PERFORM 8000-SEND-ERR-MSG
                         THRU 8000-SEND-ERR-EXIT.
     PERFORM 9200-CICS-RETURN THRU 9200-EXIT.
```

Figure 2.8 Setting up standard error-handling procedures in your program (part 2).

It is interesting to note how certain standard routines are perceived and executed in this program. Look at the following example:

```
PERFORM 9280-CALL-I-O-MODULE THRU 9280-I-O-EXIT
```

This statement is used every time you need to read, process a browse, repeatedly issue a READNEXT statement based on previously supplied values, such as a record key, update code, and so on. This all-purpose assembler program is displayed in Figures 2.14 through 2.19.

Typically, a READNEXT instruction is accomplished in several layers. After setting up the necessary parameters for the above operation, the programmer calls the 9280-CALL-I-O-MODULE, after which the record is processed, the COMMAREA gets updated, and the queue is written, as depicted in Figure 2.20. A second such update is shown in Figure 2.21.

2.4 Error Handling and Error Messages

Previously in this chapter, I talked about centralizing error handling in order to restrict it to one or a number of specialized external programs. These programs should be designed to accept and decode a problem, any problem for that matter, that dispatches a potential abend using a centrally managed text. This text would inform the user about the specific nature of the error condition.

One of the more glaring mishaps in managing error messages is the inconsistency in which such messages are developed. To take an awkward situation, for example, assume that the change and add transactions, with regard to the maintenance of the Customer Master file, are coded by two different programmers. Also assume that in the procedure a data field, such as the customer's name, is a mandatory edit compo-

```
 9000-ERR-RTNE.
*
     IF  I-O-RETPGM-PTR GREATER THAN ZERO
         MOVE I-O-RETPGM (I-O-RETPGM-PTR) TO
                CA-ERR-PROGRAM
     ELSE
         MOVE WS-PROG-NAME TO CA-ERR-PROGRAM.
     MOVE 'P'                       TO CA-ERR-PROG-TYPE.
     IF  CA-ERR-TYPE EQUAL 'P' OR 'D'
         MOVE SPACES                TO CA-X-ERR-MSG
                                       CA-X-ERR-INST0
                                       CA-X-ERR-PFKEY0
         MOVE CA-ERR-TYPE           TO CA-X-ERR-TYPE
         MOVE CA-ERR-NUM-PRG        TO CA-X-ERR-NUM
         MOVE CA-INST-NUM           TO CA-X-ERR-INST-NUM
         MOVE CA-PFKEY-NUM          TO CA-X-ERR-PFKEY-NUM
         MOVE CA-ERR-PROG-TYPE      TO CA-X-ERR-PROG-TYPE
         EXEC CICS LINK PROGRAM('ISS03C')
                        RESP(CICS-RESP)
                        COMMAREA(CA-X-ERR-COMMAREA)
                        LENGTH(CA-ERR-LENGTH)
                        END-EXEC
         IF  CICS-RESP = DFHRESP(NORMAL)
             NEXT SENTENCE
         ELSE
             EXEC CICS ABEND ABCODE ('XERR')
                             NOHANDLE
                             CANCEL
                             END-EXEC
     ELSE
         IF  CA-ERR-TYPE EQUAL 'A'
             MOVE  CICS-RESP        TO CA-ERR-NUM-SYS
             MOVE  EIBRSRCE         TO CA-ERR-RSRCE
             EXEC CICS LINK PROGRAM('ISS03C')
                            RESP(CICS-RESP)
                            COMMAREA(CA-COMMAREA)
                            LENGTH(CA-ABEND-LENGTH)
                            END-EXEC
             EXEC CICS ABEND ABCODE ('AERR')
                             NOHANDLE
                             CANCEL
                             END-EXEC.
     MOVE 0                         TO CA-X-ERR-NUM
                                       CA-X-ERR-INST-NUM
                                       CA-X-ERR-PFKEY-NUM
                                       CA-ERR-NUM-PRG
                                       CA-INST-NUM
                                       CA-PFKEY-NUM.
 9000-ERR-EXIT.   EXIT.
```

Figure 2.9 Error handling through the invocation of an external program.

```
1000-FIRST-TIME-SEND.
    MOVE +602                         TO CA-LENGTH.
    PERFORM 0900-INITIALIZE-TAGALONG THRU 0900-EXIT.
    MOVE WS-QUEUE-NAME           TO    CA-QUEUE-NAME.
    MOVE WS-KEY-AREA             TO    RMK050-WIP-HDR-KEY.
    MOVE RMK050-WIP-HDR-KEY      TO    CA-RMK050-WIP-HDR-KEY.
    PERFORM 1100-READ-WIP-HDDR         THRU 1100-EXIT.
    IF I-O-NORMAL
       MOVE RECORD-AREA          TO    RMK050, CA-RMK050-REC
       MOVE RMK050-DOCMT-NBR     TO    RMK060-DOCMT-NBR
       PERFORM 1200-STARTBR-WIP-DTL       THRU 1200-EXIT.
    IF I-O-NORMAL
       MOVE 'Y'                  TO    KEY-MATCH-SW
       PERFORM 1300-READ-NEXT-DTL  THRU 1300-EXIT VARYING
               WS-ITEM FROM 1 BY 1 UNTIL KEY-NOT-MATCHED
       PERFORM 1350-ENDBR-WIP-DTL  THRU 1350-EXIT.
    PERFORM 1500-BUILD-MAP             THRU 1500-EXIT.
1000-EXIT.  EXIT.
```

Figure 2.10 Building a temporary (TS) storage for the first time.

```
01  CA-COMMAREA.
*--------------------------------------------------------------*
*- RM STANDARD CICS/VS COMMAREA - LENGTH 375 BYTES.  01/90 -*
*--------------------------------------------------------------*
    05  STANDARD-COMMAREA.
        10  CA-USERID                        PIC X(08).
        10  CA-TRMID                         PIC X(04).
        10  CA-ATTN-KEY                      PIC X(01).
        10  CA-TRNID                         PIC X(04).
        10  CA-USER-AUTH                     PIC X(01).
            88  USER-AUTHORIZED                  VALUE 'Y'.
        10  CA-MENU-PTR                      PIC 9(01).
        10  CA-MENU-STACK.
            15  CA-MENU-PGM
                OCCURS 8 TIMES               PIC X(08).
        10  CA-PGM-PTR                       PIC 9(01).
            88  CA-FROM-MENU                     VALUE 1.
            88  CA-JUMPED-TO                     VALUE 2 THRU 9.
        10  CA-PGM-STACK.
            15  CA-PGM-NAME
                OCCURS 8 TIMES               PIC X(08).
        10  CA-TEMPQ-PTR                     PIC 9(01).
```

Figure 2.11 Layout of the standard communication area (part 1).

nent. Because it is possible to "blank out" the above name field amid a change transaction (just as it is possible not to enter it during an add), both programs must have verification procedures to reflect the potential error.

In this environment, program 1 issues an error message, such as *customer name field missing, please resubmit!* Program 2, on the other hand, will describe the above problem as *one or a number of mandatory fields omitted, please resubmit!* As you can see, the text for an identical error condition was developed by two different programmers. One of the messages is clear and to the point, informing the operator what needs to be done to resolve the problem. The second text is unfortunately confusing and much too generalized. Are you talking about a single error or a number of them? Which one(s) are in error?

In developing centralized error messages, it is quite important to remove any ambiguity from the text and to standardize the contents of such text to always be identical under identical circumstances. This, again, is best done through a central approach.

```
       10  CA-TEMPQ-STACK.
           15  CA-TEMPQ-NAME
               OCCURS 8 TIMES.
               20  CA-TEMPQ-ID.
                   25  CA-TEMPQ-TRMID PIC X(04).
                   25  CA-TEMPQ-TRNID PIC X(04).
               20  CA-TEMPQ-KEY       PIC S9(04) COMP.
               20  CA-TEMPQ-ALPHA-KEY REDEFINES
                   CA-TEMPQ-KEY       PIC X(02).
       10  CA-KEY-AREA                PIC X(40).
       10  CA-MAPSET                  PIC X(08).
       10  CA-MAPNAME                 PIC X(08).
       10  CA-CURSOR-POS              PIC S9(04) COMP.
       10  CA-OPT                     PIC 9(02).
       10  CA-DEST-PGM                PIC X(08).
       10  CA-PF9-SW                  PIC X(01) VALUE 'N'.
           88  PF9-VALID                        VALUE 'Y'.
       10  CA-ERROR-DATA.
           15  CA-ERR-PROGRAM         PIC X(08).
           15  CA-ERR-RSRCE           PIC X(08).
           15  CA-ERR-TYPE            PIC X(01).
       10  CA-ERROR-NUM.
           15  CA-ERR-NUM-SYS         PIC S9(04) COMP.
           15  CA-ERR-NUM-PRG         PIC 9(05).
       10  CA-ERR-PROG-TYPE           PIC X(01).
       10  CA-QUEUE-ID.
           15  CA-QUEUE-TRMID         PIC X(04).
           15  CA-QUEUE-MAPID         PIC X(04).
       10  CA-SP                      PIC 9(01).
       10  CA-MAP-PTR                 PIC S9(04) COMP.
       10  CA-JUMP-IND                PIC X(01).
       10  CA-INST-NUM                PIC S9(04) COMP.
       10  CA-PFKEY-NUM               PIC S9(04) COMP.
       10  SERVICE-PGM-WORKAREA.
           15  FILLER                 PIC X.
               88 CA-OPT-FOUND            VALUE 'Y'.
           15  FILLER                 PIC X(12).
       10  CA-MAP-QUE-CNT             PIC S9(04) COMP.
       10  DOCMT-PROCESSING-COMMAREA.
           15  CA-MODE-SW             PIC X(01).
               88  CA-CREATE-MODE         VALUE 'C'.
               88  CA-LIMITED-CREATE      VALUE 'L'.
               88  CA-UPDATE-MODE         VALUE 'U', 'X'.
               88  CA-LIMITED-UPDATE      VALUE 'X'.
               88  CA-NORMAL-MODE         VALUE 'U', ' '.
               88  CA-SHIP-MODE           VALUE 'S'.
               88  CA-RECEIVE-MODE        VALUE 'R'.
               88  CA-PRINT-MODE          VALUE 'P'.
```

Figure 2.12 Layout of the standard communication area (part 2).

```
               15  CA-DATA-PASSED.
                   20  CA-DOCM-NUMBER        PIC X(07).
                   20  CA-LINE-NUMBER        PIC X(03).
                   20  CA-PART-NUMBER        PIC X(08).
                   20  CA-PART-STATUS        PIC X(01).
               15  CA-RET-CODE               PIC X(01).
                   88  CA-I-REPAIR-ISSUED        VALUE 'I'.
                   88  CA-ITEM-REC-CHGED         VALUE 'M'.
                   88  CA-TRANSFER-ISSUED        VALUE 'T'.
      *-----------------------------*
      *->  STANDARD/COMMAREA/ENDS  <-*
      *-----------------------------*
```

Figure 2.13 Layout of the standard communication area (part 3).

```
*ASM XOPTS(NOPROLOG NOEPILOG)
         GBLC  &PROG          PROGRAM NAME
&PROG    SETC  'ISS06A'
         TITLE '   PROGRAM &PROG - AS OF &SYSDATE, &SYSTIME '
*
*        THIS ASSEMBLER ROUTINE IS THE CICS I/O INTERFACE PGM 'ISS06A'.
*        ISS06A MAY BE USED TO ISOLATE ACCESS TO ANY CICS FILE. TO USE
*        THIS I/O INTERFACE, THE APPLICATION PROGRAM REPLACES CICS I/O
*        OPERATIONS WITH CALLS TO THIS I/O INTERFACE PGM, 'ISS06A'.
*        ISS06A THEN CONVERTS AN APPLICATION PGM'S I/O CALL REQUEST
*        INTO A CICS LINK TO PGM 'ISS07C', AND CONVERTS THE PARAMETER
*        LIST INTO A TEMPORARY STORAGE QUEUE. THE ACTUAL I/O IS DONE
*        BY THE LINKED TO PGM 'ISS07C', WHICH IS WRITTEN IN COBOL.
*
*        THE 1ST STATEMENT TELLS THE TRANSLATOR NOT TO INSERT A
*        DFHEIENT OR DFHEIRET MACRO (I PUT THEM IN MYSELF).  THIS
*        ALLOWS ME TO CHOOSE MY OWN BASEREG (INSTEAD OF 3), AND IT
*        ALLOWS ME TO PASS A RETURN CODE BACK TO THE CALLING PGM
*        (THE DEFAULT IS RC=0). THE CSECT NAME IS PLACED ON THE
*        DFHEIRET MACRO - NO CSECT STATEMENT SHOULD BE CODED.  A
*        DFHEISTG/DFHEIEND PAIR MUST BE INCLUDED FOR DYNAMIC STORAGE,
*        AS SOME TAGS WITHIN THE GENERATED DSECT ARE REFERENCED BY
*        DFHEIENT/DFHEIRET.
         EJECT
R0       EQU   0
PARMS    EQU   1                  POINTER TO PARAMETERS UPON ENTRY
R2       EQU   2
R3       EQU   3
R4       EQU   4
R5       EQU   5
R6       EQU   6                  WORK REGISTER
R7       EQU   7                  WORK REGISTER
R8       EQU   8                  WORK REGISTER
EIBPTR   EQU   9                  WORK REGISTER
R10      EQU   10
R11      EQU   11                 PTR TO EXECUTE INTERFACE BLOCK (EIB)
BASEREG  EQU   12                 BASE REGISTER
R13      EQU   13                 SAVE (DYNAMICALLY ACQUIRED BY CICS)
RET      EQU   14                 RETURN ADDRESS TO CALLING PROGRAM
R15      EQU   15                 RETURN CODE, RETURNED TO CALLING CALLER
LDESC    EQU   30
X40      EQU   X'40'
X80      EQU   X'80'
XF0      EQU   X'F0'
*
&PROG    DFHEIENT CODEREG=BASEREG
         B     MAIN
PROGID   DC    C'&PROG..&SYSDATE..&SYSTIME'
EJECT
```

Figure 2.14 Assembler program for centralized procedures (part 1).

```
MAIN     DS    0H
         LR    R7,PARMS           LOAD ADDRESS TO PARMS PASSED INTO R7.
         MVC   QUEREC(8),0(R7)    MOVE THE PARMS PASSED TO STORAGE.
         L     R8,0(R7)           PUT 1ST PARM IN R8, PTR TO I-O-REQUEST.
         USING IO#REQST,R8        USE R8 TO ADDRESS I-O-REQUEST DSECT.
         LA    R6,1
         STH   R6,IO#RCPTR        PUSH I-O-RETPGM-STACK
         MVC   IO#RCSTK,=CL24' '
         MVC   IO#RCSTK(8),=CL8'ISS06A  '
         TM    ADDR2,X80          WAS A RECORD AREA PASSED BY CALLER ???
         BO    MAIN01             IF YES, CONTINUE PROCESSING REQUEST.
         LA    R6,91              IF NO, THEN STOP WITH RETURN CODE 91.
         ST    R6,IO#RC
         B     RETURN
*
MAIN01   DS    0H
         LA    R6,0               SET IO#RC TO DEFAULT RETURN CODE ZERO,
         ST    R6,IO#RC
         CLI   IO#ACF2M,C'A'    EXAMINE ACF2 MODE.
         BE    GETEIBLK         IF 'A','U','D',OR 'R' CONTINUE, ELSE
         CLI   IO#ACF2M,C'U'    RETURN TO CALLER WITH RETURN CODE 102.
         BE    GETEIBLK
         CLI   IO#ACF2M,C'D'
         BE    GETEIBLK
         CLI   IO#ACF2M,C'R'
         BE    GETEIBLK
         LA    R6,102
         ST    R6,IO#RC
         B     RETURN
*
*        SEQUENCE OF EVENTS
*        ------------------
*          1. DELETE PRIOR TS QUEUE, IF ONE EXISTS.
*          2. CHECK IF ACF2 WILL PERMIT ACCESS OF DSN REQUESTED.
*          4. LOAD CONSTANT TABLE AND RETREIVE FILE LRECL ATTRIBUTES.
*          4. WRITE I-O-REQUEST & REC-AREA ADDR & FILE ATTRIBUTES TO Q.
*          5. LINK TO I/O MODULE.
*          6. DELETE TS QUE AFTER I/O MODULE USAGE.
*          7. RETURN TO CALLING PROGRAM.
*
```

Figure 2.16 Assembler program for centralized procedures (part 2).

```
GETEIBLK DS    0H
         EXEC CICS ADDRESS EIB(DFHEIBR) RESP(RETCODE)
         USING DFHEIBLK,DFHEIBR
*
         CLC   EIBTRNID(2),=C'RM'         IS EIB AVAILABLE ???
         BE    ACF2#CHK                   IF YES, CONTINUE.
         CLC   EIBTRNID(2),=C'RP'         IS EIB AVAILABLE ???
         BE    ACF2#CHK                   IF YES, CONTINUE.
         CLC   EIBTRNID(2),=C'PO'         IS EIB AVAILABLE ???
         BE    ACF2#CHK                   IF YES, CONTINUE.
         CLC   EIBTRNID(2),=C'PS'         IS EIB AVAILABLE ???
         BE    ACF2#CHK                   IF YES, CONTINUE.
         LA    R6,94                      IF NOT, RETURN WITH RETCODE
         ST    R6,IO#RC                   94.
         B     RETURN
*
ACF2#CHK DS    0H                         CALL ACF2
         MVI   UCRSCREQ,UCRSCRIN
         MVC   UCRSCTNM,RSRCTYP
```

Figure 2.16 Assembler program for centralized procedures (part 3).

Figure 2.16 *Continued.*

```
         MVI    UCRSCNME,X'40'
         MVC    UCRSCNME+1(L'UCRSCNME-1),UCRSCNME
         MVC    UCRSCNME(8),IO#FNAME
         MVC    UCRSCAC,IO#ACF2M
         MVI    UCRSCVER,UCRSCVEY
         MVI    UCRSCABD,UCRSCABN
*
         EXEC CICS LINK                                                *
              PROGRAM('ACFAEUCC')                                      *
              COMMAREA(ACFAEUCR)                                       *
              LENGTH(328)                                              *
              RESP(IO#RC)
*
         CLC  IO#RC,DFHRESP(NORMAL)       IF NORMAL CONTINUE
         BNE  RETURN                      OTHERWISE RETURN TO CALLER.
*
         CLI    UCRSCRC,UCRSCRD           EXAMINE ACF2 RETURN CODE
         BNE    GET#TBLE
         MVC    IO#RC,ACF2ERR
         B      RETURN

GET#TBLE DS     0H                        DECIDE FILE TABLE TO LOAD,
         XR     R7,R7                     FIXED OR VARIABLE.
         LH     R7,IO#VRTYP
         LTR    R7,R7
         BZ     LDFIXTBL                  ZERO IS FIXED.
         BC     B'0010',LDVARTBL          POSITIVE IS VARIABLE.
         LA     R6,100                    OTHERWISE, RETURN TO CALLER
         ST     R6,IO#RC                  WITH RETCODE 100.
         B      RETURN
```

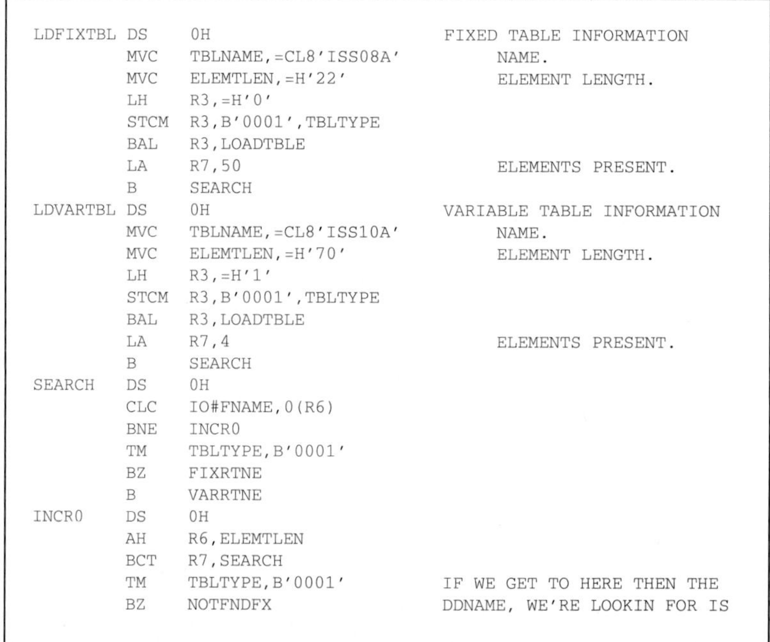

```
LDFIXTBL DS     0H                        FIXED TABLE INFORMATION
         MVC    TBLNAME,=CL8'ISS08A'           NAME.
         MVC    ELEMTLEN,=H'22'                ELEMENT LENGTH.
         LH     R3,=H'0'
         STCM   R3,B'0001',TBLTYPE
         BAL    R3,LOADTBLE
         LA     R7,50                          ELEMENTS PRESENT.
         B      SEARCH
LDVARTBL DS     0H                        VARIABLE TABLE INFORMATION
         MVC    TBLNAME,=CL8'ISS10A'           NAME.
         MVC    ELEMTLEN,=H'70'                ELEMENT LENGTH.
         LH     R3,=H'1'
         STCM   R3,B'0001',TBLTYPE
         BAL    R3,LOADTBLE
         LA     R7,4                           ELEMENTS PRESENT.
         B      SEARCH
SEARCH   DS     0H
         CLC    IO#FNAME,0(R6)
         BNE    INCR0
         TM     TBLTYPE,B'0001'
         BZ     FIXRTNE
         B      VARRTNE
INCR0    DS     0H
         AH     R6,ELEMTLEN
         BCT    R7,SEARCH
         TM     TBLTYPE,B'0001'           IF WE GET TO HERE THEN THE
         BZ     NOTFNDFX                  DDNAME, WE'RE LOOKIN FOR IS
```

Figure 2.17 Assembler program for centralized procedures (part 4).

Figure 2.17 *Continued.*

```
         LA     R4,103                        NOT FOUND IN THE TABLE THAT
         ST     R4,IO#RC                      WAS SEARCHED. IDENTIFY TABLE
         B      RETURN                        AND END WITH APPROPRIATE
NOTFNDFX DS     0H                            RETURN CODE.
         LA     R4,95
         ST     R4,IO#RC
         B      RETURN
*
FIXRTNE  DS     0H
         MVC    IO$PROGM,8(R6)
         MVC    IO#RJLEN,16(R6)
         MVC    IO#RJFLE,18(R6)
         MVC    IO#RJTYP,20(R6)
         B      TRNSCNTL
*
VARRTNE  DS     0H
         MVC    IO$PROGM,8(R6)
         ST     R6,SAVE6
         XR     R7,R7
         LH     R7,IO#VRTYP
         BCTR   R7,R0
         MH     R7,=H'2'
```

```
         LA     R6,16(R7,R6)
         MVC    IO#RJLEN,0(R6)
         L      R6,SAVE6
         LA     R7,25
         MH     R7,=H'2'
         LA     R6,16(R7,R6)
         MVC    IO#RJFLE,0(R6)
         MVC    IO#RJTYP,2(R6)
         B      TRNSCNTL
*
LOADTBLE DS    0H
         ST    R3,SAVE3
         EXEC CICS LOAD PROGRAM(TBLNAME)                              *
                HOLD                                                  *
                SET(R6)                                               *
                RESP(IO#RC)
         L      R3,IO#RC
         LTR    R3,R3
         BZ     NORMAL
         B      RETURN
*
NORMAL   DS     0H
         L      R3,SAVE3
         BR     R3
*
TRNSCNTL DS    0H
         EXEC CICS                                                    *
                LINK   PROGRAM(IO$PROGM)                              *
                       COMMAREA(QUEREC)                               *
                       LENGTH(8)                                      *
                       RESP(RETCODE)
*
         CLC   RETCODE,DFHRESP(NORMAL)
         BE    SETRCPGM
         MVC   IO#RC,RETCODE
         B     RETURN
```

Figure 2.18 Assembler program for centralized procedures (part 5).

Figure 2.18 *Continued.*

```
*
SETRCPGM DS     0H
         LA     R6,0
         C      R6,IO#RC             DID ISS07C WORK
         BE     RC000
         B      RETURN
RC000    DS     0H
         LA     R6,0
         STH    R6,IO#RCPTR
         MVC    IO#RCSTK(8),=CL8' '
RETURN   DS     0H                  RETURN TO CALLING PROGRAM
         SLR    R15,R15
         DFHEIRET RCREG=15
```

```
*
ACF2ERR  DC     F'101'
RSRCTYP  DC     C'FILE      '
*
*
IO#REQST DSECT
IO#RC    DS     F
IO#RCPTR DS     H
IO#RCSTK DS     CL24
IO#FNAME DS     CL08
IO#FKEY  DS     CL40
IO#COMND DS     CL08
IO#OPERA DS     CL05
IO#KEYLN DS     XL04
IO#GMODE DS     CL08
IO#UMODE DS     CL08
IO#UTYPE DS     CL01
IO#ACF2M DS     CL01
IO#VRTYP DS     H
IO#RJLEN DS     H
IO#RJFLE DS     H
IO#RJTYP DS     CL02
         DFHEISTG
         ACFAEUCR
PTR      DS     F
*
QUEREC   DS     0CL08
ADDR1    DS     A
ADDR2    DS     A
*
TBLNAME  DS     CL8
IO$PROGM DS     CL8
ELEMTLEN DS     H
RETCODE  DS     F
SAVE6    DS     F
SAVE3    DS     F
TBLTYPE  DS     XL1
*
QUEUEID  DS     0CL8
TRMID    DS     CL4
QNAME    DS     CL4
IORTNE   DS     CL8
         DFHEIEND
         END
```

Figure 2.19 Assembler program for centralized procedures (part 6).

```
1400-WRITE-TEMP-QUE.
    EXEC CICS
        WRITEQ TS QUEUE (WS-QUEUE-NAME) FROM (WS-QUEUE-AREA)
              LENGTH (WS-QUE-LENGTH)
                ITEM (ITEM-PTR)
                MAIN
                RESP (CICS-RESP)
    END-EXEC.
    IF  CICS-RESP = DFHRESP (NORMAL)
        NEXT SENTENCE
    ELSE
        MOVE 00315  TO CA-ERR-NUM-PRG
        MOVE 'A'    TO CA-ERR-TYPE.
1400-EXIT.  EXIT.
```

Figure 2.20 Invoking a source program, example 1.

```
7230-UPDATE-CNTL-REC.
    MOVE RMK050                TO RECORD-AREA.
    MOVE RMK050-WIP-HDR-KEY    TO I-O-FILEKEY.
    MOVE I-O-REWRITE           TO I-O-COMMAND.
    MOVE I-O-EQUAL             TO I-O-OPERATOR.
    MOVE ZEROES                TO I-O-GENERIC-KEYLEN
                                  I-O-RETCODE.
    MOVE SPACES                TO I-O-GENERIC.
    MOVE I-O-UPDATE-MODE       TO I-O-UPDATE.
    MOVE 0                     TO I-O-VREC-TYPE.
    MOVE 'C'                   TO I-O-UPD-TYPE.
    MOVE I-O-ACF2-UPDATE       TO I-O-ACF2-INTENT.
    MOVE RM-WIP-HEADER         TO I-O-FILENAME.
    MOVE WS-PROG-NAME          TO I-O-JRNL-WORKPGM.
    PERFORM 9280-CALL-I-O-MODULE THRU 9280-I-O-EXIT.
    IF  I-O-NORMAL
        GO TO 7230-EXIT.
    MOVE 'A'          TO CA-ERR-TYPE.
    MOVE I-O-RETCODE  TO CICS-RESP.
    MOVE I-O-FILENAME TO EIBRSRCE.
    MOVE 000145       TO CA-ERR-NUM-PRG.
```

Figure 2.21 Invoking a source program, example 2.

Chapter

3

Designing and Coding Advanced Tutorial Systems in Command-Level CICS

3.1 An Overview of CICS-Driven Tutorial Subsystems

This chapter will describe and highlight some of the advanced concepts in designing a help system that can be incorporated into a specific application to assist the user in resolving a problem. Help systems are built with two primary objectives in mind. The first is to find a solution to a problem by allowing you quick access to tables, values, edit rules, and a variety of things that would otherwise be difficult to memorize. A second objective is purely educational. If you are new on the job, the first piece of document you should review, as far as operational peculiarities are concerned, should be the on-line documentation of a system. This, incidentally, is synonymous with the chapter 3 topic of tutorial services. On-line documentation is designed not only to highlight a system through pages and pages of write-ups on a subject matter, but also to provide you with a working prototype.

Tutorial systems are expert systems. They should be built by someone knowledgeable in the field—by an expert rather than by a data-processing professional. That is, of course, unless the tutorial is geared to data processing. This means that tutorials should not only be built but also maintained, periodically revised, and enhanced by experts. The only role data processing should have in this is to provide the technology (the command-level source programs) that will allow the user to do all he needs to with relative ease.

This chapter is going to provide you with several aspects of a help system. First, it will show you in detail how such systems are designed and programmed. Second, it will show you how, once in place, these tutorials can be invoked by the user, and how he can return to the original panel from which assistance was originally requested.

3.2 Background for Creating Tutorial Panels

In the following frames, I would like to give you an overview of what this tutorial system is all about from the user's perspective, prior to providing you with a comprehensive technical coverage, i.e., the source code for the add/change and delete programs.

Figure 3.1 shows a Main Menu, which allows you to invoke the Help Maintenance module for maintenance of the text. This is accomplished by selecting option 6 and then pressing the Enter key.

To attain help for operational assistance, you can simply invoke it through one of the application panels by pressing PF3. This is entirely different from help maintenance, which I will describe to you in a minute.

I have selected task 01 (Invoice Header procedures) and a maintenance code of C, denoting a change. The change mechanism is actually responsible for adding new lines, as well as modifying existing lines of text, and it is shown in Figure 3.2.

If there is no tutorial available for a module, such as the prefix table maintenance (task 09 with a maintenance code of C), a blank screen containing 16 lines will appear. This is the topic of Figure 3.3. These lines simply mean that you can enter a maximum of 16 lines of interactive text and, while moving on to the second page, the first one will automatically be updated by the system.

With regard to the selection shown in Figure 3.2, note that the text was already developed by the user. One such panel is shown in Figure 3.4. Let's look at this panel briefly. Next to each line number there might be a character, such as B or W. These characters denote a specific color scheme for a particular line. In line one, for example, the number is followed by a blank and then by the character B. This character denotes the color blue (low intensification, protected mode), meaning that every line with a B prefix will be displayed in blue. Likewise, W stands for text appearing in white (high intensification, protected mode). If you want to see how each line is "colorized" after specifying the line, simply press PF3.

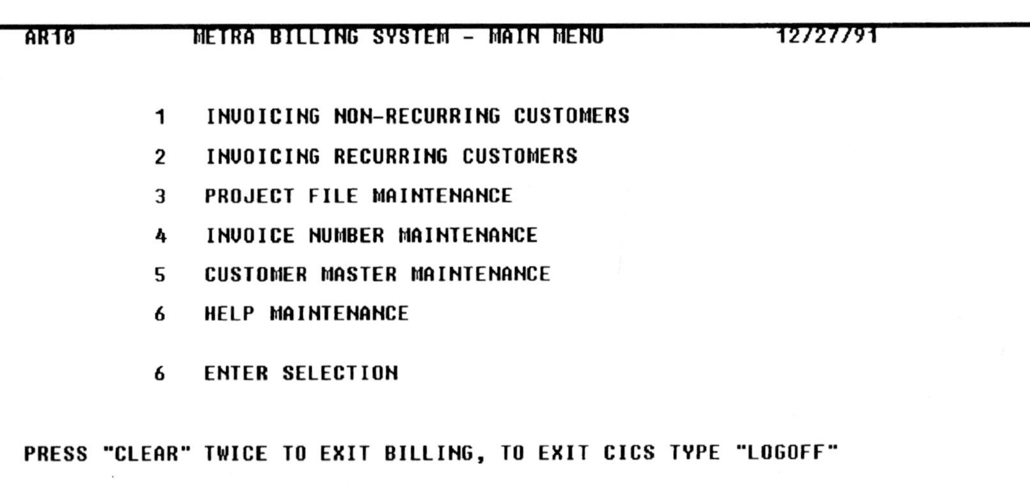

Figure 3.1 Selecting help procedures for modifying or creating text.

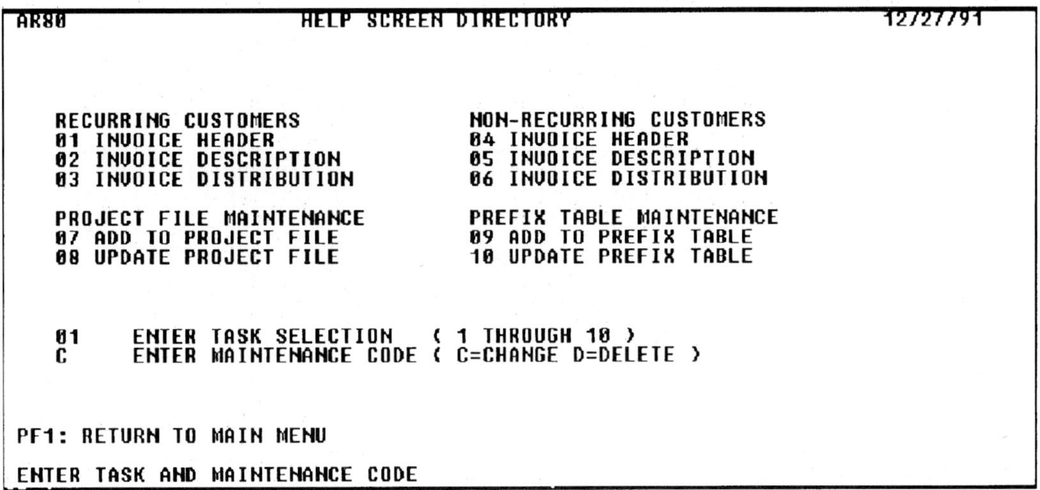

```
AR80                 HELP SCREEN DIRECTORY                        12/27/91

   RECURRING CUSTOMERS                 NON-RECURRING CUSTOMERS
   01 INVOICE HEADER                   04 INVOICE HEADER
   02 INVOICE DESCRIPTION              05 INVOICE DESCRIPTION
   03 INVOICE DISTRIBUTION             06 INVOICE DISTRIBUTION

   PROJECT FILE MAINTENANCE            PREFIX TABLE MAINTENANCE
   07 ADD TO PROJECT FILE              09 ADD TO PREFIX TABLE
   08 UPDATE PROJECT FILE              10 UPDATE PREFIX TABLE

   01     ENTER TASK SELECTION    ( 1 THROUGH 10 )
   C      ENTER MAINTENANCE CODE  ( C=CHANGE D=DELETE )

PF1: RETURN TO MAIN MENU

ENTER TASK AND MAINTENANCE CODE
```

Figure 3.2 A help screen directory with which to select a particular procedure.

```
  AR81           DEVELOP YOUR OWN HELP SCREEN(S)            12/30/91

01
02
03
04
05
06
07
08
09
10
11
12
13
14
15
16
 PF1: RETURN TO TUTORIAL MENU        PF3: TO VIEW UPDATE
 PF7: UPDATE / NEXT PAGE             PF8: PREVIOUS PAGE
```

Figure 3.3 A Tutorial Panel for accepting text for the first time.

Note that lines that do not contain a specific color attribute character always default to the previous scheme. For example, if line 01 was defined as a blue line, then line 02 will also be displayed in the identical color unless there is a redefinition of that color, such as the one shown in line 10 (white).

Without the availability of extended attribute bytes, this system displays tutorial text using a basic four-color scheme: blue (B), white (W), green (G), and red (R). Because only the view option provides you with the display of the actual color, data and text cannot be entered when in view mode. This means that when you have completed viewing the panel you have to reset each attribute byte in your program to the initial low intensity (unprotected kind), which results in green.

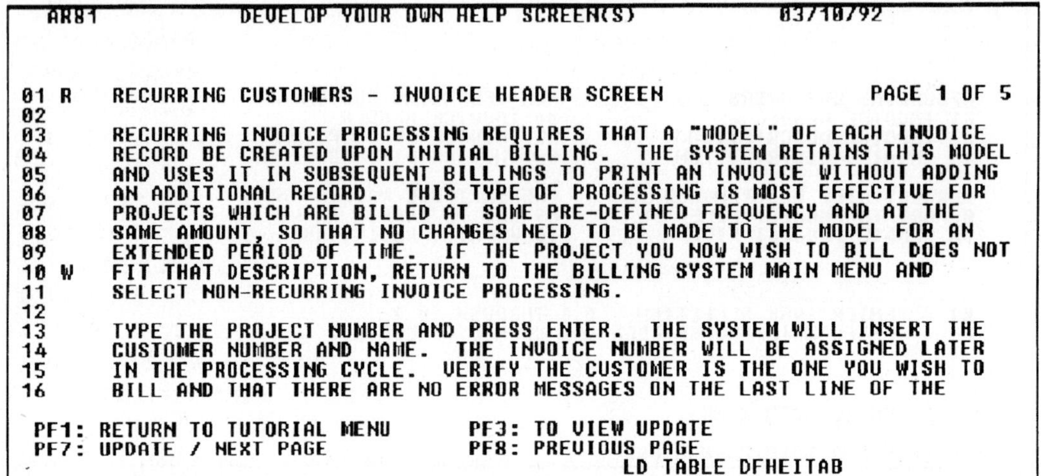

```
  AR01              DEVELOP YOUR OWN HELP SCREEN(S)              03/10/92

01 R    RECURRING CUSTOMERS - INVOICE HEADER SCREEN                 PAGE 1 OF 5
02
03      RECURRING INVOICE PROCESSING REQUIRES THAT A "MODEL" OF EACH INVOICE
04      RECORD BE CREATED UPON INITIAL BILLING.  THE SYSTEM RETAINS THIS MODEL
05      AND USES IT IN SUBSEQUENT BILLINGS TO PRINT AN INVOICE WITHOUT ADDING
06      AN ADDITIONAL RECORD.  THIS TYPE OF PROCESSING IS MOST EFFECTIVE FOR
07      PROJECTS WHICH ARE BILLED AT SOME PRE-DEFINED FREQUENCY AND AT THE
08      SAME AMOUNT, SO THAT NO CHANGES NEED TO BE MADE TO THE MODEL FOR AN
09      EXTENDED PERIOD OF TIME.  IF THE PROJECT YOU NOW WISH TO BILL DOES NOT
10 W    FIT THAT DESCRIPTION, RETURN TO THE BILLING SYSTEM MAIN MENU AND
11      SELECT NON-RECURRING INVOICE PROCESSING.
12
13      TYPE THE PROJECT NUMBER AND PRESS ENTER.  THE SYSTEM WILL INSERT THE
14      CUSTOMER NUMBER AND NAME.  THE INVOICE NUMBER WILL BE ASSIGNED LATER
15      IN THE PROCESSING CYCLE.  VERIFY THE CUSTOMER IS THE ONE YOU WISH TO
16      BILL AND THAT THERE ARE NO ERROR MESSAGES ON THE LAST LINE OF THE

 PF1: RETURN TO TUTORIAL MENU       PF3: TO VIEW UPDATE
 PF7: UPDATE / NEXT PAGE            PF8: PREVIOUS PAGE
                                              LD TABLE DFHEITAB
```

Figure 3.4 Entering narratives into the tutorial system.

In pressing PF7, I have updated the previously displayed page and invoked the second page of Tutorial Panel, which pertains to the invoice header screen. This panel is shown in Figure 3.5.

When using the system's delete features, note that this operation is designed to perform a number of objectives. To understand what I am talking about, take a look at Figure 3.6, which is a tutorial text invoked in delete mode. If you were to press PF9, it would allow you to delete a particular page and all additional (dependent) panels that follow. For example, if you had six pages of tutorial data and decided to delete page number 3, page numbers 4 through 6 would also be deleted automatically. Likewise, by deleting page number 2, all subsequent occurrences would be erased.

Contrary to this piecemeal delete, the system relies on a very powerful generic delete that allows you to erase the entire text, regardless of the number of pages, with the single action of PF3. (Actually, the same effect can be achieved by using PF9 on the first page.)

3.3 How to Use Tutorial Reference During an Application Run

So far, we have looked at the help system from the perspective of the expert who will be responsible for creating procedural text. It is probably safe to say that most employees will not have access to these components; in fact, the only thing they will be allowed to do is to invoke and page through the available procedures without having to worry about maintaining the text. This involves a single step depicted in the two frames shown in Figures 3.7 and 3.8.

The first frame, Figure 3.7, is an application screen. Suppose the cursor is on the invoice number and the operator has a question relative to the data field. Pressing PF3 will immediately trigger the first page of the corresponding tutorial, shown in Figure 3.8.

If you take a close look at this screen, you will note that there are no line numbers or color attributes corresponding to the lines. This is available only in maintenance mode. Also, by pressing the Enter key on the tutorial screen (regardless of the specific page you happened to be on at the time), the system will take you back to the initial application screen with the cursor positioned on the invoice number, which happens to be in its prior location.

Figure 3.9 provides you with an overview of the tutorial system. The upper half of the chart tells you how to build, modify, and subsequently delete Tutorial Panels in a generic fashion. Each tutorial line of text is treated by the programmer as an inde-

```
  AR81            DEVELOP YOUR OWN HELP SCREEN(S)                03/10/92


17 B    RECURRING CUSTOMERS - INVOICE HEADER SCREEN                    PAGE 2 OF 5
18
19 W    SCREEN.  CONTINUE BY TYPING THE REMAINING REQUESTED INFORMATION.
20      THE INVOICE AMOUNT MUST BE ENTERED, INCLUDING THE DECIMAL POINT AND
21      CENTS.  TYPE THE ACCOUNTING PERIOD IN THE "ACCOUNTING MM/YY"FIELD,
22      IN ALL NUMERICS, WITH NO SLASH OR DASH (I.E. 1090 FOR OCTOBER, 1990).
23      THE PERIOD DESCRIPTION SHOULD BE SPELLED OUT (SEPTEMBER, 1990).
24
25 B    FOLLOWING IS A LIST OF PROJECT NUMBERS CREATED EXCLUSIVELY FOR USE IN
26      THIS SYSTEM:
27      SELECT NON-RECURRING INVOICE PROCESSING.
28 W    LICENSE AGREEMENTS:
29      TYPE THE PROJECT NUMBER AND PRESS ENTER.  THE SYSTEM WILL INSERT THE
30 B    121C86      AMERICAN CABLE SYSTEMS            001-021-1286
31      501C84      AT&T                              005-001-1284
32      850818      AT&T                              85-08-18FP

 PF1: RETURN TO TUTORIAL MENU      PF3: TO VIEW UPDATE
 PF7: UPDATE / NEXT PAGE           PF8: PREVIOUS PAGE
                                             LD TABLE DFHEITAB
```

Figure 3.5 Entering explanation on a second panel.

```
  AR82            DELETE YOUR OWN TUTORIALS                      12/30/91


01      RECURRING CUSTOMERS - INVOICE HEADER SCREEN                    PAGE 1 OF 5
02
03      RECURRING INVOICE PROCESSING REQUIRES THAT A "MODEL" OF EACH INVOICE
04      RECORD BE CREATED UPON INITIAL BILLING.  THE SYSTEM RETAINS THIS MODEL
05      AND USES IT IN SUBSEQUENT BILLINGS TO PRINT AN INVOICE WITHOUT ADDING
06      AN ADDITIONAL RECORD.  THIS TYPE OF PROCESSING IS MOST EFFECTIVE FOR
07      PROJECTS WHICH ARE BILLED AT SOME PRE-DEFINED FREQUENCY AND AT THE
08      SAME AMOUNT, SO THAT NO CHANGES NEED TO BE MADE TO THE MODEL FOR AN
09      EXTENDED PERIOD OF TIME.  IF THE PROJECT YOU NOW WISH TO BILL DOES NOT
10      FIT THAT DESCRIPTION, RETURN TO THE BILLING SYSTEM MAIN MENU AND
11      SELECT NON-RECURRING INVOICE PROCESSING.
12
13      TYPE THE PROJECT NUMBER AND PRESS ENTER.  THE SYSTEM WILL INSERT THE
14      CUSTOMER NUMBER AND NAME.  THE INVOICE NUMBER WILL BE ASSIGNED LATER
15      IN THE PROCESSING CYCLE.  VERIFY THE CUSTOMER IS THE ONE YOU WISH TO
16      BILL AND THAT THERE ARE NO ERROR MESSAGES ON THE LAST LINE OF THE

 PF1: RETURN TO TUTORIAL MENU      PF3 DELETE RECORDS
 PF7: NEXT PAGE                    PF8: PREVIOUS PAGE   PF9: DELETE PAGE
```

Figure 3.6 Tutorial text displayed in delete mode.

```
AR24     INVOICE HEADER SCREEN FOR NON-RECURRING BILLINGS                 12/27/91


 PROJECT NO  : C71065
 CREDIT MEMO.       (Y, N)      ORIGINAL INV# :
 CUSTOMER NO: 0002              CUSTOMER NAME  : METROPOLITAN RAIL (METRA)
 INVOICE NO  : A 11666          INVOICE AMOUNT: 00002491.41
 ACCOUNTING MM/YY: 1191         BILLING DATE (MMDDYY) 122391
 PERIOD DESCRIPT.: NOVEMBER, 1991
 _________________________ SPECIAL INSTRUCTIONS _________________________


 ________________________________________________________________________


   PF1: RETURN TO MENU          PF2: INVOICE DESCRIPTION PANEL
   PF3: HELP
   TYPE IN THE CHANGES, HIT PF2 WHEN RECORD COMPLETE
```

Figure 3.7 An application screen prior to the invocation of a help function.

```
AR24              BILLING SYSTEM TUTORIAL                        12/27/91


    NON-RECURRING CUSTOMERS - INVOICE HEADER SCREEN              PAGE 1 OF 5

    TYPE IN THE PROJECT NUMBER AND PRESS ENTER.  THE CUSTOMER NUMBER AND
    NAME AND THE INVOICE NUMBER SHOULD AUTOMATICALLY APPEAR...
    OR... A MESSAGE MAY APPEAR AT THE BOTTOM OF THE SCREEN.
    IF THE PROJECT IS NOT ON FILE, ADVISE SECTION CHIEF OR DESIGNEE.  ANY
    OTHER MESSAGE SHOULD BE BROUGHT TO THE ATTENTION OF THE SECTION CHIEF.

    ENTER THE INVOICE AMOUNT, INCLUDING THE DECIMAL POINT AND CENTS.  TAB
    TO THE "ACCOUNTING MM/YY" FIELD AND ENTER THE GENERAL ACCOUNTING
    PERIOD IN WHICH THE INVOICE SHOULD BE RECORDED.  THE PERIOD SHOULD BE
    ENTERED IN NUMERICS ONLY, WITH NO SLASH OR DASH (IE. 1090 FOR OCTOBER,
    1990).  TAB PAST THE BILLING DATE FIELD; THE SYSTEM WILL AUTOMATICALLY
    INSERT THE CURRENT DATE WHEN INVOICES ARE PRINTED.  ENTER THE PERIOD
    COVERED BY THE BILL AS THE PERIOD DESCRIPTION WITH THE MONTH(S)
    SPELLED OUT.  SAVE THE RECORD BY PRESSING THE PF2 KEY.


 ENTER KEY: RETURN TO TASK     PF7: NEXT PAGE PF8: PREVIOUS PAGE
```

Figure 3.8 Tutorial text, as seen by the user.

pendent record. The concatenated key of these records starts in column 1 and encompasses a length of 6 bytes. The first four positions of this key is the transaction identifier of the add/change program. The sequence number (columns 5 through 6) contains a reference number for every line, ranging from 01 to 99. (This means that the maximum number of lines you can produce through this program is limited to 6 full pages of display per subsystem; or 6 pages times 16 lines of text per page, equaling 96 lines, plus three additional lines on the seventh page.)

Note that neither the trans I.D. nor the sequence numbers need to be entered by the operator; rather, they are system-generated. What has to be entered throughout are the color attributes of the record (the mechanics of this were already explained).

The rest of the record layout is user-developed (and maintained), including the text or a single line of explanation.

As you can see, Figure 3.9 is subdivided into two parts. The upper half of the diagram refers to the actual development of the help file. Maintenance (and therefore maintenance access to this file) should be available only to those physically involved

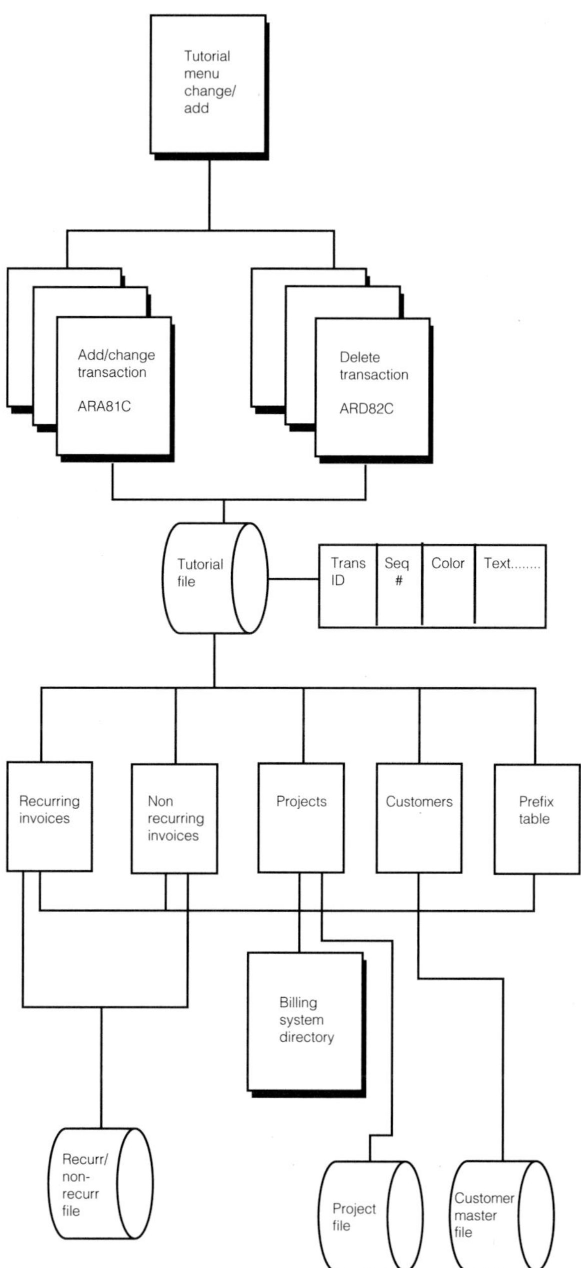

Figure 3.9 Help mechanism maintenance (top) and display access (bottom).

in the upkeep of the data set. The bottom half of the diagram, on the other hand, refers to a broad access available to the user community. All you need to do to invoke the help module (in display mode) is to depress PF3. This will trigger the source logic. Note that the current position of the cursor is accomplished by moving EIBC-POSN to a field previously defined, so the program will "remember" it upon returning (see Figure 3.10).

3.4 The Change/Add (ARA81C) and Delete (ARD82C) Tutorial Modules and Source Code

In one of my earlier publications, *Command-Level CICS Programming*, I present a tutorial environment. This was originally geared towards intermediate to advanced programmers—advanced in an academic sense, for example, students with a great deal of CICS classroom experience. This does not include industrial users for whom I decided to thoroughly enhance (or rework) the basic model in terms of source code efficiency, including two substantially better and more streamlined programs. Both modules, ARA81C (change) and ARD82C (delete), use a technique that is driven by a browse transaction. They are shown in Figures 3.11 and 3.12.

```
 PVBROWSE NTRXT.TEST.PANLIB(ARA21C) -----------------  CHARS '0220-PF3-HELP' FO
 COMMAND ===>                                                   SCROLL ===> PAGE

        0220-PF3-HELP.
            PERFORM 0610-WRITE-LINE.
            MOVE EIBCPOSN TO CURSOR-POSITION.
            EXEC CICS
                 WRITE DATASET('ARA21C')
                            FROM(INVOICE-RECORD)
                          RIDFLD(INV-KEY)
            END-EXEC.
            EXEC CICS
                XCTL  PROGRAM('ARB83C')
                      COMMAREA(COMM-AREA)
                      LENGTH(47)
            END-EXEC.

        0230-INVALID-KEY.
            MOVE 'INVALID KEY USED' TO ERMSGO.
            MOVE -1 TO PROJECTL.
            GO TO 0910-SEND-MAP-DATAONLY.

        0400-INVALID-PROJ-NUM.
            MOVE -1 TO PROJECTL.
```

Figure 3.10 Program logic to establish the current location of the cursor.

```
1PP 5740-CB1 RELEASE 2.4                                 IBM OS/VS COBOL   J
               IDENTIFICATION DIVISION.
               PROGRAM-ID.      ARA81C.
               AUTHOR.          LARRY CHEEKS.
               DATE-WRITTEN.    JUNE 14 1990.
               DATE-COMPILED. JAN  2,1992.
```

Figure 3.11 Change source program.

Figure 3.11 *Continued.*

```
       ENVIRONMENT DIVISION.
       DATA DIVISION.
       WORKING-STORAGE SECTION.
       01  COMM-AREA.
           05  FILLER                      PIC X.
           05  TASK-TRANS                  PIC X(4)   VALUE SP
           05  REC-KEY.
               10  HELP-TRANS              PIC X(4)   VALUE SP
               10  HELP-SEQ                PIC X(2).
           05  FIRST-REC-KEY.
               10  F-HELP-TRANS            PIC X(4)   VALUE SP
               10  F-HELP-SEQ              PIC X(2).
           05  LAST-REC-KEY.
               10  L-HELP-TRANS            PIC X(4)   VALUE SP
               10  L-HELP-SEQ              PIC X(2).
           05  SAVE-REC-KEY.
               10  S-HELP-TRANS            PIC X(4)   VALUE SP
               10  S-HELP-SEQ              PIC X(2).
           05  RECORD-UPDATED-SW           PIC X      VALUE 'N
               88  RECORD-UPDATED                     VALUE 'Y
           05  ATTRIB-CHANGED-SW           PIC X      VALUE 'N
               88  ATTRIB-CHANGED                     VALUE 'Y
           05  PAGE-NUM                    PIC 9(2).
           05  LINE-NUM                    PIC 9(2).
           05  LINE-NUMX REDEFINES LINE-NUM PIC X(2).

       01  TABLE-SUBS                      COMP SYNC.
           05  SUB                         PIC S9(4)    VALUE
           05  SUB2                        PIC S9(4)    VALUE

       01  CONDITION-SWITCHES.
           05  LAST-HELP-REC-SW            PIC X        VALUE
               88  LAST-HELP-REC                        VALUE
           05  COLOR-FOUND-SW              PIC X        VALUE
               88  COLOR-FOUND                          VALUE

      *------------------*  ATTRIBUTE-BYTES  *-----------------
       01  ATTRBYTE.
           05  RED                         PIC X   VALUE 'I',
           05  WHITE                       PIC X   VALUE 'Z'.
           05  BLUE                        PIC X   VALUE '/'.
           05  GREEN                       PIC X   VALUE 'A'.
           05  UNPROT-ALPHA                PIC X   VALUE ' '.
           05  UNPROT-ALPHA-MDT            PIC X   VALUE 'A'.
           05  UNPROT-ALPHA-BRT            PIC X   VALUE 'H'.
           05  UNPROT-ALPHA-BRT-MDT        PIC X   VALUE 'I'.
           05  UNPROT-NUM                  PIC X   VALUE '&'.
           05  UNPROT-NUM-MDT              PIC X   VALUE 'J'.
           05  UNPROT-NUM-BRT              PIC X   VALUE 'Q'.
           05  PROT                        PIC X   VALUE '-'.
           05  PROT-MDT                    PIC X   VALUE '/'.
           05  PROT-BRT                    PIC X   VALUE 'Y'.
           05  ASKIP                       PIC X   VALUE '0'.

      *---------------* HELP THE TUTORIAL RECORD *------------
       01  HELP-RECORD.
           05  HELP-KEY.
               10  H-REC-TRANS             PIC X(4).
               10  H-REC-SEQ               PIC X(2).
           05  H-LINE-COLOR                PIC X.
           05  H-REC-TEXT                  PIC X(70).
           05  FILLER                      PIC X(3).
```

Figure 3.11 *Continued.*

```
      *-------------* PROGRAMMER DEFINED SYMBOLIC MAP *--------
       01  HELPMAP.
           05  FILLER                           PIC X(12).
           05  IM-L-TRAN                        PIC S9(4)    COMP.
           05  IM-A-TRAN                        PIC X.
           05  IM-D-TRAN                        PIC X(4).
           05  IM-L-HDR                         PIC S9(4)    COMP.
           05  IM-A-HDR                         PIC X.
           05  IM-D-HDR                         PIC X(32).
           05  IM-L-DATE                        PIC S9(4)    COMP.
           05  IM-A-DATE                        PIC X.
           05  IM-D-DATE                        PIC X(8).
           05  IM-D-TEXT-LINES                  OCCURS 16.
               10  IM-L-SEQ                     PIC S9(4)    COMP.
               10  IM-A-SEQ                     PIC X.
               10  IM-D-SEQ                     PIC X(2).
               10  IM-L-COLOR                   PIC S9(4)    COMP.
               10  IM-A-COLOR                   PIC X.
               10  IM-D-COLOR                   PIC X(1).
               10  IM-L-TEXT                    PIC S9(4)    COMP.
               10  IM-A-TEXT                    PIC X.
               10  IM-D-TEXT                    PIC X(70).
           05  IM-L-PFMSG                       PIC S9(4)    COMP.
           05  IM-A-PFMSG                       PIC X.
           05  IM-D-PFMSG                       PIC X(19).
           05  IM-L-PFMSG2                      PIC S9(4)    COMP.
           05  IM-A-PFMSG2                      PIC X.
           05  IM-D-PFMSG2                      PIC X(28).
           05  IM-L-PFMSG3                      PIC S9(4)    COMP.
           05  IM-A-PFMSG3                      PIC X.
           05  IM-D-PFMSG3                      PIC X(17).
           05  IM-L-ERMSG                       PIC S9(4)    COMP.
           05  IM-A-ERMSG                       PIC X.
           05  IM-D-ERMSG                       PIC X(60).

       COPY DFHAID.
       01     DFHAID.
         02   DFHNULL    PIC   X   VALUE IS ' '.
         02   DFHENTER   PIC   X   VALUE IS QUOTE.
         02   DFHCLEAR   PIC   X   VALUE IS '_'.
         02   DFHCLRP    PIC   X   VALUE IS ''.
         02   DFHPEN     PIC   X   VALUE IS '='.
         02   DFHOPID    PIC   X   VALUE IS 'W'.
         02   DFHMSRE    PIC   X   VALUE IS 'X'.
         02   DFHSTRF    PIC   X   VALUE IS 'h'.
         02   DFHTRIG    PIC   X   VALUE IS '"'.
         02   DFHPA1     PIC   X   VALUE IS '%'.
         02   DFHPA2     PIC   X   VALUE IS '>'.
         02   DFHPA3     PIC   X   VALUE IS ','.
         02   DFHPF1     PIC   X   VALUE IS '1'.
         02   DFHPF2     PIC   X   VALUE IS '2'.
         02   DFHPF3     PIC   X   VALUE IS '3'.
         02   DFHPF4     PIC   X   VALUE IS '4'.
         02   DFHPF5     PIC   X   VALUE IS '5'.
         02   DFHPF6     PIC   X   VALUE IS '6'.
         02   DFHPF7     PIC   X   VALUE IS '7'.
         02   DFHPF8     PIC   X   VALUE IS '8'.
         02   DFHPF9     PIC   X   VALUE IS '9'.
         02   DFHPF10    PIC   X   VALUE IS ':'.
         02   DFHPF11    PIC   X   VALUE IS '#'.
         02   DFHPF12    PIC   X   VALUE IS '@'.
         02   DFHPF13    PIC   X   VALUE IS 'A'.
```

Figure 3.11 *Continued.*

```
           02  DFHPF14    PIC  X  VALUE IS 'B'.
           02  DFHPF15    PIC  X  VALUE IS 'C'.
           02  DFHPF16    PIC  X  VALUE IS 'D'.
           02  DFHPF17    PIC  X  VALUE IS 'E'.
           02  DFHPF18    PIC  X  VALUE IS 'F'.
           02  DFHPF19    PIC  X  VALUE IS 'G'.
           02  DFHPF20    PIC  X  VALUE IS 'H'.
           02  DFHPF21    PIC  X  VALUE IS 'I'.
           02  DFHPF22    PIC  X  VALUE IS ''.
           02  DFHPF23    PIC  X  VALUE IS '.'.
           02  DFHPF24    PIC  X  VALUE IS '<'.

       01  DFHLDVER PIC X(22) VALUE 'LD TABLE DFHEITAB 210.'.
       01  DFHEIDO PICTURE S9(7) COMPUTATIONAL-3 VALUE ZERO.
       01  DFHEIBO PICTURE S9(4) COMPUTATIONAL VALUE ZERO.
       01  DFHEICB  PICTURE X(8) VALUE IS '        '.

       01   DFHEIV16   COMP PIC S9(8).
       01   DFHB0041   COMP PIC S9(8).
       01   DFHB0042   COMP PIC S9(8).
       01   DFHB0043   COMP PIC S9(8).
       01   DFHB0044   COMP PIC S9(8).
       01   DFHB0045   COMP PIC S9(8).
       01   DFHB0046   COMP PIC S9(8).
       01   DFHB0047   COMP PIC S9(8).
       01   DFHB0048   COMP PIC S9(8).
       01   DFHEIV11   COMP PIC S9(4).
       01   DFHEIV12   COMP PIC S9(4).
       01   DFHEIV13   COMP PIC S9(4).
       01   DFHEIV14   COMP PIC S9(4).
       01   DFHEIV15   COMP PIC S9(4).
       01   DFHB0025   COMP PIC S9(4).
       01   DFHEIV5    PIC X(4).
       01   DFHEIV6    PIC X(4).
       01   DFHEIV17   PIC X(4).
       01   DFHEIV18   PIC X(4).
       01   DFHEIV19   PIC X(4).
       01   DFHEIV1    PIC X(8).
       01   DFHEIV2    PIC X(8).
       01   DFHEIV3    PIC X(8).
       01   DFHEIV20   PIC X(8).
       01   DFHC0084   PIC X(8).
       01   DFHC0085   PIC X(8).
       01   DFHC0320   PIC X(32).
       01   DFHEIV7    PIC X(2).
       01   DFHEIV8    PIC X(2).
       01   DFHC0022   PIC X(2).
       01   DFHC0023   PIC X(2).
       01   DFHEIV10   PIC S9(7) COMP-3.
       01   DFHEIV9    PIC X(1).
       01   DFHC0011   PIC X(1).
       01   DFHEIV4    PIC X(6).
       01   DFHC0070   PIC X(7).
       01   DFHC0071   PIC X(7).
       01   DFHC0440   PIC X(44).
       01   DFHDUMMY COMP PIC S9(4).
       01   DFHEIV0  PICTURE X(29).
       LINKAGE SECTION.
       01  DFHEIBLK.
       02     EIBTIME  PIC S9(7) COMP-3.
       02     EIBDATE  PIC S9(7) COMP-3.
       02     EIBTRNID PIC X(4).
```

Figure 3.11 *Continued.*

```
           02    EIBTRNID PIC X(4).
           02    EIBTASKN PIC S9(7) COMP-3.
           02    EIBTRMID PIC X(4).
           02    DFHEIGDI COMP PIC S9(4).
           02    EIBCPOSN COMP PIC S9(4).
           02    EIBCALEN COMP PIC S9(4).
           02    EIBAID   PIC X(1).
           02    EIBFN    PIC X(2).
           02    EIBRCODE PIC X(6).
           02    EIBDS    PIC X(8).
           02    EIBREQID PIC X(8).
           02    EIBRSRCE PIC X(8).
           02    EIBSYNC  PIC X(1).
           02    EIBFREE  PIC X(1).
           02    EIBRECV  PIC X(1).
           02    EIBFIL01 PIC X(1).
           02    EIBATT   PIC X(1).
           02    EIBEOC   PIC X(1).
           02    EIBFMH   PIC X(1).
           02    EIBCOMPL PIC X(1).
           02    EIBSIG   PIC X(1).
           02    EIBCONF  PIC X(1).
           02    EIBERR   PIC X(1).
           02    EIBERRCD PIC X(4).
           02    EIBSYNRB PIC X(1).
           02    EIBNODAT PIC X(1).
           02    EIBRESP  COMP PIC S9(8).
           02    EIBRESP2 COMP PIC S9(8).
           02    EIBRLDBK PIC X(1).
           01  DFHCOMMAREA                       PIC X(35).

           01  DFHBLLSLOT1 PICTURE X(1).
           01  DFHBLLSLOT2 PICTURE X(1).
           PROCEDURE DIVISION USING DFHEIBLK DFHCOMMAREA.
               CALL 'DFHEI1'.
               SERVICE RELOAD DFHEIBLK.
               SERVICE RELOAD DFHCOMMAREA.
           0000-MAIN.
               MOVE DFHCOMMAREA TO COMM-AREA.
               IF EIBTRNID NOT = 'AR81'
                   GO TO 0800-INIT-SESSION.
          *EXEC CICS
          *     HANDLE AID
          *            CLEAR(0100-RETURN-TO-MENU)
          *            PF1(0100-RETURN-TO-MENU)
          *            PF3(0535-SET-LINE-COLORS)
          *            PF7(0700-PF7-UPDATE-NEXT-REC)
          *            PF8(0300-BROWSE-BACKWARD)
          *            ANYKEY(0120-INVALID-KEY)
          *END-EXEC.
                MOVE '                      00114    ' TO DFHEIV0
               CALL 'DFHEI1' USING DFHEIV0
                GO TO  0100-RETURN-TO-MENU 0100-RETURN-TO-MENU
               0535-SET-LINE-COLORS 0700-PF7-UPDATE-NEXT-REC
               0300-BROWSE-BACKWARD 0120-INVALID-KEY DEPENDING ON D




          *EXEC CICS
          *     RECEIVE MAP('ARC81M6')
```

Figure 3.11 *Continued.*

```
      *            MAPSET('ARC81M')
      *            INTO(HELPMAP)
      *END-EXEC.
            MOVE '  }            00123    ' TO DFHEIV0
            MOVE 'ARC81M6' TO DFHC0070
            MOVE 'ARC81M' TO DFHC0071
           CALL 'DFHEI1' USING DFHEIV0  DFHC0070 HELPMAP DFHDUM
           DFHC0071.
           GO TO 0910-SEND-MAP-DATAONLY.

       0100-RETURN-TO-MENU.
      *EXEC CICS
      *        XCTL PROGRAM('ARM80C')
      *END-EXEC.
            MOVE '          00131    ' TO DFHEIV0
            MOVE 'ARM80C' TO DFHEIV1
           CALL 'DFHEI1' USING DFHEIV0  DFHEIV1.

       0120-INVALID-KEY.
           MOVE UNPROT-ALPHA-BRT-MDT TO IM-A-ERMSG.
           MOVE 'KEY IS NOT FUNCTIONAL IN TUTORIAL MODE' TO IM-
           GO TO 0910-SEND-MAP-DATAONLY.

       0200-BROWSE-FORWARD.
      *EXEC CICS
      *    HANDLE CONDITION
      *          NOTFND (0600-WRITE-PAGE)
      *          ENDFILE (0600-WRITE-PAGE)
      *END-EXEC.
            MOVE '  {                        00141    ' TO DFHEIV0
           CALL 'DFHEI1' USING DFHEIV0
            GO TO  0600-WRITE-PAGE 0600-WRITE-PAGE DEPENDING ON
           DFHEIGDI.

           PERFORM 0400-START-BROWSE.
           PERFORM 0500-READ-NEXT-RECORD.
           IF LAST-HELP-REC
               MOVE SAVE-REC-KEY TO LAST-REC-KEY
               GO TO 0600-WRITE-PAGE.
           MOVE REC-KEY TO SAVE-REC-KEY.
           PERFORM 0500-READ-NEXT-RECORD THRU 0500-READ-NEXT-EX
                VARYING SUB FROM 1 BY 1
                   UNTIL (SUB > 16) OR (LAST-HELP-REC).
           IF LAST-HELP-REC
               MOVE SAVE-REC-KEY TO LAST-REC-KEY
               GO TO 0600-WRITE-PAGE.
           GO TO 0910-SEND-MAP-DATAONLY.

       0300-BROWSE-BACKWARD.
      *EXEC CICS
      *    HANDLE CONDITION
      *          NOTFND (0605-LAST-HELP-PAGE)
      *          ENDFILE (0605-LAST-HELP-PAGE)
      *END-EXEC.
            MOVE '  {                        00161    ' TO DFHEIV0
           CALL 'DFHEI1' USING DFHEIV0
            GO TO  0605-LAST-HELP-PAGE 0605-LAST-HELP-PAGE DEPE
           DFHEIGDI.

           IF ATTRIB-CHANGED
               MOVE 'N' TO ATTRIB-CHANGED-SW
               PERFORM 0560-RESET-LINE-TO-UNPROTECTED
```

Figure 3.11 *Continued.*

```
                  VARYING SUB FROM 1 BY 1
                      UNTIL SUB > 16.
          IF PAGE-NUM > 0
              SUBTRACT 1 FROM PAGE-NUM
          ELSE
              MOVE 1 TO PAGE-NUM
              GO TO 0605-LAST-HELP-PAGE.
          MOVE FIRST-REC-KEY TO REC-KEY.
          PERFORM 0400-START-BROWSE.
          MOVE 16 TO SUB.
          PERFORM 0500-READ-NEXT-RECORD.
          IF LAST-HELP-REC
              GO TO 0605-LAST-HELP-PAGE.
          MOVE REC-KEY TO FIRST-REC-KEY SAVE-REC-KEY.
          MOVE 16 TO SUB.
          PERFORM 0510-READ-PREV-RECORD.
          IF LAST-HELP-REC
              GO TO 0605-LAST-HELP-PAGE.
          MOVE REC-KEY TO FIRST-REC-KEY SAVE-REC-KEY.
          MOVE 16 TO SUB.
          PERFORM 0510-READ-PREV-RECORD THRU 0510-READ-PREV-EX
              UNTIL (SUB = 0) OR (LAST-HELP-REC).
          IF LAST-HELP-REC
              GO TO 0605-LAST-HELP-PAGE.
          MOVE REC-KEY TO FIRST-REC-KEY.
          GO TO 0910-SEND-MAP-DATAONLY.

      0400-START-BROWSE.
          MOVE ' ' TO IM-D-ERMSG.
          MOVE UNPROT-ALPHA-MDT TO IM-A-ERMSG.
     *EXEC CICS
     *     STARTBR DATASET ('ARA81C')
     *             RIDFLD (REC-KEY)
     *END-EXEC.
           MOVE '          00199    ' TO DFHEIV0
           MOVE 'ARA81C' TO DFHEIV1
          CALL 'DFHEI1' USING DFHEIV0  DFHEIV1  DFHDUMMY DFHEI
          REC-KEY.

      0500-READ-NEXT-RECORD.
     *EXEC CICS
     *     READNEXT DATASET ('ARA81C')
     *               INTO (HELP-RECORD)
     *             RIDFLD (REC-KEY)
     *END-EXEC.
           MOVE '  M      00205    ' TO DFHEIV0
           MOVE 'ARA81C' TO DFHEIV1
          CALL 'DFHEI1' USING DFHEIV0  DFHEIV1  HELP-RECORD DF
          REC-KEY DFHDUMMY DFHEIB0.

          IF H-REC-TRANS NOT = TASK-TRANS
              MOVE 'Y' TO LAST-HELP-REC-SW
      0500-READ-NEXT-CONT.
          IF H-REC-TRANS NOT = TASK-TRANS
              GO TO 0500-READ-NEXT-EXIT.
          PERFORM 0530-SETUP-MAP.
      0500-READ-NEXT-EXIT.

      0510-READ-PREV-RECORD.
     *EXEC CICS
     *     READPREV DATASET('ARA81C')
     *               INTO (HELP-RECORD)
```

Figure 3.11 *Continued.*

```
*               RIDFLD (REC-KEY)
*END-EXEC.
      MOVE '  M       00219     ' TO DFHEIV0
      MOVE 'ARA81C' TO DFHEIV1
     CALL 'DFHEI1' USING DFHEIV0  DFHEIV1  HELP-RECORD DF
     REC-KEY DFHDUMMY DFHEIB0.

     IF H-REC-TRANS NOT = TASK-TRANS
         MOVE 'Y' TO LAST-HELP-REC-SW.
 0510-READ-PREV-CONT.
     IF H-REC-TRANS NOT = TASK-TRANS
         GO TO 0510-READ-PREV-EXIT.
     PERFORM 0530-SETUP-MAP.
 0510-READ-PREV-EXIT.

 0530-SETUP-MAP.
     IF SUB = 1
         MOVE REC-KEY TO FIRST-REC-KEY.
     IF SUB = 16
         MOVE REC-KEY TO LAST-REC-KEY.
     MOVE REC-KEY TO SAVE-REC-KEY.
     MOVE H-REC-TEXT TO IM-D-TEXT(SUB).
     MOVE H-REC-SEQ TO IM-D-SEQ(SUB) LINE-NUMX.
     MOVE H-LINE-COLOR TO IM-D-COLOR(SUB).
     IF EIBAID = DFHPF8
        SUBTRACT 1 FROM SUB
     ELSE
         MOVE H-REC-SEQ TO LINE-NUMX.

*---*  0535 - 0560 ARE RTNS. TO DISPLAY ATTRIBUTES OF LIN
 0535-SET-LINE-COLORS.
     PERFORM 0540-DISPLAY-LINE-COLORS
         VARYING SUB FROM 1 BY 1
             UNTIL SUB > 16.
     MOVE 'Y' TO ATTRIB-CHANGED-SW.
     MOVE -1 TO IM-L-COLOR(1).
     GO TO 0910-SEND-MAP-DATAONLY.

 0540-DISPLAY-LINE-COLORS.
     IF SUB > 1
         IF IM-D-COLOR(SUB) NOT = SPACES AND LOW-VALUES
             NEXT SENTENCE
         ELSE
             COMPUTE SUB2 = SUB - 1
             MOVE IM-D-COLOR(SUB2) TO IM-D-COLOR(SUB).
     IF IM-D-COLOR(SUB) = 'R'
         MOVE RED TO IM-A-TEXT(SUB)
     ELSE IF IM-D-COLOR(SUB) = 'G'
         MOVE GREEN TO IM-A-TEXT(SUB)
     ELSE IF IM-D-COLOR(SUB) = 'W'
         MOVE WHITE TO IM-A-TEXT(SUB)
     ELSE IF IM-D-COLOR(SUB) = 'B'
         MOVE BLUE TO IM-A-TEXT(SUB).
     MOVE 'Y' TO COLOR-FOUND-SW.
 0560-RESET-LINE-TO-UNPROTECTED.
     MOVE GREEN TO IM-A-TEXT(SUB).
*---------------*  END OF ATTRIBUTE ROUTINES   *----------

 0600-WRITE-PAGE.
     IF EIBTRNID = 'ARA81C'
*EXEC CICS
*      ENDBR DATASET ('ARA81C')
```

Figure 3.11 *Continued.*

```
*END-EXEC.
          MOVE '         00277    ' TO DFHEIV0
          MOVE 'ARA81C' TO DFHEIV1
         CALL 'DFHEI1' USING DFHEIV0  DFHEIV1  DFHDUMMY D
     IF EIBAID NOT = DFHPF8
        IF PAGE-NUM < 7
           MOVE TASK-TRANS TO HELP-TRANS
            MOVE SPACES TO HELP-SEQ
*EXEC CICS
*     UNLOCK DATASET ('ARA81C')
*END-EXEC
             MOVE '         00284    ' TO DFHEIV0
             MOVE 'ARA81C' TO DFHEIV1
            CALL 'DFHEI1' USING DFHEIV0  DFHEIV1
            PERFORM 0820-CREATE-HELP-RECS
                VARYING SUB FROM 1 BY 1
                    UNTIL SUB > 16
                GO TO 0900-SEND-MAP.

 0605-LAST-HELP-PAGE.
     IF EIBAID NOT = DFHPF8
         MOVE SAVE-REC-KEY TO LAST-REC-KEY
         MOVE 'THIS IS THE END OF THE FILE' TO IM-D-ERMSG
     IF EIBAID = DFHPF8
         MOVE SAVE-REC-KEY TO FIRST-REC-KEY
         MOVE 'THIS IS THE START OF THE FILE' TO IM-D-ERM
     MOVE UNPROT-ALPHA-BRT-MDT TO IM-A-ERMSG.
     GO TO 0910-SEND-MAP-DATAONLY.

 0700-PF7-UPDATE-NEXT-REC.
*EXEC CICS
*     HANDLE CONDITION
*           NOTFND (0710-UPDATE-OVER)
*           ENDFILE (0710-UPDATE-OVER)
*END-EXEC.
      MOVE '  {                    00303    ' TO DFHEIV0
     CALL 'DFHEI1' USING DFHEIV0
      GO TO  0710-UPDATE-OVER 0710-UPDATE-OVER DEPENDING
     DFHEIGDI.

     IF ATTRIB-CHANGED
         MOVE 'N' TO ATTRIB-CHANGED-SW
         PERFORM 0560-RESET-LINE-TO-UNPROTECTED
             VARYING SUB FROM 1 BY 1
                 UNTIL SUB > 16.
     ADD 1 TO PAGE-NUM.
     IF PAGE-NUM > 6
         MOVE 6 TO PAGE-NUM
         GO TO 0720-LAST-UPDATE.
     MOVE TASK-TRANS TO HELP-TRANS.
     PERFORM 0710-UPDATE-RECORD THRU 0710-UPDATE-OVER
         VARYING SUB FROM 1 BY 1 UNTIL
             (RECORD-UPDATED) OR (SUB > 16).
     MOVE 'RECORD UPFDATED HERE IS NEXT PAGE' TO IM-D-ERM
     MOVE 'N' TO RECORD-UPDATED-SW.
     MOVE UNPROT-ALPHA-MDT TO IM-A-ERMSG.
     MOVE LAST-REC-KEY TO REC-KEY.
     GO TO 0200-BROWSE-FORWARD.
 0710-UPDATE-RECORD.
     IF IM-D-SEQ(SUB) NOT NUMERIC
        MOVE 'Y' TO RECORD-UPDATED-SW
        GO TO 0710-UPDATE-OVER.
```

Figure 3.11 *Continued.*

```
           MOVE IM-D-SEQ(SUB) TO HELP-SEQ.
      *EXEC CICS
      *     READ DATASET ('ARA81C')
      *          INTO (HELP-RECORD)
      *          RIDFLD (REC-KEY)
      *          UPDATE
      *END-EXEC.
            MOVE '  }     d 00331    ' TO DFHEIV0
            MOVE 'ARA81C' TO DFHEIV1
           CALL 'DFHEI1' USING DFHEIV0  DFHEIV1  HELP-RECORD DF
           REC-KEY.


           MOVE IM-D-TEXT(SUB) TO H-REC-TEXT.
           MOVE IM-D-COLOR(SUB) TO H-LINE-COLOR.
           IF SUB > 1
               IF IM-D-COLOR(SUB) NOT = SPACES AND LOW-VALUES
                   MOVE IM-D-COLOR(SUB) TO H-LINE-COLOR
               ELSE
                   COMPUTE SUB2 = SUB - 1
                   MOVE IM-D-COLOR(SUB2) TO H-LINE-COLOR
                       IM-D-COLOR(SUB)
           ELSE
               MOVE IM-D-COLOR(SUB) TO H-LINE-COLOR.
      *EXEC CICS
      *     REWRITE DATASET ('ARA81C')
      *             FROM (HELP-RECORD)
      *END-EXEC.
            MOVE '  {       00348    ' TO DFHEIV0
            MOVE 'ARA81C' TO DFHEIV1
           CALL 'DFHEI1' USING DFHEIV0  DFHEIV1  HELP-RECORD.

       0710-UPDATE-OVER.

       0720-LAST-UPDATE.
      *EXEC CICS
      *    HANDLE CONDITION
      *          NOTFND (0710-UPDATE-OVER)
      *          ENDFILE (0710-UPDATE-OVER)
      *END-EXEC.
            MOVE '  {                        00355    ' TO DFHEIV0
           CALL 'DFHEI1' USING DFHEIV0
            GO TO  0710-UPDATE-OVER 0710-UPDATE-OVER DEPENDING
           DFHEIGDI.

           MOVE TASK-TRANS TO HELP-TRANS.
           PERFORM 0710-UPDATE-RECORD THRU 0710-UPDATE-OVER
               VARYING SUB FROM 1 BY 1 UNTIL
                   (RECORD-UPDATED) OR (SUB > 16).
           MOVE 'N' TO RECORD-UPDATED-SW.
           MOVE UNPROT-ALPHA-MDT TO IM-A-ERMSG.
           GO TO 0605-LAST-HELP-PAGE.

       0800-INIT-SESSION.
      *EXEC CICS
      *    HANDLE CONDITION
      *          NOTFND (0600-WRITE-PAGE)
      *          ENDFILE (0600-WRITE-PAGE)
      *END-EXEC.
            MOVE '  {                        00369    ' TO DFHEIV0
           CALL 'DFHEI1' USING DFHEIV0
            GO TO  0600-WRITE-PAGE 0600-WRITE-PAGE DEPENDING ON
```

Figure 3.11 *Continued.*

```
          DFHEIGDI.

     *EXEC CICS
     *     UNLOCK DATASET ('ARA81C')
     *END-EXEC.
           MOVE '          00374    ' TO DFHEIV0
           MOVE 'ARA81C' TO DFHEIV1
          CALL 'DFHEI1' USING DFHEIV0  DFHEIV1.
          MOVE SPACES TO IM-D-PFMSG3.
          MOVE 'AR81' TO IM-D-TRAN.
          MOVE CURRENT-DATE TO IM-D-DATE.
          MOVE 1 TO PAGE-NUM.
          MOVE 0 TO LINE-NUM.
          MOVE TASK-TRANS TO HELP-TRANS F-HELP-TRANS.
          MOVE SPACES TO HELP-SEQ.
          PERFORM 0400-START-BROWSE.
          PERFORM 0500-READ-NEXT-RECORD THRU 0500-READ-NEXT-EX
              VARYING SUB FROM 1 BY 1
                  UNTIL (SUB > 16) OR (LAST-HELP-REC).
          IF (SUB < 16) AND (LAST-HELP-REC)
              MOVE 0 TO LINE-NUM
     *EXEC CICS
     *     ENDBR DATASET ('ARA81C')
     *END-EXEC
               MOVE '          00390    ' TO DFHEIV0
               MOVE 'ARA81C' TO DFHEIV1
              CALL 'DFHEI1' USING DFHEIV0  DFHEIV1  DFHDUMMY D
     *EXEC CICS
     *    UNLOCK DATASET ('ARA81C')
     *END-EXEC
               MOVE '          00393    ' TO DFHEIV0
               MOVE 'ARA81C' TO DFHEIV1
              CALL 'DFHEI1' USING DFHEIV0  DFHEIV1
              PERFORM 0820-CREATE-HELP-RECS
                  VARYING SUB FROM 1 BY 1
                      UNTIL SUB > 16.
          MOVE 16 TO LINE-NUM.
          MOVE '01' TO F-HELP-SEQ.
          MOVE REC-KEY TO LAST-REC-KEY.
          GO TO 0900-SEND-MAP.

      0820-CREATE-HELP-RECS.
          IF LINE-NUM NOT NUMERIC
              MOVE 1 TO LINE-NUM.
          ADD 1 TO LINE-NUM.
          MOVE SPACES TO IM-D-TEXT(SUB) IM-D-COLOR(SUB) IM-D-S
          MOVE TASK-TRANS TO HELP-TRANS H-REC-TRANS.
          MOVE LINE-NUMX TO HELP-SEQ H-REC-SEQ IM-D-SEQ(SUB).
          MOVE IM-D-TEXT(SUB) TO H-REC-TEXT.
          IF SUB > 1
              IF IM-D-COLOR(SUB) NOT = SPACES AND LOW-VALUES
                  MOVE IM-D-COLOR(SUB) TO H-LINE-COLOR
              ELSE
                  COMPUTE SUB2 = SUB - 1
                  MOVE IM-D-COLOR(SUB2) TO H-LINE-COLOR
                      IM-D-COLOR(SUB)
          ELSE
              MOVE IM-D-COLOR(SUB) TO H-LINE-COLOR.
     *EXEC CICS
     *     WRITE DATASET ('ARA81C')
     *           FROM (HELP-RECORD)
```

Figure 3.11 *Continued.*

```
      *           RIDFLD(REC-KEY)
      *END-EXEC.
            MOVE '  }      00421    ' TO DFHEIV0
            MOVE 'ARA81C' TO DFHEIV1
           CALL 'DFHEI1' USING DFHEIV0  DFHEIV1  HELP-RECORD DF
           REC-KEY.

           IF SUB = 1
               MOVE REC-KEY TO FIRST-REC-KEY.
           IF SUB = 16
               MOVE REC-KEY TO LAST-REC-KEY.

       0900-SEND-MAP.
           IF EIBTRNID = 'AR81'
               GO TO 0910-SEND-MAP-DATAONLY.
           MOVE -1 TO IM-L-COLOR(1).
      *EXEC CICS
      *     SEND MAP('ARC81M6')
      *          MAPSET('ARC81M')
      *              FROM(HELPMAP)
      *     ERASE
      *     CURSOR
      *END-EXEC.
            MOVE '  J        S     00435    ' TO DFHEIV0
            MOVE 'ARC81M6' TO DFHC0070
            MOVE 'ARC81M' TO DFHC0071
            MOVE -1 TO DFHEIV11
           CALL 'DFHEI1' USING DFHEIV0  DFHC0070 HELPMAP DFHDUM
           DFHC0071 DFHDUMMY DFHDUMMY DFHDUMMY DFHEIV11.

           GO TO 0920-RETURN-TRANSID.

       0910-SEND-MAP-DATAONLY.
           MOVE -1 TO IM-L-COLOR(1).
      *EXEC CICS
      *     SEND MAP('ARC81M6')
      *          MAPSET('ARC81M')
      *              FROM(HELPMAP)
      *     DATAONLY
      *     CURSOR
      *END-EXEC.
            MOVE '  J              00446    ' TO DFHEIV0
            MOVE 'ARC81M6' TO DFHC0070
            MOVE 'ARC81M' TO DFHC0071
            MOVE -1 TO DFHEIV11
           CALL 'DFHEI1' USING DFHEIV0  DFHC0070 HELPMAP DFHDUM
           DFHC0071 DFHDUMMY DFHDUMMY DFHDUMMY DFHEIV11.

       0920-RETURN-TRANSID.
      *EXEC CICS
      *       RETURN TRANSID('AR81')
      *              COMMAREA(COMM-AREA)
      *              LENGTH(35)
      *END-EXEC.
            MOVE '  \      00454    ' TO DFHEIV0
            MOVE 'AR81' TO DFHEIV5
            MOVE 35 TO DFHEIV11
           CALL 'DFHEI1' USING DFHEIV0  DFHEIV5  COMM-AREA DFHE

           STOP RUN.
           GOBACK.
```

Figure 3.11 *Continued.*

```
 *STATISTICS*      SOURCE RECORDS =    684      DATA DIVISION STATEMENTS =
 *OPTIONS IN EFFECT*      SIZE =  524288  BUF =    20480  LINECNT = 57  SP
 *OPTIONS IN EFFECT*      NODMAP, NOPMAP, NOCLIST, NOSUPMAP, NOXREF,    SX
 *OPTIONS IN EFFECT*      NOTERM, NONUM, NOBATCH, NONAME, COMPILE=01, NOS
 *OPTIONS IN EFFECT*      NOOPTIMIZE, NOSYMDMP, NOTEST,    VERB,    ZWB, SY
 *OPTIONS IN EFFECT*      NOLST , NOFDECK,NOCDECK, LCOL2,  L120,    DUMP ,
 *OPTIONS IN EFFECT*      NOCOUNT, NOVBSUM, NOVBREF, LANGLVL(1)
                                            CROSS-REFERENCE DICTIONARY


 DATA NAMES                         DEFN      REFERENCE


 ASKIP                              000058
 ATTRBYTE                           000043
 ATTRIB-CHANGED                     000027    000312  000479
 ATTRIB-CHANGED-SW                  000026    000313  000411  000480
 BLUE                               000046    000429
 COLOR-FOUND                        000040
 COLOR-FOUND-SW                     000039    000430
 COMM-AREA                          000009    000230  000681
 CONDITION-SWITCHES                 000036
 DFHAID                             000105
 DFHBLLSLOT1                        000223
 DFHBLLSLOT2                        000224
 DFHB0025                           000162
 DFHB0041                           000149
 DFHB0042                           000150
 DFHB0043                           000151
 DFHB0044                           000152
 DFHB0045                           000153
 DFHB0046                           000154
 DFHB0047                           000155
 DFHB0048                           000156
 DFHCLEAR                           000108
 DFHCLRP                            000109
 DFHCOMMAREA                        000221    000230
 DFHC0011                           000181
 DFHC0022                           000177
 DFHC0023                           000178
 DFHC0070                           000183    000257  000259  000648  00065
 DFHC0071                           000184    000258  000259  000649  00065
 DFHC0084                           000172
 DFHC0085                           000173
 DFHC0320                           000174
 DFHC0440                           000185
 DFHDUMMY                           000186    000259  000351  000362  00038
 DFHEIBLK                           000189
 DFHEIB0                            000145    000351  000362  000381  00044
 DFHEICB                            000146
 DFHEID0                            000144
 DFHEIGDI                           000195    000244  000284  000309  00047
 DFHEIV0                            000187    000242  000243  000256  00025
                                              000349  000351  000360  00036
                                              000474  000475  000508  00051
                                              000568  000570  000587  00058
                                              000665  000669  000678  00068
 DFHEIV1                            000168    000268  000269  000350  00035
                                              000451  000452  000509  00051
                                              000594  000595  000627  00062
 DFHEIV10                           000179
 DFHEIV11                           000157    000650  000651  000668  00066
```

Figure 3.11 *Continued.*

```
DFHEIV12        000158
DFHEIV13        000159
DFHEIV14        000160
DFHEIV15        000161
DFHEIV16        000148
DFHEIV17        000165
DFHEIV18        000166
DFHEIV19        000167
DFHEIV2         000169
DFHEIV20        000171
DFHEIV3         000170
DFHEIV4         000182
DFHEIV5         000163  000679  000681
DFHEIV6         000164
DFHEIV7         000175
DFHEIV8         000176
DFHEIV9         000180
DFHENTER        000107
DFHLDVER        000143
DFHMSRE         000112
DFHNULL         000106
DFHOPID         000111
DFHPA1          000115
DFHPA2          000116
DFHPA3          000117
DFHPEN          000110
DFHPF1          000118
DFHPF10         000127
DFHPF11         000128
DFHPF12         000129
DFHPF13         000130
DFHPF14         000131
DFHPF15         000132
DFHPF16         000133
DFHPF17         000134
DFHPF18         000135
DFHPF19         000136
DFHPF2          000119
DFHPF20         000137
DFHPF21         000138
DFHPF22         000139
DFHPF23         000140
DFHPF24         000141
DFHPF3          000120
DFHPF4          000121
DFHPF5          000122
DFHPF6          000123
DFHPF7          000124
DFHPF8          000125  000401  000443  000459  00046
DFHPF9          000126
DFHSTRF         000113
DFHTRIG         000114
EIBAID          000198  000401  000443  000459  00046
EIBATT          000208
EIBCALEN        000197
EIBCOMPL        000211
EIBCONF         000213
EIBCPOSN        000196
EIBDATE         000191
EIBDS           000201
EIBEOC          000209
EIBERR          000214
```

Figure 3.11 *Continued.*

```
EIBERRCD           000215
EIBFIL01           000207
EIBFMH             000210
EIBFN              000199
EIBFREE            000205
EIBNODAT           000217
EIBRCODE           000200
EIBRECV            000206
EIBREQID           000202
EIBRESP            000218
EIBRESP2           000219
EIBRLDBK           000220
EIBRSRCE           000203
EIBSIG             000212
EIBSYNC            000204
EIBSYNRB           000216
EIBTASKN           000193
EIBTIME            000190
EIBTRMID           000194
EIBTRNID           000192   000231   000436   000637
F-HELP-SEQ         000017   000600
F-HELP-TRANS       000016   000576
FIRST-REC-KEY      000015   000322   000328   000333   00033
GREEN              000047   000425   000432
H-LINE-COLOR       000065   000400   000515   000518   00052
H-REC-SEQ          000064   000399   000404   000610
H-REC-TEXT         000066   000398   000514   000611
H-REC-TRANS        000063   000365   000368   000384   00038
HELP-KEY           000062
HELP-RECORD        000061   000362   000381   000510   00053
HELP-SEQ           000014   000446   000501   000577   00061
HELP-TRANS         000013   000445   000488   000546   00057
HELPMAP            000070   000259   000651   000669
IM-A-COLOR         000086
IM-A-DATE          000079
IM-A-ERMSG         000101   000272   000344   000465   00049
IM-A-HDR           000076
IM-A-PFMSG         000092
IM-A-PFMSG2        000095
IM-A-PFMSG3        000098
IM-A-SEQ           000083
IM-A-TEXT          000089   000423   000425   000427   00042
IM-A-TRAN          000073
IM-D-COLOR         000087   000400   000417   000421   00042
                            000521   000524   000608   00061
IM-D-DATE          000080   000573
IM-D-ERMSG         000102   000273   000343   000461   00046
IM-D-HDR           000077
IM-D-PFMSG         000093
IM-D-PFMSG2        000096
IM-D-PFMSG3        000099   000571
IM-D-SEQ           000084   000399   000498   000501   00060
IM-D-TEXT          000090   000398   000514   000608   00061
IM-D-TEXT-LINES    000081
IM-D-TRAN          000074   000572
IM-L-COLOR         000085   000412   000639   000657
IM-L-DATE          000078
IM-L-ERMSG         000100
IM-L-HDR           000075
IM-L-PFMSG         000091
```

Figure 3.11 *Continued.*

```
IM-L-PFMSG2                    000094
IM-L-PFMSG3                    000097
IM-L-SEQ                       000082
IM-L-TEXT                      000088
IM-L-TRAN                      000072
L-HELP-SEQ                     000020
L-HELP-TRANS                   000019
LAST-HELP-REC                  000038    000289   000293   000296   00032
LAST-HELP-REC-SW               000037    000366   000385
LAST-REC-KEY                   000018    000290   000297   000396   00046
LINE-NUM                       000029    000575   000583   000599   00060
LINE-NUMX                      000030    000399   000404   000610
PAGE-NUM                       000028    000317   000318   000320   00044
PROT                           000055
PROT-BRT                       000057
PROT-MDT                       000056
REC-KEY                        000012    000292   000322   000328   00033
                                         000397   000495   000510   00060

RECORD-UPDATED                 000025    000489   000547
RECORD-UPDATED-SW              000024    000493   000499   000550
RED                            000044    000423
S-HELP-SEQ                     000023
S-HELP-TRANS                   000022
SAVE-REC-KEY                   000021    000290   000292   000297   00032
SUB                            000033    000293   000314   000324   00032
                                         000400   000402   000408   00041
                                         000425   000426   000427   00042
                                         000501   000514   000515   00051
                                         000579   000582   000596   00060
                                         000617   000620   000631   00063
SUB2                           000034    000420   000421   000520   00052
TABLE-SUBS                     000032
TASK-TRANS                     000011    000365   000368   000384   00038
UNPROT-ALPHA                   000048
UNPROT-ALPHA-BRT               000050
UNPROT-ALPHA-BRT-MDT           000051    000272   000465
UNPROT-ALPHA-MDT               000049    000344   000494   000551
UNPROT-NUM                     000052
UNPROT-NUM-BRT                 000054
UNPROT-NUM-MDT                 000053
WHITE                          000045    000427
PROCEDURE NAMES                DEFN      REFERENCE


0000-MAIN                      000229
0100-RETURN-TO-MENU            000263    000244
0120-INVALID-KEY               000271    000244
0200-BROWSE-FORWARD            000276    000496
0300-BROWSE-BACKWARD           000301    000244
0400-START-BROWSE              000342    000287   000323   000578
0500-READ-NEXT-CONT            000367
0500-READ-NEXT-EXIT            000371    000293   000369   000579
0500-READ-NEXT-RECORD          000354    000288   000293   000325   00057
0510-READ-PREV-CONT            000386
0510-READ-PREV-EXIT            000390    000335   000388
0510-READ-PREV-RECORD          000373    000330   000335
0530-SETUP-MAP                 000392    000370   000389
0535-SET-LINE-COLORS           000407    000244
0540-DISPLAY-LINE-COLORS       000415    000408
0560-RESET-LINE-TO-UNPROTECTED 000431    000314   000481
```

Figure 3.11 *Continued.*

```
0600-WRITE-PAGE               000435   000284  000291  000298  00056
0605-LAST-HELP-PAGE           000458   000309  000321  000327  00033
0700-PF7-UPDATE-NEXT-REC      000468   000244
0710-UPDATE-OVER              000533   000476  000489  000500  00054
0710-UPDATE-RECORD            000497   000489  000547
0720-LAST-UPDATE              000535   000487
0800-INIT-SESSION             000554   000232
0820-CREATE-HELP-RECS         000604   000453  000596
0900-SEND-MAP                 000636   000456  000602
0910-SEND-MAP-DATAONLY        000656   000261  000274  000299  00034
0920-RETURN-TRANSID           000672   000654
```

```
ARD82C   Delete Source Program

IDENTIFICATION DIVISION.
PROGRAM-ID. ARD82C.
DATE-WRITTEN.   JUNE 13 1990.
DATE-COMPILED. JAN  2,1992.
ENVIRONMENT DIVISION.
DATA DIVISION.
WORKING-STORAGE SECTION.
01  COMM-AREA.
    05  FILLER                              PIC X.
    05  TASK-TRANS                          PIC X(4).
    05  REC-KEY.
        10  HELP-TRANS                      PIC X(4).
        10  HELP-SEQ                        PIC X(2).
    05  FIRST-REC-KEY.
        10  F-HELP-TRANS                    PIC X(4).
        10  F-HELP-SEQ                      PIC X(2).
    05  LAST-REC-KEY.
        10  L-HELP-TRANS                    PIC X(4).
        10  L-HELP-SEQ                      PIC X(2).
    05  SAVE-REC-KEY.
        10  S-HELP-TRANS                    PIC X(4).
        10  S-HELP-SEQ                      PIC X(2).
    05  DELETE-RECORD-SW                    PIC X      VALUE '
        88  READY-TO-DELETE                            VALUE 'R
        88  DELETE-COMPLETED                           VALUE 'D
    05  NO-HELP-RECS-FOUND-SW               PIC X      VALUE 'N
        88  NO-HELP-RECS-FOUND                         VALUE 'Y

01  SUB-COUNTERS                            COMP SYNC.
    05  SUB                                 PIC S9(4) VALUE +0

01  LINE-COUNTERS.
    05  LINE-NUM                            PIC 9(02).
    05  LINE-NUMX REDEFINES LINE-NUM        PIC X(02).

01  LAST-HELP-REC-SW                        PIC X     VALUE 'N'
    88  LAST-HELP-REC                                 VALUE 'Y'
```

Figure 3.12 Delete source program.

Figure 3.12 *Continued.*

```
       *------------*  ATTRIBUTE-BYTES  *-----------------------
        01  ATTRBYTE.
            05  RED                             PIC X    VALUE 'I'.
            05  WHITE                           PIC X    VALUE 'Y'.
            05  BLUE                            PIC X    VALUE '-'.
            05  GREEN                           PIC X    VALUE 'A'.
            05  UNPROT-ALPHA                    PIC X    VALUE SPAC
            05  UNPROT-ALPHA-MDT                PIC X    VALUE 'A'.
            05  UNPROT-ALPHA-BRT                PIC X    VALUE 'H'.
            05  UNPROT-ALPHA-BRT-MDT            PIC X    VALUE 'I'.
            05  UNPROT-NUM                      PIC X    VALUE '&'.
            05  UNPROT-NUM-MDT                  PIC X    VALUE 'J'.
            05  UNPROT-NUM-BRT                  PIC X    VALUE 'Q'.
            05  UNPROT-NUM-BRT-MDT              PIC X    VALUE 'R'.
            05  UNPROT-NUM-DRK-MDT              PIC X    VALUE ')'.
            05  PROT                            PIC X    VALUE '-'.
            05  PROT-MDT                        PIC X    VALUE '/'.
            05  PROT-BRT                        PIC X    VALUE 'Y'.
            05  PROT-BRT-MDT                    PIC X    VALUE 'Z'.
            05  ASKIP                           PIC X    VALUE '0'.

       *---------------* HELP THE TUTORIAL RECORD *------------
        01  HELP-RECORD.
            05  HELP-KEY.
                10  H-REC-TRANS-ID              PIC X(4).
                10  H-REC-SEQ                   PIC X(2).
            05  H-LINE-COLOR                    PIC X.
            05  H-REC-TEXT                      PIC X(70).
            05  FILLER                          PIC X(3).

       *--------------* PROGRAMMER INSERTED SYMBOLIC MAP  *-----
        01  HELPMAP.
            05  FILLER                          PIC X(12).
            05  IM-L-TRAN                       PIC S9(4)   COMP.
            05  IM-A-TRAN                       PIC X.
            05  IM-D-TRAN                       PIC X(4).
            05  IM-L-HDR                        PIC S9(4)   COMP.
            05  IM-A-HDR                        PIC X.
            05  IM-D-HDR                        PIC X(32).
            05  IM-L-DATE                       PIC S9(4)   COMP.
            05  IM-A-DATE                       PIC X.
            05  IM-D-DATE                       PIC X(8).
            05  IM-D-TEXT-LINES                 OCCURS 16.
                10  IM-L-SEQ                    PIC S9(4)   COMP.
                10  IM-A-SEQ                    PIC X.
                10  IM-D-SEQ                    PIC X(2).
                10  IM-L-COLOR                  PIC S9(4)   COMP.
                10  IM-A-COLOR                  PIC X.
                10  IM-D-COLOR                  PIC X(1).
                10  IM-L-TEXT                   PIC S9(4)   COMP.
                10  IM-A-TEXT                   PIC X.
                10  IM-D-TEXT                   PIC X(70).
            05  IM-L-PFMSG                      PIC S9(4)   COMP.
            05  IM-A-PFMSG                      PIC X.
            05  IM-D-PFMSG                      PIC X(19).
            05  IM-L-PFMSG2                     PIC S9(4)   COMP.
            05  IM-A-PFMSG2                     PIC X.
            05  IM-D-PFMSG2                     PIC X(28)
```

Figure 3.12 *Continued.*

```
                                              VALUE 'PF7: NEXT P
            05  IM-L-PFMSG3                   PIC S9(4)   COMP.
            05  IM-A-PFMSG3                   PIC X.
            05  IM-D-PFMSG3                   PIC X(17)
                                             VALUE 'PF9: DELETE
            05  IM-L-ERMSG                    PIC S9(4)   COMP.
            05  IM-A-ERMSG                    PIC X.
            05  IM-D-ERMSG                    PIC X(60).

        COPY DFHAID.
C       01    DFHAID.
C         02  DFHNULL    PIC  X  VALUE IS ' '.
C         02  DFHENTER   PIC  X  VALUE IS QUOTE.
C         02  DFHCLEAR   PIC  X  VALUE IS '_'.
C         02  DFHCLRP    PIC  X  VALUE IS ''.
C         02  DFHPEN     PIC  X  VALUE IS '='.
C         02  DFHOPID    PIC  X  VALUE IS 'W'.
C         02  DFHMSRE    PIC  X  VALUE IS 'X'.
C         02  DFHSTRF    PIC  X  VALUE IS 'h'.
C         02  DFHTRIG    PIC  X  VALUE IS '"'.
C         02  DFHPA1     PIC  X  VALUE IS '%'.
C         02  DFHPA2     PIC  X  VALUE IS '>'.
C         02  DFHPA3     PIC  X  VALUE IS ','.
C         02  DFHPF1     PIC  X  VALUE IS '1'.
C         02  DFHPF2     PIC  X  VALUE IS '2'.
C         02  DFHPF3     PIC  X  VALUE IS '3'.
C         02  DFHPF4     PIC  X  VALUE IS '4'.
C         02  DFHPF5     PIC  X  VALUE IS '5'.
C         02  DFHPF6     PIC  X  VALUE IS '6'.
C         02  DFHPF7     PIC  X  VALUE IS '7'.
C         02  DFHPF8     PIC  X  VALUE IS '8'.
C         02  DFHPF9     PIC  X  VALUE IS '9'.
C         02  DFHPF10    PIC  X  VALUE IS ':'.
C         02  DFHPF11    PIC  X  VALUE IS '#'.
C         02  DFHPF12    PIC  X  VALUE IS '@'.
C         02  DFHPF13    PIC  X  VALUE IS 'A'.
C         02  DFHPF14    PIC  X  VALUE IS 'B'.
C         02  DFHPF15    PIC  X  VALUE IS 'C'.
C         02  DFHPF16    PIC  X  VALUE IS 'D'.
C         02  DFHPF17    PIC  X  VALUE IS 'E'.
C         02  DFHPF18    PIC  X  VALUE IS 'F'.
C         02  DFHPF19    PIC  X  VALUE IS 'G'.
C         02  DFHPF20    PIC  X  VALUE IS 'H'.
C         02  DFHPF21    PIC  X  VALUE IS 'I'.
C         02  DFHPF22    PIC  X  VALUE IS ''.
C         02  DFHPF23    PIC  X  VALUE IS '.'.
C         02  DFHPF24    PIC  X  VALUE IS '<'.

        01  DFHLDVER PIC X(22) VALUE 'LD TABLE DFHEITAB 210.'.
        01  DFHEID0 PICTURE S9(7) COMPUTATIONAL-3 VALUE ZERO.
        01  DFHEIB0 PICTURE S9(4) COMPUTATIONAL VALUE ZERO.
        01  DFHEICB  PICTURE X(8) VALUE IS '        '.

        01   DFHEIV16  COMP PIC S9(8).
        01   DFHB0041  COMP PIC S9(8).
        01   DFHB0042  COMP PIC S9(8).
        01   DFHB0043  COMP PIC S9(8).
        01   DFHB0044  COMP PIC S9(8).
        01   DFHB0045  COMP PIC S9(8).
        01   DFHB0046  COMP PIC S9(8).
        01   DFHB0047  COMP PIC S9(8).
```

Figure 3.12 *Continued.*

```
       01    DFHB0048   COMP PIC S9(8).
       01    DFHEIV11   COMP PIC S9(4).
       01    DFHEIV12   COMP PIC S9(4).
       01    DFHEIV13   COMP PIC S9(4).
       01    DFHEIV14   COMP PIC S9(4).
       01    DFHEIV15   COMP PIC S9(4).
       01    DFHB0025   COMP PIC S9(4).
       01    DFHEIV5    PIC X(4).
       01    DFHEIV6    PIC X(4).
       01    DFHEIV17   PIC X(4).
       01    DFHEIV18   PIC X(4).
       01    DFHEIV19   PIC X(4).
       01    DFHEIV1    PIC X(8).
       01    DFHEIV2    PIC X(8).
       01    DFHEIV3    PIC X(8).
       01    DFHEIV20   PIC X(8).
       01    DFHC0084   PIC X(8).
       01    DFHC0085   PIC X(8).
       01    DFHC0320   PIC X(32).
       01    DFHEIV7    PIC X(2).
       01    DFHEIV8    PIC X(2).
       01    DFHC0022   PIC X(2).
       01    DFHC0023   PIC X(2).
       01    DFHEIV10   PIC S9(7) COMP-3.
       01    DFHEIV9    PIC X(1).
       01    DFHC0011   PIC X(1).
       01    DFHEIV4    PIC X(6).
       01    DFHC0070   PIC X(7).
       01    DFHC0071   PIC X(7).
       01    DFHC0440   PIC X(44).
       01    DFHDUMMY COMP PIC S9(4).
       01    DFHEIV0  PICTURE X(29).
       LINKAGE SECTION.
       01  DFHEIBLK.
       02     EIBTIME   PIC S9(7) COMP-3.
       02     EIBDATE   PIC S9(7) COMP-3.
       02     EIBTRNID PIC X(4).
       02     EIBTASKN PIC S9(7) COMP-3.
       02     EIBTRMID PIC X(4)
       02     DFHEIGDI COMP PIC S9(4).
       02     EIBCPOSN COMP PIC S9(4).
       02     EIBCALEN COMP PIC S9(4).
       02     EIBAID    PIC X(1).
       02     EIBFN     PIC X(2).
       02     EIBRCODE PIC X(6).
       02     EIBDS     PIC X(8).
       02     EIBREQID PIC X(8).
       02     EIBRSRCE PIC X(8).
       02     EIBSYNC   PIC X(1).
       02     EIBFREE   PIC X(1).
       02     EIBRECV   PIC X(1).
       02     EIBFIL01 PIC X(1).
       02     EIBATT    PIC X(1).
       02     EIBEOC    PIC X(1).
       02     EIBFMH    PIC X(1).
       02     EIBCOMPL PIC X(1).
       02     EIBSIG    PIC X(1).
       02     EIBCONF   PIC X(1).
       02     EIBERR    PIC X(1).
       02     EIBERRCD PIC X(4).
       02     EIBSYNRB PIC X(1).
```

Figure 3.12 *Continued.*

```
            02    EIBNODAT PIC X(1).
            02    EIBRESP  COMP PIC S9(8).
            02    EIBRESP2 COMP PIC S9(8).
            02    EIBRLDBK PIC X(1).
            01  DFHCOMMAREA                       PIC X(31).
            01  DFHBLLSLOT1 PICTURE X(1).
            01  DFHBLLSLOT2 PICTURE X(1).
            PROCEDURE DIVISION USING DFHEIBLK DFHCOMMAREA.
                CALL 'DFHEI1'.
                SERVICE RELOAD DFHEIBLK.
                SERVICE RELOAD DFHCOMMAREA.
            0000-MAIN.
                IF EIBCALEN > ZERO
                    MOVE DFHCOMMAREA TO COMM-AREA.
                IF EIBTRNID NOT = 'AR82'
                    GO TO 0800-INIT-SESSION.
           *EXEC CICS
           *     HANDLE AID
           *            CLEAR(0100-RETURN-TO-MENU)
           *            PF1(0100-RETURN-TO-MENU)
           *            PF3(0700-DELETE-6-PAGES)
           *            PF7(0200-BROWSE-FORWARD)
           *            PF8(0300-BROWSE-BACKWARD)
           *            PF9(0710-DELETE-PAGE)
           *            ANYKEY(0905-INVALID-PFKEY)
           *END-EXEC.
                 MOVE '                      00118    ' TO DFHEIV0
                CALL 'DFHEI1' USING DFHEIV0
                 GO TO  0100-RETURN-TO-MENU 0100-RETURN-TO-MENU
                0700-DELETE-6-PAGES 0200-BROWSE-FORWARD 0300-BROWSE-
                0710-DELETE-PAGE 0905-INVALID-PFKEY DEPENDING ON DFH
           *EXEC CICS
           *     RECEIVE MAP('ARC81M6')
           *             MAPSET('ARC81M')
           *             INTO(HELPMAP)
           *END-EXEC.
                 MOVE '  }           00128    ' TO DFHEIV0
                 MOVE 'ARC81M6' TO DFHC0070
                 MOVE 'ARC81M' TO DFHC0071
                CALL 'DFHEI1' USING DFHEIV0  DFHC0070 HELPMAP DFHDUM
                DFHC0071.
                GO TO 0910-SEND-MAP-DATAONLY.
            0100-RETURN-TO-MENU.
           *EXEC CICS
           *        XCTL PROGRAM('ARM80C')
           *END-EXEC.
                 MOVE '          00136    ' TO DFHEIV0
                 MOVE 'ARM80C' TO DFHEIV1
                CALL 'DFHEI1' USING DFHEIV0  DFHEIV1.
            0200-BROWSE-FORWARD.
           *EXEC CICS
           *    HANDLE CONDITION
```

Figure 3.12 *Continued.*

```
*        NOTFND (0600-LAST-PAGE)
*        ENDFILE (0600-LAST-PAGE)
*END-EXEC.
      MOVE '  {                   00141    ' TO DFHEIV0
     CALL 'DFHEI1' USING DFHEIV0
      GO TO  0600-LAST-PAGE 0600-LAST-PAGE DEPENDING ON D
     MOVE ' ' TO DELETE-RECORD-SW
     IF NO-HELP-RECS-FOUND
         GO TO 0810-NO-HELP-RECS.
     IF DELETE-COMPLETED
         MOVE RED TO IM-A-ERMSG
         MOVE 'RECORDS DELETED, HIT PF1 TO EXIT' TO IM-D-
         GO TO 0910-SEND-MAP-DATAONLY.
     MOVE LAST-REC-KEY TO REC-KEY.
     PERFORM 0400-START-BROWSE.
     MOVE 1 TO SUB.
     PERFORM 0410-READ-NEXT-RECORD
     IF LAST-HELP-REC
         GO TO 0600-LAST-PAGE.
     MOVE REC-KEY TO SAVE-REC-KEY.
     PERFORM 0410-READ-NEXT-RECORD
         THRU 0410-READ-NEXT-EXIT
             VARYING SUB FROM 1 BY 1
                 UNTIL (SUB > 16) OR (LAST-HELP-REC).
     IF LAST-HELP-REC
         GO TO 0600-LAST-PAGE.
     GO TO 0910-SEND-MAP-DATAONLY.

 0300-BROWSE-BACKWARD.
*EXEC CICS
*    HANDLE CONDITION
*          NOTFND (0600-LAST-PAGE)
*          ENDFILE (0600-LAST-PAGE)
*END-EXEC.
      MOVE '  {                   00169    ' TO DFHEIV0
     CALL 'DFHEI1' USING DFHEIV0
      GO TO  0600-LAST-PAGE 0600-LAST-PAGE DEPENDING ON D
     IF NO-HELP-RECS-FOUND
         GO TO 0810-NO-HELP-RECS.
     IF DELETE-COMPLETED
         MOVE 'RECORDS DELETED, HIT PF1 TO EXIT' TO IM-D-
             GO TO 0910-SEND-MAP-DATAONLY.
     MOVE ' ' TO DELETE-RECORD-SW
     MOVE FIRST-REC-KEY TO REC-KEY.
     PERFORM 0400-START-BROWSE.
     MOVE 16 TO SUB.
     PERFORM 0410-READ-NEXT-RECORD.
     IF LAST-HELP-REC
         GO TO 0600-LAST-PAGE.
     MOVE REC-KEY TO SAVE-REC-KEY.
     MOVE 16 TO SUB.
     PERFORM 0420-READ-PREV-RECORD
     IF LAST-HELP-REC
         GO TO 0600-LAST-PAGE.
     MOVE REC-KEY TO SAVE-REC-KEY.
     MOVE 16 TO SUB.
     PERFORM 0420-READ-PREV-RECORD
```

Figure 3.12 *Continued.*

```
         THRU 0420-READ-PREV-EXIT
             UNTIL (SUB = 0) OR (LAST-HELP-REC).
     IF LAST-HELP-REC
         GO TO 0600-LAST-PAGE.
     MOVE REC-KEY TO FIRST-REC-KEY.
     GO TO 0910-SEND-MAP-DATAONLY.

 0400-START-BROWSE.
     MOVE ' ' TO IM-D-ERMSG.
     MOVE GREEN TO IM-A-ERMSG.
*EXEC CICS
*     STARTBR DATASET ('ARA81C')
*              RIDFLD (REC-KEY)
*END-EXEC.
      MOVE '          00204    ' TO DFHEIV0
      MOVE 'ARA81C' TO DFHEIV1
     CALL 'DFHEI1' USING DFHEIV0  DFHEIV1  DFHDUMMY DFHEI
     REC-KEY.

 0410-READ-NEXT-RECORD.
*EXEC CICS
*     READNEXT DATASET ('ARA81C')
*                INTO (HELP-RECORD)
*              RIDFLD (REC-KEY)
*END-EXEC.
      MOVE '  M       00210    ' TO DFHEIV0
      MOVE 'ARA81C' TO DFHEIV1
     CALL 'DFHEI1' USING DFHEIV0  DFHEIV1  HELP-RECORD DF
     REC-KEY DFHDUMMY DFHEIB0.

     IF H-REC-TRANS-ID NOT = TASK-TRANS
         MOVE 'Y' TO LAST-HELP-REC-SW.
 0410-READ-NEXT-CONT.
     IF H-REC-TRANS-ID NOT = TASK-TRANS
         GO TO 0410-READ-NEXT-EXIT.
     PERFORM 0500-SETUP-MAP.
 0410-READ-NEXT-EXIT.

 0420-READ-PREV-RECORD.
*EXEC CICS
*     READPREV DATASET('ARA81C')
*                INTO (HELP-RECORD)
*              RIDFLD (REC-KEY)
*END-EXEC.
      MOVE '  M       00224    ' TO DFHEIV0
      MOVE 'ARA81C' TO DFHEIV1
     CALL 'DFHEI1' USING DFHEIV0  DFHEIV1  HELP-RECORD DF
     REC-KEY DFHDUMMY DFHEIB0.

     IF H-REC-TRANS-ID NOT = TASK-TRANS
         MOVE 'Y' TO LAST-HELP-REC-SW.
 0420-READ-PREV-CONT.
     IF H-REC-TRANS-ID NOT = TASK-TRANS
         GO TO 0420-READ-PREV-EXIT.
     PERFORM 0500-SETUP-MAP.
 0420-READ-PREV-EXIT.

 0500-SETUP-MAP.
     IF SUB = 1
         MOVE REC-KEY TO FIRST-REC-KEY.
     IF SUB = 16
```

Figure 3.12 *Continued.*

```
                 MOVE REC-KEY TO LAST-REC-KEY.
             IF H-LINE-COLOR = 'R'
                 MOVE RED TO IM-A-TEXT(SUB)
             ELSE IF H-LINE-COLOR = 'W'
                 MOVE WHITE TO IM-A-TEXT(SUB)
             ELSE IF H-LINE-COLOR = 'B'
                 MOVE BLUE TO IM-A-TEXT(SUB).
             MOVE H-REC-TEXT TO IM-D-TEXT(SUB).
             MOVE H-REC-SEQ TO IM-D-SEQ(SUB).
             MOVE REC-KEY TO SAVE-REC-KEY.
             IF EIBAID = DFHPF8
                SUBTRACT 1 FROM SUB.

         0600-LAST-PAGE.
             IF EIBAID NOT = DFHPF8
                 MOVE SAVE-REC-KEY TO LAST-REC-KEY
                 MOVE 'THIS IS THE END OF THE FILE' TO IM-D-ERMSG
             IF EIBAID = DFHPF8
                 MOVE SAVE-REC-KEY TO FIRST-REC-KEY
                 MOVE 'THIS IS THE START OF THE FILE' TO IM-D-ERM
             MOVE RED TO IM-A-ERMSG.
             GO TO 0910-SEND-MAP-DATAONLY.

         0700-DELETE-6-PAGES.
             IF NO-HELP-RECS-FOUND
                 GO TO 0810-NO-HELP-RECS.
             IF DELETE-COMPLETED
                 MOVE RED TO IM-A-ERMSG
                 MOVE 'RECORDS DELETED, HIT PF1 TO EXIT' TO IM-D-
                 GO TO 0910-SEND-MAP-DATAONLY.
             IF READY-TO-DELETE
                 NEXT SENTENCE
             ELSE
                 MOVE 'R' TO DELETE-RECORD-SW
                 MOVE 'DELETE CONFIRMED, HIT PF3 ONCE MORE TO DEL
                     TO IM-D-ERMSG
             GO TO 0910-SEND-MAP-DATAONLY.
             MOVE 'D' TO DELETE-RECORD-SW
             MOVE TASK-TRANS TO HELP-TRANS.
        *EXEC CICS
        *      DELETE DATASET ('ARA81C')
        *               RIDFLD (HELP-TRANS)
        *               KEYLENGTH(4)
        *               GENERIC
        *END-EXEC.
              MOVE '  q       00280    ' TO DFHEIV0
              MOVE 'ARA81C' TO DFHEIV1
              MOVE 4 TO DFHEIV11
             CALL 'DFHEI1' USING DFHEIV0  DFHEIV1  DFHDUMMY DFHDU
             HELP-TRANS DFHEIV11.

             MOVE LOW-VALUES TO HELPMAP.
             MOVE 'RECORDS DELETED HIT PF1 TO EXIT' TO IM-D-ERMSG
             MOVE WHITE TO IM-A-ERMSG.
             GO TO 0900-SEND-MAP.

         0710-DELETE-PAGE.
        *EXEC CICS
        *     HANDLE CONDITION
        *           NOTFND (0710-DELETE-END)
        *           ENDFILE (0710-DELETE-END)
```

Figure 3.12 *Continued.*

```
      *END-EXEC.
            MOVE '  {                    00292    ' TO DFHEIV0
           CALL 'DFHEI1' USING DFHEIV0
            GO TO  0710-DELETE-END 0710-DELETE-END DEPENDING ON
           DFHEIGDI.

           IF NO-HELP-RECS-FOUND
               GO TO 0810-NO-HELP-RECS.
           IF DELETE-COMPLETED
               MOVE RED TO IM-A-ERMSG
               MOVE 'RECORDS DELETED, HIT PF1 TO EXIT' TO IM-D-
               GO TO 0910-SEND-MAP-DATAONLY.
           IF READY-TO-DELETE
               NEXT SENTENCE
           ELSE
               MOVE 'R' TO DELETE-RECORD-SW
               MOVE 'DELETE CONFIRMED, HIT PF9 ONCE MORE TO DEL
                   TO IM-D-ERMSG
           GO TO 0910-SEND-MAP-DATAONLY.
           MOVE IM-D-SEQ(1) TO LINE-NUMX.
           PERFORM 0710-DELETE-CONT
                   VARYING SUB FROM LINE-NUM BY 1
                       UNTIL SUB > 96.
       0710-DELETE-END.
           MOVE 'D' TO DELETE-RECORD-SW
           MOVE TASK-TRANS TO HELP-TRANS.
           MOVE LOW-VALUES TO HELPMAP.
           MOVE 'RECORDS DELETED HIT PF1 TO EXIT' TO IM-D-ERMSG
           MOVE WHITE TO IM-A-ERMSG.
           GO TO 0900-SEND-MAP.
       0710-DELETE-CONT.
           MOVE SUB TO LINE-NUM
           MOVE  LINE-NUMX TO HELP-SEQ
      *EXEC CICS
      *     DELETE DATASET ('ARA81C')
      *              RIDFLD (REC-KEY)
      *END-EXEC.
            MOVE '          00324    ' TO DFHEIV0
            MOVE 'ARA81C' TO DFHEIV1
           CALL 'DFHEI1' USING DFHEIV0  DFHEIV1  DFHDUMMY DFHDU
           REC-KEY.

       0800-INIT-SESSION.
      *EXEC CICS
      *    HANDLE CONDITION
      *          NOTFND (0810-NO-HELP-RECS)
      *          ENDFILE (0810-NO-HELP-RECS)
      *END-EXEC.
            MOVE '  {                    00330    ' TO DFHEIV0
           CALL 'DFHEI1' USING DFHEIV0
            GO TO  0810-NO-HELP-RECS 0810-NO-HELP-RECS DEPENDIN
           DFHEIGDI.

      *EXEC CICS
      *    UNLOCK DATASET ('ARA81C')
      *END-EXEC.
            MOVE '          00335    ' TO DFHEIV0
            MOVE 'ARA81C' TO DFHEIV1
           CALL 'DFHEI1' USING DFHEIV0  DFHEIV1.
           MOVE TASK-TRANS TO HELP-TRANS F-HELP-TRANS.
           MOVE SPACES TO HELP-SEQ.
```

Figure 3.12 *Continued.*

```
           PERFORM 0400-START-BROWSE.
           PERFORM 0410-READ-NEXT-RECORD
               THRU 0410-READ-NEXT-EXIT
                   VARYING SUB FROM 1 BY 1
                       UNTIL (SUB > 16) OR (LAST-HELP-REC).
           IF LAST-HELP-REC
              GO TO 0810-NO-HELP-RECS.
           MOVE '01' TO F-HELP-SEQ.
           MOVE REC-KEY TO LAST-REC-KEY.
           GO TO 0900-SEND-MAP.

       0810-NO-HELP-RECS.
           MOVE 'Y' TO NO-HELP-RECS-FOUND-SW.
           MOVE SAVE-REC-KEY TO FIRST-REC-KEY
           MOVE 'NO TUTORIAL FOR THIS TRANSACTION, HIT PF1 TO E
               TO IM-D-ERMSG.
           MOVE RED TO IM-A-ERMSG.
           GO TO 0900-SEND-MAP.

       0900-SEND-MAP.
           MOVE 'AR82' TO IM-D-TRAN.
           MOVE 'PF3 DELETE RECORDS' TO IM-D-PFMSG.
           MOVE CURRENT-DATE TO IM-D-DATE.
           MOVE 'DELETE YOUR OWN TUTORIALS       ' TO IM-D-HDR.
           MOVE -1 TO IM-L-TEXT(1).
      *EXEC CICS
      *     SEND MAP('ARC81M6')
      *          MAPSET('ARC81M')
      *             FROM(HELPMAP)
      *     ERASE
      *     CURSOR
      *END-EXEC.
            MOVE '  J        S     00365    ' TO DFHEIV0
            MOVE 'ARC81M6' TO DFHC0070
            MOVE 'ARC81M' TO DFHC0071
            MOVE -1 TO DFHEIV11
           CALL 'DFHEI1' USING DFHEIV0  DFHC0070 HELPMAP DFHDUM
           DFHC0071 DFHDUMMY DFHDUMMY DFHDUMMY DFHEIV11.

           GO TO 0920-RETURN-TRANSID.

       0905-INVALID-PFKEY.
           MOVE RED TO IM-A-ERMSG.
           MOVE 'KEY IS NOT FUNCTIONAL IN TUTORIAL MODE' TO IM-
           GO TO 0910-SEND-MAP-DATAONLY.

       0910-SEND-MAP-DATAONLY.
           MOVE -1 TO IM-L-TEXT(1).
      *EXEC CICS
      *     SEND MAP('ARC81M6')
      *          MAPSET('ARC81M')
      *             FROM(HELPMAP)
      *     DATAONLY
      *     CURSOR
      *END-EXEC.
            MOVE '  J              00381    ' TO DFHEIV0
            MOVE 'ARC81M6' TO DFHC0070
            MOVE 'ARC81M' TO DFHC0071
            MOVE -1 TO DFHEIV11
           CALL 'DFHEI1' USING DFHEIV0  DFHC0070 HELPMAP DFHDUM
           DFHC0071 DFHDUMMY DFHDUMMY DFHDUMMY DFHEIV11.
```

Figure 3.12 *Continued.*

```

         0920-RETURN-TRANSID.
        *EXEC CICS
        *        RETURN TRANSID('AR82')
        *               COMMAREA(COMM-AREA)
        *               LENGTH(31)
        *END-EXEC.
              MOVE '  \       00389    ' TO DFHEIV0
              MOVE 'AR82' TO DFHEIV5
              MOVE 31 TO DFHEIV11
             CALL 'DFHEI1' USING DFHEIV0  DFHEIV5  COMM-AREA DFHE

             STOP RUN.
             GOBACK.


*STATISTICS*     SOURCE RECORDS =    598      DATA DIVISION STATEMENTS =
*OPTIONS IN EFFECT*      SIZE =  524288  BUF =    20480  LINECNT = 57  SP
*OPTIONS IN EFFECT*      NODMAP, NOPMAP, NOCLIST, NOSUPMAP, NOXREF,   SX
*OPTIONS IN EFFECT*      NOTERM, NONUM, NOBATCH, NONAME, COMPILE=01, NOS
*OPTIONS IN EFFECT*      NOOPTIMIZE, NOSYMDMP, NOTEST,    VERB,    ZWB, SY
*OPTIONS IN EFFECT*      NOLST , NOFDECK,NOCDECK, LCOL2,  L120,    DUMP ,
*OPTIONS IN EFFECT*      NOCOUNT, NOVBSUM, NOVBREF, LANGLVL(1)
                                           CROSS-REFERENCE DICTIONARY


DATA NAMES                     DEFN     REFERENCE


ASKIP                          000058
ATTRBYTE                       000040
BLUE                           000043   000408
COMM-AREA                      000008   000234  000595
DELETE-COMPLETED               000025   000291  000323  000428  00047
DELETE-RECORD-SW               000023   000288  000326  000435  00043
DFHAID                         000107
DFHBLLSLOT1                    000225
DFHBLLSLOT2                    000226
DFHB0025                       000164
DFHB0041                       000151
DFHB0042                       000152
DFHB0043                       000153
DFHB0044                       000154
DFHB0045                       000155
DFHB0046                       000156
DFHB0047                       000157
DFHB0048                       000158
DFHCLEAR                       000110
DFHCLRP                        000111
DFHCOMMAREA                    000223   000234
DFHC0011                       000183
DFHC0022                       000179
DFHC0023                       000180
DFHC0070                       000185   000263  000265  000557  00056
DFHC0071                       000186   000264  000265  000558  00056
DFHC0084                       000174
DFHC0085                       000175
DFHC0320                       000176
DFHC0440                       000187
DFHDUMMY                       000188   000265  000357  000368  00038
DFHEIBLK                       000191
```

Figure 3.12 *Continued.*

```
DFHEIB0                        000147   000357   000368   000387
DFHEICB                        000148
DFHEID0                        000146
DFHEIGDI                       000197   000249   000285   000318   00046
DFHEIV0                        000189   000247   000248   000262   00026
                                        000355   000357   000366   00036
                                        000500   000502   000511   00051
                                        000592   000595
DFHEIV1                        000170   000274   000275   000356   00035
                                        000501   000502   000520   00052
DFHEIV10                       000181
DFHEIV11                       000159   000449   000450   000559   00056
DFHEIV12                       000160
DFHEIV13                       000161
DFHEIV14                       000162
DFHEIV15                       000163
DFHEIV16                       000150
DFHEIV17                       000167
DFHEIV18                       000168
DFHEIV19                       000169
DFHEIV2                        000171
DFHEIV20                       000173
DFHEIV3                        000172
DFHEIV4                        000184
DFHEIV5                        000165   000593   000595
DFHEIV6                        000166
DFHEIV7                        000177
DFHEIV8                        000178
DFHEIV9                        000182
DFHENTER                       000109
DFHLDVER                       000145
DFHMSRE                        000114
DFHNULL                        000108
DFHOPID                        000113
DFHPA1                         000117
DFHPA2                         000118
DFHPA3                         000119
DFHPEN                         000112
DFHPF1                         000120
DFHPF10                        000129
DFHPF11                        000130
DFHPF12                        000131
DFHPF13                        000132
DFHPF14                        000133
DFHPF15                        000134
DFHPF16                        000135
DFHPF17                        000136
DFHPF18                        000137
DFHPF19                        000138
DFHPF2                         000121
DFHPF20                        000139
DFHPF21                        000140
DFHPF22                        000141
DFHPF23                        000142
DFHPF24                        000143
DFHPF3                         000122
DFHPF4                         000123
DFHPF5                         000124
DFHPF6                         000125
DFHPF7                         000126
DFHPF8                         000127   000412   000416   000419
```

Figure 3.12 *Continued.*

```
DFHPF9              000128
DFHSTRF             000115
DFHTRIG             000116
EIBAID              000200  000412  000416  000419
EIBATT              000210
EIBCALEN            000199  000233
EIBCOMPL            000213
EIBCONF             000215
EIBCPOSN            000198
EIBDATE             000193
EIBDS               000203
EIBEOC              000211
EIBERR              000216
EIBERRCD            000217
EIBFIL01            000209
EIBFMH              000212
EIBFN               000201
EIBFREE             000207
EIBNODAT            000219
EIBRCODE            000202
EIBRECV             000208
EIBREQID            000204
EIBRESP             000220
EIBRESP2            000221
EIBRLDBK            000222
EIBRSRCE            000205
EIBSIG              000214
EIBSYNC             000206
EIBSYNRB            000218
EIBTASKN            000195
EIBTIME             000192
EIBTRMID            000196
EIBTRNID            000194  000235
F-HELP-SEQ          000016  000531
F-HELP-TRANS        000015  000522
FIRST-REC-KEY       000014  000327  000345  000400  00042
GREEN               000044  000350
H-LINE-COLOR        000065  000403  000405  000407
H-REC-SEQ           000064  000410
H-REC-TEXT          000066  000409
H-REC-TRANS-ID      000063  000371  000374  000390  00039
HELP-KEY            000062
HELP-RECORD         000061  000368  000387
HELP-SEQ            000013  000495  000523
HELP-TRANS          000012  000440  000450  000488  00052
HELPMAP             000070  000265  000453  000489  00056
IM-A-COLOR          000086
IM-A-DATE           000079
IM-A-ERMSG          000103  000292  000350  000422  00042
IM-A-HDR            000076
IM-A-PFMSG          000092
IM-A-PFMSG2         000095
IM-A-PFMSG3         000099
IM-A-SEQ            000083
IM-A-TEXT           000089  000404  000406  000408
IM-A-TRAN           000073
IM-D-COLOR          000087
IM-D-DATE           000080  000546
IM-D-ERMSG          000104  000293  000324  000349  00041
                            000490  000538  000567
IM-D-HDR            000077  000547
```

Figure 3.12 *Continued.*

```
IM-D-PFMSG                      000093   000545
IM-D-PFMSG2                     000096
IM-D-PFMSG3                     000100
IM-D-SEQ                        000084   000410   000482
IM-D-TEXT                       000090   000409
IM-D-TEXT-LINES                 000081
IM-D-TRAN                       000074   000544
IM-L-COLOR                      000085
IM-L-DATE                       000078
IM-L-ERMSG                      000102
IM-L-HDR                        000075
IM-L-PFMSG                      000091
IM-L-PFMSG2                     000094
IM-L-PFMSG3                     000098
IM-L-SEQ                        000082
IM-L-TEXT                       000088   000548   000571
IM-L-TRAN                       000072
L-HELP-SEQ                      000019
L-HELP-TRANS                    000018
LAST-HELP-REC                   000037   000299   000302   000306   00033
LAST-HELP-REC-SW                000036   000372   000391
LAST-REC-KEY                    000017   000295   000402   000417   00053
LINE-COUNTERS                   000032
LINE-NUM                        000033   000483   000494
LINE-NUMX                       000034   000482   000495
NO-HELP-RECS-FOUND              000027   000289   000321   000426   00046
NO-HELP-RECS-FOUND-SW           000026   000536
PROT                            000054
PROT-BRT                        000056
PROT-BRT-MDT                    000057
PROT-MDT                        000055
READY-TO-DELETE                 000024   000432   000475
REC-KEY                         000011   000295   000301   000327   00033
                                         000402   000411   000502   00053
RED                             000041   000292   000404   000422   00042
S-HELP-SEQ                      000022
S-HELP-TRANS                    000021
SAVE-REC-KEY                    000020   000301   000333   000338   00041
SUB                             000030   000297   000302   000329   00033
                                         000408   000409   000410   00041
SUB-COUNTERS                    000029
TASK-TRANS                      000010   000371   000374   000390   00039
UNPROT-ALPHA                    000045
UNPROT-ALPHA-BRT                000047
UNPROT-ALPHA-BRT-MDT            000048
UNPROT-ALPHA-MDT                000046
UNPROT-NUM                      000049
UNPROT-NUM-BRT                  000051
UNPROT-NUM-BRT-MDT              000052
UNPROT-NUM-DRK-MDT              000053
UNPROT-NUM-MDT                  000050
WHITE                           000042   000406   000455   000491
PROCEDURE NAMES                 DEFN     REFERENCE


0000-MAIN                       000232
0100-RETURN-TO-MENU             000269   000249
0200-BROWSE-FORWARD             000277   000249
0300-BROWSE-BACKWARD            000310   000249
0400-START-BROWSE               000348   000296   000328   000524
0410-READ-NEXT-CONT             000373
```

Figure 3.12 *Continued.*

```
0410-READ-NEXT-EXIT           000377   000302  000375  000525
0410-READ-NEXT-RECORD         000360   000298  000302  000330  00052
0420-READ-PREV-CONT           000392
0420-READ-PREV-EXIT           000396   000340  000394
0420-READ-PREV-RECORD         000379   000335  000340
0500-SETUP-MAP                000398   000376  000395
0600-LAST-PAGE                000415   000285  000300  000307  00031
0700-DELETE-6-PAGES           000425   000249
0710-DELETE-CONT              000493   000483
0710-DELETE-END               000486   000466
0710-DELETE-PAGE              000458   000249
0800-INIT-SESSION             000505   000236
0810-NO-HELP-RECS             000535   000290  000322  000427  00047
0900-SEND-MAP                 000543   000456  000492  000533  00054
0905-INVALID-PFKEY            000565   000249
0910-SEND-MAP-DATAONLY        000570   000267  000294  000308  00032
                                       000568
0920-RETURN-TRANSID           000586   000563
CARD   ERROR MESSAGE
```

Chapter

4

Introduction to ACF2 & DOCU/TEXT Architecture

In this chapter, I'd like to present to you a pair of topics which will be helpful in designing, coding, and providing a secure environment for your applications. The first is the ACF2 (Access Control Facility 2) security software, an acquired product of the CA corporation. A second topic is a comprehensive JCL "analyzer" and flowcharting technique called DOCU/TEXT, by Diversified Software Systems. Allow me to provide you with some background on each of these productivity tools.

The DOCU/TEXT software allows you to scan job control for consistency rather than for syntax alone. Scanning JCLs in the conventional sense (like using the TYPRUN=SCAN option on your job-control statement) will in fact buy you very little. It will show you misspellings of your keywords, missing commas, or simply a forgotten continuation. Conventional JCL scanning through the TYPRUN option will tell you if you accidentally typed DISB in place of DISP, but not much else.

4.1 The Major Components of ACF2

The purpose of ACF2 is to protect your installation against unauthorized destruction, disclosure, or modification of data and resources. This means that ACF2 should preferably be handled by an administrator specifically assigned to this task of security maintenance, whose full-time job is producing rules that allow or disallow you access to a particular production system.

The idea is that the security needs of an installation can be tailored by an authorized person or persons through the definition of specific access rules. By writing rules, you can pretty much establish a user's perspective, his security profile in terms of file access, and the scope and latitude of his querying abilities. For example, user A can browse only a particular file or database, while user B has a whole array of administrative maintenance at his disposal.

In a variety of cases, an ACF2 administrator is an application-oriented analyst; in some cases, especially with larger organizations, the job is handled by systems rather than application personnel. In certain (infrequent) cases, however, establishing and maintaining security is the full-time responsibility of a quality-assurance group.

ACF2 handles both the production and test phases of an application. Although the primary purpose of ACF2 is production-oriented, it is also used extensively even in test situations to provide safeguards because some of the data used in those test systems might be the direct result of capturing live transactions from an already existing application. (More on this in chapter 9.)

Think of ACF2 as an extension of your operating system. From an administrative point of view, this software is tailored to individual users, data sets, and resources in the following manner:

- You can access the system via a logon ID, or more specifically via logonid records. The logonid essentially identifies you and other users and the system you need to access in terms of status; privileges; access history attributes related to TSO, CICS, IMS, IDMS, DB2, and VM violation statistics; and a great deal more.
- You can access the system via access rules. These access rules define the entire working environment for accessing a particular data set, and determine whether access will be granted or disallowed for a user or a particular user group. This "group" philosophy is an important concept because administrators always seek a common ground among a particular type of users and then write rules for them rather than establish individualized procedures for each and every user of an application. Access rules in ACF2 are developed in a high-level language, like state ments describing the circumstances for the access.
- You can access the system via generalized resource rules, which specifically allow or disallow you or your group of users access to generalized resources, such as TSO accounts and procedures, IMS, DB/2 applications and transactions, CICS files, programs, transactions, transient data, temporary storage, including DL/I calls, and a lot more.
- You can access the system via entry record. This methodology enables you to define access only from specific input resources or group of input resources, such as a specific terminal or group of terminals. More on this in a minute.
- You can access the system via scope records, which limit the authority a specifically privileged user has over logonid records, access rules, and other ACF2 records.
- You can access the system via shift records. This methodology simply allows or disallows you to sign on the application within a specific time. This can also be accomplished through GSO (Global System Option), which specifies the option profile of the entire computer installation.
- You can access the system via the identification record, which contains extended user authentication information.

All of these components can be maintained through the use of TSO/ISPF commands, ISPF screens, and batch utilities.

4.2 Other Components of the ACF2 Software

In addition to the above major ACF2 components (or more specifically, databases), other components include a number of topics that need to be discussed up front. The first one among these is the ACF command and subcommand structure under TSO, which allow you to create and maintain all the major ACF2 components I have talked about. A Report Generator module is designed to produce reports for you when you are initially implementing the required security so that you can closely monitor a particular access and security violations.

Your password is a unique string of characters. Just like in ISPF or in CICS, you need to enter it in addition to your logonid to verify your identity to the system. Note that once you have entered your password it is one-way encrypted, so that it is not stored as it was initially entered. Unlike the logonid, you can change your password periodically—whatever you do, make sure you remember your password!

Another important aspect of the ACF2 structure is the User Identification (UID) string. The UID exists for each user of your system. This string is scanned during the validation process because it usually contains not only the logonid, but other vital information about the user. Based on this information, ACF2 allows or disallows you access to data and other resources according to company name, department code, site, branch, responsibility code, or however you want to set up the system. I cannot be more specific than this because your installation has the option to define the amount and the type of information that will be resident in this UID string.

The ACF2 Field Definition Record, or ACFFDR, defines and establishes control for each field of data in the logonid record. Essentially, it contains the same fields for all users of the system. If you need to change any specific field on this record, you need to reassemble the ACFFDR assembler program.

4.3 What Is the Logonid Record and How Is It Used?

The Logonid record or database identifies each user to the ACF2 software through certain fields that define a user's attribute or characteristics. These attributes are clustered together in sections, some of which are as follows:

An identification section contains information such as your logon identifier, name, phone, and a previously mentioned (and setup) UID string. A cancel/suspend section includes information about the status of your logonid, whether it is cancelled and suspended, and, if so, a corresponding date of such a cancellation or suspension.

The record also contains a privileges section to describe you to ACF2 in terms of what you can and cannot access. For example, can you access TSO? Can you submit a batch job? This section also provides you with the authority to process logonid records, access rules, shift records, and so on. The access section keeps statistics on how many times you have accessed a particular system, including the date, time, and source of the last access.

ACF2 also maintains a password section that contains a violation count and date, a password expiration date, and a date when the password was last modified. Other sections are also available to you according to your needs, e.g., A CICS section, a DB2 section, an IMS or IDMS section, etc.

Consider the example in Figure 4.1. Note that the identification section highlights the name of the user (ALEX VARSEGI), logonid (USER01), and phone-number extension (223). The entry MARKTFRDUSER01 is his expanded UID or user-identification string. This is like concatenating a key. MARKT is the department reference for Varsegi, while FRD designates his function. His logonid record is a temporary one because it will expire on 11/20/93.

With regards to certain privileges, Varsegi is not allowed to modify any of the existing ACF2 rules, records, or system options, which is reflected through the AUDIT option. Also, he can run TSO batch jobs (jobs) and use the TSO, or Time Sharing Option.

Varsegi has accessed the system some 210 times, according to the exhibit. The last access was made at 10:08 on 7/12/92 using a terminal that is defined as TR720. The PSWD-VIO is going to be automatically reset at midnight on 7/15/92. The user's last invalid password attempt was made on 11/20/92. The last time he modified his password was on 5/28/92 at 8:07. He has made 2 invalid password attempts (PSDW-VIO); hopefully it was an accident on both occasions.

Varsegi's default TSO prefix is the same as his logonid (USER01). His default sysout and message classes (DFT-SOUT and DFT-SUBM) are A, and he can receive messages from other TSO users (INTERCOM). He can submit jobs from TSO (JCL) and specify any region size at the time he logs on the system (LGN-SIZE).

As of today, he had a total of only two security violations (SEC-VIO) and his logonid record was last updated 6/11/92 at 10:08. Last, the PREFIX field is the only ACF2 field in this exhibit. The user's prefix is USER01, the same as his logonid. This field gives Varsegi ownership of all data sets with a high-level index of USER01.

```
USER01              MARKTFRDUSER01      ALEX VARSEGI    EXT.223
                    DEPT(MARKT) FUNCTION(FRD)

CANCEL/SUSPEND      EXPIRE 11/20/93

PRIVILEGES          AUDIT JOB TSO

ACCESS              ACCT-CNT(210) ACC-DATE(7/12/92) ACC-SRCE(TR720)
                    ACCT-TIME(10:08)

PASSWORD            RSWD-DAT(7/15/92) PSWD-TOD(5/28/92-8:07)
                    PSWD-VIO(2)

TSO                 DFT-PFX(USER01) DFT-SOUT(A) DFT-SUBM(A)
                    INTERCOM JCL LGN-SIZE LINE(ATTN) MAIL MSGID
                    NOTICES TSOPROC(IKJACCNT) TSORGN(1,024)
                    TSOSIZE(8,172) WTP

STATISTICS          SEC-VIO(2) UPD-TOD(6/11/92-10:08)

RESTRICTIONS        PREFIX(USER01)
```

Figure 4.1 Sample Logonid record.

4.4 Categories of User Privilege Levels

Certain fields on the logonid record allow you a set of privileges, or privilege levels. These privilege levels give you access to an application (files as well as resources) and ACF2 rules. There are, overall, six privilege levels in ACF2: Account, Security, Audit, Consult, Leader, and User.

If you have account-level security, you can insert, delete, and change the contents of logonid records within the limits defined by the user scope. For example, you can add, change, and delete logonid records. With an assigned scope, however, you might be restricted to a certain group of people. Also, with account privileges, you have no authority to write rules or process other ACF2 records.

Security privileges indicate that a user is an installation security officer who has access to data sets, programs, and other resources. If you have security privileges, you can add, change, list, and delete access to generalized rules. With this kind of authority, you are also allowed to list and change certain fields on the logonid record. There are also certain restrictions (e.g., adding or deleting records on the logonid database) unless you also have account privileges.)

With audit privileges, you can look at just about anything (including a set of ACF SHOW subcommands), but without the ability to modify anything on the system.

If you are a consultant, you can display most fields on the logonid records, but update only certain nonsecurity-related fields relative to TSO. Listing most fields in a consultant capacity, of course, does not include someone else's password, account, or trace fields.

If you have leader privileges, your level of authority encompasses that of the consultant, including maintenance access to additional fields on the logonid database.

Finally, the user privilege level is the basic attribute that is automatically assigned to every ACF2 system user. It allows you to display your logonid record. An installation can determine whether a user who has only user privileges can write access rules for his own data sets by means of the central option of the GSO OPTS records.

As you probably noticed from this discussion, you might be allowed more than a single level of authority. Keep in mind that, as I explained earlier (see the previous discussion of account privileges), while privilege fields grant you certain authorities to access data, ACF2 rule sets, logonid records, and other ACF2 records, scope records are designed to restrict some of that authority.

4.5 CICS and ACF2 Security

ACF2 provides security for a CICS system by intercepting resource requests before the actual access takes place. After ACF2 CICS performs the necessary validation, control is returned to the normal CICS processing routines.

In using ACF2, your logon identifier becomes the focal point of what you can access in a CICS system. When you sign on, ACF2 verifies that you have entered a valid logon ID and the associated password. The system also checks if you have signed on from an authorized terminal, and might check valid sign-in times as well. Thus, for example, you can sign on the system only from terminal TERMJH017, which is located in the Payroll Department. You might also be further restricted to sign on between the hours of 10 A.M. through 12:30 P.M. In addition, ACF2 checks to make sure that your password is a current one and that you are authorized to use a group name. A group approach is used to primarily simplify an authorization scheme.

Password verification (in addition to checking your logon I.D.) is also part of the ACF2 access procedures. Password verification ensures that people are who they say they are. ACF2 does this by issuing a password prompt when it determines that a password is required from the terminal operator. The system determines whether such a password is a correct one and permits processing to continue as opposed to suspending and cancelling the transaction. You can customize password verification by specifying ACF2/CICS parameters and using the VERIFY keyword as one of the resource commands used by the system. Also, you can use the application program interface to directly incorporate password verification into your program. ACF2 provides the following types of protection for your data:

- Protection at the data-set name level for all data sets that reside on a DASD (Direct-Access Storage Device), including the volume table of contents, or VTOC.
- Protection at the volume name level for all direct-access (and tape) volumes.
- Protection for tape data sets at the data-set level or at the volume level.

You can easily develop several criteria for accessing a file under ACF2 through a set of generalized rules. Access simply refers to the control of transactions, programs, files, records, DL/I calls, transient data, temporary storage, and user-defined resources. (A resource can be a single terminal, file storage, part of the CPU memory, and so on.) Each resource is assigned a unique name (using the keyword &KEY) and each resource belongs to a logical group called TYPE.

ACF2 enables you to rely on a set of language-like procedures to state your access rules. Before you can write an access rule, however, you must "own" the data (along with other users) or be either a security officer or someone who has unlimited access to the system. To write effective access rules, you need to ask the following questions:

What data do I want to share? What is the high-level index of the data set, the data-set name, and possibly the name of the volume on which the data set resides? Who do I want to share the data set with? Can they be grouped together in some logical fashion? Can I mask them? How do I want others to use the data? Do I want them to be able to read and write to the data sets? Can they allocate new data sets on the volume?

A rule set is a group of related ACF2 access rules. Rule entries specify the access environments, types, and permissions. ACF2 maintains a rule set for each data-set name (DSN) although some rule sets can apply for entire volumes of DASD or tape data sets. Software stores rule sets on the access rule database by their key or high-level index. These rule sets need to be compiled and stored much like programs. The following is a rule set:

```
$KEY(PAYROLL)
MASTER.FILE UID(PAYJCL) READ(A) WRITE(A)
MASTER.FILE UID(SPACEMGR) ALLOC(A)
```

This rule set, for example, permits PAYROLL jobs to read and write to the MASTER.FILE and permits the SPACEMGR to create it. This rule set contains the following elements:

- Control statements
- Access environments
- Access types
- Access permissions

Control statements are parameters that begin a rule set. They specify conditions that apply to the whole rule set or rule entries. In ACF2, you can use two types of control statements: those that begin with a dollar sign and others using a percent sign. The only required element is $KEY, which identifies the high-level qualifier of the data set.

Access environments are statements that specify conditions for sharing, such as the name of the data set you want to share and the user(s) you want to share it with.

Access types are parameters in a rule entry that specify the type of access a user can have. A rule can specify that users have read-only (READ), read-write (WRITE), allocate (ALLOC), and execute-only (EXEC) access to the data. Allocate access means that the user can create, delete, rename, and catalog data sets. You can use a one-character abbreviation for the access type, such as R for read-only, W for read/write, A for allocate, and E for execute-only.

Access permissions are parameters in a rule entry that specify the action that ACF2 should take when all the required conditions are met. Rules can instruct ACF2 to enforce one of the following access types:

Allow (A). Grant the user access to the data.

Log (L). Grant the user access to the data, but record the access so that you can create an audit trail. You might specify this for sensitive data sets and programs.

Prevent (P). Do not grant the user access to this data but log the attempt to create an audit trail.

Permissions are matched with type to fully describe the access you want to grant. For example, R(A), W(L), and ALLOC(P) means read and write access to the data, but a log to prevent allocating new data sets for this high-level index.

In the previous PAYROLL example, UIDs that begin with PAYROLL can read and write to the data set. By default, all other UIDs are denied access. SPACEMGR can allocate PAYROLL.MASTER.FILE data sets. All other UIDs are prevented by default.

4.6 Introduction to DOCU/TEXT Techniques

The primary function of DOCU/TEXT is to process JCLs, produce reports based on those JCLs, and verify that the JCLs will execute properly once submitted.

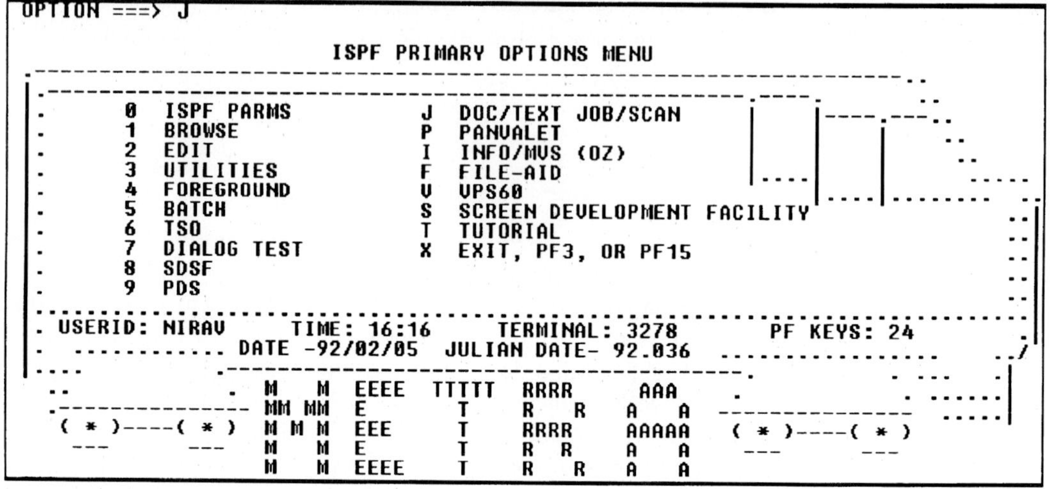

Figure 4.2 Invoking DOCU/TEXT JOB/SCAN from the ISPF main menu.

DOCU/TEXT is made up of a number of modules, each designed for a particular purpose in mind. One of these modules contains a utility product called JOB/SCAN that reads and analyzes job streams in order to determine whether a job will execute. Scanning invokes a series of consistency checks—not merely syntax checks, which you can use via a TYPRUN=SCAN JCL option. Besides scanning and submitting a job, this software can also be used to double check the proper use of your local shop standards. The result of this can then be routed to a printer or simply displayed on your CRT.

Analysis Document is another module in the DOCU/TEXT family. This module produces a number of selectable reports, including cross-reference reports, other I/O listings, flowcharts of each step within a job, and a structured JCL listing (including overrides, refer backs, and symbolics).

A third module is referred to as Operations Documents. Operations Documents produces a number of selectable reports that supplement or manually replace prepared forms used by operations and production control. One of a number of functions of this software is to document the resource requirements of your production systems and to provide setup, restart, scheduling, and report distribution information. Input to Operations Documents can be one or a number of jobs, coming from a single or multiple systems.

Two other features are also available in the DOCU/TEXT software: extended functions and on-line querying abilities. Extended functions represent certain groups of features in the system you can use to add a short description—for example, to any of the DOCU/TEXT reports, as well as some user text material. The system also allows you to store and display reports on disk (PDSOUT) files and provide query facilities for operations documentation. The on-line query features combine the capabilities of an extended function module, allowing you instant, on-line access to crucial job information.

Let me give you some examples about some of the capabilities in this software using a series of frames. Note, looking at the primary menu shown in Figure 4.2, I entered the character J to invoke DOCU/TEXT JOB/SCAN directly from the ISPF Primary Options Menu. Once the selection is made and you have pressed Enter, a DOCU/TEXT primary menu screen is prompted, showing an array of selections (Figure 4.3). At this point I have entered option 1 (JOB/SCAN) - Execute Job Scan, thereby prompting the next panel in the series.

The first detailed panel attained through selection 1 on the primary DOCU/TEXT panel is an Execution W/Standards screen (Figure 4.4) to run and analyze an actual run-stream part of the daily general-ledger processing, which underwent a great number of changes only recently. As you can see, I requested a job scan of runstream

```
---------------------------  Primary Option Menu  ------------------- DOCU/TEXT
Select Option ==> 1

     0  JOB CARD   - Job Statement and TSO Output Parms        Userid - NIRAV
     1  JOB/SCAN   - Execute JOB/SCAN                          Prefix - NIRAV
     2  OJD QUERY  - Online Job Documentation                  Time   - 16:19
     3  CREATE     - Analysis Documents                        Date   - 92/02/05
     4  CREATE     - Operations Documents                      Julian - 92.036
     5  CREATE     - All Documents
     6  DISPLAY    - Analysis Documents
     7  DISPLAY    - Operations Documents
     8  DISPLAY    - All Documents
     9  USER TEXT  - User Text Maintenance Facility
    10  SELECTION  - Selection Lists Maintenance Facility
    11  SDF MENU   - Short Description Facility
    UT  USERFUNC1  - User Function 1
    U2  USERFUNC2  - User Function 2
     X  EXIT       - EXIT


     Copyright (c) 1991. Diversified Software Systems, Inc. Release 5.5.1B
```

Figure 4.3 Primary Docutext Panel to invoke JOB/SCAN.

```
---------------------------  EXECUTION W/STANDARDS  ------------------ JOB/SCAN
Command ==> F

F - Foreground check for errors          P - Processing variables
S - Submit after checking                L - Library specification
B - Batch execution mode                 E - Edit member
R - Reformat JCL                        BR - Browse member
C - Change JCL

Input Lib ==> STANDARD.CNTL
  Select Members    ==> GLE70
  Exclude Members   ==>

List Lib   ==>
  Name (? for Dir) ==>

Report Heading      ==>

Select additional Options below:
  CRT Display       ==> Y   (Y/N/E)
  Hardcopy          ==> N   (Y/N/E/S) Options in Effect  ==> N (Y/N)
  Exitname          ==>               Exitparm  ==>
```

Figure 4.4 Execution with the Standards Panel to request a JOB/SCAN of GLE70.

GLE70, which is temporarily set up as a member on my partitioned data set NIRAV.STANDARD,CNTL, or more specifically, NIRAV.STANDARD.CNTL(GLE70).

I really need to highlight two different areas of activities at this point. The first one is the actual JCL part of the GLE70 runstream prior to the requested JOB/SCAN. This is highlighted in Figures 4.5 through 4.8.

In short, these JCLs will be analyzed not only for conventional syntax problems, but for logical inconsistencies as well. The Execute W/Standard panel (Figure 4.4) is used to perform any of the JOB/SCAN functions. It is necessary to place the required command in the command line and then press the Enter key. Note that I've entered

```
//NIRLCG7A JOB  (9000,AGLP),MSGLEVEL=(1,1),MSGCLASS=X,NOTIFY=NIRLC,
//  REGION=2048K
//*
//*********************************************************************
//*         I N P U T   P R O C E S S O R   P R O C E D U R E        *
//*********************************************************************
//*
//IP100SCR EXEC PGM=IDCAMS
//SYSPRINT DD SYSOUT=*
//SYSIN    DD DSN=NIRXT.TEST.PARMLIB(GLE70SCR),DISP=SHR
//*
//INIT     EXEC PGM=IDCAMS
//SYSPRINT DD SYSOUT=*
//SYSIN    DD DSN=NIRXT.TEST.PARMLIB(GLEDEL),DISP=SHR
//*
//*
//IP110STP EXEC PGM=IP110
//STEPLIB  DD DSN=NIRXP.PROD.LOADLIB,DISP=SHR
//SYSOUT   DD SYSOUT=X
//SYSDBOUT DD SYSOUT=X
//SORTMSG  DD SYSOUT=X
//SYS006   DD SYSOUT=L
//SYS008   DD DUMMY
//SYS011   DD DSN=NIRVT.GL70.NEWTRANS,DISP=SHR
//SYS013   DD DSN=&&DATETP,
//            UNIT=TEMP,DISP=(NEW,DELETE,DELETE),
//            SPACE=(TRK,(5,1)),
//            DCB=(RECFM=FB,LRECL=80,BLKSIZE=80)
//SYS014   DD DSN=&&DATEWK,
//            UNIT=TEMP,DISP=(NEW,DELETE,DELETE),
//            SPACE=(TRK,(30,30),RLSE),
//            DCB=(RECFM=FB,LRECL=80,BLKSIZE=80)
//SYS015   DD DSN=&&CTLTP,
//            UNIT=TEMP,DISP=(NEW,DELETE,DELETE),
//            SPACE=(TRK,(30,30),RLSE),
//            DCB=(RECFM=FB,LRECL=120,BLKSIZE=1200)
//SYS016   DD DSN=&&CTLWK,
//            UNIT=TEMP,DISP=(NEW,DELETE,DELETE),
//            SPACE=(TRK,(30,30),RLSE),
//            DCB=(RECFM=FB,LRECL=120,BLKSIZE=1200)
//SYS018   DD DSN=NIRLC.GL70.DATEFILE,
//            UNIT=3380,VOL=SER=GL0001,
//            DISP=(NEW,CATLG),
//            SPACE=(TRK,(3,3),RLSE),
//            DCB=(RECFM=FB,LRECL=80,BLKSIZE=80)
```

Figure 4.5 JCL runstream to be scanned via JOB/SCAN, Frame 1.

```
//SYS020    DD DSN=NIRLC.GL70.OPERCNTL,
//             UNIT=3380,VOL=SER=GL0001,
//             DISP=(NEW,CATLG),
//             SPACE=(TRK,(5,1),RLSE),
//             DCB=(RECFM=FB,LRECL=80,BLKSIZE=80)
//SYS021    DD DSN=NIRLC.GL70.CONTROL,
//             UNIT=3380,VOL=SER=GL0001,
//             DISP=(NEW,CATLG),
//             SPACE=(TRK,(5,1),RLSE),
//             DCB=(RECFM=FB,LRECL=80,BLKSIZE=80)
//SORTWK01 DD UNIT=TEMP,SPACE=(CYL,(10),RLSE)
//SORTWK02 DD UNIT=TEMP,SPACE=(CYL,(10),RLSE)
//SORTWK03 DD UNIT=TEMP,SPACE=(CYL,(10),RLSE)
//SORTWK04 DD UNIT=TEMP,SPACE=(CYL,(10),RLSE)
//SORTWK05 DD UNIT=TEMP,SPACE=(CYL,(10),RLSE)
//SORTWK06 DD UNIT=TEMP,SPACE=(CYL,(10),RLSE)
//SYS005    DD DSN=NIRXT.AR.JVGLFILE,DISP=SHR
//*
//STEP03    EXEC PGM=EASYTREV
//SYSOUT    DD SYSOUT=*
//SYSPRINT DD SYSOUT=L
//SORTWK01 DD UNIT=TEMP,SPACE=(CYL,(10),RLSE)
//SORTWK02 DD UNIT=TEMP,SPACE=(CYL,(10),RLSE)
//SORTWK03 DD UNIT=TEMP,SPACE=(CYL,(10),RLSE)
//FILEA     DD DSN=NIRVT.GL70.NEWTRANS,DISP=SHR
//FILISAM   DD DSN=NIRVP.GLE.VALIDM,DISP=SHR
//NEWFILE   DD DSN=NIRLC.GL70.NEWTRA1,UNIT=SYSDA,
//             SPACE=(CYL,(2,1),RLSE),DISP=(,CATLG,DELETE),
//             DCB=(LRECL=80,BLKSIZE=800,RECFM=FB)
//SYSIN     DD DSN=NIRXT.TEST.PARMLIB(APGG),DISP=SHR
//*
//STEP04    EXEC PGM=IDCAMS
//SYSPRINT DD SYSOUT=*
//DD1       DD DSN=NIRLC.GL70.NEWTRA1,DISP=SHR
//DD2       DD DSN=NIRVT.GL70.NEWTRA1,DISP=OLD
//SYSIN     DD DSN=NIRXT.TEST.PARMLIB(GLREPRO),DISP=SHR
//*
//*********************************************************************
//*         GENERAL LEDGER EDIT PROCEDURE                             *
//*********************************************************************
//*
//*         SELECT VOUCHER TRANSACTIONS FROM INPUT
//*         PROCESSOR FILE  AND SORT PRIOR EDITING
//*
```

Figure 4.6 JCL runstream to be scanned via JOB/SCAN, Frame 2.

the character F (foreground check for errors). This function is used to execute the JOB/SCAN program. When JOB/SCAN executes, unlike your typical TYPRUN=SCAN subparameter, the software performs over 500 checks (see Figure 4.9), both syntax and logical. It verifies that programs and files are available, resulting in a structured JCL listing.

If you were to submit this request using an S option, JOB/SCAN would be executed, but the system would physically execute the job, provided that no errors were detected at the time. Likewise, if you were to enter a B, JOB/SCAN would be executed in batch mode.

The character P (next to the option slot ===>>) will simply change the run-time

```
//GL100     EXEC PGM=GL100
//STEPLIB   DD DSN=NIRXP.PROD.LOADLIB,D SP=SHR
//SORTMSG   DD SYSOUT=*
//SYSDBOUT  DD SYSOUT=*
//SYSOUT    DD SYSOUT=*
//SYS006    DD SYSOUT=L
//SYS008    DD DSN=NIRVT.GL70.NEWTRA1,DISP=SHR
//SYS014    DD DSN=&GL@VCHRS,
//             UNIT=TEMP,DISP=(NEW,PASS),
//             SPACE=(TRK,(8,1),RLSE),
//             DCB=(RECFM=FB,LRECL=80,BLKSIZE=800)
//SORTWK01 DD UNIT=TEMP,SPACE=(CYL,(10),RLSE)
//SORTWK02 DD UNIT=TEMP,SPACE=(CYL,(10),RLSE)
//SORTWK03 DD UNIT=TEMP,SPACE=(CYL,(10),RLSE)
//SORTWK04 DD UNIT=TEMP,SPACE=(CYL,(10),RLSE)
//SORTWK05 DD UNIT=TEMP,SPACE=(CYL,(10),RLSE)
//SORTWK06 DD UNIT=TEMP,SPACE=(CYL,(10),RLSE)
//*
//*         EDIT INPUT VOUCHERS FOR GENERAL LEDGER
//*
//GL110     EXEC PGM=GL110,REGION=3072K
//STEPLIB   DD DSN=NIRXP.PROD.LOADLIB,DISP=SHR
//SYSDBOUT  DD SYSOUT=*
//SYSOUT    DD SYSOUT=*
//SYS006    DD SYSOUT=L
//SYS014    DD DSN=&GL@VCHRS,
//             UNIT=TEMP,DISP=(OLD,DELETE)
//SYS015    DD DSN=&GL@BALCD,
//             UNIT=TEMP,DISP=(NEW,PASS),
//             SPACE=(CYL,(2,2),RLSE),
//             DCB=(RECFM=FB,LRECL=72,BLKSIZE=720)
//SYS016    DD DSN=&GL@EDITD,
//             UNIT=TEMP,DISP=(NEW,PASS),
//             SPACE=(CYL,(2,5),RLSE),
//             DCB=(RECFM=FB,LRECL=209,BLKSIZE=2090)
//SYS018    DD DSN=NIRLC.GL70.DATEFILE,DISP=SHR,
//             UNIT=3380,VOL=SER=GL0001
//SYS019    DD DSN=NIRVT.AR.COMPMAST,DISP=SHR
//*
//*         CREATE EDITED AND BALANCED TRANSACTION FILE
//*
//GL120     EXEC PGM=GL120,REGION=3072K
//STEPLIB   DD DSN=NIRXP.PROD.LOADLIB,DISP=SHR
//SYSDBOUT  DD SYSOUT=*
//SYSOUT    DD SYSOUT=*
//SYS006    DD SYSOUT=L
```

Figure 4.7 JCL runstream to be scanned via JOB/SCAN, Frame 3.

options, such as whether to access the system catalog or access control-statement libraries. L will specify the library or libraries from which JOB/SCAN will extract JCLs for the purpose of verification. You can also use this option to specify a list library, a special PROC LIB, or the name of the user-written routine to preprocess your job-control statements. Other options used are E for editing and BR for browsing.

REFORMATTER (R) will execute a program that restructures the JCLs into a standard, easy-to-read format. Prior to pressing the Enter key, make sure the library specifications pointing to the input data set contain the JCLs to be reformatted.

The CHANGE JCL subparameter (C) is used to execute a JCL change program that enables the user to conditionally change JCL values. If you were to use a C, also make sure you specify a Y or an N in the CRT or hardcopy fields to indicate whether you want your JCL change output to be routed to a display terminal or simply to the printer.

Once processing is initiated, DOCU/TEXT starts listing all inconsistencies and problem areas in the runstream. In Frame 1 (Figure 4.10), DOCU/TEXT cannot locate one of the key data sets (HLDVCHRS) in the catalog.

As you scroll down (PF8) and view the processed document, step by step, you will encounter a number of problems. There is a problem, for instance, locating a second data set (Frame 2 in Figure 4.11). When this happens, DOCU/TEXT also provides you with the error message you need in order to look up further interpretation. The error message reads DSS4050E DATA SET NOT FOUND. If you were to look this up in the JCL messages guide, it would list *Related IBM message - EIF283I*. The data set specified in the DD statement with a DISP of OLD or SHR could not be found in the catalog. This could be caused by a misspelled DSN or the fact that the data set

```
//SYS013    DD DSN=&GL@TRANS,
//             UNIT=TEMP,DISP=(NEW,PASS),
//             SPACE=(CYL,(10,5),RLSE),
//             DCB=(RECFM=FB,LRECL=150,BLKSIZE=1500)
//SYS015    DD DSN=&GL@BALCD,
//             UNIT=TEMP,DISP=(OLD,DELETE)
//SYS016    DD DSN=&GL@EDITD,
//             UNIT=TEMP,DISP=(OLD,DELETE)
//*
//TRANSFLE EXEC PGM=IDCAMS
//SYSPRINT DD SYSOUT=*
//DD1       DD DSN=&GL@TRANS,
//             UNIT=TEMP,DISP=(OLD,PASS)
//DD2       DD DSN=NIRVT.GL70.TRANS,DISP=OLD
//SYSIN     DD DSN=NIRXT.TEST.PARMLIB(GLREPRO),DISP=SHR
//*
//*         LOAD ACCEPTED VOUCHERS TO GL MONTHLY MASTER
//*
//GL130     EXEC PGM=GL130,REGION=3072K
//STEPLIB   DD DSN=NIRXP.PROD.LOADLIB,DISP=SHR
//SYSDBOUT DD SYSOUT=*
//SYSOUT    DD SYSOUT=*
//SYS006    DD SYSOUT=L
//SYS008    DD DSN=NIRVT.GL70.HLDVCHRS.OLD,DISP=SHR
//SYS011    DD DSN=&GL@135I,
//             UNIT=TEMP,DISP=(NEW,PASS),
//             SPACE=(CYL,(1,5),RLSE),
//             DCB=(RECFM=FB,LRECL=150,BLKSIZE=1500)
//SYS013    DD DSN=&GL@TRANS,
//             UNIT=TEMP,DISP=(OLD,DELETE)
//SYS015    DD DSN=NIRVT.GL70.HLDVCHRS.NEW,DISP=SHR
//SYS018    DD DSN=NIRLC.GL70.DATEFILE,DISP=SHR,
//             UNIT=3380,VOL=SER=GL0001
//SYS019    DD DSN=NIRVT.AR.COMPMAST,DISP=SHR
//*
//*ENDSTEP   EXEC PGM=IDCAMS
//*SYSPRINT DD SYSOUT=*
//*SYSIN     DD DSN=NIRXT.TEST.PARMLIB(GLEALDEL),DISP=SHR
//*
```

Figure 4.8 JCL runstream to be scanned via JOB/SCAN, Frame 4.

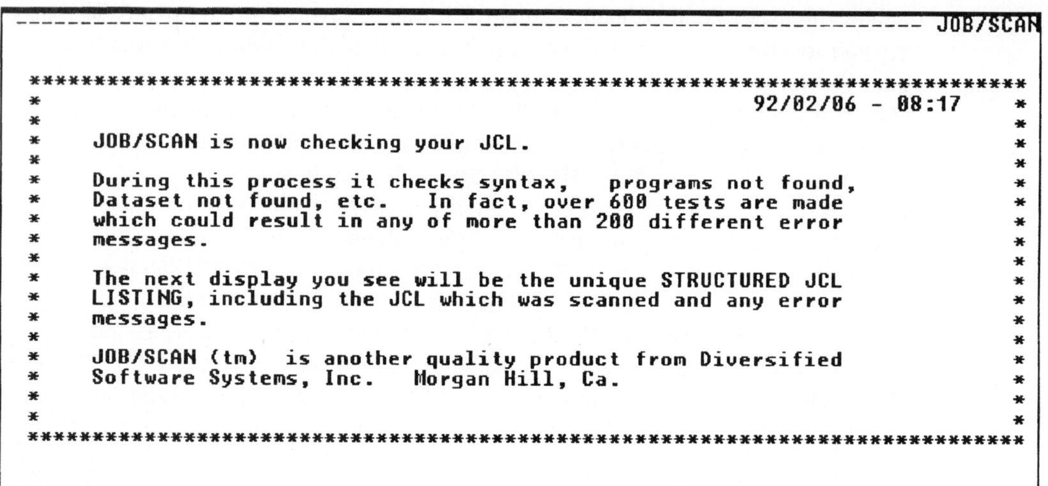

```
------------------------------------------------------------------- JOB/SCAN

****************************************************************************
*                                                   92/02/06 - 08:17       *
*                                                                          *
*    JOB/SCAN is now checking your JCL.                                    *
*                                                                          *
*    During this process it checks syntax,   programs not found,           *
*    Dataset not found, etc.   In fact, over 600 tests are made            *
*    which could result in any of more than 200 different error            *
*    messages.                                                             *
*                                                                          *
*    The next display you see will be the unique STRUCTURED JCL            *
*    LISTING, including the JCL which was scanned and any error            *
*    messages.                                                             *
*                                                                          *
*    JOB/SCAN (tm)  is another quality product from Diversified            *
*    Software Systems, Inc.   Morgan Hill, Ca.                             *
*                                                                          *
*                                                                          *
****************************************************************************
```

Figure 4.9 Panel to notify processing, syntax, and logic checking.

```
 BROWSE -- NIRAV.WORK.JLSCRN ------------------------ LINE 00000000 COL 001 078
 COMMAND ===>                                                   SCROLL ===> PAGE
********************************* TOP OF DATA **********************************
JOB/SCAN           3. STRUCTURED JCL LISTING     5.5.1B        02/06/92  08:17:35
---------------------------------------------------------------------------------
//NIRLCG7A JOB  (9000,AGLP),MSGLEVEL=(1,1),MSGCLASS=X,NOTIFY=NIRLC,        000100
//  REGION=2048K                                                           000200
//*                                                                        000300
//***********************************************************************000400
//*        I N P U T    P R O C E S S O R    P R O C E D U R E           *000500
//***********************************************************************000600
//*                                                                        000700
//IP100SCR EXEC PGM=IDCAMS                                                 000800
//SYSPRINT DD SYSOUT=*                                                     000900
//SYSIN    DD DSN=NIRXT.TEST.PARMLIB(GLE70SCR),DISP=SHR                    001000
    ----+----1----+----2----+----3----+----4----+----5----+----6----+----7----
     DEL NIRXT.AR.OPERCNTL                                                     00
     DEL NIRXT.AR.CONTROL                                                      00
     DEL NIRXT.AR.DATEFILE                                                     00
     DEL NIRXT.AR.NEWTRA1                                                      00
     DEL NIRXT.AR.HLDVCHRS                                                     00
**WARNING - DSS5825W - DATASET NOT FOUND IN CATALOG
     SET MAXCC = 0                                                             00
//*                                                                        001100
```

Figure 4.10 Frame 1 of the JOB/SCAN analysis— dataset HLDVCHRS not found.

might have been uncataloged previously in the set of jobs being scanned. Let's continue our investigation. Consider the frame in Figure 4.12.

Frame 3 highlights the beginning of an Easytrieve program called APGG, triggered via the //SYSIN statement. The panel shown in Figure 4.13 (Frame 4) is invoked when you scroll down the report via PF8, as you'd normally do in an ISPF session.

Note the following. Underneath the //SYSIN DD DSN=NIRVT.NEWTRANS statement, another error message in reference to NIRVT.NEWTRANS, ***ERROR - DSS4050E Data Set Not Found in Catalog, is displayed. In addition to this error condition, an advisory (message) is also shown (DSS8900A), which is a "self reference" to the error message.

Allow me to review some basic DOCU/TEXT conventions as part of explaining the structure of the above error message. Consider the format shown in Figure 4.14. The error code is the result of severity level associated with the error message. Severity levels are as follows:

0–3	Advisory
4–7	Warning
8–19	Errors
20–*n*	Catastrophic (processing suspended)

```
 BROWSE -- NIRAU.WORK.JLSCRN ------------------------ LINE 00000110 COL 001 078
 COMMAND ===>                                                   SCROLL ===> PAGE
//               SPACE=(TRK,(5,1),RLSE),
//               DCB=(RECFM=FB,LRECL=80,BLKSIZE=80)
//SORTWK01 DD UNIT=TEMP,SPACE=(CYL,(10),RLSE)
//SORTWK02 DD UNIT=TEMP,SPACE=(CYL,(10),RLSE)
//SORTWK03 DD UNIT=TEMP,SPACE=(CYL,(10),RLSE)
//SORTWK04 DD UNIT=TEMP,SPACE=(CYL,(10),RLSE)
//SORTWK05 DD UNIT=TEMP,SPACE=(CYL,(10),RLSE)
//SORTWK06 DD UNIT=TEMP,SPACE=(CYL,(10),RLSE)
//SYS005    DD DSN=NIRXT.AR.JUGLFILE,DISP=SHR
***ERROR  - DSS4050E - DATA SET NOT FOUND IN CATALOG
*ADVISORY - DSS8900A - DSN = "NIRXT.AR.JUGLFILE "
//*
//STEP03    EXEC PGM=EASYTREV
//SYSOUT    DD SYSOUT=*
//SYSPRINT DD SYSOUT=L
//SORTWK01 DD UNIT=TEMP,SPACE=(CYL,(10),RLSE)
//SORTWK02 DD UNIT=TEMP,SPACE=(CYL,(10),RLSE)
//SORTWK03 DD UNIT=TEMP,SPACE=(CYL,(10),RLSE)
//FILEA     DD DSN=NIRVT.GL70.NEWTRANS,DISP=SHR
***ERROR  - DSS4050E - DATA SET NOT FOUND IN CATALOG
*ADVISORY - DSS8900A - DSN = "NIRVT.GL70.NEWTRANS "
//FILISAM   DD DSN=NIRVP.GLE.VALIDN,DISP=SHR
```

Figure 4.11 Frame 2, additional problems.

```
 BROWSE -- NIRAU.WORK.JLSCRN ------------------------ LINE 00000132 COL 001 078
 COMMAND ===>                                                   SCROLL ===> PAGE
//NEWFILE   DD DSN=NIRLC.GL70.NEWTRA1,UNIT=SYSDA,
//               SPACE=(CYL,(2,1),RLSE),DISP=(,CATLG,DELETE),
//               DCB=(LRECL=80,BLKSIZE=800,RECFM=FB)
//SYSIN     DD DSN=NIRXT.TEST.PARMLIB(APGG),DISP=SHR
    ----+----1----+----2----+----3----+----4----+----5----+----6----+----7----
    FILE FILEA VS
    KEYINFO W-1 16 A COMP W-1 3 A REC W-4 1 A VEN W-5 10 A PAYIND W-15 1 A
    RECTYPE W-16 1 A VENDNUM 21 10 A VENDNUM2 21 17 A ALLREC 1 80 A
    CONUM 1 5 A MESSAGE W 25 A RECODE 20 1 A
    VEND 21 17 A BATCH 16 4 A JOUN 10 6 A AMOUNT 62 11 N2 9999
    FILE FILISAM IS
    RECA 1 200 A RECODE 17 1 A SORTFLD 139 17 A NAME 18 35 A 9999
    FILE PSTFILE FB-80-800
    RECNUM 1 7 N 9999
    FILE NEWFILE FB-80-800
    9999
    MESSAGE = *
    IF RECODE NQ 1
       PUT NEWFILE FROM FILEA
       FLUNK
    IF CONUM NQ 60290
       PUT NEWFILE FROM FILEA
```

Figure 4.12 Frame 3, part of an EASYTRIEVE program.

```
BROWSE -- NIRAU.WORK.JLSCRN ------------------------ LINE 00000066 COL 001 078
COMMAND ===>                                                 SCROLL ===> PAGE
                                                                          00
     IF MAXCC LE 8 THEN DO                                                00
        SET MAXCC = 0                                                     00
//*                                                                   001500
//*                                                                   001600
//IP110STP EXEC PGM=IP110                                             001700
//STEPLIB   DD DSN=NIRXP.PROD.LOADLIB,DISP=SHR                        001800
//SYSOUT    DD SYSOUT=X                                               001900
//SYSDBOUT  DD SYSOUT=X                                               002000
//SORTMSG   DD SYSOUT=X                                               002100
//SYS006    DD SYSOUT=L                                               002200
//SYS008    DD DUMMY                                                  002300
//SYS011    DD DSN=NIRVT.GL70.NEWTRANS,DISP=SHR                       002400
***ERROR   - DSS4050E - DATA SET NOT FOUND IN CATALOG
*ADVISORY  - DSS8900A - DSN = "NIRVT.GL70.NEWTRANS "
//SYS013    DD DSN=&&DATETP,                                          002500
//             UNIT=TEMP,DISP=(NEW,DELETE,DELETE),                    002600
//             SPACE=(TRK,(5,1)),                                     002700
//             DCB=(RECFM=FB,LRECL=80,BLKSIZE=80)                     002800
//SYS014    DD DSN=&&DATEWK,                                          002900
//             UNIT=TEMP,DISP=(NEW,DELETE,DELETE),                    003000
//             SPACE=(TRK,(30,30),RLSE),                              003100
```

Figure 4.13 Frame 4, additional "logic" problems highlighted.

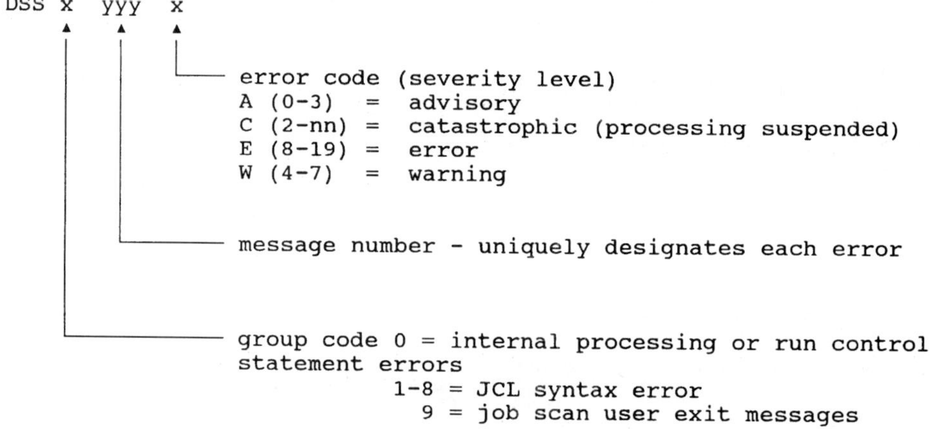

Figure 4.14 Structure for DOCU/TEXT error messages.

The error summary, part of the structured JCL listing, summarizes the total number of advisories, warnings, and errors that have occurred during a current execution. Figure 4.15, Frame 5 shows the next block of JCLs that are correct both in terms of syntax and consistency (logical) checks.

Figure 4.16 (Frame 6) continues the analysis while highlighting two error conditions during the process. NIRXT.GL70.NEWTRANS already appeared in a prior frame, but because the data set is used in a number of places, this error will propagate throughout the list. Frame 7 (Figure 4.17) continues with the analysis and finds another data set, NIRVT.GL70.NEWTRA1, incompatible.

Figure 4.18 (I've omitted a number of frames that highlight some of the undefined data sets in the system) presents some of the final statistics, which are a direct result of the scan. This error summary lists problems in four categories to be investigated by the analyst:

10 Advisory level problems
1 Warning level
10 Error level, a total of 21 occurrences

```
 BROWSE -- NIRAV.WORK.JLSCRN ------------------------ LINE 00000088 COL 001 078
 COMMAND ===>                                                  SCROLL ===> PAGE
//              DCB=(RECFM=FB,LRECL=80,BLKSIZE=80)                      003200
//SYS015     DD DSN=&&CTLTP,                                            003300
//              UNIT=TEMP,DISP=(NEW,DELETE,DELETE),                     003400
//              SPACE=(TRK,(30,30),RLSE),                               003500
//              DCB=(RECFM=FB,LRECL=120,BLKSIZE=1200)                   003600
//SYS016     DD DSN=&&CTLWK,                                            003700
//              UNIT=TEMP,DISP=(NEW,DELETE,DELETE),                     003800
//              SPACE=(TRK,(30,30),RLSE),                               003900
//              DCB=(RECFM=FB,LRECL=120,BLKSIZE=1200)                   004000
//SYS018     DD DSN=NIRLC.GL70.DATEFILE,                                004100
//              UNIT=3380,VOL=SER=GL0001,                               004200
//              DISP=(NEW,CATLG),                                       004300
//              SPACE=(TRK,(3,3),RLSE),                                 004400
//              DCB=(RECFM=FB,LRECL=80,BLKSIZE=80)                      004500
//SYS020     DD DSN=NIRLC.GL70.OPERCNTL,                                004600
//              UNIT=3380,VOL=SER=GL0001,                               004700
//              DISP=(NEW,CATLG),                                       004800
//              SPACE=(TRK,(5,1),RLSE),                                 004900
//              DCB=(RECFM=FB,LRECL=80,BLKSIZE=80)                      005000
//SYS021     DD DSN=NIRLC.GL70.CONTROL,                                 005100
//              UNIT=3380,VOL=SER=GL0001,                               005200
//              DISP=(NEW,CATLG),                                       005300
```

Figure 4.15 Frame 5, in which the block of JCLs are correct.

```
 BROWSE -- NIRAV.WORK.JLSCRN ------------------------ LINE 00000110 COL 001 070
 COMMAND ===>                                                  SCROLL ===> PAGE
//              SPACE=(TRK,(5,1),RLSE),                                 005400
//              DCB=(RECFM=FB,LRECL=80,BLKSIZE=80)                      005500
//SORTWK01 DD UNIT=TEMP,SPACE=(CYL,(10),RLSE)                           005600
//SORTWK02 DD UNIT=TEMP,SPACE=(CYL,(10),RLSE)                           005700
//SORTWK03 DD UNIT=TEMP,SPACE=(CYL,(10),RLSE)                           005800
//SORTWK04 DD UNIT=TEMP,SPACE=(CYL,(10),RLSE)                           005900
//SORTWK05 DD UNIT=TEMP,SPACE=(CYL,(10),RLSE)                           006000
//SORTWK06 DD UNIT=TEMP,SPACE=(CYL,(10),RLSE)                           006100
//SYS005   DD DSN=NIRXT.AR.JVGLFILE,DISP=SHR                            006200
***ERROR   - DSS4050E - DATA SET NOT FOUND IN CATALOG
*ADVISORY - DSS8900A - DSN = "NIRXT.AR.JVGLFILE "
//*                                                                     006300
//STEP03     EXEC PGM=EASYTREV                                          006400
//SYSOUT   DD SYSOUT=*                                                  006500
//SYSPRINT DD SYSOUT=L                                                  006600
//SORTWK01 DD UNIT=TEMP,SPACE=(CYL,(10),RLSE)                           006700
//SORTWK02 DD UNIT=TEMP,SPACE=(CYL,(10),RLSE)                           006800
//SORTWK03 DD UNIT=TEMP,SPACE=(CYL,(10),RLSE)                           006900
//FILEA    DD DSN=NIRVT.GL70.NEWTRANS,DISP=SHR                          007000
***ERROR   - DSS4050E - DATA SET NOT FOUND IN CATALOG
*ADVISORY - DSS8900A - DSN = "NIRVT.GL70.NEWTRANS "
//FILISAM  DD DSN=NIRVP.GLE.VALIDM,DISP=SHR                             007100
```

Figure 4.16 Frame 6, two additional problems.

The error summary listing that appears at the end of the structured JCL listing is a compilation of all the JCL errors found during the scanning process. The error messages in the error summary are tied back to the JCLs that caused the error, either by relative line number (for on-line execution) or by the page number on which the error is found (primarily for batch execution). Problems encountered when using the

```
 BROWSE -- NIRAV.WORK.JLSCRN ------------------------ LINE 00000176 COL 001 078
 COMMAND ===>                                                  SCROLL ===> PAGE
              AMOUNT MESSAGE
//*                                                                      007600
//STEP04    EXEC PGM=IDCAMS                                              007700
//SYSPRINT DD SYSOUT=*                                                   007800
//DD1       DD DSN=NIRLC.GL70.NEWTRA1,DISP=SHR                           007900
//DD2       DD DSN=NIRVT.GL70.NEWTRA1,DISP=OLD                           008000
***ERROR  - DSS4050E - DATA SET NOT FOUND IN CATALOG
*ADVISORY - DSS8900A - DSN = "NIRVT.GL70.NEWTRA1 "
//SYSIN     DD DSN=NIRXT.TEST.PARMLIB(GLREPRO),DISP=SHR                  008100
     ----+----1----+----2----+----3----+----4----+----5----+----6----+----7----
       REPRO INFILE(DD1) OUTFILE(DD2)                                        00
//*                                                                      008200
//***********************************************************************008300
//*         GENERAL LEDGER EDIT PROCEDURE                               *008400
//***********************************************************************008500
//*                                                                      008600
//*         SELECT VOUCHER TRANSACTIONS FROM INPUT                       008700
//*         PROCESSOR FILE  AND SORT PRIOR EDITING                       008800
//*                                                                      008900
//GL100     EXEC PGM=GL100                                               009000
//STEPLIB   DD DSN=NIRXP.PROD.LOADLIB,DISP=SHR                           009100
//SORTMSG   DD SYSOUT=*                                                  009200
```

Figure 4.17 Frame 7, another undefined dataset in the catalog.

```
 BROWSE -- NIRAV.WORK.JLSCRN ------------------------ LINE 00000286 COL 001 078
 COMMAND ===>                                                  SCROLL ===> PAGE
//SYS019    DD DSN=NIRVT.AR.COMPMAST,DISP=SHR                            016900
***ERROR  - DSS4050E - DATA SET NOT FOUND IN CATALOG
*ADVISORY - DSS8900A - DSN = "NIRVT.AR.COMPMAST "
//*                                                                      017000
//*ENDSTEP  EXEC PGM=IDCAMS                                              017100
//*SYSPRINT DD SYSOUT=*                                                  017200
//*SYSIN    DD DSN=NIRXT.TEST.PARMLIB(GLEALDEL),DISP=SHR                 017300
//*                                                                      017400
*** ERROR SUMMARY AND COUNTS ***
   10  ADVISORY LEVEL
    1  WARNING LEVEL
   10  ERROR LEVEL
   21  TOTAL ISSUED          0 SUPPRESSED.
     THE HIGHEST SEVERITY CODE ENCOUNTERED WAS    08.
REL LINE SV MSG.NO.    ERROR MESSAGE
-------- -- --------   ------------------------------------------------
     18   4 DSS5825W - DATASET NOT FOUND IN CATALOG
     78   8 DSS4050E - DATA SET NOT FOUND IN CATALOG
     79   0 DSS8900A - DSN = "NIRVT.GL70.NEWTRANS "
    118   8 DSS4050E - DATA SET NOT FOUND IN CATALOG
    119   0 DSS8900A - DSN = "NIRXT.AR.JVGLFILE "
    128   8 DSS4050E - DATA SET NOT FOUND IN CATALOG
```

Figure 4.18 Frame 8, final statistics of the scan operation (part 1).

```
BROWSE -- NIRAU.WORK.JLSCRN ------------------------ LINE 00000308 COL 001 078
COMMAND ===>                                                  SCROLL ===> PAGE
   129     0 DSS8900A - DSN = "NIRUT.GL70.NEWTRANS "
   181     8 DSS4050E - DATA SET NOT FOUND IN CATALOG
   182     0 DSS8900A - DSN = "NIRUT.GL70.NEWTRA1 "
   201     8 DSS4050E - DATA SET NOT FOUND IN CATALOG
   202     0 DSS8900A - DSN = "NIRUT.GL70.NEWTRA1 "
   234     8 DSS4050E - DATA SET NOT FOUND IN CATALOG
   235     0 DSS8900A - DSN = "NIRUT.AR.COMPMAST "
   258     8 DSS4050E - DATA SET NOT FOUND IN CATALOG
   259     0 DSS8900A - DSN = "NIRUT.GL70.TRANS "
   272     8 DSS4050E - DATA SET NOT FOUND IN CATALOG
   273     0 DSS8900A - DSN = "NIRUT.GL70.HLDUCHRS.OLD  "
   281     8 DSS4050E - DATA SET NOT FOUND IN CATALOG
   282     0 DSS8900A - DSN = "NIRUT.GL70.HLDUCHRS.NEW  "
   286     8 DSS4050E - DATA SET NOT FOUND IN CATALOG
   287     0 DSS8900A - DSN = "NIRUT.AR.COMPMAST "
XPJ60K  - END OF REPORT   JOB/SCAN      5.5.1B (C) DIVERSIFIED SOFTWARE SYSTEMS
******************************** BOTTOM OF DATA ********************************
```

Figure 4.19 Frame 9, end of the JCL scan (part 2).

ISPF panels are indicated by a short message displayed in the upper right-hand corner of the current panel. You can invoke more detailed instructions and tutorial information by using the help facility (PF1).

Figure 4.19 (Frame 9) concludes the scan-generated statistics with a detailed list of those data sets that were in error during the analysis.

Chapter 5

The New JCLs: OS/MVS/ESA

5.1 Overview

This chapter is built on the premise that you are an OS/MVS/XA shop and looking at the possibility of converting to an advanced OS/MVS ESA environment. So the topics presented in this chapter primarily focus on some of the idiosyncrasies of the new Enterprise System Architecture. I assume that you are already proficient in coding the necessary job control given an OS/MVS XA environment.

Generally speaking, the new features now available in an ESA environment (especially those in release 4 and later, using SMS) represent a great deal of improvements—looking at things rather conservatively and forgetting for a moment all the sophistication that is already available in a microcomputer environment.

Let me start by giving you some historical background on the OS/MVS operating system. XA, or Extended Architecture, is an advanced operating system introduced by IBM Corporation back in 1983 using a 31-bit addressing scheme with an address space of two megabytes. However efficient Extended Architecture seemed at the time, as larger applications were developed, address space (as has so often happened in the past) became once more a crucial issue. To resolve this problem, IBM released a new technology referred to as MVS/ESA, which gave the user multiple two-megabyte address spaces.

Being able to use multiple 2Mb address spaces does two things. First, it gives you more space for your processing requirements. Second, with special emphasis placed upon CICS, the system will place your data and the application into two different segments so your application will not clobber someone else's data as so often happens in an XA environment.

Interestingly, the dramatic changes in the new ESA architecture to achieve faster input/output operations require relatively few changes with regards to the application programmer, even though these modifications are a great deal more extensive

for the systems programmer. The new idiosyncrasies pertaining to the ESA environment is the focal point of the following sections.

5.2 The REGION SIZE

One of these changes encompasses REGION SIZE, which tells the system how much storage a particular job requires to run. Likewise, REGION SIZE with regards to an EXEC statement tells the system to allocate a certain amount of storage to a single step. The limit, of course, is set by your job statement and you can express it in terms of megabytes or kilobytes. If you were to omit the region size, it would default to whatever is defined in your installation standards. If the internal requirements for processing a job are greater than those requested on your REGION statement (or whatever is set up as a default value) the job simply abends with an 80A or an 804 condition.

There might be some difficulty in estimating the proper region size due to the fact that internal storage requirements are assigned dynamically, thus requirements for storage space constantly change during the processing cycle. One way to make sure that there is sufficient storage is to provide some kind of safety margin in your estimate. This concerns especially large jobs where storage needs to be allocated above the 16Mb line. "Above the line" describes a program that runs in an address space higher than 16Mb. If an application program, for example, requires to be run above 16Mb, it is an unusually large program, although the likelihood for this is slim. However, in an on-line CICS environment, not one but quite a number of programs need to use the same address space, so that a single, relatively small application program might end up running above the 16Mb line.

When you use the REGION parameter in an MVS/ESA environment, you are in fact referring to both the normal size REGION, which is the application address space, as well as the extended REGION, which happens to be the data space and can be allocated more than once, very much like separate address spaces.

REGION can be coded as #K (K meaning 1024 bytes of storage and # denoting a multiple of 1024 bytes). Note that storage is allocated in 2K increments and that odd numbers are rounded up to an even number. So 31K, or 31,744 bytes, would be automatically rounded to 32K, equivalent to 32,768 bytes of requested storage. In place of kilobytes, you can also utilize megabytes. REGION=#M or REGION=2M (note that this can be odd or even) is equivalent to 2,048,000 bytes of requested storage, where M denotes 1000 kilobytes times 2.

REGION in your EXEC statement, as I mentioned earlier, refers to that particular step on your JCLs. Consider the following:

```
//PAYCLC EXEC PGM=PRL100BC,REGION=32K
```

In this example, I have allocated 32 kilobytes of storage. The following:

```
//COMPPGM EXEC COB2UCLG,REGION=960K
```

simply means that each step, with regard to the above procedure, is allocated 960 kilobytes. Assume that a job contains 6 steps with the following requirements:

```
Step 1   REGION=32K
Step 2   REGION=64K
Step 3   REGION=96K
Step 4   REGION=36K
Step 5   REGION=48K
Step 6   REGION=22K
```

The largest REGION parameter on the job statement would be 96K, involving the largest step, step 3, shown on the EXEC statement.

5.3 Changes Affecting the Data Control Block (DCB)

One of the idiosyncrasies affecting the new DCB statement is the treatment of the BLKSIZE subparameter. Blocking has to do with how records are stored on an input/output device, such as a DASD or a tape. In order to differentiate the end of one and the beginning of the next record, the system creates a gap between the two. Because this inter-record gap takes up a great deal of space (230 bytes on a tape versus 185 on a disk), it is necessary to combine those records into a single unit, referred to as a *block*.

There are several reasons for blocking. First of all, the process saves you a great deal of storage space. Second, by blocking, the computer can read and write records faster and process them far more efficiently. The way you block depends very much on the particular I/O device that's available in your shop. In the past, many installations paid little or no attention to efficient blocking techniques. With fixed-length records, for example, the programmer would simply take an arbitrary multiple of the record length. With variable-length records, the formula is a bit more complicated. Here, the length of the record needs to be at least as long as the longest record on file, plus 4 additional bytes. The block size also needs to be at least as long as the longest record on file, including 8 additional bytes. The purpose of these extra bytes is to store record-length and block-size information of a particular file.

Because the calculation of efficient block sizes is a fairly involved computation, ESA will compute them for you if you omit the BLKSIZE subparameters from your DCB. This is recommended for two major reasons. First, the system can do a far better job than you can. Second, even if you could come up with the most efficient block size, your shop might decide to install new I/O devices, which would require you to rework all the existing blocking factors from scratch.

Strictly from the perspective of coding your DCB parameters, ESA now allows you to treat each subparameter within that DCB as an independent parameter. For example, you can conventionally say:

```
DCB=(RECFM=FB,LRECL=200,KEYLEN=16)
```

but now you can also state the above without the DCB parameter, like this:

```
RECFM=FB,LRECL=200,KEYLEN=16
```

One of the few instances in which you must code a BLKSIZE is when you process an unlabeled tape.

5.4 The COND Parameter and New Features

The COND parameter was initially used to enable the programmer to execute a particular step based on the outcome of a previous step. MVS communicates with you on two levels. For example, when you run an application program, the operating system might return a code at the end of each step to be tested by a following program. This code, which can be referred to as either a completion or a return code, is the first level of communication. On the second level, MVS can also provide you with a system completion code, which is composed of three digits, starting with the character S.

The COND parameter provides for a conditional execution of a job. This is done via the return codes made available by the MVS operating system in each step of the job. Every time a step is completed, it returns to MVS a code ranging from 0 to 4095. This numerical code is stored by MVS until the completion of the entire job. So any time prior to the completion of the job you can test each step for a specific condition code and decide whether to skip or continue with the next step.

Suppose that the first step of a job is executed and the compiler detects fatal errors in the program, thus there is no reason to continue the process. The COBOL compiler, for example, provides you with a set of return codes that correspond to the level of severity of the error. Figure 5.1 describes such return codes.

Most of the time programs will execute with warning-level errors, but anything beyond that (C or E) will not. So when the return code happens to be greater than a 4, you want to skip linking and executing the step.

To understand and appreciate the new capabilities of ESA, let me discuss the mechanics of the COND parameter. The COND parameter has three subparameters: code, operator, and step name. While the step name is an optional subparameter, the code and the operator fields are mandatory. The code is a number, ranging from 0 to 4,095. The operator is the condition for the comparison, such as:

Code	Means
0	No errors were detected
4	Minor errors were found, but a compiled program or load module was produced. Execution might be successful (warning messages are produced).
8	Major errors were found, but a compiled program or load module was produced. Execution will probably not be successful (caution level).
12	Serious errors were found. A compiled program or load module was not produced (error level)
16	Fatal error; execution cannot continue.

Figure 5.1 COBOL-compiler-generated return codes.

EQ equal
NE not equal
GT greater than
LT less than
GE greater than or equal to
LE less than or equal to

Let's review some examples. The following:

```
COND=(4,LT)
```

means that the job will terminate only if the return code of any step is greater than 4. The following:

```
COND=(4,LE)
```

is what to code if you want to continue processing only if no errors occur. The job will terminate if the return code of any step is greater than or equal to 4. In the next example:

```
//PAYROLLJ   job   ,'ALEX VARSEGI',COND=((10,GT),(20,LT))
```

you ask "is 10 greater than the return code or is 20 less than the return code?" If either is true, the system will skip all remaining job steps. If both are false, the system will execute all job steps. This example:

```
//PAYJ   job  COND=((5,GT),(8,EQ),(12,EQ),(17,EQ),(19,EQ),(21,EQ),
//    (23,LE))
```

shows a maximum of eight return code tests. The job continues only if the return codes are: 5, 6, 7, 9, 10, 11, 13, 14, 15, 16, 18, 20, or 22.

With MVS/ESA 4, you can still rely on this COND statement, but in addition the system provides you with IF/THEN/ELSE/ENDIF logic. Purely from a functional perspective, the new logic does not give you any additional capabilities, but it is much easier to use IF/THEN/ELSE/ENDIF logic than the COND parameter.

In constructing IF statements, note that the keywords THEN and ENDIF are mandatory, while ELSE is optional. Let's run through an example of this new JCL methodology. The following:

```
// IF (STEP10.RC GT 4 AND STEP10.RC LT 12) THEN
//STEP12 EXEC PGM=AR102C
```

executes program AR102C if and only if the return code from STEP10 is between 5 and 11 (greater than 4 and less than 12). This one:

```
// IF STEP10.RC EQ 12 THEN
//STEP13 EXEC PGM=AR111C
```

will execute program AR111C if the return code from STEP20 is equal to 8. The following:

```
// ENDIF
```

completes the IF statement prior to STEP13, and then STEP14 is executed if STEP12 is not executed:

```
// ELSE
//STEP14   EXEC PGM=AR207C
// ENDIF
```

As you can see, I used mnemonic operators as part of the IF statements. You can also use symbols to achieve the same effect. For example, you can say RC LT 4 or RC <4. Figure 5.2 highlights a table explaining these mnemonic and symbol or character operators. A more complicated IF statement is the following:

```
// IF ((STEP2.RC GT 4 AND STEP2.RC LT 8) OR (STEP2.RC GT 12
//    AND STEP2.RC LE 20)) THEN  ========>
```

Notice the relatively free form of the continuation. In comparing the return code with a previous step, the result of this comparison will always be false as if the step didn't execute. Also, in order to determine if an ABEND took place during execution, say ABEND=TRUE or simply ABEND. To test that an ABEND did not in fact occur, you may say ABEND=FALSE.

5.5 SMS-Managed Datasets

5.5.1 The AVGREC parameter, uses and examples

SMS or Storage Management System (see chapter 1 for more details) is an optional feature. One of the many functions of this system is to facilitate the use of various

Mnemonic	Symbolics	Explanation
NOT	¬	logical not
EQ	=	equal to
NE	¬ =	not equal to
GT	>	greater than
LT	<	less than
GE	> =	greater than or equal to
NL	¬ <	not greater than
LE	< =	less than or equal to
NG	¬ >	not greater than
AND	&	logical and
OR	¦	logical or

Figure 5.2 Table of mnemonic and symbolic operators.

classes for data sets and then store these data sets on tapes for future reference and retrieval. The storage and frequency by which these data sets migrate back and forth to tapes is based on several criteria, such as how often a particular data set is retrieved and its particular storage class.

Another function of the Storage Management System is to consolidate fragmented disk space—that is, to eliminate waste and optimize DASD usage. This, of course, is transparent to the programmer as long as he knows the whereabouts of the files he is directly accountable for.

Data sets that are created via SMS are referred to as SMS-managed data sets. To create them, you need to do the following:

- Code a STORCLAS parm on your DD statement.
- Establish a default class in case the programmer decides to skip the above class, which happens frequently.
- Unlike nonSMS data sets, an SMS data set is cataloged immediately at the time of its creation and not upon the completion of a particular step. Also, rather than utilizing VSAM or CVOL, SMS essentially relies on the Integrated Catalog Facility, or ICF.

Note that if SMS is not installed or happens to be inactive in your shop, the system syntax will check and then ignore commands related to the subsystem.

The purpose of the AVGREG parameter is to request space in terms of number of records, as opposed to blocks. You can use the AVGREC parameter when you define a new data set, and units of allocation requested for storage space are records. Also, the primary and secondary space quantity specified on the SPACE parameter represents units, which are thousands or millions of records. Consider the following:

```
//ARAG01   DD   DSN=NIRVT.STANDARD.CNTL(ARAG001),        X
//  DISP=(NEW,CATLG),UNIT=DISK,                          X
//  DCB=(RECFM=FB,LRECL=100),                            X
//  AVGREC=U,SPACE=(100(8000,2000),RLSE)
```

Let me explain the fourth line of this DD statement shown in bold. AVGREC=K means that both the primary and secondary space requirements are requested in terms of number of records. In the SPACE parameter, the number 100 denotes the average length of the record, which is in bytes. The number 8000 is the primary space for 8,000 records, and 2000 denotes a secondary allocation of 2,000 records. Other values for AVGREC might be a K, meaning that both the primary and secondary units are in units of kilobytes or 1,024 bytes, while M represents a megabyte of requested storage. Let's look at another example:

```
//FILE10   DD   DSNAME=NIRAV.PAYFILE,DATACLAS=CLAS1A,      C
//     DISP=(NEW,KEEP),SPACE=(128,(5,2)),AVGREC=K
```

In this example, the space allocation defined in the CLAS1A data class (set by your installation standards) is overridden by the SPACE and AVGREC parameters, which indicate an average record length of 128 bytes, a primary quantity of 5K (5,120) records and a secondary quantity of 2K, or 2,048 records.

5.5.2 The DATACLAS parameter, what it is all about

There are a number of parameters under SMS that enable you to use default values primarily for cataloged (disk) data sets. Among these are the DATACLAS, STORCLAS, MGMTCLAS, SECMODEL, and a number of other parameters. Through this concept, a data center can more efficiently control the utilization of its disk space and at the same time simplify coding and maintaining job control for DASD.

The reason for using the DATACLAS parameter is to specify a certain data class for a new data set. Data classes are normally defined by a designated person (especially in a large organization), which includes a number of viable classes. Whatever is set up, your DATACLAS parameter will be ignored by SMS if it is in reference to an existing data set or a data set that is not supported by the SMS subsystem. DATACLAS is actually available not only for VSAM, but for sequential files and for partitioned data sets or PDSs.

The term DATACLAS is a collective term that defines a number of data-set allocation attributes. These are:

- Data set organization
  - ~ Record organization (RECORG)
  - ~ Record format (RECFM)
- Record length
- Key length (KEYLEN)
- Key offset (KEYOFF)
- Type, PDS, or PDSE (DSNTYPE)
- Space allocation (AVGREC and SPACE)
- Retention period (RETPD) or expiration date (EXPDT)
- Volume count (VOLUME)
- VSAM data sets (IMBED or REPLICATE, CISIZE, FREESPACE, and SHAREOPTIONS)

For tape data sets, only the following limited number of attributes apply: EXPDT, LRECL, RECFM, RETPD, and volume count (on VOLUME). Let's look at a relatively simple example:

```
//POMASTR   DD  DSN=NIRAV.PO.MASTER,DATACLASS=CLAS2A,        C
//    DISP=(NEW,KEEP),LRECL=300,EXPDT=1992/216
```

In this example, the logical record length of 300 and the expiration date of August 3, 1992 override the corresponding attributes defined in the data class for the data set.

5.5.3 STORCLAS and the MGMTCLAS parameters

The STORCLAS parameter replaces the UNIT and VOL parameters when you create a new data set, whether temporary or permanent. Normally, your shop or an administrator will develop these specific classes and, by referring to them on your DD statement, you can omit both your VOL and UNIT parameters. If you don't specify STORCLAS for a new data set, and provided that the above mentioned administrator did set up a viable installation-written automatic class selection (ACS) routine, the ACS routine will select a particular storage class for your data set. Let's look at two examples of STORCLAS:

```
//PAYFILE  DD  SDN=NIRAV.AR.TRANSACT,STORCLAS=NSX001,      C
//    DISP=(NEW,KEEP)
```

In this example, SMS uses the attributes in the storage class named NSX001 for the storage service level of the data set: In the next example:

```
//PAYFILE2  DD  DSN=NIRAV.AR.TRANS2,STORCLAS=NSX001,      C
//    VOL=SER=(111111,200000)
```

SMS uses the attributes in the storage class named NSX001 for the storage service level of the data set. Also, allowing how the storage class was specified, VOL=SER can be coded and the data set will reside on the specific volumes.

MGMTCLAS assigns a management class to a new data set strictly for administrative purposes. This will then allow for the migration, for example, of a data set to the archives if it is inactive. It also controls a number of additional activities, such as file backups and the frequency of such backups, the release of unused space, and the deletion of data sets based on an expiration date. Again, at the risk of being redundant, this parameter is functional only if you are an SMS shop; if not, the system will routinely check for and ignore the MGMTCLAS parameter.

Like STORCLAS and DATACLAS values, this is normally the responsibility of an administrator, if there is one onboard. Consider the following example:

```
//ARFILE  DD  DSNAME=NIRAV.ARMAST,DATACLASS=XC100X,      C
//     STORCLAS=NSX001,MGMTCLASS=MIGRCLS1,DISP=NEW,KEEP)
```

In this example, SMS uses the MSGRCLS1 subparameter to handle the migration and the backup of the SMS-managed data sets. Note that MIGRCLS1 is defined by your installation.

5.5.4 The SECMODEL and the project statements

SECMODEL is coded only in an SMS installation. However, if you aren't an SMS installation, you need to rely on the DD PROJECT parameter, which I'll describe to you in a second. The purpose of the SECMODEL parameter is to specify the name of an existing RACF (short for Resource Access Control Facility) data-set profile that is copied to a new data-set profile. Thus, DD PROJECT is RACF- rather than SMS-dependent.

The PROJECT parameter is used to protect a particular data set on a DASD device. You can also protect a tape data set, provided it has the following attributes:

- Specified or implied VOLUME=PRIVATE
- Specified or implied DISP=NEW, DISP=OLD, or SHR; it must not specify or imply DISP=MOD.
- Specified, in the LABEL parameter, a label type such as SL or SUL, or NSL for nonstandard labels.

Let's look at some examples of this parameter. The following DD statement has an RACF-protected data set on direct access called NIRAV.WORKFILE:

```
//DASDFILE  DD  DSN=NIRAV.WORKFILE,DISP=(,CATLG),       C
//    VOL=SER=111111,UNIT=DISK,PROTECT=YES,             C
//    SPACE=(TRK,4)
```

The following DD statement requests RACF protection for NIRAV.TAPEF.WORKFILE, which happens to be the second data set on volume 123456:

```
//TAPEFILE  DD  DSN=NIRAV.TAPEF.WORKFILE,DISP=(NEW,CATLG),      C
//    LABEL=(2,SUL),VOL=SER=123456,UNIT=DISK,                   C
//    PROTECT=YES
```

Because a specific tape volume is requested, it automatically has the PRIVATE attribute. The volume has IBM-standard and user labels.

5.5.5 The LIKE and the REFDD parameters

You can use either of these statements to copy any SMS attribute to a data set or a DD statement. The purpose of the LIKE parameter is to let you copy DD information from a cataloged data set that's DASD-resident. REFDD, on the other hand, is used to copy DD information off a prior DD statement, unlike the LIKE parameter.

One important aspect of REFDD is that it copies information contained on a DD statement, not information the DD statement describes. The LIKE parameter overrides all the corresponding attributes shown on a DATACLAS statement. Consider the following example, which illustrates the LIKE and REFDD parameters:

```
  //AR100  EXEC  PGM=AR100AG
//AGFILE  DD     DSN=NIRAV.STANDARD.CNTL, UNIT=DISK,        C
//     DCB=(RECFM=FB,LRECL=200),                            C
//     SPACE=(TRK,(70,20),RLSE),                            C
//     DISP=(NEW,CATLG)
//AR200B  EXEC  PGM=AR200AGX
//SEVERFLE DD   DSN=NIRAV.STD2.CNTL,DISP=(NEW,CATLG),       C
//     UNIT=DISK,LIKE=NIRAV.STANDARD.CNTL         1
//AR300B  EXEC  PGM=AR300STM
//STAT050  DD  DSN=AGFILE.STANDARD.RECRDS,                  C
//     DISP=(NEW,CATLG),UNIT=DISK,                          C
//     REFDD=*.AR100B.AGFILE                      2
```

Let me explain the parts of this statement shown in bold. In the first area, 1, the DCB=(RECFM=FB,LRECL200) and SPACE=(TRK,(70,20),RLSE) information is copied from NIRAV.STANDARD.CNTL. In the second area, 2, both the DCB and SPACE statements are copied from AGFILE DD in step AR100B, which happens to be the first step in this partially presented runstream. Note, however, that any parm coded on your DD will override the copied parm statement. An example of this is as follows:

```
//AR200B   EXEC PGM=AR200AGX
//SEVERFLE DD   DSN=NIRAV.STD2.CNTL,DISP=(NEW,CATLG),      C
//    UNIT=DISK,DCB=LRECL=800,                             C
//    LIKE=NIRAV.STANDARD.CNTL
```

Attributes attained through the LIKE statement will override the corresponding attributes or subparameter part of a DATACLAS statement. If you don't code it on your DD statement, the following information will be copied:

- RECFM or REORG, depending on the type of data set
- DSNTYPE for a partitioned data set or PDS
- LRECL, regardless of the type of records
- KEYLEN or KEYOFF, the latter used for VSAM (KSDS) data sets
- SPACE and AVGREC, if any

5.5.6 The REORG and KEYOFF parameters

SMS enables you to create and delete VSAM clusters through job control. This is achieved through two previously mentioned parameters, REORG and KEYOFF. KEYOFF specifies the offset of the keys in a Key Sequenced Data Set (KSDS). REORG simply denotes a VSAM file organization. Code REORG=KS, which designates the creation of a KSDS data set. REORG=ES refers to an Entry Sequenced Dataset, or ESDS. Relative Record Data Sets are coded as RR (short for RRDS) and LS, meaning Linear Space Data Set (also LSDS), is used primarily in data in virtual, a topic I discuss in length in chapter 1.

5.5.7 The DSNTYPE statement for PDSs

DSNTYPE is available in SMS to specify a new partitioned data set or PDS, or a new partitioned data set extended (PDSE). A PDSE is similar to a PDS with one exception: it can contain only data rather than a load module. So the DSNTYPE parameter is used when you need to specify a partitioned data set or PDSE, or when you need to override the DSNTYPE attribute defined in your data class.

Note several things about PDSE. First, it doesn't need to be compressed. If you were to delete such a data set, the space previously taken up will be reused. Also, a PDSE can have 123 extents as opposed to the conventional 16. When you use a PDSE, you'll see that it's a great deal faster than accessing a PDS. Last, you can also concurrently update PDSE members.

A PDSE can exist at both the data-set and library level. If you specify DISP=SHR (share) on the DD statement for a PDSE, SHR applies to both the data set as well as the member.

In order to create a PDSE, all you have to do is to specify DSNTYPE=LIBRARY. Although the system will calculate your space requirements, you should not omit this parameter simply because, by using the SPACE parameter in requesting so many directory blocks, you are telling the operating system that you are in the process of creating a PDSE. Consider the following example:

```
//POMASTER  DD  DSN=AR.BACK(STATEMENT),DISP=(NEW,KEEP),      C
//    DATACLAS=XDATA10,DSNTYPE=LIBRARY
```

In this example, POMASTER DD defines the member statement in the PDSE named AR.BACK.DSNTYPE=LIBRARY, overriding the DSNTYPE attributes in the data class XDATA10.

5.6 The Queue Parameter

When you use the QNAME parameter on your DD statement, you are simply telling the system that the data set in reference uses the Telecommunication Access Method (TCAM). QUEUE defines a destination queue (such as in CICS) for transient data sets. There are some restrictions you need to be aware of when you use this parameter, such as you can code it only with LIKE, LRECL, RECFM and REFDD. Likewise, the only subparameters you can associate with the QUEUE are BLKSIZE, BUFL, LRECL, OPTCD, and RECFM. Consider the following example:

```
//QUEDATA   DD   QNAME=TEMPQ,                       C
//    DCB=(RECFM=FB,LRECL=100,BLKSIZE=500)
```

This example defines a data set containing TCAM messages. TEMPQ specifies the destination queue to which the messages are routed. The DCB parm supplies information normally not supplied in the DCB macro instruction for the data control block.

5.7 DD Statements for Input/Output Devices

5.7.1 Instream data sets

The reason I have included this section is to highlight some of the DD statements essential to read and write data (or data sets) in three major categories:

- Reading input data
- Writing output data other than unit record equipment
- Writing or processing data via unit record equipment such as the printer.

When you use a SYSIN DD statement, you do so to begin an instream data set. Instream data sets begin with a DD * or DD DATA statement. For example, you might say:

```
//STEP01   EXEC   PGM=READPGM
//SYSIN     DD     *
. . . data stream starts here . . .
```

If you need to terminate this instream data set, all you have to do is to specify a delimiter. This delimiter assignment is done via a DLM (short for a delimiter) statement that can include standard values, such as /* and //, in the data. In a JES2 system, when the DLM delimiter appears on a DD * statement, either the assigned delimiter or // ends the input data set. This is different from a typical JES3 system where only the assigned delimiter ends the input data set.

5.7.2 Output stream data sets

First of all, let me talk about the SYSOUT parameter, which identifies a data set as a system output data set. Note that you cannot use the SYSOUT parameter for an SMS-managed data set (one with an assigned storage class).

One of the aspects of the SYSOUT statement is that it assigns a data set to an output class. Actually, your installation should maintain a list of all available output classes and their attributes. Thus, some of these classes should be used for printing, but others should be reserved for special processing. Note that each class is processed by an output writer.

In viewing some of the parameters in conjunction with the SYSOUT statement, let me briefly review four of these for you in the following sections. These are the HOLD, DEST, COPIES and OUTLIM components.

5.7.2.1 The HOLD parameter

The purpose of the HOLD parameter is to tell the system to hold a sysout data set until it is released by the operator. When the above data set is ready to be processed, notify the system operator to release it via a TSO NOTIFY parameter.

If you are a TSO user, all you have to specify is HOLD=YES to retrieve a system data set and display it on your terminal. Note that if you don't code a SYSOUT parameter on your DD statement while indicating a HOLD, the statement will be ignored by the operating system. The following is an example of the HOLD parameter:

```
//jobAR          job     ,'VARSEGI',MSGLEVEL=1
//START1         EXEC    PGM=ARC70C
//ARMSTR         DD      SYSOUT=B,DEST=RMT1,HOLD=YES
```

5.7.2.2 The DEST parameter and its uses

DEST, the destination parameter, is used when you need to specify a target or destination for a particular SYSOUT data set. A destination parameter enables you to send your SYSOUT data set to a remote or local terminal—for example, to a node or workstation.

When you code the DEST parameter, code it only on a DD statement with a SYSOUT parameter; otherwise, the system will check the DEST parameter for syntax and then ignore it. The following is an example of DEST:

```
//ANYjob  job  ,'ALEX VARSEGI',MSGCLASS=B
//STEP1   EXEC  PGM=ART120C
//WORK1   DD   SYSOUT=A
//WORK2   DD   SYSOUT=A,DEST=R223
//WORK3   DD   SYSOUT=A,DEST=(ABCD,'9102932')
```

In this example, the system sends the SYSOUT data set defined by the DD statement WORK1 to the workstation that submitted the job. Then the data set is defined by the DD statement WORK2 to the remote terminal R223, and the data set defined by the DD statement WORK3 to a VM (Virtual Machine), userid 9102932 at node ABCD.

5.7.2.3 COPIES, OUTLIM, FREE, SEGMENT, and SPIN parameters

The third aspect of the SYSOUT parameter I need to discuss is the COPIES statement. This parameter is used to specify how many copies of the SYSOUT data set need to be printed. The printed output is in page sequence for each copy. If you do not code a COPIES statement, code it incorrectly, or code COPIES=0, the system will use a default of 1.

A fourth parameter, referred to as OUTLIM, limits the number of logical records in the SYSOUT data set that is being defined by a DD statement. Format for the OUTLIM parameter is OUTLIM=*n*, where *n* represents the number of logical records. For example:

```
//OUTDD  DD  DYDOUT=F,OUTLIM=2000
```

A fifth parameter, called FREE, is used when a system is to deallocate the resources used for a data set. The resources can be a number of things, such as devices, volumes, or even the exclusive use of a data set.

If you were to specify FREE=CLOSE, JES will print the SYSOUT data set before the job is completed. Thus, one of the subparameters used with FREE is CLOSE, which simply requests the system to deallocate the data set at the end of the step. An example of the FREE command is as follows:

```
//FILEAR  DD  DSN=AR.MSTR,DISP=OLD,FREE=CLOSE
```

A sixth parameter, SEGMENT, pertains only to JES2. Essentially, SEGMENT enables you to print while the job step is still running, even if you have any ongoing additions or other types of maintenance for a particular file.

The best way to use the SEGMENT parameter is when you have a large amount of printing and you can safely begin to print portions of a file while additional maintenance or calculations are being performed.

A seventh parameter, SPIN, is also a JES2-related statement. SPIN allows you to start printing a data set while it is in the process of deallocation. If you specify SPIN=NO (which happens to be the default), the job will start printing only at the end.

5.7.3 Reference to unit-record equipment

While some unit-record equipment, such as a card reader and card punch, have been long since phased out by most data centers, others, such as the impact printer, are still fully operational. The problem with most unit-record equipment is that it takes forever to process data compared to the phenomenal speed of a CPU or even retrieving data from primary or auxiliary devices. Because of their obsolescence, card punches are now allocated to writers while card readers simply point to the readers. Let's see how all this translates into coding a DD statement.

One of the parameters used in dealing with this type of equipment is the record length, or LRECL subparameter. With regards to the printer, use the PRTSP subparameter to control spacing, e.g., DCB=PRTSP=2. As for a card reader (or card punch), the keyword STACK refers to a particular stack, and you can code FUNC for the 3505/25 card reader/punches. If you were to say FUNC=T, for example, you would be printing with a two-line option. FUNC=W, on the other hand, will print the entire data set from start to finish.

There are two additional parameters also used in conjunction with certain unit-record equipment models. The Universal Character Set parameter (UCS) assigns a particular character set to a printer, such as the IBM 1403, 3203, and 3211. The second parameter, the Forms Control Buffer (FCB), is used to assign the forms control image to the IBM 3211 and 3800 printers. This is important when you need to set up preprinted forms, such as those used for W2 processing, quarterly-statement billing invoices, and so on.

In using this type of printer mechanism, there are several additional parameters available to the operator. One of them, the COPIES statement, has already been discussed. Other parameters, to mention a few, are BURST, CHAR, MODIFY, and FLASH.

BURST specifies the use of a 3800 printer, that is that the output will end up either in a burster trimmer stacker to be burst into separate sheets, or in a continuous form stacker to be left in a continuous fanfold.

When you specify BURST=Y (you can spell it out as BURST=YES), you are requesting that the printed output be burst into several sheets. When you specify BURST=N or BURST=NO, you are requesting that the printed output is to be in a continuous fanfold.

Note that the burster/trimmer/stacker can be requested using the BURST parameter on the OUTPUT JCL statement. Also, you can use the STACKER option on a JES3//*FORMAT PR statement or on a JES2/*OUTPUT statement. An example of the BURST command is shown as follows:

```
//RECORD DD SYSOUT=A,BURST=Y
```

```
MODIFY = module-name
         module-name [,trc]
```

```
* you must code the module name
* The trc subparameter is optional. If you omit it, you can
  omit the parentheses. However, if you omit it, you must
  not code it as a null; MODIFY=(TAB1,) is invalid.
```

Figure 5.3 Syntax for the MODIFY parameter.

The CHAR option is used to specify the name of one or more character-arrangement tables for printing this SYSOUT data set on an IBM 3800 printer. If you don't code the DD CHAR parameter, JES will use the following order:

1. The CHAR parameter on an output JCL statement, if referenced by the DD statement.
2. The DD UCS parameter value, if coded.
3. The UCS parameter on an OUTPUT JCL statement, if referenced.

You can request a high-density dump on the 3800 through two DD parameters for the dump data set, or an output JCL statement referenced by the dump DD statement:

* FBC=STD3

This parameter produces dump output at 8 lines per inch. The following parameter:

* CHAR=DUMP

produces 204 characters per print line. Consider the following example:

```
//SYSABEND  DD  UNIT=3800,CHARS=DUMP,FCB=STD3
```

In this example, the CHARS parameter on this SYSABEND DD statement specifies a high-density dump with 204 characters per line. The FCB parameter requests the dump output at 8 lines per inch.

The reason you need to use the MODIFY parameter is to specify a copy modification module that tells JES how to print a SYSOUT data set on the 3800 printer. This module is stored in a SYS1.IMAGELIB using the EIBIMAGE utility program.

Syntax for the MODIFY parameter is presented in Figure 5.3. The module name on the chart identifies a copy modification module in SYS1.IMAGELIB. Place the module name in columns 1 through 4 using alphanumeric or national ($, #, @) characters.

TRC identifies which table name in the CHARS parameter is to be used. This table-reference character is 0 for the first table name specified, 1 for the second, 2 for the third, and 3 for the fourth. The CHARS parameter is presented to you in override order, as follows:

1. The DD statement.
2. A referenced OUTPUT JCL statement.
3. A statement in the library member specified on the PAGEDEF parameter.
4. A statement in the SYS1.IMAGELIB member obtained by default.
5. A JES initialization statement.

Here is an example to clarify these specifications:

```
//PAYTRANS  DD  UNIT=3800,MODIFY=(A,0),CHARS=(GS15,GS10)
```

In this example, the MODIFY parameter requests that the data in the copy modification module named A replace variable data in the data set to be printed on the 3800 printer. Module A defines which positions are to be replaced and which copies are to be modified.

The second subparameter in MODIFY specifies that the first character arrangement table in the CHARS parameter, GS15, be used.

A third option is the FLASH parameter. The purpose of this option is to identify the forms overlay to be used in printing the SYSOUT data set on the 3800 printer, and optionally to specify the number of copies on which the forms overlay is to be printed. Figure 5.4 shows the syntax structure for the FLASH parameter.

In this example, overlay-name identifies the forms overlay frame that the operator is to insert into the printer before printing begins. The name must be placed in columns 1 through 4, containing alphanumeric or national ($, #, @) characters.

COUNT specifies a number, 0 through 255, which represents the amount of copies that JES is to flash with the overlay, beginning with the first copy printed. Code a count of 0 to flash all copies. When you specify NONE, the system suppresses flashing for the sysout data set. If FLASH=NONE is coded on the DD statement in the job to be executed at a remote node, JES3 sets the overlay name to zero before sending the job to the node.

Note that there is a relationship between FLASH and COPIES. If the particular DD statement or a referenced OUTPUT JCL statement also contains a COPIES parameter, JES will print with the forms overlay the number of copies specified in one of the following:

- COPIES=n, if the FLASH count is larger than n. For example, if COPIES=10 and FLASH=(LTHD,12), JES will print 10 copies, all with the forms overlay.
- The sum of the group values specified in the COPIES parameter, if the FLASH count is larger than the sum. For example, if COPIES=(,(2,3,4)) and FLASH=(LTHD,12), for example, JES will print nine copies in groups, all with the forms overlay.
- The count subparameter in the FLASH parameter, if the FLASH count is smaller than n or the sum from the COPIES parameter. For example, if COPIES=10 and FLASH=(LTHD,7), JES will print seven copies with the forms overlay and three copies without.

```
FLASH   = overlay-name
          overlay-name [,count]
          none
```

```
* This COUNT subparameter is optional. If you omit it, you
  can omit the parentheses. However, if you omit it, you
  must not code it as a null; FLASH=(ABCD,) is invalid.
```

Figure 5.4 Syntax for the FLASH parameter.

The following is an example of the FLASH parameter:

```
//PAYTRANS  DD  SYSOUT=A,COPIES=10,FLASH=(ABCD,5)
```

In the above example, JES issues a message to the operator requesting that the forms overlay ABCD be inserted into the printer. Then, JES prints the first five copies of the data set with the forms overlay and the last five copies without.

5.8 What Else is New in MVS/ESA JCL Conventions

There are several new functions in the form of output parameters that have been added to the new environment. Among these are ADDRESS, BUILDING, DEPT, NAME, ROOM, TITLE, and OUTDISP. Let me describe these to you as briefly as possible.

First of all, let's talk about the ADDRESS parameter. The purpose of ADDRESS is to print a delivery address on a separate page so that the operator can distribute the printed report as required in any specific order. ADDRESS allows you to use a maximum of four lines for describing an address. To use this feature, you must be using at least release 4, which also applies to all subsequently covered material. Make sure you enclose the contents of the ADDRESS in apostrophes, like this: '1127 W 31ST, CHICAGO, IL., 60606'.

A second feature, BUILDING (i.e., 'INFIRMARY') describes the particular building for distribution, using a single line. Like ADDRESS, the BUILDING parameter must also be enclosed in apostrophes.

A third feature to identify or clarify the location parameter is DEPT. The sole purpose of this qualifier is to provide you with some specifics with regards to a department address on the separator page, such as 'ACCOUNTING' or 'INFO SYSTEMS'.

The DEPT parameter can also be further qualified via the NAME parameter, which is the fourth feature available under release 4 and up aimed at separating q report based on the name of an individual. Thus, his name will show on the page separator in order to expedite the distribution process. You are restricted to a single line enclosed in apostrophes.

If you need additional location indicators, you can use the ROOM parameter, which is the fifth parameter in this structure. The sole purpose of this parameter is to point you to the right room or workstation for the individual receiving your report ('ACCOUNTS RECEIVABLE - ROOM 1278'). You can also enclose a TITLE for the report (which happens to be the sixth parameter), which will show up on the separator page, such as 'AGING RECEIVABLES REPORT FOR JANUARY, 1993.'

Last, the seventh feature, OUTDISP, gives you a chance to decide what you want to do when the job runs OK, as opposed to an abnormal termination. Note that you can refer to the following DISPOSITION in coding your OUTDISP statement:

DISP=WRITE. Prints your output and then deletes the data set.

DISP=HOLD. Holds the output data set until the operator releases it.

DISP=LEAVE. Having released the output, the operator will change the disposition of the data set to KEEP.

DISP=KEEP. Prints the report and changes the disposition of the data set to KEEP.

DISP=PURGE. This feature is used when you want to delete a report data set without printing.

Chapter

6

ISPF/Program Development Facility

6.1 What is ISPF?

Because of the extensive material presented in this chapter, I will provide a chart throughout the chapter to help you visualize the topics covered in the discussion. Each time you see the chart, the **shaded areas** represents the topics currently being discussed. The first of these is shown in Figure 6.1.

ISPF, or Interactive System Productivity Facility, is a multifacet productivity tool. Primarily, it is a dialog manager. A dialog is a conversation between a person using an interactive display terminal such as a CRT and a computer, while using an application program. For example, you might develop a program that will access and update your inventory files—this is a dialog. There are, actually, several dialog elements of the ISPF productivity tool, some that appear in every dialog and some that are optional. Among these elements are the functions, such as CLIST command procedures, programs (COBOL, PL/1, FORTRAN, etc.), panel definitions, message definitions, tables (usually in the form of two-dimensional arrays to store dialog elements), file-tailoring skeletons, and dialog variables. Figure 6.2 gives you some idea how each of these elements interact with ISPF.

Dialog begins either with the display of a screen or through the invocation of a function. So when you develop a dialog, you have the flexibility to custom-tailor it to fit the particular application. Dialogs are managed by a dialog manager, which provides various services to the dialog. It is sort of an extension of the host operating system. ISPF, for one, can edit, process, and store input data, create output, request the display of a screen, and perform functions very much like a data-management system does. Figure 6.3 shows the various service categories and dialog elements with which they interact.

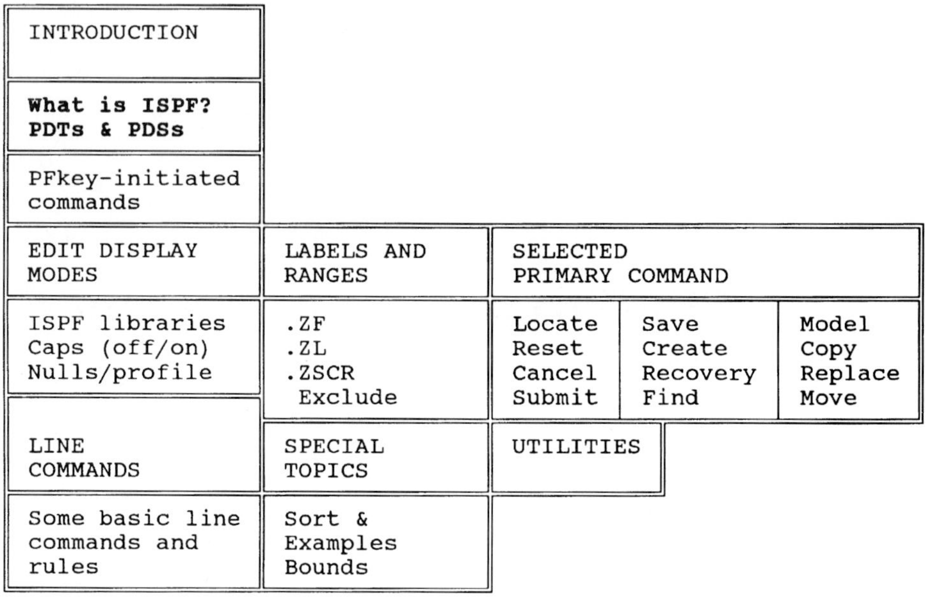

INTRODUCTION				
What is ISPF? **PDTs & PDSs**				
PFkey-initiated commands				
EDIT DISPLAY MODES	LABELS AND RANGES	SELECTED PRIMARY COMMAND		
ISPF libraries Caps (off/on) Nulls/profile	.ZF .ZL .ZSCR Exclude	Locate Reset Cancel Submit	Save Create Recovery Find	Model Copy Replace Move
LINE COMMANDS	SPECIAL TOPICS	UTILITIES		
Some basic line commands and rules	Sort & Examples Bounds			

Figure 6.1 The introductory topic chart.

The ISPF productivity tool has a very broad use in the industry. For a detailed understanding of the software, you need to acquaint yourself with an existing body of literature published by both IBM Corporation as well as independent sources. This chapter will focus on a relatively narrow aspect of the software under ISPF/PDF (PDF stands for Program Development Facility), which is a dialog that runs under ISPF control, like the dialog you create. Consider the chart shown in Figures. 6.4 and 6.5. PDF provides you with library-access services that help you perform system utility functions on ISPF libraries or data sets. An edit-recovery service allows you a recovery of the changes you made to a data set before a system failure. The edit and browse interface services enable you to provide I/O (input/output) operation to edit or browse data that is neither a sequential nor partitioned data set.

6.2 A First Glance at PDF

Let's look at a standard ISPF Primary Options Menu, which can be invoked by entering PDF following a TSO ready prompt. However, you might also consider having your installation follow a different prompt sequence in arriving at the display of this panel. The Primary Options Menu is displayed in Figure 6.6.

Note that it is customized to fit a particular installation, and thus might be different from the Primary Options Menu you rely on in your organization.

What is standard on the Primary Options Menu is the short message area located in the upper right-hand corner of the screen, containing a command line following the Option ===> subheader, and a long message area displayed on line 3. Whenever there is an error message, it is normally displayed in the short message area first.

The particular error message in Figure 6.6, for example, was caused by the erroneous selection of 15 because there are altogether only 14 valid options. If this does not clarify things for you, press PF1 to see some additional information on the problem. This panel is displayed in Figure 6.7.

Note that in requesting on-line help from ISPF, the contents on display are not cursor sensitive. What specific panel gets invoked depends largely on what part of the product you happen to be using at the time. If you are in browse mode (OPTION 1), for example, you will be restricted to a view that is only a browse-related narrative. To exit a particular module in ISPF, press PF3, which will take you back to the Primary Options Menu.

Dialog element	Description
Function	Functions direct the dialog's processing sequence. They can be written as: * CLIST command procedures * Programs FORTRAN COBOL PL/1 Pascal APL/2
Panel definition	An ISPF dialog can use several kinds of panel definitions: * Selection panels display a list of processing options you can choose from * Data-entry panels allow you to enter information to be processed by the dialog * Table display panels show you some or all of the data stored in the table * Information-only and tutorial panels give you information about dialog processing or provide help.
Message definition	ISPF's messages relay information about processing and call attention to input errors.
Table	Tables are two-dimensional arrays that store dialog data. They can be for temporary use, or they can be stored for use in future ISPF sessions. Not all dialogs use tables--it depends on the application's requirements.
File-tailoring Skeletons	Some ISPF dialogs use file skeletons to produce output. File skeletons work like a fill-in-the-blank exercise; they take dialog variables from a table and put them into a data set containing statements that control the output format.
Dialog variable	Dialog variables pass information among dialog functions and ISPF services.

Figure 6.2 A chart showing dialog elements. (*Courtesy of IBM Corp.*)

ISPF service category	Dialog element
Display	Panels, messages, and dialog variables
Select	Panels and functions
Table	Tables
File tailoring	File skeletons
Variable	Dialog variables

Figure 6.3 General ISPF dialog management service categories.

Option	Description
Option 0 - ISPF Parms	Lets you display and change ISPF parameters, such as PF key definitions and terminal characteristics at any time during an ISPF session.
Option 1 - BROWSE	Displays program code, test data, and documentation; a convenient way to scan large files, such as compiler listings.
Option 2 - EDIT	Helps you create or change program code and test data or documentation. Special features include edit macros that eliminate repetitive editing tasks and models that help you create dialog elements.
Option 3 - UTILITIES	Helps you perform system utilities and data-set management functions, including printing, renaming, deleting, cataloging, and uncataloging a data set.
Option 4 - FOREGROUND	Interactively executes language-processing programs, including assembler, COBOL, VS/FORTRAN, PL/1, Pascal, and SCRIPT/VS.
Option 5 - BATCH	Generates and submits appropriate host-system job statements and command streams for batch execution of language-processing programs.
Option 6 - COMMAND	Lets you enter TSO commands, including CLIST command procedures, while PDF is running.
Option 7 - DIALOG TEST	Helps you test individual dialog elements or whole dialogs to make sure everything works the way you want it.
Option 8 - LM UTILITIES	Helps you make sure you're working with the latest level of your development libraries and controls who's updating what.

Figure 6.4 Description of the PDF Primary Options Menu, part 1.

As you can see, PF1 is a standard tutorial key. PF3, on the other hand, is a standard exit or end key. So ISPF uses certain function keys to trigger a procedure, or a command, which can be customized in your respective installation. To find out what the default PF key setting is, type PFSHOW on the command line of the PDF Option menu and then press the Enter key. The result of this request is shown in Figure 6.8. Note that PFSHOW created two lines of a footnote, lines 23 and 24 on the bottom of

Option	Description
Option 9 - IBM PRODUCTS	Provides an interface to other IBM products that you can select while you are still in an ISPF session (if those products are installed on your system. The products are: * CSP/AD Cross System Product/Application Development * CSP/AE - Cross System Product/Application Execution * INFO/SYS - Information System * COBOL/SF-F - COBOL Structuring Facility Foreground * COBOL/SF-F - COBOL Structuring Facility Background
Option C - CHANGES	Keeps you up to date on changes that have been made to PDF since version 1 of the product.
Option T - TUTORIAL	Gives you step-by-step assistance while you are learning to use PDF, or when you need to refresh your memory.
Option X - EXIT	Ends a PDF session.

Figure 6.5 Description of the PDF Primary Options Menu, part 2.

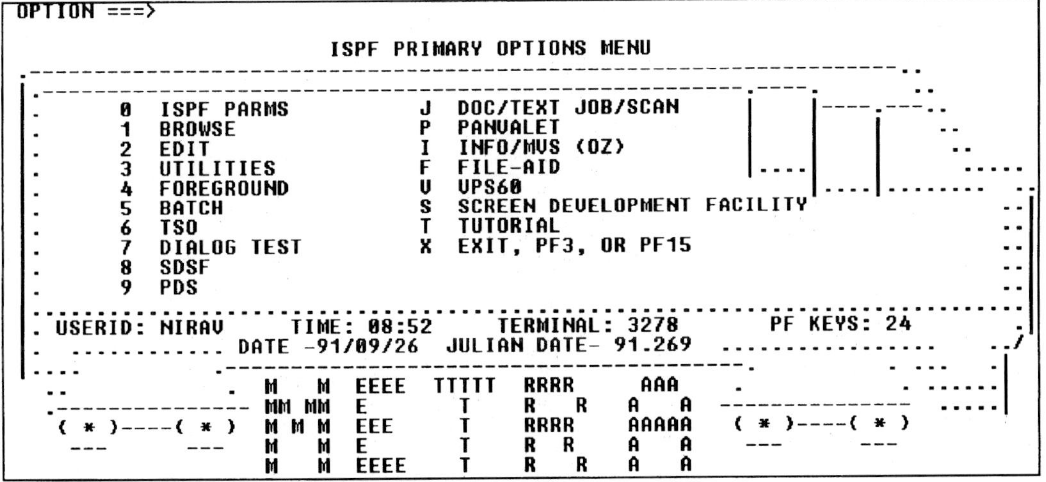

Figure 6.6 A customized ISPF Primary Options Menu.

```
TUTORIAL --------------- LIBRARY UTILITY - COMPRESS ------------------ TUTORIAL
COMMAND ===>

  Compress uses the MVS utility "IEBCOPY" to perform an in-place
  compression.  A system failure during this operation could result in
  the loss of one or more members.  Therefore, it is recommended that a
  backup copy of the data set be made before the compress is attempted.

  The output listing from the "IEBCOPY" program is placed in a temporary
  data set named SPFTEMP1.LIST or SPFTEMP2.LIST depending upon which logical
  screen is active.

  If the compress is successful, a success message is displayed in the
  short message field of the screen (upper right corner).

  If the compress fails, the return code from the IEBCOPY program is
  displayed in the short message field of the screen.

  In either case (success or failure), you may enter the HELP command to
  find out the name of the data set containing the listing from the
  IEBCOPY program.  You may then select browse to view the listing.

PF13=HELP       14=SPLIT      15=END        16=RETURN     17=RFIND      18=RCHANGE
PF19=UP         20=DOWN       21=SWAP       22=LEFT       23=RIGHT      24=CURSOR
```

Figure 6.7 A Tutorial Panel.

```
------------------------- UTILITY SELECTION MENU ----------------------------
OPTION  ===> pfshow

     1  LIBRARY    - Compress or print data set.  Print index listing.
                       Print, rename, delete, or browse members
     2  DATASET    - Allocate, rename, delete, catalog, uncatalog, or
                       display information of an entire data set
     3  MOVE/COPY  - Move, copy, or promote members or data sets
     4  DSLIST     - Print or display (to process) list of data set names
                       Print or display VTOC information
     5  RESET      - Reset statistics for members of ISPF library
     6  HARDCOPY   - Initiate hardcopy output
     8  OUTLIST    - Display, delete, or print held job output
     9  COMMANDS   - Create/change an application command table
    10  CONVERT    - Convert old format menus/messages to new format
    11  FORMAT     - Format definition for formatted data Edit/Browse
    12  SUPERC     - Compare data sets (Standard dialog)
    13  SUPERCE    - Compare data sets (Extended dialog)
    14  SEARCH-FOR - Search data sets for strings of data


PF13=HELP       14=SPLIT      15=END        16=RETURN     17=RFIND      18=RCHANGE
PF19=UP         20=DOWN       21=SWAP       22=LEFT       23=RIGHT      24=CURSOR
```

Figure 6.8 Utility selection menu to invoke PF key displays.

the Primary Option Menu. Incidentally, to turn off the function-key display, all you have to do is to enter PFSHOW OFF (two words) and the caption will disappear.

Note that Figure 6.8 provides information about these function keys. Note that PF keys are displayed in paired sets. The first set ranges from 1 to 12 and the other ranges from 13 to 24. Consequently, PF1 and PF13 will both display the same error message and tutorial information, unless, of course, you decide to reset the initial ISPF definition through the PARM OPTION, option 0. Because of the enormous popularity of ISPF, note that other packages (File AID, InterTest, Panvalet, etc.) also rely on the same function-key scheme as does IBM in this software product.

The reason for using PF keys is simply that they will save you time when you would otherwise have to enter sometimes lengthy search commands. But even in the most simplistic situations you can split a cursor-sensitive screen either through a command or via a function key, which gives you tremendous flexibility.

6.3 The ISPF Library

6.3.1 How to create a partitioned data set

It makes a great deal of sense to talk about some limited utility functions before reviewing some of the edit commands more extensively. So let me highlight some of the procedures you need to follow in order to create a data set (see Figure 6.9). This is done through the invocation of option 2, or more specifically, through option 3.2 (*3* representing the ISPF generic utility section and *2* denoting the data set to be created as part of your library). The ISPF library is made up of individual members (like books in a library), each being part of that library, thus the term *members* or *partitioned data set*.

Each member in this partitioned data set or library is maintainable through option 1 (or option 3.1), which is also known as the library utility. Library utilities are no different from other standard utilities in that you use them extensively to perform various maintenance functions, e.g., to compress, print, allocate, rename, delete,

INTRODUCTION				
What is ISPF? PDTs & PDSs				
PFkey-initiated commands				
EDIT DISPLAY MODES	LABELS AND RANGES	SELECTED PRIMARY COMMAND		
ISPF libraries Caps (off/on) Nulls/profile	.ZF .ZL .ZSCR Exclude	Locate Reset Cancel Submit	Save Create Recovery Find	Model Copy Replace Move
LINE COMMANDS	SPECIAL TOPICS	UTILITIES		
Some basic line commands and rules	Sort & Examples Bounds			

Figure 6.9 The topic chart, highlighting ISPF Libraries.

catalog, uncatalog, move, copy, browse members of a data set or the data set itself, and do all that quickly, efficiently, and without the frustration of having to write separate code for each requirement.

ISPF uses a library structure to name and organize a data set. According to the standards, ISPF requires a three-part nomenclature for defining a library, plus a member name, which is to be enclosed in parentheses. For example:

```
NIRAV.STANDARD.LIB(ARA71C)
```

where NIRAV is referred to as a project name, STANDARD denotes the group name, and LIB refers to a type suffix. Together, this is what you call a partitioned data set, including one of its members, ARA71C. Note that the ISPF project name normally contains the user I.D., but the rest of the library definition does not require any restriction in its naming-convention scheme, unless it is dictated by certain installation standards.

Before you can use the ISPF/PDF productivity tool, you need to allocate a library. This is done by selecting option 2 on the Utility Selection Menu and invoking the Data Set Utility screen shown in Figure 6.10.

Now enter the character A in the upper left-hand corner next to the OPTION ===> subheading. This panel is the one where you are required to define to ISPF all the characteristics pertinent to a new library (or data set). Make sure the entry corresponding to the DIRECTORY BLOCKS is not zero, which would mean a *sequential* rather than *partitioned* data set.

Once you have supplied the initial definition to the Data Set Utility Panel and pressed the Enter key, a message will appear in the upper right-hand corner of the screen: DATA SET ALLOCATED. So in the future, as you start creating new members to be placed on this library, refer to this library by its previously established name, which is NIRAV.STANDARD.CNTL.

```
---------------------------- DATA SET UTILITY -------------------------------
OPTION  ===> A

   A - Allocate new data set                  C - Catalog data set
   R - Rename entire data set                 U - Uncatalog data set
   D - Delete entire data set                 S - Data set information (short)
   blank - Data set information

ISPF LIBRARY:
   PROJECT ===> NIRAV
   GROUP   ===> STANDARD
   TYPE    ===> CNTL

OTHER PARTITIONED OR SEQUENTIAL DATA SET:
   DATA SET NAME  ===>
   VOLUME SERIAL  ===>          (If not cataloged, required for option "C")

DATA SET PASSWORD ===>          (If password protected)


PF13=HELP     14=SPLIT    15=END     16=RETURN    17=RFIND     18=RCHANGE
PF19=UP       20=DOWN     21=SWAP    22=LEFT      23=RIGHT     24=CURSOR
```

Figure 6.10 Data Set Utility Panel, used to allocate a partitioned dataset.

```
---------------------------  EDIT - ENTRY PANEL  ------------------------------
COMMAND ===>

ISPF LIBRARY:
   PROJECT ===> NIRAV
   GROUP   ===> STANDARD  ===>          ===>          ===>
   TYPE    ===> CNTL
   MEMBER  ===> DOCUMENT        (Blank or pattern for member selection list)

OTHER PARTITIONED OR SEQUENTIAL DATA SET:
   DATA SET NAME  ===>
   VOLUME SERIAL  ===>          (If not cataloged)

DATA SET PASSWORD ===>          (If password protected)

PROFILE NAME      ===>          (Blank defaults to data set type)

INITIAL MACRO     ===>          LOCK       ===> YES     (YES, NO or NEVER)

FORMAT NAME       ===>          MIXED MODE ===> NO      (YES or NO)

PF13=HELP     14=SPLIT    15=END     16=RETURN   17=RFIND    18=RCHANGE
PF19=UP       20=DOWN     21=SWAP    22=LEFT     23=RIGHT    24=CURSOR
```

Figure 6.11 A "blank" Edit Panel for creating a member.

Note that although you have a library defined, there are not yet any members in it. This activity, along with a number of maintenance functions, will be the topic of a more extensive review later on in this chapter.

Because you have created a library through the allocation of a data set, temporarily return to the edit module to see how to further use this data set. You can do this by entering an equal sign followed by the number 2 (=2), where 2 corresponds to the ISPF edit functions.

Once you have entered =2 and pressed the Enter key, a blank edit screen will appear, the result of the above jump command.

6.3.2 How to create and edit a member

Figure 6.11 shows the Edit Panel. The primary objective of this panel is to create a new member. To do that, expand your previously defined library to include a member name in addition to the Project, Group, and Type definitions highlighted earlier. For example, by entering:

```
ISPF LIBRARY:
     PROJECT   ===>  NIRAV
     GROUP     ===>  STANDARD
     TYPE      ===>  LIB
     MEMBER    ===>  DOCUMENT
```

you are instructing ISPF/PDF to create a new member on the library, called DOCUMENT. When you press the Enter key, a panel similar to the one presented in Figure 6.11 will be shown. Because the member DOCUMENT did not exist before, the panel will be blank and you can start entering text into it, e.g., data, JCLs, source programs, a physical map layout. In order to understand some of the capabilities of ISPF/PDF, let me present you a chart showing standard key assignments (Figure

```
TUTORIAL ------------------ COMMANDS AND PF KEYS --------------------- TUTORIAL
COMMAND ===>
                              DEFAULT ASSIGNMENT
                             PROGRAM FUNCTION KEYS

                          |----------|----------|----------|
  Listed on the           | PF1/13   | PF2/14   | PF3/15   |
  next panel are          |  HELP    |  SPLIT   |  END     |
  the system-wide         |          |          |          |
  ISPF commands.          |----------|----------|----------|
  Many of these           | PF4/16   | PF5/17   | PF6/18   |
  have default PF         |  RETURN  |  RFIND   | RCHANGE  |
  key assignments,        |          |          |          |
  shown on the            |----------|----------|----------|
  right.                  | PF7/19   | PF8/20   | PF9/21   |
                          |  UP      |  DOWN    |  SWAP    |
                          |          |          |          |
                          |----------|----------|----------|
                          | PF10/22  | PF11/23  | PF12/24  |
                          | LEFT     | RIGHT    | RETRIEVE |
                          |          |          |          |
                          |----------|----------|----------|
PF13=HELP      14=SPLIT     15=END       16=RETURN    17=RFIND     18=RCHANGE
PF19=UP        20=DOWN      21=SWAP      22=LEFT      23=RIGHT     24=CURSOR
```

Figure 6.12 ISPF PF key assignments using the PARM option.

```
EDIT ---- NIRAV.STANDARD.CNTL(DOCUMENT) - 01.00 -------------- COLUMNS 001 072
COMMAND ===>                                                   SCROLL ===> PAGE
****** ***************************** TOP OF DATA ******************************
000001 The Pay History screen is invoked through PF6 on the Claims
''''''  Entry/Update panel shown in Fig. 1.3. This panel allows you to
''''''  enter any transaction associated with a payment. If you need to
''''''  update the file through the screen, press PF12. If an entry was
''''''  keyed in erroneously, you may overlay it with the correct data or
''''''  you may use the space bar to erase a desired line.
''''''
''''''  If you need more than a single screen entry, you may scroll forward
''''''  to continue the recording of additional transaction on subsequent
''''''  screens. Page deletion is possible by entering the character "Y" next
''''''  to the delete page header on the bottom of the screen shown if Fig.
''''''  1.6.
''''''
''''''
''''''
''''''
''''''
''''''
PF13=HELP      14=SPLIT     15=END       16=RETURN    17=RFIND     18=RCHANGE
PF19=UP        20=DOWN      21=SWAP      22=LEFT      23=RIGHT     24=CURSOR
```

Figure 6.13 Entering and maintaining text into ISPF/PDF.

6.12) and a brief overview of what each of them does. I'm going to show you how to create a member on this panel and manipulate the contents, as described in Figure 6.13.

Before entering the text, you might want to enter the command CAPS OFF next to the COMMAND ===> subheader. This will allow you to use lowercase as well as uppercase text, thus rendering the display a bit more legible.

Once you have entered the text and pressed Enter, the data will be highlighted with all unused spaces eliminated, and the lines initially presented as '''''' will now be replaced with valid sequence numbers. Before continuing the editing process, you might want to save what you have entered so far. Do this by entering the command

SAVE next to the command arrow and pressing the Enter key. (You can also press PF3, but this would take you out of the current procedure in addition to saving the updated document.)

To take a close look at the way to edit a particular data set, you might want to study your edit profile. For example, you can set up your profile to edit data either in capital or in mixed letters. PDF will generate a default edit profile for you based on the ISPF library type of data set you are editing. To look at your profile and see the specific defaults, type PROFILE on the command line. The profile will appear in the first four lines of your file, similar to the one shown in Figure 6.14.

Most of these commands have to do with the display of data or text on screen, whether such a display is in upper- or lowercase, whether you need to view a file in hexadecimal (for packed decimals, for example) or in various other formats involving specific commands and procedures. Here is a brief summary of what they do for you. (Incidentally, to do away with the lines generated by the PROFILE command, type RESET next to the COMMAND ===> line and press the Enter key.)

The NULLS command, for example, has to do with initiating or discontinuing all trailing blanks by zeros. TABS indicated whether you need hardware or logical tabbing to be in effect. STATS sets the statistics mode on or off. If STATS is on, ISPF will generate the required statistics for members of a partitioned data set. AUTONUM is designed to turn the auto-numbering mode on or off. AUTOLIST works in conjunction with the AUTONUM by displaying the list.

6.3.3 PF-key-initiated commands

PF-key-initiated commands are those where a standard ISPF/PDF command is invoked through the use of a function key (see Figure 6.15). Keep in mind that, while you can associate a specific command with any of the 24 function keys on your key-

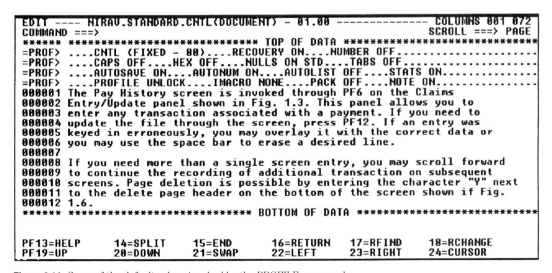

```
EDIT ---- NIRAV.STANDARD.CNTL(DOCUMENT) - 01.00 -------------- COLUMNS 001 072
COMMAND ===>                                                   SCROLL ===> PAGE
****** ***************************** TOP OF DATA ******************************
=PROF> ....CNTL (FIXED - 80)....RECOVERY ON....NUMBER OFF......................
=PROF> ....CAPS OFF....HEX OFF....NULLS ON STD....TABS OFF.....................
=PROF> ....AUTOSAVE ON....AUTONUM ON....AUTOLIST OFF....STATS ON...............
=PROF> ....PROFILE UNLOCK....IMACRO NONE....PACK OFF....NOTE ON................
000001 The Pay History screen is invoked through PF6 on the Claims
000002 Entry/Update panel shown in Fig. 1.3. This panel allows you to
000003 enter any transaction associated with a payment. If you need to
000004 update the file through the screen, press PF12. If an entry was
000005 keyed in erroneously, you may overlay it with the correct data or
000006 you may use the space bar to erase a desired line.
000007
000008 If you need more than a single screen entry, you may scroll forward
000009 to continue the recording of additional transaction on subsequent
000010 screens. Page deletion is possible by entering the character "Y" next
000011 to the delete page header on the bottom of the screen shown if Fig.
000012 1.6.
****** **************************** BOTTOM OF DATA ****************************

PF13=HELP      14=SPLIT     15=END       16=RETURN    17=RFIND     18=RCHANGE
PF19=UP        20=DOWN      21=SWAP      22=LEFT      23=RIGHT     24=CURSOR
```

Figure 6.14 Some of the default values invoked by the PROFILE command.

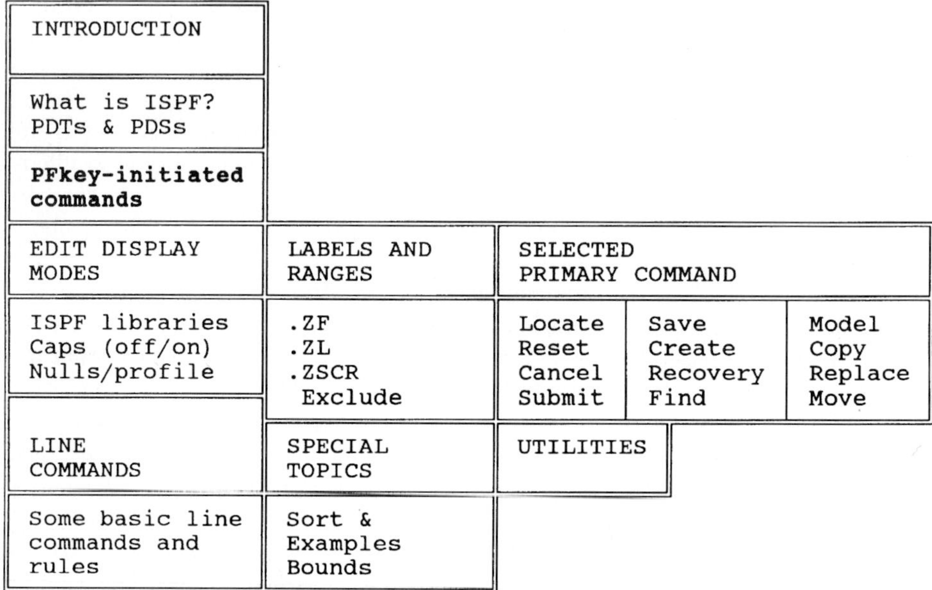

INTRODUCTION
What is ISPF?
PDTs & PDSs
PFkey-initiated commands
EDIT DISPLAY MODES
LABELS AND RANGES
SELECTED PRIMARY COMMAND
ISPF libraries
Caps (off/on)
Nulls/profile
.ZF
.ZL
.ZSCR
Exclude
Locate
Reset
Cancel
Submit
Save
Create
Recovery
Find
Model
Copy
Replace
Move
LINE COMMANDS
SPECIAL TOPICS
UTILITIES
Some basic line commands and rules
Sort &
Examples
Bounds

Figure 6.15 The topic chart, with PF-key-initiated commands highlighted.

board (you might have 12 or less), ISPF highlights a set of initial key definitions that you probably will not want to redefine. For example, PF8 allows you the downward movement on your screen by a full, half page, or any number you specify. You can also accomplish this by using the keyword DOWN and then, stating the number of lines you want, shift your display towards the bottom. If you have 24 keys on your keyboard, I strongly urge you to leave the first 12 of them intact, the way they are originally defined by ISPF, and modify only the second set. Use the second set of PF keys consistently!

So in the original scheme of things, PF1 is a help key that triggers a set of tutorial panels whenever you need to look things up or when learning the system.

PF2, or the split command, will divide a panel into two logical areas, allowing you to monitor the execution of two different tasks. The split command is cursor-sensitive, meaning it causes a split at the cursor location. You need to assign a PF key to this function, therefore, because issuing the command by its name (split) just won't do. Let me illustrate this point.

Figure 6.16 shows the display of two separate panels consolidated into a single display. This was accomplished through the following steps:

1. Display the first member on the screen, which is the ARC24C, a CICS application program. Place the cursor in line 000011 past the PIC X clause, and press PF2. This will split the screen into two halves: the upper portion, allowing you a partial view of the member, and the lower portion, highlighting a list of available members in the NIRAV.STANDARD.CNTL library.
2. Browse the library member list until you find an associated member correspond-

ing to ARC24C, which happens to be the physical map of the program, and select it from the list by placing the character S next to it and pressing the Enter key.

3. The result of this should be the simultaneous display of two members: the application program ARC21C, and the ARC24M map. Note that both of these members can be viewed or manipulated and checked for consistency to correct an existing or potential problem. If you were to press PF3 with the cursor positioned on the first (upper) half of the panel, it would cause an exit from the current display and ISPF would highlight the preceding step. This is exhibited in Figure 6.17.

```
EDIT ---- NIRAV.STANDARD.CNTL(ARC24C) - 01.07 ---------------- COLUMNS 001 072
COMMAND ===>                                                   SCROLL ===> PAGE
****** ***************************** TOP OF DATA ******************************
000001        IDENTIFICATION DIVISION.
000002        PROGRAM-ID. ARC24C.
000003        DATE-COMPILED. OCTOBER 23 1990.
000004        ENVIRONMENT DIVISION.
000005        DATA DIVISION.
000006        WORKING-STORAGE SECTION.
000007        01  BILL-DATE.
000008            05  BILL-MONTH      PIC XX.
000009            05  FILLER          PIC X.
000010            05  BILL-DAY        PIC XX.
000011            05  FILLER          PIC X.
EDIT --- NIRAV.STANDARD.CNTL ------------------------------ ROW 00025 OF 00074
COMMAND ===>                                                   SCROLL ===> PAGE
   NAME                  VV.MM  CREATED       CHANGED      SIZE  INIT   MOD   ID
  ARDS100C               01.16 90/06/28 90/07/16 15:45      266   230     0 NIRAV
  ARDS101C               01.03 90/06/22 90/06/25 15:10      221   203     0 NIRAV
  ARDS107C               01.67 90/06/28 90/08/13 08:43       47   230     0 NIRAV
  ARD73C                 01.82 90/03/15 90/05/04 14:54      140    39   117 NIRAV
  ARD73M                 01.26 90/03/15 90/03/22 16:10       47    28    47 NIRAV
  ARD82C                 01.14 90/06/11 90/06/12 15:45      344   345     0 NIRLC
```

Figure 6.16 Split-screen accessing a library member and the NIRAV.STANDARD.CNTL library member list simultaneously.

```
EDIT --- NIRAV.STANDARD.CNTL ------------------------------ ROW 00014 OF 00074
COMMAND ===>                                                   SCROLL ===> PAGE
   NAME                  VV.MM  CREATED       CHANGED      SIZE  INIT   MOD   ID
  ARC24C                 01.07 90/10/23 90/10/25 14:30      580   562     0 NIRAV
  ARC24M                 01.08 90/05/07 90/05/23 15:37       78    76     0 NIRAV
  ARC26C                 01.07 90/10/16 90/10/25 08:47      684   721     0 NIRAV
  ARC72C                 01.99 90/03/15 90/04/12 08:56      241    39   218 NIRAV
  ARC72M                 01.29 90/03/15 90/04/09 08:58       45    28    45 NIRAV
  ARC81M                 01.16 90/02/28 90/06/12 11:28      115    66   110 NIRLC
  ARC92C                 01.99 90/03/15 90/05/31 08:35      374    39     0 NIRAV
  ARC92M                 01.45 90/03/15 90/04/12 10:30       68    28    68 NIRAV
  ARC92MB
  ARDP114C               01.84 90/06/28 90/08/14 11:18      104   230     0 NIRAV
  ARDP120C               01.34 90/06/28 90/08/03 08:41      119   230     0 NIRAV
EDIT ---- NIRAV.STANDARD.CNTL(ARC24M) - 01.08 ---------------- COLUMNS 001 072
COMMAND ===>                                                   SCROLL ===> PAGE
****** ***************************** TOP OF DATA ******************************
000001          PRINT NOGEN
000002 ARC24M   DFHMSD  TYPE=&SYSPARM,MODE=INOUT,CTRL=FREEKB,LANG=COBOL,       C
000003                  TIOAPFX=YES
000004 ARC24M2  DFHMDI   SIZE=(24,80)
000005 TRANS    DFHMDF POS=(01,02),LENGTH=04,INITIAL='AR28',                  C
000006                 ATTRB=(BRT,ASKIP)
```

Figure 6.17 Split screen after a PF3-issued exit for the upper half of the screen.

This latter step of using the PF3 key to exit a current procedure and return to a previous step is just what the function key is used for. When splitting screens, use PF9 to move the cursor from one logical screen to another.

PF4 is used by ISPF to enable you to return to the previous Primary Options Menu without displaying intervening levels of panels, even if you were to split the screen on your previous instructions and happen to be several levels into the text editor.

In order to illustrate the use of PF5, I need to talk about an ISPF/PDF command called FIND. If you need to find a particular word or words in your text editor, you need to issue a FIND command on the command line, with the word or words you are looking for. The FIND command, however, is only a single-occurrence command; that is, it finds the first occurrence of a particular text. To move on to the next occurrence of the word, you need to press PF5 a second time—then a third time to highlight the third occurrence, and so on.

In using PF5, remember that it "wraps around" the document. If you have a word that appears three times in a given text, and if you were to give the command FIND DSNAME= and press Enter, ISPF would find the first occurrence of the above term and display a message in the upper right-hand corner of your screen, CHAR 'DSNAME=' FOUND. This message would display two more times until the bottom of the document is reached. At that point, ISPF will display BOTTOM OF DATA SEARCHED. The wraparound comes into play when you press PF5 following the message, which takes you back up to the beginning of the document to start the process over again.

PF6 is similar to PF5 in usage, except that it works in conjunction with the CHANGE command. Actually, you can specify CHANGE ALL DSN DSNAME, for example, which would automatically change all the occurrences of DSN to DSNAME throughout your document.

In the example in Figure 6.18, I wanted to correct some of the errors that a data-entry clerk made in entering my map. In place of DFHMDF, some of the op codes were entered as DFHMDX. To play it safe, I decided to correct every one of them. So I issued the command CHANGE DFHMDX DFHMDF. Simply put, I want to change the first occurrence of the DFHMDX operation code to read DFHMDF. The rest is history. To get to the second and subsequent occurrences, I simply used PF6. However, you can also issue a CHANGE ALL command, CHANGE ALL DFHMDX DFHMDF, and the system will perform the change without any further PF key intervention.

The PF7 through PF10 keys allow you to navigate about a screen. For example, PF7 will cause the display on your screen to shift toward the top, depending on the number of lines requested. You can also specify PAGE, which will move you upward by a total of 24 lines (an equivalent of a full-screen page) at a time, or HALF, which will move you only half a page at a time. Finally, by specifying CURSOR or CSR, ISPF allows you a cursor-sensitive move (somewhat similar to a split command without physically splitting the screen).

PF8 works like PF7, except it moves the display downward. PF10 and PF11 are designed to move horizontally in case your display has more than the conventional 80 characters.

```
EDIT ---- NIRAU.STANDARD.CNTL(ARD73M) - 01.26 ---------------- COLUMNS 001 072
COMMAND ===> change dfhmdx dfhmdf                              SCROLL ===> PAGE
****** ***************************** TOP OF DATA ******************************
000100            PRINT NOGEN
000200 ARD73M     DFHMSD   TYPE=&SYSPARM,MODE=INOUT,CTRL=FREEKB,LANG=COBOL,      C
000300                  TIOAPFX=YES
000400 ARD73M5    DFHMDI    SIZE=(24,80)
000500 TRID       DFHMDx POS=(01,02),LENGTH=04,ATTRB=(BRT,ASKIP)
000600            DFHMDx POS=(01,07),LENGTH=12,ATTRB=(BRT,ASKIP)
000700            DFHMDx POS=(01,20),LENGTH=31,ATTRB=(PROT,ASKIP),               C
000800                  INITIAL='PREFIX AND INVOICE MAINTENANCE'
000900            DFHMDF POS=(04,23),LENGTH=27,ATTRB=(BRT,ASKIP),                C
001000                  INITIAL='CURRENT   MINIMUM   MAXIMUM'
001100            DFHMDF POS=(05,05),LENGTH=44,ATTRB=(BRT,ASKIP),                C
001200                  INITIAL='PREF   ACCOUNT#     COUNT      RANGE      RANGE'
001300            DFHMDF POS=(05,55),LENGTH=07,ATTRB=(BRT,ASKIP),                C
001400                  INITIAL='T Y P E'
001500 PREF       DFHMDF POS=(07,06),LENGTH=01,ATTRB=(UNPROT,IC)
001600            DFHMDF POS=(07,08),LENGTH=02,ATTRB=ASKIP
001700 ACCOUNT    DFHMDF POS=(07,11),LENGTH=08,ATTRB=UNPROT
001800            DFHMDx POS=(07,20),LENGTH=02,ATTRB=ASKIP
001900 CURRCNT    DFHMDx POS=(07,23),LENGTH=05,ATTRB=UNPROT
002000            DFHMDF POS=(07,29),LENGTH=03,ATTRB=ASKIP
002100 MINRNG     DFHMDF POS=(07,33),LENGTH=05,ATTRB=UNPROT
```

Figure 6.18 CHANGE and PF6 commands.

Lastly, PF12 moves the cursor to the first input field on your current panel (usually the option selection or command field at the top of the screen) and retrieves or "plays back" the last command entered.

6.4 Labels and Ranges

The reason to use labels is to create a range within which you can perform a particular procedure or operation (see Figure 6.19). For example, if you have created a data file containing 5,200 lines, you might want to limit the scope of a FIND or EXCLUDE command between lines 2,200 and 4,800—leaving the rest of the data set untouched. This can be done by symbolic labeling. Symbolic labels are called so because, instead of line numbers, you use your own naming conventions or those available in the system. You can, thus, reference these labels via a number of primary (or other) commands. I will show you how to apply symbolic labels in a SORT operation in the following section.

The most common use of labels is specifying a range of lines within data being edited. Start your labeling process (which is nothing but a character string) with a period, followed by one or a number of alphabetic characters—a total of five bytes. Once you have assigned a symbolic label, it is going to stay with the line, even if the line is moved. You can then assign the label merely by typing a valid character string into the line command field of the data line. For example:

```
(before assignment)  000111   this is where it starts...
(after assignment)   .START   this is where it starts...
```

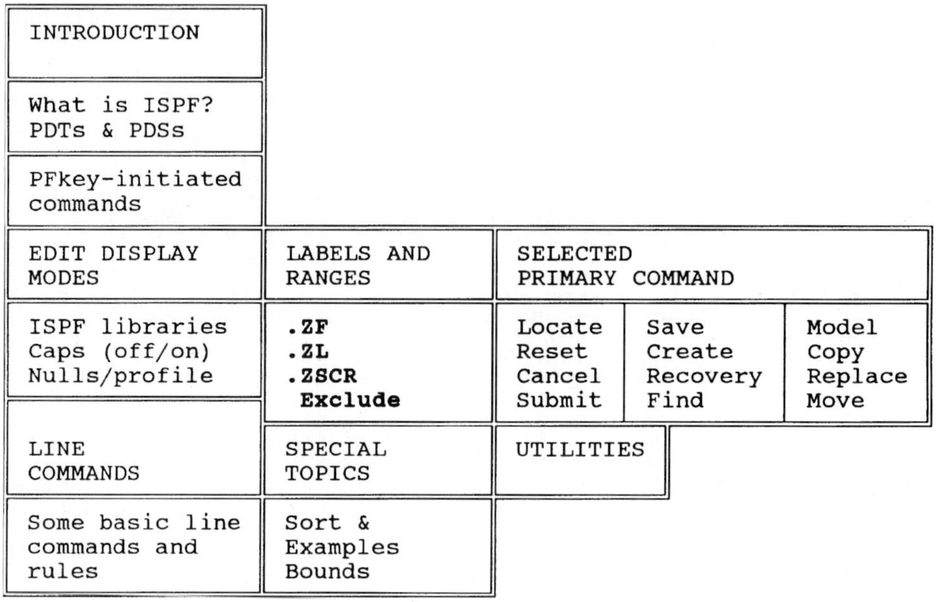

INTRODUCTION				
What is ISPF? PDTs & PDSs				
PFkey-initiated commands				
EDIT DISPLAY MODES	LABELS AND RANGES	SELECTED PRIMARY COMMAND		
ISPF libraries Caps (off/on) Nulls/profile	**.ZF** **.ZL** **.ZSCR** **Exclude**	Locate Reset Cancel Submit	Save Create Recovery Find	Model Copy Replace Move
LINE COMMANDS	SPECIAL TOPICS	UTILITIES		
Some basic line commands and rules	Sort & Examples Bounds			

Figure 6.19 Label and ranges topic chart.

Note that labels can be assigned only to data lines. They cannot be assigned to specific lines, e.g.:

```
=COLS>,  =MASK,   =TABS,
```

If you want to remove a symbolic label, all you have to do is to blank out the label characters (.START) or simply overtype them with a new label. In addition, you can also unassign a label by deleting the line that contains the label or by using the RESET LABEL command.

Overlaying a label with a line command is acceptable and does not unassign a label. Thus, the label will appear at the completion of the command and remain displayed in the line command field. Also, you can move a label to another line by typing the same label on a new line. If you don't take an explicit action to unassign a label, it's going to remain assigned until the user terminates the edit.

There are several special labels that are automatically assigned and maintained by the editor. They all begin with the letter Z and are reserved by the editor. The editor-assigned labels available to the end user are:

.ZCSR. The data line on which the cursor is currently positioned.

.ZFIRST. The first data line (relative line number 1).

.ZLAST. The last data line, which can be abbreviated as .ZL.

As previously indicated, you can limit the range of lines within the data being edited that will be processed by certain primary commands. Do this by entering a pair of labels indicating the first and the last lines to be processed, and naming those labels in the range operand of the appropriate command. The data then will be processed if it is contained within the designated (inclusive) range. The following command:

```
COMMAND ===> FIND JCL .START .ZLAST
```

means to find the first occurrence of JCL from the label .START to the end of the data. This command:

```
COMMAND ===> DEL ALL X .FROM .TO
```

means to delete all excluded (X) lines in the range of lines from label .FROM to label .TO (inclusive).

6.5 How to Use the ISPF Sort Feature

Let's talk about the kind of SORT you can perform using the ISPF text editor and how such a powerful procedure can help you develop several prototypes for testing (see Figure 6.20). Consider the following examples:

```
SORT 1 15
```

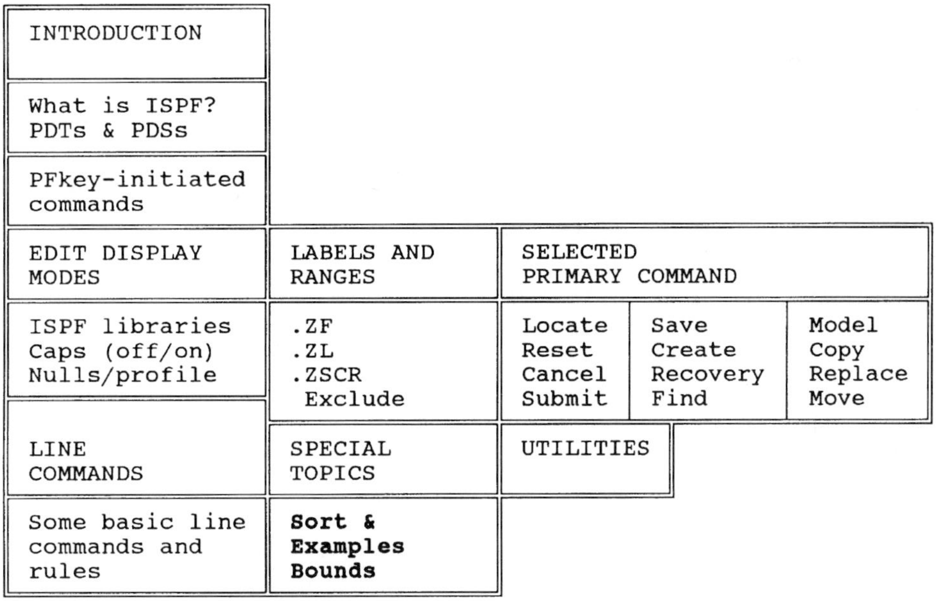

INTRODUCTION

What is ISPF?
PDTs & PDSs

PFkey-initiated commands

EDIT DISPLAY MODES	LABELS AND RANGES	SELECTED PRIMARY COMMAND		
ISPF libraries Caps (off/on) Nulls/profile	.ZF .ZL .ZSCR Exclude	Locate Reset Cancel Submit	Save Create Recovery Find	Model Copy Replace Move
LINE COMMANDS	SPECIAL TOPICS	UTILITIES		
Some basic line commands and rules	**Sort & Examples Bounds**			

Figure 6.20 SORT topic chart.

This statement simply means to sort the data that resides between columns 1 and 15. The operation will assume ascending order, which is the default order. When coding SORT parameters, make sure to place an embedded blank between 1 and 15. This command:

```
SORT 1 15 A 30 35 D
```

will sort the contents of the file using two components. The major SORT field will be located in columns 1 through 12, and will be presented in ascending order (A). The minor SORT will address columns 30 through 35, and this time the order of the SORT will be descending (D). Note that a general range for the SORT can be described through a BOUNDS statement. The BOUNDS statement (abbreviated as BNDS) can define a range for your SORT. For example, if you were to say BOUNDS 1 20 and then try to sort a field located outside the assigned boundaries (column 1 through 20), a message like the one in Figure 6.21 (triggered by PF1 action) would be displayed.

You can limit your SORT to exclude (or not exclude) certain lines of data from your display. Let me run through the whole scenario from the exclusion of certain lines (based on your own criterion), including the actual SORT operation. For example, assume the file presented in Figure 6.22.

The first criterion defined on the command line is to exclude all those employees who work in department 1127. There are three fields shown on these and subsequent panels: a name field (columns 1 through 15), a department field (columns 17 through 20), and a social security number or employee identifier field (columns 25 through 35). In excluding a line or lines from the display, I used the following ISPF command:

```
EXCLUDE ALL "1127" 17 20
```

```
EDIT ---- NIRAV.STANDARD.CNTL(XXX) - 01.07 ------------------- INVALID COLUMN
COMMAND ===> SORT NX 17 20 A                                  SCROLL ===> CSR
SORT COLUMNS MUST BE BETWEEN THE LEFT AND RIGHT BOUNDS (1-15)
=COLS> ----+----1----+----2----+----3----+----4----+----5----+----6----+----7--
000001 FLEMING, JOHN Q 1127    109-30-7049
000002 SOBOTKA, BILL   4432    112-03-4049
000003 POREBSKI, CAROL 4432    113-40-5812
000004 KEMP, SUSAN     4432    123-30-4984
000005 CHANG, VICKY    3345    124-17-0928
000006 FRAZIER, DAVID  3345    193-40-4093
000007 KONRICK, STAN   1127    199-09-0192
000008 SULLIVAN, MARY  3345    210-20-3948
000009 HAMILTON, ALEX  4432    223-30-4958
000010 MUELLER, JEFF   1127    233-03-0394
000011 SCOTT, GREGORY  4432    234-40-5986
000012 RIDER, CHRIS    3345    309-78-2039
000013 VARSEGI, ALEX   3345    310-20-3948
000014 SHER, DEBBY     4432    311-19-2039
000015 PIPER, BRIAN    1127    311-20-3000
000016 AMBROSE, FRANK  2278    345-04-5847
000017 SANDERS, DIANE  1478    450-70-9384
000018 NEWSOME, ANN    3345    456-70-6059
000019 LOUGHLIN, JOHN  4432    887-20-3048
000020 GREEN, PAT      4432    998-01-2039
```

Figure 6.21 SORT without specifying a BOUNDS command.

```
EDIT ---- NIRAV.STANDARD.CNTL(XXX) - 01.06 ----------------- INCOMPLETE STRING
COMMAND ===> EXCLUDE ALL "1127" 17 20                          SCROLL ===> CSR
****** ***************************** TOP OF DATA ******************************
000001 GREEN, PAT        4432     123-30-4984
000002 CHANG, VICKY      3345     124-17-0928
000003 HAMILTON, ALEX    4432     345-04-5847
000004 KONRICK, STAN     1127     311-19-2039
000005 MUELLER, JEFF     1127     234-40-5986
000006 AMBROSE, FRANK    2278     311-20-3000
000007 KEMP, SUSAN       4432     113-40-5812
000008 LOUGHLIN, JOHN    4432     223-30-4958
000009 RIDER, CHRIS      3345     310-20-3948
000010 SANDERS, DIANE    1478     210-20-3948
000011 SULLIVAN, MARY    3345     109-30-7049
000012 VARSEGI, ALEX     3345     309-78-2039
000013 FRAZIER, DAVID    3345     450-70-9384
000014 NEWSOME, ANN      3345     112-03-4049
000015 PIPER, BRIAN      1127     193-40-4093
000016 POREBSKI, CAROL   4432     456-70-6059
000017 SCOTT, GREGORY    4432     233-03-0394
000018 SHER, DEBBY       4432     199-09-0192
000019 SOBOTKA, BILL     4432     887-20-3048
000020 FLEMING, JOHN Q   1127     998-01-2039
****** **************************** BOTTOM OF DATA ****************************
```

Figure 6.22 Original file layout.

```
EDIT ---- NIRAV.STANDARD.CNTL(XXX) - 01.06 -------------------- 4 CHARS '1127'
COMMAND ===>                                                   SCROLL ===> CSR
****** ***************************** TOP OF DATA ******************************
000001 GREEN, PAT        4432     123-30-4984
000002 CHANG, VICKY      3345     124-17-0928
000003 HAMILTON, ALEX    4432     345-04-5847
- - -  - - - - - - - - - - - - - - - - - - -  2 LINE(S) NOT DISPLAYED
000006 AMBROSE, FRANK    2278     311-20-3000
000007 KEMP, SUSAN       4432     113-40-5812
000008 LOUGHLIN, JOHN    4432     223-30-4958
000009 RIDER, CHRIS      3345     310-20-3948
000010 SANDERS, DIANE    1478     210-20-3948
000011 SULLIVAN, MARY    3345     109-30-7049
000012 VARSEGI, ALEX     3345     309-78-2039
000013 FRAZIER, DAVID    3345     450-70-9384
000014 NEWSOME, ANN      3345     112-03-4049
- - -  - - - - - - - - - - - - - - - - - - -  1 LINE(S) NOT DISPLAYED
000016 POREBSKI, CAROL   4432     456-70-6059
000017 SCOTT, GREGORY    4432     233-03-0394
000018 SHER, DEBBY       4432     199-09-0192
000019 SOBOTKA, BILL     4432     887-20-3048
- - -  - - - - - - - - - - - - - - - - - - -  1 LINE(S) NOT DISPLAYED
****** **************************** BOTTOM OF DATA ****************************
```

Figure 6.23 Results of the EXCLUDE command.

This resulted in the redefinition of the panel, now shown in Figure 6.23. Now, let's issue a SORT command, as follows:

```
SORT NX A 17 20 A 1 15
```

This command will sort all nonexcluded lines (other than those having 1127 for department number), the major being the department number and the minor the name (both first and last) requested, in ascending order.

```
EDIT ---- NIRAV.STANDARD.CNTL(XXX) - 01.06 -------------------- 4 CHARS '1127'
COMMAND ===> SORT NX 17 20 A 1 15 A                              SCROLL ===> CSR
****** ***************************** TOP OF DATA ******************************
000001 GREEN, PAT       4432     123-30-4984
000002 CHANG, VICKY     3345     124-17-0928
000003 HAMILTON, ALEX   4432     345-04-5847
- - -  - - - - - - -  - - - -  - - - - - - - - - - - 2 LINE(S) NOT DISPLAYED
000006 AMBROSE, FRANK   2278     311-20-3000
000007 KEMP, SUSAN      4432     113-40-5812
000008 LOUGHLIN, JOHN   4432     223-30-4958
000009 RIDER, CHRIS     3345     310-20-3948
000010 SANDERS, DIANE   1478     210-20-3948
000011 SULLIVAN, MARY   3345     109-30-7049
000012 VARSEGI, ALEX    3345     309-78-2039
000013 FRAZIER, DAVID   3345     450-70-9384
000014 NEWSOME, ANN     3345     112-03-4049
- - -  - - - - - - -  - - - -  - - - - - - - - - - - 1 LINE(S) NOT DISPLAYED
000016 POREBSKI, CAROL  4432     456-70-6059
000017 SCOTT, GREGORY   4432     233-03-0394
000018 SHER, DEBBY      4432     199-09-0192
000019 SOBOTKA, BILL    4432     887-20-3048
- - -  - - - - - - -  - - - -  - - - - - - - - - - - 1 LINE(S) NOT DISPLAYED
****** **************************** BOTTOM OF DATA ****************************
```

Figure 6.24 File status prior to a SORT EXCLUDE operation.

I mentioned the use of the BOUNDS statements a few paragraphs earlier. You need to use the BOUNDS statement to set up an initial range for your operation. If you were to specify:

```
BOUNDS 1 15
```

you're saying that the range or boundary of your activities (such as SORT) will encompass the first 15 bytes of each line. Consequently, in order to sort a field containing columns 17 through 20, you need to set the bounds or the limits, such as:

`BOUNDS 17 20` or `BOUNDS 1 20`

depending on the specific requirements. The two frames shown in Figures 6.24 and 6.25 show a before and after SORT status.

You can also use SORT ranges (see section on labels and ranges) to limit your SORT to a particular area on your file. Consider the example in Figure 6.26. In this particular example, I have limited my SORT to a range bounded by .START and .END labels. Thus, everything within this range (columns 1 through 15) will be sorted in a descending sequence. The result of this SORT is shown in Figure 6.27.

6.6 Selected Primary Commands

See Figure 6.28.

6.6.1 How to locate data elements

The primary reason for using the LOCATE command (not to be confused with the FIND command) is to find and display a specific line in the data being edited. LOCATE can be abbreviated as LOC or simply L. Consider the following set of examples:

```
EDIT ---- NIRAV.STANDARD.CNTL(XXX) - 01.06 ------------------ COLUMNS 001 072
COMMAND ===>                                                  SCROLL ===> CSR
****** ***************************** TOP OF DATA ******************************
000001 SANDERS, DIANE  1478      123-30-4984
000002 AMBROSE, FRANK  2278      124-17-0928
000003 CHANG, VICKY    3345      345-04-5847
- - -  - - - - - - - - - - - - - - - - - - - - 2 LINE(S) NOT DISPLAYED
000006 FRAZIER, DAVID  3345      311-20-3000
000007 NEWSOME, ANN    3345      113-40-5812
000008 RIDER, CHRIS    3345      223-30-4958
000009 SULLIVAN, MARY  3345      310-20-3948
000010 VARSEGI, ALEX   3345      210-20-3948
000011 GREEN, PAT      4432      109-30-7049
000012 HAMILTON, ALEX  4432      309-78-2039
000013 KEMP, SUSAN     4432      450-70-9384
000014 LOUGHLIN, JOHN  4432      112-03-4049
- - -  - - - - - - - - - - - - - - - - - - - - 1 LINE(S) NOT DISPLAYED
000016 POREBSKI, CAROL 4432      456-70-6059
000017 SCOTT, GREGORY  4432      233-03-0394
000018 SHER, DEBBY     4432      199-09-0192
000019 SOBOTKA, BILL   4432      887-20-3048
- - -  - - - - - - - - - - - - - - - - - - - - 1 LINE(S) NOT DISPLAYED
****** **************************** BOTTOM OF DATA ****************************
```

Figure 6.25 File status after a SORT EXCLUDE operation.

```
EDIT ---- NIRAV.STANDARD.CNTL(XXX) - 01.09 ------------------ COLUMNS 001 072
COMMAND ===> SORT 1 15 D .START .END                          SCROLL ===> CSR
****** ***************************** TOP OF DATA ******************************
000001 AMBROSE, FRANK  4432      112-03-4049
000002 CHANG, VICKY    4432      113-40-5812
000003 FLEMING, JOHN Q 4432      123-30-4984
000004 FRAZIER, DAVID  3345      124-17-0928
.START GREEN, PAT      3345      193-40-4093
000006 HAMILTON, ALEX  1127      199-09-0192
000007 KEMP, SUSAN     3345      210-20-3948
000008 KONRICK, STAN   4432      223-30-4958
000009 LOUGHLIN, JOHN  1127      233-03-0394
000010 MUELLER, JEFF   4432      234-40-5986
000011 NEWSOME, ANN    3345      309-78-2039
.END12 PIPER, BRIAN    3345      310-20-3948
000013 POREBSKI, CAROL 4432      311-19-2039
000014 RIDER, CHRIS    1127      311-20-3000
000015 SANDERS, DIANE  2278      345-04-5847
000016 SCOTT, GREGORY  1478      450-70-9384
000017 SHER, DEBBY     3345      456-70-6059
000018 SOBOTKA, BILL   4432      887-20-3048
000019 SULLIVAN, MARY  4432      998-01-2039
000020 VARSEGI, ALEX   1112      122-20-3948
****** **************************** BOTTOM OF DATA ****************************
```

Figure 6.26 Setting up labels or ranges prior to a sort.

COMMAND ===> LOC 500. Displays line 500.

COMMAND ===> LOC .ZFIRST. Displays the first data line.

A second form of the LOCATE command can be used to display special lines, excluded lines, or data lines containing special flags, line commands, or labels. You can delimit the range of lines searched and specify the direction or starting point of the search.

COMMAND ===> LOC NEXT SPECIAL. Displays the next special line, such as COLS, PROF, TABS, MASK, BNDS, and NOTE.

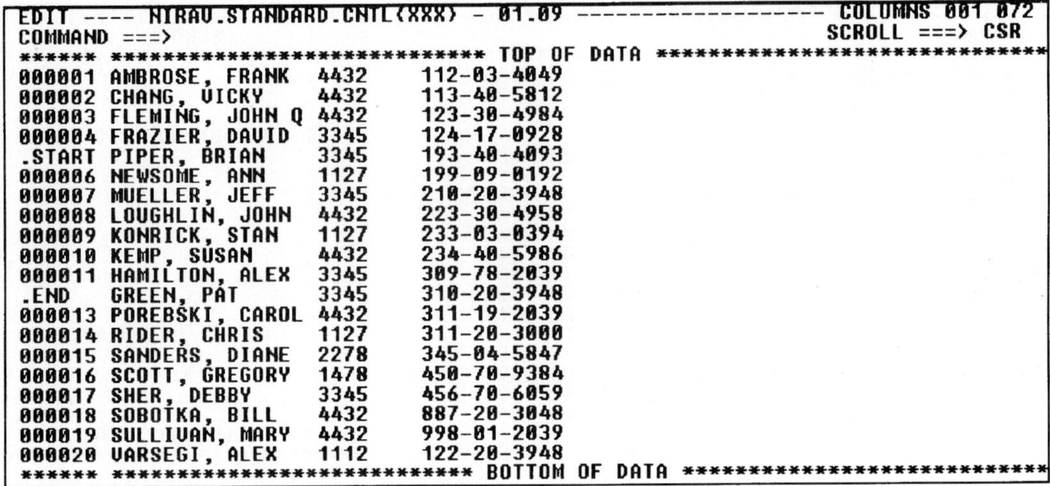

```
EDIT ---- NIRAU.STANDARD.CNTL(XXX) - 01.09 ------------------ COLUMNS 001 072
COMMAND ===>                                                  SCROLL ===> CSR
****** ***************************** TOP OF DATA ******************************
000001 AMBROSE, FRANK  4432      112-03-4049
000002 CHANG, VICKY    4432      113-40-5812
000003 FLEMING, JOHN Q 4432      123-30-4984
000004 FRAZIER, DAVID  3345      124-17-0928
.START PIPER, BRIAN    3345      193-40-4093
000006 NEWSOME, ANN    1127      199-09-0192
000007 MUELLER, JEFF   3345      210-20-3948
000008 LOUGHLIN, JOHN  4432      223-30-4958
000009 KONRICK, STAN   1127      233-03-0394
000010 KEMP, SUSAN     4432      234-40-5986
000011 HAMILTON, ALEX  3345      309-78-2039
.END   GREEN, PAT      3345      310-20-3948
000013 POREBSKI, CAROL 4432      311-19-2039
000014 RIDER, CHRIS    1127      311-20-3000
000015 SANDERS, DIANE  2278      345-04-5847
000016 SCOTT, GREGORY  1478      450-70-9384
000017 SHER, DEBBY     3345      456-70-6059
000018 SOBOTKA, BILL   4432      887-20-3048
000019 SULLIVAN, MARY  4432      998-01-2039
000020 VARSEGI, ALEX   1112      122-20-3948
****** **************************** BOTTOM OF DATA ****************************
```

Figure 6.27 The range marked by the .SORT and .END labels is sorted.

INTRODUCTION				
What is ISPF? PDTs & PDSs				
PFkey-initiated commands				
EDIT DISPLAY MODES	LABELS AND RANGES	SELECTED PRIMARY COMMAND		
ISPF libraries Caps (off/on) Nulls/profile	.ZF .ZL .ZSCR Exclude	**Locate** **Reset** **Cancel** **Submit**	**Save** **Create** **Recovery** **Find**	**Model** **Copy** **Replace** **Move**
LINE COMMANDS	SPECIAL TOPICS	UTILITIES		
Some basic line commands and rules	Sort & Examples Bounds			

Figure 6.28 LOCATE topic chart.

COMMAND ===> LOC PREV X .A .B. Displays the previous excluded line in the range, from label .A to label .B.

COMMAND ===> LOC FIRST ERR. Displays the first line flagged ==ERR>>.

COMMAND ===> LOC LAST CHG. Displays the last line flagged ==CHG>>.

COMMAND ===> LOC CMD .A .B. Displays the next pending line command in the range, from label .A to label .B.

COMMAND ===> LOC LABEL. Displays the next line that contains the label.

6.6.2 RESET, SUBMIT, SAVE, CANCEL, and RECOVERY commands

The purpose of the RESET command is to clean up a cluttered edit display. This means resetting all special lines, for example, such as those invoked by =COLS>, =BNDS>, =MASK>, =TABS>, =NOTE>, =PROF>, as well as removing line flags such as ==CHG> and ==ERR>. If you had excluded lines prior to issuing a RESET command, all those excluded lines will now be redisplayed.

Allow me to give you a few examples of using the RESET (abbreviated as RES) command:

COMMAND ===> RESET LABEL. This command clears all labels in the data.

COMMAND ===> RESET COMMAND. Deletes all pending commands. Pending commands can be triggered through a MOVE or a COPY command, among other things.

COMMAND ===> RESET ERROR. Removes all line-error flags (==ERR>).

COMMAND ===> RESET CHANGE. Removes all line-change flags (==ERR>).

COMMAND ===> RESET EXCLUDED. Redisplays all excluded lines.

COMMAND ===> RESET SPECIAL. Deletes all special lines, such as BNDS, TABS, MASK, PROF, COLS, and NOTE. Note that the word *special* is a reserved system keyword.

COMMAND ===> RES CMD .A .B. Deletes pending line commands, from .A to .B inclusive. If you need to redisplay excluded lines in the range, specify:

```
COMMAND ===> RES X .A .B
```

COMMAND ===> RES LAB CMD X. Resets labels, line commands, and excluded lines (special lines and line flags are not reset, however).

COMMAND ===> RES ERR CNG. Resets just the error and change flags.

The SUBMIT command is used (see the utility section in this chapter) to submit a job stream, or one or more jobs. The data being edited is stored in a temporary data set, and the TSO SUBMIT command is invoked. The same requirements that exist when using the TSO SUBMIT command apply directly to the SUBMIT command. Again, you can use a range by specifying the labels for the first and last lines of the data to be submitted. Data with a logical record length (LRECL) greater than 80 is truncated to 80 bytes before being passed to the TSO SUBMIT command. On the other hand, data with a logical record length less than 80 will be padded with blanks before being passed to the TSO SUBMIT command.

The SAVE command forces data to be stored back into the data set without printing the data or terminating the edit. Note that an END command (PF3) will automatically save the contents of a data file. The CANCEL command (you can use the abbreviation CAN) terminates the process of editing, but without saving the data. When you specify CANCEL, the entry panel or member list is displayed and any pending commands or error messages are purged.

The RECOVERY command turns the recovery mode on and off. If the recovery mode is on when a system crash occurs, automatic recovery will take place the next time you attempt to edit. The recovery mode setting is recorded in your edit profile. The default recovery setting for a new edit profile is off.

COMMAND ===> REC. Sets recovery on.

COMMAND ===> REC ON. Sets recovery on.

COMMAND ===> REC OFF. Sets recovery off.

If any changes have been made to the data, turning the recovery mode on causes the data to be written to a temporary backup file. Otherwise, turning the recovery mode on simply changes the current edit profile. When the first change is made to the data, it is then written to a backup file.

6.6.3 Using the Find Primary command

If you are familiar with ISPF, you have probably used the FIND command hundreds of times. This section will give you some examples, including some of the more infrequent uses of this command. The FIND command is used to find a certain character string and display it in a text you happen to be browsing or editing. In its most simple form, you can issue a FIND at the command line and press the Enter key. (Incidentally, you can abbreviate FIND as F.) In this situation, the cursor is placed at the beginning of a string. Consider the following:

```
FIND ALL 'DDNAME'
```

This command will locate the first occurrence of the term DDNAME, even though you have defined all occurrences. In order to get to the second and subsequent occurrences, you need to continually press PF5. The ALL expression is necessary, because without it the function that would normally take you to the next occurrence is inoperable. The following command:

```
FIND 'DDNAME' FIRST
```

is designed to take you to the first occurrence of DDNAME, and this command:

```
FIND ALL 'EXEC' 17 20
```

enables you to access the first occurrence of the JCL term EXEC, but only if it occurs between positions 17 and 20. The ALL specification allows you to activate PF5 in order to jump to the first and subsequent occurrences. ISPF also allows you to find a particular hexadecimal string (which comes in handy when viewing core dumps). For example, the string:

```
FIND X'00'
```

refers to finding hex 00, which is a low value. The use of the PICTURE string is a bit more complicated. It describes the type of string instead of the exact character to be found. A PICTURE string is a quoted string that is preceded or followed by the letter P. It can contain blanks, numeric or alphabetic characters that represent themselves, or any of the special characters listed in Figure 6.29, each of which represents a class of characters. Let's look at some examples now of the PICTURE string:

```
FIND P '.' 19 23
```

This particular instruction finds all invalid characters located in columns 19 through 23.

```
FIND P '###'
```

The expression # refers to a numeric byte, or digit. Thus ### tells ISPF to find a three-digit number, such as 222. Thus, 23 would be an invalid number, but 233 would fully satisfy the above search.

Note that FIND is compatible with a number of previously mentioned topics, such as ranges, exclusions, binds, and so on. For example, the statement FIND ANY .ZCSR .ZLAST will find the first ANY in the range of lines from the current cursor position to the end of the data. (I have previously explained the use of the FIRST and

```
=  any character
.  invalid character
@  alphabetic characte
-  nonnumeric character
#  numeric character
<  lowercase alphabetic
>  uppercase alphabetic
-  nonblank character

Figure out the following statements:

   FIND P '<'
   FIND '@1'P 1
```

Figure 6.29 Valid picture-string characters.

ALL parameters.) You can append other terms to a FIND statement, such as NEXT, PREV, and LAST.

When you enter optional keyword parameters or search boundaries (as part of your FIND command), you can specify them in any order and separate them by either blanks or commas. Although you are normally not required, you can always use quotation marks or apostrophes to enclose a character string, thereby avoiding any confusion with the keyword or boundaries. Consider the following example:

```
COMMAND ===> F ING PREV SUFFIX 10 70
```

This command will find a particular term (word) that has a suffix of ING, located between columns 10 and 70.

6.6.4 The CREATE and MODEL primary commands (Replace/Copy/Move)

Use the CREATE primary command to specify a member to be written from the data you are editing. CREATE adds a member only if a member of the same name does not exist. Use the REPLACE command if the member already exists. As the following command shows:

```
CREATE [member-name] [line-range]
CRE
```

you need to know two pieces of information to create data. The first parameter is the name of the member you want to add to a partitioned data set that is currently being edited. As far as the line range is concerned, there are two ways to indicate which lines are to be put into a new member. So specify two labels to indicate the beginning and the ending of those lines or group of lines that will represent the new member. Actually, you can get by with block moves (MM) or even block copies (CC).

If you use the M in a LINE command, the line(s) you have specified will be deleted from the data you are editing after the lines are successfully written. If you do not specify a member name, a panel will be displayed that lets you specify any partitioned data set member (or sequential data) as the destination of the operation. However, this panel appears only after you have specified the line(s) to be copied or moved. If you do not specify any lines, a CREATE IS PENDING message will appear in the upper right-hand corner of the screen. You must then specify lines and press Enter one more time. An overview of this is shown in Figure 6.30. Note that the beginning and the ending of the block is marked by MM. This represents the material that will be created in another data set.

When using the CREATE command, you can issue the following return codes:

0	Normal completion
8	Member already exists, so member not created
12	Member name not found or BLDL error
20	Syntax or I/O error

```
EDIT ---- NIRAV.STANDARD.CNTL(ARJCL) - 01.05 ----------------- COLUMNS 001 072
COMMAND ===> CREATE                                            SCROLL ===> CSR
****** ***************************** TOP OF DATA ******************************
000100 //NIRAVGL JOB  (9000,AGLP),MSGLEVEL=(1,1),MSGCLASS=X,NOTIFY=NIRAV,
000200 //   REGION=8192K
000300 //*
000400 //CLOSFILE EXEC PGM=COMMAND,
000500 //         PARM='F PAYRDEVO,CEMT SET DAT(AR*) CLO'
000600 //*
MM     //PGMJCL   EXEC PGM=ARDS100C
000800 //STEPLIB  DD DSN=NIRXT.TEST.LOADLIB,DISP=SHR
000900 //SYSPRINT DD SYSOUT=*
001000 //SYSOUT   DD SYSOUT=*
001100 //SYSCOUNT DD SYSOUT=*
001200 //SYSDBOUT DD SYSOUT=*
001300 //PRTREP   DD SYSOUT=*
001400 //REINV    DD DSN=NIRVT.AR.ARA41C,UNIT=SYSDA,VOL=SER=TOPS01,
MM     //         DISP=OLD
001600 //RETRANS  DD DSN=NIRVT.AR.ARA43C,UNIT=SYSDA,VOL=SER=GL0001,
001700 //         DISP=OLD
001800 //RECOMB   DD DSN=NIRXT.AR.RECOMB,UNIT=SYSDA,VOL=SER=GL0001,
001900 //         DISP=OLD
002000 //*
002100 //OPENFILE EXEC PGM=COMMAND,
```

Figure 6.30 How to code a CREATE primary command.

The REPLACE command has mechanics similar to that of the CREATE command. REPLACE is used to add or replace data in a partitioned data set, or it rewrites a complete sequential data set from the data you are editing. The member name in the current library represents the member to be replaced. If the member does not exist, it is automatically created.

Use the COPY command to specify a member of a partitioned data set to be copied into a data set being edited. Consider the following format:

```
ISREDIT COPY member-name {AFTER} lptr [linenum-range]
                         {BEFORE}
```

Let me explain what this means. Member-name represents the name of the member in the current library. AFTER and BEFORE denotes the relative position of the new data to the insertion point. Lptr (line pointer) indicates where the data is to be copied to. A line pointer can be a label or a relative line number. Finally, linenum-range indicates the line numbers of the member being copied. Two line numbers are required to indicate a range of lines. Specifying only one line number is incorrect. When using the COPY command, you can issue the following return codes:

0	Normal completion
8	End of data reached before last record read
12	Invalid line pointer (lptr); member not found or BLDL error
16	End of data reached before first record of specified range was reached
20	Syntax or I/O error

Let's look at some examples of the COPY command. To copy all of the member

MEM1 at the end of the data, specify:

```
ISREDIT COPY MEM1 AFTER .ZLAST
```

To copy all of the member MEM1 before the first line of data, specify:

```
ISREDIT COPY MEM1 BEFORE .ZFIRST
```

Finally, to copy the first three lines of the member MEM1 at the beginning of the current member, issue the following command:

```
ISREDIT COPY MEM1 BEFORE .ZF 1 3
```

Use the MOVE statement to specify a member of a partitioned data set (or a sequential data set) to be moved into the data being edited. The member is deleted following a successful read. Consider the following two examples of a MOVE macro:

```
ISREDIT MOVE ABC AFTER .ZF
```

This will move the contents of the member ABC after the first line in the current data. Consider a second example to move the contents of the member DEF before the line where the cursor is currently positioned:

```
ISREDIT MOVE DEF BEFORE .ZCSR
```

Last, let's talk about the MODEL command, which copies a specified dialog development model before or after a specified line. A MODEL is a predefined data segment you can include in the data you are editing. When you enter the MODEL command, you can select the correct segment for the data type being edited. The MODEL command allows you to specify either the logical name of the model to be copied, and optionally the destination or the class models to be searched when retrieving models. Consider the following format:

```
ISREDIT  MODEL model-name {AFTER}  lptr  [NOTE]
                          {BEFORE}       [NONOTE]
ISREDIT  MODEL CLASS class-name
```

Model-name stands for the name of the model to be copied, and BEFORE and AFTER indicates just where the operation should begin. Because a line pointer must be used to specify where the model should be copied, this can be a label or a relative line number. With the NOTE option, you can provide an explanation of what the model is all about.

Models are organized into a hierarchy based on the type and version of the dialog element they represent. This hierarchy is represented by a logical name for each model, where each part of the name corresponds to a level in the hierarchy. The first

```
EDIT ---- NIRAV.STANDARD.CNTL(ARJCL) - 01.05 ----------------- COLUMNS 001 072
COMMAND ===> CREATE                                          SCROLL ===> CSR
****** ***************************** TOP OF DATA ******************************
000100 //NIRAVGL JOB  (9000,AGLP),MSGLEVEL=(1,1),MSGCLASS=X,NOTIFY=NIRAV,
000200 //   REGION=8192K
000300 //*
000400 //CLOSFILE EXEC PGM=COMMAND,
000500 //          PARM='F PAYRDEVO,CEMT SET DAT(AR*) CLO'
000600 //*
MM     //PGMJCL   EXEC PGM=ARDS100C
000800 //STEPLIB  DD DSN=NIRXT.TEST.LOADLIB,DISP=SHR
000900 //SYSPRINT DD SYSOUT=*
001000 //SYSOUT   DD SYSOUT=*
001100 //SYSCOUNT DD SYSOUT=*
001200 //SYSDBOUT DD SYSOUT=*
001300 //PRTREP   DD SYSOUT=*
001400 //REINV    DD DSN=NIRVT.AR.ARA41C,UNIT=SYSDA,VOL=SER=TOPS01,
MM     //            DISP=OLD
001600 //RETRANS  DD DSN=NIRVT.AR.ARA43C,UNIT=SYSDA,VOL=SER=GL0001,
001700 //            DISP=OLD
001800 //RECOMB   DD DSN=NIRXT.AR.RECOMB,UNIT=SYSDA,VOL=SER=GL0001,
001900 //            DISP=OLD
002000 //*
002100 //OPENFILE EXEC PGM=COMMAND,
```

Figure 6.31 A list of available model classes.

part of the logical name is the model class. There is a model class for each data-set type qualifier that can store a dialog element. Figure 6.31 lists the classes, for example, that have been defined for the models distributed by PDF. This panel prompts you when you need to set the desired model class, if you do not name the class explicitly.

6.7 Utilities

Earlier, in introducing to you the ISPF software, I briefly highlighted the mechanics of creating a library. ISPF, however, is a very powerful utility tool (see Figure 6.32), and it does a great deal more than simply letting you create a library. Some of the utility functions are summarized in Figure 6.33.

My objective in presenting the following exercise is to look at the VTOC (Volume Table of Contents) to see what particular volumes my accounts receivable files are residents of. A generic term for them is an AR prefix with a NIRVT qualifier in front of them.

To attain such information, I entered =3.4 on the ISPF Utility Menu and pressed the Enter key. This enabled me to look at a Data Set Utility Panel shown in Figure 6.34. Next to DSNAME LEVEL, I entered NIRVT.AR because most if not all files in the A/R system begin with these qualifiers.

When I pressed the Enter key, a third panel was displayed by ISPF, showing all data sets beginning with the NIRVT.AR qualifier. In the rightmost portion of the panel is the volume of each file, each of them residing on the same VSAM04 volume. This frame is shown in Figure 6.35. Once I attained the specific volume of the AR files, it was relatively easy to get volume statistics (see Figure 6.36).

Press PF3 to return to the previous Data Set Utility Panel and, in addition to the DSNAME LEVEL, also key in the specific volume, which happens to be VSAM04.

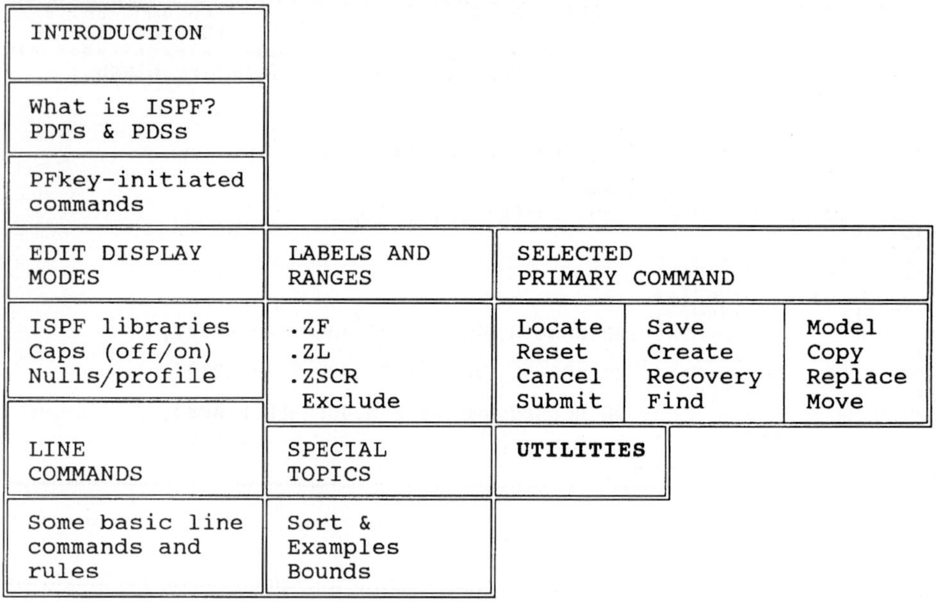

INTRODUCTION		
What is ISPF? PDTs & PDSs		
PFkey-initiated commands		
EDIT DISPLAY MODES	LABELS AND RANGES	SELECTED PRIMARY COMMAND
ISPF libraries Caps (off/on) Nulls/profile	.ZF .ZL .ZSCR Exclude	Locate, Reset, Cancel, Submit Save, Create, Recovery, Find Model, Copy, Replace, Move
LINE COMMANDS	SPECIAL TOPICS	**UTILITIES**
Some basic line commands and rules	Sort & Examples Bounds	

Figure 6.32 Utility topic chart.

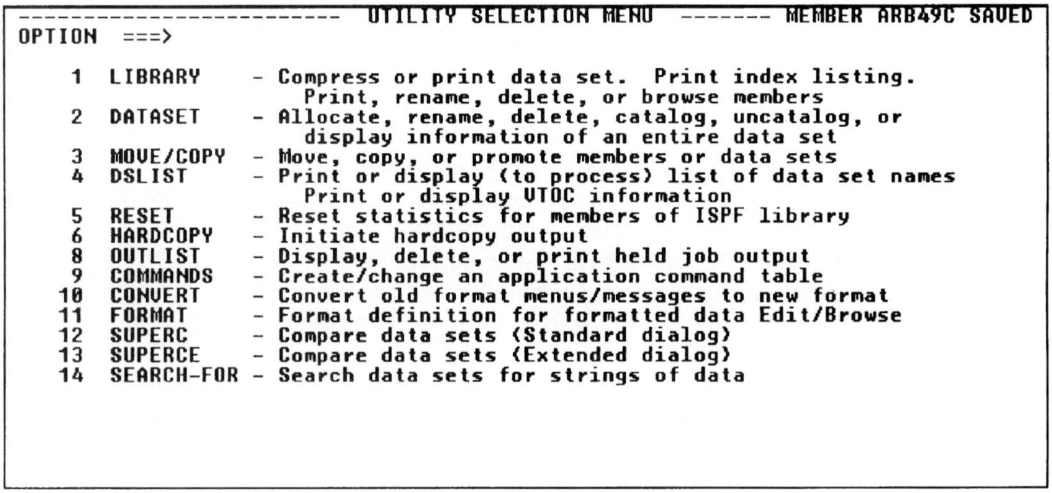

```
------------------------  UTILITY SELECTION MENU  ------- MEMBER ARB49C SAVED
OPTION  ===>

    1  LIBRARY    - Compress or print data set.  Print index listing.
                      Print, rename, delete, or browse members
    2  DATASET    - Allocate, rename, delete, catalog, uncatalog, or
                      display information of an entire data set
    3  MOVE/COPY  - Move, copy, or promote members or data sets
    4  DSLIST     - Print or display (to process) list of data set names
                      Print or display VTOC information
    5  RESET      - Reset statistics for members of ISPF library
    6  HARDCOPY   - Initiate hardcopy output
    8  OUTLIST    - Display, delete, or print held job output
    9  COMMANDS   - Create/change an application command table
   10  CONVERT    - Convert old format menus/messages to new format
   11  FORMAT     - Format definition for formatted data Edit/Browse
   12  SUPERC     - Compare data sets (Standard dialog)
   13  SUPERCE    - Compare data sets (Extended dialog)
   14  SEARCH-FOR - Search data sets for strings of data
```

Figure 6.33 A snapshot of the ISPF Utility Menu.

6.8 How to Submit a Job

One of the important functions available under ISPF is the user's ability to submit and process a request. To initiate a batch job, for example, whether you are in a test or production environment, you can create three partitioned data set members, each with a unique assignment:

Member 1 will contain a source program that needs to be compiled through ISPF if it is not already in a load module form.

Member 2 will contain the necessary job-control statements that will invoke the first member through job submission simply by issuing a SUB command.

Member 3 will contain a sequential batch file for the testing required by both the source program (member 1) and the job control (member 2).

Assume that it is necessary for you to recompile your application program because some of the statements in it were altered earlier to accommodate changes in the program logic. Obviously, if the program contains syntax or other diagnostic-triggered

```
--------------------------- DATA SET LIST UTILITY ----------------------------
OPTION  ===>

  blank - Display data set list *           P  - Print data set list
  V     - Display VTOC information only     PV - Print VTOC information only

Enter one or both of the parameters below:
  DSNAME LEVEL  ===> NIRVT.AR
  VOLUME        ===>

  INITIAL DISPLAY VIEW     ===> VOLUME    (VOLUME,SPACE,ATTRIB,TOTAL)
  CONFIRM DELETE REQUEST   ===> YES       (YES or NO)

* The following line commands will be available when the list is displayed:

B - Browse data set       C - Catalog data set       F - Free unused space
E - Edit data set         U - Uncatalog data set     = - Repeat last command
D - Delete data set       P - Print data set
R - Rename data set       X - Print index listing
I - Data set information  M - Display member list
S - Information (short)   Z - Compress data set      TSO command or CLIST
```

Figure 6.34 The Data Set Utility Panel for entering a generic dataset qualifier.

```
DSLIST - DATA SETS BEGINNING WITH NIRVT.AR ---------------------- ROW 1 OF 33
COMMAND ===>                                                 SCROLL ===> PAGE

COMMAND        NAME                                        MESSAGE      VOLUME
-------------------------------------------------------------------------------
            NIRVT.AR.ARA21C                                             VSAM04
            NIRVT.AR.ARA21C.D                                           VSAM04
            NIRVT.AR.ARA21C.I                                           VSAM04
            NIRVT.AR.ARA26C                                             VSAM04
            NIRVT.AR.ARA26C.DATA                                        VSAM04
            NIRVT.AR.ARA26C.INDEX                                       VSAM04
            NIRVT.AR.ARA41C                                             VSAM04
            NIRVT.AR.ARA41C.D                                           VSAM04
            NIRVT.AR.ARA41C.I                                           VSAM04
            NIRVT.AR.ARA43C                                             VSAM04
            NIRVT.AR.ARA43C.D                                           VSAM04
            NIRVT.AR.ARA43C.I                                           VSAM04
            NIRVT.AR.ARA61C                                             VSAM04
            NIRVT.AR.ARA61C.DATA                                        VSAM04
            NIRVT.AR.ARA61C.INDEX                                       VSAM04
            NIRVT.AR.ARA71C                                             VSAM04
            NIRVT.AR.ARA71C.D                                           VSAM04
            NIRVT.AR.ARA71C.I                                           VSAM04
            NIRVT.AR.ARA81C                                             VSAM04
```

Figure 6.35 DSLIST showing all datasets with the NIRVT.AR qualifier.

error messages, you need to have them fixed before you can move on to the next stage. If the compile is clean, however, you can go ahead and complete the rest of the test.

If you need to do processing in an on-line environment, you will also need to allocate three or possibly four PDS members for the process, even though testing an interactive system, such as CICS, is not part of the ISPF process.

The first three such members are: a source program to be tested in a CICS region, a set of JCLs to compile the program, and a third member that contains the map. A fourth PDS member comes into play as you reassemble your map due to some changes in the original appearance of that map. In this case, you also need the a PDFS member containing the JCLs initially used to assemble the map.

This is really not all you need to do to go "interactive." As an expansion of the above requirements, you also need to complete your CICS tables (either you or your systems programmer) to accommodate members such as PPT, PCT, FCT, and DCT.

Suppose you need to recompile your on-line program. Also assume that there is a requirement to modify the current layout of the map. To do that, consider the following frame-by-frame description of the procedure:

1. Assemble the map. This process requires two PDS members. The first member (BMSJCL) is the required JCL for the assembly and is as follows:

```
//NIRAVBM1  JOB (9000,AART),MSGLEVEL=(1,1),MSGCLASS=X,REGION=6144K,
//     CLASS=A,NOTIFY=NIRAV
/*JOBPARM PROCLIB=PROC01
//MAPASM  EXEC TOPSBM2,MAPNAME=SS001
//COPY.SYSUT1 DD DSN=NIRAV.STANDARD.CNTL(SS001),DISP=SHR
```

The second member refers to SS001, a PDS member that contains the source program; it is shown in Figure 6.37.

```
VTOC SUMMARY INFORMATION FOR VOLUME VSAM04 ----------------------------------
COMMAND ===>

UNIT:   3380

VOLUME DATA:                  VTOC DATA                    FREE SPACE:    TRACKS     CYLS
   TRACKS:        26,550        TRACKS:           15           SIZE:      10,816      713
   %USED:             59        %USED:            36           LARGEST:    7,095      473
   TRKS/CYLS:         15        FREE DSCBS:      510
                                                           FREE EXTENTS:      75
```

Figure 6.36 VTOC summary information for a specific (VSAM04) volume.

```
EDIT ---- NIRAV.STANDARD.CNTL(SS001) - 01.29 ----------------- COLUMNS 001 072
COMMAND ===>                                                   SCROLL ===> PAGE
****** ***************************** TOP OF DATA ******************************
000001              PRINT NOGEN
000002 SS001        DFHMSD   TYPE=&SYSPARM,MODE=INOUT,CTRL=FREEKB,LANG=COBOL,       C
000003                    TIOAPFX=YES
000004 CUSINQ       DFHMDI    SIZE=(24,80)
000005              DFHMDF POS=(01,02),LENGTH=04,ATTRB=(BRT,ASKIP),                 C
000006                    INITIAL='TC01'
000007              DFHMDF POS=(01,23),LENGTH=35,ATTRB=ASKIP,                       C
000008                    INITIAL='MASTER  FILE   INQUIRY'
000009              DFHMDF POS=(06,11),LENGTH=14,ATTRB=ASKIP,                       C
000010                    INITIAL='INQUIRY KEY    '
000011 CUST         DFHMDF POS=(06,30),LENGTH=6,ATTRB=(BRT,UNPROT,IC)
000012              DFHMDF POS=(06,37),LENGTH=1,ATTRB=ASKIP
000013              DFHMDF POS=(08,11),LENGTH=14,ATTRB=(ASKIP),                     C
000014                    INITIAL='NAME          '
000015 CUSTNM       DFHMDF POS=(08,30),LENGTH=10,ATTRB=UNPROT
000016              DFHMDF POS=(12,11),LENGTH=12,ATTRB=(BRT,ASKIP),                 C
000017                    INITIAL='ZIP  CODE     '
000018 CUSTZIP      DFHMDF POS=(12,30),LENGTH=5,ATTRB=UNPROT
000019 ERROR        DFHMDF POS=(24,2),LENGTH=20,ATTRB=(BRT,PROT)
000020              DFHMSD TYPE=FINAL
000021              END
```

Figure 6.37 The BMS member SS001 to be submitted by the JCLs.

```
U1R3M1 ------------------  SDSF PRIMARY OPTION MENU  ------------------------
COMMAND ===> h                                             SCROLL ===> PAGE

 Type an option or command and press Enter.

    DA         - Display active users of the system
    I          - Display jobs in the JES2 input queue
    O          - Display jobs in the JES2 output queue
    H          - Display jobs in the JES2 held output queue
    ST         - Display status of jobs in the JES2 queues

    TUTOR      - Short course on SDSF (ISPF only)
    END        - Exit SDSF

    Use Help key for more information.

    5665-488 (C) COPYRIGHT IBM CORP. 1981, 1990. ALL RIGHTS RESERVED
```

Figure 6.38 Displaying JES2-held output queue.

2. To check the result of the assembly, switch to SDSF (=8) from the current =2 edit mode. Three additional frames are presented in sequence at this point. The first one is shown in Figure 6.38 where, in order to display the job in the JES2-held output queue, you need to enter the character H on the command line. This selection criterion prompts the next sequential frame, displayed in Figure 6.39.

```
SDSF HELD OUTPUT DISPLAY ALL CLASSES          417 LINES LINE 1-1 (1)
COMMAND ===>                                               SCROLL ===> PAG
NP JOBNAME TYPE JNUM  DN  CRDATE   C FORMS     FCB  DEST       TOT-REC  TOT-PAG
s  NIRAVBM1 JOB  9255  7 10/09/91 X STD       **** LOCAL          417
```

Figure 6.39 Selecting a member for reviewing the results of the compile.

```
SDSF OUTPUT DISPLAY NIRAVBM1 JOB 9255  DSID   104 LINE 15       COLUMNS 02- 81
COMMAND ===>                                                 SCROLL ===> PAGE
                                      16          DFHMDF POS=(06,37),LENGTH=1,ATT
                                      17          DFHMDF POS=(08,11),LENGTH=14,AT
                                                        INITIAL='NAME          '
                                      18 CUSTNM   DFHMDF POS=(08,30),LENGTH=10,AT
                                      24          DFHMDF POS=(12,11),LENGTH=12,AT
                                                        INITIAL='ZIP CODE      '
                                      25 CUSTZIP  DFHMDF POS=(12,30),LENGTH=5,ATT
                                      31 ERROR    DFHMDF POS=(24,2),LENGTH=20,ATT
                                      37          DFHMSD TYPE=FINAL
                                      48          END

                                  DIAGNOSTIC CROSS REFERENCE AND ASSEMBLER SUMMA

    NO STATEMENTS FLAGGED IN THIS ASSEMBLY
  OVERRIDING PARAMETERS-  SYSPARM(DSECT),DECK,NOLOAD
  OPTIONS FOR THIS ASSEMBLY
   DECK, NOOBJECT, LIST, XREF(FULL), NORENT, NOTEST, NOBATCH, ALIGN, ESD, RLD,
   LINECOUNT(55), FLAG(0), SYSPARM(DSECT)
  NO OVERRIDING DD NAMES
      21 CARDS FROM SYSIN      5552 CARDS FROM SYSLIB
      35 LINES OUTPUT            32 CARDS OUTPUT
******************************** BOTTOM OF DATA ********************************
```

Figure 6.40 The results of the map assembly.

3. Having selected the job (containing the result of the compile), scroll to the bottom of the display (PF8 and the character M, or maximum, on the command line) to review any messages or other pieces of communications generated during the assembly. This panel is shown in Figure 6.40.

Repeat this process when compiling the program, where two additional PDS members will be referenced. Finally, switch to CICS, issue a new copy for the program, and you're ready to start testing.

Chapter

7

The File-AID Productivity System

7.1 What Is File-AID?

File-AID is an interactive productivity tool that is designed to enhance the capabilities of ISPF (Interactive System Productivity Facility, an IBM-engineered text editor and productivity tool discussed earlier). Primarily, File-AID accommodates additional access methods, as well as record sizes and record formats that cannot be handled through the more conventional ISPF environment.

If you were to look at the majority of the panels available in this Compuware system, they are reminiscent of those used in ISPF. This is due to the fact that File-AID is an ISPF dialog application designed to emulate and extend the capabilities of the IBM product. As you have seen in chapter 6, ISPF can process only sequential or partitioned data sets, with a substantially limited record length for editing.

The File-AID screens are designed to mimic ISPF for a more standardized approach, but File-AID functions independently from ISPF. In order to coordinate the two systems, all you need is an entry point, an interface so to speak, between the two products, which is an initial function to be defined at installation time—one that remains very much transparent to File-AID users. The entry point to File-AID from a standard TSO (ISPF/PDF) panel (PDF stands for Program Development Facility) can be denoted by the character F unless your installation already has that task allocated to another product integrated into ISPF. The Primary Options Menu is displayed in Figure 7.1.

The F selection invokes the File-AID Primary Options Menu displayed in Figure 7.2, which provides you with a list of all available functions within the File-AID system. You'll probably notice that File-AID uses the same naming and numbering conventions as does ISPF. So, as in ISPF, when you select a specific number or letter, it will display a subsequent panel representing that function.

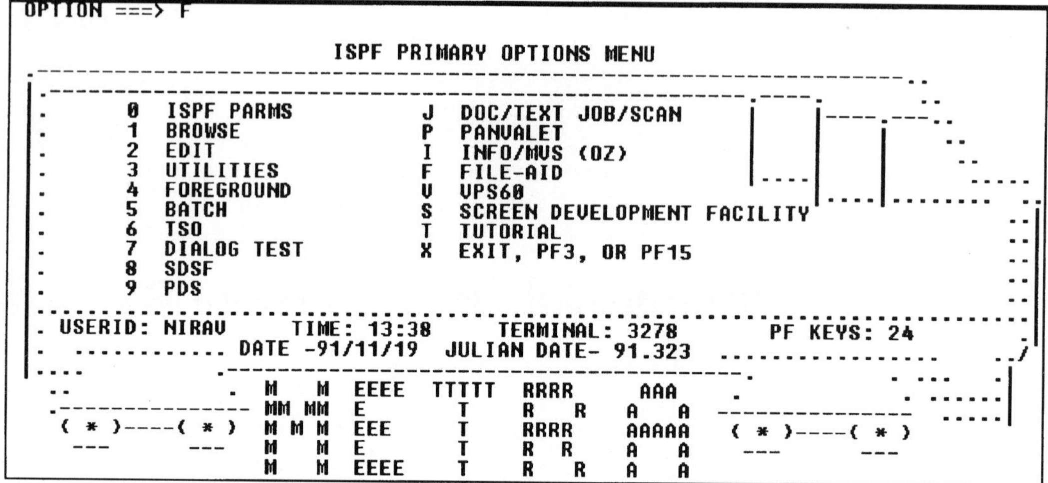

Figure 7.1 The ISPF Primary Options Menu, showing the selection F.

```
------------------ File-AID VL-6.4.1 - PRIMARY OPTION MENU ------------------
OPTION ===>                                                       USERID NIRAV

        0  - DEFAULT OPTIONS FOR FILE-AID
        1  - BROWSE
        2  - EDIT
        3  - UTILITIES
             3.1 - LIBRARY     - Manage PDS/CSECT directory information
             3.2 - DATASET     - Allocate/manage non-VSAM datasets
             3.3 - COPY        - Copy datasets without using record layouts
             3.4 - CATALOG     - Display catalog entries
             3.5 - VSAM        - Allocate/manage VSAM datasets
             3.7 - VTOC        - Find files and manage DASD
             3.8 - FORMAT      - Maintain maps and selection tables
             3.9 - COPY/RFMT   - Copy/reformat using record layouts
        4  - FILE-AID/BATCH    - Interactive
        5  - FILE-AID/BATCH    - Submission
        C  - NEW FILE-AID RELEASE FEATURES
        T  - TUTORIAL FOR FILE-AID


    Use END key to exit File-AID
```

Figure 7.2 The File-AID Primary Options Menu.

7.2 File-AID General Features and Major Functions

Any files that you create under the MVS operating system can be processed through the File-AID productivity tool. This resolves some of the restriction inherent in ISPF architecture. In addition, File-AID accommodates the IAM access method, a product I have briefly reviewed in chapter 1.

To expand on my previous statement, File-AID handles any particular record format, including fixed and variable length (spanned and unformatted) records. Each record can occupy up to 32,767 bytes of storage, or roughly 32 kilobytes.

You can process job-control statements under File-AID both as physical records or as logical statements. Processing is bidirectional, meaning that you can read and process both sequential or VSAM files forward and backward. This type of approach enables you to retrieve data at the end of the file just as quickly as you can at the very beginning.

The way File-AID works is that it scans a partitioned data set (PDS) either on a record or member level. Because you can specify one or a number of conditions for retrieval, you can produce a selected list of these members, containing only those members that conform to the requirements.

Similar to the ISPF conventions described in the previous chapter, File-AID relies in part on line-command processing. The number of available line commands depend on the function in use. For example, for a member list, only the S (SELECT) command is legitimate. For data lists, multiple commands such as B (BROWSE), E (EDIT), and D (DELETE) can be processed. Also, as with ISPF, you can navigate internally from function to function using the equal sign (=) plus a reference number. For example, if you were to allocate a VSAM data set, you might say =F.3.2 on the ISPF Primary Options Menu, or simply =3.2 anywhere within the File-AID productivity system.

Let me summarize now some of the major functions available in the File-AID productivity software:

BROWSE. This function is available so you can view but not change the contents of a particular data set. You can browse selectively or nonselectively, depending on the specific criterion defined.

EDIT. This function gives you the ability to modify the contents of a particular data set using any MVS-supported access method. When in edit mode, you can verify the changes before they become permanent.

UTILITIES. File-AID utilities, strictly from a design point of view, encompass most of those available in ISPF. In addition, they allow you to process VSAM clusters. The major utilities handled by File-AID are made up of library, data set, copy, catalog, VSAM, VTOC, and format modules. An overview of this is presented in Figure 7.3, which is the File-AID Utility Selection Menu.

LIBRARY. This utility displays directory information.

DATA SET. The data-set utility is similar to those in the ISPF software, except that you can primarily allocate and display information for ISAM and BDAM data sets. (Note that VSAM is available under the VSAM module, such as =F.5). A free-space option is also provided, along with delete and rename processing, for data sets of all MVS access methods.

COPY. When you use the File-AID copy utility, the system enables you to copy and process a record selectively (based on some predefined criteria) or nonselectively, meaning all.

```
---------------------- File-AID - UTILITY SELECTION MENU ----------------------
SELECT OPTION ===>

 1  LIBRARY    - Display and modify directory entries; display load
                 module CSECT maps; Browse, Delete, Rename PDS members
 2  DATASET    - Display dataset information; Allocate non-VSAM datasets;
                 Catalog, Uncatalog, Delete, or Rename datasets
 3  COPY       - Copy entire datasets; Copy selected records; Copy PDS members
                 based on content
 4  CATALOG    - Display generic catalog entries or VSAM datasets on a volume
                 in list form and do dataset list processing
 5  VSAM       - Allocate, Display, Delete, Modify, or Rename VSAM clusters,
                 alternate indexes, and paths
 7  VTOC       - Display and process datasets on a volume(s)
 8  FORMAT     - Compile COBOL and PL/I maps and specify map selections
 9  COPY/RFMT  - Copy while reformatting fields, using record layouts
```

Figure 7.3 The File-AID Utility Selection Menu.

CATALOG. Using this utility, you can select and list data-set names from the catalog based on index-level searching (otherwise known as a generic search), or you can select all VSAM data sets that reside on a particular volume, including those within suballocated space (volume list).

VSAM. This module lets you define a VSAM data set rather than using the lengthy and somewhat complicated IDCAMS method. Through this module you can allocate, rename and delete clusters, and alternate indexes as well as paths.

VTOC. The Volume Table of Contents utility runs a great deal faster than its ISPF equivalent and provides you with more DASD information. Data sets can be listed by name or in a physical pack order. You can process single or multiple packs. When you process interactively (Interactive Execution), you can process File-AID batch commands at the terminal to verify the logic, for example, of large batch jobs before submitting them. The background submission function, on the other hand, gives you a skeletal framework to submit any batch job for execution.

7.3 The File-AID Edit Function

In order to condense rather extensive material such as File-AID into a single chapter, I need to approach it in a summarized fashion. As with most software packages, you can spend a relatively small portion of your time on topics that in reality represent 80% of what File-AID is all about. The rest, special topics and techniques, are a great deal more time-consuming and in a way impractical for an initial review.

This chapter will give you what I've determined to be the most practical and thus most extensively used set of topics in this productivity system, such as data editing. Also, I will cover three additional topics:

- The process of cataloging
- Building and allocating VSAM Clusters
- The Volume Table of Contents or VTOC

Figure 7.4 shows the standard Edit Panel. The EDIT function allows you to make global updates to a particular data set. The term *global* simply means that a single change will apply throughout the system wherever this data set is referenced. The two options available under global changes are:

B (BROWSE). Allows you to preview your changes.

U (UPDATE). Physically implements those changes.

When you perform global changes to a particular data set, you can update just one or a number of selected members, and your JCLs are no exception. Option M, for example, will build you a member selection list matching your specific selection criteria.

Two other options are also available in the File-AID/XA or Extended Edit mode for partitioned data-set members: F and S. You can, for example, display them in F mode (meaning a full or complete display) or S mode (meaning the display of only a selected number that conforms to some predefined criteria).

7.3.1 Update Mode Edit (U)

As previously mentioned, the UPDATE function (U) is designed to update records of a data set. Because update is transparent to the user, I recommend that you also use a BROWSE function (B) in order to verify those changes. Let me illustrate this mechanism in the following five frames.

```
------------------------------ File-AID - EDIT --------------------------------
OPTION ===> S

 F - Entire file                              M - PDS member list processing
 S - Selected records
                                              Global change options:
Use record layouts ===> N (Y or N)              B - Preview global changes (BROWSE)
                                                U - Apply global changes   (UPDATE)

Specify edit dataset:
   Dataset name    ===> 'NIRUT.MSA9005.ARB701.RKCOL'
   Volume serial   ===>                (If not cataloged)
   Password        ===>                (If password protected)
   Disposition     ===> OLD            (SHR or OLD)

Specify record layout/map dataset:    (For record mapping with F or S options)
   Dataset name    ===>
   Member name     ===>                (Blank for member selection list)
   Volume serial   ===>                (If not cataloged)
   Selection       ===> NO             (Extract record layout (Y or N))

Use END key to exit EDIT mode
```

Figure 7.4 The File-AID standard Edit Panel.

```
EDIT ---- NIRAV.STANDARD.CNTL(NEWFILE) - 01.04 --------------- COLUMNS 001 07
COMMAND ===>                                                   SCROLL ===> PAG
****** ***************************** TOP OF DATA *****************************
=COLS> ----+----1----+----2----+----3----+----4----+----5----+----6----+----7
000001 HENDERSON, JACK     10100  12039409587T48737 GGRY47387   123
000002 KROLL, PETER Q      10102  019283745H1111878901387 590   334
000003 LEONARD, JAMES      10103  029320985091847509814750985   222
000004 NORBERT, ELISABETH 10104  D09837409283049837230984779   143
000005 VARSEGI, ALEX       10175  J0983709870918309567348GRT4   233
000006 GRAY, DAVID L       10176  4U901280H098Y0T094353485743   123
000007 WARNER, PAUL G      14000  108874873103874019823734389   333
000008 CAMPBELL, JOHN      10103  029320985091847509814750985   222
000009 TORRENCE, F. AL     10104  D09837409283049837230984779   143
000010 FISHER, BETTY       10175  J0983709870918309567348GRT4   233
000011 CONNOR, PATRICK     10176  4U901280H098Y0T094353485743   123
****** **************************** BOTTOM OF DATA ***************************
```

Figure 7.5 A file (PDS) containing some control numbers to be changed.

```
------------------------------ File-AID - EDIT --------------------------------
OPTION ===> B

  F - Entire file                          M - PDS member list processing
  S - Selected records
                                           Global change options:
Use record layouts ===> N (Y or N)           B - Preview global changes (BROWSE)
                                             U - Apply global changes   (UPDATE)

Specify edit dataset:
    Dataset name    ===> 'NIRAV.STANDARD.CNTL(NEWFILE)'
    Volume serial   ===>             (If not cataloged)
    Password        ===>             (If password protected)
    Disposition     ===> OLD         (SHR or OLD)

Specify record layout/map dataset:    (For record mapping with F or S options)
    Dataset name    ===>
    Member name     ===>             (Blank for member selection list)
    Volume serial   ===>             (If not cataloged)
    Selection       ===> NO          (Extract record layout (Y or N))

Use END key to exit EDIT mode
```

Figure 7.6 Using a B for a subsequent preview and the full name of the partitioned data set.

Frame 1 in Figure 7.5 shows you a partitioned data-set member named NEWFILE, which uses the COL option to highlight the exact columns of the fields to be referenced. Starting in column 20, note a five-position-long field, the first four positions of which represent a valid department number.

In the second frame, Figure 7.6, I entered a B, or BROWSE, and the name of the partitioned data set to be previewed: NIRAV.STANDARD.CNTL(NEWFILE). The reason for using the BROWSE rather than the UPDATE command is simply that, once the desired changes are described to File-AID, they will be made only on a temporary basis until they are overridden through the update command.

In the third frame, Figure 7.7, I have stated all the required conditions for changing the department number. Accordingly, starting in location 20 on the file (locations 20 through 24 contain the department numbers to be modified), I intend to transform all those departments whose first four positions equal 1010 to 7777. Again, the change is not a real change; it is merely a display showing the criteria affecting the contents of the current data set.

The fourth frame, Figure 7.8, represents all the records that would be affected by the change and their new contents. If this looks satisfactory, you can press PF3 (the End key) signaling to File-AID that you are now physically ready to apply those changes. This is done in frame 5.

```
File-AID EDIT - NIRAU.STANDARD.CNTL(NEWFILE) --------------------- ROW 1 OF 3
COMMAND ===>                                                  SCROLL ===> CSR
Enter/verify edit processing options for sequential datasets:
   Include record information   ===> N        (browse mode only)
   Number of records to skip    ===> 0        (0 = none)
   Number of records to search  ===> 0        (0 = all)
   Number of records to select  ===> 250      (browse mode only)

Enter/verify change elements below: (will be done in BROWSE mode)
  Location  ===> 20     Length or Operator ===> EQ   Change all? ===> N (Y or N)
  From data ===> '1010'
  To data   ===> '7777'

     AND/OR ===> AND
  Location  ===>        Length or Operator ===> EQ   Change all? ===> N (Y or N)
  From data ===>
  To data   ===>

     AND/OR ===> AND
  Location  ===>        Length or Operator ===> EQ   Change all? ===> N (Y or N)
  From data ===>
  To data   ===>

     AND/OR ===> AND
```

Figure 7.7 The conditions for the change.

```
BROWSE -- NIRAU.D91291.T091320.FILEAID ------------- LINE 00000000 COL 001 080
COMMAND ===>                                                   SCROLL ===> PAGE
Records/read=11 listed=6 with 6 changes
==>NIRAU.STANDARD.CNTL(NEWFILE) OPENED AS PO,RECFM=FB,LRECL=80,BLKSIZE=6160,VOL=
********************************MEMBER  NEWFILE ********************************
HENDERSON, JACK      77770  12039409587T48737 GGRY47387    123
KROLL, PETER Q       77772  019283745H1111878901387 590    334
LEONARD, JAMES       77773  0293209850918475098147509 85   222
NORBERT, ELISABETH   77774  D0983740928304983723098477 9   143
CAMPBELL, JOHN       77773  0293209850918475098147509 85   222
TORRENCE, F. AL      77774  D0983740928304983723098477 9   143
******************************** BOTTOM OF DATA ********************************
```

Figure 7.8 The records that can be changed under the command.

```
------------------------------ File-AID - EDIT ------------------------------
OPTION ===> U
Records/read=11 listed=6 with 6 changes
 F - Entire file                               M - PDS member list processing
 S - Selected records
                                               Global change options:
Use record layouts ===> N (Y or N)               B - Preview global changes (BROWSE)
                                                 U - Apply global changes   (UPDATE)

Specify edit dataset:
   Dataset name    ===> 'NIRAV.STANDARD.CNTL(NEWFILE)'
   Volume serial   ===>                (If not cataloged)
   Password        ===>                (If password protected)
   Disposition     ===> OLD            (SHR or OLD)

Specify record layout/map dataset:   (For record mapping with F or S options)
   Dataset name    ===>
   Member name     ===>                (Blank for member selection list)
   Volume serial   ===>                (If not cataloged)
   Selection       ===> NO             (Extract record layout (Y or N))

Use END key to exit EDIT mode
```

Figure 7.9 U, or Update, is requested on a previously presented Edit Panel.

```
------------------------------ File-AID - EDIT ------------ FUNCTION COMPLETED
OPTION ===> M

 F - Entire file                               M - PDS member list processing
 S - Selected records
                                               Global change options:
Use record layouts ===> N (Y or N)               B - Preview global changes (BROWSE)
                                                 U - Apply global changes   (UPDATE)

Specify edit dataset:
   Dataset name    ===> 'NIRAV.STANDARD.CNTL'
   Volume serial   ===>                (If not cataloged)
   Password        ===>                (If password protected)
   Disposition     ===> OLD            (SHR or OLD)

Specify record layout/map dataset:   (For record mapping with F or S options)
   Dataset name    ===>
   Member name     ===>                (Blank for member selection list)
   Volume serial   ===>                (If not cataloged)
   Selection       ===> NO             (Extract record layout (Y or N))

Use END key to exit EDIT mode
```

Figure 7.10 Using option M to locate a specific piece of information.

The final frame, shown in Figure 7.9, allows you to enter a U for UPDATE and press the Enter key. Upon pressing the Enter key, no additional display is invoked by the system; all that has been accomplished earlier in BROWSE or PREVIEW mode.

7.3.2 Update Mode Edit (M)

If you want to generate a list of partitioned data-set members and want to find some specific information in them, you can use the File-AID M command. Let me give you specific examples of this technique through four additional frames.

In Figure 7.10, I displayed the File-AID edit screen (=F.2). My objective is to scan and display every one of those members on my NIRAV.STANDARD.CNTL library (or data set) that contains the EXEC command in column 10. (You might think of a more creative application, such as finding the device, such as UNIT=TAPE, and overriding it with SYSDA in a typical MVS device-independent environment.) Thus, I entered the data-set name coupled with the M option and pressed Enter.

This invoked a panel shown in Figure 7.11. Note that the command portion of the screen was left blank. Also, I did not specify . . . *scan members beginning* . . .; rather I wanted to go ahead and search the entire library. You might want to restrict your search to a specific member or members in your instructions. In addition, I did the following:

- Indicated that the location of the EXEC command was in position 10 (thus an EXEC starting in position 11 would be ignored)
- Used the EXEC command for the search argument, and pressed the Enter key

The result of this was a list of all the partitioned data-set members that conformed with the stated condition. This is displayed in Figure 7.12.

Note that a total of five members are displayed by File-AID. Out of this, I selected a member named ALEX, which happens to be a JCL list. Note that, in addition to the size of the library member, a column entitled HITS represents the number of times the requested condition was satisfied. Again, if EXEC should start in column 11 or 12, or anywhere except in column 10, the condition would simply disqualify.

Figures 7.13A through 7.13C show two examples where the stated conditions were met. As you can see, most conditions did not conform because the EXEC command in those situations were listed in different locations.

```
File-AID EDIT MEMBER SELECTION FOR NIRAV.STANDARD.CNTL ----------- ROW 1 OF
COMMAND ===>                                                SCROLL ===> CSR

Enter/verify member processing options:
   Process in JCL format        ===> N      (Y=yes, N=no)
   Scan members beginning with ===>           (up to eight characters)

Enter/verify record parameters for member selection:
  Location  ===> 10     Length or Operator ===> EQ
      Data  ===> EXEC

    AND/OR ===> AND
  Location  ===>        Length or Operator ===> EQ
      Data  ===>

    AND/OR ===> AND
  Location  ===>        Length or Operator ===> EQ
      Data  ===>

    AND/OR ===> AND
***************************** END OF SELECTIONS ****************************
```

Figure 7.11 Defining conditions on the Edit Member Selection screen.

7.4 The File-Aid Utility Functions

In this section, I would like to discuss some practical situations with regards to the File-AID utility environment. This brief overview is going to contain five of the nine

```
//SYSLIB DD    DSN=NIRXT.TEST.COPYLIB,DISP=SHR
//        DD   DSN=CICS211.COBLIB,DISP=SHR
//SYSPRINT DD DSN=&&INPUT,DISP=(,PASS),UNIT=TEMP,
//   SPACE=(TRK,(15,5)),
//   DCB=(DSORG=PS,LRECL=121,BLKSIZE=2420,RECFM=FBA)
//SYSIN DD DSN=&&SYSCIN,DISP=(OLD,PASS)
//SYSLIN DD DSN=&&LOADSET,DISP=(MOD,PASS),
//        UNIT=TEMP,SPACE=(80,(250,100))
//SYSUT1 DD UNIT=TEMP,SPACE=(460,(350,100))
//SYSUT2 DD UNIT=TEMP,SPACE=(460,(350,100))
//SYSUT3 DD UNIT=TEMP,SPACE=(460,(350,100))
//SYSUT4 DD UNIT=TEMP,SPACE=(460,(350,100))
//*
//*****************************************************************
//* INTERTEST - GENERATE PARMS
//*****************************************************************
//*
//GENPARM  EXEC PGM=IN25PARM,COND=(4,LT),
//             PARM=('ARA21C,CUTPRINT=ALL,LISTER=MAP')
//STEPLIB  DD DISP=SHR,DSN=CICS211.INT312.LOADLIB
//CARDS    DD DSN=&&CARDS,DISP=(,PASS),UNIT=SYSDA,SPACE=(TRK,(1,1)
//*
//*****************************************************************
//* INTERTEST POST PROCESSOR
//*****************************************************************
//*
//POSTCOB  EXEC PGM=IN25SYMC,COND=(4,LT),REGION=512K
//STEPLIB  DD DISP=SHR,DSN=CICS211.INT312.LOADLIB
//SYSUDUMP DD SYSOUT=*
//INPUT    DD DISP=(OLD,PASS),DSN=&&INPUT
//OUTPUT   DD SYSOUT=*,DCB=(RECFM=FBA,LRECL=121,BLKSIZE=2420)
//MESSAGE  DD SYSOUT=(*,,RMIS)
//PROTSYM  DD DISP=SHR,DSN=CICS211.INT312.PROTSYM
//CARDS    DD DSN=&&CARDS,DISP=(OLD,DELETE)
//*
//DMAPSTEP EXEC  PGM=CWPCDRVR,REGION=4M COND=(4,LT)
//STEPLIB  DD  DSN=CICS211.ABAID410.LOAD,DISP=SHR
//CWPPRTI  DD  DSN=&&INPUT,DISP=(OLD,PASS)
//CWPERRM  DD  SYSOUT=(*,,RMIS)
//CWPPRTO  DD  SYSOUT=(*,,RMIS)
//SYSOUT   DD  SYSOUT=(*,,RMIS)
//SORTWK01 DD  DSN=&&SRTWRK1,DISP=(NEW,DELETE,DELETE),
//             SPACE=(TRK,(60,30)),UNIT=SYSDA,
//             DCB=(LRECL=300,BLKSIZE=304)
//CWPWRK0  DD  DSN=&&WORK0,DISP=(NEW,DELETE,DELETE),
//             DCB=(BLKSIZE=19000),
//             SPACE=(TRK,(60,30)),UNIT=SYSDA
//CWPWRK1  DD  DSN=&&WORK1,DISP=(NEW,DELETE,DELETE),
//             DCB=(BLKSIZE=19000),
```

Figure 7.13B No hit on this page.

7.4 The File-Aid Utility Functions

In this section, I would like to discuss some practical situations with regards to the File-AID utility environment. This brief overview is going to contain five of the nine

```
//SYSLIB DD    DSN=NIRXT.TEST.COPYLIB,DISP=SHR
//       DD    DSN=CICS211.COBLIB,DISP=SHR
//SYSPRINT DD DSN=&&INPUT,DISP=(,PASS),UNIT=TEMP,
//  SPACE=(TRK,(15,5)),
//  DCB=(DSORG=PS,LRECL=121,BLKSIZE=2420,RECFM=FBA)
//SYSIN DD DSN=&&SYSCIN,DISP=(OLD,PASS)
//SYSLIN DD DSN=&&LOADSET,DISP=(MOD,PASS),
//       UNIT=TEMP,SPACE=(80,(250,100))
//SYSUT1 DD UNIT=TEMP,SPACE=(460,(350,100))
//SYSUT2 DD UNIT=TEMP,SPACE=(460,(350,100))
//SYSUT3 DD UNIT=TEMP,SPACE=(460,(350,100))
//SYSUT4 DD UNIT=TEMP,SPACE=(460,(350,100))
//*
//*****************************************************************
//* INTERTEST - GENERATE PARMS
//*****************************************************************
//*
//GENPARM  EXEC PGM=IN25PARM,COND=(4,LT),
//            PARM=('ARA21C,CUTPRINT=ALL,LISTER=MAP')
//STEPLIB  DD DISP=SHR,DSN=CICS211.INT312.LOADLIB
//CARDS    DD DSN=&&CARDS,DISP=(,PASS),UNIT=SYSDA,SPACE=(TRK,(1,1)
//*
//*****************************************************************
//* INTERTEST POST PROCESSOR
//*****************************************************************
//*
//POSTCOB  EXEC PGM=IN25SYMC,COND=(4,LT),REGION=512K
//STEPLIB  DD DISP=SHR,DSN=CICS211.INT312.LOADLIB
//SYSUDUMP DD SYSOUT=*
//INPUT    DD DISP=(OLD,PASS),DSN=&&INPUT
//OUTPUT   DD SYSOUT=*,DCB=(RECFM=FBA,LRECL=121,BLKSIZE=2420)
//MESSAGE  DD SYSOUT=(*,,RMIS)
//PROTSYM  DD DISP=SHR,DSN=CICS211.INT312.PROTSYM
//CARDS    DD DSN=&&CARDS,DISP=(OLD,DELETE)
//*
//DMAPSTEP EXEC  PGM=CWPCDRVR,REGION=4M COND=(4,LT)
//STEPLIB   DD  DSN=CICS211.ABAID410.LOAD,DISP=SHR
//CWPPRTI   DD  DSN=&&INPUT,DISP=(OLD,PASS)
//CWPERRM   DD  SYSOUT=(*,,RMIS)
//CWPPRTO   DD  SYSOUT=(*,,RMIS)
//SYSOUT    DD  SYSOUT=(*,,RMIS)
//SORTWK01 DD  DSN=&&SRTWRK1,DISP=(NEW,DELETE,DELETE),
//              SPACE=(TRK,(60,30)),UNIT=SYSDA,
//              DCB=(LRECL=300,BLKSIZE=304)
//CWPWRK0   DD  DSN=&&WORK0,DISP=(NEW,DELETE,DELETE),
//              DCB=(BLKSIZE=19000),
//              SPACE=(TRK,(60,30)),UNIT=SYSDA
//CWPWRK1   DD  DSN=&&WORK1,DISP=(NEW,DELETE,DELETE),
//              DCB=(BLKSIZE=19000),
```

Figure 7.13B No hit on this page.

```
//              SPACE=(TRK,(60,30)),UNIT=SYSDA
//CWPWRK2  DD   DSN=&&WORK2,DISP=(NEW,DELETE,DELETE),
//              DCB=(BLKSIZE=19000),
//              SPACE=(TRK,(60,30)),UNIT=SYSDA
//CWPWRK3  DD   DSN=&&WORK3,DISP=(NEW,DELETE,DELETE),
//              DCB=(BLKSIZE=19000),
//              SPACE=(TRK,(60,30)),UNIT=SYSDA
//CWPWRK4  DD   DSN=&&WORK4,DISP=(NEW,DELETE,DELETE),
//              DCB=(BLKSIZE=19000),
//              SPACE=(TRK,(60,30)),UNIT=SYSDA
//CWPLOAD  DD   DUMMY
//CWPDDIO  DD   DISP=SHR,DSN=CICS211.ABAID410.LISTING
//SYSUDUMP DD   SYSOUT=*
//SYSPRINT DD   SYSOUT=*
//*
//* THE POST-PROCESSOR PARAMETERS COME FROM THE FOLLOWING PDS
//*
//CWPPRMO  DD   DSN=CICS211.ABAID410.SORCMAC(CCACBLO),DISP=SHR
//*WPPRMO  DD   DSN=NIRXT.RM.TEST.CNTL(CCACBLO),DISP=SHR
//*
//*
//PRINT EXEC PGM=IEBGENER,COND=(35,NE,C)
//SYSPRINT DD SYSOUT=*
//SYSIN DD DUMMY
//SYSUT1 DD DSN=&&INPUT,DISP=(OLD,DELETE)
//SYSUT2 DD SYSOUT=(*,,RMIS)
//*
//[LKED   EXEC PGM=IEWL,REGION=513K,]
//       PARM='XREF,LIST,LET',COND=(5,LT,C)
//SYSLIB DD  DSN=CICS211.DEVO.LOADLIB,DISP=SHR
//        DD   DSN=SYS1.VSCLLIB,DISP=SHR
//SYSLMOD DD DSN=NIRXT.TEST.CICS.LOADLIB(ARA21C),DISP=SHR
//SYSUT1 DD    UNIT=TEMP,DCB=BLKSIZE=1024,
//       SPACE=(1024,(200,20))
//SYSPRINT DD   SYSOUT=(*,,RMIS)
//SYSLIN DD    DSN=CICS211.COBLIB(DFHEILIC),DISP=SHR
//       DD DSN=&&LOADSET,DISP=(OLD,DELETE)
//*      DD    DDNAME=SYSIN
//
//*
```

Figure 7.13C The thirteenth line from the bottom represents a hit.

options listed on the File-AID Utility Selection Menu. These are, in order:

- LIBRARY
- DATA SET
- CATALOG
- VSAM DATA SET
- VOLUME TABLE OF CONTENTS, or VTOC

7.4.1 The LIBRARY utility

You can use the utility subsystem when you need to display information about different types of PDSs. A Utility Panel, which is accessible via the File-AID Utility Selection Menu (option 1), is displayed in Figure 7.14.

Note that there are seven options to choose from on utility screen. You can enter any of these options next to the SELECT OPTION ===> field. You can also use "blank" option (display member list) by entering a name in the DATA-SET NAME field. File-AID at this point will display a comprehensive list of the library members (NIRAV.STANDARD.CNTL). Note that a subsequent list triggered through the blank option is shown in Figure 7.15.

Figure 7.16 shows the result of the BROWSE request, which is a protected display of the PDS member ARA23C. Two other functions need to be described at this point: DELETE and RENAME. If you were to delete the wrong member for some reason,

```
------------------------- File-AID - LIBRARY UTILITY -----------------------
SELECT OPTION ===>

   A - Map CSECTs in address order            B - Browse member
   N - Map CSECTs in name order               D - Delete member
   S - Display directory entry of member      R - Rename member
   blank - Display member list

   Dataset name   ===> 'NIRAV.STANDARD.CNTL'

   Member name    ===>

   New name       ===>

   Volume serial ===>         (if not cataloged)

   Password       ===>         (if password protected)

   Disposition    ===> SHR     (SHR or OLD)

Use END key to end File-AID/SPF library utility
```

Figure 7.14 The File-AID Library Utility screen.

```
File-AID LIBRARY UTILITY - NIRAV.STANDARD.CNTL ------------------   ROW 4 OF 75
COMMAND ===>                                                     SCROLL ===> CSR
  Name      Rename   VV.MM  Created  Last Modified  Size  Init  Mod  ID
B ARA23C             01.03 91/09/17 91/10/02 08:17  797   797     0 NIRLC
  ARA71C             01.51 90/03/15 90/03/22 09:49  227    39   199 NIRAV
  ARA71M             01.23 90/03/15 90/03/21 12:22   47    28    47 NIRAV
  ARA81C             01.02 90/06/14 90/06/14 08:00  480   467     0 NIRLC
  ARA91C             01.99 90/03/15 91/02/26 09:54  319    39     0 NIRAV
  ARA91M             01.43 90/03/15 90/04/23 09:45   68    28    68 NIRAV
  ARB1               01.01 90/12/21 90/12/21 08:53  122   122     1 NIRAV
  ARB49C             01.02 90/05/10 91/10/08 15:46  162   160     0 NIRAV
  ARB49M             01.12 90/03/26 90/05/11 11:11   76    76     0 NIRAV
  ARB83C             01.35 90/05/07 90/06/14 12:53  408   459     0 NIRLC
  ARCHIVE            01.20 90/12/13 90/12/14 08:59  195   195    31 NIRAV
  ARC24C             01.07 90/10/23 90/10/25 14:30  580   562     0 NIRAV
  ARC24M             01.08 90/05/07 90/05/23 15:37   78    76     0 NIRAV
  ARC26C             01.07 90/10/16 90/10/25 08:47  684   721     0 NIRAV
  ARC72C             01.99 90/03/15 90/04/12 08:56  241    39   218 NIRAV
  ARC72M             01.29 90/03/15 90/04/09 08:58   45    28    45 NIRAV
  ARC81M             01.16 90/02/28 90/06/12 11:28  115    66   110 NIRLC
  ARC92C             01.99 90/03/15 90/05/31 08:35  374    39     0 NIRAV
  ARC92M             01.45 90/03/15 90/04/12 10:30   68    28    68 NIRAV
  ARC92MB
  ARDP114C           01.84 90/06/28 90/08/14 11:18  104   230     0 NIRAV
```

Figure 7.15 A detailed Library Panel showing PDS member of that library.

```
BROWSE -- NIRAV.STANDARD.CNTL(ARA23C) - 01.03 ------ LINE 00000000 COL 001 080
COMMAND ===>                                                 SCROLL ===> PAGE
********************************* TOP OF DATA **********************************
00001   IDENTIFICATION DIVISION.                                        08/14/91
00002   PROGRAM-ID. ARA23C.                                             ARA23C
00003   DATE-COMPILED.  JULY 15 1991.                                      LV005
00004   ENVIRONMENT DIVISION.                                              CL**3
00005   DATA DIVISION.                                                     CL**3
00006   WORKING-STORAGE SECTION.                                           CL**3
000065 77  PAN-VALET PICTURE X(24) VALUE '005ARA23C       08/14/91'.       CL**3
00007   77  PAN-VALET PICTURE X(24) VALUE '002ARA23C       05/07/91'.      CL**3
00008   01  COMM-AREA.                                                     CL**3
00009       05  ENTRY-SW                PIC X    VALUE '0'.                CL**3
00010           88  RETURNING-FROM-TUTORIAL      VALUE 'T'.                CL**3
00011       05  TR-KEY.                                                    CL**3
00012           10  TR-PRE-KEY          PIC X.                             CL**3
00013           10  TR-NUM              PIC X(5).                          CL**3
00014           10  FILLER              PIC X(24).                         CL**3
00015       05  PRJ-KEY.                                                   CL**3
00016           10  ZT-NUM              PIC X(02).                         CL**3
00017           10  FILLER              PIC X(04).                         CL**3
00018       05  WRITE-RECORD-SW         PIC X    VALUE 'N'.                CL**3
00019           88  WRITE-RECORD                 VALUE 'Y'.                CL**3
00020       05  RECORD-WROTE-SW         PIC X    VALUE 'N'.                CL**3
```

Figure 7.16 A library member showing a detailed overview following a browse instruction.

which is fairly easy to do, File-AID enables you to recover such a member through the U or UNDO command. (This is somewhat like deleting through the asterisk function in dBASE.)

Place the character U next to the PDS member to be recovered. Do it immediately and don't wait until the next day for restoration. When the DELETE operation is completed, File-AID will provide you with a brief message: *DELETED. When using the UNDO option, the resulting message will be *ADDED.

With regard to renaming conventions, the new name of a PDS can be up to eight characters long and must begin with any alphabetic character, including $, #, and @. These characters are also referred to as global characters. If you have a very extensive library with hundreds of members, you can use the LOCATE command to find or locate a specific PDS member very much like in ISPF mode.

In using the S option, you will obtain the member's directory entry. Two other options are also available through the Library Utility Panel. These are the A option of MAP CSECT which is displayed in address and the N option denoting MAP CSECT in name order. The purpose of either one of the above options is to display the component CSECTs of a load module including overlays.

7.4.2 The CATALOG utility

The File-AID utility can display cataloged data sets. Listing can be accomplished one of two ways. One way is to perform a specific volume search, in which case you need to specify the particular volume and indicate your choice by entering the character V next to the SELECT OPTION ===> slot. Some other procedures pertaining to volume searches include a value in the TRANSLATE DSNAME field, which is either a Yes or a No. Y means that the listed data set names be translated from the catalog names into the cluster name. N means that the listed names are the catalog names.

Another way of displaying cataloged data sets is to search generically. This does not require that you enter a specific volume because File-AID, under the circumstances, will search all available volumes. Also, the SELECT OPTION ===> field must be left blank. An overview of the Catalog Utility Panel is presented in Figure 7.17.

When you use the blank option on the above panel, note the values associated with the SEARCH NAME field are grouped into five types of qualifiers, which can include wildcard characters after the high-level qualifiers. These qualifiers are discussed in the following order:

- Explicit level
- Skeletal name
- Single-level wildcard
- Multilevel wildcard
- Last-level wildcard

The explicit-level qualifier represents an explicit (inquiry-like) value without using any wild characters. At this point, you can list only data sets that match the exact key. Remember, this type of qualifier needs to be specified as one qualifier less than that of the particular name(s) to be searched. Let me give you an example. Consider the following:

```
NIRAV.STANDARD
```

File-AID is going to display data-set names with a high-level qualifier of NIRAV and a second-level qualifier of STANDARD. However, both levels combined, such as NIRAV.STANDARD, will not be either recognized or processed.

```
------------------------- File-AID - CATALOG UTILITY ----- 0 DATASETS PROCESSED
SELECT OPTION ===>

   V - produce volume list of VSAM datasets (non-ICF catalogs only)
   BLANK - generic catalog search

Generic catalog search function:
   Search name    ===> NIRAV
   Format option ===> QUICK   (Quick, Short, Long)
   Clusters Only ===> Y       (Y or N)

Volume dataset list function:
   Volume serial ===>         (required for option "V")
   Translate DSN ===> N       (Y OR N)

Catalog to search if other than default system catalog:
   Catalog name      ===>
   Catalog password ===>           (if catalog is password protected)

Delete function options:
   Display confirm screen: ===> Y (Y=yes, N=no)
```

Figure 7.17 The layout for the Catalog Panel.

A second-level qualifier, such as the skeletal name qualifier, uses at least one or a number of underline characters as location-dependent wildcard characters. For example, if you were to search for the qualifier AR1007 (as part of NIRAV.AR1007 member definition) with the definition AR___7, AR1007 would clearly qualify. So would AR67B7. Note that a single-level qualifier using an asterisk (*) as a wildcard character can denote up to eight characters that are location-dependent. For example, NIRAV.STANDARD.CNTL can be coded as NIRAV.*.CNTL. In this instance, File-AID will process any data set name with a primary qualifier of NIRAV and a tertiary qualifier of CNTL, while ignoring any other qualifiers in between.

Another search method is referred to as a multilevel wildcard qualifier, using an addition sign to denote zero or more levels of qualifications. So the search name NIRAV.+.CNTL can be interpreted as NIRAV.STANDARD.CNTL, NIRAV.STANDARD AR44.CNTL, or even NIRAV.STANDARD.1R44.CVX.CNTL.

The last level qualifier uses a slash to specify the number of levels in a data-set name that must be searched. NIRAV.*/, for example, will cause File-AID to list any data-set name that starts with NIRAV, has any value in the second qualifier, and has only two qualifier levels.

When dealing with catalog procedures, you can use both the FIND and LOCATE commands, described earlier, in conjunction with ISPF. In addition, you should refer to some of the line commands described in detail in chapter 6. Figure 7.18 shows a catalog utility line command table for your reference.

7.4.3 The VSAM utility

If you create VSAM clusters through IDCAMS, File-AID's VSAM utility will be a great help to you. In fact, one of the greatest advantages of using File-AID is the ease with which you can allocate and maintain a VSAM data set, and the quickness and efficiency through which you can allocate alternate indexes, define VSAM space, and allocate a particular path.

Command	Description	Limitation
B	Browse	Sequential, PDS
E	Edit	Sequential, PDS
R	Rename	All access methods
U	Uncatalog	All nonVSAM access methods
D	Delete	All access methods
M	Modify	VSAM
I	Display info.	All access methods
S	Display info. short	All access methods
F	Free unused space	Sequential, PDS, BDAM
1	File-AID Browse	All access methods
2	File-AID Edit	All access methods

Figure 7.18 The catalog utility line-command table.

```
-------------------------- File-AID - VSAM UTILITY ---------- REQUEST CANCELLED
SELECT OPTION ===>

   A     - Allocate VSAM cluster          D - Delete dataset
   S     - Allocate VSAM space            T - Delete VSAM space
   X     - Allocate alternate index       P - Allocate path
   B     - Build alternate index          R - Rename Component
   M     - Modify component
   BLANK - Display dataset information

Object name if required:
   Dataset name  ===> 'NIRAV.VSAM.CNTL'
   Volume serial ===>             (if not cataloged, required for option "S")
   Password      ===>             (if dataset is password protected)

Catalog to use if other than default system catalog:
   Catalog name     ===>
   Catalog password ===>          (if catalog is password protected)

Model dataset name:
   Dataset name ===>

   For dataset allocations only, the optional model dataset is used to
   prefill the allocation information on the allocation panel.
```

Figure 7.19 The File-AID VSAM Utility Panel to allocate, maintain, and delete VSAM clusters.

Let me start out by explaining to you some of the conventions used throughout this subsystem. (Realistically, you might look at the File-AID as a productivity tool made up of several programs or component modules, each designed to do certain tasks.) To select the VSAM utility, enter the number 5 next to the SELECT OPTION field on the File-AID Utility Selection Menu. When you press the Enter key, the File-AID VSAM utility screen will pop up, as shown in Figure 7.19. As you can see, this panel is organized to accommodate two sets of information. The upper area lists all the utility options available, while the lower area represents approximately 65% to 70% of the screen, and is designed for data set and catalog specifications.

There are altogether nine options presented on this screen, including a blank character to display data-set information. The "blank" option, as well as options D (delete) and R (rename component), can be used on data sets of all access methods. All other options can be used only on VSAM files.

In order to execute a particular function, enter the name of the data set in the DATA-SET NAME field. When you need to allocate VSAM space, place a value in the VOLUME SERIAL field (and not in the DATA-SET NAME field.)

The MODEL DATA SET option is a shortcut method to create a new cluster with attributes identical to those already in existence.

This method is also referred to as a shell process.

7.4.3.1 How to allocate VSAM clusters

Let's talk about allocating a new VSAM cluster and what it entails. Using conventional IBM utilities, such as IDCAMS, might be a time-consuming experience—like anything else that involves the use of JCLs. JCLs by nature are error-prone and quite slow in communicating fatal errors. One of the many strengths of File-AID is that you can automate this entire process to the point where you can allocate and create a VSAM cluster simply by answering some basic questions about a data set, or by al-

```
-------------------- File-AID - ALLOCATE NEW VSAM CLUSTER --------------------
COMMAND ===>
Component names:
 Cluster NIRAV.VSAM.CNTL
 Data... NIRAV.VSAM.CNTL.DATA
 Index.. NIRAV.VSAM.CNTL.INDEX
   Dataset type       ===> KSDS     (KSDS,ESDS,RRDS)
                                     Specify only one of the following two fields
   Volume serial      ===> TSOWK2      (blank for authorized default volume)
   Generic unit       ===>             (Generic group name or unit)
   Reuseable          ===> YES         (Y=yes N=no)
   Type               ===> UNIQUE      (U=unique S=sub-allocate)
   Expiration date    ===>             (YYYY/MM/DD or blank)
Space allocation:   DATA component      INDEX component (Blank for default)
      Units           ===> CYLS           ===>            (TRKs,CYLs,RECs)
      Primary         ===> 3              ===> 0          (amount in above units)
      Secondary       ===> 1              ===> 0          (amount in above units)

 Average Recordsize ===> 80
 Maximum Recordsize ===> 6160
 Key length         ===> 0          (1 - 255 - KSDS only)
 Key position       ===> 0          (0 - maximum record - KSDS only)
Extended allocate   ===> NO         (Y=yes, N=no)
```

Figure 7.20 Allocating a new VSAM Cluster Panel.

lowing the system to default to some of the available standard options. You can also produce clusters with a modeling technique where you use an existing cluster as a starting point for another in terms of overall attributes, record size, and other mandatory criteria that would have to be redefined on every single occasion in a conventional environment.

To define a VSAM cluster through File-AID, use option A on the VSAM Utility Panel (refer back to Figure 7.19). Note that File-AID supports all three access methods used by VSAM: KSDS, ESDS, and RRDS. Actually, the allocation process encompasses the use of several panels. Having entered A to initiate the allocation process, type in a data-set name, assuming that no model data-set cloning is required, and then press Enter. The response by File-AID is highlighted in Figure 7.20. Several aspects of the file need to be defined on this level.

On the top of the ALLOCATE VSAM CLUSTER screen, Figure 7.20, File-AID displays the component names of the cluster specified on the VSAM Utility Panel. The names are generated based on a naming-exit routine in which File-AID appends the DATA or INDEX last-level qualifier to the cluster name to create the data-set names of the data and index component. So File-AID generates three names when a VSAM cluster is allocated, such as:

```
NIRAV.VSAM.CNTL
NIRAV.VSAM.CNTL.DATA
NIRAV.VSAM.CNTL.INDEX
```

Notice that, when the allocation panel is displayed, it contains attribute values left over from the previous allocation (and thus, has nothing to do with the current allocation process). Actually, it is also possible that they are associated with a model, but for the time being we are going to discount that possibility. So to proceed with the new attribute definition, simply specify the new values. The three types of data sets included here are:

- KSDS, or Key-Sequenced Data Set
- ESDS, or Entry-Sequenced Data Set
- RRDS, or Relative-Records Data Set

Enter a data-set location either through the VOLUME SERIAL or GENERIC UNIT field. If neither of these are entered, File-AID is going to use a default volume. Assuming you are familiar with conventional VSAM nomenclature, specify whether the cluster is a reusable one (Yes or No), the location type, and whether it is unique (V) or suballocated (S). Note that the current date is optional and if you enter it it has to be in a YYYY/MM/DD format.

The units of allocation can be expressed in terms of TRKS or tracks, CYLs or cylinders, and RECS or records. Note that the term RECS is also associated with AVERAGE RECORD SIZE field for the unit quantity.

Next, specify the unit quantity for the PRIMARY and SECONDARY fields, relative to both data and index components. For keyed data sets, enter values in the KEY-LENGTH and KEY-POSITION fields. For KSDS clusters, the key length must be at least one position long, but cannot exceed 255 positions on high (which shouldn't be much of a problem). If you want to have the key start in column 1, use a key position value of zero.

In order to display VSAM information, File-AID uses two (sometimes three) consecutive panels. These panels are shown in Figures 7.21 and 7.22, and they are the result of the blank OPTION field in the File-AID VSAM Utility Panel.

Let's review some of the options on these screens. Figure 7.21 is arranged in two

```
----------------- File-AID VSAM INFORMATION - (PAGE 1 OF 2) ------------------
COMMAND ===>
Catalog.. CATALOG.MVSICF1.VTSOWK1
Cluster.. NIRAV.VSAM.CNTL
Data..... NIRAV.VSAM.CNTL.DATA
Index.... NIRAV.VSAM.CNTL.INDEX
- - - - - - - - - - - - - - - - - - - - - - - - - - - - - - - - - - - - - - -
Data component information:                Current allocation options:
 Volume serial:            TSOWK2                 RACF protected:          NO
 Device type:                3380                 Write check:             NO
 Organization:               KSDS                 Buffer space:         45568
 KSDS key length:               9                 Erase on delete:         NO
 KSDS key location:             0                 Imbedded index:          NO
 Average record size:          80                 Replicated index:        NO
 Maximum record size:        6160                 Reuse option:           YES
 Allocated space: Unit      Primary   Secondary   Share options:          1-3
     Data -       cylinders       3           1   Spanned records:         NO
     Index   -    tracks          1           1   MSS binding:         STAGED
Dataset date information:                         MSS-destage wait:        NO
 Creation date:         1991/10/23                Key ranges present:      NO
 Expiration date:                                 AIX-unique keys:
 Modification date:                               AIX-upgrade:
 Modification time:                               Load option:       RECOVERY
 >>>>> Press ENTER to go to page 2; END key to return to utility menu <<<<<
```

Figure 7.21 Panel 1 for cluster definition.

```
----------------- File-AID VSAM INFORMATION - (PAGE 2 OF 2) -----------------
COMMAND ===>
Related Datasets - NIRAV.VSAM.CNTL
CLUSTER    - NIRAV.VSAM.CNTL                                  +-----------+
                                                              | owner-id  |
                                                              | NIRAV     |
                                                              +-----------+
- - - - - - - - - - - - - - - - - - - - - - - - - - - - - - - - - - - - - - -
Current allocations in tracks:          Current utilization in tracks:
   Allocated space:             45         Used data space:         0 (   0 %)
   Allocated extents:            1         Used extents:            0 (   0 %)
   Allocation type:         UNIQUE         Prime records:
KSDS index allocation in tracks:           Deleted records:                 0
   Allocated space:              1         Inserted records:                0
   Number of records:            0         Updated records:                 0

- - - - - - - - - - - Current Reorganization Information - - - - - - - - - - -
Control area information:               Control interval information:
   Physical record size:    22528          Size-data:    22528 index:     512
   Records per track:           2          Number CIs:                     30
   Tracks per CA:              15          Number free CIs/CA:              0
   Retrieved records:           0          Percent free CIs/CA:             0
   Max record number            0          Percent free bytes/CI:           0
   Number CA splits:            0          Number CI splits:                0
 >>>>> Press ENTER to go to page 1; END key to return to utility menu <<<<<
```

Figure 7.22 Panel 2 continues to define a VSAM cluster.

parts. The top portion of the screen displays the CATALOG field, as well as the CLUSTER, DATA, and INDEX fields. A tabular overview of this screen is presented to you in Figure 7.23. If you were to press the Enter key at this point, the second panel (Figure 7.22) would appear. This panel, overall, provides you with data on what was allocated earlier and tells you how much of it was physically used. The panel also contains reorganization-related information. Field descriptions pertaining to Figure 7.22 are shown in Figure 7.24.

When you allocate a VSAM cluster, it will be necessary for you to enclose the data-set name in apostrophes. If you don't (and there will be no diagnostics generated by File-AID), the system will simply default to duplicating the I.D. portion of the data set. For example, if you were to allocate the data set NIRAV.VSAM.CNTL without the apostrophes, the next panel in the allocation process would display:

```
NIRAV.NIRAV.VSAM.CNTL
NIRAV,NIRAV.VSAM.CNTL.DATA
NIRAV.NIRAV.VSAM.CNTL.INDEX
```

In the previous steps I presented to you the mechanics required to allocate a VSAM data set. If you somehow defined a wrong VSAM cluster or a cluster that is no longer required, perhaps, you need to use File-AID's delete-cluster procedures. This is a simple technique. Just place the character D next to the SELECT OPTION slot on the File-AID VSAM Utility Panel, shown in Figure 7.25, and press the Enter key. This will invoke and display the following confirmation delete screen shown in Figure 7.26.

The so-called confirmation panel shows the names of all the data sets to be deleted. In the current situation, of course, this refers to the NIRAV.VSAM/CNTL data set. There are two courses of action you can pursue at this point. If you press Enter, the process of deletion will be completed, meaning that all data sets below the broken line will be erased. If you were to press PF3, which is the exit key, however, the deletion will be canceled.

7.4.3.2 How to allocate/delete an alternate index

This function is similar to those described for the allocation of a VSAM cluster. However, instead of coding an A in the SELECT OPTION field, you need to code an X.

FIELD	DATA COMPONENT INFORMATION
VOLUME SERIAL	Name of the device on which data is stored
DEVICE TYPE	Type of the device on which data is stored
KSDS LENGTH KEY	Length of field within each record that contains key information
KSDS KEY LOCATION	Location relative to zero of key field
AVERAGE RECORD SIZE	Estimated average size of data record specified at allocation
MAXIMUM RECORD SIZE	Largest possible record that data set can contain
ALLOCATED SPACE: UNIT PRIMARY/SECONDARY	
DATA	Data space units (CYLs, TRKs, and RECORDS) specified at data-set allocation.
INDEX	Index units: same as Data
	DATA-SET DATE INFORMATION
CREATION DATE	Date on which the data set was allocated
EXPIRATION DATE	Date after which deletion or update of data set is permitted
MODIFICATION DATE	Date on which data set was last modified
MODIFICATION TIME	Time at which data set was last modified
	CURRENT ALLOCATION OPTION
RACF PROTECTED	YES/NO
WRITE CHECK	YES/NO
BUFFER SPACE	Minimum amount of space required for buffers
ERASE ON DELETE	YES/NO
IMBEDDED INDEX	YES/NO
REPLICATED INDEX	YES/NO
REUSE OPTION	YES/NO
SHARE OPTIONS	Options for sharing a data set across region and system
SPANNING RECORDS	YES/NO
MSS BINDING	Current value of mass-storage staging option (STAGE, BIND, CYLINDER, DEFAULT)
MSS DESTAGE WAIT	YES/NO
KEY RANGES PRESENT	YES/NO
AIX-UNIQUE KEYS	YES/NO
AIX UPGRADE	YES/NO
LOAD OPTION	SPEED/RECOVERY

Figure 7.23 File-AID VSAM field-description table for Figure 7.21.

When you use this option, File-AID will provide you with two consecutive panels in which to enter all the required attribute information. Consider the panel displayed in Figure 7.27.

When allocating a secondary or alternate index through File-AID, make sure you

FIELD	CURRENT ALLOCATION INFORMATION IN TRACKS
ALLOCATED SPACE	Total space in tracks allocated to data component
ALLOCATED EXTENTS	Number of extents allocated to data component
ALLOCATION TYPE	Allocated space unit type (CYL, TRK, or REC)
	KSDS INDEX ALLOCATION INFORMATION IN TRACKS
ALLOCATED SPACE	Total space in specified units allocated to index component
NUMBER OF RECORDS	Number of index records
	CURRENT UTILIZATION INFORMATION IN TRACKS
USED DATA SPACE	Space in use less free space in tracks
USED EXTENTS	Number of extents in specified units currently in use for data component
PRIME RECORDS	Number of data records in file
DELETED RECORDS	Number of data records deleted since file was defined or modified
INSERTED RECORDS	Number of data records inserted since file was defined or modified
UPDATED RECORDS	Number of data records updated since file was either defined or modified
Control Area Information	CURRENT REORGANIZATION INFORMATION
PHYSICAL RECORD SIZE	Number of bytes in a physical record
RECORDS PER TRACK	Number of physical records in one track
TRACKS PER CA	Number of tracks in a control area
RETRIEVED RECORDS	Number of data records read since file was was defined or modified
MAX RECORD NUMBER	Highest number of data records that file contained since it was defined or modified
NUMBER CA SPLITS	Number of times a control area was split to make room to insert new data
Control Interval Info.	
SIZE -- DATA and INDEX	Control interval size for data and index comp.
NUMBER CIs	Number of control intervals in control area
NUMBER FREE CIs/CA	Number of control intervals kept free when loading a control area
PERCENT FREE CIs/CA	% of control area kept free when loaded
PERCENT FREE BYTES/CI	% of control interval kept free when loaded
NUMBER CI SPLITS	Number of times control intervals were split to make room for new data

Figure 7.24 File-AID VSAM field-description table for Figure 7.22.

```
-------------------------- File-AID - VSAM UTILITY ----------- REQUEST CANCELLED
SELECT OPTION ===> D

   A      - Allocate VSAM cluster              D - Delete dataset
   S      - Allocate VSAM space                T - Delete VSAM space
   X      - Allocate alternate index           P - Allocate path
   B      - Build alternate index              R - Rename Component
   M      - Modify component
   BLANK  - Display dataset information

Object name if required:
   Dataset name  ===> 'NIRAV.VSAM.CNTL'
   Volume serial ===>               (if not cataloged, required for option "S")
   Password      ===>               (if dataset is password protected)

Catalog to use if other than default system catalog:
   Catalog name     ===>
   Catalog password ===>            (if catalog is password protected)

Model dataset name:
   Dataset name ===>

   For dataset allocations only, the optional model dataset is used to
   prefill the allocation information on the allocation panel.
```

Figure 7.25 File-AID VSAM Utility Menu for defining a "delete" operation of a VSAM cluster.

```
------------------------ File-AID CONFIRM DATASET DELETE -----------------------
COMMAND ===>
Dataset name:  NIRAV.VSAM.CNTL
Volume:        TSOWK2
Creation date: 1991/10/24

 R =>    --------------------------------------------------------
 E =>    CLUSTER    - NIRAV.VSAM.CNTL
 L =>
 A =>
 T =>
 E =>
 D =>
   =>
 O =>
 B =>
 J =>
 C =>
 T =>
 S =>
 Press ENTER to confirm delete request
       All related objects below the line will be deleted and uncataloged
 Press END key to cancel the delete function
```

Figure 7.26 A File-AID Confirm Delete Panel.

define the base cluster, NIRAV.VSAM.CNTL, as either REUSABLE=NO or simply nonreusable. Use these steps:

1. Enter the code X next to the SELECT OPTION field to tell File-AID that a secondary or alternate index is about to be created. If the alternate index pertains to the previously defined NIRAV.VSAM.CNTL cluster, then NIRAV.VSAM.CNTL will be the base cluster.
2. When allocating an alternate index, make sure that the name of that data set will be different from that given to the base cluster. I used NIRAV.VSAM.SECOND for

that purpose. The second panel used in creating this base cluster is shown in Figure 7.28. You are now ready to identify your alternate index. Note that File-AID retains all prior attributes associated with the primary index.

3. The only thing you are required to enter on this panel is your definition of the base cluster, unless, of course, you want to change some of the current attributes on this panel. You will most probably need to change the key position and probably the key length of the new index (otherwise it would make little sense to create an alternate index in the first place). Thus, the base cluster of the NIRAV.VSAM.SECOND data set will be the previously defined primary cluster of NIRAV.VSAM.SECOND.

```
------------------------- File-AID - VSAM UTILITY ---------- DATASET ALLOCATED
SELECT OPTION ===> X

   A     - Allocate VSAM cluster              D - Delete dataset
   S     - Allocate VSAM space                T - Delete VSAM space
   X     - Allocate alternate index           P - Allocate path
   B     - Build alternate index              R - Rename Component
   M     - Modify component
   BLANK - Display dataset information

Object name if required:
   Dataset name  ===> 'NIRAV.VSAM.SECOND'
   Volume serial ===>            (if not cataloged, required for option "S")
   Password      ===>            (if dataset is password protected)

Catalog to use if other than default system catalog:
   Catalog name     ===>
   Catalog password ===>         (if catalog is password protected)

Model dataset name:
   Dataset name ===>

   For dataset allocations only, the optional model dataset is used to
   prefill the allocation information on the allocation panel.
```

Figure 7.27 Procedures necessary for the allocation of a secondary index.

```
------------------ File-AID - ALLOCATE VSAM ALTERNATE INDEX -------------------
COMMAND ===>
Component names:
 AIX.... NIRAV.VSAM.SECOND
 Data... NIRAV.VSAM.SECOND.DATA
 Index.. NIRAV.VSAM.SECOND.INDEX
      Volume serial ===> TSOWK2   (blank for authorized default volume)
      Upgrade       ===> Y        (Y=yes N=no)
      Unique keys   ===> Y        (Y=yes N=no)
      Base cluster  ===>
  Space allocation for data component:
      Type          ===> UNIQUE   (U=unique S=sub-allocate on above volume)
      Units         ===> CYLS     (TRKS,CYLS,RECS)
      Primary       ===> 3        (amount in above units)
      Secondary     ===> 1        (amount in above units)
      Reuseable     ===> NO       (Y=yes  N=no)
  Data component record/alternate key information:
      Average       ===> 80
      Maximum       ===> 6160
      Key length    ===> 30       (1 - 255 in base cluster)
      Key position  ===> 20       (relative to zero in base cluster)

  Extended allocate ===> NO       (Y=yes, N=no)
```

Figure 7.28 Alternate Cluster Definition Panel.

```
------------------------- File-AID - VSAM UTILITY ----------------------------
SELECT OPTION ===> P

   A     - Allocate VSAM cluster           D - Delete dataset
   S     - Allocate VSAM space             T - Delete VSAM space
   X     - Allocate alternate index        P - Allocate path
   B     - Build alternate index           R - Rename Component
   M     - Modify component
   BLANK - Display dataset information

Object name if required:
   Dataset name  ===> 'NIRAV.VSAM.PATH'
   Volume serial ===>              (if not cataloged, required for option "S")
   Password      ===>              (if dataset is password protected)

Catalog to use if other than default system catalog:
   Catalog name     ===>
   Catalog password ===>           (if catalog is password protected)

Model dataset name:
   Dataset name ===>

   For dataset allocations only, the optional model dataset is used to
   prefill the allocation information on the allocation panel.
```

Figure 7.29 Panel required to define a path.

Note that the key length on the alternate index is now 30 bytes (employee name rather than employee I.D. number) and that the KSDS key starts in position 20.

7.4.3.3 Allocating a path

A path logically relates the base cluster and each of its alternate indexes. It provides a way to gain access to the base data through a specific alternate index. So the path name subsequently refers to the base cluster/alternate index pair. This means that when you refer to a path, both the base cluster and the alternate indexes are affected.

1. To allocate a new VSAM path, fill in the fields on the VSAM Utility Panel, as I did in Figure 7.29. Enter the character P, short for path, next to the SELECT OPTION field on the VSAM Utility Panel. Also enter the name of the data set, which is NIRAV.VSAM.PATH. You can also enter a catalog and a password, but these components are strictly optional.
2. When you press the Enter key, File-AID will trigger the next logical panel, shown in Figure 7.30. This is the Allocate VSAM Panel. Here, the only entry required is the name of the related data set that this path will describe. The related data set can either be an alternate index or a base cluster name for which the path will be an alias. You can also specify whether or not alternate indexes associated with the base cluster are to be opened and updated. UPDATE specifies associated alternate indexes to be opened and updated. NOUPDATE specifies that only the path and the base cluster are to be opened and updated.
3. Once you have pressed the Enter key, File-AID conveys the final message: PATH ALLOCATED.

```
------------------------ File-AID - ALLOCATE VSAM PATH -------------------------
COMMAND ===>

Path name: NIRAV.VSAM.PATH

Related alternate index or cluster:
     Name ===> 'NIRAV.VSAM.SECOND'

     Update(Y/N) ===> N

Catalog to use if other than default system catalog:
   Catalog name     ===>
   Catalog password ===>          (if catalog is password protected)
```

Figure 7.30 Panel required to define an alternate path.

7.3.4 Renaming conventions

This option (place the character R in the SELECT OPTION field of the VSAM utility screen) allows you to rename the data set regardless of the access method used by that particular data set. The process of renaming is done via the File-AID Rename VSAM Data Set Panel. The panel lists the catalog name, the current cluster name, and the components. The TYPE field displays the type of data set being renamed.

7.5 The VTOC (Volume Table of Contents) Utility

The purpose of the VTOC utility screen is two-fold: it allows you to display volume information by volume or by data-set list. You can list two types of data sets; the first one is ordered by data-set name sequence, and the second is in location sequence of the volume. To create a selective list, you need to use a generic search, which will provide the list for you whether accommodating a single- or multivolume list.

To select the VTOC utility, enter the number 7 in the SELECT OPTION field of the File-AID Utility Selection Menu. This will trigger the VTOC Utility screen shown in Figure 7.31. Note that I have left the OPTION field blank, which represents a valid selection criterion, such as listing VTOC Entries in data-set-name sequence. This list is displayed in Figure 7.32, including track, usage, and a percent of usage.

You can also select two other options on the VTOC Utility Panel. These are option M (map VTOC entries in pack location sequence) and option I (to list volume information). Volume information requires an I.D. in the VOLUME SERIAL field or a generic volume in the UNIT NAME field. The VOLUME STATUS field can contain one of four group of values, such as PUB meaning public, PRV meaning private, and

STG denoting storage. The fourth value means that all of the above can be requested by leaving the VOLUME STATUS field blank. The value in the VOLUME SERIAL field can be a six-character name or a mask value that accommodates up to 42 characters. In the example shown in Figure 7.33, a comprehensive display relative to all volume status with a value of PUB is displayed.

```
---------------------------- File-AID - VTOC UTILITY ---- 0 DATASETS PROCESSED
SELECT OPTION ===>

   I - List volume information
   M - Map VTOC entries in pack location sequence (CCCC-HH)
   BLANK - List VTOC entries in dataset name sequence

Enter volume selection parameters below:
   Volume serial   ===> TSOWK2
   Unit name       ===>
   Volume status   ===>        (PUB=public, PRV=private, STG=storage)

Generic search function:
   Search dataset name   ===>
   Max number of names   ===> 1000   (for multi volume operations)

Catalog to use if other than default system catalog:
   Catalog name      ===>
   Catalog password ===>          (if catalog is password protected)

Display confirm delete   ===> Y     (Y=yes, N=no)

Use END key to end File-AID/SPF VTOC function
```

Figure 7.31 The File-AID VTOC Utility Panel.

```
File-AID - Utility VTOC list for TSOWK2 (3380) ----------- 155 DATASETS LISTED
COMMAND ===>                                                  SCROLL ===> CSR
 VTOC:      15 Tracks (  20 %Used)      635 Free DSCB'S           155 Data sets
 VOL:    13290 Tracks (  60 %Used)       15 Tracks/cylinder        15 ALT Tracks
 FREE:     332 Cyls (MAX= 68)          5339 Trks (MAX= 1020)        72 Free Xtnts
  --------- D A T A S E T   N A M E ---------- Org   Trks %Used XTS=  Status
  ACC01.SPFLOG1.LIST                           PS       1   100    1
  ACC02.LIB.CNTL                               PO       6   100    2
  ACC21.GL91.CNTL                              PO     105    93    1
  BUD02.LIB.CNTL                               PO      45    91    2
  BUSJJ.SPFTEMP0.CNTL                          PS       1   100    1
  FDRABR.VTSOWK2                               ??       0     0    0
  GA01.DOWNLOAD.DATA                           PS       1   100    1
  GA01.LIB.CNTL                                PO      71    87    1
  GA01.PM.PCDOWN                               PS       6   100    1
  GA04.DOWNLOAD.DATA                           PS       6    17    2
  GA04.LIB.CNTL                                PO       6   100    2
  HUR00.HR.HRRANDOM.STEP1                      PS       9   100    1
  HUR00.HR.HRRANDOM.STEP3                      PS       9   100    1
  HUR00.HR.HRRANDOM.STEP5B                     PS       9   100    1
  HUR00.HR.HRRANDOM.STEP6                      PS       1   100    1
  HUR00.PR.PROY89.EMPMAST                      PS     302   100    1
  HUR00.PR.PROY90.EMPMAST                      PS     343   100    1
  ISPCB.ISPF.ISPPROF                           PO       2   100    1
```

Figure 7.32 A utility VTOC list for volume TSOWK2 on a 3380 DASD.

```
File-AID - Volume list for STATUS=PRV---------------------      47 VOLUMES LISTED
COMMAND ===>                                                     SCROLL ===> CSR
  --- V O L U M E ---   %    --- V T O C ---      ------------ F R E E -----------
  Serial type    stat used   size %used INDX      DSCB'S   Cyls  (Max) Tracks  (Max)
  BUS001 3380     PRV   37     15    15    Y         672    543    181   8358   2715
  BUS002 3380     PRV   30     30    44    Y         898   1200    568  18536   8520
  CICSDL 3380     PRV   81     30    12    N        1398    327    155   5132   2326
  CICS01 3380     PRV   86     15    12    Y         698    127    121   1924   1816
  EM5PAK 3380     PRV   87     15     1    Y         789    220    220   3326   3312
  EM6PAK 3380     PRV  100     10     2    Y         521      6      3    104     45
  FA0001 3380     PRV   57     15    11    Y         711    378    243   5726   3654
  GL0001 3380     PRV   60     30     8    Y        1468    697    383  10649   5745
  GL0002 3380     PRV   83     15    49    Y         407    268    131   4580   1965
  INFOPK 3380     PRV   25     12     3    Y         610    663    404   9968   7260
  INF089 3380     PRV   99     15     4    N         760      8      3    142     45
  KOMAND 3380     PRV   81     15    12    Y         697    327    279   4937   4185
  MVSALT 3380     PRV   82     30    10    N        1426    319    208   4856   3126
  MVSCAT 3380     PRV   45     30     2    N        1556    978    895  14683  13425
  MVSDFP 3380     PRV   94     30    12    Y        1395     99     93   1517   1395
  MVSNCP 3380     PRV   61     30     9    Y        1454    682    172  10250   2580
  MVSRES 3380     PRV   85     30    11    N        1423    266    228   4058   3440
  MVSSCR 3380     PRV   82     15    27    N         579    306    251   4740   3779
  MVSSMP 3380     PRV   89     30     8    Y        1458    197     36   3004    540
  MVS001 3380     PRV   46     15    15    N         672    945    268  14328   4020
```

Figure 7.33 Vol status listing of the VTOC for the PUB.

Chapter 8

Introduction to Test Environments and CA-InterTest

8.1 The General Categories of Testing

The intensity of testing and the overall quality of a program are directly linked. In developing your source code, you need to rely on a number of steps to verify that:

- You understand what needs to be included in your program is indeed identical to the mechanics described in the specifications.
- Contingent upon your understanding of the problem presented in these "specs," you need to see for yourself whether the requested program is doable within the allotted time frame, whether it is optimally modularized, and most importantly if it is clearly explained and documented.

Optimal modularization is an especially important aspect in testing environments, where the programmer verifies that the criteria he is expected to perform in an application program are doable; doable in terms of efficiency, whether each task to be performed should be further decomposed, for example, in a couple of smaller-sized programs.

Many programs, placed in a realistic setting, are not optimally modularized—they either attempt to handle too many functions at once or else they're single-threaded, meaning that they are far too simplistic. Given a typical test environment, the programmer, and later on a quality-assurance group (if there is such a body in place), will perform the following steps:

1. Perform unit testing, which is a reiterative process.
2. Perform debugging (contingent upon the failure of the unit test).

3. Do integration testing to consolidate the various parts, or modules, of the system.
4. Perform system testing to collectively verify the finished product.
5. Complete the cycle by performing volume testing to see and evaluate what stress can do to operating efficiency, response time, etc. by introducing a heavy but nonetheless realistic operational load.

While steps 1 and 2 (unit testing and debugging) are tools in the hands of the programmer to whom the specifications are assigned, steps 3 through 5 (integration, system, and volume testing) can be performed by a quality-assurance group, as well as other individuals, such as analysts or project leaders in charge of the particular project.

Unit testing is an activity in which the programmer completes a set of requirements. The term *unit* is identical to a single program, thus unit testing means testing a single program according to a set of criteria. This process is integrated with a set of ongoing debugging activities, that is, activities designed to address a specific problem or procedure internal to a program that the program does not do or does incorrectly. Only when this outstanding problem is resolved will the programmer return to unit test the rest of his program.

Unit testing is a hierarchical process where not all the components required by a unit (program) are usually present at the time the programmer starts his activities. Consider the exhibit presented in Figure 8.1 characteristic of a typical batch environment.

In this particular segment, which happens to be a standard accounts-receivable application, there are four program assignments (steps 2 through 5) and a utility sort. Steps 2 through 5 represent four units or application programs, each of which is handled by a different programmer given the relative complexity of the application and the amount of experience possessed by each programmer.

Assume that both the A/R transaction and the A/R master files are currently available and that they are both input to step 3. Also assume that programmers working on step 2 (Validating and Updating Corporate Policy Transactions) and step 5 (Processing A/R Activities) complete their respective assignments ahead of time, that is, ahead of the programmer working on the batch-edit procedures (step 4). Because both steps 2 and 5 expect some of their input requirements from step 4, the delay in developing step 4 will negatively impact the ability of the programmers to unit test (and debug) the policy validation and the processing of A/R activities related procedures.

Unit testing should always be viewed as an activity that must be made independent from external activities if it is to be successful. The best way to accomplish such an ambitious objective is for the programmer to create his own "complete" environment, which requires that all incomplete files (files unavailable at the time the programmer is ready to start unit testing) be created on a limited basis, consisting a half a dozen to a dozen records to be discarded when step 4 is ready to generate both the valid A/R transactions and the updated suspense files. (To create a more comprehensive test environment, you can use CICS Playback, or CA-Verify, both of which will be discussed in subsequent chapters.)

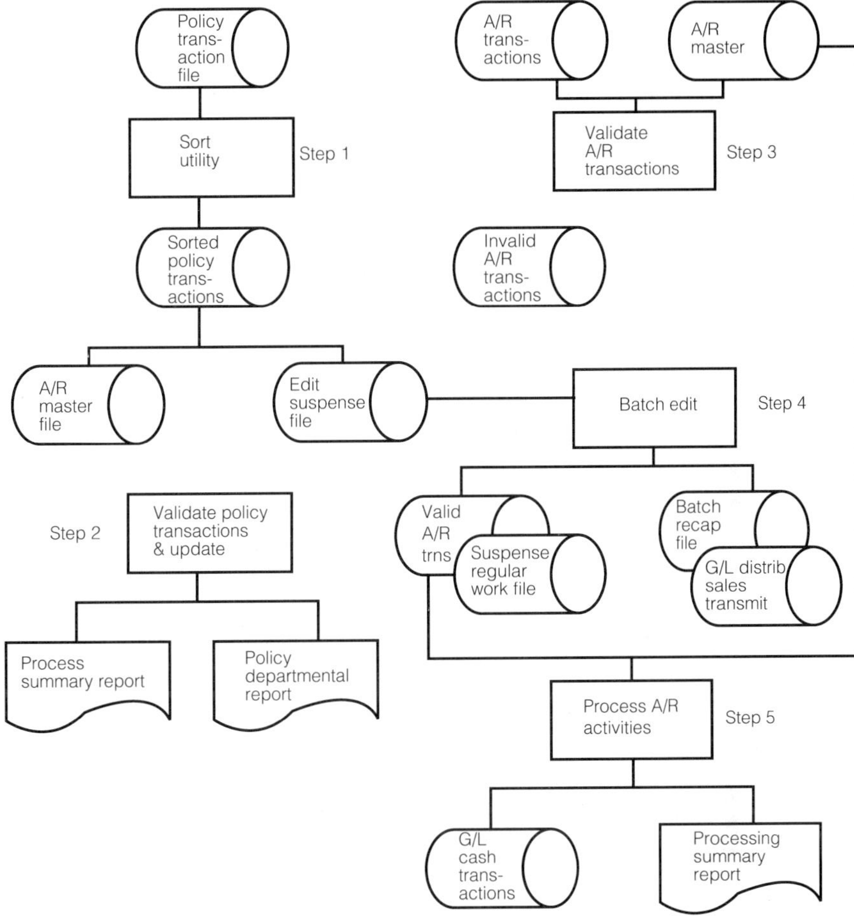

Figure 8.1 Hierarchical testing environment.

Integration testing. Integration testing is in place to consolidate a number of previously completed and tested units (programs) into a logical module or subsystem. The primary directive of the integration test is to verify the anticipated relationship(s) and a mandatory coexistence among the various program units.

The criteria set for integration-testing procedures assumes that each program is fully operational in its own individual environment; thus, it is the relationship among the units that is being heavily emphasized in this cycle—hidden problems that tend to surface, for example, in one program that passes data to another. Integration testing, in essence, is a miniature system test where a module or a subsystem is being reviewed for consistency and procedural integrity.

For example, in a payroll system, you might want to test the deduction cycle, which might include as many as 15 to 20 application programs, as opposed to testing the entire payroll system.

System testing. System testing requires an environment in which all the components of a system, as verified by the results of the integration test cycle, are fully operational. System tests are designed for verification purposes and not for uncovering major flaws in the design of the system. While a comprehensive system test will underscore such a deficiency, it might be too late to remedy problems that are just too pervasive.

System testing is merely a tool to test and verify the results of an integration test, how all the parts work jointly (encompassing both batch and on-line systems and subroutines), and call programs external interfaces even the operating system. A top-down diagram of these various test environments is presented in Figure 8.2.

In this diagram, the testing of the entire payroll system can begin only when there is a "green light" from prior test results, primarily from the integration test cycle, which assumes the completion of all the planned units: the federal and state tax cycle, programs handling all the professional dues, the gross-to-net register, voluntary and involuntary deductions, etc. Because the success and the apparent cohesiveness of the integration test depends largely on the individual units, it is necessary, better yet, mandatory that each program be functionally complete at this time.

Volume testing. Volume testing is critical because it emulates typical production environments in terms of the volume and often times the complexity of the incoming data. Volume testing is also referred to as a "stress test" because of the stress that a heavy load places upon the new system. In real-time environments, for example, this means that instead of a lone terminal providing data input, there is a full-blown production complement with tens, maybe hundreds of CRT operators (depending on the size of the corporation) bombarding the new system—just like in a real-life situation.

One of the most crucial goals of real-time volume testing is the verification of response time, given this stressful but nonetheless real (production-oriented) environment. Response time is crucial because it is one of the few items that is visible to the user. Unexpectedly lengthy response time can scrap a system even this late in

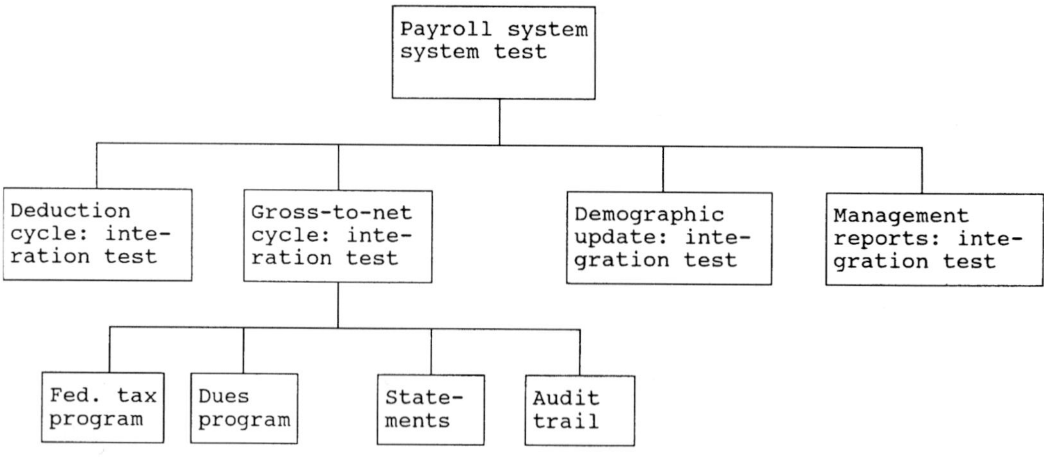

Figure 8.2 Top-down test environments.

the process, especially if it cannot be fine-tuned in retrospect. In batch systems, the heavy reliance on CPU cycles may be due to a number of internal problems, such as poorly designed VSAM clusters, a program typically trying to do too many things beyond its operational modularity, and so on.

Think of the process of paralleling two systems as a complete test environment, in which the results of all tests are comparatively evaluated and the discrepancies discussed and consequently resolved. Does the new system perform as accurately as the old? Do the modified or updated procedures in the new system yield satisfactory results, not just in comparison with the old system, but in a broad general sense?

The results of the parallel test are compared, but they might not truly measure the efficiency of the new system. After all, the old system could have been reasonably deficient in certain aspects, which is the very reason for its replacement.

8.2 What CA-InterTest Will Buy You

CA-InterTest, a product initially of On-Line Software International, now owned by Computer Associates, is an interactive testing productivity tool for CICS applications written in COBOL, COBOL II, PL/1, and Basic Assembler (BAL) languages. What CA-InterTest buys you is a system with which you can debug your application program effectively. It will prevent crashes by automatically detecting and preventing application errors before they damage CICS. When compared to the Execute Diagnostics Facility software, a broad user-based IBM product (see chapter 19 for more detail on CICS-supplied transactions), CA-InterTest is clearly a much more comprehensive (and also a great deal more expensive) product for several reasons:

CA-InterTest and CA-InterTest/Batch help programmers test and debug not only CICS-command and macro-level transactions, but also conventional batch COBOL programs—those that in reality have nothing to do with interactive processing. This is quite important because programmers are just as vulnerable to producing erroneous logic in their conventional batch programs as in a purely interactive environment.

When CA-InterTest monitors a COBOL program, for example, it detects and thus prevents storage violations and CICS abends, the abnormal termination of tasks, and potential crashes that might occur in a command- or macro-level program. Because CA-InterTest will not permit errors to execute that could damage CICS, it keeps both test and production systems stable. Also, it will prevent a program error from damaging other programs executing in the same region.

One of the big pluses of the product is that it enables you to correct errors on the fly (correct them dynamically, so to speak) so that you can continue the process of uninterrupted testing. When an error occurs, you normally need to correct and recompile the program, which is a conventional way to do business, but with CA-InterTest you can correct or go around errors and continue testing. This means many errors can be detected in a single debugging session.

CA-InterTest automatically suspends the execution of an application program through an automatic breakpoint when it detects:

- Any storage violation
- Any CICS abend in a command-level program

- Any improper or invalid CICS request
- Any statement that would cause a program check or other abend
- Any illegal or invalid instruction (e.g., STOP RUN)
- Any wild branch
- Any violation of CICS standards

Breakpoints can also be set by you, the programmer, to suspend the continued execution of a program at any location in your source code. Breakpoints are quite easy to set; you can do them through a command line, through a menu, and even by entering a character next to a source statement. You can set these breakpoints symbolically (by paragraph name) if you're a COBOL programmer, or by PL/1 or BAL labels. When you need to reset the breakpoints, CA-InterTest will do it for you, and also reset all the monitoring options in the new version of the program so you can resume testing exactly where you left off.

Actually, breakpoints are very useful because you can set them conditionally or unconditionally. For example, you might want to stop the processing of an application program at a specific paragraph only if a data field in working storage has a specific value. You can also request breakpoints prior to all CICS commands and macros, calls to DL/1 and DB2, and calls to subroutines. This means that you can set breakpoints at all CICS requests or just at a specific type, such as at all READ and WRITE requests. You can also single-step; that is, stop the execution of your program after one or a specified number of COBOL verbs have executed.

When program execution is suspended, CA-InterTest explains why the program was halted and provides much useful information, including:

- What program statement triggered the breakpoint
- The reason for the stoppage
- A trace history of the latest branches of the program
- An explanation of the error and how to use CA-InterTest to continue testing

You can resume program execution from the point of suspension, or you can start executing from a completely different location in your program. The advantage of this kind of flexibility is that you can "go around" any error without correcting it permanently.

Because you can reference all program locations symbolically (rather than by hexadecimal address locations), that is by the names you have defined in your program, you don't have to worry about calculating (or miscalculating, as the case may be) the locations of certain key data fields. So symbolic support means you don't have to perform an old systems-software activity: looking at core dumps. When you want to display the value of a data item, CA-InterTest will present a structured main-storage display that indicates the name of the data item and its character and hexadecimal representation.

You can test and debug composite modules, that is modules consisting of separately compiled (or assembled) parts, and link edited modules into one load module, even if the separate modules are written in different languages. Thus, you can test each subprogram as if it were a separate unit, so complex programs can be more efficiently debugged.

Last, you can display or change auxiliary storage such as VSAM and BDAM files; DL /1, DB2, and SQL/DS databases; temporary storage; and transient data. You can also use this facility to generate test data and add, update, and delete records.

8.3 The Interactive Test Mechanism

The system's interactive mechanism is highlighted in Figure 8.3. Allow me to briefly summarize each of the components or transactions (in addition to the chart in 8.3) and then provide you with some "live" examples of how to invoke and use them.

The LIST transaction allows you to display source listing and compiler information on-line. This is helpful because it enables you to have access to information, such as maps, cross reference tables, and messages—information your on-line editor cannot provide for you. Also, the source listing display is available whether or not a program is executing or is stopped at a breakpoint. There are, of course, a number of advantages in dealing with source listing. First and foremost is that there is a considerable amount of time you can save by not having to wait for a time-consuming printout. Directly from the source listing, you monitor a program, set and remove breakpoints, change the location from which to resume program execution, and access main and auxiliary storage.

In the two frames shown in Figures 8.4 and 8.5, I have requested and received a source listing through the LIST option. I entered the program (ID) and ARM70C next to the Program= heading (Figure 8.4), then pressed the Enter key. CA-InterTest displayed the source listing, illustrated in Figure 8.5.

The CNTL transaction, short for Controlling Program Monitoring, controls the way CA-InterTest monitors a particular application program. Monitoring is the process by which CA-InterTest detects and prevents errors. Monitoring options include break-

LIST	Display on-line COBOL, COBOL II, PL/1, and BAL source listings and compiler output, and invoke other CA-InterTest functions
CNTL	Control program monitoring
CORE	Inspect and modify main storage
FILE	Display and update CICS files (VSAM, BDAM), DL/I, DB2, and SQL/DS databases, temporary storage, and transient data
HELP	Obtain on-line HELP in using CA-InterTest and in resolving common CICS abends
SymDump	Analyze dumps on-line using a program's symbolic listing, and manage the dump data set

Figure 8.3 CA-InterTest's interactive mechanism.

```
                  OSI INTERTEST - SOURCE LISTING DISPLAY

Program= arm70c    Option #        Stmt #                             Margin= 01
                   Label/Search Arg=
OPTS 1 Procedure div   2 Working-storage   3 Linkage sect  4 D-map 5 Clist/Pmap
     6 Xref      7 Procedure names     8 Error msgs     9 Search fwd 10 Search bwd
PFKS 1 Help      2 Cntl Menu 3 End     4 List Profile  5 Set Monitor 6 Core Menu
     7 Backward 8 Forward    9        10                11            12 File
--------------------------------------------------------------------------------

                          InterTest Release 3.1

                              COPYRIGHT 1985
                    On-Line Software International, Inc.
                            ALL RIGHTS RESERVED
                   800-TECHOSI (USA)      800-257-9426 (CANADA)
```

Figure 8.4 Panel to enter the name of a module for listing.

```
                  CA-INTERTEST - SOURCE LISTING DISPLAY

Program= ARM70C  Option #       Stmt #                              Margin= 01
                  Label/Search Arg=
OPTS 1 Procedure div   2 Working-storage   3 Linkage sect  4 D-map 5 Clist/Pmap
     6 Xref      7 Procedure names     8 Error msgs     9 Search fwd 10 Search bwd
PFKS 1 Help      2 Cntl Menu 3 End     4 List Profile  5 Set Monitor 6 Core Menu
     7 Backward 8 Forward    9        10                11            12 File
--------------------------------------------------------------------------------
   00001 ID DIVISION.
   00002 PROGRAM-ID. ARM70C.
   00003 ENVIRONMENT DIVISION.
   00004 DATA DIVISION.
   00005 WORKING-STORAGE SECTION.
   00006 77   S999-FIELD1            PIC S9(3).
   00007 77   S999-FIELD2            PIC S9(3)         VALUE +50.
   00008 77   999-FIELD1             PIC 9(3).
   00009 77   999-FIELD2             PIC 9(3)          VALUE 50.
   00010 77   COMMAREA-LEN           PIC S9(4) COMP   VALUE +59.
   00011 77   LINK-COMMAREA-LEN      PIC S9(4) COMP   VALUE +10.
   00012 77   TSQ-LEN                PIC S9(4) COMP   VALUE +59.
   00013 77   REC-LEN                PIC S9(4) COMP.
   00014 77   NUP-LEN                PIC S9(4) COMP   VALUE +28.
   00015 77   RFC-OFF-LEN            PIC S9(4) COMP   VALUE +43.
```

Figure 8.5 The listing of a source program.

points and other features that let you create testing scenarios to meet the needs of your program.

I recommend that you experiment with CA-InterTest at your leisure. Instruct CA-InterTest to monitor your program. Set breakpoints at the beginning of the Procedure Division and at key paragraph names. If CA-InterTest detects an error and automatically halts program execution, simply press PF1 to get tutorial assistance. When the program is stopped at a breakpoint (either automatically invoked by CA-InterTest because it detected an error, or set by you), you can examine and modify main storage, examine and modify files and databases, page through the source listing, set additional breakpoints and other options, and resume execution from any program location.

In order to use CA-InterTest, compile or assemble your program in CA-InterTest mode. The JCL shown in Figures 8.6A through 8.6C allows you to compile a COBOL

```
//NIRAV70C JOB (9000,PPOT),'ARM70C TO DEVO',
//         MSGLEVEL=(1,1),
//         MSGCLASS=X,
//         NOTIFY=NIRAV,
//         CLASS=A
/*OUTPUT RMIS F=ZX01
//PANSTEP  EXEC PGM=PAN#1,PARM='OPEN=INP'
//PANDD1    DD  DSN=NIRXT.TEST.PANLIB,DISP=SHR
//PANDD11   DD  DSN=NIRXP.PROD.PANLIB,DISP=SHR
//SYSPRINT DD   SYSOUT=*
//PANDD2    DD  DSN=&&SOURCE,UNIT=SYSDA,DISP=(NEW,PASS),
//              SPACE=(CYL,(2,2),RLSE),
//              DCB=(LRECL=80,RECFM=FB,BLKSIZE=6000)
//SYSIN DD *
++WRITE WORK,ARM70C
/*
//*
//*******************************************************************
//* COMMAND LEVEL TRANSLATION
//*******************************************************************
//*
//TRANS     EXEC   PGM=DFHECP1$
//STEPLIB   DD   DSN=CICS211.DEVO.LOADLIB,DISP=SHR
//SYSPRINT DD SYSOUT=(*,,RMIS)
//SYSPUNCH DD DSN=&&SYSCIN,DCB=BLKSIZE=400,
//             DISP=(,PASS),UNIT=3380,
//             SPACE=(CYL,(1,1))
//*
//SYSIN DD DSN=&&SOURCE,DISP=(OLD,DELETE)
//C       EXEC PGM=IKFCBL00,REGION=512K,
// PARM=(NONUM,DMAP,VERB,CLIST,SXREF,L120,LCOL1,
//      NOSEQ,LIB,'SIZE=512K,BUF=20K,LANGLVL(1)',APOST,NOADV)
//SYSLIB DD    DSN=NIRXT.PO.TEST.COPYLIB,DISP=SHR
//        DD   DSN=NIRXT.TEST.COPYLIB,DISP=SHR
//        DD   DSN=CICS211.COBLIB,DISP=SHR
//SYSPRINT DD DSN=&&INPUT,DISP=(,PASS),UNIT=TEMP,
//  SPACE=(TRK,(15,5)),
//  DCB=(DSORG=PS,LRECL=121,BLKSIZE=2420,RECFM=FBA)
//SYSIN DD DSN=&&SYSCIN,DISP=(OLD,PASS)
//SYSLIN DD DSN=&&LOADSET,DISP=(MOD,PASS),
//        UNIT=TEMP,SPACE=(80,(250,100))
//SYSUT1 DD UNIT=TEMP,SPACE=(460,(350,100))
//SYSUT2 DD UNIT=TEMP,SPACE=(460,(350,100))
//SYSUT3 DD UNIT=TEMP,SPACE=(460,(350,100))
//SYSUT4 DD UNIT=TEMP,SPACE=(460,(350,100))
//*
```

Figure 8.6A JCLs required to compile a COBOL program using PANLIB and CA-InterTest, page 1.

```
//*****************************************************************
//* CA-InterTest - GENERATE PARMS
//*****************************************************************
//GENPARM  EXEC PGM=IN25PARM,COND=(4,LT),
//            PARM=('ARM70C,CUTPRINT=ALL,LISTER=MAP')
//STEPLIB  DD DISP=SHR,DSN=CICS211.INTRTST.LOADLIB
//CARDS    DD DSN=&&CARDS,DISP=(,PASS),UNIT=SYSDA,SPACE=(TRK,(1,1))
//*****************************************************************
//* CA-InterTest POST PROCESSOR
//*****************************************************************
//POSTCOB  EXEC PGM=IN25SYMC,COND=(4,LT),REGION=512K
//STEPLIB  DD DISP=SHR,DSN=CICS211.INTRTST.LOADLIB
//SYSUDUMP DD SYSOUT=*
//INPUT    DD DISP=(OLD,PASS),DSN=&&INPUT
//OUTPUT   DD SYSOUT=*,DCB=(RECFM=FBA,LRECL=121,BLKSIZE=2420)
//MESSAGE  DD SYSOUT=(*,,RMIS)
//PROTSYM  DD DISP=SHR,DSN=CICS211.INTRTST.PROTSYM
//CARDS    DD DSN=&&CARDS,DISP=(OLD,DELETE)
//*
//DMAPSTEP EXEC  PGM=CWPCDRVR,REGION=4M COND=(4,LT)
//STEPLIB  DD   DSN=CICS211.ABAID410.LOAD,DISP=SHR
//CWPPRTI  DD   DSN=&&INPUT,DISP=(OLD,PASS)
//CWPERRM  DD   SYSOUT=(*,,RMIS)
//CWPPRTO  DD   SYSOUT=(*,,RMIS)
//SYSOUT   DD   SYSOUT=(*,,RMIS)
//SORTWK01 DD   DSN=&&SRTWRK1,DISP=(NEW,DELETE,DELETE),
//              SPACE=(TRK,(60,30)),UNIT=SYSDA,
//              DCB=(LRECL=300,BLKSIZE=304)
//CWPWRK0  DD   DSN=&&WORK0,DISP=(NEW,DELETE,DELETE),
//              DCB=(BLKSIZE=19000),
//              SPACE=(TRK,(60,30)),UNIT=SYSDA
//CWPWRK1  DD   DSN=&&WORK1,DISP=(NEW,DELETE,DELETE),
//              DCB=(BLKSIZE=19000),
//              SPACE=(TRK,(60,30)),UNIT=SYSDA
//CWPWRK2  DD   DSN=&&WORK2,DISP=(NEW,DELETE,DELETE),
//              DCB=(BLKSIZE=19000),
//              SPACE=(TRK,(60,30)),UNIT=SYSDA
//CWPWRK3  DD   DSN=&&WORK3,DISP=(NEW,DELETE,DELETE),
//              DCB=(BLKSIZE=19000),
//              SPACE=(TRK,(60,30)),UNIT=SYSDA
//CWPWRK4  DD   DSN=&&WORK4,DISP=(NEW,DELETE,DELETE),
//              DCB=(BLKSIZE=19000),
//              SPACE=(TRK,(60,30)),UNIT=SYSDA
//CWPLOAD  DD   DUMMY
//CWPDDIO  DD   DISP=SHR,DSN=CICS211.ABAID410.LISTING
//SYSUDUMP DD   SYSOUT=*
//SYSPRINT DD   SYSOUT=*
//*
```

Figure 8.6B JCLs required to compile a COBOL program using PANLIB and CA-InterTest, page 2.

source program in such a manner. The CA-InterTest postprocessor step executes after the compiler step and writes the program information to its symbolic file.

The following JCLs are merely a "shell" that most likely will require customizing to conform to your specific operational environment. Once the compile is successful, update your CICS program by issuing a NEWCOPY statement (see chapter 19 for more detail on this), and then start by entering CNTL.

The CORE transaction enables you to display and modify data in CICS main storage. Using the various CORE functions and displays, you can modify and correct application software, and fine-tune your CICS system without having to wait for and wade through time-consuming dumps. For example, you can set a breakpoint to stop the execution of your program at a specified place and then change the values of data items through the CORE transaction. For example, CORE allows you to initialize an internal WORKING-STORAGE counter in order to avoid a potential ASRA (data exception) situation. Of course, changes to main storage are temporary changes. In order to make the changes permanent, you must change your source code and recompile the program.

The CORE facility enables you to change variable and constant data internal to your program. You can also use it to access and modify CICS control blocks and table entries. When you have completed looking at the various snapshots, CORE allows you to analyze each problem in detail.

In Figure 8.7, I requested a structured CORE display of the PPT (Program Processing Table) by specifying PPT on the System-Related Areas menu, and pressing PF12. CA-InterTest responded with the formatted display shown in Figure 8.8.

As you can see in Figure 8.8, when you issue a CORE request, the appropriate areas of main storage appear on your terminal in a structured, easy-to-read format. The traditional dump format is also available. You can quickly see the character and hexadecimal representation of each field. The hexadecimal display area looks at each byte as two hexadecimal values. Each line is 16 bytes long and, for conve-

```
//* THE POST-PROCESSOR PARAMETERS COME FROM THE FOLLOWING PDS
//*
//CWPPRMO   DD   DSN=CICS211.ABAID410.SORCMAC(CCACBLO),DISP=SHR
//*WPPRMO   DD   DSN=NIRXT.RM.TEST.CNTL(CCACBLO),DISP=SHR
//*
//*
//PRINT EXEC PGM=IEBGENER,COND=(35,NE,C)
//SYSPRINT DD SYSOUT=*
//SYSIN DD DUMMY
//SYSUT1 DD DSN=&&INPUT,DISP=(OLD,DELETE)
//SYSUT2 DD SYSOUT=(*,,RMIS)
//*
//LKED     EXEC PGM=IEWL,REGION=512K,
//         PARM='XREF,LIST,LET',COND=(5,LT,C)
//SYSLIB DD   DSN=CICS211.DEVO.LOADLIB,DISP=SHR
//         DD   DSN=SYS1.VSCLLIB,DISP=SHR
//SYSLMOD DD DSN=NIRXT.TEST.CICS.LOADLIB(ARM70C),DISP=SHR
//SYSUT1 DD   UNIT=TEMP,DCB=BLKSIZE=1024,
//         SPACE=(1024,(200,20))
//SYSPRINT DD   SYSOUT=(*,,RMIS)
//SYSLIN DD    DSN=CICS211.COBLIB(DFHEILIC),DISP=SHR
//         DD DSN=&&LOADSET,DISP=(OLD,DELETE)
//*        DD   DDNAME=SYSIN
//
//*
```

Figure 8.6C JCLs required to compile a COBOL program using PANLIB and CA-InterTest, page 3.

```
      OSI InterTest CORE COMMAND BUILDER - SYSTEM-RELATED AREAS  (CORE=Syst)
Specify AREA, ADDRESS, TABLE or PROGRAM to be displayed or changed:
  CICS AREA:  ppt_      CSA, PCT, PPT, FCT, TCT, DCT, SIT      ADDRESS: ________
                        PAM, TRT, OPFL, ATRT, ADCH, SDCH
  CICS TABLE entry:     PPT ________  FCT ________  PCT ____  TCT ____  DCT ____
  To display PROGRAM:   ________      ENTER L to load, D to delete or M for map: _
Optional offset: ______________________________
Scan value: ___________________________________                 Data  Formats
Scan range: ______          B to scan backwards: _         ----------------
                                                           | P' ' = Packed |
To VERIFY and/or CHANGE data:                              | X' ' = Hex    |
Existing data: ______________________________              | C' ' = Char   |
     New data: ______________________________              ----------------
Press PF12 (structure display) or ENTER (dump display), or select PF key:
1 Help       2 CNTL        3 End       4 Source     5 CORE=Task     6 CORE=Bkpt
7 FILE       8             9 BMSG     10           11 CORE=Syst    12 Structure
```

Figure 8.7 CA-InterTest responds with a formatted display (shown in Figure 8.8).

```
             CA-InterTest - MAIN STORAGE UTILITY - Termid = A01I
   Name      Address  Disp              Hexadecimal                  Character

DFHPPTDS     1364A4    0 |
PPTPI        1364A4    0 | C1C4C7C1 C3D6D4D7                        | ADGACOMP
PPTDASA      1364AC    8 | 00000000                                 | ....
PPTCSA       1364B0    C | 00000000                                 | ....
PPTSAR       1364B4   10 | 00000000                                 | ....
PPTENTD      1364B8   14 | 00000000                                 | ....
PPTENL       1364BC   18 | 0028                                     | ..
PPTDSRSL     1364BE   1A | 00                                       | .
PPTTLR       1364BF   1B | 00                                       | .
PPTTLR2      1364C0   1C | 60                                       | -
PPTFLGS      1364C1   1D | 00                                       | .
PPTTYPE      1364C2   1E | 80                                       | .
PPTFLGS2     1364C3   1F | 00                                       | .
PPTVSPLI     1364C3   1F | 00                                       | .
PPTRCC       1364C4   20 | 000C                                     | ..
PPTFCH       1364C6   22 | 0000                                     | ..
-----------------------------------------------------------------------------
PFKEYS 1 Help  2 Cntl Menu  3 End  4 Source  5 File  6 Core Menu
7 Backward 8 Forward  9 Caps Off 10 Next Entry 11 Redisplay 12 Structure
  CORE=PPT
```

Figure 8.8 Structured display of the PPT.

nience and readability, a space is inserted between every four bytes. The character-display area shows the same 16 bytes as characters. Nondisplayable bytes are shown as periods.

Suppose you need to change some value or values in CORE. For example, suppose I need to change the value of the STATE data field corresponding to a particular customer on file, from Illinois to Indiana (IL to IN).

Figure 8.9 shows an unconditional breakpoint that was set earlier in the program to suspend operation at the paragraph 008-MOVE-FIELDS. (More on this in the following section dealing with the setting and the removal of breakpoints.) To display the contents of CUSTOMER-STATE, simply key in D (for display) next to any statement referencing the data item, place the cursor under any character in the data item, and press Enter, as illustrated in Figure 8.9.

CA-InterTest will then display the contents of the data item and all items below it in the same COBOL, PL/1, or Assembler DSECT structure, as shown in Figure 8.10. Now you can simply overtype the IL with IN to change the value of CUSTOMER-STATE. Either the character or hexadecimal representation can be changed.

```
                    CA-INTERTEST - SOURCE LISTING BREAKPOINT

Program= ARM70C   Option #       Stmt #                        Margin= 01
                  Label/Search Arg=
OPTS 1 Procedure div   2 Working-storage   3 Linkage sect  4 D-map 5 Clist/Pmap
     6 Xref      7 Procedure names     8 Error msgs     9 Search fwd 10 Search bwd
PFKS 1 Help      2 Cntl Menu 3 End     4 List Profile   5 Set Monitor 6 Core Menu
     7 Backward 8 Forward   9          10              11            12 File
-------------------------------------------------------------------------------
   01187          MOVE 'DMAP05' TO MAPNAME
   01188          GO TO SEND-REWRITE-RETURN.
 U 01189 008-MOVE-FIELDS.
 d 01190      MOVE CUSTOMER-STATE TO STATEO.
   01191      MOVE CUSTOMER-NAME TO CUSTNAMO.
   01192 CICS-LOOP.
   01193*EXEC CICS ASKTIME
   01194*          END-EXEC.
   01195       MOVE '          00976     ' TO DFHEIV0
   01196      CALL 'DFHEI1' USING DFHEIV0.
   01197
   01198 MXS-OPTION.
   01199      IF  TASK-SWITCH3 EQUAL SPACE
   01200          MOVE 'A' TO TASK-SWITCH3
   01201          MOVE 'DMAP06' TO MAPNAME
```

Figure 8.9 Requesting a structured display of CUSTOMER-STATE.

```
          CA-InterTest - MAIN STORAGE UTILITY - Termid = A01I
   Starting at Address = 05D0B7        Hexadecimal                 Character

 02 CUSTOMER-STATE       | C9D3                               | IL
 02 CUSTOMER-NAME        | C1D3D3C9 C5C4                      | ALLIED
                         |                                    |
----------------------------------------------------------------------------

PFKEYS 1 Help     2 Cntl Menu 3 End       4 Source       5 File        6 Core Menu
       7 Backward 8 Forward   9 Caps Off 10 Next Entry 11 Redisplay 12 Structure
         CORE='CUSTOMER-STATE'
```

Figure 8.10 Structured main storage display of CUSTOMER-STATE.

```
                    CA-INTERTEST - SOURCE LISTING BREAKPOINT

Program= ARM70C   Option #        Stmt #                          Margin= 01
                  Label/Search Arg=
OPTS 1 Procedure div   2 Working-storage   3 Linkage sect  4 D-map 5 Clist/Pmap
     6 Xref      7 Procedure names    8 Error msgs    9 Search fwd 10 Search bwd
PFKS 1 Help      2 Cntl Menu 3 BKPT   4 List Profile  5 Continue    6 Core Menu
     7 Backward 8 Forward   9 Abend 10 Do    1 Verb  11 Backtrace  12 File
-----------------------------------------------------------------------------

MOVE ZERO______________________________ to COUNTER

Overtype Underscores with a Data-Name, Figurative Constant,
Alphanumeric Literal, or Numeric Literal
```

Figure 8.11 Using the MOVE command to change the value of a date item.

```
                    CA-INTERTEST - SOURCE LISTING BREAKPOINT

Program= ARC92C   Option #        Stmt #                          Margin= 01
                  Label/Search Arg=
Command ===>                                                      PF4=Profile
 -----------------------------------------------------------------------------
|  COUNTER                   |          000000                 |              |
 -----------------------------------------------------------------------------
   00880 CONTINUE-TASK.
   00881**** COUNTER *NOTE* FIELD MUST BE INITIALIZED
 A    ==>       ADD +1 TO COUNTER.
   00883        IF COUNTER = 1
   00884            MOVE 'DMAPASR'  TO MAPNAME.
   00885        IF COUNTER = 2
   00886            MOVE 'DMAPSUM'  TO MAPNAME.
   00887        IF COUNTER GREATER 2
   00888            GO TO SEND-END-MSG.
   00889        GO TO REWRITE-TSQ.
   00890 REWRITE-TSQ.
   00891*EXEC CICS WRITEQ TS
   00892*           REWRITE
   00893*           QUEUE(TSQ-NAME)
   00894*           FROM(TASK-STRUCTURE)
   00895*           LENGTH(TSQ-LEN)
```

Figure 8.12 Viewing a data item in the Keep Window.

Another easy way to change main storage is via the MOVE command. With the MOVE command, you don't have to know the type of data (binary, packed, etc.) or its length. CA-InterTest takes care of all the details for you. To access the command, type M next to any statement referencing a data item, place the cursor under a character in the data item, and press Enter. CA-InterTest will display the MOVE statement, as illustrated in Figure 8.11.

A third way to view and change the value of a data item is to put it in the Keep Window of the source-listing display, as illustrated in Figure 8.12. Up to six items can be displayed in the Keep Window. The Keep Window lets you observe how the values of data items change as the program executes, without leaving the source-listing display. Also, you can overtype the character or hexadecimal representation of a data item in the Keep Window to change its value. For example, to initialize the data item COUNTER displayed in the Keep Window of Figure 8.12, simply replace the last 0 with C.

The CA-InterTest HELP module provides on-line tutorial assistance. HELP is designed to help you learn the system from scratch or to answer a specific question. To invoke the HELP module, simply press PF1 from any CA-InterTest screen.

Whenever your program is halted at an automatic breakpoint, you can press PF1 to see why the error occurred. Normally, the tutorial will suggest some corrective measures and how to use CA-InterTest in particular situations. Figure 8.13 shows the introductory CA-InterTest screen that lets you access any CA-InterTest function. Figure 8.14 is the CA-InterTest Help Facility Master Menu that provides you with

```
                    CA-InterTest TRANSACTION CODES

CA-InterTest is a productivity tool that will make your CICS testing faster,
easier, and more effective. The following transactions are available:

LIST    To display compiler and assembler output, set and remove breakpoints,
        view and modify data variables, and control program execution
CNTL    To set and remove breakpoints and monitoring options, control
        program execution, and report on monitoring activity
CORE    To display or modify main storage
FILE    To display or modify any CICS file, or DL/I or DB2 database
HELP    To obtain assistance in using InterTest
SYMD    To display transaction dumps symbolically

                                            CA-InterTest Release 4.2
 Please enter any transaction code                  COPYRIGHT 1985
 or press ENTER for HELP menu:
                                         Computer Associates International
                                                ALL RIGHTS RESERVED
```

Figure 8.13 Introductory CA-InterTest Panel.

```
                  CA-INTERTEST - INTERACTIVE HELP FACILITY
              TUTORIAL: CA-InterTest HELP Facility Master Menu

                        01 Program Monitoring
                        02 The BREAKPOINT Facility
                        03 The FILE Facility
                        04 The CORE Facility
                        05 The SOURCE LISTING Facility
                        06 The SYMBOLIC DUMP Facility - SYMDUMP
                        07 The CNTL and CORE MENUS
                        08 Miscellaneous
                        09 New Release Features

-------------------------------------------------------------------------------
ENTER A SELECTION CODE FROM THE MENU, OR N FOR NEXT PAGE, P FOR PRECEDING PAGE,
 M FOR RETURN TO PREVIOUS MENU. PRESS CLEAR TO EXIT.          SELECTION ==> 01
```

Figure 8.14 CA-InterTest Help Facility Master Menu.

specific information for each function. You can browse the entire HELP system or select specific topics for viewing.

You can use the FILE transaction to provide a quick and easy way of updating files or creating test data without having to write a utility program. You can use the FILE transaction to display and modify CICS files as well as temporary storage and transient data sets. CA-InterTest is also functional with databases such as DB/2 or IMS.

You can use the FILE transaction when the program you are testing stops at a breakpoint. In addition, you can also use FILE to view, add, update, and delete records even when a program is not executing. In Figure 8.15, I have entered the DD name for the file RK501 and pressed the Enter key to access basic information on the file.

In order to browse a few records in that file, starting with the first record, and to continue in a forward (browse) manner, press PF2 and then PF4 to begin the browse operation. The result of this request is shown in Figure 8.16.

You can browse forward or backward, just like in a CICS browse transaction. You can use PF7, PF8, PF10, and 11 to scan either up or down the panel or left and right to attain a full view of the file.

The best way to understand the FILE transaction is to think of it as a generalized application program that issues CICS macros and operates in a conversational mode. Thus, you can use the FILE transaction at any time—even when CA-InterTest is inactive.

When you are using the FILE transaction, you do your processing in a work area, not to be confused with a data record. It is simply a working storage area owned by the FILE transaction, which stores and provides current data as needed. The work area does not exist when you first activate the FILE transaction. It is created in re-

```
DATATYPE= FC FILEID= RK501     MODE=           LOG=OFF TODEST=          PASSWORD=
FUNC=        SUBFUNC=       RETMETH=           ARGTYP=      SRCHTYP=
MESSAGE=
 RETNRCID=                                                                CHGLEN=
    RCID=
    DATA=                                                                 SIZE= 0000
FORMAT= D 00112233 44556677 8899AABB CCDDEEFF  *0123456789ABCDEF*
LOC 0000  ........ ........ ........ ........   ................
                                                                          DSORG=VSKS
                                                                          RECFM=FB
                                                                          LRECL=044C
                                                                          BLKSIZE=0000
                                                                          KEYPOS=0001
                                                                          KEYLEN=23
                                                                          STRNO=02

                                                                          READ
                                                                          ADD
                                                                          UPDATE
                                                                          BROWSE
                                                                          DELETE
--------------------------------------------------------------------------------
1 Help       2 Format C   3 End        4 BEGB        5              6 DataType DL
7 Page bwd   8 Page fwd   9 Caps Off  10 Top        11 Bottom      12
```

Figure 8.15 Displaying file information for RK501.

```
DATATYPE= FC FILEID= RK501     MODE=BROWSELOG=OFF TODEST=          PASSWORD=
FUNC= NEXT SUBFUNC=       RETMETH=         ARGTYP=      SRCHTYP=
MESSAGE=
 RETNRCID=                                                          CHGLEN=
    RCID=
    DATA=                                                           SIZE= 00681
FORMAT= C 00000000011111111112222222222333333333344444444445
LOC 00001 12345678901234567890123456789012345678901234567890
          ..................................................       DSORG=VSKS
 00001             THIS IS NOT A NAME  D  1                        RECFM=FB
 00051                                     S...............S...    LRECL=044C
 00101    .A..........S.....A.........S......A........S.....       BLKSIZE=00000
 00151    ..A.......S.........Z......S.........Z.....S.......      KEYPOS=0001
 00201    ...Z..............................................       KEYLEN=23
 00251    ..................................................       STRNO=02
 00301    ..................................................
 00351    ..................................................       READ
 00401    ..................................................       ADD
 00451    ..................................................       UPDATE
 00501    ..................................................       BROWSE
 00551    ..................................................       DELETE
-------------------------------------------------------------------------------
1 Help        2 Format V    3 End        4 ENDB        5 PREV        6 DataType DL
7 Page bwd    8 Page fwd    9 Caps Off  10 Top        11 Bottom     12
```

Figure 8.16 Displaying a record in character format.

sponse to your first successful input operation, like reading a file record or a temporary storage queue. Then, on each succeeding input operation, the data portion of the record is moved into the work area, replacing the previous work area.

Records and DL/1 segments can be viewed in character, dump, vertical, or structured format. Structured format, like the CORE main storage display, displays the record or segment on a field-by-field basis using COBOL or PL/1 01-level data names or Assembler DSECT names. A sample record in structured format is shown in Figure 8.17.

8.3.1 CA-SymDump

CA-SymDump is an optional CA-InterTest component that provides symbolic dump analysis for OS users. CA-SymDump allows users to view dumps symbolically. The statement that triggers the abend is automatically highlighted. All the facilities of CA-InterTest are available to help you resolve the abend. In addition, you can view formatted system areas, formatted trace table, and registers and displacement at the time of the abend.

CA-SymDump was designed to complement CA-InterTest, primarily in production systems where you do not want to monitor every task processed by the system. CA-SymDump lets you bring a dump “back to life.” CICS production dumps can be analyzed symbolically from any region. For example, you can debug production abends from your test region.

CA-SymDump also provides the tools you need to manage your dump data set. You can retain the dumps you want to view and print and discard the ones you don’t need.

```
DATATYPE= FC FILEID= PROTCPF  MODE=BROWSELOG=OFF TODEST=         PASSWORD=
FUNC= NEXT SUBFUNC=       RETMETH=         ARGTYP=      SRCHTYP=
MESSAGE= RECORD OBTAINED FOR VIEWING
RETNRCID=40C3D2D7E300000001                                       CHGLEN=
    RCID=
    DATA=                                                          SIZE= 02A9
FORMAT= S USE= COBDEMO.VSAM-AREA
LOC 0000             Name                      Hexadecimal          Character
--------------------------------------------------------------------------------
 01 VSAM-AREA                       |                                  |
 02 VSAM-KEY                        | 40C3D2D7 E3000000 01             |  CKPT....
 02 VSAM-NAME                       | 40404080 FE002C00 00003800       |   .........
                                    | 1C0000C3 D5E3D37E                | ...CNTL=
 02 FILLER                          | E2E3C1D9 E36BD7D9 D6D47EF0       | START,PROM=0
                                    | F2F06BD7 D9D6E77E F0F1F040       | 20,PROX=010
                                    | 40404080 FE002000 00005800       |   .........
                                    | 100000C3 D5E3D37E C9E3E3D9       | ...CNTL=ITTR
                                    | C1C3C56B                         | ACE,
 02 FILLER                          | D6C6C640 40404080 FE001800       | OFF    .....
                                    | 00007000 0B0000C3 D5E3D37E       | .......CNTL=
                                    | C1C2D76B D6D54080 FE002400       |  ABP,ON .....
--------------------------------------------------------------------------------
1 Help       2 Format D   3 End        4 ENDB        5 PREV        6 DataType DL
7 Page bwd   8 Page fwd   9 Caps Off  10 Top        11 Bottom     12
```

Figure 8.17 A record displayed in structured (field-by-field) format.

8.4 Setting and Removing Breakpoints

The purpose of this overview is to show you, in a step-by-step fashion, how a breakpoint is set in your COBOL program that will temporarily suspend the execution of that program.

In this case study, you will set both conditional and unconditional breakpoints, each of which can be used at different times and under varying circumstances. It will also highlight how to handle an abnormal termination of an application program, such as an AEIL (data set I.D. exception error) and get help in resolving a particular problem. Finally, I am going to show you how to remove one or a set of breakpoints once you have completed the task.

My first objective is to set an unconditional breakpoint in ARC92C, which is a change/update transaction program. Briefly, an unconditional breakpoint is one that causes a suspension during the execution process whenever execution reaches the specified location. Setting such a breakpoint lets you closely examine the code and the values of data items. You can slow down the execution process in your program to a pace where you can carefully analyze every statement for the soundness of its logic.

When the program stops at a breakpoint, you'll have access to vital resources, such as the contents of main storage and file records, to help you debug the problem. Let me walk you through this process of setting a breakpoint at a paragraph name.

In CICS, clear the screen and display the program's source listing by entering LIST=*program-name*, in this case LIST=ARC92C. CA-InterTest will display the program's source code, as illustrated in Figure 8.18.

To set an unconditional breakpoint at the SEND-MAP00 paragraph, specify 9 in the OPTION # field and the paragraph name in the LABEL/SEARCH ARG field. Thus, you will display the location in the listing, as illustrated in Figure 8.19. To set an unconditional breakpoint at this paragraph name, simply enter U next to the paragraph name and press Enter.

```
Program= ARC92C    Option #        Stmt #                                Margin= 01
                   Label/Search Arg=
OPTS 1 Procedure div   2 Working-storage   3 Linkage sect  4 D-map 5 Clist/Pmap
     6 Xref      7 Procedure names     8 Error msgs    9 Search fwd 10 Search bwd
PFKS 1 Help      2 Cntl Menu 3 End     4 List Profile  5 Set Monitor 6 Core Menu
     7 Backward 8 Forward   9        10               11              12 File
-------------------------------------------------------------------------------
   00001 ID DIVISION.
   00002 PROGRAM-ID. ARC92C.
   00003 ENVIRONMENT DIVISION.
   00004 DATA DIVISION.
   00005 WORKING-STORAGE SECTION.
   00006 77  S999-FIELD1              PIC S9(3).
   00007 77  S999-FIELD2              PIC S9(3)         VALUE +50.
   00008 77  999-FIELD1               PIC 9(3).
   00009 77  999-FIELD2               PIC 9(3)          VALUE 50.
   00010 77  COMMAREA-LEN             PIC S9(4) COMP    VALUE +59.
   00011 77  LINK-COMMAREA-LEN        PIC S9(4) COMP    VALUE +10.
   00012 77  TSQ-LEN                  PIC S9(4) COMP    VALUE +59.
   00013 77  REC-LEN                  PIC S9(4) COMP.
   00014 77  NUP-LEN                  PIC S9(4) COMP    VALUE +28.
   00015 77  RFC-OFF-LEN              PIC S9(4) COMP    VALUE +43.
```

Figure 8.18 Program source code.

```
                        CA-INTERTEST - SOURCE LISTING DISPLAY

Program= ARC92C    Option # 9      Stmt #                                Margin= 01
                   Label/Search Arg= SEND-MAP00
OPTS 1 Procedure div   2 Working-storage   3 Linkage sect  4 D-map 5 Clist/Pmap
     6 Xref      7 Procedure names     8 Error msgs    9 Search fwd 10 Search bwd
PFKS 1 Help      2 Cntl Menu 3 End     4 List Profile  5 Set Monitor 6 Core Menu
     7 Backward 8 Forward   9        10               11              12 File
-------------------------------------------------------------------------------
   00968*    CRITERIA. 01 IS FIRST ENTRY, 02 IS SECOND ... ETC.
   00969
 u 00970 SEND-MAP00.
   00971     IF  TASK-SWITCH2 LESS NUM-CHOICES
   00972         ADD 1, TASK-SWITCH2 GIVING REQCDI
   00973     ELSE
   00974         MOVE '01' TO REQCDO.
   00975     MOVE 99 TO TASK-SWITCH2.
   00976     MOVE SPACE TO TASK-SWITCH3.
   00977*EXEC CICS SEND
   00978*          MAP ('DMAP00')
   00979*          MAPSET ('IN25CMP')
   00980*          ERASE
   00981*          END-EXEC.
   00982      MOVE '  }       S     00807    ' TO DFHEIV0
```

Figure 8.19 Setting an unconditional breakpoint.

```
                    CA-INTERTEST - SOURCE LISTING DISPLAY

Program= ARC92C    Option #        Stmt #                              Margin= 01
                   Label/Search Arg=
OPTS 1 Procedure div   2 Working-storage    3 Linkage sect   4 D-map 5 Clist/Pmap
     6 Xref       7 Procedure names     8 Error msgs     9 Search fwd 10 Search bwd
PFKS 1 Help       2 Cntl Menu 3 End     4 List Profile   5 Set Monitor 6 Core Menu
     7 Backward 8 Forward    9          10               11              12 File
--------------------------------------------------------------------------------
   PROCEDURE NAMES                  DEFN      REFERENCE
   AFTER-REWRITE                    01313
   CICS-LOOP                        01192  01190
u  CONTINUE-TASK                    00880  00809 00873
   DATA-NAME                        01065
   DO-READ-VAR                      01084  01081
   EXPANDED-DEMO                    00956  00806 00877 00878
   GEN-ERR                          01274  00787 00839 01032
u  GETMAIN-LOOP                     01211  01209
   INITIALIZE-TABLE                 01059  01046
   LAST-SCREEN                      00939  00932
   LINK-COBDEML                     01366  01357
   LOOP-RTN                         01189
   MOVE-RECORD                      01133
u  MXR-OPTION                       01184  01357
```

Figure 8.20 Setting breakpoints at selected paragraph names.

To set breakpoints at multiple paragraph names, you can display a list of paragraph names (Option 7) and then type U next to all the names at which you want to set breakpoints, as illustrated in Figure 8.20.

Now you are ready to initiate the transaction that will execute ARC92C. Once the program is stopped at a breakpoint, you can do things in "slow motion," for example, look at the program instruction by instruction. This kind of analysis is very useful. You can also inspect and modify the contents of main storage or files or databases and inspect the backtrace.

When ARC92C executes and reaches SEND-MAP00, CA-InterTest halts execution at the unconditional breakpoint and displays the panel illustrated in Figure 8.21.

There are several options now at your disposal. You can simply "single-step" through ARC92C, executing it verb by verb (PF10), and review the results (and the associated logic) of each statement. Of course, you can change the step amount to execute more than one verb at a time. This is a powerful tool and it gives you all sorts of flexibility.

Suppose you decide to set a conditional breakpoint. A conditional breakpoint will halt execution at a specified location only when a condition is met; for example when a COUNTER exceeds a specified number. It is like an IF statement in a COBOL application program.

To set a conditional breakpoint, simply type C next to the statement or paragraph name where you want to halt execution. CA-InterTest will display the screen illustrated in Figure 8.22, on which you can specify the condition. In Figure 8.23, the condition MONTH NE MAY is specified. This means the breakpoint will occur only when the data item MONTH is not equal to MAY.

When an unconditional or conditional breakpoint is set, CA-InterTest displays a U or C next to the program location. To remove the breakpoint, just overtype the U or C with an X.

When a program is about to abnormally terminate, CA-InterTest will intercept and suspend the operation at an automatic breakpoint. This is important because before

```
                  CA-INTERTEST - SOURCE LISTING BREAKPOINT

Program= ARC92C   Option #      Stmt #                        Margin= 01
                  Label/Search Arg=
OPTS 1 Procedure div   2 Working-storage   3 Linkage sect   4 D-map 5 Clist/Pmap
     6 Xref      7 Procedure names     8 Error msgs     9 Search fwd 10 Search bwd
PFKS 1 Help      2 Cntl Menu 3 BKPT    4 List Profile   5 Continue     6 Core Menu
     7 Backward 8 Forward    9 Abend 10 Do     1 Verb   11 Backtrace  12 File
-------------------------------------------------------------------------------
   00968*    CRITERIA. 01 IS FIRST ENTRY, 02 IS SECOND ... ETC.
   00969
 U  ===> SEND-MAP00.
   00971      IF  TASK-SWITCH2 LESS NUM-CHOICES
   00972          ADD 1, TASK-SWITCH2 GIVING REQCDI
   00973      ELSE
   00974          MOVE '01' TO REQCDO.
   00975      MOVE 99 TO TASK-SWITCH2.
   00976      MOVE SPACE TO TASK-SWITCH3.
   00977*EXEC CICS SEND
   00978*           MAP ('DMAP00')
   00979*           MAPSET ('IN25CMP')
   00980*           ERASE
   00981*           END-EXEC.
   00982       MOVE '  }        S     00807    ' TO DFHEIV0
```

Figure 8.21 Halting execution at an unconditional breakpoint.

```
         CA-InterTest MONITORING COMMAND BUILDER - CONDITIONAL BREAKPOINT

Enter LEFT SIDE
    Data Name MONTH_________________________

Enter OPERATOR (EQ, NE, GT, LT, GE, LE):  NE

Enter RIGHT SIDE
    Data Name ______________________________
       OR
    Literal MAY_______________________________________________________________

          Press PF9 to go to complex conditional screen if necessary

Press ENTER key with data to process command or select PF key:
1 Help        2 CNTL        3 End         4 Source      5 CORE=Task      6 CORE=Bkpt
7 FILE        8 Prev        9 Complex    10            11 CORE=Syst     12 Status
```

Figure 8.22 Specifying the condition.

```
                    CA-INTERTEST - SOURCE LISTING BREAKPOINT

Program= ARA21C   Option #        Stmt #                          Margin= 01
                  Label/Search Arg=
OPTS 1 Procedure div   2 Working-storage   3 Linkage sect  4 D-map 5 Clist/Pmap
     6 Xref      7 Procedure names    8 Error msgs    9 Search fwd 10 Search bwd
PFKS 1 Help      2 Cntl Menu 3 BKPT   4 List Profile  5 Continue    6 Core Menu
     7 Backward 8 Forward    9 Abend 10 Do    1 Verb  11 Backtrace  12 File
--------------------------------------------------------------------------------
   01111      MOVE '         00916    ' TO DFHEIV0
   01112      MOVE 'PROTH' TO DFHEIV1
 A   ==>     CALL 'DFHEI1' USING DFHEIV0  DFHEIV1  DFHDUMMY DFHEIB0
     ==>
     ==> CICS abend intercepted. Abend code = AEIL,  EXEC CICS request was
     ==> STARTBR. Now stopped AFTER the CALL.
     ==>
     ==>      Press PF1 for a detailed description.
     ==>
   01114      RECORD-KEY.
   01115     MOVE +1 TO SUB.
   01116*EXEC CICS READNEXT DATASET('PROTH') SET(REC-POINTER)
   01117*          LENGTH(REC-LEN) RIDFLD(RECORD-KEY) END-EXEC.
   01118      MOVE '  4      00919    ' TO DFHEIV0
   01119      MOVE 'PROTH' TO DFHEIV1
```

Figure 8.23 Halting execution at an AEIL abend.

```
   CA-INTERTEST - INTERACTIVE HELP FACILITY - TUTORIAL: ERROR MESSAGE AEIL

 The data-set name referred to in the DATASET option cannot be found in the FCT.
 Your program did not have a Handle Condition for this error. Or a second Handle
 Condition without a routine for this error superseded the one that had a
 routine for this error.

 WHAT YOU CAN DO: If the named file was entered incorrectly and the one you
 wanted exists, you may use the Replace File Option to dynamically replace the
 filename and then use the resume task facilities to execute the CICS request
 again. To perform the above functions from the Source Listing Breakpoint screen
 you would:

 1. Key =20s in the Option # field and press ENTER.
 2. Tab to Replace Filename and key in the incorrect filename.
 3. In the next field, key in the correct filename and press ENTER.
 4. Press CLEAR to return to your Source Listing Breakpoint screen.
 5. Key in G to resume execution at the beginning of the EXEC CICS command
    and press ENTER.

 ------------------------------------------------------------------------------
ENTER N FOR NEXT PAGE, P FOR PRECEDING PAGE, F FOR FIRST PAGE, OR M
FOR RETURN TO PREVIOUS MENU. PRESS CLEAR TO EXIT.          SELECTION ==> N
```

Figure 8.24 Help Information on an AEIL abend.

you begin testing you might not know if and where the program has errors. For example, CA-InterTest halts program ARA21C before an AEIL abend can take place.

This panel in Figure 8.23 indicates that the AEIL occurred following an EXEC CICS STARTBR command. Press PF1 (HELP) to get more information on this "bomb out." The Help screen is illustrated in Figure 8.24.

Another useful tool is the backtrace, which lists the path of the most recently executed code. Each entry lists a pair of program locations, identifying the first and last statement numbers for a section of sequentially executed code. The number after the decimal point indicates the COBOL verb in the statement that was executed. Each entry represents a break in sequential execution; for example, a call to CICS or a branch to another program location. A sample backtrace is shown in Figure 8.25.

```
  in .... out
#775.0 ->#776.0
#776.0 ->#786.0
#786.0 ->#787.0
#789.0 ->#789.0
#797.0 ->#798.0
#786.0 ->#787.0
#814.0 ->#815.0
#815.0 ->#816.0
#821.0 ->#823.0
#823.0 ->#833.0
#833.0 ->#838.0
#838.0 ->#839.0
#841.0 ->#851.0
#851.0 ->#866.0
#866.0 ->#872.0
#872.0 ->#873.1
#882.0 to here.
```

Figure 8.25 Sample backtrace.

Chapter

9

Testing with CICS Playback

9.1 What CICS Playback Will Buy You

CICS Playback is a productivity tool developed by the Compuware Corporation to eliminate problems traditionally associated with putting CICS systems into a production environment. The system enables you to completely test new and revised programs and systems while offering facilities to:

- Capture live CICS transactions
- Execute captured transactions
- Edit and replicate captured transactions
- Test a program's ability to handle concurrent transactions
- Generate test data for "what if" questions
- Compare transaction output

CICS Playback eliminates problems associated with the following circumstances:

- A minor change to one program that creates a problem after it is put into production
- A program or operating system release that causes problems under peak load conditions
- Major changes to a CICS application that result in errors

CICS Playback is characterized by three architectural features. The first of these has to do with the various test environments. Among these are unit and concurrency testing, integration testing, and regression and stress testing. While these topics are also covered under CA-Verify, let me provide you with an overview from Compuware's perspective:

Unit testing involves the testing of a single program at the programmer's terminal. Concurrency testing pertains to the programmer's ability to perform concurrent processing of transactions entered simultaneously from several terminals. Integration testing entails the simultaneous testing of all programs in an application when integrated into a full-blown system. Regression testing uses CICS Playback to ensure users that a change made to one part of the system does not cause an undesired result in another part. Stress testing is performed to test the entire system under peak volume conditions to measure system stress.

A second architectural feature has to do with Playback's ability to recreate a production environment in test mode without using the physical network. The idea here is to capture all or a portion of the production workload and then play it back in test mode without having to rely on the physical environment. This particular ability of the product lends itself to other aspects, such as debugging unmanageable production problems. In Playback, you can capture data in production until a problem occurs, take the data to a particular test region, and recreate the problem repeatedly until it is resolved.

A third architectural aspect or feature of the product is simply that it is designed to support broad ranges of terminals because terminals used in production differ significantly from organization to organization. Transactions can be viewed or edited on-line in full-screen format (3270 terminals), or in character or hexadecimal format regardless of the type of compatible terminals involved.

CICS Playback captures logical groups of CICS transactions, called *scripts*, and stores them in a file. Captured transactions can be modified before they are played back (executed) to create scripts that emulate other CICS environments. CICS Playback contains the following major components:

Data capture. Captures transactions to a VSAM data set or CICS user journal.

Script playback. Plays back scripts in interactive or unattended mode.

Script modification. Changes and replicates scripts from captured transactions in an on-line or batch environment.

Script comparison. Compares input and output messages from any two scripts in on-line or batch mode (such as a data capture with script Playback session or two script Playback sessions).

Utilities. Provide on-line and batch capabilities to browse, manage, and print scripts. The CICS Playback architecture is illustrated in Figure 9.1. A Playback Primary Menu screen is displayed in Figure 9.2.

As an added feature to the Playback productivity tool, let me mention to you the CICS Simulcast option, which might already be part of your CICS environment. This

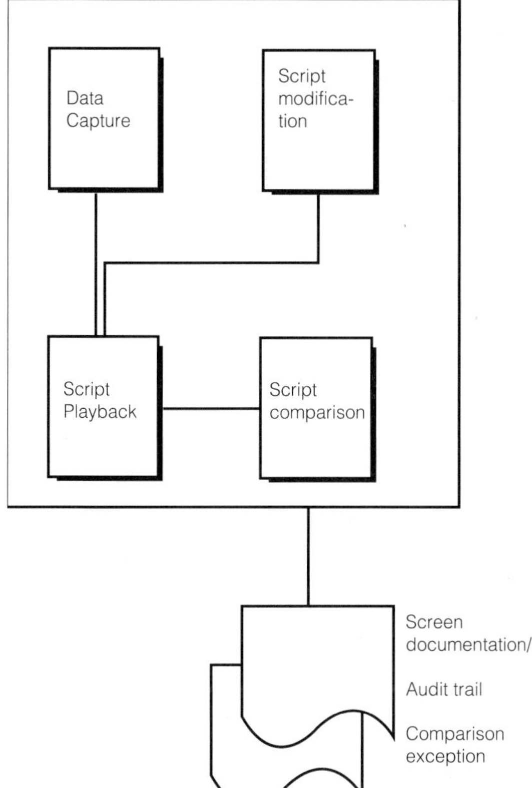

Figure 9.1 CICS Playback architecture.

```
PLAYP                   CICS PLAYBACK - PRIMARY MENU                 VER: 04.04.04
COMMAND ==>

Functions:        1  DATA CAPTURE   -  Capture messages to a script
                  2  U/A PLAYBACK   -  Unattended Playback
                  3  COMPARE        -  Compare scripts
                 12  I/A PLAYBACK   -  Interactive Playback

Utilities:        4  BROWSE         -  Browse a script
                  5  EDIT           -  Edit a script
                  6  UTILITIES      -  Copy, rename, delete scripts
                  7  STATUS         -  Session status
                  8  DIRECTORY      -  Script directory
                  9  RESOURCES      -  Available resources
                 10  GLOBAL PARMS   -  Global parameters maintenance

                  X  EXIT
                OFF  EXIT & SIGNOFF


TERM: 0000          LU: LAN004A          DATE: 10/28/91          TIME:  9.06.45
          COPYRIGHT (C) 1986 BY COMPUWARE CORP. ALL RIGHTS RESERVED
```

Figure 9.2 CICS Playback Primary Menu screen.

module is made up of two facilities. The first one, referred to as a *conference facility*, provides you with certain capabilities to establish a screen conference between users and technical personnel at different locations. The second facility, the so-called *broadcast facility*, provides the ability to present CICS sessions simultaneously to multiple terminals with the CICS region. There are three broadcast modes available in this mode: echo, script, and text.

Echo broadcasts transmit input and output application screens from the source terminal to the receiving terminals. Transactions entered at the source terminal are executed in CICS. Script broadcasts send previously captured scripts from the source terminal to all receiving terminals. Finally, text broadcasts are used to enter free-form text at the source terminal and send to other terminals.

9.2 Why Is It Necessary to Capture Data?

The first step in this process is creating test data. In conventional CICS testing, transactions are manually entered by programmers or terminal operators to create the test data. Because of the transient nature of all on-line transactions, the test transactions must be repeatedly entered. So the first objective of the Playback apparatus is to capture "live" transactions as they are entered into the system and store them in a script file for subsequent testing. This script file is automatically created by CICS Playback.

The capture process is not affected by the size or complexity of testing. An application programmer can use Playback to capture data for unit testing, a test coordinator can capture an end user's testing session, and a member of technical support staff can capture all or a portion of the production workload. Thus, the script can be edited and used as a consistent input for repeated testing.

You can initiate data capture either on-line or via autostart. Both methods, in essence, provide you with an unattended capability, so that the user can enter the actual test transactions or perform other tasks while the data capture session is in process.

Let's talk about the on-line data capture first. The basic-level data capture screen is shown in Figure 9.3. To initiate a data capture that captures all of the transactions from your terminal, type the option code 1 in the command field in the upper left corner of the Primary Menu (see Figure 9.2). Then press the Enter key to display the above data-capture screen.

1. Enter the character I, meaning Initiate, in the command field.
2. Enter USERNAME or a user I.D. in the user ID field.
3. Type in a script identifier in the script field. Note that I have entered the script identifier DEMO, which is Compuware's own presentation of the data capture mechanism. You can also enter the version number, which is optional, and a brief description to describe what the particular data capture is all about.
4. Press the Enter key. If all data previously entered is valid, the system will display a message like the following:

```
PLA0442 - CAPTURE STARTED - PRESS CLEAR AND BEGIN
```

```
PLAC5                                         DATA CAPTURE
COMMAND ==>          PLA0444 - SCRIPT TO CAPTURE SUCCESSFULLY RETRIEVED

I - INITIATE         T - TERMINATE         B - BROWSE


SCRIPT TO CAPTURE:
  FILE........ PLAYDT1
  USER ID..... USERNAME
  SCRIPT...... DEMO
  VERSION..... 0001

DESCRIPTION... DATA CAPTURE DEMO



PF1 = HELP    PF3 = RETURN    PF4 = PRIMARY MENU    PF9 = EXTENDED LEVEL
PF13 = TO TERMINATE CAPTURE WITHOUT RE-ENTERING CICS PLAYBACK
```

Figure 9.3 Data or Transaction Capture screen.

```
PLAS 11111 - ENTER EMPLOYEE NUMBER

   *** COMPUWARE CORPORATION ***
   CICS PLAYBACK SAMPLE TRANSACTION

   ENTER DESIRED EMPLOYEE NUMBER ABOVE:
   VALID EMPLOYEE NUMBERS ARE:
         11111
         22222
         33333
         44444
         55555



   DATE: 10/28/91
   TIME: 10:33:56



   COPYRIGHT (C) 1986 COMPUWARE CORP. ALL RIGHTS RESERVED
```

Figure 9.4 Data / Transaction Capture Panel.

indicating to you that data capture has now been initiated. At this point, Playback is set up to capture transactions as they are entered into the system.

5. Press Clear, and type in the transaction identifier PLAS, which is assigned to the demo system. Press Enter and review the screen that appears in Figure 9.4, which is a transaction initial screen.

As you can see, there are five transactions emulated on this particular system for simplicity. Enter the first employee identifier on the screen (11111) and press the Enter key. This will invoke a Transaction Completed Panel, shown in Figure 9.5.

```
PLAS

    *** COMPUWARE CORPORATION ***
    CICS PLAYBACK SAMPLE TRANSACTION

    EMPLOYEE NUMBER: 11111
    EMPLOYEE NAME:   MR. JOHN DOE
    HOURS WORKED:          10
    HOURLY RATE:            9.50
    GROSS PAY:             95.00




    DATE: 10/28/91
    TIME: 10:35:31


    *** TRANSACTION COMPLETE ***
        PRESS ENTER TO CONTINUE
           OR CLEAR TO END
```

Figure 9.5 Transaction Completion screen.

Once you have captured all the required transactions, press PF13 to stop the process. This will trigger a previously displayed panel (Figure 9.3), including the message:

```
PLA0076 - STOP HAS BEEN SCHEDULED FOR THE REQUEST in the command field
```

If you want to view some of the statistics generated through this process of data capture, type the character A in the command field of the data-capture screen. The data-capture statistics screen is displayed in Figure 9.6.

This data-capture statistics panel provides you with vital statistics regarding the data-capture process. Note that there was a single terminal used in the operation (terminal mask), including all the transactions entered. The total number of transactions captured was 20, for both input and output. The total number of characters involved in the operation (300) represents the number of transactions times the size of each transaction. Duration for the capture was 21 seconds, attained by subtracting start time from stop time.

As I mentioned earlier, there are two types of data captures in CICS Playback. The first kind is on-line data capture. The second one is an autostart data-capture type, which is initiated through the CICS Program Load Table (PLT). Thus, data capture can begin without the programmer being present. Because the data capture begins before any operator can sign on the system, every transaction is captured. This method is ideal for capturing data from the production environment.

This mechanism is important in situations in which all data must be retained. CICS Playback captures data efficiently in user journals that handle large volumes of data. The system can also be set to not capture output messages. This feature further reduces the impact of data capture on production applications. An overview of the data-capture mechanism is shown in Figure 9.7.

9.3 How to Play Back Captured Reports

Once scripts are captured, they can be "played back"—immediately, if necessary. There are two types of Playback mechanisms in this software; an interactive one and an unattended Playback type, the latter of which includes on-line unattended and autostart unattended Playback. Essentially, these methods serve different needs in

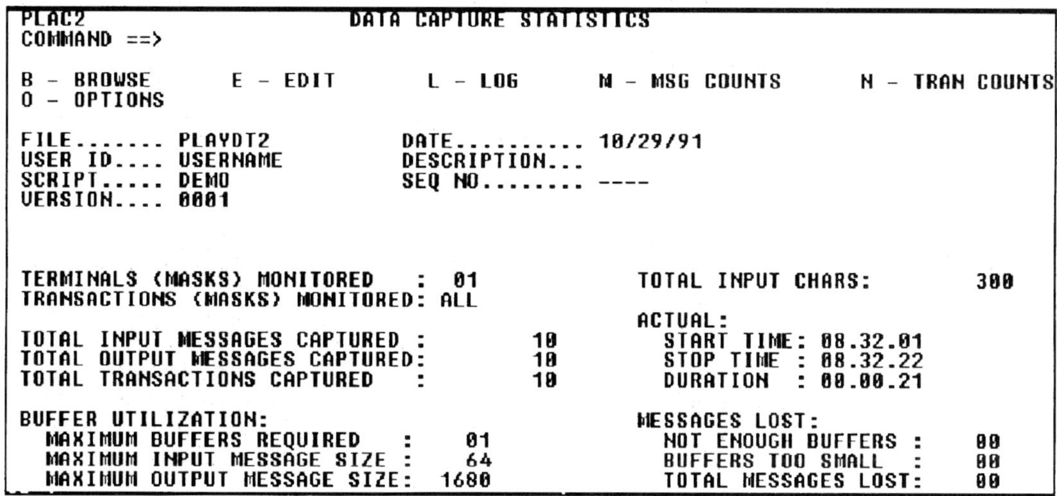

Figure 9.6 Data Capture Statistics screen.

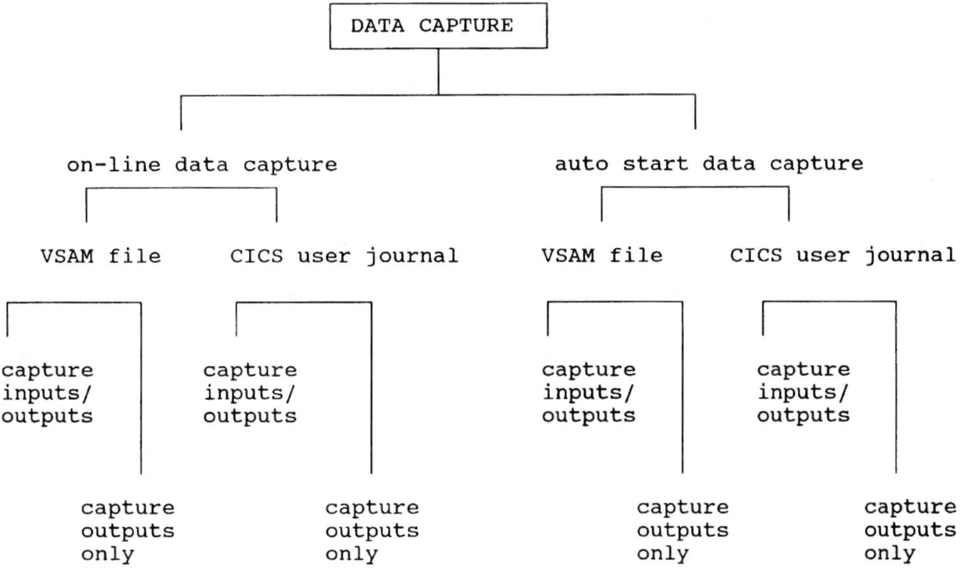

Figure 9.7 Overview of the data-capture mechanism.

```
PLAR5                              INTERACTIVE PLAYBACK
COMMAND ==>

I - INITIATE        B - BROWSE


SCRIPT TO PLAY BACK:
  FILE........ PLAYDT1
  USER ID..... USERNAME
  SCRIPT...... DEMO
  VERSION..... 0001

DESCRIPTION... PLAYS BACK CAPTURED SCRIPTS



PF1 = HELP              PF3 = RETURN              PF05 = SUSPENDS PLAYBACK
PF4 = PRIMARY MENU      PF9 = EXTENDED LEVEL      PF06 = CAPTIONS ON/OFF
```

Figure 9.8 Interactive Playback screen.

the testing cycle, but very much support each other. With CICS Playback, the output of playing back a data-capture script is a new script called a Playback script. This Playback script can then be changed to a data-capture script, which can be used as input script for the next Playback execution.

9.3.1 Interactive Playback

Interactive Playback is designed so a programmer can test his program. With this type of mechanism, he can single-step through the entire script, or change any input transaction before it is submitted to CICS. The programmer can also suspend and resume a script Playback session at any point in a script.

Figure 9.8 shows the Interactive Playback Panel. In order to execute Interactive Playback, specify a complete script name on this panel and then enter the character I (Initiate).

Interactive Playback allows you to suspend and resume transactions at a given point in the script. When Playback is suspended, CICS Playback displays a suspended Playback screen. Having suspended Interactive Playback, you can insert a new transaction, discard messages in the script, or simply purge the current transactions—after which you can exit the system. At your option, you can then resume the previously suspended session interactively, terminate it, or convert it to an online unattended Playback session. If you need to resume a Playback session, keep in mind that this can be accomplished either at the point of suspension or at any previous or subsequent message.

9.3.2 Unattended Playback

Unattended Playback addresses the repetitive nature of CICS testing. It provides the ability to execute scripts of various sizes and complexity in a repetitive fashion. An

Unattended Playback session can be initiated through the On-Line Unattended Playback screen. The system allows you to start a session simultaneously. The specific panel used in conjunction with the unattended session looks very much like the one presented in Figure 9.9, with some minor differences in layout.

In order to execute Unattended Playback, you need to specify the file, user ID, script, and version (make sure that the file has a valid entry in the File Control Table or else it won't run). Then enter I for initiate. The result of this will be stored in a new script marked by a new qualifier.

Along with the basic functions, you can also use the software's extended features, which provide you with the full capabilities of the product. The extended functions can be divided into four major areas:

- Accessing extended data capture
- Accessing extended Unattended Playback
- Performing concurrency testing
- Accessing extended comparison

The Extended Data-Capture Panel is shown in Figure 9.10. Allow me to explain some of the features that appear on the screen.

TERMINAL TO CAPTURE specifies certain available options. As you might have noticed in Figure 9.10, there are three available options enclosed in parentheses: HERE, meaning that the terminal in use is currently captured; ALL, indicating that the terminals in the CICS system are captured; and LIST, which is designed to include (or exclude) certain terminals. If you were to specify TR, for example, you would be specifying a mask that would capture only terminals that start with TR.

TRANSACTIONS TO CAPTURE specifies the transaction to be captured. In this particular situation, you might use only the ALL and LIST options, which would give

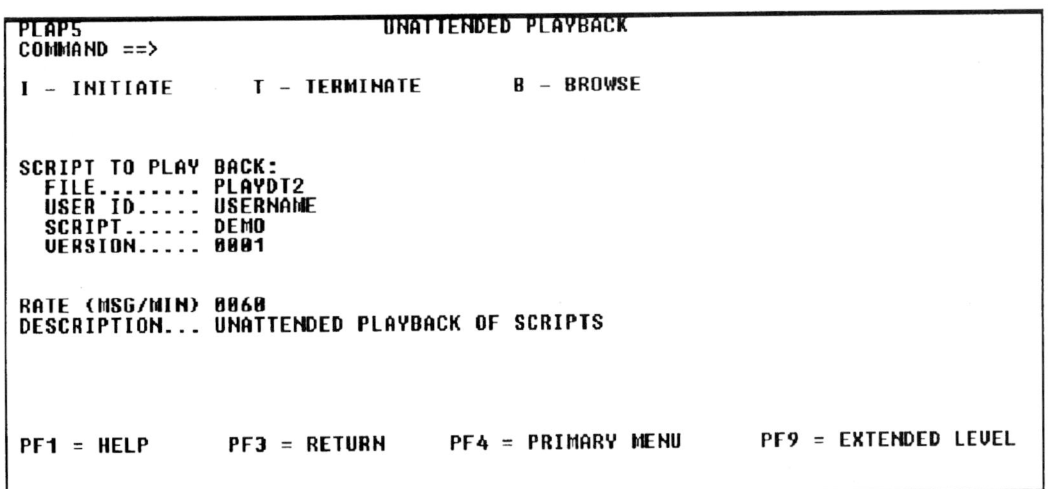
```
PLAP5                               UNATTENDED PLAYBACK
COMMAND ==>

I - INITIATE        T - TERMINATE        B - BROWSE


SCRIPT TO PLAY BACK:
  FILE........ PLAYDT2
  USER ID..... USERNAME
  SCRIPT...... DEMO
  VERSION..... 0001


RATE (MSG/MIN) 0060
DESCRIPTION... UNATTENDED PLAYBACK OF SCRIPTS



PF1 = HELP       PF3 = RETURN      PF4 = PRIMARY MENU       PF9 = EXTENDED LEVEL
```

Figure 9.9 Unattended Playback screen.

```
PLAP1                    EXTENDED UNATTENDED PLAYBACK
COMMAND ==>

A - STATISTICS     B - BROWSE       I - INITIATE     L - LOG      M - MSG COUNTS
N - TRAN COUNTS    O - ADD'L OPTS   R - RETRIEVE     S - SAVE     T - TERMINATE


FILE.......... PLAYDT2    CAPTURE OUTPUT...... YES     SECURITY........ NO
USER ID....... USERNAME   RATE (MSG/MIN)...... 0060    VIRTUAL TERMS... YES
SCRIPT........ DEMO       SERIAL.............. NO      VIRTUAL MASK.... VT--
VERSION....... 0001       STALL INTERVAL...... 030
DESCRIPTION... UNATTENDED PLAYBACK OF SCRIPTS
DATE.......... 10/29/91

TERMINALS TO PLAYBACK...... ALL   (ALL,LIST) PLAYBACK CRITERIA.... -- (EQ, NE)
---- ---- ---- ---- ---- ---- ---- ---- ---- ---- ---- ---- ---- ---- ---- ----
---- ---- ---- ---- ---- ---- ---- ---- ---- ---- ---- ---- ---- ---- ---- ----
---- ---- ---- ---- ---- ---- ---- ---- ---- ---- ---- ---- ---- ---- ---- ----
---- ---- ---- ---- ---- ---- ---- ---- ---- ---- ---- ---- ---- ---- ---- ----
TRANSACTIONS TO PLAYBACK... ALL   (ALL,LIST) PLAYBACK CRITERIA.... -- (EQ, NE)
---- ---- ---- ---- ---- ---- ---- ---- ---- ---- ---- ---- ---- ---- ---- ----
---- ---- ---- ---- ---- ---- ---- ---- ---- ---- ---- ---- ---- ---- ---- ----
---- ---- ---- ---- ---- ---- ---- ---- ---- ---- ---- ---- ---- ---- ---- ----
---- ---- ---- ---- ---- ---- ---- ---- ---- ---- ---- ---- ---- ---- ---- ----
```

Figure 9.10 Extended Data Capture Panel.

```
PLAP6                     ADDITIONAL PLAYBACK OPTIONS

FILE........ PLAYDT1                     ALTERNATIVE I/O OPTIONS:
USER ID..... USERNAME                           INPUT JOURNAL ID......... --
SCRIPT...... DEMO                               INPUT TD QUEUE NAME...... ----
VERSION..... 0001                               OUTPUT TD QUEUE NAME..... ----

                                         PLT-STARTUP OPTIONS:
MAX TERMINALS................ 7500              ISSUE SHUTDOWN........... NO
MAX BUFFERS.................. 0016              SHUTDOWN IMMEDIATE....... NO
BUFFERSIZE................... 32700             SHUTDOWN DUMP............ NO
SIGNOFF REAL TERMS........... YES               START TRACE.............. NO
O/P TO REAL TERMS............ NO                AUXTRACE IND............. NO
ORIG TERM-ID FOR VIRT........ NO                SNAP DUMP................ NO
MDT MERGE.................... NO                PURGE.................... YES
BYPASS LU NAME CHGS.......... NO
                                         AUTO-INSTALL OPTIONS:
                                                AUTO-INSTALL TERMINALS... YES
COPY TCTUA................... NO                MIN TIOA LENGTH.......... 1024
USER EXIT.................... OFF               MAX TIOA LENGTH.......... 4096
USER EXIT NAME............... PLAPBEXT          TIMEOUT INTERVAL......... 0000
BYPASS DYNAMIC EXITS......... 00                TCT USER AREA LEN........ 255
                                                MASK..................... PM--
                         PF3 = END ADDITIONAL OPTIONS
```

Figure 9.11 Additional Playback Options Panel.

you a time frame for a capture operation. You might, for instance, define a stop time to terminate data capture. TRANSACTIONS TO CAPTURE specifies journal and filenames used when capturing very large amounts of data, and controls the modes of execution available for a Playback. When you set this to YES, messages are sent to CICS one at a time in exactly the same sequence in which they were captured.

The STALL INTERVAL determines if the transaction has gone into a stall condition. If no terminal input/output occurs within the specified time, CICS Playback assumes that this transaction is in a stall condition and purges the transaction.

The RATE specifies the way security is handled for the Playback. When set to YES, the system restores security exactly as it was during the capture. When set to NO, security will not be restored and CICS might require a sign on.

VIRTUAL TERMINALS specifies whether the process of Playback occurs on a virtual terminal, not tying up a real terminal. In conjunction with this, VIRTUAL MASK determines which pool of virtual terminals is used for the Playback.

One additional panel affects the additional Playback options presented in Figure 9.11. You can invoke this by specifying an O and ADD'L OPTS in the command line on the Extended Playback screen.

Actually, the path to the extended panels shown in Figures 9.10 and 9.11 are accessible from the CICS Playback Primary Menu. Enter 1E next to the command ===>> field. This will trigger the Extended Data-Capture screen. Afterwards, enter 2E on the Extended Data-Capture Panel and press the Enter key one more time. This will trigger a secondary screen, which is the Extended Unattended Panel. Select O to get to the Additional Playback Option Panel. A couple of items on this panel need to be explained:

O/P TO REAL TERMS is an option that indicates whether the messages written by an application during a Playback are physically written to the original real terminal captured.

ORIG TERM-ID FOR VIRT specifies whether the virtual terminal I.D. used during the Playback is changed to the original terminal I.D. that was captured.

MDT MERGE specifies whether output message fields with the modified data-tag bit turned on will replace the corresponding previous input message fields.

PLT STARTUP OPTIONS is where CICS Playback allows an Unattended Playback to be auto-started through the CICS Program Load Table (PLT).

AUTO-INSTALL OPTIONS supports the dynamic TCT facility for both the capture and Playback mechanism.

As I mentioned before, CICS Playback allows you to use both real and virtual terminals. The major benefits of this mechanism are that the physical network is not used during testing (a major source of cost and effort invested in a conventional test environment), and that programmers can use terminals to either view the Playback or perform other tasks while Playback is running.

When messages with real terminal ID's are played back, this software takes the physical device out of service. This feature eliminates inadvertent data entries that can seriously jeopardize file integrity. The use of real terminals eliminates the need to create duplicate virtual terminal IDs for the production TCT.

In stress testing, or after reorganizing the physical terminals in the network, it is often desirable to send messages to terminals to test the validity of the network connection. With Unattended Playback, you can direct the output messages to the physical device used in the data capture. This capability is restricted to environments not using the IBM automatic installation facility. An overview of the script Playback features is presented in Figure 9.12. Also a comprehensive summary of Interactive Play-

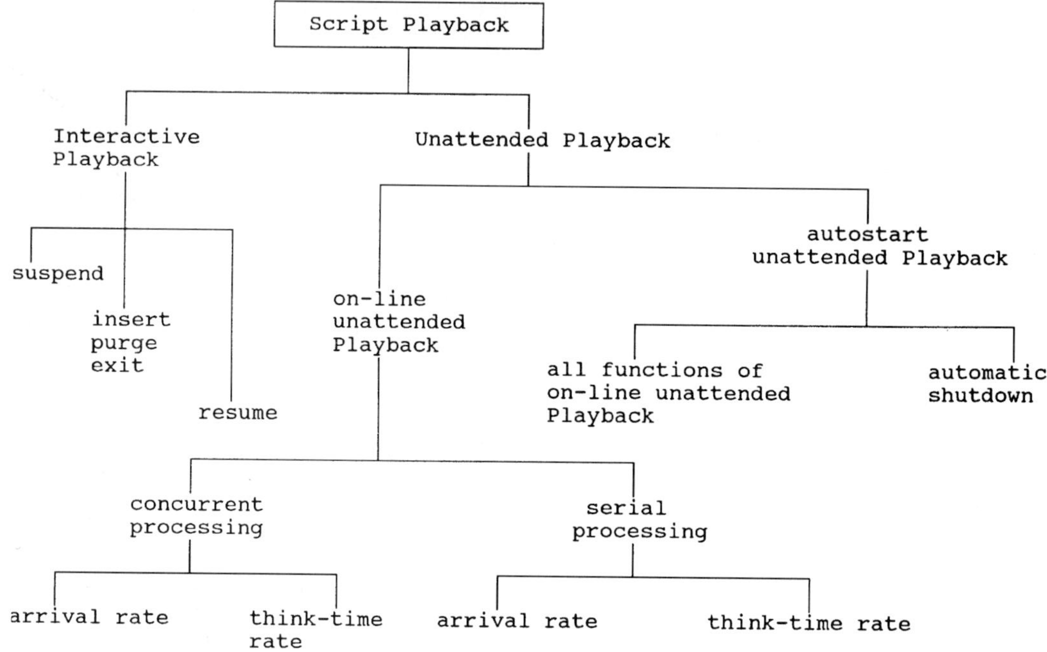

Figure 9.12 Script Playback features.

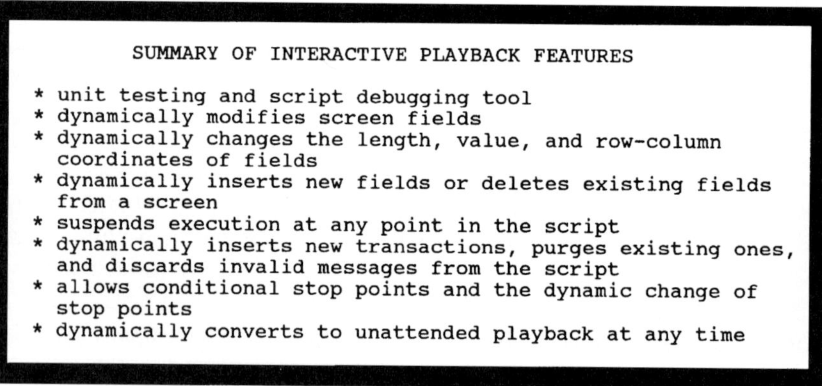

SUMMARY OF INTERACTIVE PLAYBACK FEATURES

* unit testing and script debugging tool
* dynamically modifies screen fields
* dynamically changes the length, value, and row-column coordinates of fields
* dynamically inserts new fields or deletes existing fields from a screen
* suspends execution at any point in the script
* dynamically inserts new transactions, purges existing ones, and discards invalid messages from the script
* allows conditional stop points and the dynamic change of stop points
* dynamically converts to unattended playback at any time

Figure 9.13 Interactive Playback characteristics.

back features are highlighted for you in Figure 9.13 as well as Unattended Playback features shown in Figure 9.14.

9.4 How to Modify a Script

This component module of CICS Playback enables you to use captured transactions as building blocks to generate scripts. When you capture scripts or live transactions, clearly you must have the ability to both edit and replicate them across a number of terminals to provide the environment with a proper mix.

Scripts can be developed and modified on-line via a script editor. The script editor can be accessed through the CICS Playback Script Editor Panel, displayed in Figure 9.15.

To use the script editor, type the filename for the input script on the upper panel. The vendor recommends that you also specify an output script. If you need to edit only certain terminals or transactions, you must specify an output script. By specifying such a script, note that the input script is going to remain unchanged; therefore, all modifications are made to the new script. Thus, at your option, you can keep both script or transaction types or cancel them.

In comparing scripts, the editor provides you with two types or levels of editing: the data and message levels. Let's talk about the first level, which is data-level editing. This mechanism provides editing capabilities for captured messages using a number of editing modes, such as:

- Full-screen editing
- Field editing
- Hexadecimal editing
- Character or physical editing

```
            SUMMARY OF UNATTENDED PLAYBACK FEATURES

* performs no extraneous functions, such as screen
  comparisons, which can dilute the accuracy of stress
  measurements
* allows a serial of concurrent processing mode for each
  script
* provides two ways to specify script execution rate: as
  messages per second or as a percent of think time
* supplies accurate performance characteristics needed for
  stress testing and capacity planning
* plays back messages from non3270 terminals
* allows the user of both real and virtual terminal IDs
* allows output messages to be sent to the real terminals
  as an option during a Playback
* allows for real-time terminal IDs as an option when using
  virtual terminals
* provides an MDT merge mode for testing applications that
  generates numbers internally
* accommodates the use of other Compuware products (CICS
  dBUG-AID and CICS Abend-AID) for unattended storage
  violation detection and analysis
* allows standard performance monitors to gather performance
  data
* permits specification of stall time to invoke stall
  detection and correction logic
* provides an autostart unattended Playback through the PLT
  with all the features of on-line unattended Playback
* autostart Playback can automatically shutdown CICS
  normally once the session is completed
```

Figure 9.14 Summary of Unattended Playback characteristics.

```
PLAK5                          COMPARISON REQUEST
COMMAND ==>         PLA0647 - COMPARE HAS BEEN INITIATED

I - INITIATE        B - BROWSE RESULTS


COMPARISON RESULTS:          INPUT SCRIPT A:              INPUT SCRIPT B:
FILE......... PLAYDT2        FILE......... PLAYDT2        FILE......... PLAYDT2
USER ID...... USERNAME       USER ID...... USERNAME       USER ID...... USERNAME
SCRIPT....... DEMO           SCRIPT....... DEMO           SCRIPT....... DEMO
VERSION...... 0001           VERSION...... 0001           VERSION...... 0001
                             TYPE......... P (C OR P)     TYPE......... C (C OR P)
DESCRIPTION.. ------------------------------






PF1 = HELP    PF3 = RETURN    PF4 = PRIMARY MENU    PF9 = EXTENDED LEVEL
```

Figure 9.15 CICS Playback Comparison Request Panel.

```
PLAG2         COMPARE MISMATCH AND BYPASS COUNT FOR EACH TERMINAL
COMMAND ==>

COMPARISON RESULTS:          INPUT SCRIPT A:              INPUT SCRIPT B:
FILE......... PLAYDT2        FILE......... PLAYDT2        FILE......... PLAYDT2
USER ID...... USERNAME       USER ID...... USERNAME       USER ID...... USERNAME
SCRIPT....... DEMO           SCRIPT....... DEMO           SCRIPT....... DEMO
VERSION...... 0001           VERSION...... 0001           VERSION...... 0001
DATE......... 10/31/91       TYPE......... P              TYPE......... C
DESCRIPTION..

  LINE CMDS: C - SCREEN   R - PHYSICAL   X - SCREEN HEX   Q - MESSAGE LIST

  TERM MIS  BYPS      TERM MIS  BYPS      TERM MIS  BYPS      TERM MIS  BYPS
  ---- ---- ----      ---- ---- ----      ---- ---- ----      ---- ---- ----
- 0000    0    0
```

Figure 9.16 Compare Mismatch and Bypass Count for Each Terminal screen.

These methodologies enable you to display an actual on-line transaction, modify the contents of a field, increase or decrease field lengths, change row/column positions, and insert new or delete existing fields as desired.

Message-level editing is available so you can expand the size or complexity of a script. Having entered the name of the field to be edited, the script editor will display a complete message list of captured scripts. Messages can be inserted or deleted within a script. You can use selective copying on a complete script, specific terminals or transactions, and a range of messages.

In order to initiate a comparison request, enter the character I (Initiate) on a Comparison Request Menu. Once you have initiated the process, the message *Compare has been initiated* will display on the panel until the process is terminated. As I mentioned earlier, to execute (or compare) Unattended Playback using a data-capture or a type-C script, you need to specify the four script-name qualifiers (File, User ID, Script, and Version). The result of this is stored in a new script with the same script qualifier, but with a type of P, for Playback script.

Once you have terminated the process, you can view comparison mismatch counts and results, as demonstrated in Figure 9.16 (compare mismatch and bypass count for each terminal). Briefly review this screen. If you want to review the results of the comparison in message-list format, type Q next to the terminal (TERM) field towards the lower left portion of the screen. This will trigger a Comparison Results Message-List Screen, which is shown in Figure 9.17. If you were to place the character S (Select) next to a particular message type and then press the Enter key, a previously displayed output screen from script A would appear. This is highlighted in Figure 9.18.

9.5 Batch Script Comparisons

Doing large volumes of script comparisons on-line is inefficient and uses a great deal of CICS resources. The batch script comparison function compares messages from individual script executions and reports the differences between them. This facility is better and more comprehensive than the interactive version because it provides you with hard copies of screen images of both messages when CICS detects differences from the IBM 3270 type terminals.

Batch script comparison is a viable tool because programmers cannot really compare high volumes of transactions in a timely manner. You can submit script comparison commands (Options, Exclude, Include, Tioadrop, Cmprtioa, Tioaexcl, Tioaincl) in the form of job-control statements provided by the Playback apparatus. In addition, if you rely on ISPF/PDF, you can also use the ISPF interface to run batch

```
COMPARE -------- PLAYDT2(USERNAME.DEMO.0001) -------------------- TERMID: 0000
COMMAND ==>

                         ******** SCRIPT A ********      ******** SCRIPT B ********
      ORIG  ASGN             MSG    MSG   MSG   AID            MSG    MSG   MSG   AID
STAT  TRAN  TRAN     CMD   TYPE     SEQ   LEN  /WCC     CMD   TYPE    SEQ   LEN  /WCC
----  ----  ----      -  ------    ----  ----  ----      -  ------   ----  ----  ----
EQ    PLAS            -  ATTACH       1     4  ENTR      -  ATTACH      1     4  ENTR
EQ    PLAS            -  ER,WRT       2  1680   C2       -  ER,WRT      2  1680   C2
EQ    PLAS            -  ATTACH       3     8  ENTR      -  ATTACH      3     8  ENTR
EQ    PLAS            -  ER,WRT       4  1610   C2       -  ER,WRT      4  1610   C2
EQ    PLAS            -  ATTACH       5    64  ENTR      -  ATTACH      5    64  ENTR
EQ    PLAS            -  ER,WRT       6  1680   C2       -  ER,WRT      6  1680   C2
EQ    PLAS            -  ATTACH       7     8  ENTR      -  ATTACH      7     8  ENTR
EQ    PLAS            -  ER,WRT       8  1610   C2       -  ER,WRT      8  1610   C2
EQ    PLAS            -  ATTACH       9    64  ENTR      -  ATTACH      9    64  ENTR
EQ    PLAS            -  ER,WRT      10  1680   C2       -  ER,WRT     10  1680   C2
EQ    PLAS            -  ATTACH      11     8  ENTR      -  ATTACH     11     8  ENTR
EQ    PLAS            -  ER,WRT      12  1610   C2       -  ER,WRT     12  1610   C2
EQ    PLAS            -  ATTACH      13    64  ENTR      -  ATTACH     13    64  ENTR
EQ    PLAS            S  ER,WRT      14  1680   C2       -  ER,WRT     14  1680   C2

DIFFERENCE CMDS:  C - SCREEN     R - PHYSICAL     X - SCREEN HEX
BROWSE CMDS    :  E - HEX        L - CHAR         F - FIELD          S - SCREEN
```

Figure 9.17 Comparison Results Message List screen.

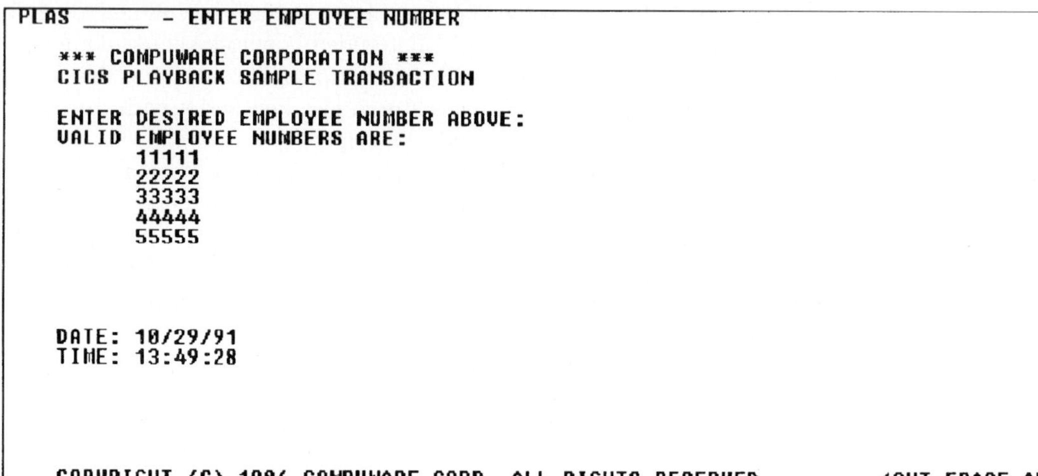

```
PLAS ______ - ENTER EMPLOYEE NUMBER

   *** COMPUWARE CORPORATION ***
   CICS PLAYBACK SAMPLE TRANSACTION

   ENTER DESIRED EMPLOYEE NUMBER ABOVE:
   VALID EMPLOYEE NUMBERS ARE:
         11111
         22222
         33333
         44444
         55555

   DATE: 10/29/91
   TIME: 13:49:28

   COPYRIGHT (C) 1986 COMPUWARE CORP. ALL RIGHTS RESERVED        <OUT-ERASE A>
```

Figure 9.18 Previously displayed panel used during the (PLAS) demo session.

```
                SUMMARY OF SCRIPT-COMPARISON FEATURES

 * Provides the flexibility to compare any two scripts--not merely
   a comparison of a Playback script with the previous data-capture
   script.
 * Compares messages from non3270-type terminals
 * Provides automatic exclusion of systems date and time fields
   from comparison
 * Allows the elimination of specific fields from the comparisons
 * Provides an on-line message list of comparisons
 * Permits scrolling back and forth through any number of on-line
   comparison screen
 * Provides unique on-line global-parameter library functions
 * Facilitates high-volume batch comparisons.
 * Provides print facilities for batch script comparisons
```

Figure 9.19 Summary of script-comparison features.

script comparisons. This interface provides a set of screens that can be used to access all the capabilities of the batch script comparison program. A summary of script comparison features are presented in Figure 9.19.

9.6 CICS Playback Utilities

Playback is enhanced with a variety of batch and on-line utility programs for viewing and modifying scripts. Among these utilities are: on-line browse, on-line modification, batch VSAM, and batch screen list. You can access a browse function for data-capture and Playback scripts from the Primary Options Menu screen. As with the script editor, you can also access a complete message list for all terminals in the script. Note that on-line (interactive) utilities can be executed from a single screen to append, copy, delete, and rename, scripts, as highlighted in Figure 9.20.

The batch VSAM utility allows you to perform file reorganization and maintenance function for VSAM scripts. This particular batch utility has five major functions:

- Reorganizing and comparing script data sets
- Creating a script directory list for a data set
- Renaming, copying, and deleting scripts within a data set by generic or specific search
- Copying and moving scripts between data sets by generic or specific name
- Appending a script to the end of single or multiple scripts

The batch screen-list utility is used to print input and output messages either in screen or record images or in hexadecimal.

9.7 CICS Simulcast

CICS Simulcast is designed to streamline communications throughout the network, visually link many users at different locations, facilitate training of new applications, and improve help desk and technical support.

Simulcast sends screen images from one terminal to other terminals and allows users to receive screen images from another terminal. With Simulcast, it is possible to view the same screen image at the same time as other users. You can send screen images of CICS transactions as they occur to multiple users anywhere in the network. You can also receive screen images of CICS transactions as they occur from any other terminal in the network. In addition, you can:

- Present "live" demos of new CICS applications to users at remote locations without leaving your terminal
- Send captured training or demo sessions to remote users
- Capture a CICS Simulcast session and store, browse, and print it to document a problem or training session
- Send text bulletins to some or all users throughout the network

One of a number of features included in the Simulcast module is the system's conference facility. A conference facility enables you to receive screen images from any terminal in the region. Because multiple users can receive and view the same screen image simultaneously, you can establish a screen conference", visually linking technical personnel and users at different locations. Simulcast offers a capture option that you can use to capture and store screen images received during a conference as a script on a VSAM file. This script, then, can be browsed on-line at a later time, printed in screen format for problem documentation, or broadcast to other users to alert them of the problem.

The Broadcast facility is designed to allow you to send screens from a terminal to one or more terminals simultaneously in a CICS region, regardless of the dis-

```
PLAU1                           CICS PLAYBACK UTILITIES
COMMAND ==>

A - APPEND      C - COPY      D - DELETE      G - REGENERATE      R - RENAME

*** FROM SCRIPT ***                   **** TO SCRIPT ****
FILE......... PLAYDT2                 FILE......... --------
USER ID...... USERNAME                USER ID...... --------
SCRIPT....... DEMO                    SCRIPT....... --------
VERSION...... 0001                    VERSION...... ----
TYPE......... - (C)APTURE/(P)LAYBACK  TYPE......... - (C)APTURE/(P)LAYBACK

IF COPY, REPLACE EXISTING "TO" RECORDS? --- (YES/NO)

TERMINALS TO COPY......... ALL   (ALL,LIST)   COPY CRITERIA..... -- (EQ,NE)
---- ---- ---- ---- ---- ---- ---- ---- ---- ---- ---- ---- ---- ---- ---- ----
---- ---- ---- ---- ---- ---- ---- ---- ---- ---- ---- ---- ---- ---- ---- ----
---- ---- ---- ---- ---- ---- ---- ---- ---- ---- ---- ---- ---- ---- ---- ----
---- ---- ---- ---- ---- ---- ---- ---- ---- ---- ---- ---- ---- ---- ---- ----
TRANSACTIONS TO COPY...... ALL   (ALL,LIST)   COPY CRITERIA..... -- (EQ,NE)
---- ---- ---- ---- ---- ---- ---- ---- ---- ---- ---- ---- ---- ---- ---- ----
---- ---- ---- ---- ---- ---- ---- ---- ---- ---- ---- ---- ---- ---- ---- ----
---- ---- ---- ---- ---- ---- ---- ---- ---- ---- ---- ---- ---- ---- ---- ----
---- ---- ---- ---- ---- ---- ---- ---- ---- ---- ---- ---- ---- ---- ---- ----
```

Figure 9.20 CICS Playback Utilities Panel.

tance. This methodology gives you three different modes of communication. Broadcast allows you to conduct training sessions and on-line demons from your terminal to other terminal locations. The three different modes of communications are as follows:

Echo broadcast. This means that CICS transactions entered at a source terminal are sent to all receiving terminals.

Script broadcast. This is used to broadcast a previously captured script to other terminals in the CICS region. In this particular mode, the transactions in the script are not executed by CICS. This is a practical way to increase the flexibility and comfort level of trainer and programmers conducting a demo session.

Text broadcast. Allows you to enter free-form text on the terminal, and broadcast it to all receiving terminals (e.g., sending text bulletins).

9.8 How Playback Operates in Various Test Modes

The purpose of this section is to show you how CICS Playback handles testing and quality assurance in various test environments. To do this, I have established a format with three major criteria in mind.

I will describe a particular test mode, such as unit or concurrency testing, and explain how it works. I will also describe some of the potential problems associated with that particular test mode when placed in a conventional environment. Finally, I will provide you with some guidelines as to what CICS Playback does and, more importantly, how it handles each of these situations.

As you recall, I initially described five modes of testing based on the continuous development (and refinement) of the application in the beginning of this chapter. These were, as you recall:

- Unit testing
- Concurrency testing
- Integration testing
- Regression testing
- Stress testing

A thorough approach to CICS program testing requires a series of tests that employ both the volume of transactions and the variety of terminals typically encountered in a CICS network. It is important to note that the phased approach to CICS testing is intended only as a model. Actual testing standards and procedures will vary from one installation to another. It is, thus, appropriate to assume that the actual applications of CICS Playback will also vary.

Testing, as I previously indicated, starts with a unit test (see CA-InterTest) from a single terminal, and includes and represents the operation of the production environment in which the test program will function. Each phase has its own objectives and problems.

9.8.1 Playback and unit testing

Unit testing accommodates only as a single program (a program being synonymous with a unit) with several objectives in mind. First of all, it ensures that the application program will process individual programs correctly to predefined programming standards and specifications. Because a program might handle several transaction types, each test execution must process all possible combinations to test the processing logic.

This means that you have to create and use a standard set of transactions to check the logic of each program. Once unit testing is completed in this manner, you need to compare the results of the above unit test with predefined objectives. This can be facilitated through the interaction of a quality-assurance group, if there is such a group in place, to make sure that each program is thoroughly tested. If there is no such group, some other arrangement needs to be made to provide the necessary “outside” verification.

Some of the problems associated with unit testing are:

- Making sure that proper transactions are submitted. Each program module has different testing requirements and, therefore, the programmer must segregate the transactions needed to test an individual module.
- Having to exit a test in order to perform other tasks (like recompiling), and then return to the same point in the test. During the exit-and-return cycle, the programmer might not return to the same point to resume the rest of the test.
- The costly nature of repetitive testing and creating screen documentation.

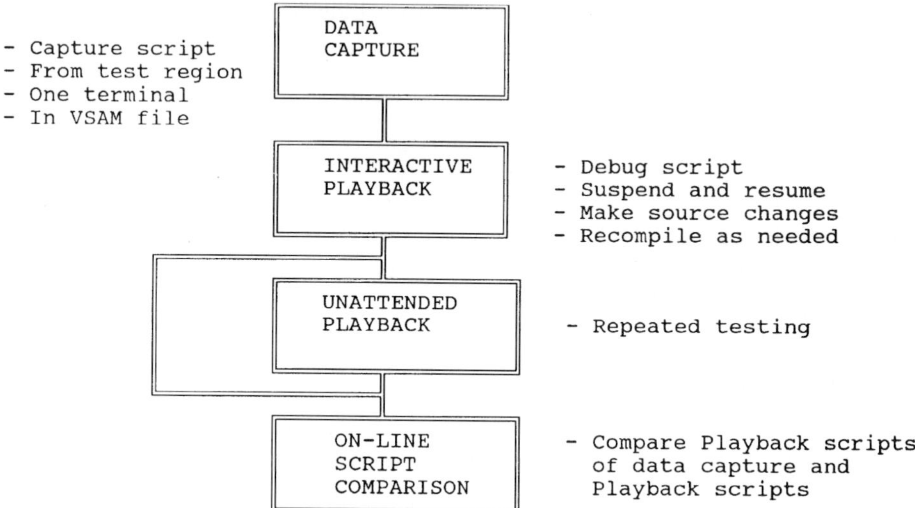

Figure 9.21 Unit testing flow diagram.

When using Playback, you can capture all the appropriate transaction types for a particular program. Afterwards, you can modify and execute them as frequently as necessary. Each test execution uses exactly the same input from the captured transactions and eliminates repetitive reentry. Also, Playback allows you to exit a particular test session to make changes to the source program in question, recompile the program, and resume testing at the appropriate point in the program. Once the test session is over, you can compare the results of your test with those of the standard criteria. An overview of the unit testing mechanism is presented in Figure 9.21.

9.8.2 Playback and concurrency testing

Concurrency, by definition, is when CICS attempts to process two or a number of transactions of the same type simultaneously. The objectives are as follows:

You want to make sure that the program can indeed handle all the required transactions concurrently. Also, you want to verify that the program is fully operational under conditions that closely resemble a full-blown production environment.

The problem with this approach is that it is quite difficult to recreate concurrency situations. Without knowing if two or more transactions can be processed concurrently, a question of quality assurances comes into play. What happens if this situation occurs in production? Errors experienced during the concurrency phase of the system might prove to be fatal—resulting in incorrect transaction processing, corrupted data, abnormal terminations, and storage violations. In more severe cases, the entire CICS region could lose integrity. Because these types of problems are likely to increase as you introduce more and more volume to the processing cycle, they normally occur during peak load when it is least affordable.

As I mentioned earlier, Playback does not rely on physical network conditions. Rather, the system employs a "parallel processing logic," referred to as a *transac-*

tion driver, that can release multiple transactions to CICS at the same time. This process forces the tested program to process multiple transactions simultaneously. An overview of the concurrency-testing flow is shown in Figure 9.22.

9.8.3 Integration testing

You probably have experience with situations where a program seems fully operational when treated individually, yet does not seem to be that way when placed into a more integrated environment where all the individual units need to coexist.

The objectives of integration testing are to make sure that the program being tested does not conflict with other programs in the region. It maintains a standard set of benchmark transactions in order to recreate the same test at a later date. Integration testing needs to modify the standard benchmark set of transactions to permit the entry of new transaction types, the deletion of obsolete transaction types, etc. Finally, the most important objective of integration testing is to ensure the quality of the entire system being tested before placing it into a production environment.

Some of the problems associated with integration testing are:

- The difficulty of recreating production problems in a test mode
- The inability to meet total system quality assurance when the system is tested in a less-than-production environment
- The testing of new situations after hours or on weekends, the only time a complete CICS environment can be used
- Coping with file contentions and storage violations that occur when more than one program is operating in a region

With Playback, a benchmark set of transactions are captured for integration testing during peak load. This data-capture script can be modified to include new transactions for new programs. The modified script is then played back in the new system. You can execute this Playback script because it does not conflict with any production system. Playback allows production situations to be created for the integration test without affecting the actual production environment. Transaction dependencies

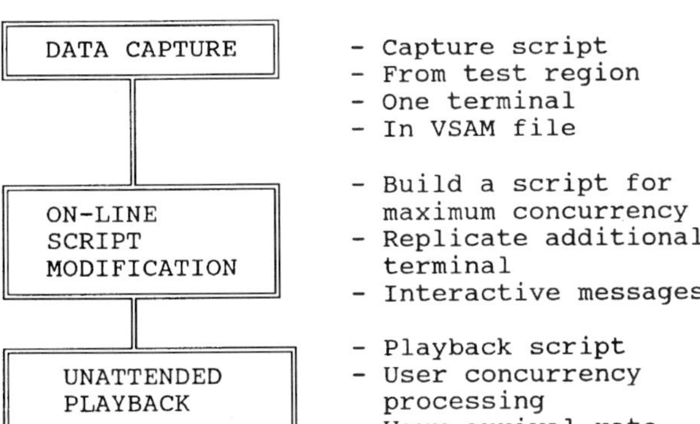

Figure 9.22 Concurrency-testing flow diagram.

can be discovered, problems can be fixed, and the script can be played back as often as needed for total quality assurance. An overview of the integration test cycle is illustrated in Figure 9.23.

The first method captures the test data from users' CICS sessions. The second method builds the script in a test environment by capturing the data from one or a number of terminals and then replicating and editing the captured script.

9.8.4 Regression testing

When you need to make a change to an otherwise static system, you want to make sure that such a change does not adversely affect the system in terms of response time, in addition to a number of other detectable ways. This is done through regression analysis or regression testing. Here, the objective is to recreate the current production environment including the recently implemented change. Again, you will compare the results of your test to anticipated test results, which means that you need to maintain a standardized test for any given system or application program.

Some of the problems associated with regression testing include:

- Pressure to put a new program into production as soon as possible, resulting in shortcuts in standard testing procedures
- The problem of comparing two different sets of tests
- The difficulty in maintaining a standardized set of transactions
- Test situations with which to test each new version of CICS, the operating system, or an application package

Using the Playback mechanism, it is relatively easy to build and maintain a standard set of transactions for a program. This standard script can be executed without in-

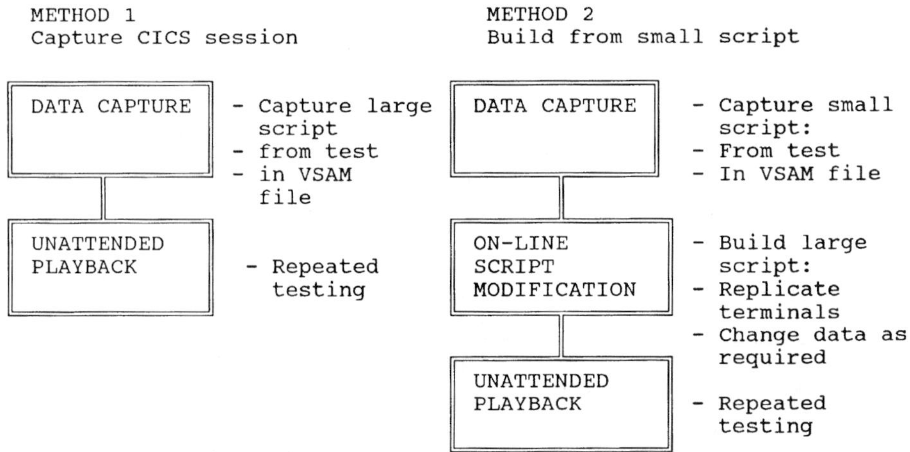

Figure 9.23 Integration-testing flow diagram.

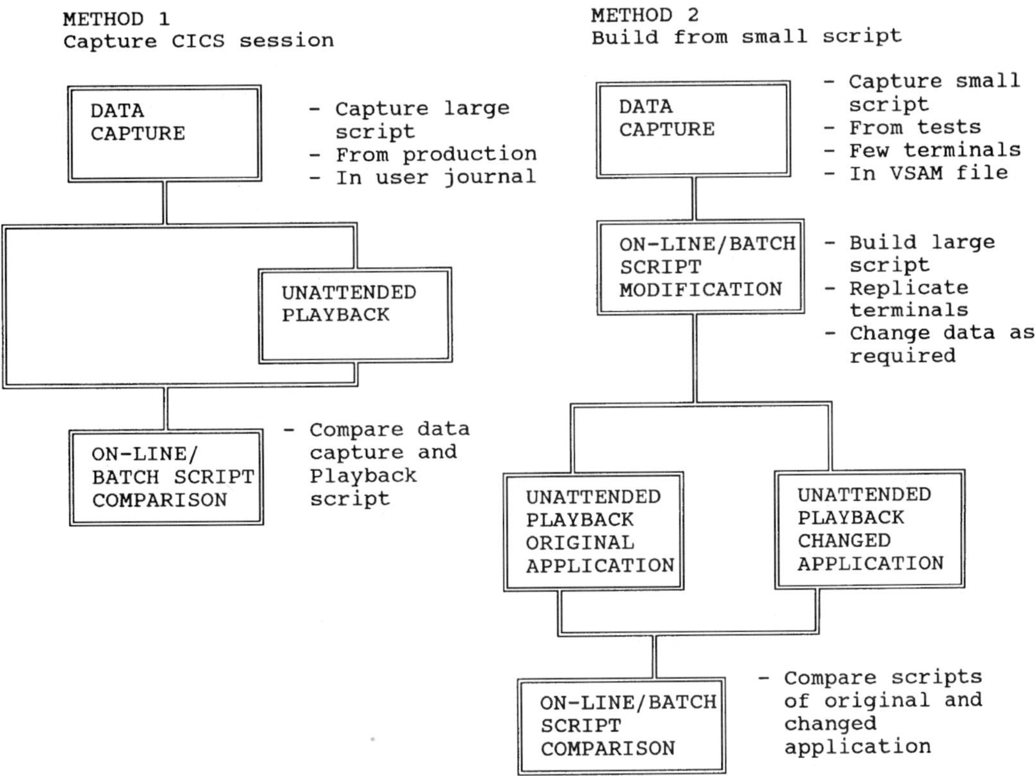

Figure 9.24 Regression-testing flow diagram.

terrupting the production environment, as often as you see fit. An overview of regression testing procedures are shown in Figure 9.24.

The first method captures the test data from the production environment and plays it back in a test environment. The second method builds the script in the test environment by capturing the data from one or more terminals, editing the captured script, and playing it back a number of times.

9.8.5 Stress testing

Stress testing is also referred to as volume testing because of the extremely high volume of transactions processed during a stress audit. Stress testing is an emulation of the real world. Among its objectives are to determine the capacity of the actual CICS system under test conditions, or to test a proposed configuration before implementation using transaction rates that approximate actual production condition.

Other objectives are to find any points at which the system stops operating and thoroughly test the system with a high volume of transactions before putting it into production.

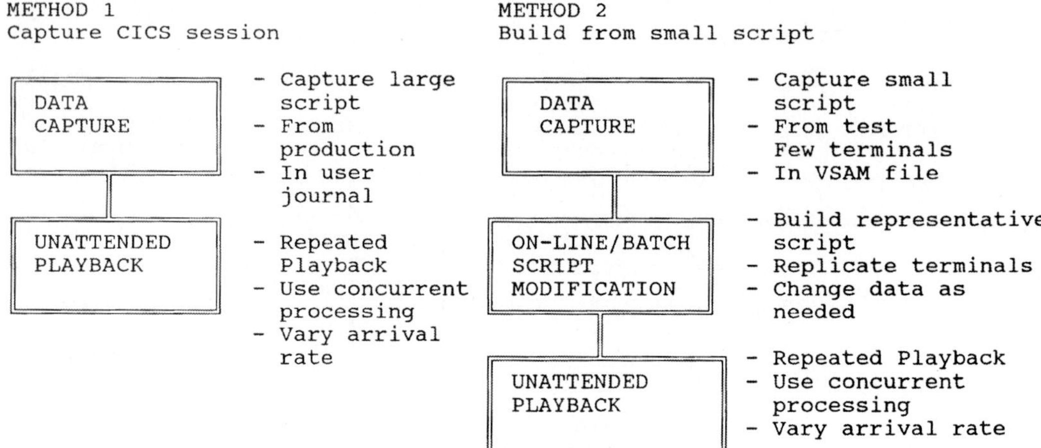

Figure 9.25 The stress-test environment.

Some of the problems typically associated with stress is that the testing is very labor-intensive, and thus costly and error-prone using conventional methods of testing. Also, it is rather difficult to maintain a proper stress environment for a prolonged period of time. Without some systematic method, it would be quite difficult—if not impossible—to create a realistic stress environment.

With Playback, you can capture all transaction types necessary for testing. You can also control the speed and method of execution in order to place the system under a predefined stress.

Figure 9.25 shows the dynamics of a stress environment. The first method captures the test data from the production environment. The second method builds the script in the test environment by capturing a data from one or more terminals, and then replicating and editing the data-capture script.

Chapter

10

The Abend-AID Productivity Tool

10.1 Introduction to Abend-AID Technology

CICS Abend-AID, like File-AID, is a product of the Compuware Corporation, and is one of the more popular productivity tools on the market today in diagnosing CICS transaction abends. Briefly, the difference between Abend-AID and InterTest (the latter is currently owned by Computer Associates) is manifested in both a conceptual and a philosophical approach.

The primary purpose of CA-InterTest is to "walk you through" a particular interactive session, command by command, if necessary, allowing you to observe a task while it is executing, similar to the EDF concept. Thus, using CA-InterTest, a program does not have to terminate abnormally. If it does, InterTest will warn you in advance and allow you to make changes that would temporarily alleviate the problem.

Abend-AID, on the other hand, does not allow you to go on when you experience a fatal error. However, it will compile for you all the essentials necessary to establish what happened in the transaction and what can be done in the future to prevent it from happening again. Abend-AID is not a substitute for CA-InterTest; nor is CA-InterTest for Abend-AID. If financially feasible, perhaps both of these packages should be purchased for higher productivity.

CICS Abend-AID, as I mentioned before, provides you with a comprehensive analysis as to the exact cause of an abend. It is an intelligent system that functions very much like expert systems do—"learning" from past experiences. In case the system doesn't find the exact cause of a problem, it will provide you with a list of probable causes. It will then suggest possible solutions that would render the program operational once more, while highlighting potential problem areas.

Abend-AID, therefore, communicates a problem in a consistent, readable format that includes an array of data required to solve the problem. Among these methodologies are trace tables and trace-table entries for the abending task, EIB-related dumps (Execute Interface Block), program summaries including communication areas, and TCA- and TWA-related information.

Abend-AID provides support for COBOL, PL/I, Assembler (BAL), DL/I, and DB2—most IBM environments.

10.2 How to Activate Abend-AID

I would like to introduce to you three Abend-AID transactions and explain each of them in detail. These are:

AAON. Designed to activate or shut down CICS Abend-AID.

AADF. Used to provide on-line access to CICS Abend-AID.

AADM. Compuware's own demo module, primarily for tutorial purposes.

Let me start out by giving you a quick example of an Abend-AID session using Compuware's demo module (AADM) and the previously mentioned AADF transaction. To arrive at the panel shown in Figure 10.1, I cleared the screen and entered the AADM demo transaction.

By entering 00001 in the appropriate spot, I selected to abend on an ASRA (data exception) error. Note the standard CICS message displayed on the bottom of the screen: DFH2206I Transaction AADM ABEND ASRA.

Next, I cleared the screen for the second time and entered the AADF transaction in order to trace the previous abend in detail. This panel is designed to inform the user that an abend occurred (date and time), resulting in an ASRA condition in program CCAADEMO. As you can see, the demo module was run twice on the same day, but at different times. On both occasions it abended with the same (data-exception) error.

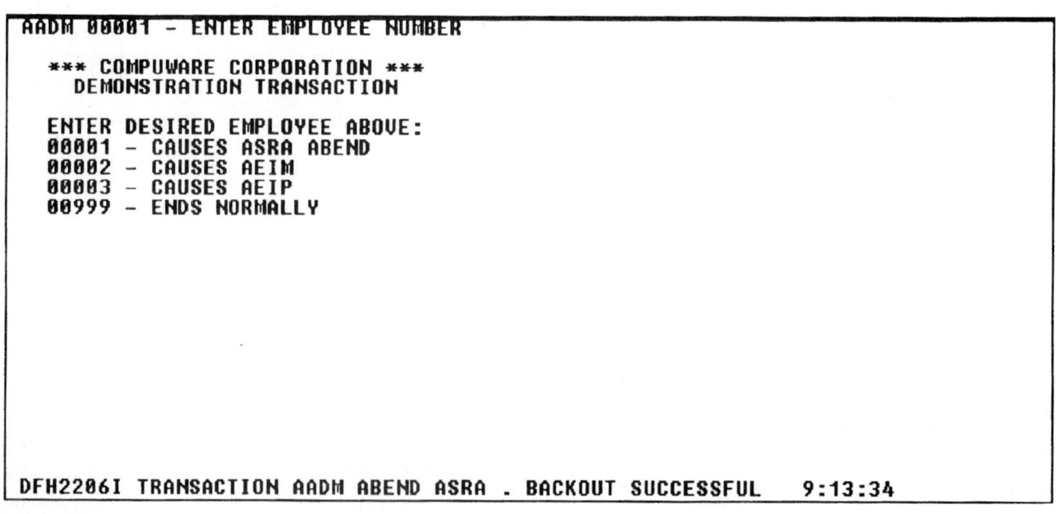

AADM 00001 - ENTER EMPLOYEE NUMBER
*** COMPUWARE CORPORATION ***
DEMONSTRATION TRANSACTION
ENTER DESIRED EMPLOYEE ABOVE:
00001 - CAUSES ASRA ABEND
00002 - CAUSES AEIM
00003 - CAUSES AEIP
00999 - ENDS NORMALLY
DFH2206I TRANSACTION AADM ABEND ASRA . BACKOUT SUCCESSFUL 9:13:34

Figure 10.1 Invoking an ASRA (data exception) termination.

```
-------------------- CICS ABEND-AID REPORT FILE DIRECTORY --------------------
COMMAND ==>                                                        SCROLL ==> CSR

  TRAN  TERM   REPORT  ABEND    DATE      TIME     PROGRAM   NETNAME   STATUS
- AADM  0000   000645  ASRA  11/08/91  09:13:32  CCAADEMO  LAN004A
- AADM  0000   000644  ASRA  11/08/91  08:57:52  CCAADEMO  LAN004A
- PLAY  0000   000643  ATNI  10/30/91  11:49:29  PLAPBREQ  LAN004A
- PLAY  0000   000642  ATNI  10/29/91  16:41:00  PLAMENU   LAN004A
- PLAY  0000   000641  ATNI  10/28/91  12:09:16  PLADCSTS  LAN004A
- CECI  0000   000640  ATNI  10/10/91  12:11:47  DFHECID   LAN004A
- AR21  0000   000639  AEIL  10/10/91  11:20:27  ARA21C    LAN004A
- AR60  0000   000638  AEIL  10/10/91  11:19:40  ARB64C    LAN004A
- AR20  0000   000637  AEIL  10/10/91  11:19:24  ARB28C    LAN004A
- AR21  R605   000636  AEIL  10/08/91  10:01:30  ARA21C    TR06J206
- MSA1  R605   000635  ASRA  10/04/91  14:19:22  LPCZZNUC  TR06J206
- MSA1  R605   000634  ASRA  10/04/91  14:17:45  LPCZZNUC  TR06J206
- MSA1  R605   000633  0813  10/04/91  14:13:43  LPCZZNUC  TR06J206
- UTAT  0000   000632  KERN  10/04/91  11:00:53  IN25PGMS  LAN004A
- AR92  0000   000631  ATNI  10/04/91  10:44:48  IN25PGMS  LAN004A
- AR92  0000   000630  ATND  10/04/91  10:44:44  IN25PGMS  LAN004A
- AR92  !!!!   000629  INTE  10/04/91  10:44:40  ARC92C
- AR92  !!!!   000628  OCKC  10/04/91  10:44:36  IN25PGMS

PF1-HELP  PF2-PRINT  PF3-END  PF4-EXIT  PF6-MENU  PF7-UP  PF8-DOWN
```

Figure 10.2 The CICS Abend-AID Report Directory Panel.

If you want to get detailed information about the problem, you can select a particular transaction by placing the cursor next to a Trans ID on the Report Directory Panel by entering an S in the corresponding column (Figure 10.2). This will invoke a series of screen sequences designed to give you a comprehensive overview describing the various parts of the program at the time the abnormal termination occurred. An in-depth analysis of such an abend will be the subject of a case study involving over two dozen frames, presented in the second half of this chapter. For this particular purpose, however, I am going to highlight only the two initial panels in Figure 10.3 and 10.4. Note that you can navigate through the analysis by continually pressing PF8, or by pressing PF7 should you decide to reverse the order of the presentation.

Figure 10.3, for example, produces a section-display panel that points to the abending statement shown in line 000399 as follows:

```
COMPUTE CURR-PAY  EQUAL WA-HOURS * WA-RATE
```

Note the concise explanation offered by the software: *The data exception is caused when a packed field has an invalid digit (not 0-9) or its last byte contains an invalid sign (not F, C, or D)*. The next frame adds more clarity to this problem by displaying the value of each field involved in the abending statement. Two of these fields, WA-HOURS and CURR-PAY, are both numeric fields containing "garbage." CURR-PAY was explained during the previous frame, and is physically responsible for the blow-up. However, if you take another look at the WA-HOURS field, you will see that it contains three asterisks (***), which are invalid in a numeric definition.

As you continue the analysis of the problem, Abend-AID provides you with accurate snapshots of the various segments in your program. Eight PF-key assignments are standard on the bottom of these panels. PF1 enables you to obtain assistance in case you have a question with regards to the procedures. PF2 will produce a hardcopy for you. PF3 and PF9, under the circumstances, will invoke the same directory

```
-------------------- CICS ABEND-AID REPORT FILE DIRECTORY --------------------
COMMAND ==>                                                      SCROLL ==> CSR

  TRAN  TERM   REPORT  ABEND    DATE      TIME     PROGRAM   NETNAME   STATUS
- AADM  0000   000645   ASRA  11/08/91  09:13:32  CCAADEMO  LAN004A
- AADM  0000   000644   ASRA  11/08/91  08:57:52  CCAADEMO  LAN004A
- PLAY  0000   000643   ATNI  10/30/91  11:49:29  PLAPBREQ  LAN004A
- PLAY  0000   000642   ATNI  10/29/91  16:41:00  PLAMENU   LAN004A
- PLAY  0000   000641   ATNI  10/28/91  12:09:16  PLADCSTS  LAN004A
- CECI  0000   000640   ATNI  10/10/91  12:11:47  DFHECID   LAN004A
- AR21  0000   000639   AEIL  10/10/91  11:20:27  ARA21C    LAN004A
- AR60  0000   000638   AEIL  10/10/91  11:19:40  ARB64C    LAN004A
- AR20  0000   000637   AEIL  10/10/91  11:19:24  ARB28C    LAN004A
- AR21  R605   000636   AEIL  10/08/91  10:01:30  ARA21C    TR06J206
- MSA1  R605   000635   ASRA  10/04/91  14:19:22  LPCZZNUC  TR06J206
- MSA1  R605   000634   ASRA  10/04/91  14:17:45  LPCZZNUC  TR06J206
- MSA1  R605   000633   0813  10/04/91  14:13:43  LPCZZNUC  TR06J206
- VTAT  0000   000632   KERN  10/04/91  11:00:53  IN25PGMS  LAN004A
- AR92  0000   000631   ATNI  10/04/91  10:44:48  IN25PGMS  LAN004A
- AR92  0000   000630   ATND  10/04/91  10:44:44  IN25PGMS  LAN004A
- AR92  !!!!   000629   INTE  10/04/91  10:44:40  ARC92C
- AR92  !!!!   000628   OCKC  10/04/91  10:44:36  IN25PGMS

PF1-HELP  PF2-PRINT  PF3-END  PF4-EXIT  PF6-MENU  PF7-UP  PF8-DOWN
```

Figure 10.3 Abend-AID Diagnostic Display Panel (one of many).

```
----------------------- CICS ABEND-AID SECTION DISPLAY ------------------------
COMMAND ==>                                                      SCROLL ==> CSR

CODE=ASRA  TASK=AADM  PROGRAM=CCAADEMO  DATE=11/08/91  TIME=09:13:32  TERM=0000
THIS STATEMENT IS CONTAINED IN PARAGRAPH "300-EMPLOYEE-PAY-RTN" OF
PROGRAM CCAADEMO.

                              COBOL INFORMATION

.                  # INDICATES FIELD CONTAINS INVALID DATA
                 CURRENT VALUES OF FIELDS ON ABENDING STATEMENT
LEVEL/FIELD NAME                  PICTURE/TYPE OFFS      VALUE
--------------------------------- ----------------- ----+----1----+----2
02 WA-RATE                        9(3)V99                00950
02 WA-HOURS                       999                    ***
77 CURR-PAY                       9(5)V99              X'0001F0F00016F0'
****************************** BOTTOM OF SECTION ******************************




PF1-HELP  PF2-PRINT  PF3-END  PF5-RFIND  PF6-MENU  PF7-UP  PF8-DOWN  PF9-DIR
```

Figure 10.4 A subsequent Abend-AID Diagnostic Display Panel.

screen. PF5 works in conjunction with a FIND command. PF7 and PF8 are standard IBM assignments (such as those used in ISPF, for example), allowing you to scan snapshot sequences forward and backward. PF6 takes you back to the functional (reporting) menu, which is shown in Figure 10.5.

To activate Abend-AID, simply enter the transaction identifier AAON on a blank CICS Panel. This transaction will dynamically modify the CICS region, giving Abend-AID control during an abnormal termination. The AAON transaction activates the system after the region is brought up.

AAON can be entered with different suffixes. Enter AAON and a single space, and then the suffix. For example, AAON ON will activate the CICS Abend-AID productivity tool. Likewise, AAON OFF will deactivate an additional Abend-AID analysis of an abnormal termination, providing a system shutdown for all other transactions running concurrently.

AAON OFFX, for example, does what AAON OFF is designed to do except it does it in a more abrupt fashion, while immediately freeing storage areas dedicated to the currently used program. Note that AAON OFFX is, as I mentioned earlier, a very drastic command and should be used only when AAON OFF does not produce the anticipated results in a reasonable length of time.

The transaction AAON CUSTINFO displays a customer information screen containing installation and product-specific data on all available options. This can be expanded through the AAON GLOBAL command, which displays a Global Options screen for viewing the current setting. Both the CUSTINFO and the GLOBAL Panels are displayed in Figures 10.6 and 10.7.

10.3 How to Use the Abend-AID Tutorial

Abend-AID provides you with two types of HELP assistance. The first one operates on a screen level and is fully interactive. The second type is an optional batch-report tutorial and prints on the front of the Abend-AID report.

When you use the on-line (screen-level) tutorials, the system provides you with both panel- and command-related information. There are two ways you can access on-line HELP: either by pressing PF1 (which is standard in an ISPF-driven (and mimicked) environment, or by entering the HELP primary command. This instruction is entered in the command field (see Figures 10.8A and 10.8B). Actually, PF13 is also available for HELP assistance within the Abend-AID module, along with other standard command keys, to scroll the display. As you will soon see in the case study

```
------------------------- CICS ABEND-AID REPORT MENU --------------------------
COMMAND ==>                                             REPORT NUM ==>  000645

      1 OR DIAG    - DIAGNOSTIC SECTION
      2 OR NSI     - NEXT SEQUENTIAL INSTRUCTION
      4 OR TRACE   - TRACE TABLE
      6 OR EIB     - EXECUTE INTERFACE BLOCK (EIB)
      7 OR PROG    - PROGRAM SUMMARY
      8 OR LIST    - PROGRAM LISTING SECTION
      9 OR PSTOR   - PROGRAM STORAGE
     10 OR LINK    - COBOL LINKAGE SECTION
     12 OR FILE    - FILE SECTION
     13 OR TCA     - FORMATTED TCA AND TWA
     14 OR TCTTE   - TERMINAL STORAGE




PF1-HELP  PF2-PRINT  PF3-END  PF4-EXIT  PF9-DIRECTORY
```

Figure 10.5 CICS Abend-AID Report Menu.

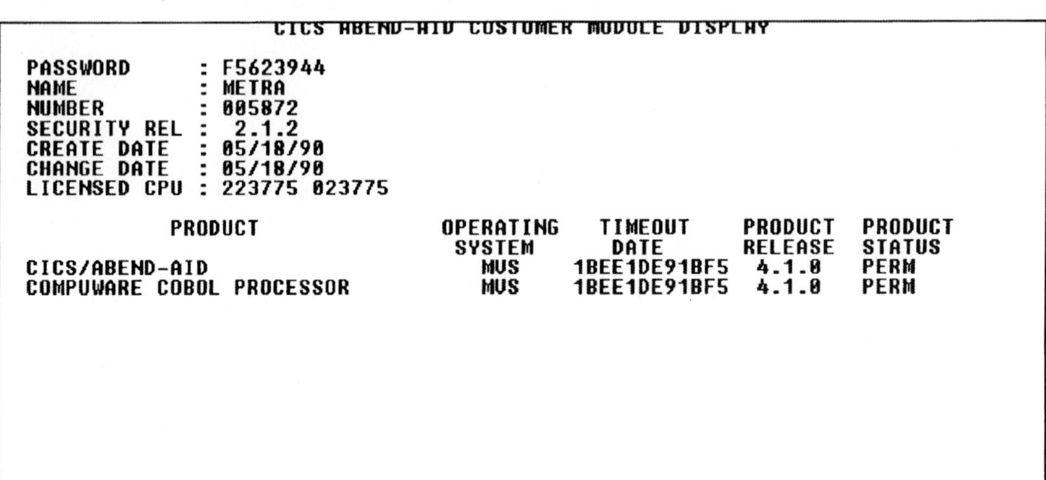

```
                    CICS ABEND-AID CUSTOMER MODULE DISPLAY

PASSWORD      : F5623944
NAME          : METRA
NUMBER        : 005872
SECURITY REL  :  2.1.2
CREATE DATE   : 05/18/90
CHANGE DATE   : 05/18/90
LICENSED CPU  : 223775 023775

          PRODUCT                    OPERATING   TIMEOUT      PRODUCT  PRODUCT
                                      SYSTEM      DATE        RELEASE  STATUS
CICS/ABEND-AID                         MVS     1BEE1DE91BF5   4.1.0    PERM
COMPUWARE COBOL PROCESSOR              MVS     1BEE1DE91BF5   4.1.0    PERM
```

Figure 10.6 The result of an AAON CUSTINFO transaction.

```
                    CICS ABEND-AID GLOBAL OPTIONS

        TRACE    :  00150                          SRCH     :  015
        DEST     :  CSMT                           SHOWTR   :  NO
        RESCT    :  024                            BLDLCT   :  014
        HELP     :  NO                             TSQNAME  :  CCA
        SNAP     :  ALL                            ONLDEL   :  YES
        FILEUSE  :  00                             DISPTYPE :  L
        AAMSG    :  N                              PRINT    :  OPERID
        SLSLIST  :  PARAGRAPH                      SLSWORK  :  PROGRAM
        SLSLINK  :  PROGRAM                        SLSEXT   :  PROGRAM
        SLSWRAP  :  YES                            SLSDDN   :  SLSF001
        NBRSLS   :  008
```

Figure 10.7 The result of an AAON GLOBAL transaction.

(which is nothing more than a walk-through of a specific problem), you can navigate from one panel to another just by pressing PF7 and PF8 (or their equivalents), entering HELP in the command field, or pressing PF1 or PF13. You can also press the following command keys for navigational purposes:

- PF3 or PF15, which returns to the previous screen
- PF8 or PF19, which scrolls up the text
- PF8 or PF20, which scrolls down the text

10.4 An Abend-AID Case Study

The purpose of this case study is to monitor and review potential problems that occur during a CICS transaction, and how Abend-AID analyzes such problems leading up to an abnormal termination.

Suppose your CICS program, ARA21C, has terminated with an AEIL condition code and you need to obtain some specific information about the problem.

```
----------------------- CICS ABEND-AID SECTION DISPLAY -----------------------
COMMAND ==> HELP                                              SCROLL ==> CSR

CODE=AEIL  TASK=AR21  PROGRAM=ARA21C   DATE=10/02/91  TIME=09:40:05  TERM=0000

                        C I C S   A B E N D - A I D
    (C) COPYRIGHT 1984 COMPUWARE CORPORATION ALL RIGHTS RESERVED
                          RELEASE 900227-R 4.1.0


        ***************************************************
        *    DIAGNOSTIC SECTION          -AEIL DSIDERR-    *
        ***************************************************

THE AEIL ABEND OCCURRED WHEN A READ REQUEST TO FILE ARA61C COULD NOT BE
SATISFIED BECAUSE THE DATA SET ID SPECIFIED WAS IN ERROR. MAKE SURE YOU
SPECIFY THE CORRECT NAME IN THE-

       EXEC CICS READ DATASET(ARA61C) COMMAND.

THE FOLLOWING IS A DISPLAY OF THE FIRST 16 CHARACTERS OF THE SEARCH

PF1-HELP  PF2-PRINT  PF3-END  PF5-RFIND  PF6-MENU  PF7-UP  PF8-DOWN  PF9-DIR
```

Figure 10.8A A HELP request on the command line.

```
----------------------- CICS ABEND-AID SECTION DISPLAY -----------------------
COMMAND ==>                                                   SCROLL ==> CSR


                 C I C S   A B E N D - A I D   H E L P
                  D I A G N O S T I C   S E C T I O N

THIS SECTION CONTAINS SPECIFIC INFORMATION RELATING TO THE ABEND.
SUCH AS:

        1) REASONS FOR THE ERROR.
        2) THE ABENDING STATEMENT ITSELF.
        3) FIELDS ON THE ABENDING STATEMENT.

THE FOLLOWING TOPICS ARE PRESENTED IN SEQUENCE.

        - PRIMARY COMMANDS
        - REPORT SECTION SELECTION COMMANDS
        - SCROLL COMMANDS
        - PF KEY COMMANDS


PF3-END  PF4-EXIT  PF5-RFIND  PF7-UP  PF8-DOWN  PF9-DIRECTORY
```

Figure 10.8B An Abend-AID HELP screen.

```
-------------------- CICS ABEND-AID REPORT FILE DIRECTORY --------------------
COMMAND ==>                                                   SCROLL ==> CSR

   TRAN  TERM   REPORT  ABEND    DATE      TIME     PROGRAM   NETNAME   STATUS
 - AR21  !!!!   000627  OCKC   10/02/91  16:34:46  IN25PGMS
 - VTAT  0000   000626  KERN   10/02/91  14:11:39  IN25PGMS  LAN004A
 - AR40  0000   000625  AEIL   10/02/91  12:24:30  ARC44C    LAN004A
 - AR21  JEFA   000624  AEIL   10/02/91  09:53:32  ARA21C    LAN007A
 - AR21  0000   000623  AEIL   10/02/91  09:48:08  ARA21C    LAN004A
 - AR21  0000   000622  AEIL   10/02/91  09:44:55  ARA21C    LAN004A    V
 S AR21  0000   000621  AEIL   10/02/91  09:43:55  ARA21C    LAN004A
 - AR21  0000   000620  AEIL   10/02/91  09:43:33  ARA21C    LAN004A
 - AR20  0000   000619  AEIL   10/02/91  09:42:25  ARC24C    LAN004A
 - AR21  0000   000618  AEIL   10/02/91  09:40:05  ARA21C    LAN004A
 - AR21  0000   000617  AEIL   10/02/91  08:55:17  ARA21C    LAN004A
 - AR21  T001   000616  AEIL   10/02/91  08:47:03  ARA21C    TAF0001
 - AR60  T002   000615  AEIL   10/02/91  07:49:23  ARB64C    TAF0002
 - AR21  T002   000614  AEIL   10/02/91  07:48:21  ARA21C    TAF0002
 - AR92  0000   000613  AED3   09/26/91  16:58:31  DFHEDFX   LAN004A
 - AR90  0000   000612  AEI9   09/26/91  15:53:32  ARM90C    LAN004A
 - AR60  0000   000611  AEIL   09/26/91  15:27:15  ARB64C    LAN004A
 - AR40  0000   000610  AEIL   09/26/91  15:26:51  ARB48C    LAN004A

PF1-HELP  PF2-PRINT  PF3-END  PF4-EXIT  PF6-MENU  PF7-UP  PF8-DOWN
```

Figure 10.9 The Abend-AID File Directory Panel.

The first response is to issuc an AADF transaction, which displays a directory panel (Figure 10.2) of not just the specific abend sought, but others as well. So when the Abend-AID File Directory is invoked, you need to know the particular program by number, the transaction identifier (AR21), whether there are more than single incidents of the same transaction, and the specific time of the "bomb out." Figure 10.9 gives you a previously described panel, allowing you to select a particular transaction by placing the character S next to it.

The selection of transaction AR21 (program ARA21C) also requires you to know the time frame (9:43:55) because, as you can see, there were other attempts during the day to submit and run the transactions—several times, in fact.

In the next frame, you'll see that an abend occurred as CICS made an attempt to read a required file, ARA61C. More specifically, the command that caused the error is displayed as:

```
EXEC CICD READ DATASET('ARA61C')
```

Note on the bottom of Figure 10.10 (the first section display panel) the statement *the following is a display of the first sixteen characters of the search*. This display is shown in Figure 10.11.

The next sequential-instruction section enables you to see where the program was executing when it abended. The software calculates the location of the next sequential instruction in the abending program. The displacement of the last call or EXEC statement is also provided, and gives you another clue as to what was happening in the program before it terminated. The displacement is used to find the program statement in the COBOL compile CLIST or PMAP (procedure map). This is highlighted in Figure 10.12 and continued in Figure 10.13.

Next, shown in Figures 10.14 through 10.16, is a trace table, which is part of

Abend-AID's Trace Table section. By definition, a trace table is a storage area into which trace information is placed. This table contains the chronological occurrences of events that take place in CICS, recorded in wrap-around fashion within the trace table. The Trace Table section shows only the entries for the abending task. It contains the name of the program from which the command was issued, the CICS command executed, the offset or address of the CICS command, the CICS response, and the information based on the type of CICS request. The most current entries are displayed first.

```
----------------------- CICS ABEND-AID SECTION DISPLAY ------------------------
COMMAND ==>                                                      SCROLL ==> CSR

CODE=AEIL  TASK=AR21  PROGRAM=ARA21C    DATE=10/02/91  TIME=09:43:55  TERM=0000

                       C I C S   A B E N D - A I D
    (C) COPYRIGHT 1984 COMPUWARE CORPORATION ALL RIGHTS RESERVED
                         RELEASE 900227-R 4.1.0


        ***************************************************
        *    DIAGNOSTIC SECTION          -AEIL DSIDERR-     *
        ***************************************************

THE AEIL ABEND OCCURRED WHEN A READ REQUEST TO FILE ARA61C COULD NOT BE
SATISFIED BECAUSE THE DATA SET ID SPECIFIED WAS IN ERROR. MAKE SURE YOU
SPECIFY THE CORRECT NAME IN THE-

       EXEC CICS READ DATASET(ARA61C) COMMAND.

THE FOLLOWING IS A DISPLAY OF THE FIRST 16 CHARACTERS OF THE SEARCH

PF1-HELP  PF2-PRINT  PF3-END  PF5-RFIND  PF6-MENU  PF7-UP  PF8-DOWN  PF9-DIR
```

Figure 10.10 A Section Display Panel specifying the reason for the AEIL.

```
----------------------- CICS ABEND-AID SECTION DISPLAY ------------------------
COMMAND ==>                                                      SCROLL ==> CSR

CODE=AEIL  TASK=AR21  PROGRAM=ARA21C    DATE=10/02/91  TIME=09:43:55  TERM=0000
ARGUMENT USED IN THE REQUEST.
LEVEL/FIELD NAME                PICTURE/TYPE OFFS      VALUE
------------------------------- ----------------- ----+----1----+----2
03 FILLER                       X(24)            X'C1D4C5D9C5E7D5D50000
                                              +10 X'0000F0F0F0F0'
****************************** BOTTOM OF SECTION ******************************











PF1-HELP  PF2-PRINT  PF3-END  PF5-RFIND  PF6-MENU  PF7-UP  PF8-DOWN  PF9-DIR
```

Figure 10.11 Continuation of the Section Display Panel.

```
----------------------- CICS ABEND-AID SECTION DISPLAY -----------------------
COMMAND ==>                                                   SCROLL ==> CSR

CODE=AEIL  TASK=AR21  PROGRAM=ARA21C   DATE=10/02/91  TIME=09:43:55  TERM=0000


           ***********************************************
           *     NEXT SEQUENTIAL INSTRUCTION SECTION     *
           ***********************************************

THE NEXT STATEMENT IS:

000837            GO TO  0510-READ-PREFIX-END DEPENDING ON DFHEIGDI.

THIS STATEMENT IS CONTAINED IN PARAGRAPH "0510-CHECK-NUMBER" OF PROGRAM
ARA21C.

LANGUAGE PROCESSOR INTERFACE RELEASE      = 03.20.04
LANGUAGE PROCESSOR POST PROCESSOR RELEASE = 03.20.04

* * * * * * * * * * * *   W A R N I N G   * * * * * * * * * * * *


PF1-HELP  PF2-PRINT  PF3-END  PF5-RFIND  PF6-MENU  PF7-UP  PF8-DOWN  PF9-DIR
```

Figure 10.12 Section Display Panel showing the next sequential instruction.

```
----------------------- CICS ABEND-AID SECTION DISPLAY -----------------------
COMMAND ==>                                                   SCROLL ==> CSR

CODE=AEIL  TASK=AR21  PROGRAM=ARA21C   DATE=10/02/91  TIME=09:43:55  TERM=0000
THE SOURCE LISTING FOR THE PROGRAM WAS CREATED ON 10/ 2/91
AT 10:05:33, AND DOES NOT MATCH THE PROGRAM COMPILE DATE AND TIME

* * * * * * * * * * * * * * * * * * * * * * * * * * * * * * * * *

THE PROGRAM WAS COMPILED ON 01/18/91 AT 15:54:09 AND IS 003FBC BYTES
LONG. IT IS PART OF LOAD MODULE ARA21C WHICH WAS LOADED FROM
NIRXT.TEST.CICS.LOADLIB.

IT WAS LINK EDITED ON 01/18/91 AND IT IS 004C60 BYTES LONG.

THE LAST CALL OR 'EXEC CICS' COMMAND WAS:

000831       *EXEC CICS
000832       *     HANDLE CONDITION
000833       *           NOTFND(0510-READ-PREFIX-END)
000834       *END-EXEC.
00083500367        MOVE '                       00465     ' TO DFHEIV0

PF1-HELP  PF2-PRINT  PF3-END  PF5-RFIND  PF6-MENU  PF7-UP  PF8-DOWN  PF9-DIR
```

Figure 10.13 Continuation of the Next Sequential Instruction Panel.

The Execute Interface Block (EIB) section formats relevant EIB information, as shown in Figure 10.17. It decodes information such as the function code, response code, and attention identifier (AID) byte. The Program section identifies all of the programs involved in the abending task, and contains two sections:

The Link Trace Summary section provides information about all programs linked to by the task. It summarizes the program-execution sequence by showing how each program was linked. The Program Summary section lists detailed information about each program contained in the Link Trace Summary. It provides compile/link edit dates, program languages, CSECT name and length, and CICS type for each program linked to or loaded by the abending task. An overview of this is shown in Figure 10.18.

The Program Listing section was developed by the vendor for COBOL programs. It shows the source code, statement by statement, of the abending program. Abend-AID allows you the flexibility to not run the entire listing; you can specify it through the SLSLIST Global option. Accordingly, you might list only the abending statement, or the paragraph in which the abnormal termination took place. You can also obtain a specific number of statements before and after the termination.

```
----------------------- CICS ABEND-AID SECTION DISPLAY ------------------------
COMMAND ==>                                                    SCROLL ==> CSR

CODE=AEIL  TASK=AR21  PROGRAM=ARA21C    DATE=10/02/91  TIME=09:43:55  TERM=0000
          ****************************************************
          *    TRACE TABLE WITH MOST CURRENT ENTRIES FIRST    *
          ****************************************************

              TYP: S=STATEMENT NUMBER, A=ADDRESS, +=OFFSET

              STATEMENT
PROGRAM  TYP ADDR/OFFS                  COMMAND/VERB
_______  ___ _________ ____________________________________________

ARA21C    S    0000831 EXEC CICS
                           HANDLE CONDITION
                           NOTFND(0510-READ-PREFIX-END)
                           END-EXEC.


                       THE RESPONSE WAS DSIDERR - DATASET NAME
                       NOT IN FCT

PF1-HELP  PF2-PRINT  PF3-END  PF5-RFIND  PF6-MENU  PF7-UP  PF8-DOWN  PF9-DIR
```

Figure 10.14 Part of Abend-AID's Trace Table section.

```
----------------------- CICS ABEND-AID SECTION DISPLAY ------------------------
COMMAND ==>                                                    SCROLL ==> CSR

CODE=AEIL  TASK=AR21  PROGRAM=ARA21C    DATE=10/02/91  TIME=09:43:55  TERM=0000

ARA21C    S    0000813 EXEC CICS
                           READ DATASET('ARA71C')
                           INTO(PREFIX-TABLE)
                           RIDFLD(I-KEY)
                           END-EXEC.


ARA21C    S    0000520 EXEC CICS
                           HANDLE CONDITION
                           NOTFND(0200-END1)
                           END-EXEC.


ARA21C    S    0000479 EXEC CICS
                           HANDLE AID
                           CLEAR(0200-PF1-MAIN-MENU)
                           PF1(0200-PF1-MAIN-MENU)

PF1-HELP  PF2-PRINT  PF3-END  PF5-RFIND  PF6-MENU  PF7-UP  PF8-DOWN  PF9-DIR
```

Figure 10.15 Commands relating the abnormal termination.

```
----------------------- CICS ABEND-AID SECTION DISPLAY -----------------------
COMMAND ==>                                                    SCROLL ==> CSR

CODE=AEIL  TASK=AR21  PROGRAM=ARA21C    DATE=10/02/91  TIME=09:43:55  TERM=0000
                          PF2(0210-PF2-EDIT-ADD)
                          PF3(0220-PF3-HELP)
                          ANYKEY(0230-INVALID-KEY)
                          END-EXEC.


           A    50303996 COMMAND LEVEL GETMAIN
                         0118 BYTES OF USER STORAGE OBTAINED
                         AT ADDRESS 0005C3B0

TRACE ENTRY (UNEXPANDED)
  ID   REG14    REQD  TASK  FIELD A  FIELD B       RESOURCE   TIME
* F1 802EDD28 0004   483 40000000 4105B704 *  *              *41424C0C

           A    802EEDB6 MACRO LEVEL UNCONDITIONAL GETMAIN
                         WITH INITIALIZATION

                         0038 BYTES OF USER STORAGE

PF1-HELP  PF2-PRINT  PF3-END  PF5-RFIND  PF6-MENU  PF7-UP  PF8-DOWN  PF9-DIR
```

Figure 10.16 Commands displayed part of the trace-table analysis.

```
----------------------- CICS ABEND-AID SECTION DISPLAY -----------------------
COMMAND ==>                                                    SCROLL ==> CSR

CODE=AEIL  TASK=AR21  PROGRAM=ARA21C    DATE=10/02/91  TIME=09:43:55  TERM=0000
                *********************************************
                *      EXECUTE INTERFACE BLOCK  (EIB)       *
                *********************************************

EIBTIME     9.43.55                       EIBDATE     91/275
EIBTRNID   AR21                           EIBTASKN      0483
EIBTRMID   0000                           EIBCPOSN      01A0
EIBCALEN   00047                          EIBAID     7D - ENTER
EIBFN      0602          - READ
EIBRCODE   010000000000 - DSIDERR
EIBDS      ARA61C                         EIBREQID   ........
EIBRSRCE   ARA61C                         EIBSYNC    00
EIBFREE    00                             EIBRECV    00
EIBATT     00                             EIBEOC     00
EIBFMH     00                             EIBCOMPL   00
EIBSIG     00                             EIBCONF    00
EIBERR     00                             EIBERRCD   00000000
EIBSYNRB   00                             EIBNODAT   00

PF1-HELP  PF2-PRINT  PF3-END  PF5-RFIND  PF6-MENU  PF7-UP  PF8-DOWN  PF9-DIR
```

Figure 10.17 Execute Interface Block section.

The purpose of the Program Storage section is to monitor and print or display all user storage areas that are associated with the abending program, and those still on the active link chain—as depicted in Figure 10.19.

For Basic Assembler programs, this section shows the Dynamic Storage Area (DSA). For PL/I programs, it shows both the dynamic and the static storage areas. For COBOL programs, if they are compiled using the vendor's postprocessor, the Program Storage section is formatted to display the WORKING STORAGE level number, field name, field type, and the value associated with each field. A Dynamic Task Global Table (TGT) is also displayed at this point.

Fields that include nondisplayable data are presented in hexadecimal format. Fields that are more than 20 bytes long are wrapped. Figure 10.20 shows additional WORKING STORAGE assignments. I selected these two panels to display WS assignments on a sample basis; Abend-AID covers the entire section unabridged.

Figures 10.21 and 10.22 highlight the beginning and the end of the TGT table. For COBOL application programs, each BLL cell (Base Linkage Locator) is formatted with displacements that match the program's data map, or DMAP. The type of storage referenced by each BLL cell is also identified. For a close look, review Figures 10.23 and 10.24.

```
----------------------- CICS ABEND-AID SECTION DISPLAY ------------------------
COMMAND ==>                                                      SCROLL ==> CSR

CODE=AEIL  TASK=AR21  PROGRAM=ARA21C    DATE=10/02/91  TIME=09:43:55  TERM=0000
                ***************************************
                *           PROGRAM SECTION           *
                ***************************************

                     ***************************
                     *   LINK TRACE SUMMARY    *
                     ***************************

  PROGRAM    CSECT                      PROGRAM    CSECT    RETURN

  ARA21C     ARA21C    **LINKED TO BY**  SYSTEM

                     ***************************
                     *     PROGRAM SUMMARY     *
                     ***************************

                       LINK     COMPILE    LOAD                       CICS
PROGRAM      CSECT     DATE      DATE      POINT    LENGTH   LANG     TYPE

PF1-HELP  PF2-PRINT  PF3-END  PF5-RFIND  PF6-MENU  PF7-UP  PF8-DOWN  PF9-DIR
```

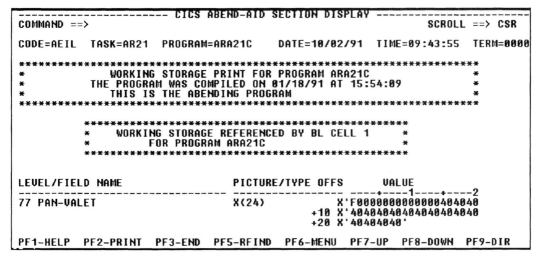

Figure 10.18 Abend-AID's Program Section table.

```
----------------------- CICS ABEND-AID SECTION DISPLAY ------------------------
COMMAND ==>                                                      SCROLL ==> CSR

CODE=AEIL  TASK=AR21  PROGRAM=ARA21C    DATE=10/02/91  TIME=09:43:55  TERM=0000

**********************************************************************
*            WORKING STORAGE PRINT FOR PROGRAM ARA21C                *
*         THE PROGRAM WAS COMPILED ON 01/18/91 AT 15:54:09           *
*            THIS IS THE ABENDING PROGRAM                            *
**********************************************************************

          ************************************************
          *    WORKING STORAGE REFERENCED BY BL CELL 1   *
          *         FOR PROGRAM ARA21C                   *
          ************************************************

LEVEL/FIELD NAME                  PICTURE/TYPE OFFS       VALUE
--------------------------------- ----------------- ----+----1----+----2
77 PAN-VALET                      X(24)                 X'F0000000000000404040
                                                    +10 X'40404040404040404040
                                                    +20 X'40404040'

PF1-HELP  PF2-PRINT  PF3-END  PF5-RFIND  PF6-MENU  PF7-UP  PF8-DOWN  PF9-DIR
```

Figure 10.19 The Program Storage section.

```
----------------------- CICS ABEND-AID SECTION DISPLAY -----------------------
COMMAND ==>                                                       SCROLL ==> CSR

CODE=AEIL  TASK=AR21  PROGRAM=ARA21C    DATE=10/02/91  TIME=09:43:55  TERM=0000
01 COMM-AREA
02 ENTRY-SW                     X                   SPACES
02 INV-KEY
03 I-KEY                        X                   SPACES
03 I-NUM                        X(5)                SPACES
03 FILLER                       X(24)             X'C1D4C5D9C5E7D5D50000
                                              +10 X'0000F0F0F0F000000000
                                              +20 X'00000000'
02 PRJ-KEY                      X(6)                LOW-VALUES
02 WRITE-RECORD-SW              X                   LOW-VALUES
02 RECORD-WROTE-SW              X                   LOW-VALUES
02 COM-ACC-PER                  X(4)                LOW-VALUES
02 CURSOR-POSITION              9(4)                LOW-VALUES
01 INVOICE-COUNTER              S9(4)    COMP       +0
01 INVOICE-RECORD
02 INVOICE-KEY
03 INVOICE-PREFIX-KEY           X                   LOW-VALUES
03 INVOICE-NUMBER               9(5)                LOW-VALUES

PF1-HELP  PF2-PRINT  PF3-END  PF5-RFIND  PF6-MENU  PF7-UP  PF8-DOWN  PF9-DIR
```

Figure 10.20 A second panel, showing additional storage assignments and values.

```
----------------------- CICS ABEND-AID SECTION DISPLAY -----------------------
COMMAND ==>                                                       SCROLL ==> CSR

CODE=AEIL  TASK=AR21  PROGRAM=ARA21C    DATE=10/02/91  TIME=09:43:55  TERM=0000
01 DFHEIV10                     S9(7)    COMP-3 X'00000000'
01 DFHEIV9                      X(1)                LOW-VALUES
01 DFHC0011                     X(1)                LOW-VALUES
01 DFHEIV4                      X(6)                LOW-VALUES
01 DFHC0070                     X(7)                LOW-VALUES
01 DFHC0071                     X(7)              X'0602D000050000'
01 DFHC0440                     X(44)             X'00F0F0F3F6F140404040
                                              +10 X'40404040404040404040
                                              +20 X'400000'
01 DFHD               FIELDS NOT AVAILABLE   COMP


                  *************************************
                  *        PROGRAM'S DYNAMIC TGT       *
                  *************************************

ADDRESS   DISPL   -------------HEX DATA--------------   --DISPLAY DATA--
0006024C  00000   00300000 0005B584 00000000 5010CD52   *.......d....&...*

PF1-HELP  PF2-PRINT  PF3-END  PF5-RFIND  PF6-MENU  PF7-UP  PF8-DOWN  PF9-DIR
```

Figure 10.21 Beginning of the TGT table, toward the bottom.

The Terminal Storage section, shown in Figures 10.25 and 10.26, highlights selected fields from the terminal control table, the terminal-control-table user area (TCTUA), and all terminal I/O areas belonging to the terminal at the time.

Last, the Abend-AID File section shows all active files remaining on the storage chain, including the access method used during the operation, such as VSAM, record and key length, and vital input/output statistics. The record data and search arguments are formatted for each current record. The example shown in Figure 10.27 tells you that no active file was available associated with the AR21 transaction.

10.5 How to Use an Abend-AID On-Line Report

You can initiate an on-line report through the AADF transaction identifier. Just like with the AAON transaction type, mentioned earlier in this chapter, you can make the following AADF transaction types valid simply by tacking a single-character suffix onto the initial transaction identifier. (Remember that AADF without a suffix will display the CICS Abend-AID Report File Directory screen.)

```
----------------------- CICS ABEND-AID SECTION DISPLAY -----------------------
COMMAND ==>                                                    SCROLL ==> CSR

CODE=AEIL  TASK=AR21  PROGRAM=ARA21C    DATE=10/02/91  TIME=09:43:55  TERM=0000
0006025C 00010   00000000 0006004C 0006050C 5010CCD6   *........<....&..O*
0006026C 00020   0010B5F8 0005B574 0005C378 0005F04C   *...8.......C...0<*
0006027C 00030   0006004C 00060454 0010DF7E 0010A050   *...<........=...&*
0006028C 00040   0010A050 0010B5E0 2042A04B 00000000   *...&.............*
0006029C 00050   00000000 002EDDE0 00000000 00000000   *.................*
000602AC 00060   00000000 00000000 00000000 00000000   *.................*
            LINE(S) 000602BC-000603EC SAME AS ABOVE
000603FC 001B0   0010A050 00000000 0010E010 E2E8E2D6   *...&.........SYSO*
0006040C 001C0   E4E34040 E300000C 0010A0D8 00000000   *UT  T.......Q....*
0006041C 001D0   00000000 00000000 00000000 00000000   *.................*
            LINE(S) 0006042C-0006043C SAME AS ABOVE
0006044C 00200   0005F04C 0006004C 00000000 00000000   *..0<...<.........*
0006045C 00210   00000000 00000000 00000000 00000000   *.................*
            LINE(S) 0006046C-0006046C SAME AS ABOVE
0006047C 00230   0005B628 0005C378 00060484 002F1000   *.......C....d....*
0006048C 00240   00000000 00000000 00000000 00000000   *.................*
            LINE(S) 0006049C-000604BC SAME AS ABOVE
000604CC 00280   00000000 00000000 0010DF28 00000000   *.................*

PF1-HELP  PF2-PRINT  PF3-END  PF5-RFIND  PF6-MENU  PF7-UP  PF8-DOWN  PF9-DIR
```

Figure 10.22 A second panel, showing the TGT.

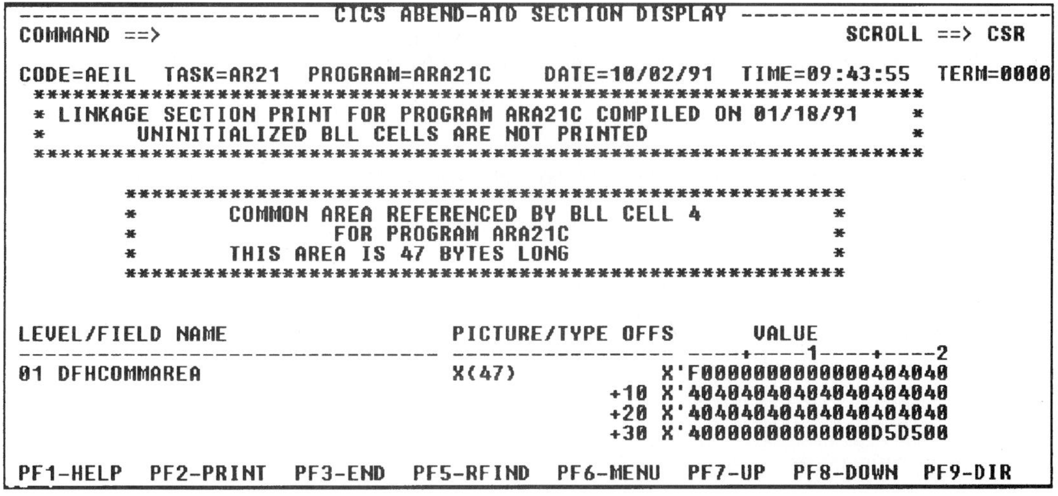

```
----------------------- CICS ABEND-AID SECTION DISPLAY -----------------------
COMMAND ==>                                                    SCROLL ==> CSR

CODE=AEIL  TASK=AR21  PROGRAM=ARA21C    DATE=10/02/91  TIME=09:43:55  TERM=0000
 **********************************************************************
 * LINKAGE SECTION PRINT FOR PROGRAM ARA21C COMPILED ON 01/18/91      *
 *       UNINITIALIZED BLL CELLS ARE NOT PRINTED                      *
 **********************************************************************

        ****************************************************
        *       COMMON AREA REFERENCED BY BLL CELL 4        *
        *              FOR PROGRAM ARA21C                   *
        *       THIS AREA IS 47 BYTES LONG                  *
        ****************************************************


LEVEL/FIELD NAME                PICTURE/TYPE OFFS       VALUE
------------------------------- ------------------ ----+----1----+----2
01 DFHCOMMAREA                  X(47)              X'F0000000000000404040
                                              +10 X'40404040404040404040
                                              +20 X'40404040404040404040
                                              +30 X'40000000000000D5D500

PF1-HELP  PF2-PRINT  PF3-END  PF5-RFIND  PF6-MENU  PF7-UP  PF8-DOWN  PF9-DIR
```

Figure 10.23 A snapshot of the Linkage Editor.

```
----------------------- CICS ABEND-AID SECTION DISPLAY -----------------------
COMMAND ==>                                                  SCROLL ==> CSR

CODE=AEIL  TASK=AR21  PROGRAM=ARA21C    DATE=10/02/91  TIME=09:43:55  TERM=0000
                                            +40 X'000000F0F0F0F0'

        *******************************************************
        *          CSA REFERENCED BY BLL CELL 6               *
        *          FOR PROGRAM ARA21C                         *
        *          THIS AREA IS 2,560 BYTES LONG              *
        *******************************************************

LEVEL/FIELD NAME                 PICTURE/TYPE OFFS      VALUE
-------------------------------- ---------------- ----+----1----+----2
01 DFHBLLSLOT2                   X(1)             LOW-VALUES
****************************** BOTTOM OF SECTION ******************************




PF1-HELP  PF2-PRINT  PF3-END  PF5-RFIND  PF6-MENU  PF7-UP  PF8-DOWN  PF9-DIR
```

Figure 10.24 A panel showing the CSA being referenced by the BLL cell.

```
----------------------- CICS ABEND-AID SECTION DISPLAY -----------------------
COMMAND ==>                                                  SCROLL ==> CSR

CODE=AEIL  TASK=AR21  PROGRAM=ARA21C    DATE=10/02/91  TIME=09:43:55  TERM=0000

              *****************************************
              *         TCA FORMATTED SECTION         *
              *****************************************

TASK IDENTIFICATION NUMBER- 00483
ORIGINAL TRANS CODE-        AR21       ORIGINAL PROGRAM-    ARA21C
CURRENT PROGRAM-            ARA21C     LANGUAGE IS-         COBOL
ORIGINAL ABEND CODE-        AEIL       CURRENT ABEND CODE-  AEIL
FACILITY CONTROL IND-       01         EVENT CTL IND-       20
USERID-                     NIRAU

NO TRANSACTION WORK AREA PRESENT FOR THIS TRANSACTION
****************************** BOTTOM OF SECTION ******************************




PF1-HELP  PF2-PRINT  PF3-END  PF5-RFIND  PF6-MENU  PF7-UP  PF8-DOWN  PF9-DIR
```

Figure 10.25 The TCA Formatted section.

AADFT. This enhanced transaction is designed to display the most current Abend-AID report generated from your terminal. A report is simply a series of screen sequences "left over" from the most current session.

AADFX. This allows you to view the most currently referenced report (or, more specifically, screen) in the Report File Directory.

The AADF transaction identifier can also be used in conjunction with a report number, such as AADF 000643, with an embedded blank segregating the transaction identifier and the report number. Note that you can obtain the report number for the CICS Abend-AID Report File Directory (third column from the left). A word of caution though—do not type the above request on the Report File Directory Panel. If you do, the system will respond with an error message. Use a blank screen by clearing the contents of the current session.

CICS Abend-AID, as you will have noticed from the previous case study, uses a standardized screen format. Each screen has a title and, in the following line, an area where you can enter a particular primary command. A primary command or com-

```
----------------------- CICS ABEND-AID SECTION DISPLAY ------------------------
COMMAND ==>                                                    SCROLL ==> CSR

CODE=AEIL   TASK=AR21   PROGRAM=ARA21C    DATE=10/02/91   TIME=09:43:55   TERM=0000

        ****************************************************
        *    TCTTE TERMINAL CONTROL TABLE TERMINAL ENTRY    *
        ****************************************************

TERMINAL ID- 0000                      TERM TYPE- 91 3277R
MODEL NUMBER- 2
VTAM NETNAME- LAN004A
TERM STATUS-  IN SERVICE
CURRENT OPERATOR ID- ALV
NUMBER OF INPUTS-    269               NUMBER OF OUTPUTS-      392
NUMBER OF TRANS-      53               NUMBER OF TRAN ERRS-      0

        ****************************************************
        *       TERMINAL CONTROL TABLE ENTRY FOLLOWS        *
        ****************************************************

ADDRESS  DISPL  -------------HEX DATA--------------  --DISPLAY DATA--

PF1-HELP  PF2-PRINT  PF3-END  PF5-RFIND  PF6-MENU  PF7-UP  PF8-DOWN  PF9-DIR
```

Figure 10.26 The Terminal Control section.

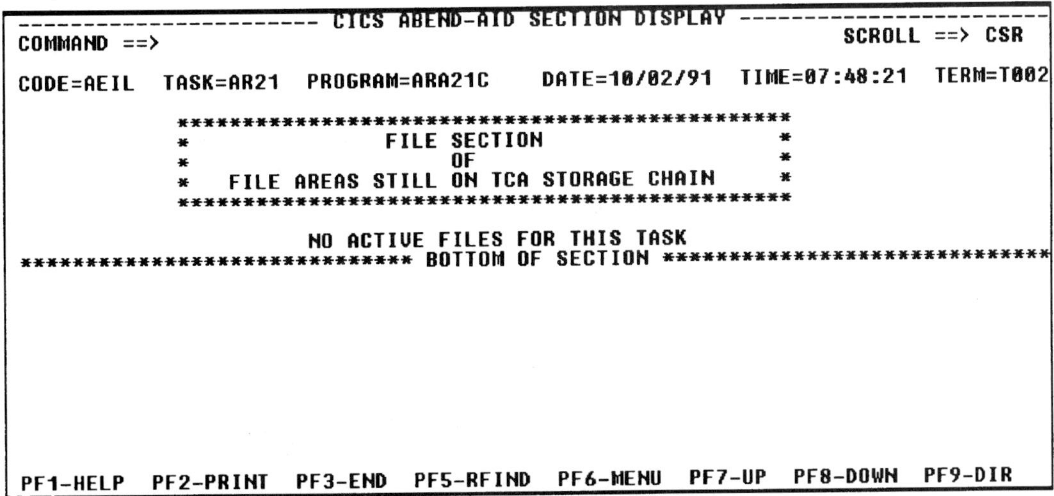

```
----------------------- CICS ABEND-AID SECTION DISPLAY ------------------------
COMMAND ==>                                                    SCROLL ==> CSR

CODE=AEIL   TASK=AR21   PROGRAM=ARA21C    DATE=10/02/91   TIME=07:48:21   TERM=T002

               **********************************************
               *               FILE SECTION                 *
               *                    OF                      *
               *   FILE AREAS STILL ON TCA STORAGE CHAIN    *
               **********************************************

                        NO ACTIVE FILES FOR THIS TASK
****************************** BOTTOM OF SECTION ******************************

PF1-HELP  PF2-PRINT  PF3-END  PF5-RFIND  PF6-MENU  PF7-UP  PF8-DOWN  PF9-DIR
```

Figure 10.27 The Abend-AID File section.

mand field, by definition, is a field that appears in the upper left-hand corner of most CICS Abend-AID screens. All CICS Abend-AID functions and screens are selected by entering the desired function or screen ID in the command line. A command itself means a request from a terminal to an operation or to execute a program.

Some primary commands are viable on all Abend-AID screens, and some appear only on specific ones during certain sessions.

The SCROLL command (upper right-hand entry) is very much like those used in the ISPF text editor. Thus, valid values include PAGE (scrolling a full page), HALF, DATA, MAX, or any number of lines desired. Also, the CSR command allows you to perform a cursor-sensitive scroll, meaning that you begin scrolling from the current location of the cursor.

PF key assignments are similar, if not identical, to the text editor. A summary of Abend-AID PF key assignments are listed in detail in Figure 10.28. I have included a number of selected primary commands that will expedite your handling of the on-line reports. Suppose your program has abended with an ASRA (data exception) return code and you would like to scan through the analysis as fast as possible. First, select a particular transaction off the Abend-AID File Report Directory by placing

```
  PF1    Displays help information for each screens.

  PF2    Displays the CICS Abend-AID Print Specification
         screens for printing a hardcopy of the report or
         directory.

  PF3    Terminates a CICS Abend-AID function and returns
         to the previous level.

  PF4    Returns to CICS.

  PF5    Repeats the previous FIND command. Valid on the
         Section Display screen.

  PF6    Displays the Report Menu screen for the selected report.

  PF7    Scrolls up a specified number of display lines. Valid
         on the Report File Directory and Section Display screens.

  PF8    Scrolls down a specified number of display lines. Valid
         on the Report File Directory and Section Display screens.

  PF9    Displays the Report File Directory screen

 PF10    Scrolls to the previous CICS Abend-AID report section.
         Valid on the Section Display screen.

 PF11    Scrolls to the previous CICS Abend-AID report section.
         Valid on the Section Display screen.

 PF13-   Equate to PF1 through PF11.
 PF14

CLEAR    Returns to CICS.
```

Figure 10.28 Standard PF key assignments in CICS Abend-AID.

the character S next to it. This will invoke the first panel, the Section Display screen, for your review.

If you want to get to the bottom of the report in a hurry, you can issue a BOTTOM command (also BOT or B) next to the command line and press the Enter key. This will take you down to the very last page of the Report File Directory being viewed. Likewise, you can issue a TOP or T command to get back to the top of the report.

If you intend to navigate only a page or a few lines up or down on the report, you can specify DOWN (DN) or UP, accordingly. Either one of these commands work in conjunction with a number (representing your target statement or page). You can also use DOWN and UP with the specifications HALF, PAGE, and MAX(imum). DATA is also acceptable, meaning scrolling down (or up) by a page less one line.

NEXT (NX) and PREV (PV) are used by Abend-AID to locate a particular report section (Linkage, Execute Interface Block (EIB), Program Storage, etc.), which comes in handy if you are interested only in locating a specific portion of your online report.

FIND (F) works in conjunction with the RFIND command. Thus, FIND will locate the first occurrence of a search argument and RFIND, which is equal to PF5, will give you all the subsequent occurrences of the data—very much like ISPF, File-AID, or other standard IBM-emulated packages.

The HELP (H) command will display help information for the display screen, as I mentioned earlier. This can also be accomplished by pressing PF1 for the first time, but to continue scrolling you must press PF7 or PF8 depending on the direction and the scroll amount specified.

In order to delete a report from the directory, all you have to do is specify DELETE and the report number to be deleted. The report number is available from the CICS Abend-AID Report File Directory (third column from the left). Once the report is deleted, Abend-AID will display the message *Specified report has been successfully deleted*. The EXIT or =X command returns control to CICS. So does the END command.

There are also the commands LOCK and UNLOCK. The LOCK primary command "locks" a specific report to protect it from deletion. The unlock does exactly the opposite, making it ready for deletion. These two commands, as well as the next two I am about to present (SORT and SELECT), are valid on the Report File Directory screen.

The SORT command sorts the members listed on the Report File Directory screen according to some specified member component, such as ABCODE (short for abnormal termination code) or TRANID (transaction identifier). ABCODE will sort the directory by abnormal termination codes, and TRANID by transaction identifiers. Figures 10.29 and 10.30 present different SORT situations. In Figure 10.29, the directory is sorted by program name using the keyword PROG. In Figure 10.30, sorting takes place by date in a descending order.

The SELECT command actually complicates things because it is so much easier to place the character S next to a particular selection. In using a SELECT command, you need to specify the keyword SELECT and the specific report to be selected off the Report File Directory screen, such as 000637. DIR allows you to return to the Report File Directory screen at your choosing.

```
-------------------- CICS ABEND-AID REPORT FILE DIRECTORY --------------------
COMMAND ==>
                                                                SCROLL ==> CSR

   TRAN  TERM   REPORT  ABEND    DATE       TIME     PROGRAM   NETNAME   STATUS
 - AR21  0000   000639   AEIL  10/10/91   11:20:27   ARA21C    LAN004A
 - AR21  R605   000636   AEIL  10/08/91   10:01:30   ARA21C    TR06J206
 - AR21  JEFA   000624   AEIL  10/02/91   09:53:32   ARA21C    LAN007A
 - AR21  0000   000623   AEIL  10/02/91   09:48:08   ARA21C    LAN004A
 - AR21  0000   000622   AEIL  10/02/91   09:44:55   ARA21C    LAN004A
 - AR21  0000   000621   AEIL  10/02/91   09:43:55   ARA21C    LAN004A
 - AR21  0000   000620   AEIL  10/02/91   09:43:33   ARA21C    LAN004A
 - AR21  0000   000618   AEIL  10/02/91   09:40:05   ARA21C    LAN004A
 - AR21  0000   000617   AEIL  10/02/91   08:55:17   ARA21C    LAN004A
 - AR21  T001   000616   AEIL  10/02/91   08:47:03   ARA21C    TAF0001
 - AR21  T002   000614   AEIL  10/02/91   07:48:21   ARA21C    TAF0002
 - AR20  0000   000637   AEIL  10/10/91   11:19:24   ARB28C    LAN004A
 - AR40  0000   000610   AEIL  09/26/91   15:26:51   ARB48C    LAN004A
 - AR40  T002   000606   AEIL  09/17/91   07:53:25   ARB48C    TAF0002
 - AR40  T002   000605   AEIL  09/17/91   07:52:20   ARB48C    TAF0002
 - AR60  0000   000638   AEIL  10/10/91   11:19:40   ARB64C    LAN004A
 - AR60  T002   000615   AEIL  10/02/91   07:49:23   ARB64C    TAF0002
 - AR60  0000   000611   AEIL  09/26/91   15:27:15   ARB64C    LAN004A

PF1-HELP  PF2-PRINT  PF3-END  PF4-EXIT  PF6-MENU  PF7-UP  PF8-DOWN
```

Figure 10.29 SORT ordered by program name.

```
-------------------- CICS ABEND-AID REPORT FILE DIRECTORY --------------------
COMMAND ==>
                                                                SCROLL ==> CSR

   TRAN  TERM   REPORT  ABEND    DATE       TIME     PROGRAM   NETNAME   STATUS
 - PLAY  0000   000643   ATNI  10/30/91   11:49:29   PLAPBREQ  LAN004A
 - PLAY  0000   000642   ATNI  10/29/91   16:41:00   PLAMENU   LAN004A
 - PLAY  0000   000641   ATNI  10/28/91   12:09:16   PLADCSTS  LAN004A
 - CECI  0000   000640   ATNI  10/10/91   12:11:47   DFHECID   LAN004A
 - AR21  0000   000639   AEIL  10/10/91   11:20:27   ARA21C    LAN004A
 - AR60  0000   000638   AEIL  10/10/91   11:19:40   ARB64C    LAN004A
 - AR20  0000   000637   AEIL  10/10/91   11:19:24   ARB28C    LAN004A
 - AR21  R605   000636   AEIL  10/08/91   10:01:30   ARA21C    TR06J206
 - MSA1  R605   000635   ASRA  10/04/91   14:19:22   LPCZZNUC  TR06J206
 - MSA1  R605   000634   ASRA  10/04/91   14:17:45   LPCZZNUC  TR06J206
 - MSA1  R605   000633   0813  10/04/91   14:13:43   LPCZZNUC  TR06J206
 - VTAT  0000   000632   KERN  10/04/91   11:00:53   IN25PGMS  LAN004A
 - AR92  0000   000631   ATNI  10/04/91   10:44:48   IN25PGMS  LAN004A
 - AR92  0000   000630   ATND  10/04/91   10:44:44   IN25PGMS  LAN004A
 - AR92  !!!!   000629   INTE  10/04/91   10:44:40   ARC92C
 - AR92  !!!!   000628   OCKC  10/04/91   10:44:36   IN25PGMS
 - AR21  !!!!   000627   OCKC  10/02/91   16:34:46   IN25PGMS
 - VTAT  0000   000626   KERN  10/02/91   14:11:39   IN25PGMS  LAN004A

PF1-HELP  PF2-PRINT  PF3-END  PF4-EXIT  PF6-MENU  PF7-UP  PF8-DOWN
```

Figure 10.30 SORT ordered by date, in a descending sequence.

10.6 File Utility

The Abend-AID FILE utility enables you to perform a number of standard functions, such as moving, copying, and deleting reports in both source listing and report files. These utilities are available to you in three major environments: TSO, CMS, and Roscoe. The utilities in this productivity tool allow you to access a report with or without the source-level support, as well as JCLs to access the source listing.

There are also a number of batch utility commands available under this productivity tool. Among these are the COPY, DELETE, DIRECTORY, DIRX, FORMAT,

MOVE, and PRINT utilities. In presenting these utilities, I have taken a standardized approach in describing each command, parameter, and a valid abbreviation, if any, corresponding to the command. As in job-control statements, each parameter must be segregated from the others by a comma, thus no embedded blanks are allowed.

Note the use of an asterisk, which is a wildcard character I described to you earlier in the chapter dealing with File-AID. For example, P TRAN=AR* is designed to print all transaction abend reports with a transid that starts with AR.

You can copy your source program from reports to source file and vice versa. The source dataset (the dataset from which you copy) is listed under FROMDD while the target or destination of the copy is denoted by the TODD parameter. The keyword REPTNUMBER is optional because you might want to copy all reports and listings, which incidentally is the default value. The specific formats for the COPY and DELETE commands are as follows:

```
COPY   [REPTNUMBER=XXXX],FROMDD=ddname,TODD=ddname
       [TRAN=XXXX*     ]
       [PROGRAM=XXXXXXXX*]

DELETE [REPTNUMBER=XXXX ][INDD=ddmame]
       [TRAN=XXXX*      ]
       [PROGRAM=XXXXXXXX]
```

Other keywords used in the COPY utility are:

TRAN (T). Specifies a report or program by a transaction identifier.

PROGRAM (P). Specifies the above by program name.

TRAN (T). Stands for *transaction identifier*.

DELETE (DEL). Is used to erase a report or source listing from the report file.

DIRECTORY (D). Displays the entries in the report or in the source listing file. To invoke the directory, for example, I used a set of vendor-developed JCLs, shown in Figure 10.31.

After submitting the job, the (partial) result is shown in Figure 10.32. Another directory command, DIRX or DX, is a function very similar to the previously mentioned DIR command with one minor exception. DIRX also displays file-attribute and allocation information. In Figures 10.33A and 10.33B, a partial directory is listed after using DX. In Figure 10.33B, the term `BLOCKS IN FILE` appears in conjunction with the DIRX command, and tells you how many blocks were allocated to the directory listing.

ALLOCATION GROUPS. Denotes the number of groups in the listing.

DIRECTORY ENTRIES. Gives you the number of programs the listing file holds in its directory. In the sample report, up to 100 programs with different names can be on the listing file, provided it has enough space.

```
//NIRAVXC  JOB (9000,SSSB),'ALEX VARSEGI',MSGLEVEL=(1,1),MSGCLASS=X,
//         REGION=4096K,CLASS=A,NOTIFY=NIRAV
//*        CCADPJCL ˇ-- BATCH JCL TO EXEC THE TMDDSUTL PROGRAM
//*
//*
//TMDDSUTL EXEC PGM=TMDDSUTL,REGION=1024K
//STEPLIB  DD  DSN=CICS211.ABAID410.LOAD,DISP=SHR
//ABNLDFIL DD  DSN=CICS211.ABAID410.LISTING,DISP=SHR
//ABNLREPT DD  SYSOUT=*
//ABNLPARM DD  *               /*ˇ--ˇ--ADD COMMAND CARDS BELOWˇ--ˇ--*/
  D
//*
```

Figure 10.31 Vendor-developed JCLs to view the directory.

```
 SDSF OUTPUT DISPLAY NIRAUXC  JOB 681    DSID     4 LINE 58        COLUMNS 02- 81
 COMMAND ===>                                                    SCROLL ===> PAGE
**********************************************************************************
IEF375I  JOB /NIRAUXC / START 91317.0910
IEF376I  JOB /NIRAUXC / STOP  91317.0910 CPU    0MIN 00.58SEC SRB    0MIN 00.02S
ENTER UTILITY COMMAND:
  D
PROGRAM    LIST NUMBER    COMP DATE   TIME     RC  LANGUAGE ---BYTES---
RMBA5C    (L)        914   11/13/91    8.56.48 00 VS COBOL       638K
VM0140C   *IL        913   11/13/91    8.49.21 20 VS COBOL        39K
RMAA4C    (L)        912   11/13/91    8.44.34 00 VS COBOL       718K
VM0110C   *IL        911   11/13/91    8.30.32 20 VS COBOL       638K
POP0100   (L)        910   11/12/91   16.39.31 00 VS COBOL       519K
TRE1ADD   (L)        902   11/12/91   15.05.32 00 VS COBOL       399K
POP0101   (L)        899   11/12/91   14.19.30 00 VS COBOL       838K
RMP91C    (L)        889   11/11/91   14.07.39 00 VS COBOL       598K
RMX47C    (L)        888   11/11/91   12.41.29 00 VS COBOL       638K
RMCA6C    *IL        866   11/07/91   10.08.35 20 VS COBOL       598K
RMI28C    *IL        846   11/06/91    9.12.28 20 VS COBOL       399K
RMC51C    (L)        844   11/06/91    8.21.37 00 VS COBOL       638K
RMP71C    *IL        836   11/05/91   14.32.52 20 VS COBOL       559K
RMI44C    *IL        828   11/05/91   12.37.28 20 VS COBOL       239K
RMC43C    (L)        826   11/05/91   12.33.44 00 VS COBOL       519K
RMX91C    *IL        825   11/05/91   12.29.42 20 VS COBOL       678K
```

Figure 10.32 A partial directory listing.

BLOCK SIZE. This is the record size for the listing file given at the time of allocation. The vendor requires a record size of 4089 for VSAM listing files.

When you issue a FORMAT command, it prepares the report or source file for use after the file is allocated, or reformats an existing file. The TYPE=CICS is mandatory, while other parameters are optional. A word of caution—this command is similar to a typical PC FORMAT command in that it erases all CICS Abend-AID reports or source listings currently available on the file. The FORMAT command is as follows:

```
FORMAT  TYPE=CICS[,SUBTYPE=SOURCE][,INDD=ddname][,REPTCOUNT=XXXX]
[,GROUPCOUNT=XXX][,BLKSIZE=XXXX]  [,AUTODELETE=YES  ]
                                  [             NO  ]
                                  [             DUPS ]
```

Note the following keywords used in this statement:

TYPE. Specifies a CICS type file. TYPE=CICS means to format a CICS Abend-AID report or source file.

SUBTYPE. Refers to a source listing file. Code this parameter as SUBTYPE= SOURCE to allow postprocessor programs to store program listings in the file.

```
 SDSF OUTPUT DISPLAY NIRAUXC  JOB 824    DSID      4 LINE 59        COLUMNS 02- 81
 COMMAND ===>                                                      SCROLL ===> PAGE
IEF375I  JOB /NIRAUXC / START 91317.1302
IEF376I  JOB /NIRAUXC / STOP  91317.1303 CPU    0MIN 00.60SEC SRB    0MIN 00.02S
ENTER UTILITY COMMAND:
  DX
FILE FORMATTED FOR CICS USE.
FILE CONTAINS SOURCE DATA.
FILE HAS AUTO/UNLOCK (DUPLICATES-ONLY) ATTRIBUTE.
64 EXTENTS MAXIMUM PER MEMBER
10 BLOCKS PER GROUP
20250 BLOCKS IN FILE
2022 ALLOCATION GROUPS
350 DIRECTORY ENTRIES
4089 IS THE BLOCK SIZE
917 IS THE CURRENT DUMP NUMBER
19 DIRECTORY ENTRIES/BLOCK
19 DIRECTORY BLOCKS
2022 ALLOCATED GROUPS
PROGRAM    LIST NUMBER    COMP DATE  TIME     RC  LANGUAGE ---BYTES---
RMBA5C     (L)      916    11/13/91  11.40.11 00 VS COBOL      638K
 GROUPS-           995    1568     1580     1582     1583     1584     1585     1587
 GROUPS-          1590    1591     1593     1594     1596     1598     1599     1601
UM0140C    *IL      913    11/13/91   8.49.21 20 VS COBOL       39K
```

Figure 10.33A DIRX command, partial attribute listing (page 1).

```
 SDSF OUTPUT DISPLAY NIRAUXC  JOB 824    DSID    102 LINE 21        COLUMNS 02- 81
 COMMAND ===>                                                      SCROLL ===> PAGE
 GROUPS-          1567
RMAA4C     (L)      912    11/13/91   8.44.34 00 VS COBOL      718K
 GROUPS-          1211    1602     1604     1605     1607     1609     1610     1611
 GROUPS-          1613    1841     1843     1845     1847     1849     1992     1994
 GROUPS-          1997    2000
UM0110C    *IL      911    11/13/91   8.30.32 20 VS COBOL      638K
 GROUPS-          1815    1816     1953     1954     1955     1956     1974     1975
 GROUPS-          1976    1977     1978     1979     1980     1981     1982     2022
POP0100    (L)      910    11/12/91  16.39.31 00 VS COBOL      519K
 GROUPS-          1683    1684     1685     1686     1687     1688     1689     1690
 GROUPS-          1691    1692     1693     1694     1695
TRE1ADD    (L)      902    11/12/91  15.05.32 00 VS COBOL      399K
 GROUPS-           985     986      987      988      989      990      991      992
 GROUPS-           993     994
POP0101    (L)      899    11/12/91  14.19.30 00 VS COBOL      838K
 GROUPS-          1793    1794     1795     1796     1797     1798     1799     1800
 GROUPS-          1801    1802     1803     1804     1805     1806     1807     1808
 GROUPS-          1809    1810     1811     1812     1813
RMP91C     (L)      889    11/11/91  14.07.39 00 VS COBOL      598K
 GROUPS-          1339    1340     1341     1342     1343     1344     1345     1346
 GROUPS-          1347    1348     1349     1350     1351     1352     1353
RMX47C     (L)      888    11/11/91  12.41.29 00 VS COBOL      638K
```

Figure 10.33B DIRX command, partial directory listing (page 2).

INDD. Refers to an alternative file ddname.

REPTCOUNT. Tells you the maximum number of directory entries or source listings to allocate.

GROUPCOUNT. Specifies the number of report file blocks to be allocated to a report or source listing member each time more space is needed.

BLKSIZE. This is the block size for a BDAM report file.

AUTODELETE. Tells you whether the oldest member in the file is automatically deleted when the file becomes full.

Two more utility functions are MOVE and PRINT. The MOVE command is designed to move reports or source listings between CICS Abend-AID report or source files, and is as follows:

```
MOVE    [REPTNUMBER=XXXX ],FROMDD=ddname,TODD=ddname
        [TRAN=XXXX*      ]
        [PROGRAM=XXXXXXXX*]
```

Please note that if CICS happens to be using the FROMDD or TODD data set, a MOVE statement is inoperable. The file must be either closed or disabled.

The purpose of the PRINT command is to list reports or source listings to your terminal, and the format is as follows:

```
PRINT   {TRAN=XXXX*         }[,LINESIZE=S][PAGESIZE=nn][INDD=ddname]
        {REPTNUMBER=XXXX         }          L
        {JOBNAME=XXXX*           }
        {PROGRAM=XXXXXXXX*       }
[,OUTDD=ddname][,STARTDATE=mm/dd/yy][,ENDDATE=mm/dd/yy]
[,SLSDD=ddname]
```

The TRANS, REPTNUMBER, and JOBNAME parameters are mandatory. The OUTDD parameter directs the output to a required device. All other parameters are optional.

Chapter

11

All About the CA-Verify Product

11.1 Product Overview

CA-Verify is a productivity tool designed to automate the testing process. The product essentially captures screen images from live CICS transactions and lets you reuse them for testing. This methodology does two things for you. First, it saves you time because it saves you from retyping a great volume of data already entered into the system at one time but not saved at the end of the CICS session. Second, the test streams that are saved via CA-Verify become available to simulate production testing.

When CA-Verify runs a test stream, it allocates virtual terminals for each terminal in the test stream. It uses terminal information, stored when the test stream was created, to synchronize the status of the virtual terminal with the real terminal. Using virtual terminals saves system resources and means that testing is not restricted to the number of physical terminals available. Moreover, users who need real terminals are not affected by the testing.

Let me describe to you a typical problem that is difficult to monitor. It is 2:30 in the morning and production CICS abends due to a transaction error on an ASRA (data exception) condition. Six hours later, the problem is reviewed by the systems programmer only to find that it is next to impossible to recreate the scenario, including the particular transaction that might be the one that momentarily disabled the production environment. Pinpointing a specific problem out of thousands of transactions, some submitted concurrently, is a major chore that is often error-prone and can render the system vulnerable.

This situation could be one of a number of instances where you would have been better off relying on some kind of a capture-and-playback mechanism such as CA-Verify, which can capture and retain sequences of input and output screens so you can rerun them under conditions you define. While rerunning a test stream, CA-Verify can compare the current output with the original output and promptly display all differences (called mismatches) interactively.

As a rule, programmers generally do their testing in test systems. However, a test system doesn't give you an accurate representation of a production environment. Test systems are much less complicated than their production counterparts. They also operate at lower volumes, have fewer users, and generally cannot simulate the full range of conditions and activities of a typical production environment. Consequently, despite hours of work, test results might still be unreliable because programs that work in a test environment could fail under the stressful conditions of a high-volume production system.

To make a long story short, manual testing is a tedious, error-prone process that's time consuming, terribly wasteful, and too mechanical because it requires data entry and comparison of before and after snapshots. Also, the methodology fails to accurately simulate production conditions, thus yielding unreliable results.

As I mentioned before, CA-Verify captures screen images, that is, terminal inputs and outputs from "live" CICS transactions. Each series of captured screen images (referred to as test streams) is stored for later use. As circumstances dictate, you can modify these test streams to fit your specific needs (or simply leave them as they are). After an application is modified, rerun the captured test stream and CA-Verify will compare the current and previous outputs and flag all differences.

CA-Verify also has an Extended Environment option that can capture any application executing under a VTAM subsystem, for example TSO, CMS, CICS, and IMS. The functions and user interfaces of CA-Verify for CICS and CA-Verify for VTAM are virtually identical.

11.2 Components of the CA-Verify Primary Options Menu

To invoke CA-Verify for CICS, clear your screen and enter the transaction identifier XTCA. Once you have pressed the Enter key, a panel identical to the one shown in Figure 11.1 will appear.

The upper right-hand corner of the menu contains the time, CICS identifier for your terminal, and your operator ID. The operator identifier is recorded by CICS in the TCT, or Terminal Control Table, at the time you sign on the system.

To select a function, enter the first character of the function in the command area.

```
VERSION x.x -------- CA-VERIFY PRIMARY OPTIONS MENU ------------     09:24:11
ENTER COMMAND ===>                                                TERMID: VNV9
                                                                  OPERID: TERM

 L    LOG A TEST STREAM
 B    BROWSE A TEST STREAM
 R    RUN A TEST STREAM
 E    EDIT A TEST STREAM
 I    INQUIRY AND TERMINATION OF ACTIVE FUNCTIONS
 U    UTILITIES
 T    CA-VERIFY TUTORIAL
 X    EXIT CA-VERIFY

              *** ENTER COMMAND "KEYS" OR PRESS PF12 AT ***
              ***  ANY TIME TO LIST PF KEY ASSIGNMENT   ***
```

Figure 11.1 The CA-VERIFY Primary Options Menu.

```
---------------------- CA-VERIFY FUNCTIONS ---------------------09:24:11
ENTER COMMAND ===>

      FROM THE CA-VERIFY PRIMARY OPTIONS MENU YOU CAN SELECT ONE OF
      THE CA-VERIFY FUNCTIONS BY ENTERING THE FIRST CHARACTER OF THE
      FUNCTION NAME IN THE COMMAND AREA. USE THE END COMMAND OR
      OPTION "X" TO EXIT CA-VERIFY.

      ENTER ONE OF THE FOLLOWING TOPIC NUMBERS IN THE COMMAND AREA,
      OR LEAVE THE COMMAND AREA BLANK TO REVIEW ALL OF THE TOPICS
      IN SEQUENCE:

      1 - COMMANDS AND PF KEYS
      2 - LOGGING TEST STREAMS
      3 - INQUIRE INTO ACTIVE FUNCTIONS
      4 - RUNNING TEST STREAMS
      5 - BROWSING TEST STREAMS
      6 - EDITING TEST STREAMS
      7 - UTILITY FUNCTIONS
      8 - BATCH FUNCTIONS
      9 - 3270 DATA STREAMS

      PRESS ENTER TO CONTINUE
```

Figure 11.2 The CA-VERIFY Tutorial, which provides HELP assistance.

You can also invoke CA-Verify and select the transaction identifier at the same time by entering XTCA followed by a space and the first character of the function. For example, XTCA T will invoke the CA-Verify Tutorial.

You can also invoke the Primary Options Menu (if you happen to be on another panel in the system) simply through an equal sign followed by the first character of the function you need to perform.

Notice that the Primary Options Menu, like all CA-Verify menus, is structurally similar to those panels used in the ISPF text editor. Thus, commands are entered on the second line next to the ENTER COMMAND ===> option. Error messages, if any, appear in the upper right-hand corner of the screen with an option to get more tutorial assistance via PF1.

If you need tutorial (HELP) assistance and have pressed PF1, the result will be a short error message, such as *Invalid option*. If this is not enough, press PF1 again for a longer error message. For specific instructions regarding the error message, press PF1 one more time to invoke the CA-Verify Tutorial module, which allows you to explore the entire system's help facilities. An overview of this panel is shown in Figure 11.2. You can return to the main menu by pressing PF3.

Let me review some of the functions that appear on the CA-Verify Primary Options Menu in detail:

L (log a test stream). Enables you to capture the input and resulting output from one or more terminals executing a CICS transaction or VTAM application.

B (browse a test stream). Lets you view the input and output screens captured during a logging or testing session. You can view any differences detected during a test run, and all the instructions given to CA-Verify during the RUN function.

R (run a test stream). Enables you to test an application with the same or edited data that was captured during logging. The system acts like an operator, sending the stored input to the application. When the application responds with its new output, CA-Verify can immediately flag any differences it finds and provides you with a number of tools to handle the situation.

E (edit a test stream). Lets you change the input and output captured during logging and testing. This is helpful if you need to change certain fields, such as dates, before running a test stream. It can also be used to create new test data and to create tutorials for user training on a new application.

I (inquiry and termination of active functions). Provides a facility for displaying current CA-Verify activities. Note that this option can also terminate a LOG function or interrupt a RUN function.

U (utilities). These are additional features allowing you to maintain your test streams. For example, you can merge or append test streams to create ones suitable for concurrency testing, stress testing, or capacity planning.

Your first task is to LOG (capture) the application screens. To do this, simply select the LOG function by typing an L on the command line (Figure 11.3). The result is shown in Figure 11.4, where CA-Verify displays a Log Options Menu, allowing you to capture your own terminal or, optionally, other terminals in the network.

11.3 Logging a Transaction Using Multiple Terminals

Let's clarify the term *logging test streams*, or simply *logging a transaction or application*. Logging allows you to capture the input an operator sends from a terminal to an application, and the output that the application responds with during a working session of the application.

```
VERSION x.x -------- CA-VERIFY PRIMARY OPTIONS MENU --------------- 09:24:11
ENTER COMMAND ===> L                                            TERMID: VNV9
                                                                OPERID: TERM

 L   LOG A TEST STREAM
 B   BROWSE A TEST STREAM
 R   RUN A TEST STREAM
 E   EDIT A TEST STREAM
 I   INQUIRY AND TERMINATION OF ACTIVE FUNCTIONS
 U   UTILITIES
 T   CA-VERIFY TUTORIAL
 X   EXIT CA-VERIFY

            *** ENTER COMMAND "KEYS" OR PRESS PF12 AT ***
            ***  ANY TIME TO LIST PF KEY ASSIGNMENT   ***
```

Figure 11.3 Requesting the Log function from the CA-VERIFY Primary Options Menu.

```
------------------------- LOG OPTIONS MENU -----------------------09:24:41
ENTER COMMAND ===> M

        T  THIS TERMINAL
        O  ANOTHER TERMINAL
        M  MULTIPLE TERMINALS

ENTER ONE OF THE ABOVE OPTIONS AND PRESS ENTER TO CONTINUE OR PF3 TO END
```

Figure 11.4 The Log Options Menu.

```
---------------------- MULTIPLE TERMINAL LOG ---------------------- 09:24:48
ENTER COMMAND ===>                                                         L3

LOG TEST STREAM AS:
    DDNAME           ===> TCADS
    APPLICATION      ===> HELPDESK
    MEMBER           ===> LOGALL
    VERSION          ===> 001

DESCRIPTION          ===> CAPTURE ALL SCREENS FROM ALL TERMINALS FOR
                     ===>
                     ===>

ENTER TERMINAL ID'S (USE "=" FOR GENERIC):               PF7-UP 8-DOWN
  ===> ====          ===>                ===>                ===>
  ===>               ===>                ===>                ===>
  ===>               ===>                ===>                ===>
  ===>               ===>                ===>                ===>

   INCLUDE OR EXCLUDE TRANSACTIONS ===>     (I OR E)  PF: 10-LEFT 11-RIGHT
   TRANSACTION IDENTIFIERS         ===>       ===>      ===>      ===>
   TEST STREAM PROTECTION          ===>     (R-READ  W-WRITE P-PRINT)
   LOG INPUT SCREEN ONLY           ===>  NO
ENTER THE ABOVE INFORMATION AND PRESS ENTER TO CONTINUE OR PF3 TO END
```

Figure 11.5 Multiple-Terminal Log Panel.

Logging can capture input and output from your terminal, from another terminal, or from a number of (multiple) terminals. Because you have already requested the LOG function in Figure 11.3, the panel shown in Figure 11.4 is a response to that request.

Note that the character M has been entered next to the command in order to log multiple terminals. An overview of the Multiple-Terminal Log Panel is highlighted in Figure 11.5. Multiple terminal logs are used to capture data from any number of terminals. This can be useful for capturing large amounts of data for a subsequent stress test or capacity planning. Another common application is to capture a production environment for help-desk purposes. When a user calls with a problem, CA-Verify has already captured the terminal session, so you have the necessary documentation to recreate the problem in a test environment.

CA-Verify's Extended Environment option has an additional LOG function: the ability to log an entire VTAM application.

Unlike the Single and Other Terminal LOG Menus, which I will be presenting in a moment, there is no stop-option support. Because multiple terminals are being logged, you must end logging manually via the inquiry function. Another difference is that multiple terminal test streams cannot be extended. However, you can use the APPEND utility function to extend multiple terminal test streams.

Test streams are named by a combination of DDNAME, APPLICATION, MEMBER and VERSION number. DDNAME is the name of the physical file into which the captured screen images will be stored. There can be many different CA-Verify files. The APPLICATION name should be used to group test streams by application, department, or project. The MEMBER name should be used to identify the specific contents of the test stream. VERSION allows you to use the same application and member for similar test streams or to archive your test streams. The DESCRIPTION field is used for comments and to document your test streams.

Next to the terminal IDs, you can type the IDs of the terminals to be captured. As with ISPF, you can use PF7 or 8 to page down and up. You can specify the terminals you want to log generically or specifically. A generic terminal identifier is one that contains an equal sign as part of the name. For example, the generic ID TRM= tells the system to log all terminals whose IDs begin with TRM, such as TRMA, TRM1, and TRMB. A generic ID of ==== directs CA-Verify to log every terminal in your CICS system, as illustrated in Figure 11.5.

Note that you can limit the transactions captured simply by including or excluding transactions. You can also use the generic character(s). Test streams can be protected by users for read, write, and print access. This feature further strengthens security. Thus, you don't have to worry about one user deleting or viewing another user's test stream. For large tests, such as stress tests, where it isn't important to compare the captured output with the new output, CA-Verify can reduce the amount of data captured by capturing only the input screens.

Press Enter at this point to start the log. Note that logging multiple terminals or an entire VTAM application is used for large-volume data captures.

11.4 Logging a Transaction Using a Single Terminal

To log test streams at your own terminal, enter the character T on the Log Options Menu next to the COMMAND arrow. A Single-Terminal Log Panel is displayed in Figure 11.6. Note that CA-Verify fills in the default values for the DDNAME, APPLICATION, VERSION, STOP, and EXTENDING TEST STREAM options. (These can be changed during the installation of CA-Verify.)

The Single-Terminal Log Menu is similar to the Multiple-Terminal Log Menu. There are two new fields on this menu. You can specify the STOP option to provide a quick method of stopping a single-terminal log by pressing a PF or PA key, or CLEAR. You can override it by typing MAN into the field. The EXTENDING TEST STREAM option allows an existing test stream to be extended.

To initiate the log, name the test stream and give an accurate description. Pressing the Enter key will display a clear screen and begin the logging process.

The example used in the remainder of this chapter is adapted from the CA-Verify

```
----------------------- SINGLE TERMINAL LOG ---------------------- 09:48:18
ENTER COMMAND ===>                                                        L1

LOG TEST STREAM AS:
   DDNAME          ===> TCADS
   APPLICATION     ===> HELPDESK
   MEMBER          ===>
   VERSION         ===> 001

DESCRIPTION        ===>
                   ===>
                   ===>

STOP OPTION        ===> PF12             (MAN, PF__, PA__, OR CLEAR)

EXTENDING TEST STREAM ===> NO

INCLUDE OR EXCLUDE TRANSACTIONS ===>   (I OR E)  PF:  10-LEFT 11-RIGHT
TRANSACTION IDENTIFIERS         ===>     ===>        ===>        ===>

TEST STREAM PROTECTION          ===>   (R-READ W-WRITE P-PRINT)
LOG INPUT SCREENS ONLY          ===>   NO

ENTER THE ABOVE INFORMATION AND PRESS ENTER TO CONTINUE OR PF3 TO END
```

Figure 11.6 Single-Terminal Log Panel.

demo. To illustrate how CA-Verify works, I will log the screens from an application, change the application, and then run the logged test stream to test the changes. I have logged the test stream as:

```
DDNAME          ===> TCADS
APPLICATION     ===> CUSTOMER
MEMBER          ===> CUSTMAST
VERSION         ===> 001
```

CA-Verify will now capture and store all the data entered at my terminal and all the data with which the application responds.

To start the demo transaction, key in the transaction ID (CUST) and press Enter. This will invoke the first panel, the main menu for the Customer Master Maintenance application. This screen is displayed in Figure 11.7.

The demo application is a simple application that has two main options. The first one is a customer inquiry and the second is a customer list. As you can see from Figure 11.7, I selected option 1 and inquired about customer 9045. Once I pressed Enter, a Customer Inquiry screen was invoked, as shown in Figure 11.8. I'm going to make two changes to this screen:

- Expand the zip code from 5 to 9 positions
- Add a new field to prompt the user for a detailed display of accounting information

Let's return now to the Application Main Menu by pressing PF3, and invoke the second option, which is a display by salesperson. This screen is shown in Figure 11.9,

```
                    CUSTOMER MASTER MAINTENANCE                    07/26/92
                            MAIN MENU                              09:53:07


                    SELECT OPTION ===>  1

                    1 - INQUIRE / CHANGE CUSTOMER
                    2 - LISTING BY SALES PERSON

               CUSTOMER NUMBER OR SALES PERSON ===>  9045

 PF3=QUIT
```

Figure 11.7 Main Menu screen for customer maintenance.

```
                    CUSTOMER MASTER MAINTENANCE                    07/26/92
                         CUSTOMER INQUIRY                          10:02:06

         SALES PERSON: ELLEN JENKINS

 CUSTOMER NAME:  ALLIED GENE SPLICING      CONTACT1:  GERONIMO DAVIS
      ADDRESS1:  TECHNOLOGIES PLAZA        CONTACT2:  WAYNE BUFORD
      ADDRESS2:  114 MCCAULEY AVENUE       CONTACT3:  HENRY MEEHAN
          CITY:  SAN ANTONIO               CONTACT4:  BRADLEY THOMAS
         STATE:  TX    ZIP:  78221

 PLEASE UPDATE DESIRED INFORMATION AND ENTER          PF3=QUIT
```

Figure 11.8 Customer Inquiry screen.

```
                    CUSTOMER MASTER MAINTENANCE                    07/26/92
                       SALES PERSON INQUIRY                        10:03:17

         SALES PERSON: ELLEN JENKINS

 NUMBER    CUSTOMER NAME        CITY         STATE  MAIN CONTACT       TOTAL AR
 _ 9045  ALLIED GENE SPLICING  SAN ANTONIO   TX    GERONIMO DAVIS       112,000
 S 2353  U.S.TIRE NOZZLES      GREENWICH     CT    ALEX SCHMELTEN     1,065,000
 _ 6028  3D COMPUTER GRAPHIC   N HOLLYWOOD   CA    HORATIO IVANOWITZ 2,331,756


   TYPE "S" NEXT TO DESIRED CUSTOMER AND ENTER          PF3=QUIT
```

Figure 11.9 Selecting a customer from the Sales Person Inquiry Panel.

and is an alpha listing of customers for the selected salesperson. Let's select customer 2353 for display, which will display the customer inquiry screen illustrated in Figure 11.8. Now you can exit from the transaction because all the necessary screens have been captured.

Remember the changes the programmer must make: zip code expanded to 9 positions, a new field asking if the user wants to see accounting information, and the new screen which displays such information.

You can now stop CA-Verify's logging by typing XTCA STOP or using the quick STOP option you selected when you initiated the log. The resulting Log Termination Panel is shown in Figure 11.10, which provides statistics regarding the test stream.

Notice the average think and response times that CA-Verify keeps. These are important for future testing. For example, the think time can be reduced or eliminated to stress the system. All the system's test streams are immediately available for testing, browsing, or any other function. To accomplish this, CA-Verify does not require any additional batch jobs, on-line jobs, or system utilities.

11.5 Invoking the BROWSE Function

To browse a test stream (to view what has been captured), enter B at the Primary Options Menu. This will result in the Browse Display Panel shown in Figure 11.11.

You can type in the name of the test stream you need to view, or leave the application or member blank in order to display a selection list. In the current example, the member name was left blank, so the Browse Test Stream Selection Panel (see Figure 11.12) positions you just before the first test stream for the specified DDNAME and APPLICATION.

Note that CA-Verify's Test Stream Selection Panel is integrated into every function of this productivity tool. If you cannot remember the test stream name, this list is always available. For a quick procedural review, let's select the test stream you just logged.

In Figure 11.11 (Test Stream Browse), the default is for CA-Verify to display the current screens. After a test, original screens can also be displayed. This allows you

```
CUSTOMER.CUSTOMER.001 --------- LOG TERMINATION ------------------ 10:30:35
ENTER COMMAND ===>                                                        L5

 DESCRIPTION: CUSTOMER MASTER MAINTENANCE SYSTEM TEST STREAM
              FOR QUALITY ASSURANCE TESTING

             LOG:          RUN:          EDIT:    TEST STREAM:      IN:    OUT:
 INVOKED BY:                                      TOTAL STREAMS:     7       7
 INVOKED ON: 07/26/92                             AVERAGE BYTES:    10     484
 START TIME: 09:53:01
 DURATION:   00:01:32
 JOB NAME:   CICS161T
 STATUS:     NORMAL
 TERMINAL:   VNV9
 VSAM CI'S:  2


 AVERAGE THINK TIME:        00:00:12.077
 AVERAGE RESPONSE TIME:     00:00:01.082
 MAXIMUM SCREEN SIZE:       24  BY   80
 PROTECTION STATUS:

 PRESS PF3 TO END
```

Figure 11.10 CA-VERIFY Log Termination Panel.

```
------------------- TEST STREAM BROWSE ------------------------ 10:30:49
ENTER COMMAND ===>                                                    B1

ENTER TEST STREAM NAME:
   DDNAME:        ===>  TCADS
   APPLICATION    ===>  CUSTOMER     LEAVE APPLICATION, MEMBER,
   MEMBER         ===>               OR VERSION BLANK AND PRESS
   VERSION        ===>  001          ENTER FOR A SELECTION LIST)

BROWSE VIEWING OPTIONS:             (YES - SELECTS, NO - BYPASSES VIEWING)
   ORIGINAL SCREENS    ===> NO
   CURRENT SCREENS:         YES
   UNEQUAL ROWS        ===> NO      (ONLY - SHOWS SCREENS ONLY WHEN MISMATCH)
   MISMATCH SIGNOFF    ===> NO
   VARIABLE FIELDS     ===> NO      (ONLY - SHOWS SCREENS ONLY WHEN VAR FLDS)

ENTER THE ABOVE INFORMATION AND PRESS ENTER TO CONTINUE OR PF3 TO END
```

Figure 11.11 CA-VERIFY Test Stream Browse screen.

```
TCADS --------------- BROWSE: TEST STREAM SELECTION -----------------10:36:13
ENTER COMMAND  ===>                                                        B2



_ CLIST    OPERATOR 001  08/01/92 RJK        3  08/03/92 NO COMP  00:00:01
                   CEMT INQUIRY OF ALL PROGRAMS AND FILES
S CUSTOMER CUSTMAST 001  07/26/92           12                    00:00:05
                   CUSTOMER MASTER MAINTENANCE SYSTEM TEST STREAM
                   FOR QUALITY ASSURANCE TESTING
_ CUSTOMER SERVICE  001  07/05/92 FJD     1273  07/17/92 NOT EQ   00:09:21
                   TEST OF ALL CUSTOMER SERVICE APPLICATIONS
_ HELPDESK LOGALL   001  08/08/92        59325                    05:15:27 M
                   CAPTURE ALL SCREENS FROM ALL TERMINALS FOR
                   HELP DESK ASSISTANCE
_ PAYROLL DOCUMENT  001  07/11/92 LCM      873                    00:06:06
                   THIS TEST STREAM CONTAINS ALL SCREENS IN
                   THE PAYROLL SYSTEMS APPLICATIONS FOR USER
                   TRAINING AND DOCUMENTATION
_ QUALITY ASSURE    001  06/14/92 DAB     2283  07/15/92 LGC EQ   00:15:45 M
                   FINAL QUALITY ASSURANCE TEST FOR ALL
                   APPLICATIONS IN THE CONVERSION FROM
                   DOS TO MVS/XA
_ SYSTEM TEST       001  07/22/92 MJF      476  08/02/92 PHY EQ   00:03:30 M
TYPE AN "S" TO SELECT A TEST STREAM AND ENTER   PF: 3-END  7-UP 8-DOWN
```

Figure 11.12 The Browse Test Stream Selection Panel. Note that the test stream just logged has been selected.

to view both the LOG and RUN versions of the screens at the same time. If you specify YES or ONLY in the UNEQUAL ROWS field, CA-Verify will compare the original to the current screen and display any mismatches. This feature is often used to perform a comparison after the test has completed. If the MISMATCH SIGNOFF or

VARIABLE FIELDS options were used during a RUN function, these options will allow you to view the information.

CA-Verify first displays the Directory Information screen, which describes LOG, RUN, and EDIT information for the selected test stream. Next, CA-Verify displays terminal information for the test stream. For a single-terminal test stream, this is the Initial Terminal Status screen (Figure 11.13); for a multiple-terminal test stream, this is the Terminal Selection Menu, which lists all the terminals in the test stream. You can select any terminal from this menu to display the Initial Terminal Status screen for the terminal.

The Initial Terminal Status screen depicted in Figure 11.13 describes the characteristics of the terminal. This information is used during the RUN function to make the virtual terminal take on the same features as the one that was logged.

After displaying terminal status information, CA-Verify displays the Browse Record Selection Menu. The menu lists the screens in the test stream and allows you to select one for browsing. This panel is displayed in Figure 11.14.

Note that the Record Selection Menu is a convenient way to review the entire test stream at a glance. CA-Verify displays a single line of descriptive information for each screen in the test stream. The default descriptive information on this screen can be changed; for example, you can display different data from the screen, the cursor position, or the date and time the record was logged or changed.

You can use PF keys to move through the data just like you do in ISPF. That means that you can also use the MAXIMUM (M) command to move all the way to the bottom or to the right, when necessary.

Let me continue my previous case study by invoking the Browse Record Selection Panel (as before), and selecting the first record from it. At this point, CA-Verify

```
CUSTOMER.CUSTMAST.001 - BROWSE: INITIAL TERMINAL STATUS ---------- 10:36:55
ENTER COMMAND  ===>                                                       B6

TERMINAL ID:  VNV9           ACCESS METHOD:  VTAM        TYPE:3277 REMOTE
OPERATOR ID:                 SECURITY KEY:   X"000001"   EXTENDED SECURITY
PAGE STATUS:  PAGE, 3270     RESOURCE KEY:   X"000000"   KEY: "0000000000"
ALT. SIZE:    NO                                         RESOURCE LEVEL: 0
SCREEN SIZE:  24 BY 80       PAGE SIZE:  24 BY 80
  ALTERNATE:   0 BY  0       ALTERNATE    0 BY  0
FEATURES:  DUALCASE,  UCTRAN
STATUS:    ATI
USER AREA ---------+---------+---------+---------+---------+---------+
     001:

     071:

     041:

     211:

                                              PRESS PF6 TO CONTINUE
```

Figure 11.13 Initial Terminal Status screen for browsing.

```
CUSTOMER.CUSTMAST.001 --- BROWSE: RECORD SELECTION -----------------10:37:07
ENTER COMMAND ===>                                                        B7



-  VNV9   CUST  00:14.614   RM       7  ENTER      1
_  VNV9   XCTA  00:00.882   W      438             2  IFY DEMONSTRATION PRO
_  VNV9   XCTA  00:14.214   RM      14  ENTER      3  IFY DEMONSTRATION PRO
_  VNV9   XCTA  00:00.613   W      476             4  IFY DEMONSTRATION PRO
_  VNV9   XCTA  00:04.766   RM       3  PF3        5  IFY DEMONSTRATION PRO
_  VNV9   XCTA  00:03.022   W      239             6  IFY DEMONSTRATION PRO
_  VNV9   XCTA  00:04.262   RM       7  ENTER      7  IFY DEMONSTRATION PRO
_  VNV9   XCTA  00:00.384   W      518             8  IFY DEMONSTRATION PRO
_  VNV9   XCTA  00:07.041   RM       9  ENTER      9  IFY DEMONSTRATION PRO
_  VNV9   XCTA  00:00.222   W      463            10  IFY DEMONSTRATION PRO
_  VNV9   XCTA  00:08.069   RM       3  CLEAR     11
_  VNV9   XCTA  00:00.007   W        1            12

                                              PF3-END   7-UP   8-DOWN
TYPE AN "S" TO SELECT A RECORD AND PRESS ENTER   9-FORMAT 10-LEFT 11-RIGHT
```

Figure 11.14 The Browse Record Selection Menu.

```
CUSTOMER.CUSTMAST.001 --- BROWSE: DISPLAY FORMAT ------------------10:38:08
ENTER COMMAND ===>                                RECORD 1                B5
          10        20        30        40        50        60        70
  ---------+---------+---------+---------+---------+---------+---------+---
 |CUST
 |
 4
 |
 |
 8
 |
 |
12
 |
 |
16
 |
 |
20
```

Figure 11.15 The first Browse Display Panel for customer records.

shows the stored record screen in display format with a ruler around it. Figures 11.15 through 11.19 show three of the screens that were captured.

The panel shown in Figure 11.16 was captured second. (You can eliminate the rulers simply by paging to the right and then down.) As you can see, the screens like the one shown in Figure 11.17 appear exactly as they did when they were logged.

You can browse a series of captured screens to familiarize yourself with transactions without actually working on the production system. Help-desk personnel can see what happened at a specific terminal to resolve a problem.

You can also use CA-Verify to demonstrate your own application. This means you don't have to worry about slip-ups in the middle of a demo (your application not behaving properly) because the system's BROWSE function is only displaying the screens. Also, you can browse screens from any particular sized terminal from any other terminal. You are not restricted to using the identical type of device.

Let's recall for a moment the necessary program changes discussed earlier. The zip code is to be expanded to 9 positions and a new field will prompt the user if he wants to see accounting information. This brings me to the Field Format Panel displayed in Figure 11.18.

Field format provides an alternative to display format. Instead of showing the logged screen, field format shows you the data stream transmitted to or from the terminal. Field format will not usually include all the fields shown in display format, because all of the fields are transmitted only on erase/write outputs or read buffer inputs.

Another available format is hex, which provides the character and hexadecimal representation of the data. Switching between display, field, and hex formats is easily accomplished by pressing PF9 or by entering the FORMAT command.

```
CUSTOMER.CUSTMAST.001 --- BROWSE: DISPLAY FORMAT -------------------10:38:08
 ENTER COMMAND ===>                                       RECORD 1            B5

                         CUSTOMER MASTER MAINTENANCE                    07/26/92
                                   MAIN MENU                            09:53:07


                           SELECT OPTION  ===> _


                            1 - INQUIRE / CHANGE CUSTOMER
                            2 - LISTING BY SALES PERSON

                   CUSTOMER NUMBER OR SALES PERSON ===>  ______
```

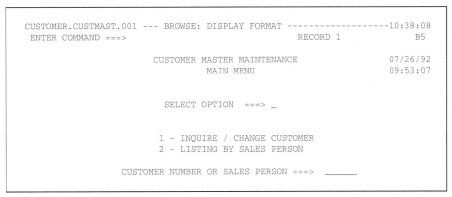

Figure 11.16 The second Browse Display Panel.

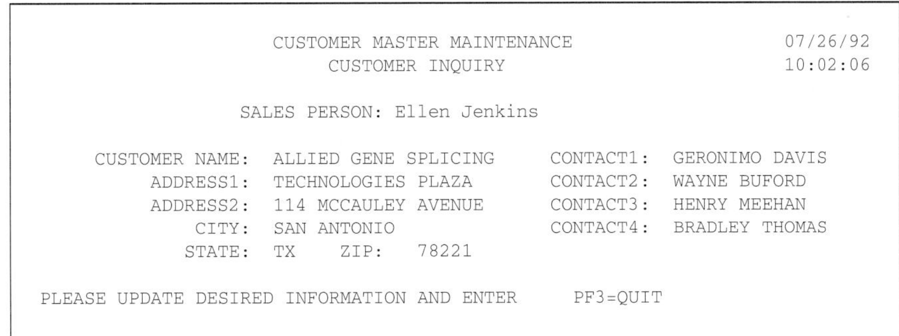

```
                      CUSTOMER MASTER MAINTENANCE                     07/26/92
                           CUSTOMER INQUIRY                           10:02:06

                   SALES PERSON: Ellen Jenkins

    CUSTOMER NAME:  ALLIED GENE SPLICING     CONTACT1:  GERONIMO DAVIS
         ADDRESS1:  TECHNOLOGIES PLAZA       CONTACT2:  WAYNE BUFORD
         ADDRESS2:  114 MCCAULEY AVENUE      CONTACT3:  HENRY MEEHAN
             CITY:  SAN ANTONIO              CONTACT4:  BRADLEY THOMAS
            STATE:  TX     ZIP:    78221

PLEASE UPDATE DESIRED INFORMATION AND ENTER     PF3=QUIT
```

Figure 11.17 The Browse Display Panel and Customer Inquiry screen.

```
CUSTOMER.CUSTMAST.001--- BROWSE: FIELD FORMAT -------------------- 10:38:54
ENTER COMMAND ===>                                                        B4

                                                     RECORD NUMBER:   4
TYPE:          OUTPUT                                DATA LENGTH:   476
OPERATION:     WRITE                                 SCREEN SIZE: 24 BY 80
RESPONSE:      00:00:00.613                          TERMINAL ID:      VNV9
WCC: C3:NL/EM/CR PRINT CNTL, KEYBOARD RESTORE, RESETMDT
ORDER ROW  COL ATTR  LENGTH ---------+---------+---------+---------+-------
 SBA    2   73            8   10:02:06
 FLD    3   32  PS       16    CUSTOMER INQUIRY
 SF             PS        0
 FLD    5   24  PSH      13    SALES PERSON:
 SF             U        13    ELLEN JENKINS
 SF             PS        0
 FLD    7    2  PSH      14    CUSTOMER NAME:
 SF             PS        0
 SF             U        20    ALLIED GENE SPLICING
 SF             PS        2
 SF             PSH       9    CONTACT1:
 SF             PS        0
 SF             U        14    GERONIMO DAVIS
 SF             PS        0
 FLD   8     7  PSH       9    ADDRESS1:
```

Figure 11.18 The Field Format Panel.

```
--------------------------- RUN OPTIONS ------------------------ 10:39:48
ENTER COMMAND ===>                                                      R1

ENTER INPUT TEST STREAM NAME:
  DDNAME        ===> TCADS
  APPLICATION   ===> CUSTOMER
  MEMBER        ===> CUSTMAST
  VERSION       ===> 001

REPLACE INPUT TEST STREAM ===> YES (FOR VARIABLE FIELDS AND CHANGES)

CREATE NEW OUTPUT TEST STREAM:      (ONLY VALID IF REPLACE INPUT IS "NO")
  DDNAME        ===>                ("*" USES NEXT AVAILABLE VERSION)
  APPLICATION   ===>
  MEMBER        ===>
  VERSION       ===>

MISMATCH TYPE TO STOP FOR ===> LOGICAL  (PHYSICAL, LOGICAL OR NONE)
MISMATCH DATA RECORDING   ===> YES      (YES REQUIRES MISMATCHES)
MISMATCH SIGNOFF          ===> NO       (YES REQUIRES MISMATCH EXPLANATION)

SIMULATED OPERATOR THINK TIME ===> NONE (NONE, NNN% OF ORIGINAL, NN SECONDS)
STATUS INTERVAL               ===> 005  (SECONDS)
CANCEL INTERVAL               ===> 001  (MINUTES)
```

Figure 11.19 The Run Options Panel.

11.6 Running/Editing Test Streams

The RUN function lets you test an application with the same data that was captured during the logging process. CA-Verify acts like a terminal operator, sending the stored input to the application, and the application responds with the output. CA-Verify then compares the output from this test session with the output from the previously logged session and flags any differences it finds. Because CA-Verify can perform the comparison while the test stream is executing, you can handle each screen change on an individual basis and also handle any possible condition as it occurs. Let's start out by keying in the name of the test stream (shaded area) you just captured.

The Run Options Panel is displayed in Figure 11.19. Note that the input test stream is the one you want to execute. You can obtain the Test Stream Selection list by leaving the APPLICATION and/or MEMBER blank. Let's place the results of the test in a new test stream—shown in Figure 11.20. Here, the same DDNAME, APPLICATION and MEMBER names are used, just new versions.

The MISMATCH TYPE option determines the type of comparison CA-Verify performs. For most test streams, you'll request a logical compare, which is the default. A logical comparison compares the corresponding rows on the original and current screen and flags any differences. A physical compare is used for non-3270 terminals or for test streams that use graphics. CA-Verify will compare 80-byte segments of the data streams. If you specify NONE, CA-Verify will not interrupt the run for mismatches. However, if you specify YES for MISMATCH DATA RECORDING, CA-Verify will store the new screens along with the original screens so you can perform the comparison later when you browse or print the test stream.

MISMATCH SIGNOFF lets you document your test and programming changes. CA-Verify will ask you to explain each mismatch it finds. SIMULATED OPERATOR THINK TIME allows you to vary the speed at which the input is sent to the applica-

```
  ------------------------ RUN OPTIONS ----------------------- 10:39:48
ENTER COMMAND ===>                                                     R1

ENTER INPUT TEST STREAM NAME:
  DDNAME       ===> TCADS
  APPLICATION  ===> CUSTOMER
  MEMBER       ===> CUSTMAST
  VERSION      ===> 001

REPLACE INPUT TEST STREAM ===> YES (FOR VARIABLE FIELDS AND CHANGES)

CREATE NEW OUTPUT TEST STREAM:      (ONLY VALID IF REPLACE INPUT IS "NO")
  DDNAME       ===> TCADS           ("*" USES NEXT AVAILABLE VERSION)
  APPLICATION  ===> CUSTOMER
  MEMBER       ===> CUSTMAST
  VERSION      ===> 002

MISMATCH TYPE TO STOP FOR ===> LOGICAL  (PHYSICAL, LOGICAL OR NONE)
MISMATCH DATA RECORDING   ===> YES      (YES REQUIRES MISMATCHES)
MISMATCH SIGNOFF          ===> NO       (YES REQUIRES MISMATCH EXPLANATION)

SIMULATED OPERATOR THINK TIME ===> NONE (NONE, NNN% OF ORIGINAL, NN SECONDS)
STATUS INTERVAL               ===> 005  (SECONDS)
CANCEL INTERVAL               ===> 001  (MINUTES)
```

Figure 11.20 A Run Options Panel defining the new output test stream.

```
---------------------------- RUN STATUS -------------------------11:01:08
                                                                       R3
TEST STREAM BEING RUN:
  CUSTOMER.CUSTMAST.001

OUTPUT TEST STREAM:
  CUSTOMER.CUSTMAST.002

CURRENTLY PROCESSING SCREEN:          1
TOTALS SCREENS TO BE PROCESSED:      14
ESTIMATED REMAINING RUN TIME:  00:00:08

STATUS INTERVAL:   5 SECONDS
CANCEL INTERVAL:   1 MINUTE

DESCRIPTION: CUSTOMER MASTER MAINTENANCE SYSTEM TEST STREAM
             FOR QUALITY ASSURANCE TESTING
```

Figure 11.21 The Run Status Panel.

```
---------------------RUN MISMATCH OPTIONS ---------------------- 11:01:32
ENTER COMMAND ===>                                                     R6

  1  DISPLAY ORIGINAL SCREEN                  6  IGNORE TEMPORARY CHANGE
  2  DISPLAY CURRENT SCREEN                   7  ACCEPT PERMANENT CHANGE
PF2  ROTATE: ORIGINAL, CURRENT, MENU          8  DISPLAY SCREEN FOR UPDATE
  3  DISPLAY PREVIOUS INPUT                      SEND IN PLACE OF NEXT INPUT
  4  DISPLAY NEXT INPUT                     OUT  SHOW OUT-OF-SYNC OPTION
  5  UPDATE VARIABLE FIELDS                AUTO  SHOW AUTOMATED MISMATCH OPTIONS
                                            PF3  VIEW TERMINATION OPTIONS

  RECORD: 4                                   RUNNING:CUSTOMER.CUSTMAST.001
                                              OUTPUT: CUSTOMER.CUSTMAST.002

                                             CURSOR     SCREEN    STREAM  TERM
           TYPE    OPERATION          WCC   ROW COL        SIZE   LENGTH  ID
ORIGINAL:  OUTPUT  WRITE              C3      8  51   24  *  80     436   VNV9
CURRENT:   OUTPUT  WRITE              C3      8  51   24  *  80     436   VV01

ONLY UNEQUAL ROW:  02                            PF:  7-UP  8-DOWN
                        .CUSTOMER MASTER MAINTENANCE.              .09:53:07
                        .CUSTOMER MASTER MAINTENANCE.              .11:01:32
                                                                    XX XX XX
```

Figure 11.22 The Run Mismatch Options Panel identifying discrepancies.

tion. Limiting the think time is one way to perform stress and concurrency testing. The STATUS INTERVAL and CANCEL INTERVAL options control the timing of status reports and opportunities to cancel the run.

Press Enter to start the test. The Run Status Panel is shown in Figure 11.21, and a Run Mismatch Options Panel is highlighted in Figure 11.22. The Run Status screen provides information on the test.

By presenting the Run Mismatch Options Panel, CA-Verify informs you that it has found a difference between the screen that was originally captured and the current output screen. The system provides you with a number of features to handle mismatches. This is one of two menus of options which are available. Notice that it has stopped on record number 4.

On the bottom of the screen, CA-Verify displays the original row first, followed by the current row, and notes any differences. You can see that CA-Verify detected a difference in the time stamp. You can use option 1 to display the current screen, or you can use PF2 simply to rotate between the original and current screens. Let's hit PF2 and rotate between the two screens. The original screen that was captured is displayed in Figure 11.23. Now press PF2 to see the current screen, the result of which is displayed in Figure 11.24. If you look at the original screen, you can see that the time has changed.

Press PF2 one more time to redisplay the Run Mismatch Options Menu, shown in Figure 11.25. As you can see, this mismatch is caused by a change in the time, as shown by the flags 1 and 2. The first time was 09:53:07, while the second time was 11:01:32. This is a valid difference, which will always occur whenever the test stream is run.

CA-Verify provides a Variable Fields capability (option 5) that enables you to ignore specific field positions for the purpose of comparison. An Automated Mismatch Option Panel allows you to automatically resolve such mismatches on all screens or on all screens of a specific type. To define automated variable fields, enter AUTO on the command line of the Run Mismatch Options screen. CA-Verify will display the Automated Mismatch Options Panel illustrated in Figure 11.27.

Global and automated variable fields are stored with the test stream; CA-Verify will keep track of them for you. First, you must identify the screens on which CA-

```
 CUSTOMER MASTER MAINTENANCE                        07/26/92
          MAIN MENU                                 09:53:07

        SELECT OPTION  ===> _

      1 - INQUIRE / CHANGE CUSTOMER
      2 - LISTING BY SALES PERSON

CUSTOMER NUMBER OR SALES PERSON ===>  ______
```

Figure 11.23 The original Customer Master Maintenance Main Menu.

```
 CUSTOMER MASTER MAINTENANCE                        07/26/92
          MAIN MENU                                 11:01:32

        SELECT OPTION  ===> _

      1 - INQUIRE / CHANGE CUSTOMER
      2 - LISTING BY SALES PERSON

CUSTOMER NUMBER OR SALES PERSON ===>  ______
```

Figure 11.24 The current Customer Master Maintenance Main Menu.

```
----------------------RUN MISMATCH OPTIONS ----------------------- 11:01:32
ENTER COMMAND ===>                                                        R6

  1  DISPLAY ORIGINAL SCREEN                  6  IGNORE TEMPORARY CHANGE
  2  DISPLAY CURRENT SCREEN                   7  ACCEPT PERMANENT CHANGE
PF2  ROTATE: ORIGINAL, CURRENT, MENU          8  DISPLAY SCREEN FOR UPDATE
  3  DISPLAY PREVIOUS INPUT                      SEND IN PLACE OF NEXT INPUT
  4  DISPLAY NEXT INPUT                     OUT  SHOW OUT-OF-SYNC OPTION
  5  UPDATE VARIABLE FIELDS                AUTO  SHOW AUTOMATED MISMATCH OPTIONS
                                            PF3  VIEW TERMINATION OPTIONS

  RECORD: 4                                   RUNNING:CUSTOMER.CUSTMAST.001
                                              OUTPUT: CUSTOMER.CUSTMAST.002

                                             CURSOR     SCREEN     STREAM  TERM
            TYPE    OPERATION          WCC  ROW COL        SIZE    LENGTH  ID
ORIGINAL:   OUTPUT  WRITE              C3     8  51    24  *  80      436  VNV9
CURRENT:    OUTPUT  WRITE              C3     8  51    24  *  80      436  VV01

ONLY UNEQUAL ROW:  02                              PF:  7-UP  8-DOWN
                        .CUSTOMER MASTER MAINTENANCE.       1        .09:53:07
                        .CUSTOMER MASTER MAINTENANCE.       2        .11:01:32
                                                                      XX XX XX
```

Figure 11.25 A Run Mismatch Options Panel reexamined.

```
---------------------- AUTOMATED MISMATCH OPTION -----------------11:03:35
ENTER COMMAND ===>                                                      A1

   1  DISPLAY ORIGINAL SCREEN               5  AUTO VARIABLE FIELDS
   2  DISPLAY CURRENT SCREEN
 PF2  ROTATE: ORIGINAL, CURRENT, MENU
   3  DISPLAY PREVIOUS INPUT
   4  DISPLAY NEXT INPUT

 SCREEN NAME ===>  GLOBAL  1          (LEAVE BLANK FOR SELECTION LIST)

 DESCRIPTION ===>  IGNORE DATE AND TIME STAMPS ON ALL CUSTOMER MASTER
                   MAINTENANCE SYSTEM PANELS.  2

 TO IDENTIFY SCREEN:  3
   ROW       COLUMN      RELATION     VALUE                         AND/OR
   ===>      ===>        ===>         ===>                          ===>
   ===>      ===>        ===>         ===>                          ===>
   ===>      ===>        ===>         ===>

 MISMATCH STATUS:         02  MISMATCHES ARE PRESENT.
                          SPECIFY AUTO VARIABLE FIELDS TO RESOLVE MISMATCHES
                          PF3 RETURNS TO MISMATCH OPTION MENU.
```

Figure 11.26 The Automated Mismatch Options Panel.

Verify should ignore the variable fields. In Figure 11.26, the word GLOBAL in the SCREEN NAME field indicates that CA-Verify should ignore the date and time fields on all the application panels. To ignore fields on a group of screens, you can specify a comparison (3). For example, you can instruct CA-Verify to ignore fields on all screens that have the word MENU in row 3, column 50.

After you complete the Automated Mismatch Options Panel, CA-VERIFY will display the Variable Fields Panel in Figure 11.27, on which you specify the positions of the fields CA-Verify should ignore. In this case, specify the position and length of the date and time fields. Then press PF3 to instruct CA-Verify to recompare the original and current screens, this time taking into account the variable fields.

CA-Verify redisplays the Automated Mismatch Options Panel (Figure 11.28), which now indicates that the mismatch was resolved. PF3 continues the run. As the run con-

```
------------------------- RUN: VARIABLE FIELDS -------------------11:05:54
ENTER COMMAND ===>                                                      RV

  ROW       COLUMN      LENGTH           TYPE: AUTOMATED: DATETIME
  ===> 01   ===>  073   ===>  0008
  ===> 02   ===>  073   ===>  0008       TO DELETE A VARIABLE FIELD
  ===>      ===>        ===>             CLEAR THE ROW, COLUMN, AND LENGTH
  ===>      ===>        ===>
  ===>      ===>        ===>
  ===>      ===>        ===>
  ===>      ===>        ===>             PRESS PF3 TO SAVE AND RECOMPARE
  ===>      ===>        ===>
  ===>      ===>        ===>
  ===>      ===>        ===>
  ===>      ===>        ===>
  ===>      ===>        ===>
  ===>      ===>        ===>
  ===>      ===>        ===>
  ===>      ===>        ===>
  ===>      ===>        ===>
  CURSOR    WCC         SIZE
  ===> N    ===> N      ===> N           (Y IF VARIABLE, N IF NOT)
```

Figure 11.27 Specifying variable fields.

```
---------------------- AUTOMATED MISMATCH OPTION ----------------11:03:35
ENTER COMMAND ===>                                                      A1

    1  DISPLAY ORIGINAL SCREEN              5  AUTO VARIABLE FIELDS   (DONE)
    2  DISPLAY CURRENT SCREEN
  PF2  ROTATE: ORIGINAL, CURRENT, MENU
    3  DISPLAY PREVIOUS INPUT
    4  DISPLAY NEXT INPUT

 SCREEN NAME ===>  GLOBAL              (LEAVE BLANK FOR SELECTION LIST)

 DESCRIPTION ===>  IGNORE DATE AND TIME STAMPS ON ALL CUSTOMER MASTER
                   MAINTENANCE SYSTEM PANELS.

 TO IDENTIFY SCREEN:
   ROW      COLUMN     RELATION    VALUE                         AND/OR
   ===>     ===>       ===>        ===>                          ===>
   ===>     ===>       ===>        ===>                          ===>
   ===>     ===>       ===>        ===>

 MISMATCH STATUS:    99  ALL MISMATCHES ARE RESOLVED BY AUTOMATED MISMATCH
                         OPTIONS.  PF3 WILL CONTINUE THE RUN.
```

Figure 11.28 The Automated Mismatch Options Panel, showing that the mismatch was resolved by the automated variable fields.

```
---------------------------- RUN STATUS ------------------------11:06:24
                                                                      R3
  TEST STREAM BEING RUN:
    CUSTOMER.CUSTMAST.001

  OUTPUT TEST STREAM:
    CUSTOMER.CUSTMAST.002

  CURRENTLY PROCESSING SCREEN:                 5
  TOTAL SCREENS TO BE PROCESSED:              14
  ESTIMATED REMAINING RUN TIME:         00:00:03

  STATUS INTERVAL:  5 SECONDS
  CANCEL INTERVAL:  1 MINUTE

  DESCRIPTION:  CUSTOMER MASTER MAINTENANCE SYSTEM
                FOR QUALITY ASSURANCE TESTING
```

Figure 11.29 A Run Status screen showing current statistics.

```
----------------------RUN MISMATCH OPTIONS ---------------------- 11:01:26
ENTER COMMAND ===>                                                      R6

  1  DISPLAY ORIGINAL SCREEN                 6  IGNORE TEMPORARY CHANGE
  2  DISPLAY CURRENT SCREEN                  7  ACCEPT PERMANENT CHANGE
PF2  ROTATE: ORIGINAL, CURRENT, MENU         8  DISPLAY SCREEN FOR UPDATE
  3  DISPLAY PREVIOUS INPUT                     SEND IN PLACE OF NEXT INPUT
  4  DISPLAY NEXT INPUT                    OUT  SHOW OUT-OF-SYNC OPTION
  5  UPDATE VARIABLE FIELDS               AUTO  SHOW AUTOMATED MISMATCH OPTIONS
                                           PF3  VIEW TERMINATION OPTIONS

  RECORD: 6                                 RUNNING:CUSTOMER.CUSTMAST.001
                                            OUTPUT: CUSTOMER.CUSTMAST.002


                                          CURSOR     SCREEN     STREAM   TERM
           TYPE    OPERATION        WCC   ROW COL        SIZE   LENGTH   ID
ORIGINAL:  OUTPUT  WRITE            C3      5  39    24  *  80    476    VNV9
CURRENT:   OUTPUT  WRITE            C3      5  39    24  *  80    520    VV01

ONLY UNEQUAL ROW:  02
FIRST UNEQUAL ROW:  11  UNEQUAL ROWS: 02        PF:  7-UP  8-DOWN
.          .STATE:..TX.  .ZIP:..78221
.          .STATE:..TX.  .ZIP:..78221-2481.
                                    XXXXXX
```

Figure 11.30 A Run Mismatch Options Panel indicating a second discrepancy.

tinues, another Run Status screen is displayed, shown in Figure 11.29. This screen is updated to reflect the state of the test. Are we done evaluating the mismatches? Figure 11.30 shows that CA-Verify has found another mismatch on record 6.

There are actually two mismatches indicated on the panel in Figure 11.30. The first one is currently displayed; the second one is shown in Figure 11.31. These mismatches look like the programming changes you made. Let's take a look at both the original and current screens to validate them. The original screen is displayed in Figure 11.32, while the current screen is highlighted in Figure 11.33. Notice the zip code field and the new field.

Both these mismatches reflect valid programming changes, so select option 7 on the Run Mismatch Options Panel (Figure 11.30). This instructs CA-Verify to accept the changes as permanent. The next time you test the system, CA-Verify will use this new screen with the programming changes.

Note that CA-Verify did not flag the date field as a mismatch on record 6. The global variable fields defined in Figures 11.27 and 11.28 instructed CA-Verify to ignore date and time mismatches on all Customer Master Maintenance Panels.

When you accept the changes, CA-Verify will resume the run. Because there are no other mismatches, the run completes and CA-Verify displays a Run Completion Panel that provides statistics on the run.

11.7 Inquiry and Termination

You can invoke the INQUIRY function by entering I on the CA-Verify Primary Options Panel. The Inquiry/Termination Panel indicates the status of all CA-Verify functions, and is shown in Figure 11.34.

```
CUSTOMER.CUSTMAST.001 ------- RUN: ALL UNEQUAL ROWS ---------------11:06:33
ENTER COMMAND ===>                                                        RL

 PF:  2-ROTATE  3-END  7-UP  8-DOWN                                  RECORD 6

          10        20        30        40        50        60        70
ROW: 11--+---------+---------+---------+---------+---------+---------+------

.        .STATE:..TX.    .ZIP:..78221.
.        .STATE:..TX.    .ZIP:..78221-2481.
                                    XXXXX

ROW: 15--+---------+----------+--------+----------+---------+---------+-----

                  .ACCOUNTING INFORMATION (Y/N) ===> .N.
                  XXXXXXXXXXX XXXXXXXXXXX XXXXX XXXXXXX
***   END OF UNEQUAL ROWS   ***
```

Figure 11.31 Reviewing all mismatches.

```
                       CUSTOMER MASTER MAINTENANCE                  07/22/92
                           CUSTOMER INQUIRY                         10:02:06

                    SALES PERSON: Ellen Jenkins

     CUSTOMER NAME:  ALLIED GENE SPLICING      CONTACT1:  GERONIMO DAVIS
          ADDRESS1:  TECHNOLOGIES PLAZA        CONTACT2:  WAYNE BUFORD
          ADDRESS2:  114 MCCAULEY AVENUE       CONTACT3:  HENRY MEEHAN
              CITY:  SAN ANTONIO               CONTACT4:  BRADLEY THOMAS
             STATE:  TX     ZIP:    78221

PLEASE UPDATE DESIRED INFORMATION AND ENTER      PF3=QUIT
```

Figure 11.32 The original screen.

The Inquiry/Termination Panel indicates the active and suspended functions, and the terminal at which they were invoked. You can use this panel to terminate a LOG function or to suspend a RUN function.

When you suspend a function, you can exit from CA-Verify to use other transactions or utilities. For example, if you are a CA-InterTest user, you can use the LIST function in the middle of a CA-Verify test session to review your program's source code on-line. In addition, you can also use the FILE transaction to take a look at your Customer Master file.

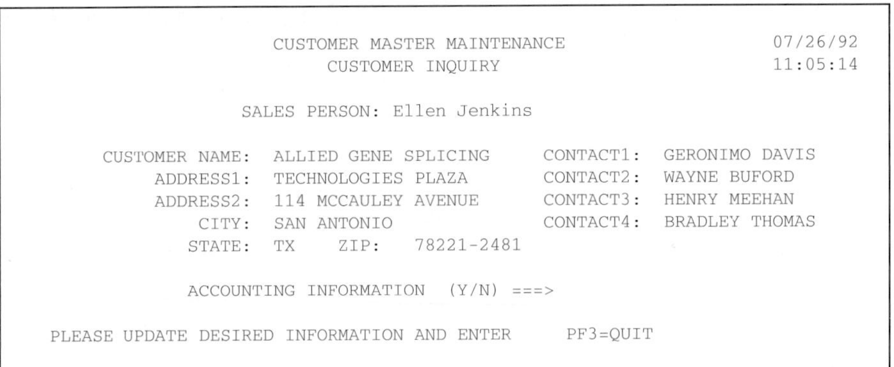

```
                         CUSTOMER MASTER MAINTENANCE                    07/26/92
                              CUSTOMER INQUIRY                          11:05:14

                      SALES PERSON: Ellen Jenkins

          CUSTOMER NAME:  ALLIED GENE SPLICING      CONTACT1:  GERONIMO DAVIS
               ADDRESS1:  TECHNOLOGIES PLAZA        CONTACT2:  WAYNE BUFORD
               ADDRESS2:  114 MCCAULEY AVENUE       CONTACT3:  HENRY MEEHAN
                   CITY:  SAN ANTONIO               CONTACT4:  BRADLEY THOMAS
                  STATE:  TX     ZIP:    78221-2481

                  ACCOUNTING INFORMATION   (Y/N) ===>

     PLEASE UPDATE DESIRED INFORMATION AND ENTER      PF3=QUIT
```

Figure 11.33 The current screen.

```
 ---------------------- INQUIRY/TERMINATION ---------------------11:08:34
 ENTER COMMAND ===>                                                     I1


             INVOKED                                    USING        SCREENS
 FUNCTION    BY        TERM    DATE        TIME        TERMINAL      PROCESSED
_INQUIRY     TEM       VNV9    08/08/92    10:48:34
_EDIT        RJK       VSVJ    08/08/92    10:41:44
_RUN         TEM       VNV9    08/08/92    10:48:31     VV01          SUSPENDED
_LOG         TEM       VNV9    08/08/92    10:23:23     983              3162

    DATA CAPTURE BUFFERS  00% FULL, NO SECONDARY BUFFERS ALLOCATED


TYPE AN "S" NEXT TO A LOG FUNCTION TO STOP IT
TYPE AN "I" NEXT TO A RUN FUNCTION TO INTERRUPT IT (CANCEL OPTION APPEARS)

PRESS ENTER TO INVOKE STOP OR INTERRUPT, PRESS PF3 TO END INQUIRY
```

Figure 11.34 The Inquiry/Termination Panel.

Chapter

12

CICS dBUG-AID and the XPEDITER Product

12.1 Product Description and Integration

"A CICS debugging product is a necessity, not a luxury," says Harvey Bookman, authority on COBOL II and author of *COBOL II*, a J. Ranade IBM Series book. "Without a debugging product, some programming errors may nearly be unsolvable."

With XPEDITER/CICS, you can interactively test and debug your CICS programs, resolve CICS problems beyond your terminal or program, tailor the product's capabilities to your specific debugging needs, and resolve production problems.

You interact directly with your program, at the source level, as it executes. The program source is displayed, breakpoints can be set to pause the program on any statement, variables can be displayed and modified, and abends trapped and prevented from occurring. Problems can be analyzed and repaired, and the program can either proceed at the point of the error or go around the problem. Working storage can be accessed and modified. Data (including temporary storage and databases) can be browsed, displayed, and modified.

There is also a special systems programmer's transaction used to implement global storage protection, which prevents transactions from corrupting storage and possible crashing of the region. This transaction allows authorized users to access and modify CICS areas either in dump format or by formatted DSECT. The systems transaction also provides basic monitoring capabilities, which allow investigation into suspended transactions and testing parameters to be set by programmers. This transaction is covered at the end of the chapter.

12.2 Integration of XPEDITER and dBUG-AID

This chapter explains in detail how to debug COBOL programs using Compuware's debugger, XPEDITER/CICS Release 6.0.1. Release 6.0.1 is the first integration release combining Centura's XPEDITER/CICS with Compuware's dBUG-AID. The Compuware/Centura merger occurred in August of 1990.

XPEDITER has long been application programmers' preferred debugger. First released in 1979, it was a pioneer in providing a rich suite of functions in an easy-to-learn format. Because of its source-based debugging approach, it was immediately familiar, yet powerful enough to handle complex debugging needs. It provided a single tool for multiple environments: batch, CA-ROSCOE, IMS/DC, CICS, and multiple databases.

dBUG-AID has provided industrial-strength debugging support for CICS specialists since 1985. Its architecture permitted dBUG-AID to protect the CICS region from storage violations and provide CICS-specific debugging functionality, while freeing the region of restrictive resource overhead that could prohibit its use.

The combination of these two products now provides an efficient CICS debugger for both applications and systems programmers alike.

12.3 Technical Definition

XPEDITER/CICS source-level support is available for COBOL, Assembler, and PL/I programs. XPEDITER can also be used to debug programs that do not have an available source (more on this later), and has special support for many vendor packages, such as HOGAN, Cybertek, and Dunn & Bradstreet. The system supports CICS 1.7 through CICS/ESA 3.3., and can be used to debug both command-level and macro-level programs.

XPEDITER does not require special compile parameters and does not modify the load module. When source-level debugging is preferred (and this is by far the most common debugging method), a postcompile step is added to the compile JCL. This step processes the output from the compile and stores a copy of the source listing in the data set allocated for this purpose.

The installer can allocate multiple data sets (so if one fills up you have a spare available), and they will all automatically be searched for the proper listing. Automatic batch maintenance procedures can be set up so that old listings are periodically deleted. These features make the listing data set more or less maintenance-free so that there are no unnecessary disruptions to the testing environment.

There are two categories of debugging. Each category has its own set of unique requirements. The first one is reactive debugging, which is when a problem has already occurred or incorrect results have been obtained. The second is proactive debugging, which is when the programmer needs to do some investigation or analysis prior to the actual debugging session. XPEDITER can handle both of these situations.

In reactive debugging, a test or production abend might have already occurred, or a storage violation might be suspected. The programmer is reacting to a preexisting condition, and frequently needs only to reexecute the transaction to recreate the problem. The source might not be available, and solving the problem might be a high priority. When the programmer enters the XPEDITER testing transaction, all abends and, optionally, all storage violations will automatically be trapped, prevented from occurring, and presented on the screen for analysis, repair, or circumvention. There is no set-up required.

In proactive debugging, the programmer will first view the source listing, analyze the logic, and then set breakpoints to pause the program at predetermined locations and select variables for constant display. During proactive debugging, the programmer might also create or modify data prior to the test to exercise specific areas or conditions of the program.

Note that later on in this chapter I am going to show you how to debug a COBOL program. Just like ISPF, there are three ways to communicate with the product. You can enter primary commands on the command line that is available on every screen, as shown in Figure 12.1. You can also enter the equivalent line command in the line-number area. There are also tailorable PF keys, which will execute stored commands automatically. The product is shipped with the most common commands already preset in PF keys 1 through 12. These defaults match the rest of the XPEDITER product line, but can be changed and stored in the user's profile so that your preferred settings will be available whenever you sign-on.

The line under the command line is divided into two areas. The first area allows you to enter or change the name of the program that is to be displayed. The second area will display the program date/time stamp and also informational messages. These messages could be simply conformation of a command that is processed, or very important messages such as data-access return codes that are received during testing. Whenever a message is surrounded by plus signs, that is your indication that there is specific help information available by entering the HELP command or pressing the appropriate PF key.

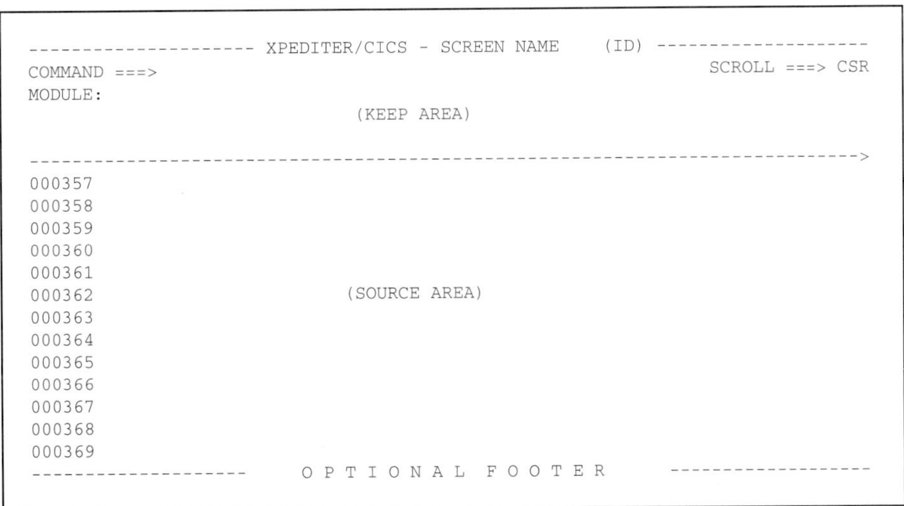

Figure 12.1 The XPEDITER/CICS Screen Name Menu, showing a command line.

The next area on the screen is where the variables and source of your program will be displayed. Prior to starting a debugging session, the Variables window, or Keep window, will be suppressed because no data can be displayed. The Keep window is sizable, so the more variables you choose to display, the less source will show on the screen. There is a profile setting that lets you take advantage of large display terminals.

There is an optional display area at the bottom of the screen that can be used during testing to tailor the displayed data. This area can be turned off to display more source lines, or can display status information about the transaction being tested and current source statements when working on nonsource screens, PF key settings, menu choices, and data. These options are explored more completely in the *Advanced Functions* section later in this chapter.

A quick reference card is available and contains all commands, abbreviations, and syntax. A reference manual contains extensive detail for each command. You can also use the provided user's guide to step through the demonstration programs provided during installation. There is an on-line help facility, which provides on-line access to the reference manual while you are using the product and also contains command-usage examples.

Before actually starting a debugging session, you should review the profile options and PF key settings, and use the PF keys whenever possible. In the following examples, the entire command will be shown to prevent confusion.

12.4 How to Debug a COBOL Program

This section is an example of a typical COBOL debugging session. A program has been changed, the compile has been run successfully, and the program has been newcopied.

First, the debugging transaction for this CICS region is entered. The supplied default transaction is XPED, although this might have been changed at your site. The Primary Menu shown in Figure 12.2 will appear on the terminal. By entering the debugging transaction, three important functions will automatically be set at your terminal. Abend trapping is turned on, an XPEDITER trace is turned on, and storage protection is turned off. These are the defaults that are shipped with the product; you can review them by selecting 0 from the Primary Menu. These three functions are defined in the following paragraphs.

Abend trapping means that any abend that occurs at your terminal will be trapped, prevented, and presented for analysis. Trapping will occur regardless of whether the program has been precompiled or not.

XPEDITER's trace facility automatically begins to collect the program's execution history. This execution history is available during and after the test session is complete. XPEDITER's trace is independent of the CICS trace, which is frequently disabled in test regions.

Storage protection prevents instructions being executed from accessing or altering storage areas that do not belong to the transaction. You can tailor the storage protection in many ways to suit the needs of your installation, and globally turn stor-

```
---------------------- XPEDITER/CICS  6.0.1- PRIMARY MENU --------------------
COMMAND ===>
PROGRAM:            MODULE:

   0  SESSION PROFILE       - Set default session attributes
   1  SESSION CONTROL       - Analyze summary of session events
   2  DEBUGGING FACILITIES  - Interactively debug application programs
   5  FILE UTILITY          - Access datasets, temp stg, trans data, DLI, DB2
   7  CICS ABEND-AID        - Interface to CICS Abend-AID

   X  EXIT                  - Exit XPEDITER


      To set STOPs in your program or KEEP specific data fields,
      enter your program name and use either the SOURCE command or PF key.

   Copyright (C) 1984, 1991 by Compuware Corporation.  All rights reserved.
```

Figure 12.2 The XPEDITER/CICS Primary Menu.

age protection off or on, depending on your site's standards. You can set storage protection at the program or transaction level during testing.

Because XPEDITER's interception of abends is automatic and not just set for specific transactions or programs, it is also very important to understand the need to turn that interception off when testing is finished. Just as you would in ISPF, the =X command entered on the command line will take you to the exit screen, where you can then turn the abend interception off by typing in a YES to end the session and release testing resources.

To begin the test, simply clear the XPEDITER/CICS screen and enter the program transaction. The program will run just as it would without the debugger, except that all abends will be automatically trapped and prevented from occurring.

Figure 12.3 shows the default screen that will appear if a problem is encountered. This is the standard XPEDITER Source Listing screen. Notice that the compile date and time are displayed. XPEDITER automatically compares the date/time stamps in the load module and source listing member to be sure that the dates match. Another advantage to this date/time checking is that you will immediately know that it is the version of the program you expected. If the date/time stamp does not match, pressing PF1 for help would give you specific information about the mismatch.

Next on the source listing screen is the Keep window. This window can be sized to show from 5 to 11 variables at a time, and you can scroll it by tabbing the cursor to the Keep window and pressing the scroll keys. You can, therefore, examine an unlimited number of variables at any time during the debugging session.

Notice that an ASRA has been trapped and prevented at statement 427. The offending COMPUTE statement is highlighted and indicated by the execution arrow on the left. It contains 3 variables that need to be investigated to determine the cause of the ASRA. These variables are automatically displayed in the Keep window along with their definitions and their values from WORKING-STORAGE. The values are over-type-able; there is no need to go to the WORKING-STORAGE screen to modify the data.

```
-------------------- XPEDITER/CICS - SOURCE LISTING (2.L) -------------------
COMMAND ===> GO 1                                              SCROLL ===> CSR
PROGRAM: CWDEMCBL   MODULE: CWDEMCBL  COMP DATE: 11/ 1/91  COMP TIME: 12.54.57
  LV ----- COBOL DATANAME ---------- -- ATTRIBUTES -- ----+---10----+---20--->
  77 CURR-PAY                         9(5)V99          0000000
  02 WA-HOURS                         999              040
  02 WA-RATE                          9(3)V99          00950
  **END**

------ ------------------------------------- ASRA AT STMT 00427 IN CWDEMCBL->
000425 300-EMPLOYEE-PAY-RTN.
000426        IF WA-TYPE EQUAL 'N' OR 'I' OR 'S'
=====>            COMPUTE CURR-PAY   EQUAL WA-HOURS * WA-RATE
000428            COMPUTE CURR-TAXES EQUAL CURR-PAY * WA-TAX-RAT
000429            ADD CURR-PAY   TO WA-YTD-GRS
000430            ADD CURR-TAXES TO WA-YTD-TAX.
000431
000432        IF PAYEMP1 EQUAL '00001'
000433            MOVE WORK-AREA TO PAYROLL-DATA-EMP001.
000434
000435        IF PAYEMP1 EQUAL '00999'
000436            MOVE WORK-AREA TO PAYROLL-DATA-EMP999.
000437
000438 400-TRANSACTION-COMPLETE.
```

Figure 12.3 XPEDITER/CICS Source Listing screen, part 1.

When an abend is trapped, the programmer has a number of alternatives of how to continue the debugging session. With XPEDITER, the programmer can choose the appropriate action from the following.

By typing in the SKIP primary command or the SK line command, the current statement will be skipped both in the current transaction and during any subsequent executions of the program. When the cause of the problem is not immediately correctable, this method allows the programmer to continue the test, execute the rest of the program statements, and uncover multiple problems without additional compiles and reexecutions of the program.

By overtyping the value of the incorrect variable in the Keep window, the programmer can retest the COMPUTE statement with the new value and continue the test. XPEDITER automatically positions the program at the beginning of the abending statement so that it can easily be executed again with the new value.

The execution point can also be changed to force the program down a different logic path. This method is very valuable for testing multiple edit criteria or complicated, nested IF statements.

After the appropriate corrective action is taken, the program can resume processing. To continue execution, simply enter the GO primary command. The program will continue to execute without interruption until the transaction is complete or until another abend attempts to occur.

Note that in a simple, reactive debugging session, the debugger is turned on, an abend prevented and corrected, and the rest of the program executed. Only one primary command is required for the execution of this test—GO.

In real life, the problem is seldom so simple. The following section describes a more proactive debugging session, where more of XPEDITER's facilities are explored.

XPEDITER can be invoked and used before the debugging session is started. The earlier automatic abend trap was sufficient for the first test of a new program change, but it is frequently necessary to examine the program source before starting the test transaction. This is especially useful before testing an unfamiliar program and presetting breakpoints in the program.

For a new user, set-up is simple. Enter the XPEDITER transaction XPED, fill in the program name on the Primary Menu, and select Debugging Facilities by typing a 2 on the command line. Figure 12.4 will then be displayed.

Because this is an extremely common function, a shorthand command has been added to speed the process. From a blank screen, typing the XPEDITER transaction followed by a space and the name of the program will take you directly to the source listing screen shown in Figure 12.4.

XPEDITER will keep track of where you are when you leave a program, and automatically position you within the program at the statement last accessed. Otherwise, you will be positioned at the procedure division. Because the program is not executing at this time, the Keep window is suppressed to show more source. If, during a debugging session, your primary concern is the source and you prefer this view of the program, simply enter the SET KEEP OFF primary command.

In the previous example, the WA-HOURS field somehow became corrupted. To get a more concise picture of the program logic, start with the EXCLUDE ALL command to suppress the display of the source. Then, by entering the FIND ALL WA-HOURS command, you will cause all statements directly referencing the WA-HOURS field to

```
-------------------- XPEDITER/CICS - SOURCE LISTING (2.L) -------------------
COMMAND ===>                                                  SCROLL ===> CSR
PROGRAM: CWDEMCBL   MODULE: CWDEMCBL   COMP DATE: 11/ 1/91  COMP TIME: 12.54.57
----------------------------------------------------------------------------->
 PROCEDURE DIVISION USING DFHEIBLK DFHCOMMAREA.
     CALL 'DFHEI1'.
     SERVICE RELOAD DFHEIBLK.
     SERVICE RELOAD DFHCOMMAREA.
     SERVICE RELOAD BLLCELLS.
 000-BEGIN-PROGRAM.
*EXEC CICS HANDLE AID
*           CLEAR (800-RETURN-TO-CICS)
*END-EXEC.
      MOVE '                         00283    ' TO DFHEIV0
     CALL 'DFHEI1' USING DFHEIV0
      GO TO  800-RETURN-TO-CICS DEPENDING ON DFHEIGDI.
     IF EIBCALEN EQUAL ZERO
         NEXT SENTENCE
     ELSE
         GO TO 200-RECEIVE-INPUT.

 100-SEND-INITIAL-SCREEN.
     MOVE WS-13                           TO PAY13.
     MOVE '_____'                         TO PAYEMP1.
```

Figure 12.4 XPEDITER/CICS Source Listing screen, part 2.

```
--------------------- XPEDITER/CICS - SOURCE LISTING (2.L) --------------------
COMMAND ===>                                                      SCROLL ===> CSR
PROGRAM: CWDEMCBL   ************** 0000003 OCCURRENCES OF OBJECT **************
------------------------------------------------------------------------------->
- - -   - - - - - - - - - - - - - - - - - - 84 LINE(S) NOT DISPLAYED
000085       05  WA-HOURS      PIC 999.
- - -   - - - - - - - - - - - - - - - - - 341 LINE(S) NOT DISPLAYED
000427           COMPUTE CURR-PAY    EQUAL WA-HOURS * WA-RATE
- - -   - - - - - - - - - - - - - - - - - - 13 LINE(S) NOT DISPLAYED
000441       MOVE WA-HOURS  TO  HRSWRKD.
- - -   - - - - - - - - - - - - - - - - - 263 LINE(S) NOT DISPLAYED
 *************************** BOTTOM OF DATA ***************************
```

Figure 12.5 XPEDITER/CICS Source Listing screen, part 3.

be displayed on the screen. Figure 12.5 shows the definition statement, as well as two programming statements.

The FIND command works similar to the way it does in ISPF. You can find data strings by typing FIND data-name. The RFIND command will then repeat the command from the current position.

Because the WA-HOURS field is of obvious interest, a manual KEEP will now be set on the field. Remember, during testing, that all variables referenced will be automatically displayed with their values in the Keep window. To add variables to the Keep window, either enter the primary command, KEEP WA-HOURS, or tab down to the line-number area next to the definition statement and type in the line command, K. K1 will set a KEEP on the first variable of a source line, K2 will set a KEEP on the second variable, etc.

As a shortcut to this procedure, the line command K* will set a KEEP on all of the variables on a statement. You can also set breakpoints in the program prior to its execution—before the execution of a statement, after the execution of the statement, or generically using keywords.

BEFORE breakpoints will pause the program before the statement is executed and display the variables along with their values. AFTER breakpoints pause the program after the execution of the statement and display the variables just affected by the execution of the statement. Also, the next logical statement executed is noted at the top of the screen, because if it is in another part of the program it might not be displayed. AFTER breakpoints are extremely useful for programs that jump back and forth through the logic of the program.

Generic breakpoints allow the setting of multiple breakpoints using just one command. Examples of generic breakpoints are AFTER ALL EXEC, which would pause the program after all CICS EXEC statements, or BEFORE ALL WA-HOURS, which would pause the program before all statements that directly refer to the field WA-HOURS.

A useful generic breakpoint is the AFTER ALL CICS RECEIVE command. This sets breakpoints to be taken only after the CICS screen has been received from the terminal. This command is extremely useful when testing a pseudo-conversational program which processes data from an input screen.

Frequently, breakpoints are set by statement number. For example, to set a breakpoint after statement 328 is executed, specify AFTER 328. Use the same syntax for the BEFORE breakpoint. When a breakpoint has been set, the breakpoint indicator will appear at the beginning of the line-number area (SA for STOP AFTER, SB for STOP BEFORE).

You can also use XPEDITER and CEDF together. Turn on CEDF (see chapter 19 for more on CEDF) to pause before and after each EXEC statement in all command-level programs processed before the program of interest. Turn on XPEDITER to pause programs between EXEC statements through the use of breakpoints, and to trap and prevent abends. (Remember, CEDF does not allow you to resume execution after an abend occurs.) Also, to simulate the CEDF style, use the generic BEFORE ALL CICS EXEC command.

So far in this section, the KEEP, EXCLUDE, FIND, BEFORE and AFTER commands have been explored, all prior to the execution of the program. Remember that in the FIND ALL WA-HOURS display, there are only two direct references to the WA-HOURS field. After setting a KEEP on WA-HOURS and typing in the AFTER ALL CICS RECEIVE command, you can then perform your functions.

To quickly display KEEPs and breakpoints that you have set, use the SHOW KEEPS and SHOW STOPS commands. You can delete the KEEPs and breakpoints from this screen with the D line command. The rest of the source will be suppressed and the settings displayed. The RESET command will redisplay the source.

To start the debugging session, clear the screen and enter the test transaction. Remember, the AFTER ALL CICS RECEIVE command will pause the program only after the screen data has been filled in, so the program will run uninterrupted until then.

After the data is entered, the program will pause. Notice, in Figure 12.6, that the

```
-------------------- XPEDITER/CICS - SOURCE LISTING (2.L) --------------------
COMMAND ===>                                                      SCROLL ===> CSR
PROGRAM: CWDEMCBL   ************* NEXT LOGICAL STATEMENT IS 00405 *************
  LV ----- COBOL DATANAME ---------- -- ATTRIBUTES -- ----+---10----+---20--->
K 02 WA-HOURS                          999            'X 000000
  01 DFHEIV0                           X(31)          'X 0402C000050000014000040
  01 DUMMY-EMP                         GROUP          'X 1140C6F0F0F0F0F1
  77 DUMMY-LEN                         S9(4)             +8
  **END**
---------------------------------------- STOPPED AFTER STMT 00402 IN CWDEMCBL->
000399 *           LENGTH (DUMMY-LEN)
000400 *END-EXEC.
000401       MOVE '                    00308    ' TO DFHEIV0
SA==>>      CALL 'DFHEI1' USING DFHEIV0  DUMMY-EMP DUMMY-LEN.
000403
000404
000405      MOVE DUMMY-PAYEMP1 TO PAYEMP1.
000406      IF PAYEMP1 EQUAL '00001'
000407           MOVE PAYROLL-DATA-EMP001 TO WORK-AREA
000408           GO TO 300-EMPLOYEE-PAY-RTN.
000409      IF PAYEMP1 EQUAL '00002'
000410           GO TO 900-PROCESS-00002-SELECTION.
000411      IF PAYEMP1 EQUAL '00003'
000412           GO TO 950-PROCESS-00003-SELECTION.
```

Figure 12.6 XPEDITER/CICS Source Listing screen, part 4.

data in WA-HOURS has been initialized to low values. The x in front of the value specifies that the field is defined to display in character format, but rather than SHOW "...", the current value is displayed automatically in hex.

Again, there are a number of ways that this problem can be resolved. Because the WA-HOURS field will always be displayed in the Keep window, you could repeatedly enter the GO 1 (or PF9 key) command to execute one statement and then pause the program. You could then examine the value of WA-HOURS to see if any change had occurred. In a small program, this solution would work just fine.

Normally, this program will contain hundreds of statements. To automate the manual process described previously, use the GO UNTIL WA-HOURS command. This command will cause the program to execute at normal speed, while XPEDITER examines the WA-HOURS field for any changes. Figure 12.7 shows the result of the GO UNTIL WA-HOURS command.

The program pauses after statement 407 has executed. Notice the information message and also the message indicating the next logical statement that will be executed. This message is displayed because the next logical statement could possibly be far away from the statement that caused the corruption of the field in question.

The GO UNTIL command will pause the program wherever the value of WA-HOURS is changed, even when the change is caused indirectly, as in the previous example. There are also conditional breakpoints that test the condition only at specific points in the program.

Entering the AC line command for AFTER CONDITIONAL will open up a line on the screen, where a specific condition can be entered. In Figure 12.8, the program will be paused after statement 427 only if the condition is true. The conditional

```
-------------------- XPEDITER/CICS - SOURCE LISTING (2.L) ------------------
COMMAND ===> GO UNTIL WA-HOURS                                  SCROLL ===> CSR
PROGRAM: CWDEMCBL    ****** "UNTIL" CONDITION MET, STEP EXECUTION HALTED *******
  LV ----- COBOL DATANAME ---------- -- ATTRIBUTES -- ----+---10----+---20--->
K 02 WA-HOURS                          999              $$$
  01 PAYROLL-DATA-EMP001               GROUP            NMR. DAVID ABEND456 MAIN
  01 WORK-AREA                         GROUP            NMR. DAVID ABEND456 MAIN
  **END**

------------------------------------- STOPPED AFTER STMT 00407 IN CWDEMCBL->
000399 *          LENGTH (DUMMY-LEN)
000400 *END-EXEC.
000401         MOVE '             00308     ' TO DFHEIV0
SA            CALL 'DFHEI1' USING DFHEIV0  DUMMY-EMP DUMMY-LEN.
000403
000404
000405        MOVE DUMMY-PAYEMP1 TO PAYEMP1.
000406        IF PAYEMP1 EQUAL '00001'
====>>            MOVE PAYROLL-DATA-EMP001 TO WORK-AREA
000408            GO TO 300-EMPLOYEE-PAY-RTN.
000409        IF PAYEMP1 EQUAL '00002'
000410            GO TO 900-PROCESS-00002-SELECTION.
000411        IF PAYEMP1 EQUAL '00003'
000412            GO TO 950-PROCESS-00003-SELECTION.
```

Figure 12.7 XPEDITER/CICS Source Listing screen, part 5.

```
-------------------- XPEDITER/CICS - SOURCE LISTING (2.L) -------------------
COMMAND ===>                                                  SCROLL ===> CSR
PROGRAM: CWDEMCBL    ****** STATEMENT 00408 EXECUTED          STEP=00003 *******
  LV ----- COBOL DATANAME ---------- -- ATTRIBUTES -- ----+---10----+---20--->
K 02 WA-HOURS                        999              040
  02 WA-TYPE                         X                N
  **END**

------------------------------------- STOPPED BEFORE STMT 00426 IN CWDEMCBL->
000423       GO TO 600-SEND-PAY-MAP.
000424
000425   300-EMPLOYEE-PAY-RTN.
=====>       IF WA-TYPE EQUAL 'N' OR 'I' OR 'S'
AC                COMPUTE CURR-PAY   EQUAL WA-HOURS * WA-RATE
-COND-   IF WA-HOURS = '$$$'
000428            COMPUTE CURR-TAXES EQUAL CURR-PAY * WA-TAX-RAT
000429            ADD CURR-PAY    TO WA-YTD-GRS
000430            ADD CURR-TAXES TO WA-YTD-TAX.
000431
000432       IF PAYEMP1 EQUAL '00001'
000433            MOVE WORK-AREA TO PAYROLL-DATA-EMP001.
000434
000435       IF PAYEMP1 EQUAL '00999'
```

Figure 12.8 XPEDITER/CICS Source Listing screen, part 6.

breakpoint is valuable for those times when only a particular value causes the desired result. At this point in the test it is quite clear that statement 407, MOVE PAYROLL-DATA-EMP001 TO WORK-AREA, is the true culprit. The resolution at this point can be simple, but I want to further demonstrate XPEDITER functionality.

Earlier in this chapter, I explained program positioning. The same positioning can quickly display group items in WORKING-STORAGE. Remember that you can scroll the Keep window by placing the cursor in the window. By placing the cursor under a variable in the window and then scrolling that variable to the top of the window, you can use automatic positioning for a shortcut to the location of a variable. Now that PAYROLL-DATA-EMP001 is at the top of the Keep window, entering the WS command, shorthand for WORKING-STORAGE, will not only take you to the WORKING-STORAGE display screen, but also automatically positions the display at variable PAYROLL-DATA-EMP001, as shown in Figure 12.9.

Working storage is displayed and can be modified. It can be scrolled and variables can be located using the LOCATE primary command. The SOURCE command transfers back to the Source Listing screen. When data is changed in working storage, the change will automatically be displayed on the Source Listing screen.

In the previous example, the MOVE statement has already been executed and so the data is already corrupted. Because the change was entered in WORKING-STORAGE, the location of the current execution arrow could be changed, causing the re-execution of the MOVE statement. The line command of GT can be entered on line 406, which will cause two things to happen. First the execution arrow will be positioned on statement 406. But the variables in statement 406 will also be redisplayed, as shown in Figure 12.10. The primary command GOTO or the line command can be used to temporarily redisplay variables at any time during testing.

```
-------------------- XPEDITER/CICS - VARIABLE STORAGE (2.3) -------------------
COMMAND ===>                                                       SCROLL ===> CSR
PROGRAM: CWDEMCBL   MODULE: CWDEMCBL  COMP DATE: 11/ 1/91  COMP TIME: 12.54.57


  LV ----- COBOL DATANAME ---------- -- ATTRIBUTES -- ----+---10----+---20--->
  01 PAYROLL-DATA-EMP001             GROUP
  02 PAY001-TYPE                     X                N
  02 PAY001-NAME                     X(15)            MR. DAVID ABEND
  02 PAY001-ADDRESS                  GROUP
  03 PAY001-STREET                   X(12)            456 MAIN ST.
  03 PAY001-CITY                     X(8)             HOMETOWN
  03 PAY001-STATE                    XX               MI
  03 PAY001-ZIP                      X(5)             48010
  02 PAY001-RATE                     9(3)V99          00950
  02 PAY001-DATE-EFF                 GROUP
  03 PAY001-DTEFF-MM                 XX               01
  03 PAY001-DTEFF-DD                 XX               01
  03 PAY001-DTEFF-YY                 XX               84
  02 PAY001-LST-PCT                  9(3)V9           0110
  02 PAY001-TAX-RAT                  9(3)V9           0200
  02 PAY001-YTD-GRS                  S9(5)V99         +1500000
  02 PAY001-YTD-TAX                  S9(5)V99         +0300000
  02 PAY001-HOURS                    XXX              $$$
```

Figure 12.9 Variable Storage table.

```
-------------------- XPEDITER/CICS - SOURCE LISTING (2.L) --------------------
COMMAND ===>                                                       SCROLL ===> CSR
PROGRAM: CWDEMCBL   ***************** GOTO STATEMENT 00406 ******************
  LV ----- COBOL DATANAME ---------- -- ATTRIBUTES -- ----+---10----+---20--->
K 02 WA-HOURS                        999              $$$
  03 PAYEMP1                         X(5)             00001
  **END**

------------------------------------- STOPPED BEFORE STMT 00406 IN CWDEMCBL->
000399 *          LENGTH (DUMMY-LEN)
000400 *END-EXEC.
000401         MOVE '            00308     ' TO DFHEIV0
SA             CALL 'DFHEI1' USING DFHEIV0  DUMMY-EMP DUMMY-LEN.
000403
000404
000405         MOVE DUMMY-PAYEMP1 TO PAYEMP1.
=====>         IF PAYEMP1 EQUAL '00001'
000407             MOVE PAYROLL-DATA-EMP001 TO WORK-AREA
000408             GO TO 300-EMPLOYEE-PAY-RTN.
000409         IF PAYEMP1 EQUAL '00002'
000410             GO TO 900-PROCESS-00002-SELECTION.
000411         IF PAYEMP1 EQUAL '00003'
000412             GO TO 950-PROCESS-00003-SELECTION.
```

Figure 12.10 Source Listing screen.

At any time during and after testing an application, the XPEDITER/CICS trace is available. In Figure 12.11, not only is the statement number shown, so is the actual statement that was executed. This allows you to redisplay the logic of the program, and view only the statements that were executed. This trace display is available across the execution of multiple programs. The size of the trace table is set at installation time and can be increased when large programs are being tested.

12.5 File Utility

XPEDITER/CICS's File utility allows access to VSAM and BDAM data sets, Temporary Storage and Transient Data Queues, and DL/1 and DB2 databases. The File utility is included in the base product and can be used both during the debugging of a program and as a stand-alone program to set up test data or correct problems. The File Utility Menu is shown in Figure 12.12.

```
--------------------- XPEDITER/CICS - PROGRAM TRACE (2.4) --------------------
COMMAND ===>                                                     SCROLL ===> CSR
PROGRAM: CWDEMCBL   MODULE: CWDEMCBL  COMP DATE: 11/ 1/91  COMP TIME: 12.54.57
TERM: 2004 ------------------------------- STOPPED AFTER STMT 00402 IN CWDEMCBL
=======>  TASK(00376)     PROGRAM(CWDEMCBL)    LANGUAGE(COBOL) COMMAND
00366               GO TO  800-RETURN-TO-CICS DEPENDING ON DFHEIGDI.
00367              IF EIBCALEN EQUAL ZERO
<BRANCH>
00370                  GO TO 200-RECEIVE-INPUT.
<BRANCH>
00390          200-RECEIVE-INPUT.
00391         *EXEC CICS HANDLE CONDITION
00392         *          LENGERR (500-MAPERR)
00393         *END-EXEC.
00394               MOVE '......................00305    ' TO DFHEIV0
00395              CALL 'DFHEI1' USING DFHEIV0
00396               GO TO  500-MAPERR DEPENDING ON DFHEIGDI.
<BRANCH>
00401               MOVE '........... ...00308    ' TO DFHEIV0
00402              CALL 'DFHEI1' USING DFHEIV0  DUMMY-EMP DUMMY-LEN.
00403
00404
00405              MOVE DUMMY-PAYEMP1 TO PAYEMP1.
******************************** BOTTOM OF DATA ********************************
```

Figure 12.11 XPEDITER/CICS Program Trace screen.

```
-------------- XPEDITER/CICS - FILE UTILITY MENU (5) -------------
COMMAND ===>
PROGRAM:MODULE:


1 CICS DATASETS       - Access CICS datasets
2 TEMPORARY STORAGE   - Access CICS temporary storage
3 TRANSIENT DATA      - Access CICS transient data queues
4 DL/1 DATABASES      - Access local DL/1 databases
5 DB2 EASY QUERY      - Access DB2 tables
```

Figure 12.12 File Utility Menu.

The only exception to using the File utility during a debugging session is that, because there are a limited number of DB2 threads available in each CICS region, each debugging session is allowed only one thread. This means that if you are debugging a DB2 program and are using the DB2 thread, you cannot simultaneously access the DB2 File utility.

XPEDITER/CICS's File utility always provides a list for the programmer to choose from. For instance, Figure 12.13 displays a list of all of the VSAM and BDAM data sets defined to the CICS region. You can use the LOCATE command to position the list at the appropriate data set.

Although the programmer can access the update screen immediately by typing an S, for Select, the most common method is to type a B for Browse instead. The reason is that in full-screen browse mode, as shown in Figure 12.14, you can use the FIND command to search for data strings within the records, whether in the key or contained in the record. When the desired record is found, simply enter an S to immediately access the update screen directly from browse mode.

The update screen is shown in Figure 12.15. You can view the chosen record in character mode, hex, hex dump format, and also formatted by an 01 level from a COBOL program, as shown in Figure 12.16. The record can be updated or used as a model for a new test record.

Temporary storage can be accessed in exactly the same manner as a data set. Remember that temporary storage queues are created by the program, written to by a program, and hopefully deleted by a program. It is therefore important to be able to display a list of the existing temporary storage queues, as shown in Figure 12.17. The

```
----------------- XPEDITER/CICS - CICS DATASET LIST (5.1.1) -----------------
COMMAND ===>                                                    SCROLL ===> CSR
PROGRAM:              MODULE:

LINE COMMANDS:  B (Browse)  S (Select)

ACCESS         CURRENT      SERVICE                               REMOTE
CMD    NAME   METHOD TYPE   STATUS        REQUESTS         OPTIONS    ID      NAME
-----------------------------------------------------------------------------------
_   BDAMFBLB  BDAM DA-REL   CLO ENA REA UPD ADD BRO EXC
_   BDAMFBLD  BDAM DA-REL   CLO ENA REA UPD ADD BRO EXC
_   BDAMFBLH  BDAM DA-REL   CLO ENA REA UPD ADD BRO EXC
_   BDAMFBLM  BDAM DA-REL   CLO ENA REA UPD ADD BRO EXC
_   BDAMFIXB  BDAM DA-UNB   CLO ENA REA UPD ADD BRO EXC
_   BDAMFIXD  BDAM DA-UNB   CLO ENA REA UPD ADD BRO EXC
_   BDAMFIXH  BDAM DA-UNB   CLO ENA REA UPD ADD BRO EXC
_   BDAMFIXM  BDAM DA-UNB   CLO ENA REA UPD ADD BRO EXC
_   BDAMKEYB  BDAM DA-UNB   CLO ENA REA UPD     BRO EXC
_   BDAMKEYD  BDAM DA-UNB   CLO ENA REA UPD     BRO EXC
_   BDAMKEYH  BDAM DA-UNB   CLO ENA REA UPD     BRO EXC
_   BDAMKEYM  BDAM DA-UNB   CLO ENA REA UPD     BRO EXC
_   BDAMVARB  BDAM DA-UNB   CLO ENA REA UPD ADD BRO EXC
_   BDAMVARD  BDAM DA-UNB   CLO ENA REA UPD ADD BRO EXC
_   BDAMVARH  BDAM DA-UNB   CLO ENA REA UPD ADD BRO EXC
```

Figure 12.13 CICS Dataset List screen.

```
--------------- XPEDITER/CICS - BROWSE CICS DATASET (5.1.2) ----------------
COMMAND ===>                                                    SCROLL ===>CSR
PROGRAM:         MODULE:

                      ACCESS METHOD: VSAM         TYPE: KSDS
FILENAME: PLAYDT1                                              MAX RECLN: 08026
                                      RECFM: V KEYLN: 00026         RKP: 00000
KEY FIELD: ----+---10----+---20----26
          ..........................
          00000000000000000000000000
          00000000000000000000000000

LINE COMMANDS:  D (Delete)  S (Select)

CMD RECLN ----+---10----+---20----+---30----+---40----+---50----+---60----+-->
_   00050 ..........................<---LOW VALUE RECORD--->
_   02544 1ALDEN   USER     0001C    04.03...................................
_   02544 1BALDEN  CD9P     0001C    04.03...................................
_   02544 1BALDEN  FILEABND     C    04.03...................................
_   02544 1BALDEN  FILEABND0001C     04.03...................................
_   02544 1BALDEN  USER     0001C    04.03...................................
_   02544 1DUCHANANSMUTTEST     C    04.03...................................
_   02544 1CWX0030 DB2TEST 0001C     04.03...................................
_   02544 1DPLKTEST             C    04.03...................................
```

Figure 12.14 Browse CICS Dataset screen.

```
-------------- XPEDITER/CICS - EDIT CICS DATASET RECORD (5.1.3) -------------
COMMAND ===>                                                   SCROLL ===> CSR
PROGRAM:           MODULE:
VALID COMMANDS: READ  DELETE  WRITE  REWRITE NEXT  PREV  CLOSE
                      ACCESS METHOD: VSAM          TYPE: KSDS
FILENAME: PLAYDT1                                  RECLN: 02544  MAX RECLN: 08026
DEC-OFFSET: 000000 ADD-OFFSET: ______      RECFM: V KEYLN: 00026          RKP: 00000
KEY FIELD: ----+---10----+---20----26
          1CWX0030 DB2TEST 0001C
          FCEEFFFF4CCFECEE4FFFFC4444
          13670030042235230000130000
----+---10----+---20----+---30----+---40----+---50----+---60----+---70----+--->
1CWX0030 DB2TEST 0001C    04.03..............................................
----+---10----+---20----+---30----+---40----+---50----+---60----+---70----+--->
```

Figure 12.15 Edit a CICS Dataset Record screen.

appropriate queue can then be created, displayed, browsed, updated, or deleted.

Transient data queues are available for reading and updating, but not browsing. (Remember that CICS deletes transient data queue records after they are read.)

DL/I databases are available and a list of the available PSBs is displayed. After choosing the desired PSB, a list of the available PCBs is displayed. The list is displayed until the desired segments are chosen. A skeleton SSA is provided to access a specific SSA.

For DB2, a list of the available tables and views is displayed. The list can be limited by creator, database, just tables or just views, or by table space. DB2 controls security and limits access to authorized objects. After a table is selected, it is available in

```
----------------- XPEDITER/CICS - EDIT QUEUED RECORD (5.2.3) ----------------
COMMAND ===>                                                    SCROLL ===>CSR
PROGRAM: CWDEMCBL MODULE:
VALID COMMANDS: READ  DELETE  WRITE  WRAUX  REWRITE NEXT
                                                  TYPE:  MULTIPLE RECORD QUEUE
QUEUE NAME:PRINTER       RECORD NUMBER:00001       RECLN: 02544 MAX RECLN:32755
          DDCDECD4                                RECFM: V
          79953590
DEC-OFFSET:  000000      ADD-OFFSET:_______

 FIELD LEVEL/NAME               PICTURE       ----+---10----+---20----+---30
 01 REPORT01                    GROUP
 05 REPORT-NUM                  X(21)         REPORT #698
 05 REPORT-CO                   X(35)         ABC COMPANY
 05 REPORT-DATE                 X(18)         AUGUST 1, 1991
 10 REPORT-MONTH                X(6)          AUGUST
 10 REPORT-DAY                  X(2)          1
 10 FILLER                      X(2)
 10 REPORT-YEAR                 X(4)          1991
 05 PAGE-NUM                    X(8)          PAGE 1
```

Figure 12.16 Edit Queued Record screen.

```
------------- XPEDITER/CICS - TEMPORARY STORAGE QUEUE LIST (5.2.1) ------------
COMMAND ===>                                                    SCROLL ===>CSR
PROGRAM:         MODULE:

 T/S TYPE       CI SIZE    TOTAL CI'S      MAX USED     PCT        IN USE     PCT
-------------  ----------  ----------    ----------     ---     ----------   ----
AUX.  (CI)         4096       300           8  2          8  2
MAIN  (BYTES)

LINE COMMANDS: B(Browse) S(Select)
OUTPUT
CMD          NAME           TYPE      GROUP       BY      RECORDS
--------------------------------------------------------------------------------
_            ABRF           AUX       QUEUED      PUTQ    0000007          4.55  1.5
_            BACF           MAIN      QUEUED      PUTQ    0000001        2568     7
_            PRINTER        MAIN      QUEUED      PUTQ    0000007       17976    50
_            TNGOVC04       MAIN      QUEUED      PUTQ    0000006       15408    42
**END**
```

Figure 12.17 Temporary Storage Queue List screen.

full-screen browse, just like a data set. FINDs can be done on data strings and, when the desired row is found, it is displayed by column and definition, and the data is formatted out for easy modification.

There is another mode for selecting from DB2 tables, called DB2 Easy Query. This facility allows you to manipulate the columns through an ISPF-like set of line commands, order the columns selected, and type in the appropriate WHERE clause, as shown in Figure 12.18. A SELECT statement will be generated from your selections, and it can be executed and saved to be accessed from TSO—all without extensive knowledge of SQL. The resulting table is then displayed, and updating can take place as usual.

12.6 Advanced Functions

The previous sections have discussed the most common usage of the product. When working in the CICS environment, however, there are frequently more complex tasks that also need to be performed. These tasks are briefly detailed in the following sections.

12.6.1 Single stepping automatically

Single-stepping is the ability to slow-step automatically through the program. The command GO 15 3, for instance, will execute 15 statements, pausing 3 seconds between each statement. This command is extremely valuable, especially for unfamiliar programs. This command allows you to concentrate on the variables and their values (remember the automatic KEEPs) while getting a mental picture of the logic of the program.

12.6.2 Remote trapping

You can use XPEDITER/CICS to debug programs that do not run on a terminal. These include programs that run on printers, asynchronous programs that run as background tasks, and LU6.2 programs, where the terminal ID is selected from a pool of available terminals.

Remember that by turning on XPEDITER/CICS, abends are automatically trapped and prevented on the terminal that you are running a program on. In Figure 12.19, the remote-trap screen is shown with the automatic trap set by XPEDITER/CICS

```
 -------------------- XPEDITER/CICS - BUILD SQL "EASY QUERY (5.5.2) -----------
COMMAND ==>                                                       SCROLL ==> CSR
PROGRAM:                MODULE:

CREATOR: DSN8130  TABLE: TEMPL                                ROW      1 OF 12
                                                         POSITION      1 OF 254

PREFIX COMMANDS:  A AFTER    B BEFORE   M/MM MOVE    S/SS SELECT    X/XX EXCLUDE
PRIMARY COMMANDS: SHOW RESULT DISPLAY QUERY RESULT  RESET EXPAND EXCLUDED LINES
                  SHOW SQL    DISPLAY GENERATED SQL END    LIST OF TABLES/VIEWS
                  CHECK       WHERE CLAUSE SYNTAX CHECK

                                             ORDER-BY           WHERE CLAUSE
      COLUMN  NAME       ATTRIBUTES     SEQ A/D        VALUES AND OPERATORS
   ------------------ --------------- --- ---  ----+---10----+---20----+---30---
S_ EMPNO              CHAR(6)         __  _
S_ FIRSTNME           VARCHAR(12)     02  A
S_ MIDINIT            CHAR(1)         __  _
S_ LASTNAME           VARCHAR(15)     01  A
S_ WORKDEPT           CHAR(3)         __  _
S_ PHONENO            CHAR(4)         __  _
S_ HIREDATE           DATE            __  _   > '1975-05-01'
__ JOBCODE            DECIMAL(3,0)    __  _
__ EDUCLVL            SMALLINT        __  _
```

Figure 12.18 Build SQL Easy Query screen.

```
---------------------- XPEDITER/CICS - TRAP SUMMARY (1.6) ---------------------
COMMAND ===>                                                       SCROLL ===> CSR
PROGRAM:                MODULE:                                       ENTRY 000001
LINE COMMANDS:  A (After) B (Before) C (Copy) D (Delete) I (Insert) M (Move)

                 CMD        TERM       TRAN       PROGRAM
                 -----------------------------------------
                  _         2100       ****       ********
                  _         ****       ****       CWDEMCBL
                  _         ____       ____       ________
                  _         ____       ____       ________
                  _         ____       ____       ________
                  _         ____       ____       ________
                  _         ____       ____       ________
                  _         ____       ____       ________
                  _         ____       ____       ________
                  _         ____       ____       ________
                  _         ____       ____       ________
                  _         ____       ____       ________
                  _         ____       ____       ________
                  _         ____       ____       ________
                  _         ____       ____       ________
```

Figure 12.19 XPEDITER/CICS Trap Summary screen.

and an additional trap for program CWDEMCBL. Any mix of terminal, transaction, and program can be entered by using asterisks as wildcards.

XPEDITER/CICS can be only as selective as your testing session. What this means is that if your transaction will run on an unknown terminal ID, then you might have to set up a conditional breakpoint to trap your test and not someone else's. An example of the condition to check would be AFTER 328 IF USERID = "CWDEM45". If you intercept a transaction that is not the one you want to test, simply enter the GO command to allow it to continue processing and intercept the next one.

12.6.3 Memory display

You can use the Memory Display screen to display and modify areas of your program and the load module of your program. This screen can also display CICS areas and tables. XPEDITER/CICS will allow you to view CICS tables and areas, but allows changes only to areas that belong to your program or testing session.

12.6.4 Tailoring the foot area

The last five lines of the screen can optionally be used to display additional information on all screens. The SET FOOT command can be used to display menu selections, the analysis summary from the COUNT facility, the PF-key settings, current lines of source, and data. This is an area that you can tailor to suit your programming needs.

12.6.5 The SKIP command

I mentioned the SKIP command briefly in the debugging scenario as a way to skip certain lines of code. There is also a conditional SKIP command that works similarly to the conditional BREAKPOINT command. An example would be when your program works just fine until a particular part number is encountered. The command SKIP IF PART-NUMBER = "45393" would execute the statement every time except when part number 45393 is encountered. Another use is to generically skip all CICS updates or rewrites when no file updating is required. The SKIP command can be used to avoid database updates as well as updates to data sets.

12.6.6 Storage protection

Storage protection will prevent a program from accessing or modifying storage that does not belong to it. The systems programmer can set up global storage protection, which is defined at the end of this chapter. The storage protection that is set is specific to the transaction and programs being tested.

Remember that you can also set storage protection for your entire session through the defaults of the product. This is not usually the case, however, for test regions.

12.6.7 Test-coverage analysis

At the end of the testing cycle, it is frequently necessary to check that all the statements in a program have been thoroughly tested. There might be, for example, particular conditions that get executed only when an error occurs or only at the end of the year. Rather than cross your fingers and wait, you can use XPEDITER/CICS to keep track of the statements that have been executed, how many times they were executed, and—sometimes most important of all—which statements did not get executed.

You can use the ANALYZE (or COUNT) feature to set counters with either the line commands of COUNT or the generic COUNT ALL PARA statement. The COUNT ALL PARA command will set a counter on each paragraph and increment it each time a paragraph is executed. These counts are maintained across the repeated execution of a program, so if multiple transactions need to be entered to test all the paragraphs in the program the counts will remain until the COUNT OFF command erases them.

XPEDITER/CICS also has a SET FOOT ANALYZE command that will display the percentage of programs executed, percentage not executed, and paragraph executed the most times (for loop detection).

12.6.8 Debugging programs without a source

Sometimes the program source is not available. This can be because the program trapped was not the one being tested and thus not precompiled, or the debugging might be taking place in production, where source-based debugging is not always allowed. Whatever the reason, programs can be debugged in this manner. All of the basic debugging functions are available, and XPEDITER/CICS will provide as much information as it can to help with this process.

Figure 12.20 shows the screen that is displayed when an abend is trapped for a program that does not have source. You can see that the abend code is still displayed on the right side of the header area—in this case, an AEIP has been prevented. The offset and the address of the instruction causing the problem is displayed along with the disassembled instruction from the load module. If you have a compiled listing for this program, you can translate the information back to the related source code and proceed with the necessary correction. If that is not possible, you can still perform the following functions:

- Go around the offending instruction by changing the offset
- Use the offset on the working storage screen to display or modify the data in working storage
- Single-step through the program, using the GO 1 command
- Display the trace (by offset) to find out how you got to this part of the program
- Display the Last 3270 Screen(=2.8) to view the last application program map sent to or received from the program

12.7 Systems Programmer Functions

Years ago when the first debuggers appeared, they were systems programmer tools first and application debuggers second. Although the number of application programmers using debuggers today is much higher than the number of systems programmers using the product, the system functions are still important and necessary to a debugger.

The functions available for the systems programmer are divided into two categories: dynamic region maintenance and storage protection. The features of the two categories are listed in the following sections. If you have access to a CICS monitor product, the region maintenance utilities might already be provided. But only an "industrial-strength" debugger can provide the rest.

```
----------------- XPEDITER/CICS - ASSEMBLER STOP/ABEND (2.20) -----------------
COMMAND ===> =2.4                                               SCROLL ===> CSR
PROGRAM: CWDEMCBL   +++++++++++ NO SOURCE AVAILABLE.  PF1 OR "HELP" +++++++++++
CAUSE: "INVREQ" INVALID REQUEST         (TRACED)               ABEND CODE: AEIP
CICS SYSTEM: CICSCWZP       TERM ID: 2018    NETNAME: LU102018     TRANS ID: XCBL
INTERRUPT OFFSET: 001B8E    ADDRESS: 001D3BC6    PSW:
RESUME     OFFSET: 001B8E    ADDRESS: 001D3BC6    LAST CICS MACRO/EXEC:   01B8E

INSTRUCTION: 05EF               BALR    14,15
REGISTERS:

       R0       R1       R2       R3       R4       R5       R6       R7
    00000000 0033FFC8 0033F103 0000001E 0033F100 8033EEA8 0033EF0C 0033FF7B

       R8       R9       R10      R11      R12      R13      R14      R15
    0033FF7C 001D4320 001D2038 001D2038 001D31B8 0033FD74 501D3BC8 00000000
```

Figure 12.20 Assembler Stop/Abend Panel.

```
------------------ XPEDITER/CICS - SYSTEM FACILITIES MENU (9) ----------------
COMMAND ===>
PROGRAM:                MODULE:

  1  VIEW SINGLE TASK     - View a selected task
  2  MEMORY               - Display/modify memory
  3  TASK LIST            - List all Tasks in the CICS region/partition
  4  EXCLUSIONS           - Display/modify trace and protection exclusions
  5  CSECT EXCLUSIONS     - Display/modify CSECT exclusions
  6  TRAP SUMMARY         - Display/modify global ABEND traps
  7  STORAGE EXCEPTIONS   - Display/modify global storage protection exceptions
  8  STORAGE PROTECTION   - Display/modify global storage protection entries
  9  SYSTEM LABELS        - Create system labels for storage areas
  D  CICS DSECTS          - Display formatted CICS DSECTs
  P  RESOURCE SUMMARY     - Display/remove global STOPs/KEEPs
```

Figure 12.21 Systems Facilities Menu.

12.7.1 Dynamic region maint

- Dynamic alteration of CICS tables without cycling the region
- Dynamic application of ZAPs without cycling the region

12.7.2 Storage protection (and utilities)

- Global storage protection
- Global storage exception
- Global trapping of abend
- Dynamic review and resetting of debugging parameters
- Ability to trap and debug problems in DFH modules (with or without source)

Because this chapter is specifically intended for applications programmers, I will discuss the systems utilities only briefly.

Within the XPEDITER/CICS product, there is a separate transaction reserved for the systems programmer (or CICS specialist) authorized to perform CICS region maintenance. The default transaction is XPSP, and this transaction has all the capabilities mentioned in the previous sections, plus the ability to alter CICS storage and set global storage protection. The Systems Facilities Menu is shown in Figure 12.21.

Global storage protection prevents storage violations before they occur. You can set this protection permanently through the PLT so that it is reset each time the region is cycled, or dynamically by typing in the required settings. Storage protection can be set by terminal, transaction, program, or any mix of the three parameters using asterisks as wildcards.

The following are some of the procedures pertaining to systems programmers alone—what is available to them, as opposed to application programmers. You can:

- Dynamically display and change any CICS storage area, CICS tables in memory, and CICS control blocks.

- Easily "chase" CICS storage chains—when viewing a storage area (such as the CSA), just position the cursor under an address and press the PF9 key. XPEDITER will automatically take you to that address, and also keep track of each address visited for later reselection.
- Turn storage protection on at CICS start-up (through the PLT) or dynamically for any transaction, terminal, program, or mix of all three through the use of wildcards. Transactions attempting to cause a storage violation will be abended with a STOR abend code and prevented. Also, the storage exception table can allow necessary but nondestructive violations to occur. The systems programmer can, for instance, allow updates to the EIB on a system-wide basis, while preventing other forms of violations from occurring.
- Use DSECT support—XPSP gives access to storage by DSECT name, and formats the area so you can overtype areas of storage without the danger of missing by a byte or two.
- Undo anything the programmers can do. For example, the programmer can set KEEPs and BREAKs in the programs they are debugging. The XPSP transaction can set or remove KEEPs and BREAKs for all programs in the region, and turn on protection for all transactions and programs.
- Dynamically apply ZAPs to any programs in the region. If a ZAP needs to be applied, you can display and modify the load module in storage, and then test to be sure the change is as expected. If the results are incorrect, you can NEWCOPY the program to remove the changes. If the ZAP is correct, you can then permanently update the load module.
- Use Hung-Task Analysis, which is available from the XPSP transaction. You can use this feature to display the transactions running in a region. If an abend has been intercepted through remote trapping, the transaction can be selected for analysis. If a transaction is suspended for any reason, the task can be selected and the reason for its suspension will be displayed.
- Use the XPSP transaction, which can exclude programs or modules from trace. If there are areas of sensitivity, such as security modules, they can be excluded from display during the debugging process to prevent circumvention.

Chapter

13

IBM's Approach to Debugging: COBTEST

13.1 Product Overview

COBTEST, or COBOL TEST, is a productivity tool designed to debug and diagnose problems in your VS COBOL II programs. The software operates both in batch mode or under MVS or CMS interactively in line or full-screen mode. With COBTEST, just like with CA-InterTest or CICS dBUG-AID, you can suspend the execution of your application program using breakpoints, skip sections of your code, correct errors, set up displays, and perform other useful techniques.

The power, effectiveness, and flexibility of COBTEST are perhaps best demonstrated when used in ISPF (Interactive System Productivity Facility) in full-screen mode. In this sort of environment, you can set and highlight breakpoints, for example, at your convenience. A breakpoint allows you to suspend processing of your code at a certain location in your program so that you can closely examine values, storage contents, and other scenario leading to a possible abend. But there are other techniques you can use in this productivity tool, as well. You can monitor a RUN, for example, as it performs dynamically, and highlight a currently executing line. You can also change window configurations throughout the session to suit your debugging needs. All this while you display your source listing throughout the test.

When you use COBTEST in a full-screen debugging session, you can rely on menus and subdirectories to change a particular design feature, such as color attributes, intensity, and brightness; change area sizes; and display a different source listing.

Because COBTEST runs under ISPF, you have access to ISPF functions, such as splitting a screen in half; you can also browse and edit portions of it, or run a recompile. Incidentally, these sessions require that you have both ISPF and PDF (Program Development Facility) fully installed and operational.

13.2 TESTCOB, the Old Productivity Tool

The forerunner of the current IBM productivity tool was called TESTCOB. The IBM OS COBOL Interactive Debug was also a command-processing program that operated under the control of the Time-Sharing Option (TSO), and Conversational Monitoring System (CMS) in a virtual-machine environment.

The term TESTCOB, just like the new version, had its own command language, which included the TESTCOB command and a set of subcommands. To run TESTCOB, you were responsible for performing the following procedures:

- Creating and editing a source-program data set.
- Compiling the program with the TEST compiler option in order to create an object module.
- Linking and editing the program, which creates a load module.
- Creating and editing all required data sets.
- Allocating all required data sets.

Once the above steps were completed, you could begin debugging your program by entering the TESTCOB command.

There were several problems, both technical and marketing-oriented, that added to the unpopularity and eventual obsolescence of TESTCOB. First of all, it was quite difficult to set up and use. In addition, IBM charged for the product, which placed the software into direct competition with more comprehensive and easy-to-use vendor packages. With CICS dBUG-AID and CA-InterTest already on the market, IBM had to go back to the drawing board to concentrate on a better productivity tool. This gave rise to COBTEST.

13.3 COBTEST in Line Mode

COBTEST is one of the better productivity tools when it comes to a debugging session. The system operates in line mode, batch mode, and full-screen mode. This section will highlight for you some of the features involved in line mode.

If a full-screen terminal is not available, you can still use some of the interactive capabilities of COBTEST in line mode. In this particular environment, input and output are presented to you sequentially, one line at a time, rather than in full-screen mode, when the entire screen is controlled and used by this debugging productivity tool. However, some users would be quick to point out that using COBTEST in line mode is the exception rather than the rule, and is intended primarily for users with access to only a typewriter-like terminal or when, of course, ISPF is not installed. The following is a step-by-step session; each set of commands is followed directly by an explanation of what those commands accomplish:

```
cobtest  INV0200C
INV0200C.000125.1
COBTEST
```

Request line-mode debugging for program INV0200C. COBTEST will accept the request and start at statement 125 (the first verb in the program). COBTEST will then wait for the next command.

```
trace name
COBTEST
```

Request COBTEST to display the name and the number of each procedure in the program. COBTEST acknowledges this request and waits for the next command.

```
at 400
COBTEST
```

Request COBTEST to set a breakpoint at statement 400. COBTEST accepts the command and waits for the next instruction.

```
go
TRACING INV0200C
000132  ADD ITEMS
AT INV0200C.000400.1
COBTEST
```

Request COBTEST to start executing the program via a GO command. COBTEST begins executing program INV0200C, acknowledges that it is executing an ADD-ITEMS procedure, stops at the first verb in statement 400, as requested, and waits for the next command.

```
list MASTER-INVENTORY
000027 01   REC-NAME AN...
   54776  125   SMITH
COBTEST
```

Request COBTEST to display information about the record MASTER-INVENTORY. COBTEST displays the definition and the contents of MASTER-INVENTORY and waits for the next command.

At this point in the debugging session, you might have enough information to alter the program. For example, it might be evident that the format or content of the record is wrong and can be corrected immediately or; if not, you can continue the dialog.

13.4 COBTEST in Batch Mode

When you run COBTEST in batch mode, you need to enter all the requests in a data set before you run your program. This means that some debugging requests that, in interactive mode, would return control to the programmer return control to the program instead. Because of this obvious limitation, when debugging in batch mode you cannot stop the execution of a program and check its status, as you can during a dBUG-AID or CA-InterTest session, and then dynamically respond to the conditions revealed. Instead, COBTEST lets you specify a set of instructions to be carried out if certain conditions occur. For instance, the following request directs COBTEST to perform three separate actions if and when the item VALUE-1 in the program equals the item SUM-1:

```
WHEN TST1 (VALUE-1 EQ SUM-1) (FLOW(5); SET REC1 = REC2; GO)
```

Planning is crucial when you are using commands in batch mode. Because all commands are entered at the beginning of the debugging session, you must plan them more carefully than in interactive mode. As you prepare the commands you want to use in batch mode, remember that all the commands you have specified will take effect immediately. For example, QUIT will stop all testing and debugging as soon as it is read in.

The commands will be executed in the same sequence in which they occur in the SYSDBIN data set (CSCOxxxx for CICS and SYSIPT for VSE). If any severe syntax errors are introduced, your debugging session will terminate. Also, you cannot make any changes in the command sequence while the test is executing. The most useful commands in batch mode are shown in Figure 13.1.

Note that the timing of these commands is quite significant when used in batch mode. Some commands, such as LIST, take effect and complete their function as soon as they are entered (as primary commands). Other commands, such as TRACE or FLOW, take effect as soon as they are entered; however, they set up some continuing action. Yet other commands, such as AT, do nothing when first entered, but set up a condition that must be satisfied before they are acted upon.

The difference in timing between WHEN and IF is illustrated by the following examples: First, when you enter IF (condition) (LIST dataname), the test for the condition is made at once. If the condition is true, the LIST function takes place. Second, when you enter WHEN C1 (condition) (LIST dataname), no test is made and no LIST occurs. The WHEN condition is entered into a table and the command string (LIST) is saved. When the execution of the COBOL program takes place, the WHEN condition is tested at every COBOL statement, and if true, the LIST occurs. Like the AT command, the WHEN condition is not exhausted by one true condition, but continues to be tested during the life of the program (or until you turn it off explicitly with OFFWN).

The notion of timing is crucial for batch mode also, because in batch mode all the commands will be processed before the first instruction in the COBOL program is executed. To get the most out of batch mode, you will want to make use of the delayed-action commands to control the timing of your other commands. This is possible because the command list of delayed commands (see the table in Figure 13.2)

```
AT      LISTBRKS   PROC
FLOW    LISTEQ     QUALIFY
FREQ    LISTFREQ   TRACE
LINK    NEXT       WHEN
LIST    ONABEND
```

Figure 13.1 Most frequently used batch commands.

```
Immediate commands with no further effect:

DUMP      LISTBRKS      WHERE
IF        LISTEQ
LIST      LISTFREQ

Immediate commands that affect further execution
of the program:

DROP      OFF            RECORD
EQUATE    OFFWN          RUN
FLOW ON   PRINTDD        SET
FREQ      QUALIFY        STEP
GO        QUIT           TRACE
LINK

Delayed commands: The operation of the following
commands takes place only after the condition is
met.

AT        ONABEND        WHEN
NEXT      PROC
```

Figure 13.2 Immediate and batch commands.

are activated only when the initial or primary command in a string of commands is true. Therefore, in the command:

```
WHEN C1 (condition) (SET dataname = value)
```

the SET function occurs every time the WHEN condition is true. Immediate commands (Figure 13.2) are those commands that are completed immediately after the issuance of such a command.

13.5 COBTEST in Full-Screen Mode

When COBTEST runs under ISPF, TSO, or CMS, it executes in full-screen mode. This means that, like in InterTest or CICS dBUG-AID, the entire screen becomes available for the software. Because COBTEST executes in ISPF, it uses ISPF panels and services.

Using ISPF, you can simultaneously view the source program, contents of variables, and log of your interactions and communications with the COBTEST. In full-screen mode, you can dynamically step through your program, monitor program variables, display the source listing in a window, and even split the physical screen into two logical screens. (Note that I have covered the process of splitting panels in chapter 6.) Using a split screen, you can browse, edit, and recompile (TSO only) a source listing while debugging; however, to take advantage of these functions in split-screen mode, you must also have PDF installed.

Having invoked ISPF/PDF, you will be presented with the Primary Options Menu. At this point, select the FOREGROUND option. You will then be presented with the Foreground Selection Panel. On this panel, select the option associated with VS COBOL II debug. You will be further presented with the full-screen Debug Invocation

Panel. (Another way to proceed is to enter 4.*nn* on the Primary Option Menu command line, where *nn* is the number associated with the VS COBOL II debug option on the Foreground Selection Panel.

If you are invoking COBTEST in full-screen mode using TSO (Time-Sharing Option), you will be presented with the full-screen TSO Invocation Panel shown in Figure 13.3. Specify the main debugging unit and its runtime parameters on this panel. When you invoke COBTEST in full-screen mode, the system allocates a SYSABOUT and SYSDBOUT data set for you. Note that some of these parameters were discussed in the chapter dealing with the ISPF text editor. Others, however, need some additional clarification.

VS COBOL II Program Parameters represent input parameters and runtime options for the program to be debugged. The input parameters cannot exceed 130 characters in length. If you use runtime options in the parameter string, you must list your COBOL program parameters first, followed by a slash (/), followed by your runtime parameters—as shown in the following example:

```
00AABBCC/NOSSR, SPOUT
```

The two-position field at the beginning of the parameter string is added by the debug tool. Be sure your COBOL program allows for insertion of this two-byte field.

The DDNAME field allows you to specify a previously allocated DDNAME. All data sets allocated to this ddname will be concatenated to the data set where the program unit resides. This lets you concatenate several program libraries to the ddname.

If you want to create a log data set, specify YES. The default value of this option is NO. LOGON DSN is used so that the data set, should you request it, contains the ses-

```
----------- VS COBOL II DEBUG INVOCATION ----------------
COMMAND ===>

 ISPF LIBRARY:
  PROJECT ===>
  TYPE    ===>
  GROUP   ===>
  MEMBER  ===>          (BLANK FOR MEMBER SELECTION LIST)

 OTHER PARTITIONED DATA SET:
  DATA SET NAME  ===>

 PASSWORD ===>          MIXED MODE ===>    (YES OR NO)

 VS COBOL II PROGRAM PARAMETERS:
  ===>
  ===>

 DDNAME  ===>
 LOG     ===>     (YES OR NO)
 LOG DSN ===>
 RESTART ===>     (YES OR NO)
 RESTART DSN ===>
```

Figure 13.3 Full-screen TSO Invocation Panel.

```
COBTEST     WHERE:  SAMPLE.000031.1                                SCROLL ===> PAGE
COMMAND ===>
AUTO 0----+----1----+----2----+----3----+----4----+----5----+--LINE 1 OF 2
00001 000026 77  SAMPLE.E-O-F-FLAG                                 X
00002         DISP    ===>N     1
************************* BOTTOM OF AUTO ***********************************

SOURCE----+----1----+----2----+----3----+----4----+----5----+--LINE 28 OF 53
   28         77   INVENT-STATUS                  PIC XX.
   29         PROCEDURE DIVISION    2
   30         0000-MAIN-LINE.
   31                Open Input Inventory
   32                 If Invent-Status Not Equal Zero
   33                   Then Display "Open Error On"
   34                      "File Inventory" Upon Console
   35                   Goback
   36                  End-If
   37                Initialize Inventory-Record
   38                  Invent-Status
LOG  0----+----1----+----2----+----3----+----4----+----5----+--LINE 0 OF 6
00001 IGZ100I PP - 5668-958 VS COBOL II DEBUG FACILITY -- REL 3.2
00002 IGZ100I LICENSED MATERIAL - PROPERTY OF IBM    3
```

sion log. It is created with a fixed record format (RECFM) and a logical record length (LRECL) of 80. If you want to use a restart data set, specify YES; otherwise, the system will assume NO. RESTART DSN is used if you request that the data set be read upon invocation of the debug tool. The restart data set must have a fixed record format (RECFM) and a logical record length (LRECL) of 80.

Having invoked COBTEST in full-screen mode, the system will display a full-screen panel similar to the one displayed in Figure 13.4. The Main Full-Screen Panel contains a permanent log area and could contain a source area. Note the following three distinct areas in Figure 13.4:

Auto. When opened, the auto monitoring area appears immediately below the command line.

Source. The source area is always opened with the currently executing line highlighted. If, however, a source line is excluded from the listing (via the compiler directive LIST OFF), COBTEST will display the following line in its place in the source listing:

Figure 14.2A TRAILERS subparameter format chart, part 1.

- - - STATEMENT *nnnnn.n* EXCLUDED - - -

where *nnnnn.n* is the statement number of the line excluded from the source listing. When stepping through the program, the excluded line will still be executed.

Log. If you don't open either the auto or the source area, the log area will cover the entire display portion of the panel. If the source area is opened to its full column width, the log area will be overlaid by the source area and will appear immediately below the source area display. However, if you display the source listing using a half-screen width (Figure 13.5), the source area will overlay the top portion of the log area.

Note that the labeled header line for each panel area contains a scale and a line counter. If you scroll a panel area horizontally, the scale will also scroll so that it indicates the columns displayed in the panel area. The line counter indicates the line number at the top of the panel area and the total number of lines in that area.

You can enter a command or modify what is on the main full-screen panel in four areas. These four areas are indicated in Figure 13.5. The command line is where you can enter all debug tool commands (except for the COBTEST command), ISPF commands, and TSO or CMS systems commands. 2 and 3 represent the prefix and suffix areas, and the log area lists input lines marked by an asterisk, which can be modified and placed on the command line.

13.6 Debugging and Maintenance

Abend information is available for all active VS COBOL II programs in case of an abend. The abend information contains all the data you need to find useful items in a dump.

COBTEST produces formatted dumps. The FDUMP compiler option specifies that a formatted dump will be produced if a program abnormally ends. You can also produce a VS COBOL II formatted dump for a program running under the control of CICS. The dump is directed to a CICS temporary storage queue and can be printed or displayed using a CICS browse transaction. The information VS COBOL II uses to build the dump is part of the object code for the program. You do not need

```
COBTEST    WHERE:  SAMPLE.000031.1                           SCROLL ===> PAGE
COMMAND ===>     1
AUTO 0----+----1----+----LINE 0 OF 18  | SOURCE ---+---1---+---LINE: 47 OF 53
00001 IGZ100I  PP - 5668-958 VS COBOL  | 47                "File Inv    ....
00002 IGZ100I LICENSED MATERIAL - PP   |  2                 3
00003 IGZ100I (C) COPYRIGHT IBM CORPO  | 49              End-If
00004 IGZ100I US GOVERNMENT USERS RES  | AT              Display Inven 0025
00005 IGZ100I RESTRICTED BY GSA ADP S  | 51          End-Perform        ....
00006 IGZ102I SAMPLE.00005.1           | 52          Close Inventory    0000
00007 * AT 50 count (26)               | 53          Goback.            0000
00008 * freq                           |**********BOTTOM OF SOURCE***********
00009 * go     4                       |
00010 IGZ105I AT SAMPLE.00005.1        |
00011 * list inventory-record: invent  ------------------------------------
00012 000024 01 SAMPLE.INVENTORY-RECORD X(80)
00013          DISP  ===>  00026ZZZZZZZZZZZZZZZZZZZZZZZZZZZZZZZZZZZZZZZZZZZZ
00014                ===>  ZZZZZZZZZZZZZZZZZZZZZZZZZZZZZZ
00015 0000026 77 SAMPLE.E-O-F-FLAG X
00016           DISP ===>N
00017 000028  77 SAMPLE.INVENT-STATUS XX
00018           DISP ===>00
************************** BOTTOM OF LOG ****************
```

Figure 14.13 Control statements for an Outstanding Payments report.

```
--- VS COBOL II Formatted Dump at ABEND ---
Program = 'SAMPLE'    1  <=====
Completion Code = '01035'.
PSW at ABEND = '000400CA60F39A78'.
The ABEND address was outside of mainline COBOL code.    2 <=====
Optimization was in effect for this program.
The relative address of the next instruction to be executed:
'00F19A78'
The GP registers at entry to ABEND were      3 <=======
     Regs  0 - 3   -  80000000  8000040B  0000040B  00042164
     Regs  4 - 7   -  00030DA8  00045B98  00042170  000422E2
     Regs  8 - 11  -  00024BBC  00045B98  00026894  0003EF80
     Regs 12 - 15  -  40045D9A  00030D60  50045DF6  00035920
Data Division dump of 'SAMPLE1'
000180 FD SAMPLE1.FILE-1 FD
FILE SPECIFIED AS:
  ORGANIZATION=SEQUENTIAL   ACCESS MODE=SEQUENTIAL
  RECMF=FIXED BLOCK
CURRENT STATUS OF FILE IS:
  QSAM STATUS CODE=35
000240 01 SAMPLE1.RECORD-1 X(80)              ADDRESS CANNOT BE CALCULATED
000264 01 SAMPLE1-FILLER AN-GR
000265 02 SAMPLE1.ABEND-ITEM1 S9999
      CMP3    ===> +0010    4  <===
000266 02 SAMPLE1.ABEND-ITEM2 S9999
      CMP3    ===> +0000
000270 01 SAMPLE1.EOF-SW X
      DISP    ===>
000295 01 SAMPLE.WORK-RECORD AN-GR   <=== 5
000300 02 SAMPLE1.W-EMPLOYEE-NO 9(6)
                                           INVALID DATA FOR THIS DATA TYPE
      DISP    HEX=00000000
                  00000000
000305 02 SAMPLE1.NAME-FIELD AN-GR   <===  6
000310 03 SAMPLE.FIRST-NAME X(10)
:
--- End of VS COBOL II Formatted Dump at ABEND ---
```

Figure 13.6 The VS COBOL II debugging mechanism.

to make an external file available to capture this information when the program runs. An example of this formatted dump is highlighted in Figure 13.6. Note the following explanation:

1. Indicates the name of the program that abnormally terminated.

2. Displays the relative address of the next instruction when the address is available.

3. Displays the contents of the general-purpose registers (and the floating-point registers, if any are used in the program).

4. Indicates the values in the data items at abnormal termination.

5. This section shows the data items defined in the program.

6. Indicates the type of data (AN=alphanumeric, GR=group item, and FD=file definition).

The VS COBOL II compiler produces, on request, a number of listings that provide information about a program and its compilation. In addition, VS COBOL II provides you with an embedded map report containing condensed data map information along with the compiler-generated listing. You can also request a procedure map of an object code listing. Note that in the listings in Figures 13.7A and 13.7B, the SAMPLE1 program is presented in mixed-case letters.

1. Indicates the product description at the top of each page of the compiler listing. (Using the TITLE statement, you can generate individual headings for each page of the listing produced during compilation. However, the TITLE statement is not printed on the source listing).
2. The LVLINFO installation option allows user-supplied "compiler-level" information to be displayed in the listing.
3. Displays the Date/Time format in mixed case.
4. Indicates statement numbers that were specified in the program preceded either by compiler-assigned numbers for out of sequence statements (SEQUENCE compiler option) or by compiler-assigned numbers for all statements (NUMBER compiler option).
5. Shows program (PL) and statement (SL) nesting levels of a program line.
6. Produces partial listings of a source program using *CBL statements. For example, you can use a *CBL statement to suppress the listing of all statements in the program except statements 380 through 600.
7. Displays diagnostic messages immediately below statements in error and also in the diagnostic list. Using the FLAG compiler option, you can control the level of

```
LineID  PL SL  ----+-*A-1 B--+----2----+----3----+----4----+----5----+----6--
               000010 Identification Division.
     4         000040 Program-ID.   Sample1.
000041**       000030 Author.       A. V.
               000050 Date-Written. January 10, 1992.
               000070
000071**       000070 Environment Division.
               000080 Configuration Section.
               000090 Source-Computer. IBM-370.
               000100 Object-Computer. IBM-370.
               000105 Special-Names.
               000106        Sysout is S2.
```

Figure 13.7A Source code using mixed-case letters and diagnostics, part 1.

```
LineID  PL SL ----+-*A-1 B--+----2----+----3----+----4----+----5----+----6----
        5                                              Map & Cross Reference  8
                 6
                 000380 Procedure Division Using Table-Record.             345
                 000400 000-Mainline.
                 000405      Display Starting Upon S2                   UND 106

                    7
==000405==> IGYPS2121-S "STARTING" was not defined as a data name.
            The statement was discarded.
                 .
                 .
                 .
                 000600      Move Employee-No to W-Employee-No          350 300
                    7

==006000==>  IGYPS2028-E    "EMPLOYEE-NO" was a table item but was not
             subscripted or indexed. The first occurrence of the table
             was assumed.

          2      000740      Display "I'm in X1"
          2      000750      Call "X11"                                     790
          2      000760      CALL "X12"                                     850
          2      000770      Exit Program.
          3      000780      ID Division.
                 .
                 .
                 .
```

Figure 13.7B Source code using mixed-case letters and diagnostics, part 2.

diagnostic messages displayed in the source listing, and the level displayed at the end of the listing.

8. Indicates the statement number at which the item is defined. Using the XREF compiler option, embedded cross reference information can be printed on the same line as the original line of the source program (DUP=duplicately defined, EXT=external program name, IMP=implicitly defined, UND=undefined.)

The procedure for producing a cross-reference listing is shown in Figure 13.8, as follows:

1. Highlights the statement number at which the procedure is defined.

2. Depicts the statement number at which the procedure is used in the specified context (in this case P). Context-usage codes precede this section of the listing.

Let's quickly review a data-division map. A data-division map illustrates the structure of defined data in a program, and provides other pertinent information such as where the data is defined and what its attributes are. Figure 13.9 highlights such a map. Note the areas numbered on the exhibit.

1. Shows the statement number at which the data item is defined.

2. Displays data items with indentation to show the hierarchy of the data structure.

3. Indicates where storage has been allocated for the data item in base-locator format.

4. Indicates where storage has been allocated for the data item in hexadecimal-displacement format.

5. Indicates how far the data item is located from the beginning of a structure in hexadecimal format.

6. Indicates the attributes of a defined data item. The data attribute codes precede this portion of the listing.

7. Indicates the beginning of a data map for a nested program. Note that using *CBL statements (not shown here), you can produce a partial data-division map. For instance, you can produce a map of only the WORK-RECORD structure.

Another feature of this productivity tool is the system's ability to display nested program maps. This technique displays the nested program structure of a program. Such a map is displayed in Figure 13.10.

1. Indicates the statement number at which the program is defined.

2. Highlights the program nesting level.

3. Displays the nested program structure using indentation.

4. Depicts the program attributes of the nested program. The program attribute codes precede this section of the listing.

```
     .
     .
Context usage is indicated by the letter preceding a procedure name
reference. These letters and their meanings are:

     A = ALTER (procedure name)
     D = GO TO (procedure name)  DEPENDING ON
     E = End of Range of (PERFORM) through (procedure name)
     G = GO TO (procedure name)
     P = PERFORM (procedure name)
     T = (ALTER) TO PROCEED TO (procedure name)
     U = USE FOR DEBUGGING (procedure name)

Defined    Cross Reference of procedures     References
  1                                               2

000400     000-MAINLINE
000470     100-CHECK-PARA....................     P000440
```

Figure 13.8 Procedure cross reference listing.

```
  PP 5668-958 IBM VS COBOL II Release 3.2 09/05/92     SAMPLE1  Date 12/28/92  Time 10:02:23  Page  7
  Data Division Map
  Data division attribute codes (rightmost column) have the following meanings:
         D = Object of OCCURS DEPENDING    G = GLOBAL                              S = Spanned file
         E = External                      O = Has OCCURS clause                   U = Undefined-format
file
         F = Fixed-length file            OG = Group has own length definition     V = Variable-length
file
        FB = Fixed-length block size       R =  Redefines                         VB = Variable-length
block
 1        2                    3        4            5
Source  Hierarchy and         Base    Hex-Displacement  Asmblr Data
LineID  Data Name             Locator Blk Structure     Definition   Data Type
  48   PROGRAM-ID SAMPLE1 ------------------------------------------------*
 130  FD-FILE1..........................001                        QSAM    FB 6
 240  01 RECORD-1..............BLF=0000  000               DS 80C    Display
 264  01 FILLER................BLW=0000  000               DS OCL6   Group
 265     02 ABEND-ITEM1........BLW=0000  000  0 000 000    DS 3P     Packed-Dec
 266         02 ABEND-ITEM2....BLW=0000  003  0 000 003    DS 3P     Packed-Dec
 270  01 EOF-SW................BLW=0000  008               DS 1C     Display
 280  88 EOF-ON................
 296  01 WORK-RECORD...........BLW=0000  010               DSOCL80   Group
 300     02 W-EMPLOYEE-NO......BLW=0000  010  0 000 000    DS 6C     Disp-Num
 305     02 NAME-FIELD.........BLW=0000  016  0 000 000    DS 0CL38  Group
 310        03 FIRST-NAME......BLW=0000  016  0 000 006    DS 10C    Display
 313        03 FILLER..........BLW=0000  020  0 000 010    DS 1C     Display
 315        03 MIDDLE-INITIALS.BLW=0000  021  0 000 011    DS 1C     Display
 320        03 FILLER..........BLW=0000  022  0 000 012    DS 1C     Display
 325        03 LAST-NAME.......BLW=0000  023  0 000 013    DS 25C    Display
 327     02 WAGE-RATE..........BLW=0000  03C  0 000 02C    DS 6C     Dis-Num
 330     02 FILLER.............BLW=0000  042  0 000 032    DS 30C    Display
 345  01 TABLE-RECORD..........BLL=0001  000               DS OCL26  Group
 347     02 PARM-LENGTH........BLL=0001  000  0 000 000    DS 2C     Binary
 350     02-EMPLOYEE-NO........BLL=0001  002  0 000 002    DS 6C     Disp-Num  0
 352        INDEX-1............IDX=0001  000                         Index-Name
 640  PROGRAM-ID X ---------------------------------------------------------*
 720  PROGRAM-ID X1-----------------------------------------------------*  7
 720  01  XDATA................BLW=0000  060               DS 6C     Display
 790  PROGRAM-ID X11--------------------------------------------------------*
 850  PROGRAM-ID X12--------------------------------------------------------*
 920  PROGRAM-ID X2---------------------------------------------------------*
```

Figure 13.9 Data-Division map.

In running COBTEST, the system will provide you with a comprehensive listing of diagnostic messages using the FLAG option. This is highlighted in Figure 13.11. Note the following explanation:

1. Indicates a data name in the message.
2. Displays a message tally, if the same error is made more than once. The message tally appears below the message, indicating the statement number in which the error occurs.
3. Shows statistics for the compiled program.
4. Assigns a number to the program. For batch compilations, this number indicates the position of the program in the compilation.

```
Nested Program Map
Program attribute codes (rightmost column) have the following meanings:
    C = COMMON
    I = INITIAL
    U = PROCEDURE DIVISION USING ...

    1      2          3                                         4
 Source Nesting                                              Program
 LineID Level      Program Name from PROGRAM-ID paragraph    Attributes

    40             SAMPLE1...................................U
   640      1       X........................................I
   720      2         X1.....................................C
   790      3           X11..................................
   850      3           X12..................................C
   920      2         X2.....................................
```

Figure 13.10 Nested program map.

```
     IGYSC0090-W    3 sequence errors were found in this program
                    1
352  IGYSC0086-I    "INDEX-1" was specified as an informational word table.
                    The reserved word table used might be different from the
                    IBM-supplied default. Refer to VS COBOL II Application
                    Programming Language Reference for information on
                    reserved words.
                    2   Same message on line 480 555.
405  IGYPS2121-S    "STARTING" was not defined as a data name. The statement
                    was discarded.
                    Same message on line 610.
600  IGYPS2028-E    "EMPLOYEE-NO" was a table item but was not subscripted
                    or indexed. The first occurrence of the table was
                    assumed.
Messages    Total  Informational  Warning   Error   Severe   Terminating  7
Printed:      8          4           1        1       2
     3
* Statistics for COBOL program SAMPLE1:
*      Source records = 78
*      Data division statement = 15
*      Procedure division statement = 17
         4                          5               6
  End of compilation 1, program SAMPLE1,  highest severity 12
```

Figure 13.11 Diagnostic message listing.

5. Displays the name of the program.

6. Indicates the highest severity level of all messages that are issued for the program.

7. Shows, as summary information, the total number of messages and individual totals for each message level.

13.7 Tips in Avoiding Some of the Abends

IBM gives you some tips that can be useful to avoid an abnormal termination while debugging a system. These tips are compiled in three categories: those pertaining to MVS and CMS, those that have to do with VSE, and tips helpful in handling CICS-related problems.

13.7.1 MVS- and CMS-related tips

Do not call a COBOL program with ATTACH. COBTEST is not designed to function as a task separate from a COBOL program. This situation could arise if an ATTACH macro instruction is used to call the COBOL program.

Do not use the XCTL (exit-control) macro instruction. The XCTL macro should not be used in any load module that contains a COBOL program compiled with the TEST option.

Be careful about the way you use LINK and DELETE. Note that COBOL special registers and DATA DIVISION items must not be referenced in COBTEST commands when the program they are related to is no longer in storage—for example, after returning from the LINK macro instruction or after issuing a DELETE. In this case, if you were to refer to a special register, the result might be unpredictable.

There might be two or a number of copies of the same program in storage simultaneously when loading dynamically. COBTEST commands addressed to that program operate against only the first of the copies, not necessarily against the one you are running.

COBTEST uses STAE/ESTATE to control abend- and termination-handling. If there are user programs or other products, such as IMS, that set STAE/ESTATE, make sure that they give control to COBTEST when an abend occurs, or when QUIT or DUMP commands are executed. User programs or other products that issue STAE/ESTATE should not be included in a run unit under COBTEST.

If your program abends while performing a SORT operation, simply bypass it. After an abnormal termination, retry your last COBOL statement by entering GO. This might not always function correctly. You should not rely on being able to continue debugging after an abend. You can also issue a RESTART if you need to start one more time at the beginning of your program without having to reset anyone of your breakpoints.

If a VS COBOL II program is deleted by a non-VS COBOL II program during a debugging session, then an attempt to reference a data item in the delete program by means of COBTEST will probably result in an abend.

13.7.2 VSE environment tips

If your program abends while sorting, bypass the sort. Following an abend, you might be able to retry your last COBOL statement by entering GO. Do not rely, however, on being able to continue the debugging session after an abend.

You can also issue a RESTART if you need to begin one more time at the beginning of your program without having to reset anyone of the previous breakpoints.

13.8 Tips for working in CICS

The CICS instruction causes a new COBOL run unit to be created. It is best to limit the debug session to a single run unit by compiling only the programs within a single run using the TEST option.

An abend that takes place while you are debugging under CICS will end the task. The debug tool abend handler issues a message and ends the task. The instruction CICS HANDLE ABEND prevents the ONABEND command from taking effect. COBTEST issues its own abend type '?????', which will be issued in order to terminate the job after an abend of another type, or after the DUMP or QUIT commands.

Chapter

14

Programmed Sorts: the SyncSort Mechanism

14.1 Introduction to Sort Techniques

In discussing the various means of sorting a file, I need to emphasize the importance of this utility whether you are working in a batch or in an interactive (real-time) environment.

Being able to sort, or sort merge, batch files so that the output is presented to the user in a meaningful way is important. On-line files conventionally rely on the use of secondary or tertiary indexes in order to access and retrieve a record based on a different set of requirements. For example, a payroll file that has the employee's identification number for its primary key might also have to be attainable via a different set of criteria—by name or department, or possibly both using a concatenated key. It is a fact that most credit-card holders simply don't remember their customer number (which is normally the primary key to their transaction) in an inquiry/maintenance situation, so the operator needs to be able to correlate such a number with a name or zip code and other qualifiers. Alternate keys tend to lengthen response time proportionate to the increase in the number (and level) of such indexes.

Large companies in the past (those not necessarily in the software business) developed their own sorting methodologies, but the cost of such undertakings versus the marginal performance of some of the in-house products (all geared to reinvent the wheel), turned out to be unwise investments.

Sorting, by definition, is used to rearrange records in a data set in order to produce a specific reference, such as a chronological or alphabetic order. When you rely on SyncSort, you'll find that the software provides you with a number of techniques. Among these are MAXSORT, tape sort, and disk sort. These techniques will be described for you in detail in upcoming sections of this chapter.

MAXSORT, or maximum-capacity sort, is designed to sort very large amounts of data. MAXSORT breaks up the sorting process into small, individual strings, creating a breakpoint at the end of each phase. During this process, the intermediate results of the sort are written to a work file. When a breakpoint occurs, the operator can intervene to change previous programming options. When all the input required for the sort has been processed, and it thus becomes a sorted data set, it is merged with other data sets created through an identical mechanism.

Tape sort was used in the past because of the cost and limited availability of DASD. SyncSort presently recommends MAXSORT in place of tape sort, especially for large-volume applications, because of its speed and efficiency.

Disk sort is the standard way of handling a sort when it is impractical to invoke MAXSORT. You can initiate a disk sort (or anyone of the previously mentioned sort techniques) through JCLs (external sort), or invoke it from a program (internal sort) written in COBOL, PL/I, or Assembler. External, or JCL-initiated sort, is a great deal more efficient than a programmed sort because it puts SyncSort in control of sort execution, including core management and I/O handling.

SyncSort, and generally any sort operation, has four distinct phases ranging from phase 0 to phase 3.

In Phase 0, all JCL and sort parameters are validated for syntax. If there are any syntax errors that are crucial, the operation will terminate while the system produces an error message. The SyncSort diagnostic structure normally generates one of three types of messages.

An action message, which uses the suffix A (e.g., WER002A), stands for a crucial error condition. When this happens, SyncSort typically terminates in order to allow the user to correct the problems. A tuning message displays the suffix B, and allows you to make adjustments in the actual job stream. Tuning messages are printed in conjunction with a crucial error. The suffix I denotes informational messages that are not severe enough to prompt termination of the sort. If, however, there are no coding errors, this phase uses the JCL PARM options and control statements to optimize the operational parameters for the job.

In phase 1, the input data is read into core, and records are written out to work files. Each record is written out in sequence with the one immediately preceding it. This process creates sorted strings. As long as records are written in sequence, the process continues in a reiterative fashion. When a record in memory cannot sequentially follow the record previously written out, the string is considered complete and a new string is initiated. At the end of this phase, all input data will be translated into individual (small) string sizes.

The purpose of phase 2 is to further consolidate the relatively small sort strings created in phase 1 into larger, more cohesive strings. This phase is over when the remaining strings can be merged into a final string. Note that this phase can be skipped if phase 1 produces only a few strings that can be immediately absorbed in a merge process.

Phase 3 is responsible for the final merge/sort, and is completed once the sorted data is written to an output file. When performing a merge operation, phases 1 and 2 are simply bypassed. An overview of this is presented to you in Figure 14.1.

Unlike external (JCL-driven) sorts, it is practical to incorporate logic into SyncSort procedures. This gives you the power of a typical internal sort mechanism ex-

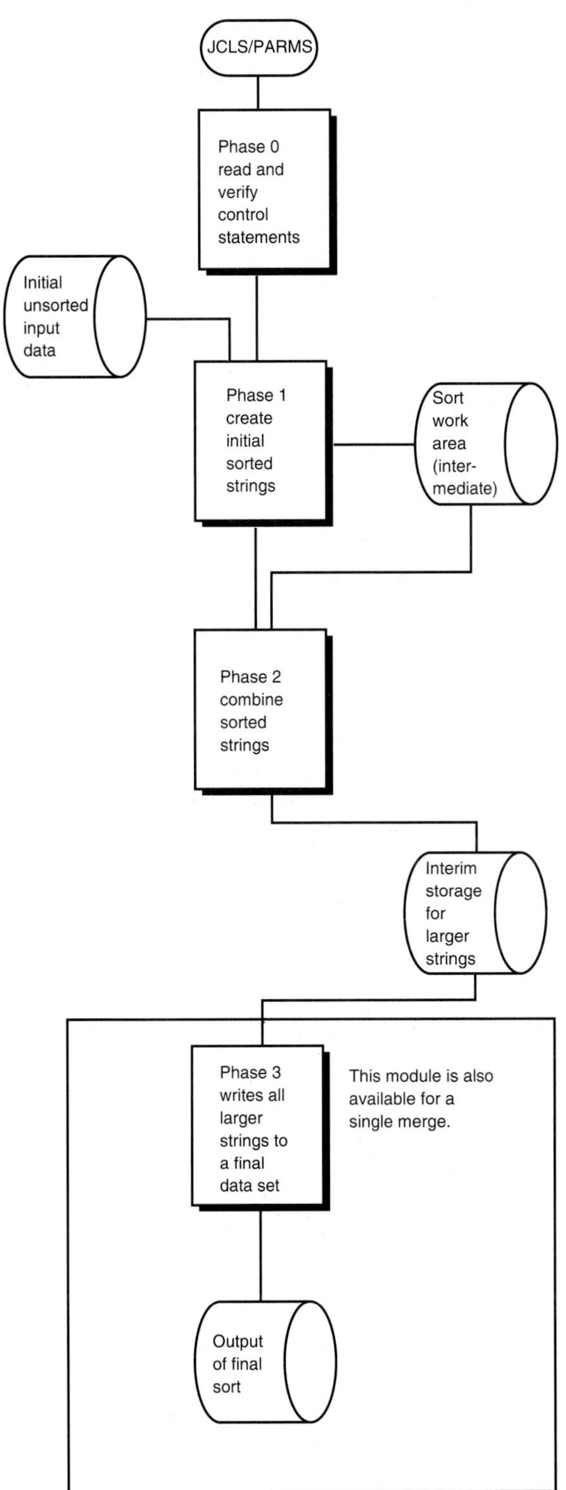

Figure 14.1 The four phases of the SORT mechanism.

cept for a substantially enhanced processing speed. Thus, you can prescreen a certain number of records based on some selection criteria, calculation, or Boolean logic before or after sorting a file. Unlike the invocation of a set of internal sort procedures, however (e.g., input/output procedures), this type of sort is normally initiated through control statements. For example, if you were to say SKIPREC=*n* (where *n* is a number), you can exclude the first *n* number of records from the sort procedure.

SyncSort includes resident or re-entrant code where all intermediate work storage (SORTWK) and output (SORTOUT) are automatically released at the end of the task—all without JCL specifications. Unless you use VSAM data sets, the minimum storage requirements to perform SyncSort is 36K; you need additional main storage for VSAM clusters.

14.2 SyncSort Control Statements

14.2.1 The INCLUDE/OMIT control statement

There are twelve control statements in SyncSort (most of which are covered in this chapter) that govern the way a file is set up and processed. Later on, using the Data utility function, I am going to show you how you can sort and generate on-demand reports using this methodology.

Let me start out by briefly describing the INCLUDE/OMIT control statement and explaining how it is used in this software. The INCLUDE/OMIT statement (either INCLUDE or OMIT, but not both) selects records from an input file based on a comparison between one of a number of fields in that record. You can compare a data field to a constant or to another field within that record. You can use only one of these control statements within an application.

In conjunction with the INCLUDE/OMIT control statement, use the parameter COND to specify the comparison in order to determine which records are to be omitted from and which records are to be included in an application. To trigger and evaluate a comparison, use Boolean logic with the following six values:

EQ	Equal to
NE	Not equal to
GT	Greater than
GE	Greater than or equal to
LT	Less than
LE	Less than or equal to

These values can be combined or segregated via an AND or an OR condition. Here is an example of the INCLUDE/OMIT control statement:

```
OMIT COND=(15,5,ZD,EQ,10000,AND,44,1,CH,NE,X'40')
```

In this particular instance, you are including records with the following criteria: a field starts in column 10 and is seven positions long must be less than the field starting in position 40 for the same length.

However, an additional condition might also satisfy the above comparison, such as: the field starting in column 10 that contains the value CHICAGO. Note that the code

CH, which stands for *character*, is one of several other formats: PD or packed decimal, BI or binary, etc. Here is another example; see if you can decode it:

```
OMIT COND=(15,5,ZD,EQ,10000,AND,44,1,CH,NE,X'40')
```

Note that ZD stands for zoned decimal, while X'40' (X meaning hexadecimal in conjunction with 40 or blank) denotes a test of a single byte for a blank value.

14.2.2 The INREC control statement

The purpose of the INREC control statement is to reformat input records. You can use this statement to delete fields prior to the records being sorted or merged. The use of INREC is recommended to delete data fields in order to improve sort performance. (The less fields you have to process, the faster SyncSort will execute.)

As you will see in the next section, just about all functions that are performed via the OUTREC statement (e.g., inserting character strings or binary zeros) can also be performed by the INREC statement. It is more practical, however, to use the OUTREC statement to expand a record in this fashion, as you will shortly see, because OUTREC processing takes place after the records are sorted and merged—very much like the OUTPUT PROCEDURE using a COBOL-driven internal sort. Here is an example of the INREC control statement:

```
INREC FIELDS=(1:10,25,26:52,5,31:63,2)
```

The first field starts in position 10 and is 25 characters long. The 1: simply means that, having reformatted the input record, the same field is going to begin in position 1 instead. The second data field, on the other hand, is shown to have originally started in position 52 and occupies a total of 5 characters. This field, when the record is reformatted, will start in column 26. Finally, the third data field is located in columns 63 and 64 and will now be relocated to start in position 31.

As you can see, the initial record has been remapped and cut down in size from 64 to 32 positions. This can be very substantial when you have a large file, not only in terms of DASD storage but when it comes to reducing execution time.

14.2.3 SORT/MERGE control statements

Let me start out with a simple SORT statement that's similar to that of an IBM JCL sort:

```
SORT FIELDS=(10,5,CH,A)
```

This statement sorts the input file by the field (or fields) starting in column 10 for 5 characters. The CH denotes the disposition of the field, which is character, and A means it is ascending.

Sorting a file simply means rearranging the existing order of a single data set. The term *merge* refers to both sorting and consolidating two or a number of files into one—all in the required sequence. Using SyncSort's merge operation, you can also perform a copy (FIELDS=COPY) with certain restrictions in mind.

14.2.4 The OUTFIL control statement

The purpose of the OUTFIL control statement is to describe the output file or files. Essentially, it is designed with three objectives in mind:

- To create multiple output files. This is done through the FILES, INCLUDE/OMIT, and OUTREC parameters.
- To use SyncSort's SortWriter facilities via a number of control parameters, such as HEADER1, HEADER2, LINES, NODETAIL, SECTIONS, TRAILER1, and TRAILER2. The SortWriter feature of OUTFIL gives you the ability to produce completely reformatted reports.
- To reformat records after E35 (E stands for Exit) processed through the OUTREC control statement.

In producing a sorted report, SyncSort provides you with a great deal of flexibility through parameters, reminiscent to a high (third-generation) language using keywords and reserved procedures. SyncSort gives you the ability to use three types of headers:

HEADER1. Provides you with a header or a title page for the entire report. It appears only once at the beginning of the report.

HEADER2. Provides a running header for each page, used in conjunction with the LINES parameter.

HEADER3. Gives a section header that appears at the beginning of each specified section.

You might want to take note of two additional subparameters: &DATE and &PAGE. &DATE is like the keyword CURRENT-DATE in COBOL, which contains the current date and is passed to you in eight bytes (including two slashes). &PAGE sequentially numbers logical pages of the output report, and requires a total of six bytes of storage.

In addition to the HEADER parameters, SyncSort gives you an ability to use TRAILERS (1, 2, and 3) to define control totals and other important summary information.

TRAILER1 produces a trailer or summary for an entire report, should that be a requirement. It appears only once at the end of the report. TRAILER2 produces a page trailer for each page defined by the LINES parameter. It appears at the end of each page. TRAILER3 gives you a section trailer, highlighted at the end of each specified section, and serves as a conclusion or summary for that section. These parameters also provide you with TOTAL, SUBTOTAL, COUNT, and SUBCOUNT capabilities at report, page, and section levels. Note that a comprehensive format chart is shown in Figures 14.2 and 14.3.

The format chart shown in Figure 14.2 illustrates and defines the available TRAILER subparameters. Each subparameter constitutes a separate field of TRAILER.

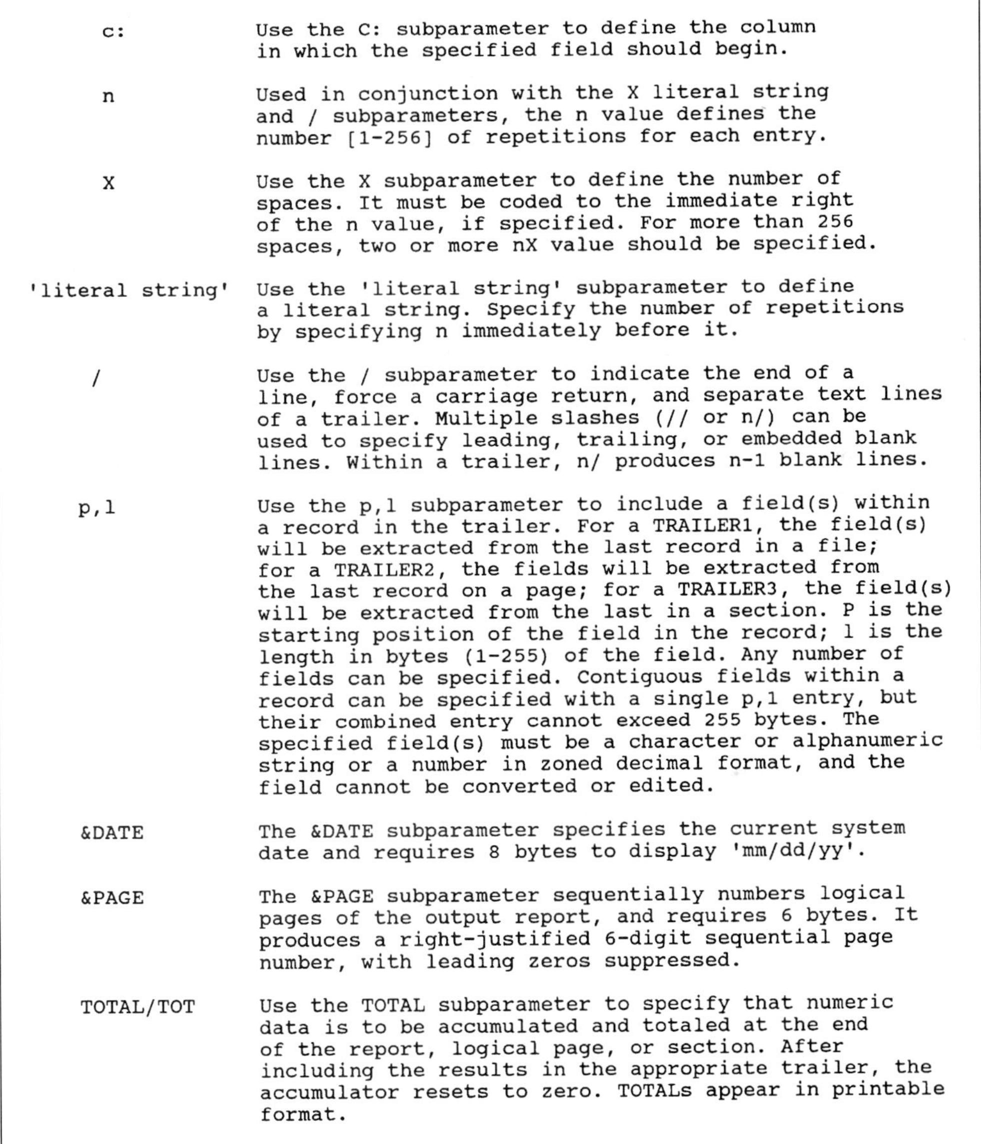

c:	Use the C: subparameter to define the column in which the specified field should begin.
n	Used in conjunction with the X literal string and / subparameters, the n value defines the number [1-256] of repetitions for each entry.
X	Use the X subparameter to define the number of spaces. It must be coded to the immediate right of the n value, if specified. For more than 256 spaces, two or more nX value should be specified.
'literal string'	Use the 'literal string' subparameter to define a literal string. Specify the number of repetitions by specifying n immediately before it.
/	Use the / subparameter to indicate the end of a line, force a carriage return, and separate text lines of a trailer. Multiple slashes (// or n/) can be used to specify leading, trailing, or embedded blank lines. Within a trailer, n/ produces n-1 blank lines.
p,l	Use the p,l subparameter to include a field(s) within a record in the trailer. For a TRAILER1, the field(s) will be extracted from the last record in a file; for a TRAILER2, the fields will be extracted from the last record on a page; for a TRAILER3, the field(s) will be extracted from the last in a section. P is the starting position of the field in the record; l is the length in bytes (1-255) of the field. Any number of fields can be specified. Contiguous fields within a record can be specified with a single p,l entry, but their combined entry cannot exceed 255 bytes. The specified field(s) must be a character or alphanumeric string or a number in zoned decimal format, and the field cannot be converted or edited.
&DATE	The &DATE subparameter specifies the current system date and requires 8 bytes to display 'mm/dd/yy'.
&PAGE	The &PAGE subparameter sequentially numbers logical pages of the output report, and requires 6 bytes. It produces a right-justified 6-digit sequential page number, with leading zeros suppressed.
TOTAL/TOT	Use the TOTAL subparameter to specify that numeric data is to be accumulated and totaled at the end of the report, logical page, or section. After including the results in the appropriate trailer, the accumulator resets to zero. TOTALs appear in printable format.

Figure 14.2A TRAILERS subparameter format chart, part 1.

If you were to specify LINES=ANSI, you could use standard control characters to define the logical pages. For example, a zero in the first position of the output record would result in double spaces on the printed report. An overview of this is presented in Figure 14.4. The NODETAIL parameter tells the SyncSort SortWriter to print a report with header and totals only while omitting all the detail.

The OUTREC parameter is primarily responsible for formatting each output file. So

SUBTOTAL/SUB	Use SUBTOTAL to generate a running total of a field at the end of a report, logical page, or section. This subparameter functions like a TOTAL subparameter except the accumulator does not reset to zero. SUBTOTALS appear in printable format.
p	Use the p subparameter to indicate the first position of the first byte of the field to be totaled.
l	Use the l subparameter to indicate the length of the field to be totaled.
f	Use the l subparameter to indicate the format of the field to be totaled. Replace f with BI, FI, PD, or ZD.
Mm	Use the Mm subparameter to indicate that one of the 10 SyncSort-supplied masks (M0-M9) be used to format the totaled field. Replace m with the mask number.
EDIT=(pattern)	Use the EDIT=(pattern) subparameter to indicate that a user-provided editing mask be used to format the totaled field.
SIGNS=(...)	Use the SUGN subparameter to specify leading and/or trailing signs that will appear before or after the edited number.
LENGTH=(n)	Use the LENGTH subparameter to alter the length of a totaled field determined by the edit pattern and the internal field format.
COUNT	Use the COUNT subparameter to obtain a count of the number of records in either the entire report or a specific part of the report. In a TRAILER1, this field will contain a count of the total number of data records in the report. In a TRAILER2, it will contain a count of the number of data records on each page. In a TRAILER3, it will contain a count of the number of data records in each section. This number will be a right-justified 8-digit-long field with leading zeros suppressed. The maximum volume is 99999999.
SUBCOUNT	Use the SUBCOUNT parameter to obtain a running or cumulative count of the number of records throughout a report. Works the same as COUNT.

Figure 14.2B TRAILERS subparameter format chart, part 2.

you can create two or a number of differently formatted files via this parameter option. Following are a couple of examples of coding the OUTFIL control statement. This will be further discussed and illustrated in section 14.3 of this chapter.

```
OUTFIL FILES=1,OUTREC=(1:40,15,16:60,5,21:70,3),OMIT=(10,7,EQ,C'CHICAGO')
OUTFIL FILES=2,OUTREC=(5:30,10,15:44,3,18:60,21),INCLUDE=(70,7,EQ,C'ONTARIO')
```

Two files are created because of the above parameters. Each will be formatted differently, using different criteria for selecting or omitting records. When creating the first type of record (output) from the available input, only records will be selected that do not contain the value CHICAGO in columns 10 through 16. If this criterion is true, then the output will be reformatted so that field 1 starts in column 1 and ends in column 15, field 2 encompasses columns 16 through 20, and field 3 starts in column 21 for a total length of three bytes.

Accordingly, the second output file will include all those records where columns 70 through 76 in the input equals the value ONTARIO, using identical reformatting. Here is one more example on using the OUTFIL parameter:

```
OUTFIL FILES=(01,02),OUTREC=(1:10,11,12:47,3)
```

In this particular example, two output files are created, and both are formatted alike. The new format is that field 1 starts in column 1 for 11 bytes (starts in column 10 on the input), and field 2 begins in column 12 and includes column 14.

```
 [n] X
 [n] 'literal string
 [n] /
  p,l
c: &DATE
   &PAGE

{TOTAL/SUBTOTAL}=p,l,f[{,  Mm     }] [, SIGNS=(...) [,LENGTH=(n)
                        [EDIT=(...)}]

COUNT
SUBCOUNT
```

Figure 14.3 Subparameter format chart.

CODE	INTERPRETATION
blank	space 1 line before printing
0	space 2 lines before printing
-	space 3 lines before printing
+	suppress space before printing
1	skip to channel 1 before printing
2	skip to channel 2 before printing
3	skip to channel 3 before printing
4	skip to channel 4 before printing
5	skip to channel 5 before printing
6	skip to channel 6 before printing
7	skip to channel 7 before printing
8	skip to channel 8 before printing
9	skip to channel 9 before printing
A	skip to channel 10 before printing
B	skip to channel 11 before printing
C	skip to channel 12 before printing
V	select stacker 1
W	select stacker 2

Figure 14.4 ANSI control character chart.

14.2.5 The OUTREC/OUTFIL control statement

The purpose of the OUTREC control statement is to reformat the output records. This control statement is quite handy, and you can use it for a number of tasks, such as:

- Deleting or repeating input record(s)
- Inserting character strings, or binary zeros between fields
- Converting numeric data, such as packed decimals, to a printable format
- Realigning a data field
- Changing the order of or completely redesigning the original input records

When you issue an OUTREC control statement, you need to realize that processing takes place after the records have been sorted or merged, but prior to an E35 processing. (For more on E35, review section 14.5.) Because you might find it somewhat confusing whether to use an INREC statement, OUTREC statement, or the OUTREC parameter of the OUTFIL control statement, allow me to provide you with some guidelines.

If you need to delete irrelevant data fields, use the INREC statement. This is desirable because deleting or weeding out certain data fields prior to a sort that you do not need will improve performance.

If you want to expand a record, reposition certain data fields, or simply convert packed fields to unpacked numeric ones, you can use either the OUTREC statement or the OUTREC parameter of the OUTFIL control statement. Think of a parameter as a subset or component of a control statement.

If all you need to do is to create multiple output files using the same (or different) output records, you can accomplish that via the OUTREC statement. Finally, use the OUTREC parameter of the OUTFIL statement when you specify the TOTAL or SUBTOTAL subparameters of the TRAILER.

One of the most important functions of OUTREC is to convert and edit numeric data so it can be printed. To convert numeric data, you need to indicate to SyncSort the format of the field.

The LENGTH subparameter (LENGTH=*n*, where *n* is equal to a number equal or less than 22) is used primarily to alter the default length of the field. Also, SyncSort gives you editing masks to simplify the more common editing formats. More on this in section 14.3. For a quick review, however, consider the following:

```
OUTREC FIELDS=(1:6Z,7:17,5,14:35,6,5X)
```

In this example, I have inserted six binary zeros in the first six positions of the record by coding 6Z. Thus, the next field will start in position 7 and is five positions long. Note that prior to OUTREC processing this field was located in positions 17 through 21. Because the last field ended in position 11, and the third field (14:35,6) starts in position 14, the system will automatically pad the record with two blank positions. The 5X simply denotes that, at the end of the above record beginning in position 20,

I have inserted five additional blank characters. This record, by the way, is 24 positions long. Let's take a bit more complicated situation:

```
OUTREC FIELDS=(1,50,64,4,PD,M2,86,6,ZD,EDIT=($I,IIT,.TTS),SIGNS=(,,+,-))
```

In this example, you are telling SyncSort that the first data field starts in position 1 for the length of 50 bytes. This, incidentally, also started in the same positions prior to the OUTREC processing. The next field, which happens to be a packed decimal, begins in position 51 (by default), which used to start in position 64, and contains four bytes of data.

After being converted and edited by editing mask M2, the resulting field will be 10 bytes long. However, the number of digits that will actually print depends on the number of leading zeros, if any, because this mask specifies that only three digits must print whether or not they are leading zeros. Moreover, this mask specifies that a minus sign be printed after the number (provided the field has a negative value), and a blank be printed after the number if it is positive.

SyncSort/OS provides editing masks to simplify the more common editing operations. If neither Mm nor EDIT is specified in the OUTREC control statement, the default mask M0 is used. An editing mask chart is presented in Figure 14.5.

The letter D represents the number of resulting digits after data conversion. The symbols indicate that only the integer part of this division should be retained. The editing mask chart illustrates the following for each of the available masks:

- Edit pattern
- Leading and trailing zeros, where appropriate
- Length

The edit patterns use the same symbolic letter part of the EDIT subparameter. Leading insignificant digits are represented by the letter I, and significant digits are represented by the letter T. Leading or trailing sign-replacement characters are represented by the letter S. All other characters print as they appear in the pattern. The SIGNS illustrated for each mask follow the format requirements of the SIGNS subparameters.

Mask	Pattern	Sign	Length
Default Mask (M0)	IIII...IITS	(,,' ',-)	d+1
M1	TTTT...TTTS	(,,' ',-)	d+1
M2	I,III,...,IIT.TTS	(,,' ',-)	d+1 + [d/3]
M3	I,III,...,IIT.TTCR		d+1 + [d/3]
M4	SI,III,...,IIT.TT	(+,-)	d+1 + [d/3]
M5	SI,III,...,IIT.TTS	(' ',(,' ',))	d+1 + [d/3]
M6	III-TTT-TTTT		12
M7	TTT-TT-TTTT		11
M8	IT:TT:TT		8
M9	IT/TT/TT		8

Figure 14.5 Editing masks.

You can specify SIGNS to selectively override those of a particular mask. For example, if you specify mask M4 and also specify SIGNS=(' '), a leading blank will print instead of a plus sign if the number is positive. However, a leading minus sign will print if the number is negative because the leading negative sign specified in the editing mask has not been overridden.

14.2.6 Additional control statements to remember

Among some of the other control statements you need to code is your definition to provide record length (thus overriding your initial DCB definition) and format information. SyncSort accommodates both fixed-length (F) and variable-length (V) records.

The SORT control statement defines the application, as a sort or sort/merge. It is possible to use logical (Boolean) operands (EQUAL and NOEQUAL) in this statement to restrict the sort to certain criteria, thus minimizing the total volume of the data to be sorted. Let's look at a simple example:

```
SORT FIELDS=(10,2,A,20,5,D,29,4,A),FORMAT=CH,CKPT
```

As you can see, this statement is similar to a typical IBM SORT statement. Note that the first control field begins in byte 10 for two positions, and A specifies ascending order. At the end of the SORT statement, note that the subparameter FORMAT=CH refers to every field in the SORT statement. The second control field starts in position 20, is five bytes long, and is to be sorted in descending order. The third control field starts in position 29 for a total of four bytes, and is sorted in an ascending order.

The CKPT next to the FORMAT parameter simply means that SyncSort will take a checkpoint. Last, but not least, is the SUM control statement. The SUM control statement does several things. It summarizes specified numeric fields and deletes fields with equal control values. Records with equal key values are processed pair by pair. If numeric fields are to be summarized, the data in the summary fields is added, the sum is placed in one of the records, and the other record is deleted. Provided arithmetic overflow does not occur, the SUM statement produces only one record per sort key in the output data set.

14.3 Data Utilities

In the previous section, I described control statements, their function, and the methodology required to invoke them. This, unfortunately, will remain abstract until I can provide some practical examples of how these control statements are used, which is the purpose of this section. Let's examine a simple case in which you are reading an input file containing one type of record only. Each of these records, as shown in Figure 14.6, are made up of ten data fields for the total length of 40 characters. What you need to do is to sort this input file by the first data field (DEPART) and create an output file with records containing only three of the ten data fields (DIV, EMPID, and DEPART), with a total length of only 13 characters.

In this example, only three fields are used in the output definition. These are the

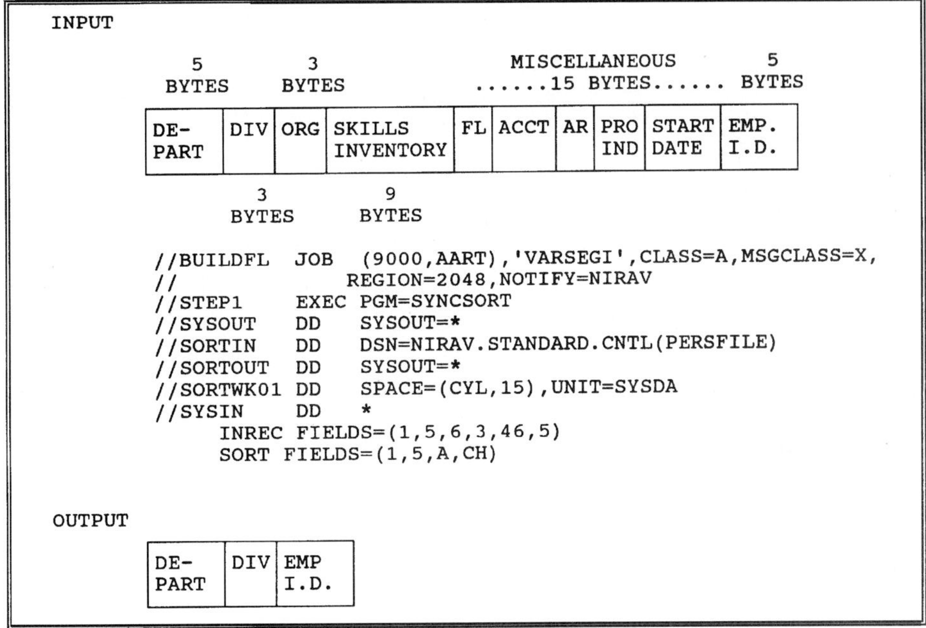

INPUT

DE-PART	DIV	ORG	SKILLS INVENTORY	FL	ACCT	AR	PRO IND	START DATE	EMP. I.D.
5 BYTES	3 BYTES	3 BYTES	9 BYTES	MISCELLANEOUS ......15 BYTES......					5 BYTES

```
//BUILDFL   JOB   (9000,AART),'VARSEGI',CLASS=A,MSGCLASS=X,
//                 REGION=2048,NOTIFY=NIRAV
//STEP1     EXEC  PGM=SYNCSORT
//SYSOUT    DD    SYSOUT=*
//SORTIN    DD    DSN=NIRAV.STANDARD.CNTL(PERSFILE)
//SORTOUT   DD    SYSOUT=*
//SORTWK01  DD    SPACE=(CYL,15),UNIT=SYSDA
//SYSIN     DD    *
     INREC FIELDS=(1,5,6,3,46,5)
     SORT FIELDS=(1,5,A,CH)
```

OUTPUT

DE-PART	DIV	EMP I.D.

Figure 14.6 Sorting and reformatting a file.

```
BROOKHOUSE, CRAIG   10000 144
BAILY, CYNTHIA      21112 344
VARSEGI, ALEX       34443 444
MUELLER, JEFF       22211 533
CHEEKS, LARRY       10000 672
MORAN, DEBORAH      33455 433
LOUGHLIN, JOHN      33456 534
SULLIVAN, MARY      11111 444
RIDER, CHRIS        21112 444
CHENG, VICKY        21112 444
SHER, DEBBY         10000 111
PEROBSKY, DIANNE    33455 234
WOOD, FRED          33455 123
WELLS, GEORGE       33345 234
WASHINGTON, JO      10000 333
CAMPBELL, JACKIE    10000 222
KENNEDY, DAVID      22232 167
O'TOOL, MARGARET    22211 345
SCOTT, GREG         22211 990
FRANCONE, EMBROSE   22211 990
```

Figure 14.7 Records prior to sort/select; bold lines represent records to be eliminated.

department number, division number, and the employee's identifier. The records are sorted by department number in an ascending order.

Now let me take you through a simple problem of sorting and selecting records. Figure 14.7 shows the actual record layout of the input to be sorted and selected. The requirements for this problem are simple. Sort the input file in an ascending order by employee name (positions 1 through 19) and omit all those records whose de-

```
//NIRAV  JOB    (9000,AART),'VARSEGI',CLASS=A,MSGCLASS=X,REGION=2048K,
//              NOTIFY=NIRAV
//STEP1  EXEC   PGM=SYNCSORT
//SYSOUT   DD   SYSOUT=*
//SORTIN   DD   DSN=NIRAV.STANDARD.CNTL(NEWFILE),DISP=SHR
//SORTOUT  DD   SYSOUT=*
//SORTWK01 DD   SPACE=(CYL,5),UNIT=SYSDA
//SYSIN    DD   *
     OMIT COND=(20,5,CH,EQ,C'100000')
     SORT FIELDS=(1,19,CH,A)
     OUTFIL OUTREC=(10:1,19,30:20,5,37:26,3)
//
```

Figure 14.8 JCL statements and SyncSort control statements for the stated requirements.

```
SDSF OUTPUT DISPLAY NIRAV1    JOB 177    DSID    102 LINE 10        COLUMNS 02- 81
COMMAND ===>                                                        SCROLL ===> PAGE
WER124I  TRK  OVER-ALLOC FACTOR= PRIM/USED=023
WER045C  END SORT PH
WER405I  SORTOUT  :  DATA RECORDS OUT        15; TOTAL RECORDS OUT        15
WER246I  FILESIZE 1,200 BYTES
WER054I  RCD IN         20, OUT         15
WER169I  TPF LEVEL      5
WER052I  END SYNCSORT:  NIRAV1   ,STEP1    ,
        BAILY, CYNTHIA       21112  344
        CHENG, VICKY         21112  444
        FRANCONE, EMBROSE    22211  990
        KENNEDY, DAVID       22232  167
        LOUGHLIN, JOHN       33456  534
        MORAN, DEBORAH       33455  433
        MUELLER, JEFF        22211  533
        O'TOOL, MARGARET     22211  345
        PEROBSKY, DIANNE     33455  234
        RIDER, CHRIS         21112  444
        SCOTT, GREG          22211  990
        SULLIVAN, MARY       11111  444
        VARSEGI, ALEX        34443  444
        WELLS, GEORGE        33345  234
        WOOD, FRED           33455  123
```

Figure 14.9 The result of the sort/select operation.

partment number equals 10000. Figure 14.8 shows the JCL set up for these requirements, and Figure 14.9 shows the result—a sorted employee file excluding all those employees with a department code of 10000.

Let's continue with a more complex problem. The objectives are as follows: read the input file shown in Figure 14.10, which contains five data fields. These are:

- NAME (positions 1 through 19)
- DEPARTMENT (positions 20 through 24)
- DIVISION (positions 26 through 28)
- ORGANIZATION (positions 35 through 37)
- EMPLOYEE SALARY (positions 50 through 55)

Sort this input file by NAME and generate a report with headers as well as trailers (final totals). The final total (EMPLOYEE SALARY) is to be edited to include a dollar sign. Figure 14.11 shows the required JCLs, including the SyncSort control statements, which I am going to explain momentarily.

The SORT FIELD statement tells SyncSort to sort the input file by the employee name in ascending sequence. It also tells the software that a summary total is to be generated on EMPLOYEE SALARY, starting in position 50 on the input file. OUTFIL OUTREC defines the format of the report. 10:1,19 means that the data field that starts in column 1 on the input file will start in position 10 on the report, etc. ZD means zoned decimal, and M2 denotes an editing format I briefly discussed earlier. The // (slashes on the header control statement) allows you to space twice. &DATE is designed to print the current date. The $I,ITT.TT) stands for the print format. The output report is depicted in Figure 14.12. Note that I have not omitted any records from the printed report.

```
BROOKHOUSE, CRAIG  10000 144       200 00000000000056567
BAILY, CYNTHIA     21112 344       200 00000000000043660
VARSEGI, ALEX      34443 444       200 00000000000044656
MUELLER, JEFF      22211 533       200 00000000000065556
CHEEKS, LARRY      10000 672       230 00000000000034000
MORAN, DEBORAH     33455 433       230 00000000000055000
LOUGHLIN, JOHN     33456 534       230 00000000000060000
SULLIVAN, MARY     11111 444       230 00000000000029890
RIDER, CHRIS       21112 444       240 00000000000033667
CHENG, VICKY       21112 444       250 00000000000033453
SHER, DEBBY        10000 111       250 00000000000043443
PEROBSKY, DIANNE   33455 234       250 00000000000055450
WOOD, FRED         33455 123       250 00000000000052000
WELLS, GEORGE      33345 234       261 00000000000039554
WASHINGTON, JO     10000 333       261 00000000000033345
CAMPBELL, JACKIE   10000 222       261 00000000000065312
KENNEDY, DAVID     22232 167       261 00000000000056112
O'TOOL, MARGARET   22211 345       262 00000000000037344
SCOTT, GREG        22211 990       262 00000000000034111
FRANCONE, EMBROSE  22211 990       262 00000000000047055
```

Figure 14.10 Input to SyncSort.

```
//NIRAV   JOB    (9000,AART),'VARSEGI',CLASS=A,MSGCLASS=X,REGION=2048K,
//               NOTIFY=NIRAV
//STEP1   EXEC   PGM=SYNCSORT
//SYSOUT    DD   SYSOUT=*
//SORTIN    DD   DSN=NIRAV.STANDARD.CNTL(NEWFILE),DISP=SHR
//SORTOUT   DD   SYSOUT=*
//SORTWK01  DD   SPACE=(CYL,5),UNIT=SYSDA
//SYSIN     DD   *
     SORT FIELDS=(1,19,CH,A)
     SUM FIELDS=(50,6,ZD)
     OUTFIL OUTREC=(10:1,19,30:20,5,37:26,3,44:35,3,60:50,6,ZD,M2),
     HEADER2=(28:'EMPLOYEE ROSTER',50:'DATE',56:&DATE,//,
              10:'EMP NAME',30:'DEPART',37:'DIV',44:'ORG',
              62:'SALARY',//),
     TRAILER2=(10:'TOTALS',52:TOT=(50,6,ZD,EDIT=($I,III.TT)))
//
```

Figure 14.11 JCLs and SyncSort control statements for generating a report.

```
WER045C  END SORT PH
WER405I  SORTOUT  :   DATA RECORDS OUT      20; TOTAL RECORDS OUT;      38
WER246I  FILESIZE 1,600 BYTES
WER054I  RCD IN          20,  OUT       20
WER169I  TPF LEVEL       5
WER052I  END SYNCSORT:    NARAV1     ,STEP1   ,

                         EMPLOYEE ROSTER           DATE    12/02/91

  EMP NAME              DEPART  DIV    ORG                SALARY

  BAILY, CYNTHIA        21112   344    200                436.60
  BROOKHOUSE, CRAIG     10000   144    200                565.67
  CAMPBELL, JACKIE      10000   222    261                653.12
  CHEEKS, LARRY         10000   672    230                340.00
  CHENG, VICTORIA       21112   444    250                334.53
  FRANCONE, EMBROSE     22211   990    262                470.55
  KENNEDY, DAVID        22232   167    261                561.12
  LOUGHLIN, JOHN        33456   534    230                600.00
  MORAN, DEBORAH        33455   433    230                550.00
  MUELLER, JEFF         22211   533    200                655.56
  O'TOOL, MARGARET      22211   345    262                373.44
  PEROBSKY, DIANNE      33455   234    234                554.50
  RIDER, CHRIS          21112   444    240                336.67
  SCOTT, GREG           22211   990    262                341.11
  SHER, DEBBY           10000   111    250                434.43
  SULLIVAN, MARY        11111   444    230                298.90
  VARSEGI, ALEX         34443   444    200                446.56
  WASHINGTON, JO        10000   333    261                333.45
  WELLS, GEORGE         33345   234    261                395.54
  WOOD, FRED            33455   123    250                520.00

  TOTALS                                               $9,201.75
```

Figure 14.12 SyncSort-generated report, as specified in Figure 14.11.

Finally, let's look at a more complex reporting structure, representing a vendor case study. Let me give you some background on this and see if you can figure out, from the examples and from the enclosed SyncSort control statements, what this problem is all about. A set of control statements are presented in Figure 14.13, and a sample report generated out of these statements is shown in Figure 14.14. Answer the following questions:

- Why are there three files defined in the control statements?
- Are there any calculations performed?
- What is being omitted from the report?
- Why was there a need to define INREC FIELDS?
- Can the control statements responsible for generating this report be simplified?

14.4 MAXSORT: What It Is and How to Use It

MAXSORT is for when you need to sort a very large database and the available conventional techniques are inefficient. What MAXSORT does is break up the bulky task into small, individual sorts. The sorted data is then written to an intermediate (work) storage. So at the end of the MAXSORT utility, you might have a number of sorted data sets that have to be combined into a final input.

The two diagrams shown in Figure 14.15 will give you a better understanding of both the control and the data flow apparatus of MAXSORT.

Some of the advantages of using MAXSORT (as opposed to a conventional IBM sort) is that MAXSORT is a great deal more economical in terms of space requirements (although this is becoming less and less of a factor) and its processing speed. The real advantage of using MAXSORT is that the original job can be interrupted for higher priority jobs without wasting processing time. This is practical because the output of each individual sort (think of MAXSORT as a conglomerate of a number of smaller-volume sorts) is a completely sorted data set. Thus, if a system or a specific program fails, whatever data sets have been produced up to that point will still be available. The job can now be restarted at the last breakpoint, including all the previously produced data sets, without having to resort them all over.

```
OMIT COND=(115,1,CH,EQ,C'F')
INREC FIELDS=(17,23,
             67,16,
             107,8)
SORT FIELDS=(1,23,CH,A)
SUM FIELDS=(24,4,PD,
            28,4,PD,
            32,4,PD,
            38,4,PD,
            40,4,PD,
            44,4,PD)
OUTFIL OUTREC=(17:1,23,
               52:24,4,PD,M2,
               63:28,4,PD,M2,
               74:32,4,PD,M2,
               85:36,4,PD,M2,
               96:40,4,PD,M2,
              107:44,4,PD,M2),
    HEADER2=(44:'OUTSTANDING PAYMENTS',
             73:'DATE',
             78:&DATE,//,
             17:'COMPANY',
             60:'INVOICE',
             84:AMT.PD',
            106:'BALANCE',/,
             53:'PRODUCT',
             67:'TAX',
             77:'PRODUCT',
             90:'TAX',
             98:'PRODUCT',
            113:'TAX',2/,
     TRAILER2=(31:'TOTALS:',
               51:TOT=(24,4,PD,EDIT=($II,ITT.TT)),
               62:TOT=(28,4,PD,EDIT=($II,ITT.TT)),
               73:TOT=(32,4,PD,EDIT=($II,ITT.TT)),
               84:TOT=(36,4,PD,EDIT=($II,ITT.TT)),
               95:TOT=(40,4,PD,EDIT=($II,ITT.TT)),
              106:TOT=(44,4,PD,EDIT=($II,ITT.TT)))
```

Figure 14.13 Control statements for an Outstanding Payments report.

OUTSTANDING PAYMENTS DATE: 03/01/92

COMPANY	INVOICE		AMT. PO		BALANCE	
	PRODUCT	TAX	PRODUCT	TAX	PRODUCT	TAX
ARLINE FRAGRANCES	7,500.00	618.75	0.00	0.00	7,500.00	618.75
BALTIC AVENUE CORP.	650.00	29.25	0.00	0.00	650.00	9.25
BATHO PRODUCTS	850.00	51.00	0.00	0.00	850.00	51.00
CARRINGTON OIL	1,600.00	64.00	0.00	0.00	1,600.00	64.00
CDR TRUST INC.	1,500.00	75.00	0.00	0.00	1,500.00	75.00
CHARACTER DATA	1,100.00	90.75	0.00	0.00	1,100.00	90.75
COUNTRY INDUSRIAL	850.00	0.00	0.00	0.00	850.00	0.00
DESIGN TECHNOLOGIES	360.00	21.60	0.00	0.00	360.00	21.60
DUNHAM INDUSTRIES	850.00	0.00	0.00	0.00	850.00	0.00
ECHO LABS INC.	1,650.00	66.00	250.00	0.00	1,400.00	66.00
EH CONSULTANTS	550.00	22.00	250.00	0.00	300.00	22.00
ESS SECURITIES	1,100.00	44.00	0.00	0.00	1,100.00	44.00
EVERMORE INDUSTR.	5,000.00	225.00	2,000.00	0.00	3,000.00	225.00
FASTEROOT EQUIP.	1,700.00	76.50	0.00	0.00	1,700.00	76.50
FEDERAL FABRICS	1,750.00	70.00	0.00	0.00	1,750.00	70.00
GARVINS PRINTERS	1,500.00	67.50	0.00	0.00	1,500.00	67.50
GOODEY FOODS	600.00	30.00	0.00	0.00	600.00	30.00
GROSS BOOKS CO.	3,000.00	180.00	0.00	0.00	3,000.00	180.00
HABSBURGH IMPORTS	750.00	45.00	0.00	0.00	750.00	45.00
HARVEY MOTORS CO.	5,000.00	225.00	2,000.00	0.00	3,000.00	225.00
RABBIT TECHNOLOGIES	400.00	50.00	0.00	0.00	300.00	26.00
ROBBINS NEST CORP.	900.00	54.00	0.00	0.00	900.00	900.00
SPENSER INDUSTRIES	650.00	26.00	0.00	0.00	650.00	26.00
SUTHERLAND CORP.	655.00	26.70	400.00	0.00	455.00	25.65
TOLLGATES EQUIP.	1,700.00	76.50	0.00	0.00	1,700.00	76.50
UNITED INTEREST CO	1,500.00	90.00	0.00	0.00	1,500.00	90.00
WEBB BROS. CORP.	600.00	36.00	0.00	0.00	600.00	36.00
WELLINGTON IMPORTS	750.00	45.00	0.00	0.00	750.00	45.00
WINIFRED INDUSTRIES	1,300.00	52.00	300.00	0.00	1,000.00	52.00
TOTALS:	$ 46,315.00	$2,457.55	$5,200.00	$0.00	$41,215.00	$3,278.50

Figure 14.14 Report generated out of the control statements in Figure 14.13.

In your job-control statement, simply specify PARM='MAXSORT' in the EXEC statement. I recommend that you also request additional space (SORTWK) when using this technique.

14.5 The Use of Exit Programs

The term *exit program* simply means a particular location in your sort where control can be passed to a user-written routine. For every record processed in your sort program, you can activate an exit point. The problem is that every time you issue an exit point, it increases the overall execution time of the task—using additional main storage that could be allocated to the sort. So it is important for you to use exit points or exit programs for tasks that cannot be done through SyncSort control statements.

Programmed exits use two-digit decimal numbers, such as E35. For example, the first digit of 35, 3, simply refers to the sort merge phase, at which point the routine is to acquire control. (An exception to this is E61, which can acquire control either

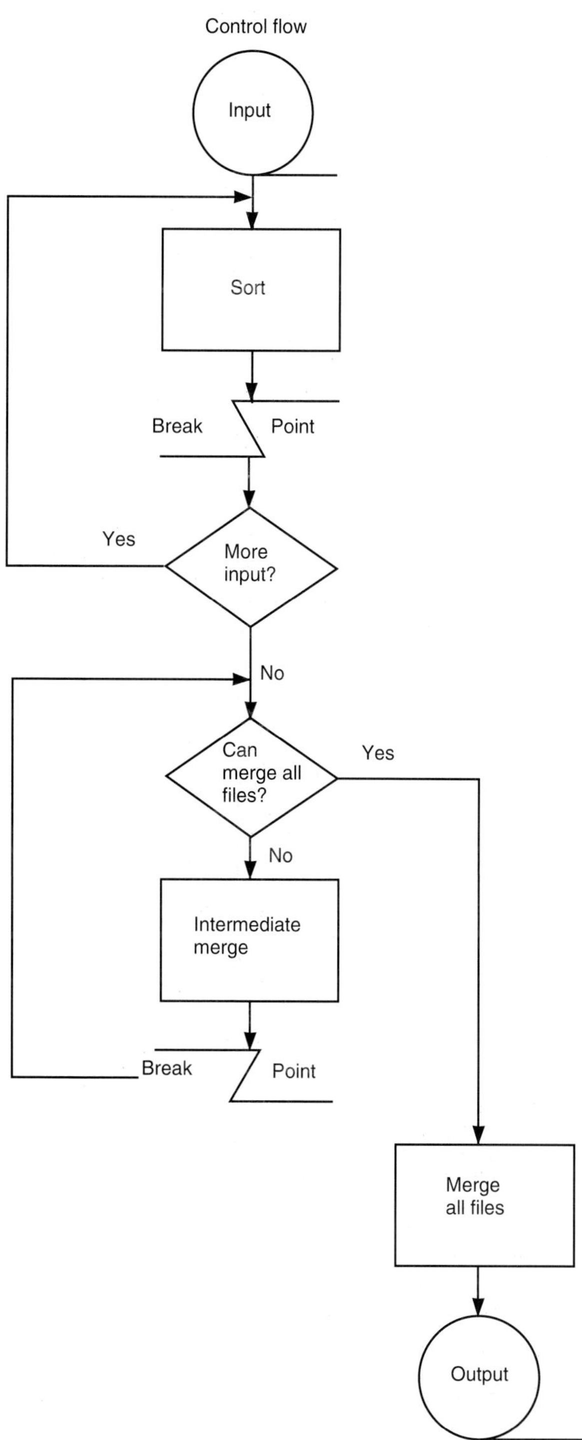

Figure 14.15 SyncSort data- and control-flow diagram.

Figure 14.15 *Continued.*

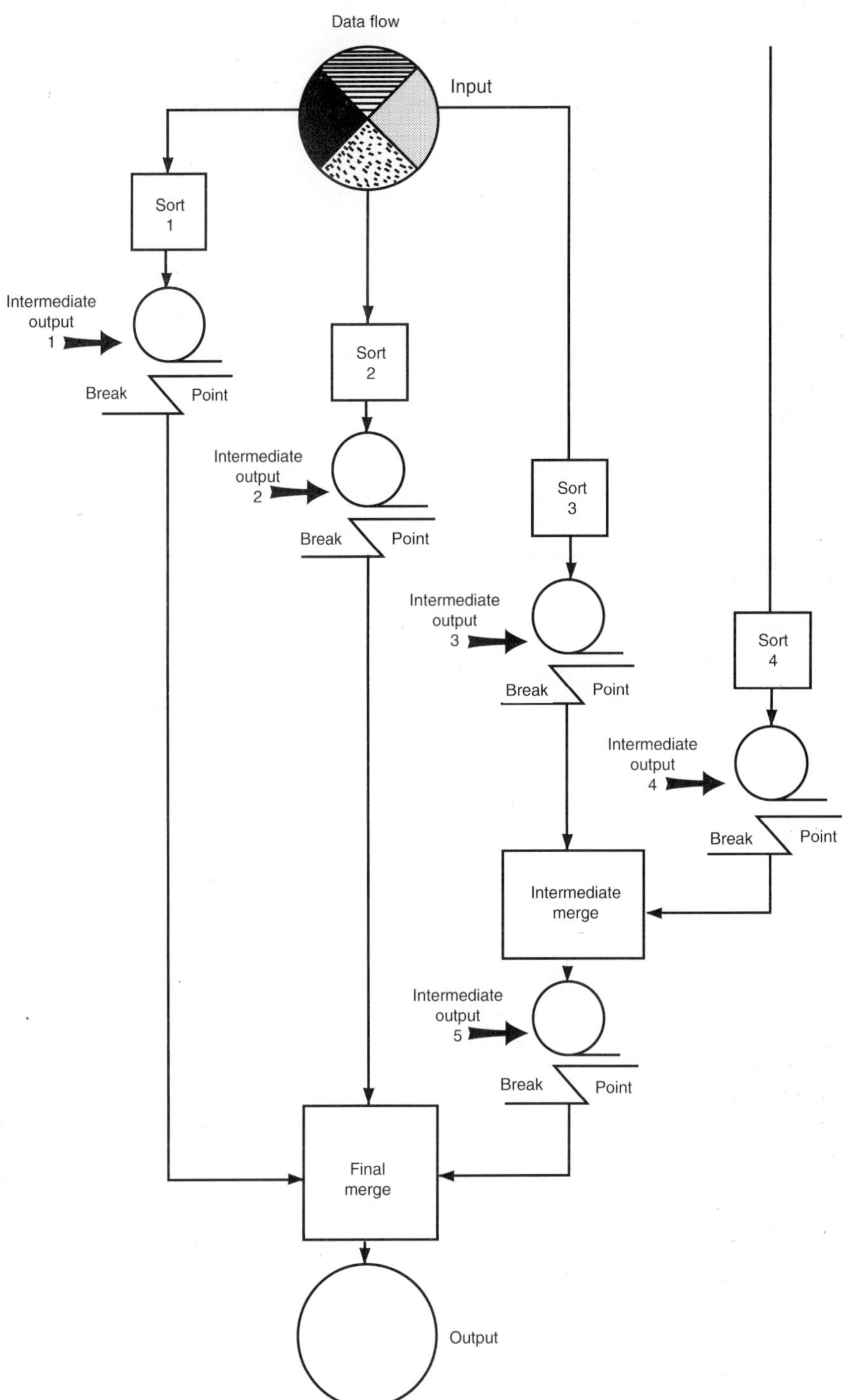

TASK	PHASE 1							PHASE 2			PHASE 3						
	E 11	E 14	E 15	E 16	E 17	E 18	E 61	E 21	E 25	E 27	E 31	E 32	E 35	E 37	E 38	E 39	E 61
Prepare for other routine	x							x			x						
Create input records for sort			x														
Create input records for merge												x					
Add records			x										x				
Delete records		x	x														
Change records		x	x						x				x				
Sum records		x	x						x				x				
Choose action if inter-mediate storage insuffic.				x													
Close other exit data sets					x						x			x			
Process read errors						x									x		
Process write errors																x	
Check labels						x									x	x	
Modify a collating sequen.							x										x

Figure 14.16 Exit routines corresponding to each sort phase.

in phase 1 or in phase 3.) The second digit refers to the number of that exit within the phase. Figure 14.16 shows how tasks and exit routines line up within a particular phase.

Let me briefly review with you the meaning of each phase that occurs during the SyncSort process, from phase 0 to phase 4. This, incidentally, is a rehash from one of the earlier sections, but, relative to the chart in Figure 14.16, is going to make a great deal more sense now.

In phase 0, all JCL and sort parameters are validated for syntax. If there are any crucial syntax errors, the operation will terminate and produce an error message.

In phase 1, the input data is read into core, and records are written out to work files. Each record is written out in sequence with the one immediately preceding it. This process creates sorted strings. As long as records are written in sequence, the process will continue in a reiterative fashion. When a record in memory cannot sequentially follow the record previously written out, the string is considered complete and a new string is initiated. At the end of this phase, all input data will be translated into individual (small) string sizes.

The purpose of phase 2 is to further consolidate the relatively small sort strings created in phase 1 into larger, more cohesive strings. This phase is over when the remaining strings can be merged into the final string at least once. Note that this phase can also be skipped if phase 1 produces only a few strings that can be immediately absorbed in the merge process.

Phase 3 is the final merge/sort and is completed once the completely sorted data is written to an output file. When performing a merge operation, phases 1 and 2 are simply bypassed.

E14, or Exit 14, can be used to change the contents of a particular data field or fields, and to summarize or delete records during phase-1 operations. (Adding a record requires another exit point, such as E15.) When the operation is completed, the system makes a return code available for the user, accessible through a register (e.g., register 15) with one of two values. When the return code is 0, for example, SyncSort is instructed to accept the record. Code 4, on the other hand, will delete the record.

E15, as I mentioned above, is used to add, modify, or analyze an input record. This exit can be used only in conjunction with a sort operation. Exit 15 has two constraints. First, if a record is to be changed, it should first be moved into a work area in your program. Second, if your input record is made up of variable-length records, the first four bytes must contain the Record Descriptor Word, giving the length of the record. In addition to the previously mentioned return codes (0 and 4), this exit also uses three other status codes.

A status code of 8 instructs SyncSort to close the exit for the remainder of the sort application; 12 tells SyncSort that the exit routine has located a record that should be added to the input data set before the record whose address appears in the parameter list; and 16 notifies SyncSort to terminate the current operation and to return to the prior program.

When an output data set is available, the user might want to incorporate an E35 exit to add, delete, or change records at the end of phase 3. In the absence of an output data set, E35 has full responsibility for output processing and, under normal conditions, will delete every record passed by the sort.

Chapter

15

DB2 Concepts and Utilities

15.1 DB2 Terms and Nomenclature

DB2, or Database 2, is a relational Database Management System, also referred to by the abbreviation DBMS. It provides you with a relational model where data is defined and accessed in terms of tables, each containing one or more columns and a number of rows. Think of columns as data fields (a bit oversimplified, perhaps) and the rows simply as records. You can also define views on these tables so that the resulting "logical" table is a subset of the original tables.

A relational database is essentially a collection of tables maintained in one or a number of VSAM (Virtual Storage Access Method) data sets, referred to as *table spaces*. Table spaces are associated with storage groups, which are residents of DASD (Direct Access Storage Device) volumes, and are automatically allocated as required.

Table spaces can be partitioned, segmented, or simple. A partitioned table space is one where the space is divided into separate units called partitions, each containing a part of the table. In this situation, the data is divided into partitions based on a range of data values of certain designated columns (fields). Segmented and simple table spaces can contain more than one table. Segmented table spaces generally provide better performance than simple table spaces.

Tables can also be indexed. When tables are indexed, they are maintained in index spaces. A clustering index is one that determines the physical order in which the rows in the table are stored. The columns used for partitioning data into a partitioned table space must be indexed by a clustering index, which is then also known as a partitioning index. Indexes can be unique or nonunique. If you define an index as nonunique, DB2 will not allow you to load or insert rows that would cause duplicate index entries. This concept is illustrated in Figure 15.1.

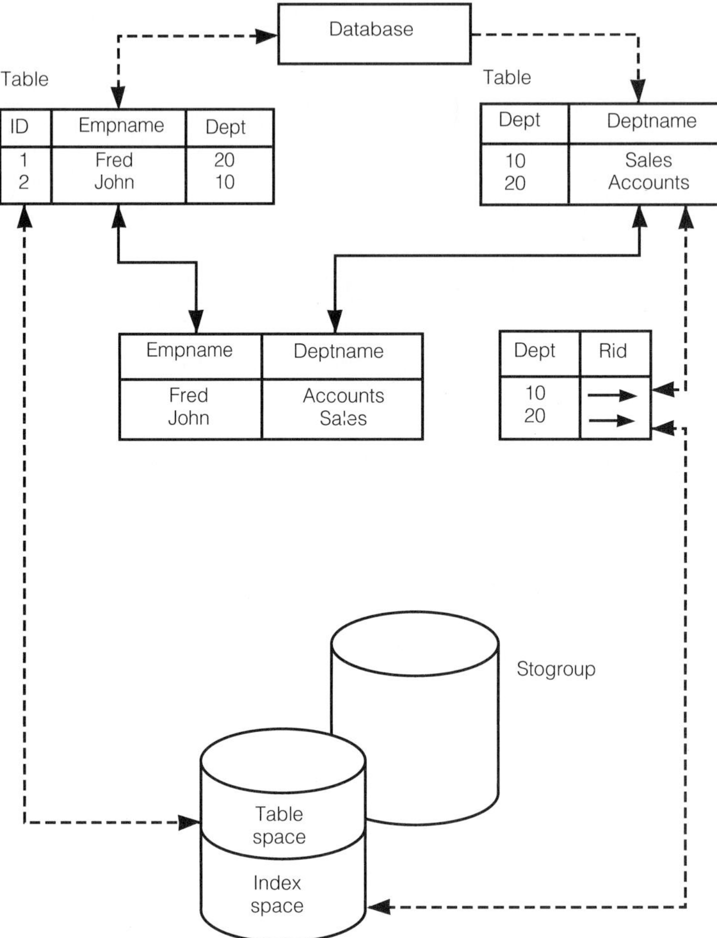

Figure 15.1 Some DB2 objects.

The term *referential integrity* is used to describe a function of DB2 that ensures the validity of relationships between two tables. For example, you can define referential constraints on the employee table in Figure 15.1 so that a row cannot be inserted into the table if the DEPT column contains a department number that does not exist in the department table. Referential constraints can also be used to control the deletion of rows; for example, you can define that a row in the department table cannot be deleted while there are still employee rows that reference that specific department.

15.2 DB2 System Data Sets and SQL

One data set, DB2 catalog, is essentially a set of tables. The purpose of this set is to contain information about all the objects defined in the system. This catalog is an active one, so any changes you make to the definition of any object are recorded immediately. You can retrieve information from the catalog using SQL (Structured Query Language) statements.

A second system data set is a DB2 directory, which is a set of control information that is used by the DB2 database-management system at start-up time, as well as during normal operation. This file, unlike the catalog data set, cannot be accessed through SQL.

A third system data set is used by DB2 for working storage; this can be used if an internal (programmed) sort is required to satisfy an order by keyword in a SELECT statement. More on this in section 15.5.

Other data sets include the Bootstrap Data Set (abbreviated as BSDS) and the log data sets. BSDS is a VSAM data set that contains control information used primarily at restart and in recovery situations. The log data sets are used to record changes so that recovery options can be performed.

Access to the database is provided by the Structured Query Language, commonly referred to as SQL. SQL contains three types of statements:

Data Definition Language, or DDL. This represents statements you use to define DB2 objects. For example, CREATE TABLE is the statement for defining a DB2 table.

Data Manipulation Language, or DML. This represents statements that are used the most frequently. Their function is to retrieve, update, insert, or delete data within a table. An example of this is the SELECT statement, which is used to retrieve data.

Data Control Language, or DCL. The purpose of this is to grant or revoke authorization for the use of some DB2 resource.

15.3 Application Programming in DB2

In order to access data stored in DB2, application programs include embedded SQL statements. Thus, you can write your application programs in COBOL, PL/I, FORTRAN, BASIC, C, or BAL, and they will include certain SQL commands. Consider the following statements:

```
EXEC SQL
UPDATE DEPT_TABLE SET MGRNO = :MGRNUM
     WHERE DEPTNO = :DEPTNUM
END SQL
```

This shows how an UPDATE statement would be embedded in a COBOL program. The statement, incidentally, will change the MGRNO field in the department table to some value contained in a host variable (:MGRNUM), which is defined in the program. The only rows that are changed are those where the department number contains a value equal to that contained in another host variable, :DEPTNUM.

Because of the relational nature of DB2, a single SQL statement might sometimes cause a set of rows to be returned. For example, if you issue the statement:

```
SELECT DEPT, DEPTNAME FROM DEPT_TABLE
     WHERE DEPT > 10
```

all the rows that have a department number greater than 10 will be returned. Obviously, a program would find it difficult to handle all the rows in the set at once. Instead, a cursor is defined in the program to FETCH one row at a time from the answer set.

The DCLGEN process allows the user to develop source-language data structures of the table definitions stored in the DB2 catalog. The definitions can then be used in the application program to define input/output areas. Before a DB2 program can be executed, it must be processed by the DB2 compiler, which analyzes the DB2 source code (very much like command-level CICS, for one), and saves the SQL statements in a DBRM (short for Database Request Module). The SQL statements are then replaced by calls to a DB2 interface module.

As I mentioned previously, if the program contains CICS commands, the initial source program must also be processed via the CICS-command language translator. This can be done either before or after processing by the DB2 precompiler. Afterwards, the program can then be compiled and link-edited. A special process called BIND analyzes the DBRM and determines the access path for the SQL requests, based on the definitions of tables, indexes, etc. in the DB2 catalog. The output of this process is stored in a DB2 catalog table as an application plan. This is illustrated in detail in Figure 15.2. In this diagram, the numbers refer to the following:

1. The output of this step is a modified source module.
2. This step can be done either before or after the DB2 precompiler.
3. The output of this step is an object module.
4. The plan is stored in a table in the DB2 catalog.

When the program is executed, the plan is loaded when the first SQL call is encountered and the tables are accessed using the strategy established during the BIND. The program is then said to be using *static SQL*. *Dynamic SQL* is the term used when the access path is determined at the time the SQL statement is executed. Dynamic SQL is sometimes used in application programs, and is always used in an interactive environment. The code that determines the access path is called DB2 Optimizer.

DB2I is an interactive ISPF-based tool. It allows you to perform such functions as invoking DB2 utilities, preparing programs for execution, and issuing DB2 commands. It also provides a facility called SPUFI, which allows you to submit and test SQL statements without writing any application code. This function could be used to test statements before an application program is developed, as well as to create tables and execute other DB2 statements. More on this in the upcoming sections.

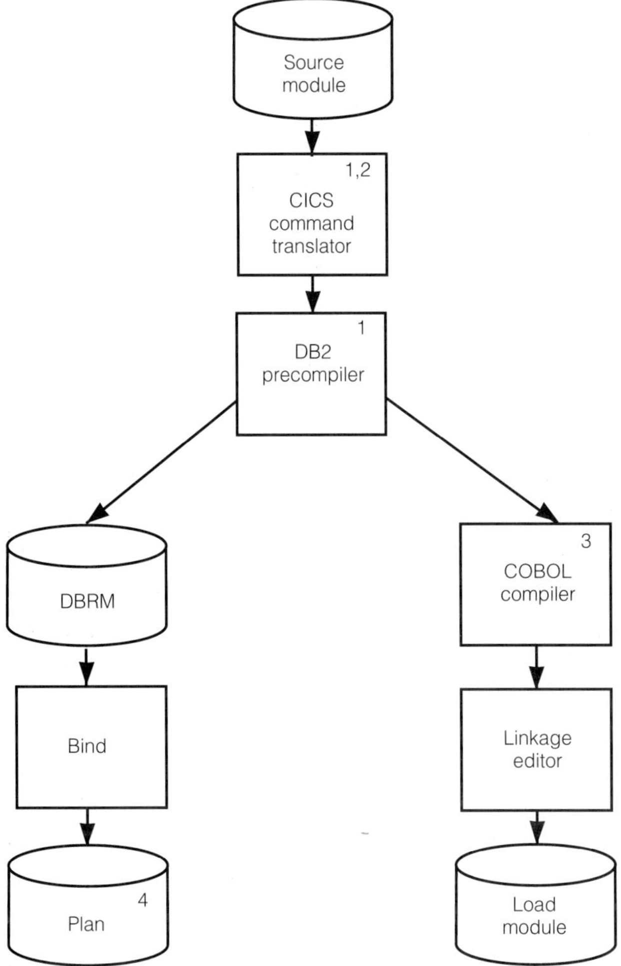

Figure 15.2 Preparing a CICS DB2 application program.

15.4 DB2 Architecture

DB2 was initially designed for an OS/MVS/XA system and runs in three address spaces:

- The Database Services address space, which provides the access to the DB2 catalog and all user tables.
- The System Services address space, which provides termination and restart processing, logging, and other operational-control services.
- The IMS/VS Resource Lock Manager (IRLM) address space, which provides locking services to permit sharing of data among users running in separate user address spaces. Note that the IRLM is used even if your installation does not have IMS installed.

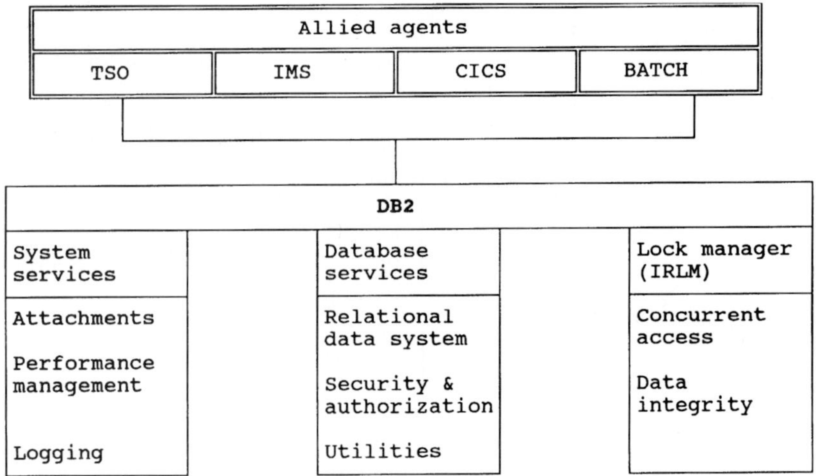

Figure 15.3 The DB2 environment.

Figure 15.3 shows the DB2 operating environment. User programs running under the control of IMS/VS, CICS, TSO foreground, and in batch can access DB2 data. DB2 provides a number of utilities that can be invoked from DB2I, a TSO CLIST, or from a batch job. The major utilities includes ones for:

- Loading data from sequential files
- Making backup copies of table space data sets
- Recovering data
- Unloading and reloading table space and index spaces (reorganizing)
- Updating catalog statistics about table spaces and index spaces

The resource limit facility can be used to control the amount of resources used for certain SQL queries.

15.5 Structured Query Language (SQL)

SQL is used primarily to manage information on the database, although the language is often used by other than DB2 shops because of its fourth-generation capabilities. In a DB2 environment, you can add, change, and delete information in a table, or request information from one or more tables in the form of a report.

This section presents an IBM case study in which a company has a database that consists of two tables. The first one is the Corporat table, which contains information about company structure and organization. The table also accommodates data for department numbers, department names, managers' numbers, and the division and location to which each department belongs. The second table, Employee, contains information about the company's employees. It holds data for ID numbers, employee names, their departments and jobs, the number of years they have been employed by the firm, and their salaries and commissions. The Corporat table is displayed in Figure 15.4, and the Employee table is shown in Figure 15.5.

Let us look at the mechanics of the SELECT statement first. With a SELECT statement, you can query your database in order to display or print the specific information. For example:

```
SELECT *
FROM CORPORAT
```

will give you a report like the one in Figure 15.6 (as well as the one in 15.4). If you want to select specific columns, use their names. For example, to select department numbers and names from the Corporat table, simply enter:

```
SELECT DEPTNAME, DEPTNUMB
FROM CORPORAT
```

DEPTNUMB	DEPTNAME	MANAGER	DIVISION	LOCATION
10	Head Office	160	Corporate	New York
15	New England	50	Eastern	Boston
20	Mid Atlantic	10	Eastern	Washington
38	South Atlantic	30	Eastern	Atlanta
42	Great Lakes	100	Midwest	Chicago
51	Plains	140	Midwest	Dallas
66	Pacific	270	Western	San Francisco
84	Mountain	290	Western	Denver

Figure 15.4 The Corporat table, one of two tables on the CONSOLID database model.

ID	NAME	DEPT	JOB	YEARS	SALARY	COMM
10	Thermond	20	Mgr	7	18357.50	-
20	Marzullo	20	Sales	8	18171.25	612.45
30	Mueller	38	Mgr	5	17506.75	-
40	O'Toole	38	Sales	6	18006.00	846.55
50	Varsegi	15	Mgr	5	17506.75	-
60	Stockton	38	Sales	-	18762.09	837.09
70	Alexander	20	Clerk	2	20928.99	-
80	Brookfield	20	Mgr	4	21029.00	987.00
90	Cunningham	66	Sales	6	19029.74	-
100	Thompson	66	Mgr	3	20918.00	-
110	Peterson	38	Sales	2	23948.00	872.00
120	Vanderbuilt	84	Sales	-	18901.98	786.00
130	Eckersley	20	Sales	1	20938.00	-
140	Dickerson	20	Mgr	5	21029.77	789.00

Figure 15.5 The Employee table, second table on the CONSOLID database model.

```
DEPTNUMB  DEPTNAME          MANAGER    DIVISION       LOCATION
--------  --------------    ----------  ------------  --------------
 10       Head Office         160      Corporate       New York
 15       New England          50      Eastern         Boston
 20       Mid Atlantic         10      Eastern         Washington
 38       South Atlantic       30      Eastern         Atlanta
 42       Great Lakes         100      Midwest         Chicago
 51       Plains              140      Midwest         Dallas
 66       Pacific             270      Western         San Francisco
 84       Mountain            290      Western         Denver
```

Figure 15.6 The result of a SELECT * SQL statement in the Corporat table.

which will display the following:

```
DEPTNAME          DEPTNUMB

-----             -----

Head Office          10
New England          15
Mid Atlantic         20
South Atlantic       38
Great Lakes          42
Plains               51
Pacific              66
Mountain             84
```

Let's now look at a specific example of eliminating duplicate rows. When using the SELECT statement to produce a report, you might not want to display or print duplicate information. The DISTINCT command eliminates duplicate rows in a report. For example, Corporat has a DEPT column in which several department values are listed more than once, and a JOB column in which several job descriptions are listed more than once. To use DISTINCT to produce a report in which a job within a department is listed only once, type:

```
SELECT DISTINCT DEPT, JOB
FROM EMPLOYEE
```

which will result in the following display:

```
15  MGR
20  CLERK
20  MGR
20  SALES
38  MGR
38  SALES
66  MGR
66  SALES
84  SALES
```

Suppose you now need to select specific rows from a table. In this situation, the WHERE clause allows you to identify a condition or a set of conditions that a row must meet in order to be selected. To select only those rows for department 20, type:

```
SELECT DEPT, NAME, JOB
FROM EMPLOYEE
WHERE DEPT = 20
```

and the result will be:

```
DEPT    NAME          JOB
---     ---            --
20      Thermond      Mgr
20      Marzullo      Sales
20      Alexander     Clerk
20      Brookfield    Mgr
20      Eckersley     Sales
20      Dickerson     Mgr
```

Note the following rules in initiating a query. You need to type each data element as it exists on the database. Lowercase characters must be presented in lowercase, otherwise no rows will be selected. Alphanumeric values must be enclosed in apostrophes, while numeric are not.

You can use a special value, such as NULL, where there is no value for a given column in a row. If you want to perform calculations in SQL (e.g., give everyone in department 20 a $100 bonus), simply specify:

```
SELECT DEPT, NAME, SALARY+100
FROM EMPLOYEE
WHERE DEPT = 20
```

Let's complicate things a bit further by selecting rows based on multiple conditions. This selection is connected via the AND and OR logic. When AND is used, only rows that satisfy both conditions are selected. For example, to select employees with five years of service and salaries over $19,000.00:

```
SELECT ID, NAME, YEARS, SALARY
FROM EMPLOYEE
WHERE YEARS = 5
AND SALARY > 19000
```

When OR is used, on the other hand, every row that satisfies either or both of the conditions will be selected. To select employees with five years of service *or* whose salaries are over $19,000, specify:

```
SELECT ID, NAME, YEARS, SALARY
FROM EMPLOYEE
WHERE YEARS = 5
OR SALARY > 19000
```

When you use both OR and AND Boolean logic in your SQL, use parentheses to make the expression clear. Another way to select rows is based on certain pre-established ranges. For example:

```
SELECT ID, NAME, SALARY
FROM EMPLOYEE
WHERE SALARY BETWEEN 19000 AND 20000.
```

Selecting rows via a list of values is also viable. Consider the following:

```
SELECT DEPTNUMB, DEPTNAME
FROM CORPORAT
WHERE DEPTNUMB IN (20, 38, 42)
```

which will locate department names and numbers, specifically for departments 20, 38, and 42.

There are times when you need to produce a report that contains information located in different tables. To produce such a report, use the SELECT statement to combine data from the tables. In database terminology, the use of one SELECT statement to combine data from more than one table is called a *join*. Two or more SELECT statements can be combined into a single SELECT statement with a SET operator. The SET operators are UNION, EXCEPT, and INTERSECT, which correspond to the relational operators UNION, DIFFERENCE, and INTERSECTION. All three operators combine rows from similar tables into one table.

Thus, you can use the SELECT statement to produce reports that contain information from two or more tables. For example, the Employee and Corporat tables can be joined to form a new table. To join two tables, specify the table names in a FROM clause and the connection between them in a WHERE clause. The connection is usually some data that is the same in both tables. To join the NAME column from the Employee table and the DEPTNAME column from the Corporat table, where the data is the same in the ID column in the Employee table and the Manager column in the Employee table, enter:

```
SELECT NAME, DEPTNAME
FROM EMPLOYEE, ORG
WHERE MANAGER = ID
```

which will produce the following display:

```
NAME          DEPTNAME
---           ------

Mueller       South Atlantic
Varsegi       New England
Thompson      Great Lakes
Dickerson     Plains
```

You can use multiple SELECT statements with SET operators to produce reports that contain information from two or more result tables. The UNION operator creates a new result tables consisting of rows from the combined result tables. For example, to select employees in the Western Division and those in the Corporate Division from the Employee table, enter the following SQL statements:

```
SELECT NAME 'Corporate'
FROM EMPLOYEE
WHERE DEPT IN
(SELECT DEPTNUMB FROM CORPORAT
WHERE DIVISION='Corporate')
UNION
SELECT NAME, 'Western'
FROM EMPLOYEE
WHERE DEPT IN
(SELECT DEPTNUMB FROM CORPORAT
WHERE DIVISION = 'Western')
```

The result of this query is as follows:

```
EXPRESSION 1  EXPRESSION 2
------- --    --------

Cunningham    Western
Thompson      Western
```

Here is an example of the EXCEPT statement:

```
SELECT DEPT
FROM EMPLOYEE
WHERE JOB = 'Sales'
EXCEPT
SELECT DEPTNUMB
FROM CORPORAT
WHERE DIVISION = 'Eastern'
```

The EXCEPT operator creates a new result table consisting of all rows in the first result table that are not in the second result table. Somewhat similar, the INTERSECT operator creates a new result table consisting of rows in the first result table that are also in the second result table. For example, to select all sales employees with less than five years of service from the Employee table, specify the following:

```
SELECT NAME
FROM EMPLOYEE
WHERE JOB='Sales'
INTERSECT
SELECT NAME
FROM CORPORAT
WHERE YEARS < 5
```

When you write a SELECT statement, you can place another SELECT statement within the WHERE clause. Each SELECT after the first SELECT starts a phrase that is called a subquery. You can use subqueries to identify conditions based on information in another table.

You can produce a report in which the condition for selecting data is based on a table other than the one from which data is selected. This is done by using a subquery in the WHERE clause. To select the division and location of the employee whose ID is 30, specify:

```
SELECT DIVISION, LOCATION
FROM CORPORAT
WHERE DEPTNUMB = (SELECT DEPT
FROM EMPLOYEE
WHERE ID = 30)
```

The result is:

```
DIVISION   LOCATION
-----      -----

EASTERN    ATLANTA
```

The subquery first selected the value of the DEPT column in the row for the employee whose ID is 30. This value is 38. Then the SELECT statement selected DIVISION and LOCATION from the row in the Corporat table in which the value of DEPTNUMB is 38.

Subqueries can draw from any table (including any tables used in the main SELECT statement). You can use more than one level of subquery, that is, you can have subqueries within subqueries. Note that the last subquery is evaluated first, the next to last second, and so on until the main SELECT statement is evaluated. A subquery generally specifies only one column in the select list, and will produce only one value from that column unless it is preceded by ANY, ALL, SOME, EXISTS, or IN. A subquery preceded by EXISTS can specify any number of columns in the select list. In writing a subquery, you can use ANY, ALL, SOME, EXISTS, or IN to return more than one value. For example, to select the NAME, ID, and YEARS of the employees who worked fewer years than all of the managers, enter:

```
SELECT NAME, ID, YEARS
FROM EMPLOYEE
WHERE YEARS < ALL
(SELECT YEARS
FROM EMPLOYEE
WHERE JOB = 'Mgr')
```

When your subquery does not need to produce a value, only find out whether a row exists that satisfies a certain condition, use the EXISTS predicate. For example, to find out which departments have employees that have been with the company more than 10 years:

```
SELECT DEPTNAME
FROM CORPORAT
WHERE EXISTS(SELECT NAME
FROM STAFF WHERE
DEPT=CORPORAT, DEPTNUMB
AND YEARS>10)
```

You can use the CREATE TABLE statement to define a table. First name the table and the columns, and then assign a data type to each column. To define a table called BRANCH, for example, with columns named ID, NAME, DEPT, JOB, YEARS, SALARY, and COMM using various data types, enter:

```
CREATE TABLE BRANCH
(ID         SMALLINT   NOT NULL,
 NAME       VARCHAR(9),
 DEPT       SMALLINT,
 JOB        CHAR(5),
 YEARS      SMALLINT,
 SALARY     DECIMAL(7,2),
 COMM       DECIMAL(7,2))
```

Note that in this table, the ID column is defined as NOT NULL so that no rows can be added to BRANCH unless data is entered in the ID column. Once a table is defined, rows of data can be entered.

The list of columns from the table must be enclosed in parentheses. If the data type for the column is CHAR or VARCHAR, the length or maximum length of the column must also be included in the parentheses. For example, in CHAR(5), the number 5 is enclosed in parentheses because it is the length or maximum length of the column. Here is how you add rows:

```
INSERT INTO BRANCH
VALUES (400, 'DONALDSON', 20, 'SALES', NULL, 18000.66, 0)
```

and here's how you change rows:

```
UPDATE BRANCH
SET JOB='CLERK', SALARY=SALARY+300) to also reflect a salary
```

(which is an increase of $300.00). Here's how to delete rows:

```
DELETE FROM BRANCH
WHERE ID=510
```

15.6 What SPUFI Is All About

To enhance program development and testing, DB2 allows you to access data interactively from TSO through SPUFI (short for Sequential Processor Using File Input) or QMF (Query Management Facility). SPUFI comes with your DB2 package and is part of IBM's DB2I (DB2 Interactive) utility program. I'll elaborate on this in a minute. QMF is not part of the standard DB2 package, although it is extensively used in this kind of environment.

SPUFI, in essence, enables you to process SQL statements interactively and gives you some limited formatting with regards to the output. QMF, which is primarily used for data retrieval, provides you with far more comprehensive formatting capabilities than does SPUFI; in fact, users often rely on QMF as a report writer or an easy way to perform a query. One of the major differences between SPUFI and QMF remains the fact that QMF is geared to the nonprofessional or those with limited experience, while SPUFI, on the other hand, is geared to the programmer analyst or the technician with prior experience.

When you access DB2 through SPUFI, you are initiating a dynamic SQL program. It is referred to as dynamic for the simple reason that the application program is not identified to the system until you have completed keying in the entire program and have pressed the Enter key upon completion. The problem with dynamic SQL queries is that the more complex ones tend to substantially slow down the system, in some cases bringing the entire system "to its knees." In reality, while you can rely on dynamic programs (SPUFI or QMF), static SQL is regarded as a great deal more common in the industry.

To reiterate, SPUFI lets you submit and dynamically execute your SQL commands, sort, and test them prior to entering them into your program. All you need to do is to place the SQL commands in a partitioned or sequential data set, which then will be dynamically submitted by SPUFI to DB2. SPUFI will provide you with messages through ISPF in the following manner: the input will be handled via ISPF edit while the output will be displayed through the Browse function. This ISPF emulation should explain why SPUFI is geared more towards the professional, the technician with prior exposure.

As I mentioned before, SPUFI is accessed through DB2 Interactive or DB2I, which describes a number of screens in conjunction with DB2 and its dynamic procedures. The DB2I Primary Options Menu is presented in Figure 15.7.

15.7 QMF (Query Management Facility)

Query Management Facility, or QMF, is not part of the DB2 package, like SPUFI. Rather, it is a supplement designed to let you dynamically submit SQL statements. SQL statements are used to maintain the various DB2 tables in your application program.

QMF differs from SPUFI in that it is more for nontechnical people, and is more user-friendly, giving you extended formatting facilities.

You can use QMF very much like a fourth-generation language to accomplish a number of objectives, such as being able to look at your data a number of different ways, producing control figures, and creating reports a great deal faster than it would using a conventional language, such as COBOL. QMF, placed into a more complex situation, does not have the power nor the flexibility of its COBOL counterpart. It is also a great deal more resource-oriented.

One of the better ways of using QMF is for producing ad-hoc queries, where you can present multidimensional criteria for retrieval.

The path I chose in this chapter focuses on describing QMF from the perspective of a data-processing professional rather than from that of the user. You can start a QMF session in either batch or interactive mode.

One of a number of ways to start a QMF session is through an SAA-callable interface from a high-level language. SAA is short for IBM's System Application Architecture, and you can use a set of QMF commands through a callable interface module

```
                      DB2I PRIMARY OPTIONS MENU

===>
Select one of the following DB2 functions and press ENTER.

 1  SPUFI                  (process SQL statements)
 2  DCLGEN                 (generate SQL and source language declarations)
 3  PROGRAM PREPARATIONS   (prepare a DB2 application to run)
 4  PRECOMPILE             (invoke DB2 compiler)
 5  BIND/REBIND/FREE       (BIND, REBIND, or FREE, application plans)
 6  RUN                    (run an SQL program)
 7  DB2 COMMANDS           (issue DB2 commands)
 8  UTILTIES               (invoke DB2 utilities)
 D  DB2I DEFAULTS          (set global parameters)
 X  EXIT                   (leave DB2I)

 PRESS:   END to exit        HELP for more information
```

Figure 15.7 The DB2I Primary Options Menu.

such as the one that exists between an application and COBOL. This interface gives you direct access between QMF and the particular application, as well as portability among most IBM systems.

Applications can be built from components of many different kinds. Some components, for example, can be EXECs to allocate or deallocate resources. They can also use all the ISPF services, including panel and message displays, file tailoring, and table services. In addition, they can execute QMF commands through a command interface, and develop those commands dynamically through EXEC logic.

You can also use EXECs as prototypes for components that you will eventually replace with program modules. This can help you test the design. Moreover, users with a pressing need for the application can use the prototype while the final version is still being developed.

When you develop an EXEC for a QMF application, remember that when the EXEC executes, it is part of an ISPF dialog. In any EXEC, you must issue your ISPF commands in an ISPF environment; do this by prefacing all your ISPF commands with ADDRESS ISPEXEC.

A third way to start a QMF session is by using program modules with a command interface. This is a different process than the one mentioned above in that callable interface modules run independently of QMF, whereas command interface modules require QMF to start before they run. Like EXECs, program modules in an application can read, write, and update sequential data sets. And like EXECs, they can use all the ISPF services. Moreover, they can execute QMF commands dynamically through the command interface by using program logic and string manipulation.

Program modules can also do things that EXECs can't. They can, for example, use embedded SQL statements. They can also invoke the command interface without help from the ISPF SELECT service. In an application with many calls to the command interface, invoking the command interface in this manner could substantially improve performance.

Deciding whether to use batch mode or interactive sessions depends on the type of application. Some applications require user interaction, running only in interactive sessions. Other applications perform time-consuming tasks with no need for user interactions. Such applications would normally run in batch mode.

15.8 DCLGEN (Declarations Generator)

As noted in my coverage of SPUFI and QMF, both of these programs enable you to dynamically access the DB2 structure. However, DB2 can also be accessed from your application program, which is what happens in the majority of cases. A table declaration is required in DB2 to define the columns in a particular table, including their attributes, such as length, data type, and so on. In COBOL, this is defined in your WORKING-STORAGE section, where you need to show a DECLARE TABLE statement for every table used or otherwise referenced.

The purpose of DCLGEN, or Declaration Generator, is to automatically provide you with accurate DECLARE TABLE code. If you were, for example, to code an SQL DECLARE TABLE yourself, you could in all likelihood compromise the accuracy of the table. DCLGEN, which is part of the DB2 environment, references the catalog and produces these copy book members, which is one of the primary reasons for using automatically generated DECLARE tables. The precompiler then extracts these copy book members (based on your SQL INCLUDE statement) and, along with other copy members, merges them into your code.

DCLGEN can be invoked from DB2 Interactive (DB2I) or simply as a job in your job-control stream. It can also be initiated through the DCLGEN subcommand of the SDN command processor.

One of a number of functions of the DCLGEN utility is to read the SYSIBM.SYSCOLUMNS catalog table, hold the requested information about the columns in a particular table (e.g., Corporat and Employee), and create the DECLARE TABLE code. Another aspect of DCLGEN is to generate and display a host language, like COBOL, and record layout for a particular row in the table.

15.9 CA's Pro-EDIT for DB2

Pro-EDIT is a DB2 testing tool by Computer Associates that enables you, the application programmer, and the database administrator to create and edit DB2 tables using a menu-driven ISPF-like interface. Thus, programmers tend to become productive relatively quickly assuming they are already familiar with the ISPF format. There are three aspects of Pro-EDIT that will be covered in this section:

- Creating DB2 tables with entity and referential integrity
- Editing DB2 tables using familiar commands
- Dynamically testing embedded SQL—with host variable and without leaving an ISPF session

15.9.1 Creating DB2 tables with entity and referential integrity

Pro-EDIT provides a way to create tables and indexes without having to write SQL statements. The system lets you define foreign keys and create unique indexes for primary keys. Using fill-in-the-blank screens, like the one shown in Figure 15.8, you can enter the column names and attributes of new tables and indexes. The result of this will be Pro-EDIT automatically generating the necessary SQL statement. While this concept is not the latest technique in developing source code, it is certainly an efficient way to define a program or a utility.

Pro-EDIT uses all DB2 release 2.2 functions. The system can create an index as easily as it can create a table. Through a COPY routine, it can duplicate existing tables and indexes, such as copying data from one table to another—even if their structure differs. The system can save SQL for use in another environment and it can create aliases to access and update data on distributed systems, as well.

When you need to create a table similar to one that already exists, you can use the system's TEMPLATE command to duplicate existing tables and indexes along with their integrity definitions. Once you have duplicated a table, you can modify it by adding, deleting, and copying columns, and by changing column attributes. You can

```
ProEDIT - CREATE TABLE ---------------------------- ROW 1 OF 8
 COMMAND ===>                                         SCROLL ===> PAGE

 Valid Commands ===> CREATE      QSAVE     TEMPLATE tablename      PROFILE
                     INTEGRITY   SQLID id  CREATE LIKE tablename   DROP

 DB2 TABLE NAME ====> TEST.TEMPL                DB2  SSN:  DSN
 DATABASE...    ====>                           SQLID   :  SMITH
 TABLESPACE.    ====>
 EDITPROC...    ====>
 VALIDPROC..    ====>     AUDIT.......===> NONE  (NONE, CHANGES, ALL)

 RCMD     COLUMN       COLUMN                          NULLS?   DEFAULT?    BIT?
(I,R,D)   NAME          TYPE    LENGTH    SCALE     (Y OR N)  (Y OR N)  (Y OR N)

  _       DEPTNO        CHAR         3       0          N         N          N
  _       DEPTNAME      VARCHAR     30       0          N         N          N
  _       MGRNO         CHAR         6       0          N         N          N
  _       ADMDEPT       CHAR         3       0          N         N          N
************************* BOTTOM OF DATA ****************************
```

Figure 15.8 Panel used to create a DB2 table.

```
                CREATING A TABLE, INDEX, OR ALIAS

With Pro-EDIT
- Familiar, ISPF-like screens
- ProEDIT generates all the necessary SQLs
- Entity and referential integrity is preserved
- Existing tables, indexes, and aliases can be duplicated
  using a single command
- Data can be copied from one table to another and across
  subsystems
- SQL can be saved for use in other environments
- DB2 wildcards are supported

Without Pro-EDIT
- SQL statements must be coded and executed
- No entity or referential integrity is incorporated
- Tables must be created from scratch - no way to
  duplicate existing tables or indexes
- Data must be keyed in - no way to copy data between tables
```

Figure 15.9 Creating a table, index, or alias.

also copy data from one table to another when the source and target tables have different structures. Using this option, simply specify which source columns will be used to populate which target columns, which allows the system to map the rows to a new format.

One of the options available in Pro-EDIT is your ability to save SQL statements in a data set for later execution. This means you can reuse the output from a Pro-EDIT session as you require it.

The system also supports DB2 wildcards, like % ans _, in order to display a list of table, view, alias, and index names that meet the generic criteria. Figure 15.9 highlights some of the major topics to consider with or without Pro-EDIT.

```
ProEdit - EDIT DATA FOR TABLE DSN82.TEMPL ————ROW 1 OF 23
 COMMAND ===>                                    SCROLL ===> PAGE
        1(C)       2(V)        3(C)      4(V)        5(C)        6(C)      7(D)
RCMD  EMPNO    FIRST NAME  MIDINIT  LASTNAME    WORKDEPT  PHONENO    HIREDATE
      000220   JENNIFER     W       LUTZ         A10       4551       680829
      000140   HARRY        A       NICHOLLS     A15       4551       761215
 i    000300   PHILIP       D       SMITH        A18       9221       830611
      000260   MARY         V       JOHNSON      A11       4551       750911
      000250   DAVID        D       SMITH        A10       8765       830611
      000240   SALVATORE    S       MARINO       A09       8021       701205
      000323   MARYBETH     S       EMERSON      A10       9221       710728
      000230   JAMES        S       JEFFERSON    A17       4265       661121
      000200   DONALD       S       BROWN        A18       9221       660303
      000190   JAMES        S       WALKER       A29       9221       740726
      000170   MASATOSHI    S       YOSHIMURA    A10       9221       780915
      000160   ELISABETH    R       PIANKA       A12       8999       771011
      000150   HARRY        S       ADAMSON      A15       9221       720212
      000100   THEODORE     S       SPENSER      A11       9221       800619
      000090   EILEEN       W       HENDERSON    A10       4551       700815
      000060   IRVING       S       STERN        A25       9221       730914
      000050   JOHN         S       GEYER        A10       9221       490817
      000030   SALLY        A       KWAN         A14       4551       750405
      000020   JACKIE       S       THOMPSON     A16       9221       731010
      000070   EVA          D       PULASKI      A23       4551       800930
```

Figure 15.10 Inserting a row in the table.

15.9.2 Editing DB2 tables using ISPF commands

As I mentioned earlier, one of the advantages of using Pro-EDIT is your ability to use standard ISPF commands. The system presents each row of a DB2 table as a line in an ISPF edit session. To change table data, you can overkey the information directly on the screen.

Use standard ISPF-like line-editing commands to edit the table—for example, to delete, insert, and copy rows. When you copy rows, Pro-EDIT lets you specify unique values for primary keys so you can maintain entity integrity. Figure 15.10 highlights the procedure to insert a row. Like "standard" ISPF, simply key in the character I where you want to insert the row. The result of this is shown in Figure 15.11, which is a blank line.

When you fill in the data and press Enter, the system will automatically insert another row for you to fill in, so you can enter row after row of information. In this fashion, you can also change multiple rows using ISPF-like block commands. Block commands help you populate and edit test tables. For example, the block command identified by the RR commands in Figure 15.12 will be replicated eight times.

Like ISPF, Pro-EDIT lets you scroll a specified number of rows or pages. You can "anchor" a specified column so when you scroll to the left or right, the column always remains on your screen.

There are times when you need to inspect or edit a subset of a table—for example, to check the effect of application changes or table updates to specific row/column values. The system will allow you to select the columns and rows you want displayed.

You can include or exclude columns, select only rows that meet specified criteria, and change the sequence of the rows that are displayed (sort the table by one or multiple columns). For example, Figure 15.13 shows just a subset of the table in Figure 15.10. In this case, only the employees in department A10 are listed, and the rows are ordered sequentially by employee number.

When you edit a DB2 table, Pro-EDIT initially displays the table in standard for-

```
ProEdit - EDIT DATA FOR TABLE DSN82.TEMPL ———————ROW 1 OF 23
 COMMAND ===>                                 SCROLL ===> PAGE
      1(C)      2(V)       3(C)      4(V)       5(C)      6(C)      7(D)
RCMD  EMPNO   FIRST NAME  MIDINIT  LASTNAME   WORKDEPT  PHONENO   HIREDATE
      000220  JENNIFER    W        LUTZ       A10       4551      680829
      000140  HARRY       A        NICHOLLS   A15       4551      761215
      000300  PHILIP      D        SMITH      A18       9221      830611
'''
      000260  MARY        V        JOHNSON    A11       4551      750911
      000250  DAVID       D        SMITH      A10       8765      830611
      000240  SALVATORE   S        MARINO     A09       8021      701205
      000323  MARYBETH    S        EMERSON    A10       9221      710728
      000230  JAMES       S        JEFFERSON  A17       4265      661121
      000200  DONALD      S        BROWN      A18       9221      660303
      000190  JAMES       S        WALKER     A29       9221      740726
      000170  MASATOSHI   S        YOSHIMURA  A10       9221      780915
      000160  ELISABETH   R        PIANKA     A12       8999      771011
      000150  HARRY       S        ADAMSON    A15       9221      720212
      000100  THEODORE    S        SPENSER    A11       9221      800619
      000090  EILEEN      W        HENDERSON  A10       4551      700815
      000060  IRVING      S        STERN      A25       9221      730914
      000050  JOHN        S        GEYER      A10       9221      490817
      000030  SALLY       A        KWAN       A14       4551      750405
      000020  JACKIE      S        THOMPSON   A16       9221      731010
```

Figure 15.11 Inserting a blank row into the table.

```
ProEdit - EDIT DATA FOR TABLE DSN82.TEMPL -----------ROW 1 OF 23
 COMMAND ===>                                 SCROLL ===> PAGE
      1(C)      2(V)       3(C)      4(V)       5(C)      6(C)      7(D)
RCMD  EMPNO   FIRST NAME  MIDINIT  LASTNAME   WORKDEPT  PHONENO   HIREDATE
      000220  JENNIFER    W        LUTZ       A10       4551      680829
      000140  HARRY       A        NICHOLLS   A15       4551      761215
      000300  PHILIP      D        SMITH      A18       9221      830611
      000260  MARY        V        JOHNSON    A11       4551      750911
      000250  DAVID       D        SMITH      A10       8765      830611
      000240  SALVATORE   S        MARINO     A09       8021      701205
      000323  MARYBETH    S        EMERSON    A10       9221      710728
      000230  JAMES       S        JEFFERSON  A17       4265      661121
      000200  DONALD      S        BROWN      A18       9221      660303
      000190  JAMES       S        WALKER     A29       9221      740726
      000170  MASATOSHI   S        YOSHIMURA  A10       9221      780915
      000160  ELISABETH   R        PIANKA     A12       8999      771011
      000150  HARRY       S        ADAMSON    A15       9221      720212
      000100  THEODORE    S        SPENSER    A11       9221      800619
      000090  EILEEN      W        HENDERSON  A10       4551      700815
      000060  IRVING      S        STERN      A25       9221      730914
      000050  JOHN        S        GEYER      A10       9221      490817
      000030  SALLY       A        KWAN       A14       4551      750405
      000020  JACKIE      S        THOMPSON   A16       9221      731010
      000070  EVA         D        PULASKI    A23       4551      800930
```

Figure 15.12 Inserting a row in the table.

```
ProEdit - EDIT DATA FOR TABLE DSN82.TEMPL ————ROW 1 OF 23
  COMMAND ===>                                      SCROLL ===> PAGE
         1(C)       2(V)        3(C)       4(V)        5(C)       6(C)        7(D)
RCMD  EMPNO    FIRST NAME  MIDINIT  LASTNAME    WORKDEPT  PHONENO   HIREDATE
      000050   JOHN        S        GEYER       A10       9221      490817
      000090   EILEEN      W        HENDERSON   A10       4551      700815
      000170   MASATOSHI   S        YOSHIMURA   A10       9221      780915
      000220   JENNIFER    W        LUTZ        A10       4551      680829
      000323   MARYBETH    S        EMERSON     A10       9221      710728
      000250   DAVID       D        SMITH       A10       8765      830611
          .
          .
          .
          .
          .
```

Figure 15.13 Displaying a subset of a sorted table.

```
ProEdit - EDIT DATA FOR TABLE DSN82.TEMPL ————ROW 1 OF 23
  COMMAND ===>                                      SCROLL ===> PAGE
   RCMD ===>     (Valid Command: R-Replicate, D-Delete, I-Insert, G-Go
   STATUS =>

   1.(C)    EMPNO        :  000220
   2.(V)    FIRSTNAME    :  JENNIFER
   3.(C)    MIDINIT      :  W
   4.(V)    LASTNAME     :  LUTZ
   5.(C)    WORKDEPT     :  C21
   6.(C)    PHONENO      :  4551
   7.(D)    HIREDATE     :  680829
   8.(D)    JOBCODE      :  55
   9.(S)    EDUCLVL      :  ?
  10.(C)    SEX          :  F
  11.(D)    BIRTHDATE    :  480319
  12.(D)    SALARY       :  5000.00
```

Figure 15.14 Displaying a single row.

mat. However, you can request that Pro-EDIT display the table one row at a time to simplify the task of browsing or editing data in a table with many columns. Figure 15.14 shows how Pro-EDIT displays a single row of data.

Use the FIND command to locate data in the table. For example, you can find the first and the last occurrence of a last name or a department code. You can use it with the conventional NEXT and PREV commands. Global changes are accommodated, as well. For example, if you need to change certain values, for example a telephone area code, you can do it via a single command. You can also change values arithmetically. For example, you can add $1,000 to each value in the SALARY column.

The system gives you an ability to commit changes, done via the AUTOCOMMIT command. With this command, you can commit changes whenever you press Enter—which is often the preferred way given a DB2 test environment. Or you can commit changes only when you explicitly save them.

The chart in Figure 15.15 describes how to edit a table with Pro-EDIT, as well as without it.

15.9.3 Dynamic testing of embedded SQL

When you use Pro-EDIT, you can develop your SQL code via the ISPF text editor. Debugging becomes relatively easy because the system allows you to test embedded instructions, including host variables. Thus, you don't have to precompile, compile, and BIND before physically testing your program. To instruct Pro-EDIT to test embedded SQL, identify the beginning and the end of the block to be tested by entering PP, as shown in Figure 15.16.

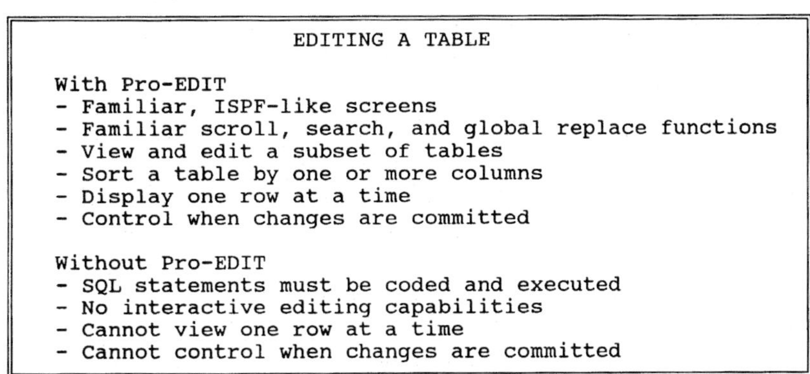

EDITING A TABLE

With Pro-EDIT
- Familiar, ISPF-like screens
- Familiar scroll, search, and global replace functions
- View and edit a subset of tables
- Sort a table by one or more columns
- Display one row at a time
- Control when changes are committed

Without Pro-EDIT
- SQL statements must be coded and executed
- No interactive editing capabilities
- Cannot view one row at a time
- Cannot control when changes are committed

Figure 15.15 Editing a table with or without Pro-EDIT.

```
EDIT ---- DA2BE.DSNSAMP(DSN88C3) - 01.03 ------------------COLUMNS 001 072
COMMAND ===> proedit                                      SCROLL ===> PAGE

001500
001600
001700
001800
001900
001000
001100 **************************************************************
001200 * CURSOR LISTS ALL EMPLOYEE NAMES WITH A PATTERN (%) OR (_)    *
001300 * FOR LAST NAME                                                *
001400 **************************************************************
001500
001600
001700
001800
001900
002000
PP   00         EXEC SQL  DECLARE TELE2 CURSOR FOR
002200                    SELECT *
002300                    FROM DSN82, VPHONE
002400                    WHERE LASTNAME LIKE   :LNAME-WORK
002500                     AND FIRSTNAME LIKE   :FNAME-WORK
PP   00              END EXEC.
002700
002800
002900
```

Figure 15.16 Testing embedded SQL statements.

```
                    TESTING EMBEDDED SQL STATEMENTS

With Pro-EDIT
- Only one step is required - identify the block to be tested
  and issue a command; Pro-EDIT tests the SQL and, if appropriate,
  displays the table
- Host variables are supported
- Switch back and forth between ISPF and Pro-EDIT mode
- DB2 EXPLAIN SQL function is supported
- Subsystem, SQLID, and other parameters can be modified

Without Pro-EDIT
- The following steps are necessary to test SQL:
   1) Strip out the embedded SQL from the source program
   2) Remove all host variable references and replace them with
      constants
   3) Insert the SQL in the file
   4) Process the statements using SPUFI and note any problems
   5) Return to ISPF to make any necessary changes
- No support for host variable
- No interactive editing capabilities
```

Figure 15.17 Testing embedded SQL statements, with or without Pro-EDIT.

When you type PROEDIT on the command line, Pro-EDIT will test all the SQL statements in the block you identify. When you test an SQL SELECT statement, the system will display the resultant table in edit mode so you can browse and edit it using any one of the previously mentioned commands. For example, you can overkey data and insert, delete, and copy rows. When you are finished, Pro-EDIT will return you to your ISPF edit session. The software also supports the DB2 EXPLAIN SQL function that displays the access path and all viable alternate paths based on the host variable values you supply. When testing or explaining embedded SQL, you can display and change the DB2 subsystem, SQLID, and other Pro-EDIT parameters.

The chart in Figure 15.17 describes testing embedded SQL statements with and without Pro-EDIT.

15.10 Miscellaneous Topics

One additional features inherent in this package is the capability to compare "before" and "after" images of DB2 data so you can verify the accuracy of your program after a test run. You can quickly confirm that the changes you intended to make with SQL were actually made. In this manner, you can compare two DB2 tables, two data sets unlocked by the system, or a DB2 table with a data set unloaded by Pro-EDIT.

Pro-EDIT also has a SPUFI emulator with editing capabilities. While you can only browse the output using conventional SPUFI, you can both browse and edit via Pro-EDIT's emulator. This means that, in this environment, you don't need to remove host variables or replace them with constants. Instead, the system will automatically prompt you for a value for each variable.

A second feature of Pro-EDIT allows you to unload table data to a sequential data set and load information from a data set to a DB2 table. This means you don't have to rekey data in a sequential file format or rely on an IBM utility, which is a great deal more cumbersome to work with.

Last, but not least, Pro-EDIT has a ZOOM command to focus on a particular column so you can view all its data on one screen. You'll find this especially helpful when you want to display or edit long VARCHAR columns.

Chapter

16

The CA-Panvalet Library System

16.1 What Is CA-Panvalet?

CA-Panvalet is a library system. Much like CA-Librarian, it allows you to maintain your source programs and the job-control statements related to those source programs. Actually, the terms *library* and *library management system* are not entirely correct. In these systems, a library system is a central storage area in the computer that eliminates your need for independent (secondary) storage facilities.

By using this storage area, you can eliminate accidental or unauthorized alteration of production programs, production JCLs, or data files invoked and used in the production process. CA-Panvalet places your source code into a security-controlled environment; at the same time it restricts access or retrieval to authorized personnel according to a method for controlling code.

Other security measures maintain the integrity of data at various levels. For example, you cannot modify a CA-Panvalet member that has a production status, nor can you change its status back to test. Also, you cannot delete a member from the library with commands available to everyone using the CA-Panvalet system. The reason? Only management can perform a DELETE function, thus requiring a reasonable amount of verification before such an operation can take place.

Safeguards like this use two ISPF commands: MOVE and REPLACE. In a typical ISPF/PDF setting, when you issue a MOVE statement the system physically copies an existing member into a specified area while erasing the member from its original location. This procedure is standard in most systems packages. However, CA-Panvalet does not use this move-and-delete approach when it comes to its own members. Instead, in executing an EDIT/MOVE command, the system copies an external member, resulting in a message that a COPY rather than a MOVE operation was performed.

This procedure, of course, applies only to CA-Panvalet members. If you specify such a move without a member name, the system would assume that your move involves an ISPF/PDF member or sequential data set, and revert back to the standard ISPF/PDF processing mode.

In a conventional ISPF environment, the REPLACE command physically replaces the designated data—whether these are a file, a source program, or job-control statements. When you issue a REPLACE in a CA-Panvalet environment, however, you need to observe an additional restriction. The target CA-Panvalet member must have a status of TEST and ENABLE. If the member you want to replace is not TEST/ENABLE (in production status), CA-Panvalet will not replace it; but it will issue an error message stating that it cannot.

The CA-Panvalet Library is a direct-access data set (DASD), not a partitioned data set. You do not need to reorganize the library because the system automatically reorganizes all unused space. Thus, when a CA-Panvalet Library is full, you need to allocate more space to a directory, or simply to create a bigger library.

16.2 ++INCLUDE and Member Status

Use CA-Panvalet's ++INCLUDE statement to store a source program or whatever else needs storing in the CA-Panvalet library as a separate member. Suppose you have a copybook stored in your production (CA-Panvalet) library. The copybook contains a number of records, and you particularly need to bring an expanded record with all data fields included into your program.

To accomplish this, you need both the copybook and the program requesting that copybook. If your program has a production status, your copybook must also have the same status; otherwise, the expansion process cannot occur.

The term *expansion* refers to the process of supplying CA-Panvalet the name of the copylib member (or subroutine) to be invoked. The system then expands the member into a physical record layout, or a source program, and places it into the driver program that issued the call. A member in test status can include members in either test or production status.

The following uses will work: A protected CA-Panvalet member includes a nonprotected member. (By protected, I simply mean a degree of access security.) A protected CA-Panvalet member includes another protected member, and their access codes are exactly the same.

The following uses will not work: A nonprotected CA-Panvalet member includes a protected member. A protected CA-Panvalet member includes another protected member, but their access codes are different.

When you retrieve a CA-Panvalet member, you can either expand or not expand an included member. The default is no expansion.

CA-Panvalet is available as the original base product, a batch system, and as a newer option—an on-line system. Batch CA-Panvalet is more complicated and cumbersome to work with than the on-line version. For example, to add a member to PanLib (or CA-Panvalet Library), you need to include even the driver program (the one that invokes all other subroutines and file layouts) the very first time around. When you change a particular statement in batch mode, you must tell CA-Panvalet the exact line to be modified (or deleted).

On-line CA-Panvalet is simpler to operate. To add a member to PanLib, simply invoke CA-Panvalet and start entering the source code on a blank screen. To change a particular statement, overlay the particular line in your source code with the revised statement.

Every CA-Panvalet member has three status attributes. Each status attribute can be in one of the following states:

- Production or Test
- Active or Inactive
- Enabled or Disabled

These states reflect that only a member with a status of Test and Enable can be modified. All three of the member's status attributes can be changed, with one exception; the Production/Test attribute cannot be changed from Production to Test (for security reasons). The Active/Inactive attribute can be used freely because it has no special meaning to CA-Panvalet. When a member with a status of Production or Disabled is retrieved for editing and you try to modify its original contents and then save it, the system will notify you that it is not permissible.

16.3 Change Levels and Member Language Format

Programmers tend to work and rework application programs a number of times before the programs perform according to exact specifications. The CA-Panvalet system accommodates this habit by providing (and automatically maintaining) a change-level number for each member. Every time you update a program, for example, the change level is incremented by 1. This number will increase until you have reached level 255, at which point the level number will return to 1. Note that the level number is also the mechanism CA-Panvalet uses to prevent two users from making changes to the same member simultaneously.

When you retrieve a program from CA-Panvalet for editing, the system records the current level of that program. So when you are about to save a member, make sure the program in the library still has that same level number. CA-Panvalet uses a conditional queue to prevent simultaneous updates of a member by multiple on-line users within a single central processor. Note that there is no such restriction when two CPUs are utilized via shared direct-access storage devices. When two users on different CPUs retrieve the same member for editing, the first user to issue a save will be the successful one. The other user will get an INCORRECT LEVEL message when he issues a save.

When you use CA-Panvalet's on-line features, the system will display the last correct level of your program. In batch mode, however, you must specifically state the level number to be worked on.

16.4 How to Display CA-Panvalet Members

Let's consider a simple procedure that involves the display of certain CA-Panvalet members. I invoked the PVEDIT - Entry panel shown in Figure 16.1, and entered a standard CA-Panvalet Library name (NIRXT.TEST.PANLIB), where I keep most of

```
----------------------  PVEDIT - ENTRY PANEL  ---- Pansophic Systems, Inc.
COMMAND ===>
                                                           VERSION - xx.xx
 STANDARD PANVALET LIBRARY:
   PROJECT  ===> nirxt
   GROUP    ===> test      ===>           ===>           ===>
   TYPE     ===> panlib

   MEMBER   ===>                (Blank for MEMBER SELECTION LIST)

 NON STANDARD PANVALET LIBRARY:
   DSNAME   ===>
   VOLSER   ===>                (If NOT Cataloged)

 PANVALET RETRIEVAL OPTIONS:
   CONTROL  ===>                (If necessary)
   ACCESS   ===>                (If necessary)
   EXPAND   ===>                (Y/N)

 PANVALET EDIT PROFILE     ===>
 INITIAL MACRO             ===>

   Press ENTER key to process; Enter END command to terminate.
```

Figure 16.1 The PVEDIT Entry Panel.

```
---------------------  PVEDIT - MSL CRITERIA   --- Pansophic Systems, Inc.
COMMAND ===>

  LIB1: PAYROLL.WORK.PANLIB
  LIB2: PAYROLL.TEST.PANLIB
  LIB3: PAYROLL.QUALITY.PANLIB
  LIB4: PAYROLL.PROD.PANLIB

  Please choose one or more of the following for the MEMBER SELECTION LIST:

  List members starting with     ===> AR
  List members with LANG TYPE    ===>
  List members with USER CODE    ===>
  List members with STATUS       ===>

  Display with COMMENT Data      ===> N  (Y/N)

  MSL DISPLAY OPTIONS:           ===> A  A - STANDARD MSL
                                         B - USER-ID of Last Update
                                         C - Last UPDATE, Current LOCK Info.

  CONTROL (if not already entered) ===>

  Press ENTER key to process; Enter END command to terminate.
```

Figure 16.2 The PVEDIT MSL Criteria Panel in use.

my source programs for display and maintenance. Then I pressed the Enter key and displayed the PVEDIT - MSL Criteria Panel, shown in Figure 16.2.

The only criterion I defined to CA-Panvalet on this panel was to list every member with an AR prefix. In practice, you can also enhance your selection with additional criteria: selecting members that are written in COBOL, those that are active or inactive, and so on.

Once I defined the criterion to CA-Panvalet, a third screen, shown in Figure 16.3, was displayed. Note that, like in ISPF, you can use PF7 and PF8 to scroll up or down on this panel.

You can select any members on this panel by positioning the cursor next to it and entering S for selection, then pressing the Enter key. There is nothing revolutionary, compared to the way things are handled in ISPF. The name or member name represents a source program or another data file, and is made up of at least 1 and up to 10 alphanumeric (national) characters. LIB, or library, denotes an area from where the member was retrieved.

LVL is a level indicator denoting the number of times you have revised and updated your program. This process, of course, requires you to submit a job to CA-Panvalet after implementing all the necessary changes, thereby incrementing the level indicator. This indicator represents a range of 1 through 255, and is automatically manipulated by CA-Panvalet. For example, the number 3 simply represents the third version of the member in discussion. User, or user code, means access protection if it contains a blank character.

A member entered in the library can be written in a specific language if it is a source program. If you do not specify a format, the member will be described as UNSPECIFIED. You can change the format type through the FORMAT command. A CA-Panvalet option enables you to format the statements of CA-Panvalet members. Suppose the member is described as a source language (COBOL, PL/I, BAL, etc.), but you don't specify the NOFORMAT parameter when you supply the information to CA-Panvalet. The sequence and identification fields will be removed from each statement before it is stored in the library, and new sequence numbers and identification fields will be generated whenever the member is subsequently retrieved.

```
------------------  PVEDIT - MEMBER SELECTION LIST  - Pansophic Systems, Inc.
COMMAND ===>                                                   SCROLL ===> PAGE
  LIB 1: NIRXT.TEST.PANLIB                                  150 SCAN HITS V 14.0
  RE-ENTER THE PANVALET RETRIEVAL OPTIONS? ===> N
--------------------------------------------------------------------------------
  NAME          LIB LVL   USER F LANG  STAT LAST     LAST       BLKS  STATMTS ACT AVG
                               M TYPE       MAINT    ACCESS
  ARA21C              3      0   COBOL TAE           02/28/91      5      619      22
  ARA21MB             1      0   DATA  TAE  02/19/91 02/27/91      2       76      53
  ARA21MC             1      0   DATA  TAE           02/27/91      2      151      27
  ARA22C              3      0   COBOL TAE           03/13/91      3      338      24
  ARA22MB             1      0   DATA  TAE  02/15/91 02/27/91      1       59      56
  ARA22MC             1      0   DATA  TAE           02/27/91      1      123      28
  ARA23MB             1      0   DATA  TAE  02/15/91 02/27/91      5      265      61
  ARA23MC             1      0   DATA  TAE           02/27/91      7      816      27
  ARA41C              1      0   COBOL TAE  03/04/91 05/09/91      5      647      23
  ARA41MB             1      0   DATA  TAE  02/19/91 02/27/91      2       99      49
  ARA41MC             1      0   DATA  TAE  02/27/91 05/09/91      1      116      27
  ARA42C              1      0   COBOL TAE           03/13/91      2      248      19
  ARA42MB             1      0   DATA  TAE  02/19/91 02/27/91      1       60      56
  ARA42MC             1      0   DATA  TAE           02/27/91      1      116      27
  ARA43C              4      0   COBOL TAE           09/17/91      7      801      28
  ARA43MB             1      0   DATA  TAE  02/19/91 02/27/91      5      268      61
  ARA43MC             1      0   DATA  TAE           02/27/91      7      823      27
```

Figure 16.3 Member Selection Panel showing relevant statistics.

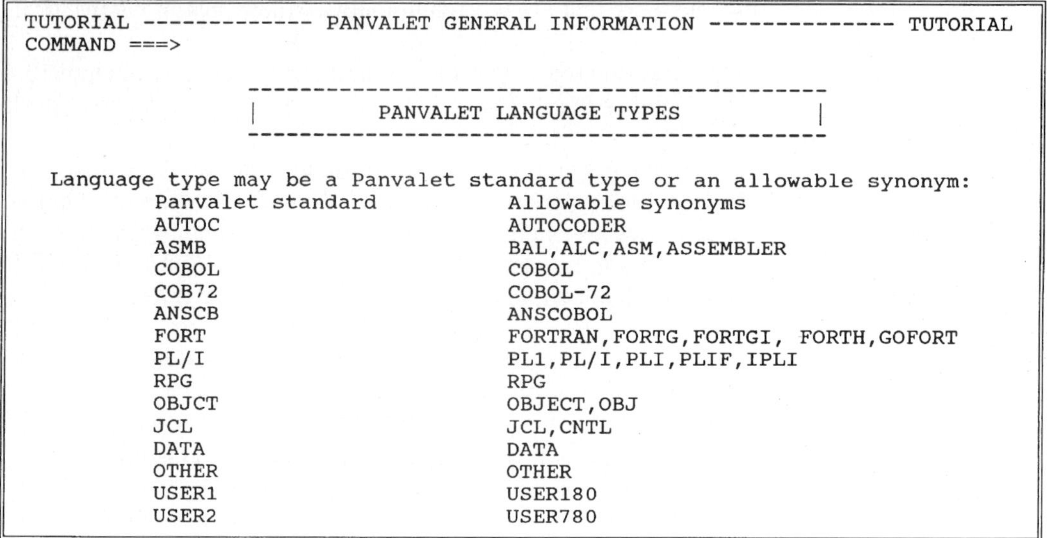

```
TUTORIAL ------------- PANVALET GENERAL INFORMATION -------------- TUTORIAL
COMMAND ===>

                 -------------------------------------------
                 |          PANVALET LANGUAGE TYPES         |
                 -------------------------------------------

  Language type may be a Panvalet standard type or an allowable synonym:
          Panvalet standard            Allowable synonyms
          AUTOC                        AUTOCODER
          ASMB                         BAL,ALC,ASM,ASSEMBLER
          COBOL                        COBOL
          COB72                        COBOL-72
          ANSCB                        ANSCOBOL
          FORT                         FORTRAN,FORTG,FORTGI, FORTH,GOFORT
          PL/I                         PL1,PL/I,PLI,PLIF,IPLI
          RPG                          RPG
          OBJCT                        OBJECT,OBJ
          JCL                          JCL,CNTL
          DATA                         DATA
          OTHER                        OTHER
          USER1                        USER180
          USER2                        USER780
```

Figure 16.4 Panvalet General Information screen.

Language type refers to the type of language a particular member is written in. Note, for example, that in Figure 16.3 the term DATA refers to a map; it could also refer to a file, such as a set of JCL statements. For a more comprehensive language, type LIST (see Figure 16.4).

The second column could have a value of A for Active, or I for Inactive. The third column could be an E for Enable, or a D for Disable.

Production and Test describe the current status of the member. The member is Production if it represents a program or file that is being actively used in your firm's data-processing operations and cannot, therefore, be modified. A member in Test represents a program or file being used for testing, which can be updated. You can use a COPY command to create a duplicate of any library member; a copied member is automatically placed in Test status.

Enable and Disable describe the activity of the member. For example, when a member is to be removed from the library because it is obsolete, it is placed in Disable status.

Active and Inactive describe how frequently you expect to reference the member. The member is Active if you reference it normally or with greater frequency. You can remove the member to a backup or low-usage file if you need more space in the library.

When the member is initially entered into the library, it is assigned a status of Test, Enable, and Active. You can use the status command of PAN#1 to alter the status (use or activity) of a member.

The two columns that follow the status bytes refer to the date when a particular member was updated and the date it was last accessed by the user. Blocks tells you the physical size of the member and the amount of storage it occupies in the library. This information is further refined by the statement (STATMTS) column, which highlights the number of statements composing such a program (or other data).

Action simply describes the last action that was performed on the member, and Average denotes the number of average bytes stored in each statement.

You have the option of assigning a security level to selected members via the USER command in PAN#1. (You can also assign it in CA-Panvalet ISPF.) Zero is the default value for all library members and implies that no special actions are necessary to protect the contents of the individual member. Specifying a value of 1, 2, or 3 as a member's security level will result in various security-controlled environments.

To access a security member, you must submit an ACCESS command with an appropriate code for that member in a PAN#1 run. A member's security level determines a number of factors (the member's security code, installation code, and library security codes); these are used to develop the appropriate code specified in the ACCESS command. Briefly, this parameter tells you what you can and cannot look at—what you can or cannot modify on the library.

Recall that you can select any member from your criteria panel (if you use the right access code) by placing an S (select flag) next to the member name. Once you have pressed the Enter key, the member is displayed; if you are in edit mode, you can begin to modify it. An overview of this is shown in Figure 16.5. Note that the change level is 1 at this point. By the time you complete all your modifications, the LVL will have increased to 2. Also note that above the level number, the current date is automatically assigned to a level, which is 02/13/91. (The example shown in Figure 16.6 represents the first page of an on-line CICS program.)

16.5 The CA-Panvalet Cycle

You can directly enter a source program into on-line CA-Panvalet. But this exercise will show you, a step at a time, how to add such a program to PanLib from a previous

```
PVEDIT - NIRXT.TEST.PANLIB(ARA42C) ---------------------- COLUMNS 007 072
COMMAND ===>                                              SCROLL ===> PAGE
****** ******************** TOP OF DATA *********************************
       *   THE FOLLOWING IS THE COBOL SAMPLE PROGRAM  'TESTRUN' *** 02/13/91
        IDENTIFICATION DIVISION.                                  COBSAMP
        PROGRAM-ID.  TESTRUN.                                       LV001
          DATE-COMPILED.
          REMARKS. THIS PROGRAM HAS BEEN WRITTEN AS A SAMPLE PROGRAM FOR
            COBOL USERS. IT CREATES AN OUTPUT FILE AND READS IT BACK AS
            INPUT.
        ENVIRONMENT DIVISION.
        CONFIGURATION SECTION.
          SOURCE-COMPUTER. IBM-370.
          OBJECT-COMPUTER. IBM-370.
        INPUT-OUTPUT SECTION.
        FILE-CONTROL.
            SELECT FILE-1 ASSIGN TO UT-2400-S-SAMPLE.
            SELECT FILE-2 ASSIGN TO UT-2400-S-SAMPLE.
        DATA DIVISION.
        FILE SECTION.
        FD  FILE-1
            LABEL RECORDS ARE OMITTED
            BLOCK CONTAINS 100 CHARACTERS
            RECORD CONTAINS 20 CHARACTERS
```

Figure 16.5 A sample screen highlighting a COBOL program for maintenance.

```
---------------------------  PANVALET PRIMARY MENU  ------ MEMBER PGMADD SAVED
OPTION ===> 2
                                                           VERSION - 14.0A

     +----------------------------------------------------------------------+
     |                                                                      |
     |  1  BROWSE     - Display PANVALET Members                            |
     |                                                                      |
     |  2  EDIT       - Modify/Create PANVALET Members                      |
     |                                                                      |
     |  3  UTILITY    - PANVALET Utilities (COPY, RENAME, STATUS, etc.)     |
     |                                                                      |
     |  4  WHAT'S NEW - In PANVALET                                         |
     |                                                                      |
     +----------------------------------------------------------------------+




     Use END key (PF3) to back out of PANVALET mode.
```

Figure 16.6 The CA-Panvalet Primary Menu.

```
---------------------------  PVEDIT - ENTRY PANEL  ---- Pansophic Systems, Inc.
COMMAND ===>
                                                           VERSION - 14.0A
 STANDARD PANVALET LIBRARY:
   PROJECT  ===> NIRXT
   GROUP    ===> TEST     ===>          ===>          ===>
   TYPE     ===> PANLIB

   MEMBER   ===> pgmadd            (Blank for MEMBER SELECTION LIST)

 NON STANDARD PANVALET LIBRARY:
   DSNAME   ===>
   VOLSER   ===>                   (If NOT Cataloged)

 PANVALET RETRIEVAL OPTIONS:
   CONTROL  ===>                   (If necessary)
   ACCESS   ===>                   (If necessary)
   EXPAND   ===> N                 (Y/N)

 PANVALET EDIT PROFILE ===>
 INITIAL MACRO         ===>

   Press ENTER key to process; Enter END command to terminate.
```

Figure 16.7 The CA-Panvalet Edit Entry Panel.

library like the one available in ISPF. Note that the ISPF member will be renamed during the transfer process from ARC92C to PGMADD. The first panel, shown in Figure 16.6, is the CA-Panvalet Primary Menu. I selected option 2 (Modify/Create CA-Panvalet Members) on this panel to invoke the PVEDIT - Entry panel for specifying the name of the member to be added to the NIRXT.TEST.PANLIB. This panel is shown in Figure 16.7.

PGMADD, a new program added to the library, is a copy of existing programs from ISPF (NIRAV.STANDARD.CNTL). Once you press the Enter key, you invoke a PVEDIT Add Panel (see Figure 16.8); this will retain the previously displayed CA-

Panvalet Library (NIRXT.TEST.PANLIB) and the name of the new program to be added to CA-Panvalet (PGMADD). In addition, you are required to enter a language type (e.g., ANSCB, meaning ANS COBOL). Press Enter again when the language type is filled in. This will invoke the next panel in the series, shown in Figure 16.9. This screen is blank because you need to perform a COPY operation (copying an existing program such as ARC92C into PANLIB under a different name, such as PGMADD). I have entered the keyword COPY next to the COMMAND ===>.

Press Enter to invoke the next frame, an Edit Copy Panel (see Figure 16.10),

```
------------------------  PVEDIT(ADD) - MEMBER OPTIONS  NEW MBR, NEED LANG TYPE
COMMAND ===>

 STANDARD PANVALET LIBRARY:
   PROJECT         : NIRXT
   GROUP           : TEST
   TYPE            : PANLIB

   MEMBER          : PGMADD

 NON STANDARD PANVALET LIBRARY:
   DSNAME          :
   VOLSER          :           (If NOT Cataloged)

 NEW MEMBER OPTIONS:
   LANG TYPE   ===> anscb      (Required)
   USER CODE   ===>            (Optional)
   PAN/TSO     ===> PAN        (Sequencing)
   NOFORMAT    ===> N          (Y/N)


   Press ENTER key to process; Enter END command to terminate.
```

Figure 16.8 PVEDIT ADD Member Option Panel.

```
PVEDIT --- NIRXT.TEST.PANLIB(PGMADD)------------------ WARNING - PROD/DISABLED
COMMAND ===> COPY                                           SCROLL ===> CSR
****** ***************************** TOP OF DATA *****************************
''''''
''''''
''''''
''''''
''''''
''''''
''''''
''''''
''''''
''''''
''''''
''''''
''''''
''''''
''''''
''''''
''''''
''''''
''''''
''''''
''''''
```

Figure 16.9 A blank panel used to copy a source code.

```
----------------------------  EDIT - COPY  --------------------------------
COMMAND ===>
"CURRENT" DATA SET: NIRXT.TEST.PANLIB

FROM ISPF LIBRARY:
   PROJECT ===> NIRAV
   GROUP   ===> STANDARD  ===>           ===>           ===>
   TYPE    ===> CNTL
   MEMBER  ===> ARC92C           (Blank or pattern for member selection list)

FROM OTHER PARTITIONED OR SEQUENTIAL DATA SET:
   DATA SET NAME  ===>
   VOLUME SERIAL  ===>           (If not cataloged)

DATA SET PASSWORD ===>           (If password protected)

LINE NUMBERS                     (Blank for entire member or seq. data set)
   FIRST LINE     ===>
   LAST LINE      ===>
   NUMBER TYPE    ===>           (STANDARD, COBOL, or RELATIVE)

Press ENTER key to copy.
Enter END command to cancel copy.
```

Figure 16.10 The EDIT/COPY Panel to define the source library.

```
PVEDIT --- NIRXT.TEST.PANLIB(PGMADD)-------------------- MEMBER ARC92C COPIED
COMMAND ===>                                                  SCROLL ===> CSR
****** ***************************** TOP OF DATA ******************************
==MSG> -CAUTION- PROFILE CHANGED TO "NUMBER OFF" (FROM "NUMBER ON COB").
==MSG>        DATA DOES NOT HAVE VALID COBOL NUMBERS.
000001        IDENTIFICATION DIVISION.
000002        PROGRAM-ID. ARC92C.
000003        DATE-COMPILED.
000004        ENVIRONMENT DIVISION.
000005        DATA DIVISION.
000006        WORKING-STORAGE SECTION.
000007        01  CONN-AREA.
000008            02  SEND-REC-FLAG  PIC X(01).
000009            02  CUST-COMPARE   PIC X(04).
000010        01  CUSTOMER-MASTER. COPY RK501.
000011        01  STORE-CUSTNO       PIC X(05).
000012        COPY DFHBMSCA.
000013        COPY DFHAID.
000014        COPY ATTRBYTE.
000015        COPY ARC92M.
000016        LINKAGE SECTION.
000017        01  DFHCOMMAREA        PIC X(05).
000018        PROCEDURE DIVISION.
000019        001-START-PROCESSING.
```

Figure 16.11 The original ARC92C program invoked and brought into a PANLIB from an ISPF library.

showing the following prerequisites: The name of the library, the original source code, and the name of the original program, ARC92C, now renamed on the CA-Panvalet Library.

Once you press the Enter key, the system displays ARC92C, shown in Figure 16.11, under PGMADD as a new PANLIB member (the original ARC92C program invoked and brought into a PANLIB from an ISPF library). Notice that COPY statements need to be replaced with ++INCLUDEs because CA-Panvalet does not use COPY statements (in lines 101, 120, 130, 140, and 150). Figure 16.12 shows COPY statements replaced by ++INCLUDE statements required by CA-Panvalet.

To render the new program PGMADD operational, you must make sure that all members referenced through the ++INCLUDE statements (a standard procedure with COPY statements, as well) were previously loaded into PANLIB. You cannot include, reference, or expand a record layout or a map that simply is not there.

16.6 How to Delete a PAN Member from a Test

Let's examine the first delete situation from PANLIB involving the previously added PGMADD member. Note that in production mode, the procedures are identical except for the security code, allowing such a deletion. Also note that, when deleting in CA Panvalet, the system will only flag the member for deletion. The member will physically remain on file, typically until the end of the day when the system is brought down for scheduled maintenance.

In Figure 16.13, a previously shown CA-Panvalet Primary Menu is displayed (this time, however, using the utility code 3). Once you have pressed the Enter key, the

```
PVEDIT --- NIRXT.TEST.PANLIB(PGMADD)-------------------------- COLUMNS 007 078
COMMAND ===>                                                  SCROLL ===> CSR
****** ***************************** TOP OF DATA ******************************
=NOTE= CAUTION:  PROFILE CHANGED TO "NUMBER ON COB" FROM "NUMBER OFF"
=NOTE=           BECAUSE OF SEQUENCE NUMBERS OR LACK OF THEM FOUND IN DATA.
000010  IDENTIFICATION DIVION.                                        01/10/92
000020  PROGRAM-ID. ARC92C.                                             PGMADD
000030  DATE-COMPILED.                                                    LV01
000040  ENVIRONMENT DIVISION.
000050  DATA DIVISION.
000060  WORKING-STORAGE SECTION.
000070  01   COMM-AREA.
000080       02   SEND-REC-FLAG    PIC X(01).
000090       02   CUST-COMPARE     PIC X(04).
000100  01   CUSTOMER-MASTER.
000101  ++INCLUDE RK501
000110  01   STORE-CUSTNO          PIC X(05).
000120  ++INCLUDE DFHBMSCA
000130  ++INCLUDE DFHAID
000140  ++INCLUDE ATTRBYTE
000150  ++INCLUDE ARC92M
000160  LINKAGE SECTION.
000170  01   DFHCOMMAREA           PIC X(05).
000180  PROCEDURE DIVISION.
```

Figure 16.12 COPY statements replaced by the ++INCLUDE statements required by CA-Panvalet.

```
----------------------- PANVALET PRIMARY MENU --- Pansophic Systems, Inc.
OPTION ===> 3

                                                        VERSION - xx.xx


       1  BROWSE      - Display PANVALET Members
       2  EDIT        - Modify/Create PANVALET Members
       3  UTILITY     - PANVALET Utilities (COPY, RENAME, STATUS, etc.)
       4  CHANGES     - WHAT'S NEW - In PANVALET


    Enter END command to terminate PANVALET.
```

Figure 16.13 Panvalet Primary Menu for selecting the utility function.

```
---------------------  UTILITY SELECTION MENU  --- Pansophic Systems, Inc.
OPTION ===> 3
                                                        VERSION - xx.xx
            1 - PANVALET MEMBER ATTRIBUTE CHANGES
                . Add/Change USER CODE
                . Change LEVEL Number
                . Add/Change COMMENT
                . Change STATUS

            2 - PANVALET MEMBER MANIPULATION
                . COPY a member
                . RENAME a member
                . PRINT a member  (in ISPF LIST data set)

            3 - PANVALET MEMBER LANGUAGE CHANGE

            4 - PANVALET MEMBER LIBRARY-TO-LIBRARY COPY

            5 - PANVALET MEMBER LOCK/UNLOCK Utility

            Enter END command to terminate.
```

Figure 16.14 The Utility Selection Menu.

```
---------------------------  CHANGES - ENTRY PANEL  --- Pansophic Systems, Inc.
FUNCTION ===> S
                                                          VERSION - 14.0A
 S - Modify the STATUS of a member          L - Modify the LEVEL of a member
 U - Add/Change a USER code                 C - Modify/Add a COMMENT to a member
                                        BLANK - Display MEMBER SELECTION LIST
 STANDARD PANVALET LIBRARY:
   PROJECT   ===> NIRXT
   GROUP     ===> TEST                      CONTROL ===>
   TYPE      ===> PANLIB                    ACCESS  ===>

   MEMBER    ===> PGMADD

 NON-STANDARD PANVALET LIBRARY:
   DSNAME    ===>
   VOLSER    ===>                   (If NOT Cataloged)

 ENTER MODIFICATION DATA BELOW:
   STATUS    ===> D                 LEVEL NUMBER   ===>
   USER CODE ===>                   SECURITY LEVEL ===>
   COMMENT   ===>

   Press ENTER key to process; Enter END command to terminate.
```

Figure 16.15 Changes in the Entry Panel.

Utility Selection Menu (shown in Figure 16.14) will appear for further specifications. At this point, I selected option 1 to disable PGMADD. This took me to the next frame, Changes-Entry Panel, presented in Figure 16.15.

You must supply four elements on this panel. First, you need to tell CA-Panvalet that the function of this operation is to modify the status (S) of one of its members. Second, identify the library where the status change is to take place (NIRXT.TEST.PANLIB). Third, identify to the system the particular member to be deleted (PGMADD). Last, identify the status of the operation (listed under ENTER MODIFICATION DATA BELOW), which is a D (for disable).

Once you press Enter, a response will appear in the upper left-hand corner of the same panel with the text PGM STAT CHANGED, meaning the operation was successful.

Become familiar with these two additional panels. The first one, which you are already familiar with, is the Criteria Panel, displayed in Figure 16.16. To return to this panel, simple press PF3 repeatedly.

Now, instead of entering a generic name or a prefix, such as AR, I have entered the full member name, PGMADD, to be disabled. Figure 16.17 shows the last character

```
---------------------------  PVEDIT - MSL CRITERIA  --- Pansophic Systems, Inc.
COMMAND ===>

   Please choose one or more of the following for the MEMBER SELECTION LIST:



          List members starting with       ===> PGMADD
          List members with LANG TYPE      ===>
          List members with USER CODE      ===>
          List members with STATUS         ===>

          Display with COMMENT Data        ===> N (Y/N)

          CONTROL (If not already entered) ===>




   Press ENTER key to process; Enter END command to terminate.
```

Figure 16.16 The CA-Panvalet Criteria Panel.

```
--------------------  PVEDIT - MEMBER SELECTION LIST  - Pansophic Systems, Inc.
COMMAND ===>                                                  SCROLL ===> PAGE
  LIB 1: NIRXT.TEST.PANLIB                                   1 SCAN HITS V 14.0
  RE-ENTER THE PANVALET RETRIEVAL OPTIONS? ===> N
-------------------------------------------------------------------------------
  NAME        LIB LVL  USER F LANG STAT LAST      LAST       BLKS  STATMTS ACT AVG
                            M TYPE      MAINT     ACCESS
  PGMADD            1     0   ANSCB TAD           01/10/92      4      374 STA  27
---------------------------- END OF MEMBER LIST -------------------------------
```

Figure 16.17 The last character of the STAT column changed to a D (TAD), meaning disabled. The previous setting of the status attribute showed TAE.

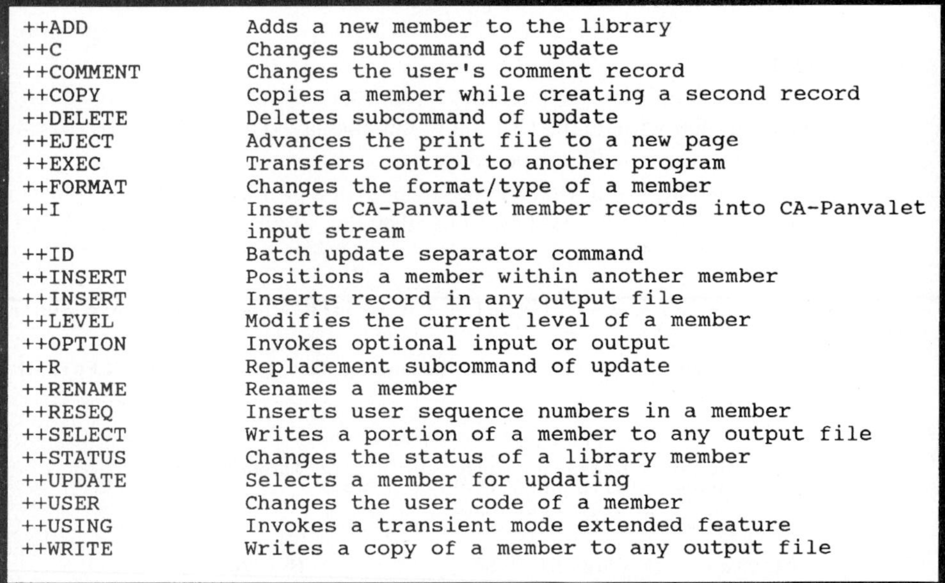

++ADD	Adds a new member to the library
++C	Changes subcommand of update
++COMMENT	Changes the user's comment record
++COPY	Copies a member while creating a second record
++DELETE	Deletes subcommand of update
++EJECT	Advances the print file to a new page
++EXEC	Transfers control to another program
++FORMAT	Changes the format/type of a member
++I	Inserts CA-Panvalet member records into CA-Panvalet input stream
++ID	Batch update separator command
++INSERT	Positions a member within another member
++INSERT	Inserts record in any output file
++LEVEL	Modifies the current level of a member
++OPTION	Invokes optional input or output
++R	Replacement subcommand of update
++RENAME	Renames a member
++RESEQ	Inserts user sequence numbers in a member
++SELECT	Writes a portion of a member to any output file
++STATUS	Changes the status of a library member
++UPDATE	Selects a member for updating
++USER	Changes the user code of a member
++USING	Invokes a transient mode extended feature
++WRITE	Writes a copy of a member to any output file

Figure 16.18 CA-Panvalet Commands for batch processing.

of the STAT column, which was changed to a D (TAD) meaning disabled. The previous setting of the status attribute showed TAE.

16.7 PAN Library Statements

Figure 16.18 provides you with a chart including all the relevant commands. These commands are primarily batch statements. While this chapter emphasizes the on-line aspect of CA-Panvalet, I need to explain the batch portion of the system (which I consider to be obsolete). To add a member to the CA-Panvalet Library, issue a command like the following:

```
++ADD AR112AC,COBOL
```

where AR112AC represents the name of the source program to be added to the PANLIB, and COBOL refers to the source language of the application. Once the program is entered (following the ++ADD), which assumes level 1 at this point, you can enter the full source code followed by a ++WRITE WORK AR112AC. Afterwards, submit the job through a set of specified JCLs to compile the program, and place it in CA-Panvalet when the compile is clean.

Adding a member to PANLIB in on-line mode requires that you simply enter your source code and then save it by pressing PF3, just like in ISPF. (For more on this, refer back to section 16.5). The JCL you need to submit such a job is shown in Figure 16.19.

When you want to change an existing program in batch mode, use the following first set of statements:

```
++UPDATE AR112AC,1
++112,129
>>>>>>put your source statement here<<<<<<
++WRITE WORK,AR112AC
```

and this second set of statements:

```
++UPDATE AR112AC,1
++D 200,205
++D 300
++WRITE WORK,AR112AC
```

In the first set of statements, I changed 18 statements, from line 112 all the way through line 129. The new source statements will then be inserted in the following lines. At the end, I issued a ++WRITE statement and submitted the latest changes to the system.

In the second set of statements (still in batch mode), I deleted lines 200 through 205, and a single line, line 300. The following is the third set of statements:

```
++UPDATE AR112AC,10
++C 0
>>>>>>>put your source statement here<<<<<<
++C 42,(8,WORKING-STORAGE)
>>>>>>>put your source statement here<<<<<<
++R 70,80,/FILE1/FILE2/
```

In this set of statements, I want to update the member AR112AC at level 10. The first C (++C 0) indicates that the following source statements are to be placed at the be-

```
//NIRAVFAR JOB (9000,APRB),'PAN COMPILE     ',CLASS=A,MSGCLASS=L,        *
//*         TYPRUN=SCAN,                                                  *
//          REGION=4M,NOTIFY=NIRAV
//*
/*JOBPARM   PROCLIB=PROC01
//*
//***********************************************************************
//*         JCL  = NIRJM.LIB.CNTL(PANCOBOL)                              *
//*         PROC = NIRXT.TEST.PROCLIB(JMCOBCMP)                          *
//*
//DPCOBCMP EXEC JMCOBCMP,PRGNAME=ARC21C
//*
//S020.PANDD1 DD DSN=NIRXT.TEST.PANLIB,DISP=SHR
//S020.SYSIN DD *
++WRITE WORK,ARC21C
//*
//S060.SYSLMOD  DD  DSN=NIRXT.TEST.LOADLIB(ARC21C),DISP=SHR
//*
```

Figure 16.19 JCLs to submit a CA-Panvalet job.

```
--------------------- UTILITY SELECTION MENU  --- Pansophic Systems, Inc.
 OPTION ===>
                                                         VERSION - xx.xx
          1 - PANVALET MEMBER ATTRIBUTE CHANGES
              . Add/Change USER CODE
              . Change LEVEL Number
              . Add/Change COMMENT
              . Change STATUS

          2 - PANVALET MEMBER MANIPULATION
              . COPY a member
              . RENAME a member
              . PRINT a member  (in ISPF LIST data set)

          3 - PANVALET MEMBER LANGUAGE CHANGE

          4 - PANVALET MEMBER LIBRARY-TO-LIBRARY COPY

          5 - PANVALET MEMBER LOCK/UNLOCK Utility

          Enter END command to terminate.
```

Figure 16.20 Utility Selection Panel for performing a RENAME command online.

ginning of the member. The second C represents a columnar update, which places the characters WORKING-STORAGE in column 8 of statement sequence number 42. The following source statements are inserted into the program after line 42. The ++R is a replacement update that scans for all occurrences of FILE1 in statements 70 through 80. All occurrences are replaced with FILE2.

16.8 Batch and On-Line Idiosyncrasies

To describe the CA-Panvalet Cycle (Section 16.5), I used the CA-Panvalet Utility Panel presented earlier.

The CA-Panvalet Utility Panel illustrates how functions in batch that you had to request via a CA-Panvalet command can now be requested on-line through the CA-Panvalet Utility Selection Menu (shown in Figure 6.20). For example, instead of issuing a ++COPY or ++RENAME command, you can request task 2 (CA-Panvalet Member Manipulation section) to achieve the same results. Actually, once you have selected task 2 on the Utility Menu, the system will prompt an additional screen for further specification. This prompted panel is highlighted in Figure 16.21.

I used the Manipulate-Entry Panel to rename an existing member from ABC to DEF. I placed the character R (for Rename) in the upper left-hand corner of the screen. When the operation is successfully performed on-line, a message ABC RENAMED will be displayed, resulting in data set ABC being deleted from the directory through a new replacement.

I'm now going to present to you with a number of problems and solutions using both batch and on-line environments. Note that, after these changes, a specific job needs to be submitted to MVS. However, jobs to submit CA-Panvalet changes vary from organization to organization.

16.8.1 Problem 1

Add two programs to CA-Panvalet. Both programs use the COBOL format. Also, list the source input and do sequence checking on the relevant columns, giving the member (ARC110C) a user code of 120. The second program to be added also lists the member, but it does not do any sequence checking.

The batch solution is as follows:

```
++ADD ARC110C,COBOL,SEQ,120
      IDENTIFICATION DIVISION.
      PROGRAM-ID. 'ARC110C'.
      ++INCLUDE ROUTN1
             |
             |
             |
      STOP RUN.
++ADD ROUTN1,COBOL,LIST
      ENVIRONMENT DIVISION.
             |
             |
             |
      INPUT-OUTPUT SECTION.
/*
```

The on-line solution is to invoke the CA-Panvalet Edit Panel, enter each program (or copy it into the CA-Panvalet Library), and either issue a SAVE command or press PF3, which will automatically save both members (a standard ISPF procedure).

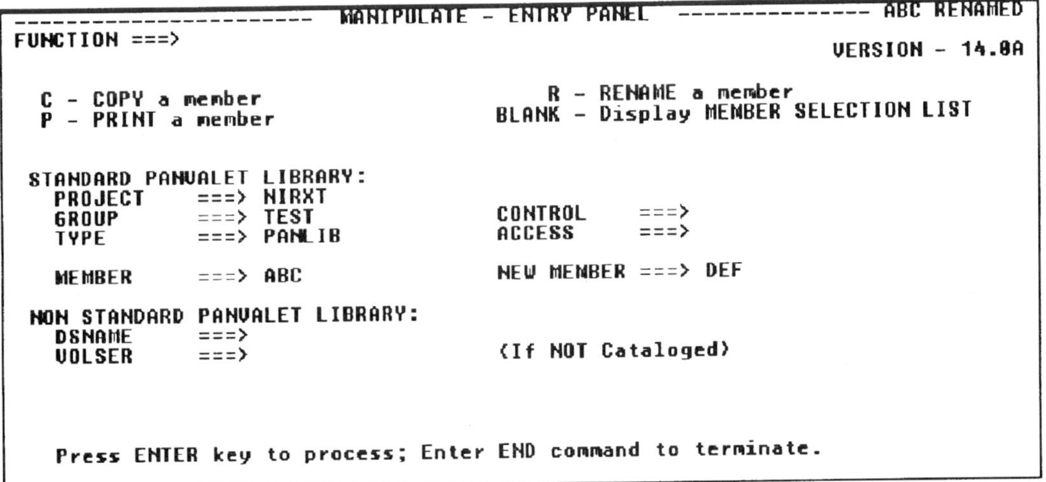

Figure 16.21 CA-Panvalet Edit Panel required to define the member (and level) to be modified.

16.8.2 Problem 2

Change the program in Problem 1 at level 15 by deleting line 90 and line 120, and replacing them with the following two statements:

```
01  COMPARE-FIELDS    PIC  X(02) VALUE SPACES.
01  LINE-COUNTR       PIC  9(05) VALUE ZEROS.
```

The batch solution is as follows:

```
++UPDATE ARC999C,15
++C 90,90
++C 120,120
      01  COMPARE-FIELDS    PIC  X(02) VALUE SPACES.
      01  LINE-COUNTR       PIC  9(05) VALUE ZEROS.
```

The on-line solution is to invoke the CA-Panvalet Edit Panel (shown in Figure 16.22) and enter the name of the program to be changed (ARC999C). Note that the library was already retained by the system from a prior entry (NIRXT.TEST.PANLIB).

When you press the Enter key in the panel containing the information, a second panel will display program ARC999C to be changed. In the upper right-hand area of the screen, note the level number (15), representing the most recent version, which is the one the system automatically triggers and increments. This panel is displayed in Figure 16.23, and is part of the current source listing prior to modification. Modification of a source program can be directly incorporated into the body of a program (in update mode) rather than with line the reference statements that characterize a typical batch environment. Note that such a revised source listing is shown in Figure 16.24.

```
---------------------------  PVEDIT - ENTRY PANEL  ---- Pansophic Systems, Inc.
COMMAND ===>
                                                            VERSION - 14.0A
 STANDARD PANVALET LIBRARY:
   PROJECT   ===> NIRXT
   GROUP     ===> TEST        ===>          ===>          ===>
   TYPE      ===> PANLIB

   MEMBER    ===> ARC999C          (Blank for MEMBER SELECTION LIST)

 NON STANDARD PANVALET LIBRARY:
   DSNAME    ===>
   VOLSER    ===>                  (If NOT Cataloged)

 PANVALET RETRIEVAL OPTIONS:
   CONTROL   ===>                  (If necessary)
   ACCESS    ===>                  (If necessary)
   EXPAND    ===> N                (Y/N)

 PANVALET EDIT PROFILE ===>
 INITIAL MACRO         ===>

   Press ENTER key to process; Enter END command to terminate.
```

Figure 16.22 Source listing prior to modification.

```
PVEDIT --- NIRXT.TEST.PANLIB(ARC999C)------------------------ COLUMNS 007 078
COMMAND ===>                                                   SCROLL ===> CSR
****** ***************************** TOP OF DATA ******************************
000010  IDENTIFICATION DIVISION.                                          05/14/91
000020  PROGRAM-ID.    ARC999C.                                           ARC999C
000030  DATE-COMPILED. MAY 29 1992.                                         LV015
000040  ENVIRONMENT DIVISION.
000050  DATA DIVISION.
000060
000070  WORKING-STORAGE SECTION.
000080  01   PGM-MSG.
000090       03   FILLER                PIC X(11) VALUE 'SELECTION   '.
000100       03   PGM-SEL               PIC X.
000110       03   FILLER                PIC X(15) VALUE '  NOT AVAILABLE'.
000120       03   FILLER                PIC X(15) VALUE '  AT THIS TIME.'.
000130
000140  01   COMM-AREA.
000150       03   ENTRY-SW           PIC X VALUE 'Y'.
000160            88   INITIAL-ENTRY       VALUE 'Y'.
000170
000180  01   END-OF-SESSION-MSG      PIC X(13) VALUE 'SESSION ENDED'.
000190
000200  ++INCLUDE ARM10MC
000210       COPY DFHBMSCA.
```

Figure 16.23 ARC999C following the required modifications described in problem 2.

```
PVEDIT --- NIRXT.TEST.PANLIB(ARC999C)------------------------ COLUMNS 007 078
COMMAND ===>                                                   SCROLL ===> CSR
****** ***************************** TOP OF DATA ******************************
000010  IDENTIFICATION DIVISION.                                          05/29/92
000020  PROGRAM-ID.    ARC999C.                                           ARC999C
000030  DATE-COMPILED. MAY 29 1992.                                         LV015
000040  ENVIRONMENT DIVISION.
000050  DATA DIVISION.
000060
000070  WORKING-STORAGE SECTION.
000080  01   PGM-MSG.
D00090       03   FILLER                PIC X(11) VALUE 'SELECTION   '.
000100       03   PGM-SEL               PIC X.
000110       03   FILLER                PIC X(15) VALUE '  NOT AVAILABLE'.
000120       02   COMPARE-FIELDS        PIC X(02) VALUE SPACES.
000130       02   LINE-COUNTR           PIC 9(05) VALUE ZEROS.
000140  01   COMM-AREA.
000150       03   ENTRY-SW           PIC X VALUE 'Y'.
000160            88   INITIAL-ENTRY       VALUE 'Y'.
000170
000180  01   END-OF-SESSION-MSG      PIC X(13) VALUE 'SESSION ENDED'.
000190
000200  ++INCLUDE ARM10MC
000210       COPY DFHBMSCA.
```

Figure 16.24 Mass change command issued at the beginning of the file.

Statement 90 carries a D in the first position of the line number, which is essentially an ISPF line command for a DELETE operation. Thus, as soon as you press Enter, line number 90 will be deleted.

Notice that line number 120 was overlayed with the new data, and line 130, which was previously a blank line, has been overlayed with the requested COBOL statement.

16.8.3 Problem 3

Update source program ARC999C at level 15 by deleting statement 160, and replacing all ANYKEY statements with PF5 (lines 305 through 307).

The batch solution is:

```
++UPDATE ARC110C,15
++D 160
++R 305,307,/ANYKEY/PF5/
```

The on-line solution is to meet the above requirements and place the character D in the first digit of the line number 000160. Issue a LOCATE statement to that end, and then go directly to line 305 and physically replace the reserved word ANYKEY with PF5. Finally, look at lines 306 and 307 and see if the changes are indeed applicable.

You can also use a number of ISPF commands (reproduced in CA-Panvalet), for example to find the first occurrence of ANYKEY and then move on to the next occurrence visually verifying the change. In Figure 16.25, I went a step beyond what was requested by changing all ANYKEY commands to PF5. I did this to demonstrate the interrelation between CA-Panvalet and ISPF commands.

16.8.4 Problem 4

Print the member ARC999C (level 15) on the system printer.

The batch solution is as follows:

```
++WRITE PRINT,ARC999C,15
```

The on-line solution involves two panels. The first one is the frequently used Utility Selection Menu (shown previously in Figure 16.20), where I selected option 2 to print

```
PVEDIT --- NIRXT.TEST.PANLIB(ARC999C)------------------------- COLUMNS 007 078
COMMAND ===> CHANGE ALL ANYKEY PF5                              SCROLL ===> CSR
****** **************************** TOP OF DATA ******************************
000010  IDENTIFICATION DIVISION.                                       0501/14/
000020  PROGRAM-ID.    ARC999C.                                         AARC999
000030  DATE-COMPILED. MAY 29 1992.                                         LV0
000040  ENVIRONMENT DIVISION.
000050  DATA DIVISION.
000060
000070  WORKING-STORAGE SECTION.
000080  01  PGM-MSG.
000090      03  FILLER                   PIC X(11) VALUE 'SELECTION  '.
000100      03  PGM-SEL                  PIC X.
000110      03  FILLER                   PIC X(15) VALUE '  NOT AVAILABLE'.
000120      03  FILLER                   PIC X(15) VALUE '  AT THIS TIME.'.
000130
000140  01  COMM-AREA.
000150      03  ENTRY-SW             PIC X VALUE 'Y'.
D00160          88  INITIAL-ENTRY          VALUE 'Y'.
000170
000180  01  END-OF-SESSION-MSG       PIC X(13) VALUE 'SESSION ENDED'.
000190
000200  ++INCLUDE ARM10MC
000210      COPY DFHBMSCA.
```

Figure 16.25 CA-Panvalet Utility Selection Menu.

```
------------------------  MANIPULATE - ENTRY PANEL  ----------- ARC999C PRINTED
FUNCTION ===> P
                                                           VERSION - 14.0A

  C - COPY a member                          R - RENAME a member
  P - PRINT a member                     BLANK - Display MEMBER SELECTION LIST


 STANDARD PANVALET LIBRARY:
   PROJECT     ===> NIRXT
   GROUP       ===> TEST                 CONTROL    ===>
   TYPE        ===> PANLIB               ACCESS     ===>

   MEMBER      ===> ARC999C              NEW MEMBER ===>

 NON STANDARD PANVALET LIBRARY:
   DSNAME      ===>
   VOLSER      ===>                      (If NOT Cataloged)


   Press ENTER key to process; Enter END command to terminate.
```

Figure 16.26 Panel to request printing a job.

a member, such as the source listing ARC999C. This prompted an additional panel, shown in Figure 16.26, where the member is ARC999C. To reproduce the subsequent message, ARC999C PRINTED, I pressed the Enter key and rekeyed the information.

16.8.5 Problem 5

Change the level of the current source program (ARC999C) from level 15 to level 17.

The batch solution is:

```
++LEVEL ARC999C 15,17
```

The on-line solution is to use the CA-Panvalet Utility Panel and select option 1, CA-Panvalet Member Attribute Changes with a subtask of Change Level Number. Once you press the Enter key, the panel will be displayed in Figure 16.27.

You must supply four pieces or components to complete the transaction. The first one is the level number (Function=L), the second is the name of the library, the third is the member name (ARC999C), and the fourth is the new level (17). Note that the system keeps track of the current level number, which is assumed to be 15.

16.8.6 Problem 6

Update source program ARC999C in the following manner:

1. Delete statements 440 through 500 at level 17.
2. Insert statements 550 through 590 in their place.
3. Replace the term STMNT1 in statement 600 with the new term STMNT2.
4. Delete statement 720 and insert statement number 1 of ARC111C (a second source program) in its place.

```
-------------------------- CHANGES - ENTRY PANEL --- Pansophic Systems, Inc.
FUNCTION ===> L
                                                          VERSION - 14.0A
 S - Modify the STATUS of a member        L - Modify the LEVEL of a member
 U - Add/Change a USER code               C - Modify/Add a COMMENT to a member
                                      BLANK - Display MEMBER SELECTION LIST
 STANDARD PANVALET LIBRARY:
   PROJECT    ===> NIRXT
   GROUP      ===> TEST                  CONTROL ===>
   TYPE       ===> PANLIB                ACCESS  ===>

   MEMBER     ===> ARC999C

 NON-STANDARD PANVALET LIBRARY:
   DSNAME     ===>
   VOLSER     ===>               (If NOT Cataloged)

 ENTER MODIFICATION DATA BELOW:
   STATUS     ===>               LEVEL NUMBER   ===> 17
   USER CODE  ===>               SECURITY LEVEL ===>
   COMMENT    ===>

   Press ENTER key to process; Enter END command to terminate.
```

Figure 16.27 Panel to trigger a level change.

The batch solution is:

```
++UPDATE ARC110C,17
++D 440 500
++I 550,590
      >>>>>>>statements<<<<<<
++R 600,,/STMNT1/STMENT2/
++D 700
++I 2540,,ARC111C,32
```

The on-line solution can be accomplished entirely through ISPF commands. Invoke source program ARC999C as you did before. The listing shows level 17, which was changed earlier to 17 from 15. Locate (L) line 440 and place a block delete (DD) character in the first two positions of that line (DD0440). Also place DD in the first two positions of 500 (DD0500).

Now, insert statements located in lines 550 through 590 (a total of five lines) in place of the deleted lines. You can do this through block moves right after line 430:

```
MM0550  MOVE - 1 TO FIELDL
000560  MOVE 'Y' TO FIELDA
000570  MOVE 'CHECK YOUR ENTRY BEFORE UPDATING' TO ERRMSGO
000580  MOVE 'Y' TO ERRMSGA
MM0590  EXEC CICS ...
```

Use the LOCATE command to locate statement 600. You can physically change STMNT1 to STMNT2 or simply issue an ISPF CHANGE command. Then delete line 700, as before. Finally, insert line 1000 of ARC998C (another source program) after line 2540 in the current (ARC999C) program. (This is an "added bonus" apart from the original batch requirements.)

To satisfy the last request, program ARC999C, which is the program receiving a single line copied from ARC998C, is already invoked. Next to the command line, enter the keyword COPY, and then position your cursor on line 2540 using the character B (before) or A (after) to denote where the COPY statement should be targeted. Press the Enter key, which will prompt a subsequent panel.

Underneath the Line section, I defined both my first and last line as 1000, because that was the only line in program ARC998C that I wanted to copy. The number type is defined as R, for Relative. (Now you can see how easy it would have been to insert the entire second source program next to the specified line, as I did in the batch problem . . .) These are all typical ISPF procedures, which are available to on-line CA-Panvalet.

Chapter

17

The CA-Librarian System

17.1 Introduction to the CA-Librarian Product

CA-Librarian, like CA-Panvalet, is a source-code management system. CA-Librarian master files can be used to store data, in the form of LIBRARIAN modules, from MVS, VSE, and VM. A master file can be simultaneously accessed by users of any of these operating environments.

Figure 17.1 provides a conceptual overview of the product. Note that some of the components in the diagram are explained in detail later on in this chapter.

Level 1 includes the three operating systems (MVS, VSE, and VM) and the Cross Operating System Sharing (COSS). COSS enables you to access the CA-Librarian master file depicted at the bottom of the diagram (level 3). COSS permits users of the three operating systems to simultaneously read from and write to the master file. A master file must be MVS-initialized for COSS.

Level 2 includes the LibAudit facility, the Comparator program, and the Change Control Facility (CCF). These components work in unison to maintain a complete audit trail of all your changes to a source program. Comparator compares two source files and reports on their similarities and differences. LibAudit identifies and date-stamps the line changes made to a module.

CCF provides an application-development environment with distinct test, production, and QA (or staging) libraries. CCF tracks and documents changes to the source code as it progresses through this environment. CCF is enhanced through information from the Source Load Audit Trail (SLAT) variables, which can be automatically inserted into each source and load module. SLAT variables enable you to verify that your source-code modules match your load modules. The LibrScan utility automates the task of comparing source to load.

CA-Librarian provides statement-level archiving, which enables you to recreate and compare different versions of a module or to back out an update. A module can

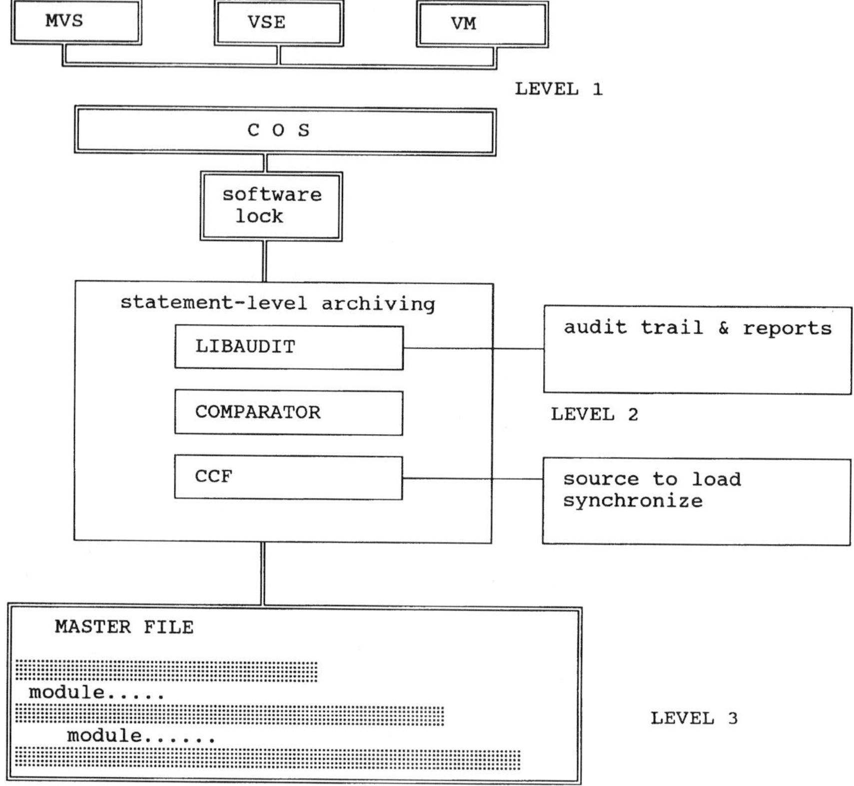

Figure 17.1 System overview.

have up to 255 archive levels. No single record is stored more than once, even if it is included in all 255 versions. This is accomplished by internally labeling each record with a two-byte field that indicates the archive levels to which the record belongs. Examples of this are shown in Figures 17.2 through 17.4. In the diagrams, the character in the rightmost column indicates the following:

Character	Explanation
*	the record remained the same
D	the record was deleted
A	the record was added or updated

Version 0 (Figure 17.2) is a new COBOL program. Note that all records have been labeled with a 0 for both the level created and the current level.

Version 1 (Figure 17.3) has been updated to include Division after Environment, Working-Storage Section, and P100-Start. Note how the level indicators have been changed to reflect the update.

Version 2 has been updated by deleting Working-Storage Section and Procedure Division, and an End has been added. Again, the level indicators are updated to reflect these changes. This is highlighted in Figure 17.4.

VERSION 0

Level Created	Current Level		
0	0	Identification Division	
0	0	Author. Alex Varsegi.	
0	0	Environment.	
0	0	Data Division.	
0	0	Procedure Division.	

Figure 17.2 New COBOL program.

VERSION 1

Level Created	Current Level		
0	1	Identification Division	*
0	0	Author. Alex Varsegi.	D
0	0	Environment.	D
1	1	Environment Division.	A
0	1	Data Division.	*
1	1	Working-Storage Section.	A
0	1	Procedure Division.	*
1	1	P100-Start.	A

Figure 17.3 First updated version.

VERSION 2

Level Created	Current Level		
0	2	Identification Division	*
0	0	Author. Alex Varsegi.	D1
0	0	Environment.	D1
1	2	Environment Division.	*
0	2	Data Division.	*
1	1	Working-Storage Section.	D
0	1	Procedure Division.	D
1	2	P100-Start.	*
2	2	End.	A

Figure 17.4 Second updated version.

Using the archive-level indicators, CA-Librarian can quickly reconstruct the archive level of the module. By not storing duplicate records, LIBAUDIT and archiving reduce DASD usage, thereby increasing efficiency.

Level 3 includes the CA-Librarian master file and the modules stored on the master file. In addition to data records, a module can include control information, such as a language code, module description, programmer name, and history records.

CA-Librarian uses data compression to reduce storage requirements. All blanks, COBOL-reserved words, and repeated characters are automatically compressed. Additionally, every eight bits is compressed to six bits.

17.2 The CA-Librarian Access Method

The CA-Librarian Access Method, abbreviated as LIB/AM, provides an interface between CA-Librarian and a range of IBM products. LIB/AM allows a program in an MVS or VSE environment to directly access a master file as though it were an IBM-Partitioned Data Set (PDS) or sequential file.

17.3 CA-Librarian Online Interfaces

CA-Librarian interfaces to CA-ROSCOE, ISPF, and CMS. CA-Librarian does not have an editor of its own. Instead, it works with the editor provided with the product to which it interfaces. For example, the ISPF interface uses the ISPF editor.

The Extended Librarian Interactive Productivity Services (ELIPS) facility provides a TSO/ISPF interface via the ISPF/PDF environment. ELIPS enables you to edit, browse, copy, print, and rename modules. ELIPS is available to sites using ISPF/PDF version 2 or above.

17.4 CA-Librarian Control Statements

You can start a CA-Librarian function through a set of control statements. These statements conform to a standard format: each statement starts with a dash (e.g., -SEL, -SCAN). Make sure you separate the commands by at least one blank character, and that every parameter field in the parameter section is also segregated by a comma. For example:

```
-SEL PAYMOD,JET,LIST
```

where -SEL means to select a module for processing, PAYMOD is the name of the module to be selected (and can contain up to 8 characters), JET is a user-established password, and LIST is simply a processing option for listing the module.

There are, overall, seven basic kinds of CA-Librarian control statements (for a more detailed review refer to Figure 17.5). These are:

Execution control statements. These have to do with the general execution of the software. They also contain options such as -OPT, -MOD, and will remain in force for the duration of an entire operation.

Type of Statement	Command	Function
Execution Control	-OPT -EMOD -END	Establish execution parameters End processing for a module End the entire control stream
Module Control	-ADD -SEL -DLM	Add a module to the master file Select a module for processing Delete an entire module
Editing Control	-SCAN -EDIT -FILL	Search module for char. string Change char. string to another Place char. string in cols n-n
Updating Control	-INS -REP -DEL	Insert a record Replace a record or records Delete a record or records
Documentary Control	-PGMR -LANG -DESC -HST -HSTD -COM	Name of the programmer Name of the programming language Describe program Describe every update Delete all history records Comment on the update rec list
Miscellaneous Control	-AUX -DATA -INC -JCL -JCLT	Add records from another file Put test data at the end of module Include another module Provide job control statement Provide temporary JCL
Utility Control	-INC -EXTRACT -PRINT -PUNCH -SCAN -SCANR -COPY	Transfer records or modules Transfer specific module level List all or part of module Punch all or part of module Search master file for string Search some modules for string Transfer modules from master

Figure 17.5 CA-Librarian control commands.

Module control statements. These are responsible for the processing of an entire module, including certain options, such as -ADD, -SEL, or -DLM.

Editing control statements. These are designed primarily for examining and changing existing records in a module, such as searching for a character string through a -SCAN statement.

Updating control statements. The sole purpose of these statements is to add, replace, or remove records in a module. They are represented by the commands -INS, -REP, and -DEL, respectively.

Documentary control statements. These are also available for adding a special record or records to a module (other than data records), each containing record-control information about the module. For example, -PGMR enables you to display the name of the programmer, and -LANG denotes the type of programming language in use.

Miscellaneous control statements. These statements allow you to combine or simply incorporate other module or modules into the current stream, such as records and generated job-control (JCL) statements. Among these commands are -AUX, used for adding records from another file, and -DATA, for placing test data at the end of a particular module.

Utility control statements. This is available primarily for transferring data records or whole modules within a master file, or searching an entire master file for a set of character strings. The -INC, -EXTRACT, -PRINT, and -COPY commands are good examples of such utility control statements. For more on this, review Figure 17.5.

Note that the chronology or sequence in which a record is updated is quite significant in a typical batch environment. It is significant for at least two reasons. The first is that in batch mode everything takes place in a given order. The second is that, once you have read and passed a particular statement, there is no mechanism to go back. This is no different than the batch portion of the CA-Panvalet system. (In an on-line environment, of course, there is no such restriction because you can "navigate" back and forth on a given panel simply by cursor movement.) Thus, to delete or insert a particular statement, you don't need to apply the command DEL or -INS, because all can be performed on the spot.

As CA-Librarian scans your batch module while applying control statements (e.g., -INS, -REP, and -DEL), it reads and updates each record type in a predefined sequence. If you were to replace (-REP) record number 30 in the stream and then try to delete (-DEL) record number 20 afterwards, CA-Librarian would give you an error message because the record had already been read, processed, and duly passed.

Editing control statements (-SCAN, -EDIT, and -FILL) are different in this respect. Unlike updating control statements, which must be arranged so that the records to which they refer are in ascending alphanumeric order, editing statements can be specified in any order.

The software highlights the location of each edit operation, but does not perform it until the record or records it refers to are read, often in response to an updating control statement. For this reason, you can edit any number of control statements before physically updating previously read records on file. But because CA-Librarian reads every record in a module, and thus sequentially processes (or ignores) them, it is not viable to edit prior records once a particular line of instruction has been passed and selectively updated. So, to avoid all "unpleasantness," you must either put the editing control statements first, or place them in sequence by record number with the updating control statements.

An example of the combined use of editing and updating statements is shown in Figure 17.6. Note that the section marked with an (A) refers to an operation performed on the entire module. (B) is limited to records 70 through 300. (C) represents operations performed on all records beginning with record 90, and (D) points to a rejected statement because CA-Librarian had already processed record 390. A resulting update record listing is presented in Figures 17.7A and 17.7B.

```
                                           Number of           Last
                                        currently active      record
                                        editing commands     processed

-SEL MIXED,ZXJP
-EDIT    /APLHA/BETA/_ ------┐                  1
-EDIT    /PAY3/PAY4/ --------->(A)              2
-FILL    /NEWPAY/            |                  3
-SCAN    /WTD-/ _____________┘                  4
-EDIT    /PIK/PIC/70,300 <-------- (B)          5
-INS  FIRST
         SELECT PAY ASSGN TO SYSUT1.
-REP  80                                                         10
         BLOCK CONTAINS 50 RECORDS
-EDIT    /DAY/PAY/90                            6                80
-EDIT    /WITH/FWTD/        <--------- (C)      7                80
-EDIT    /MASTER/PAY-MASTER/              |     8                80
-EDIT    /MVE/MOVE/90,110                 |     9                80
-EDIT    /SAVE// _________________________┘    10                80
-REP  220
         ADD WK-FWTD TO YTD-FWTD.
-EDIT    /STAY/STAX/300,360                     9               220
-INS  400
         ADD WK-FICA TO YTD-FICA.
-EDIT    /MVE/MOVE/450                          8               400
-EDIT    /MVE/MOVE/390 <---------- (D)
-EDIT    /STAY/STAX/460,490                     9               400
-EDIT    /STX/STAX/460,490                     10               400
-EDIT    /STX/STAX/620,630
-INS  500
         ADD WK-PAY TO YTD-PAY.
-REP  610                                       7               500
       .
       .
```

Figure 17.6 Control stream with both editing and updating commands.

17.5 The Include Facility

The CA-Librarian -INC statement (include) enables you to include all or some of the data records of one module in another module at compilation time. Figures 17.8A and 17.8B show the module listing with an -INC statement. Figure 17.9 is a listing of the compiled results, with the -INC statement replaced by the data records of the included module.

17.6 Comparator II

Comparator II enables you to compare two files and obtain a report on the similarities and differences between the files. Comparator II can compare modules on a master file, archive levels of the same module, IBM sequential files, or PDS members. For example, if you feel that someone has tampered with one of your archived CA-Librarian source modules, you can compare the current level to the previous level in order to see the differences.

Because the two files being compared might have different characteristics (for ex-

```
-SEL MIXED,ZXJP
-EDIT    /APLHA/BETA/
-EDIT    /PAY3/PAY4/
-FILL    /NEWPAY/
-SCAN    /WTD-/
-EDIT    /PIK/PIC/70,300
-INS  FIRST
   000010   SELECT PAY ASSGN TO SYSUT1.
          THE NEW CARDS HAVE BEEN INSERTED BEFORE THE FOLL CARD
          000010           ACCESS RANDOM

   000020       ACCESS RANDOM                              NEW FILL PERFORMED
   000030       BLOCK CONTAINS 50 RECORDS                  NEW FILL PERFORMED
   000040       NOMINAL KEY IS PSF-KEY                     NEW FILL PERFORMED
   000050       RECORD KEY IS PSF-REC-KEY                  NEW FILL PERFORMED
   000060       SELECT PDSQISAM ASSIGN TO DA-I-ISAMDSQ     NEW FILL PERFORMED
   000070       ACCESS IS RANDOM                           NEW FILL PERFORMED
   000080       NOMINAL KEY IS PDSQ-KEY                    NEW FILL PERFORMED
-REP  80
   000090  BLOCK CONTAINS 50 RECORDS

           FOLLOWING CARDS REMOVED FROM MASTER BY LAST OPER
           000080           NOMINAL KEY IS PDSQ-KEY.
-EDIT   /DAY/PAY/90
-EDIT   /WITH/FWTD/
-EDIT   /MASTER/PAY-MASTER/
-EDIT   /MVE/MOVE/90,110
-EDIT   /SAVE//
   000100       SELECT PAYLOG ASSIGN TO DA-S-XMITQLOG.     NEW FILL PERFORMED
   000110       SELECT READER ASSIGN TO DA-S-CARDIN.       NEW FILL PERFORMED
   000120       SELECT SCMV ASSIGN TO DA-S-SCMV.           NEW FILL PERFORMED
   000130       SELECT PAY-MASTER ASSIGN TO UT-S-DELETE.   NEW FILL PERFORMED
   000150  IO-CONTROL.                                     NEW FILL PERFORMED
   000160       APPLY CORE-INDEX ON PSFI PDSQI.            NEW FILL PERFORMED
   000170  DATA DIVISION.                                  NEW FILL PERFORMED
   000180  FILE-SECTION.                                   NEW FILL PERFORMED
   000190  FD  PAY-MASTER                                  NEW FILL PERFORMED
   000200       BLOCK CONTAINS 0 RECORDS                   NEW FILL PERFORMED
   000210       RECORD CONTAINS 80 CHARACTERS              NEW FILL PERFORMED
   000220       RECORDING MODE IS F                        NEW FILL PERFORMED
-REP 220
   000230  ADD-WK-FWTD.
              FOLLOWING CARDS REMOVED FROM MASTER BY LAST OPER
              000220    LABEL RECORDS ARE STANDARD
```

Figure 17.7A Result update record listing, part 1.

ample, the records on one file could be wider than those of the other file), default rules exist for performing the comparison.

Comparator II uses comparison strings to perform file comparison. A *comparison string* is a continuous string of data that is derived by extracting from a record the fields of interest that are defined either by Comparator II commands or by the default rules. In comparing two sets of files, the file attributes examined by Comparator II include data-set organization, logical record length, and record format. Data-set organization can be partitioned, sequential, or, in the case of CA-Librarian master files, direct access.

A comparison string can be either longer or shorter than the record itself, either because only part of the data in the record is significant or because the files have dif-

```
  000240       DATA RECORD IS PRODUCTS-CONTROL-CARD.     NEW FILL PERFORMED
  000250  01   PRODUCTS-CONTROL-CARD.                    NEW FILL PERFORMED
  000260       05  C-C-CTL-CHAR      PIC XXX             NEW FILL PERFORMED
  000270                             VALUE '< >'.        NEW FILL PERFORMED
  000280       05  C-C-C-CODE        PIC X.              NEW FILL PERFORMED
  000290           88  BETA          VALUE '3'.          NEW FILL PERFORMED
  000300           88  PROC          VALUE 'P'.          NEW FILL PERFORMED
  000310           88  CMNT-STAX     VALUE '+' THRU '*'. NEW FILL PERFORMED
  000320           88  CHNG          VALUE 'C'.          NEW FILL PERFORMED
  000330           88  PAY4          VALUE 'D'.          NEW FILL PERFORMED
  000340           88  MSG-BETA      VALUE 'M'.          NEW FILL PERFORMED
  000350           88  DSD-STAX      VALUE 'B'.          NEW FILL PERFORMED
  000360           88  PSD-BETA      VALUE 'S'.          NEW FILL PERFORMED
  000370           88  PAT-STAX      VALUE '2'.          NEW FILL PERFORMED
  000380  WORKING-STORAGE SECTION.                       NEW FILL PERFORMED
  000390  PROCEDURE DIVISION USING PARM-1.               NEW FILL PERFORMED
  000400  MVPG                                           NEW FILL PERFORMED
  000410       OPEN INPUT READER OUTPUT DELPRINT ERRPRINT NEW FILL PERFORMED
-INS 400
  000420       ADD WK-FICA TO YTD-FICA.
         THE NEW CARDS HAVE BEEN INSERTED AFTER THE FOLL CARD
         000400  OPEN INPUT READER OUTPUT DELPRINT
   -EDIT   /MVE/MOVE/450
   -EDIT   /MVE/MOVE/390
   -EDIT   /STAY/STAX/460,490
   -EDIT   /STX/STAX/460,490
   -EDIT   /STX/STAX/620,630
```

Figure 17.7B Result update record listing, part 2.

```
RUN NO. 49   DATE=06/14/92 TIME=0933      LISTING OF MODULE COBOLTST     PAGE 1

DESCRIPTION       COBOL TEST PROGRAM

MASTER FILE         LIBR.DEV.MAST
ADDED TO MASTER     07/03/91
LAST DATE COPIED    NONE
LAST DATE UPDATED   06/14/92  092609
ARCHIVING STATUS    ACTIVATED
NUMBER OF LEVELS    4
CURRENT LEVEL NO.   3
NUMBER OF RECORDS   24
NUMBER OF UPDATES   3
NUMBER OF ACCESSES  7
SEQUENCE PARAMS     01/6/0010/0010 - RESEQ
COMPRESS STATUS     FULL
COPYDD STATUS       NOT ACTIVATED
COBOL COPY STATUS   NOT ACTIVATED
MODULE STATUS       TEST

PASSWORD            BROWNLY
PROGRAMMER          VARSEGI
LANGUAGE            COB
PROC PARAMETER      $NOJCL

HISTORY RECORD(S) FOR THIS MODULE:
07/03/91            MODULE FOR TEST COMPILES
```

Figure 17.8A Module listing showing -INC statement, part 1.

```
000010  ID DIVISION.
000020  PROGRAM-ID. COBOLTST.                                              06/14/92
000030  ENVIRONMENT DIVISION.
000040  INPUT-OUTPUT SECTION.
000050  FILE CONTROL.
000060      SELECT INFILE ASSIGN TO UT-S-IN.
000070  DATA DIVISION.
000080  FILE SECTION.
000090  FD  INFILE
000100      DATA RECORD IS INREC.
-INC INREC                  00000110
000120  WORKING-STORAGE SECTION.
000130  77  IN-COUNT         PIC 999.
000140  77  IN-INDEX         PIC 999.
000150  77  IN-ID            PIC XXXXX.
000160  PROCEDURE DIVISION.
000170      ACCEPT IN-COUNT FROM SYSIN.
000180      OPEN INPUT INVFILE.                                            06/14/92
000190      PERFORM IN-COPY VARYING IN-INDEX FROM 1 BY 1 UNTIL             06/14/92
000200          IN-INDEX EQUAL IN-COUNT. STOP RUN.                         06/14/92
000210  IN-COPY.
000220      READ INVFILE.                                                  06/14/92
000230      MOVE INVFILE-ID TO IN-ID                                       06/14/92
000240      DISPLAY IN-ID UPON SYSOUT.
```

Figure 17.8B Module listing showing -INC statement, part 2.

```
000010  IDENTIFICATION DIVISION.
000020  PROGRAM-ID. COBOLTST.
000030  ENVIRONMENT DIVISION.
000040  INPUT-OUTPUT SECTION.
000050  FILE CONTROL.
000060      SELECT INFILE ASSIGN TO UT-S-IN.
000070  DATA DIVISION.
000080  FILE SECTION.
000090  FD  INFILE
000100      DATA RECORD IS INREC.
000010  01  INREC.  -----------------------+
000020      02  INFILE-ID    PIC  XXXXX.    | (A)
000030      02  FILLER       PIC  X(75).    |
000120  WORKING-STORAGE SECTION.     -------+
000130  77  IN-COUNT         PIC  999.
000140  77  IN-INDEX         PIC  999.
000150  77  IN-ID            PIC  XXXXX.
000160  PROCEDURE DIVISION.
000170      ACCEPT IN-COUNT FROM SYSIN.
000180      OPEN INPUT INFILE.
000190      PERFORM IN-COPY VARYING IN-INDEX FROM 1 BY 1 UNTIL
000200          IN-INDEX EQUAL IN-COUNT. STOP RUN.
000210  IN-COPY.
000220       READ INFILE.
000230       MOVE INFILE-ID TO IN-ID.
000240       DISPLAY IN-ID UPON SYSOUT.
```

Figure 17.9 Listing of the compilation file, showing -INC statements replaced by included module. The -INC statement that appears in the calling module (A) is replaced in the compilation file by the module to which it refers.

```
//COMP7    JOB  70000,VARSEGI,CLASS=X,MSGCLASS=A
//STEP1    EXEC  PGM=COMP2
//SYSPRINT DD SYSOUT=*
//SYSUT1    DD DSN=your.mst.file,DISP=SHR
//SYSUT2    DD DSN=your.pds,DISP=SHR
//SYSIN     DD *
 OLDFILE MEM=MODLE1,STRING=(7,66)
NEWFILE MEMBER=MODLE2,STRING=(7,66)
REP LST=CHG
TITLE=('PRODUCE RECEIVABLES',
'VS. TEST VERSION'),
OLDLINE=((1,'*'),(4,(1,80)),(86,'*')),
EQUILINE=((17,'*'),(20(1,80),OLD),(102,'*')),
NEWLINE=((35,'*'),(38,(1,80)),(120,'*'))
```

Figure 17.10 JCL and commands required to compare a CA-Librarian module to a PDS member specifying sequence fields.

ferent characteristics with respect to record length and format. A pair of files can consist of:

- Two non-CA-Librarian files
- One CA-Librarian member and one non-CA-Librarian file
- Two CA-Librarian members

In putting together a Comparator II control stream, you need to know not only what you want to do with it, but also the Comparator II defaults. If you specify your own comparison strings using the STRING= parameter, you must also specify REPORT OLDLINE= and NEWLINE= in order to produce any report at all.

In Figure 17.10, I compared a PDS member to a CA-Librarian module. Note that the old version is in a CA-Librarian master file. The new version is on a partitioned data set. In both versions, the sequence numbers are in column 73 through 80. Note that because the STRING= parameter was specified, the report lines must also be specified. Otherwise, no report lines are produced. In the figure, note the following relationships:

- OLDFILE points to the SYSUT1 data set YOUR.MST.FILE, member MODULE1.
- NEWFILE points to the SYSUT2 data set YOUR.PDS, member MODULE2.
- STRING specifies the fields to be used in constructing the comparison string. Col, len stands for two numbers defining the location of the field. Enclose these numbers in parentheses and separate them with commas—for example, OLDFILE STRING=(7,12), where 7 (col) represents the column number of the beginning field and 12 (len) represents the length of the field.

And the following terms:

- OLDLINE defines the layout of a unique record from the OLDFILE.
- NEWLINE defines the layout of a unique record from the NEWFILE.
- EQUILINE defines the layout of a record common to both OLDFILE and NEWFILE.

- The asterisk indicates that the field being defined is to follow immediately after the previously defined field. If this is the first description in the report line definition, it will begin in column 1.
- There are two keywords—OLD and NEW. The purpose of OLD is to select the field from the record in the OLDFILE. Likewise, NEW will select the field from the record in the NEWFILE.

In Figure 17.11, I compared two versions of a COBOL program on a CA-Librarian master file. Through this execution, I have produced a new module by applying all the changes against the existing program.

In this comparison, a name and address field is the only part of the data that needs to be compared. The STRING= parameter is used to select this field for comparison. Note that the two files being compared are formatted differently and the name and address field, while the same length in both files, appear in different locations in each.

17.7 CA-Librarian Change Control Facility (CCF)

The CA-Librarian Change Control Facility provides a way for change requests to be entered by the user, reviewed, and assigned to a programmer. There are several ways that LIB/CCF can be configured to implement a change request. Figure 17.12 shows the CCF Primary Options Menu. Refer to this in the following paragraphs.

The user of an application uses option 1 to open the change request on-line. The request is then viewed on option 2 by the programming manager in charge of that application. The manager uses option 2 to review the request, add comments, and assign the request to one of his programmers.

The programmer to whom the request is assigned uses option 3 to view the request. Using option 4, he logs out the source module from the production environment to the test environment, and makes the requested changes on the test master file.

When the changes have been completed and tested, the programmer uses option

```
//COMP2   JOB  70000,VARSEGI,CLASS=X,MSGCLASS=A
//STEP1   EXEC PGM=COMP2
//SYSPRINT DD SYSOUT=*
//SYSPUNCH DD DSN=your.dataset.name,DISP=(NEW,CATLG,DELETE),
//   SPACE=((800,(1,1),RLSE),VOL=SER=volser,
//   UIT=DISK,DCB=(RECFM=FB,LRECL=80,BLKSIZE=800)
//SYSUT1  DD   DSN=your.master.file,DISP=SHR
//SYSUT2  DD   DSN=your.master.file,DISP=SHR
//SYSIN   DD   *
OLDFILE MEMBER=FILE1
NEWFILE MEMBER=FILE2
DK PUN=YES,CLEARID=NO
REP LST=CHG,
TITLE=('COBPGM -- PROD',
'VS. TEST VERSION)
/*
```

Figure 17.11 Two versions of a COBOL program, both residing in the CA-Librarian.

```
                  CA-LIBRARIAN CHANGE CONTROL FACILITY

OPTION ===>

 0   CCF PARMS            Specify job statement/DB2 information
 1   OPEN                 Open a change request
 2   ASSIGN               Assign, reassign, reject a change request
 3   DISPLAY              Display assigned change request
 4   LOGOUT               Logout a module to test
 5   LOGIN                Login a module to production
 6   LINK                 Initiate a production linkedit or bind
 7   CLOSE                Close a change request
 8   REPORTS              Print or display LIB/CCF reports
 9   MOVEMENT STATUS      Display, process, reject, LOGOUT/REQUESTS
10   LINK STATUS          Display, process, reject, link/bind requests
11   JOB STATUS           Display, process, submit, pending jobs
12   ADMIN SERVICES       LIB/CCF administrator services
 T   TUTORIAL             Display information about LIB/CCF
 X   EXIT                 Terminate LIB/CCF
```

Figure 17.12 LIB/CCF Primary Options Menu.

5 to request that the control group log in the source modules to the production master file. Alternatively, CCF can be configured to allow the programmer to log in the module. After the member is logged in and compiled, the programmer uses option 6 to request that the control group link the members to the application system. Again, CCF can also be configured to allow the programmer to perform this function. Finally, the programmer uses option 7 to close the change request.

When an application manager assigns a change request to you, it becomes one of the change requests that you can view by selecting option 3 on the Main Menu. Each change request has a unique number, so you can find individual change requests by number by specifying FIND WO*n* or FIND *n* on the command line of option 3, where *n* is the change-request number. Alternatively, you can view the change requests one after another in numerical order by pressing the Enter key.

When you have determined which CA-Librarian modules must be changed to fulfill the change request, log them out from the production environment by using option 4. Then use option 5 to log the changed and fully tested programs back into the production environment.

Use option 6 to initiate a production link request, after verifying that the production compile is complete.

17.8 Viewing Assigned Requests

Each change request appears by itself on the screen. You can view them sequentially by specifying ENTER??, or view a specific change request by entering FIND and the change request number on the command line. The scroll forward and backward, top and bottom PF keys can be used to viewing the change results. The Assigned Change Request Panel is displayed in Figure 17.13. The coordinator is the person in the requestor's department who is assigned to coordinate requests for changes to this application. Also, the PRINT statement will print one copy of the change request that is currently being viewed, using the default print location.

```
FRI 09/09/92   ----- ASSIGNED CHANGE REQUEST ---------    10.22.51

OPTION ===>

  REQUESTOR===> Alex Varsegi   Type===> PROBLEM   ID: W0000001

      PHONE===> x4038                  MANAGER ===> Bob Cunningham
APPL/SYSTEM===> ACCT                DEPARTMENT ===> Accounting
COORDINATOR===> Ron Sullivan             PHONE ===> x7765

DESCRIPTION===>           Subroutine WR152G needs to be modified to
                          produce additional Status reports

MGR COMMENTS===>          Target date is 09/15/92 or before.

                          OPENED: 08/23/92  11.02.08 BY JOHNSTON
```

Figure 17.13 Assigned Change Request Panel.

17.9 Logging Out a Module

Once you have been assigned a change request, you can log out the production source module(s) needed to implement the change by using option 4. Option 4 displays up to three panels. Use the first one to specify the change-request number. The second panel provides a list of valid pairs of production and test master files. Enter a member name or wildcard specification and the number of the correct pair of master files from the list. Note that if you were to enter wildcard specifications, a third panel would appear.

The logout procedure copies the module(s) you have specified from the production master file to the test master file associated with it.

17.10 Adding a Member to Production

There are times when you will need to add a new member to a CCF-controlled production master file. For example, a change request might require the creation of a new program.

First, you must log out the member from option 4, even though the member does not yet exist on the production master file. This will reserve the member name you choose for the new member. During the logout of the new member, LIB/CCF will present you with a History Create/Modify Panel. This panel is shown in Figure 17.14.

Note that you must enter a description of the member, the application system to which it belongs, a detailed abstract, and the appropriate programming language. The programming language entered in this panel will determine what action takes place when the member is logged in. For example, specifying COB might cause the member to be compiled at login. Complete the History Create/Modify Panel and press the Enter key to continue. The END PF key will cancel the logout. After the information is entered, LIB/CCF will issue the message *Assuming New Member*. . . .

Because the member is new, you will have to create it on the test master file that was specified during the logout. When you have completed the work on this module, you can log it in using option 5.

17.11 Logging In a Module

When you have completed your changes to a module and are ready to return it to the production environment, use option 5 to perform the login function. Option 5 allows you to process a single member or multiple members associated with a change request. The latter is referred to as *group processing*.

The Login Function Panel (shown in Figure 17.15) displays one module-tracking record (MTR) entry for each of the modules you have logged out.

The first line of each entry shows the name of the member to be logged in, the related change-request number, the date and time the member was logged out, and the name of the programmer who initiated the logout. If this logout request was submitted to a control group and then rejected by that group for any given reason, the rejected request indicator will also be displayed in the MTR.

The second line displays the name of the production master file where the member resides. The third line shows the name of the test master file to which the mem-

```
 FRI  03/25/92   -----  HISTORY CREATE/MODIFY, NEWMOD ----14.25.15

     SYSTEM ===>                               REQUEST ID: W0000001
DESCRIPTION ===>
   LANGUAGE ===>

   ABSTRACT ===>
            ===>
            ===>
            ===>
            ===>
            ===>
            ===>
            ===>
            ===>
            ===>
            ===>
```

Figure 17.14 History Create/Modify Panel.

```
FRI  03/14/92  ------------MODULE LOGIN -------------16.12.30

COMMAND ===>
    Available Cmds: PROCESS n, DELETE n, HISTORY N, BIND n

    MODULE       MODULE TRACKING RECORD:

01)  LIBREST    CR:W0000001  LOGOUT STAMP: 03/01/92  09:32:22
                 PROD MASTER:     LIBR.PROD.MAST
                 TEST MASTER:     LIBR.TEST.MAST
                 VERS:09221201

02)  NEWMOD      CR:W0000001  LOGOUT STAMP: 03/01/92  10:51:07
                 PROD MASTER:     LIBR.PROD.MAST
                 TEST MASTER:     LIBR.TEST.MAST
                 VERS=*NEW*
```

Figure 17.15 Option 5 Module Tracking Records (MTR).

ber was copied during the logout processing. The fourth line shows the date and time to be supplied for the CA-Librarian version check during login processing. This line might also show information supplied by a site user exit.

17.12 Logging In Multiple Members to Production (Group Processing)

The group-processing facility enables you to display the status of members associated with a change request, and process those members in a group by entering one command. The members to be processed must first be selected using the SELECT command from the Login Panel. This is shown in Figure 17.16. The format of the SELECT command is as follows:

```
SELECTx cr#
```

where x designates the type of SELECT to be done, and cr# indicates the LIB/CCF change-request number to be selected. The SELECTx portion of the command can be specified in one of the following forms:

SELECT selects all members currently logged out for the specified change request. If your site is using the control group to perform logins, the display will include members rejected by the control group, but not members that the control group has pending.

SELECTF selects all members that have been logged out or logged in with this change request. This includes all members that were logged into production and those that the control group has pending. Members that were logged out then deleted will not be selected.

```
FRI  03/14/92   ----GROUP PROCESSING-CR:W0000001------16.12.30

COMMAND ===>
    MODULE     (PRTY)   PROD MASTER / CURRENT MASTER

CDINTM12 (000)  LIBR.PROD.MAST                     VERS:02261152
                LIBR.TEST.MAST
                LOGOUT: 03/16/92   14.50.53  LANGUAGE: ASSEMB
                CURRENT STATUS:  Under development

CDINTM24 (002)  LIBR.PROD.MAST                     VERS:02261243
                LIBR.TEST.MAST
                LOGOUT: 03/16/92  14.51.32         LANGUAGE: ASSEMB
                CURRENT STATUS: Under Development

CDINTM36 (002)  LIBR.PROD.MAST                     VERS: 11191810
                LIBR.REJECT.MAST
                LOGOUT: 03/16/92  14:53:35  LANGUAGE: ASSEMB
                CURRENT STATUS: Login Rejected by CNTL
```

Figure 17.16 Group Processing panel.

The change-request number can be specified as the full LIB/CCF change-request number. The following:

```
SELECT  W0000019
```

can be abbreviated to the significant digits of the change-request number, like this:

```
SELECT 19
```

The SELECTx command can also be abbreviated, as follows:

```
S 19 or SF 19
```

Group processing displays a selection list containing three lines for each member. You can scroll this list using the PF keys.

The first line of each entry includes the member name, the production master file that the member was logged out of, and the date and time to be supplied for the CA-Librarian version check during the login process. The second line will contain the master file in which the member currently resides and date (mmddyy) the member was logged out. The third line contains the member's current status and the logout time (hhmmss).

17.13 Initiating a Production Link Request (Option 6)

Once all source members for a change request are updated, it will probably be necessary to relink the application. Do this with option 6 after the login functions are completed. Site options determine whether or not you will be able to proceed with the link of a change request that has unresolved activities, such as outstanding module-movement records, module-tracking records, and job-submission records, and duplicate system-link records.

Chapter

18

The IBM Netview Product

18.1 The Communication Concept

In presenting IBM's Netview package to an application oriented audience, I have assumed a relatively inexperienced user in regards to a systems (as opposed to an application-oriented) environment. However, I have also assumed that users are familiar with some limited topics, such as switching from an active CICS session to an ISPF session or vice versa without logging off the system in the process—more of a convenience than a necessity. This chapter, therefore, will provide you with a broad, general background on some of the basics of the Netview system and elaborate on the relationship that exists between Netview and SNA, or Systems Network Architecture.

The primary function of Netview is to diagnose and correct physical and logical problems in a network. SNA, on the other hand, is IBM's way of making sure that different types of computers, terminals, and other devices can connect with each other both physically and logically in order to communicate.

Let's look at a network and talk about what it is made up of. Most networks composed of hundreds of resources. The term *resource*, essentially, means any piece of the network. Although every network uses a different number of resources and they are organized in different ways, the resources themselves do different things in any given SNA network.

18.2 Local Resource Concept

18.2.1 What is a local resource?

The network I am going to use in the upcoming example is a relatively simple one that includes only a few resources. The first topic is local resources. Consider the example shown in Figure 18.1. This network consists of host and some local resources.

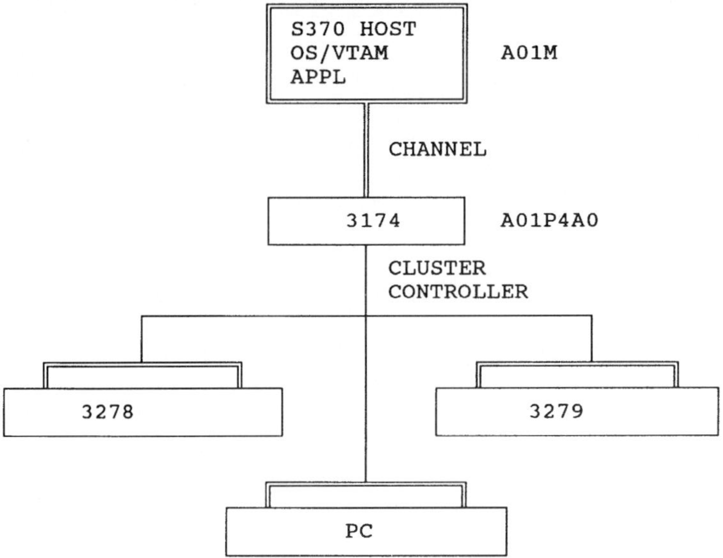

Figure 18.1 Local resource configuration.

The resources, as you can see, are local, because all resources in this network are near each other and there is no telecommunication link between the resources and the host. The host is the most important resource in the network. It manages the network by controlling which resources can communicate with each other. It does this by using the operating system (OS) and an access method, such as VTAM (Virtual Teleprocessing Access Method).

The operating system has the responsibility for managing and controlling work to be processed by the host. This involves running batch jobs, and managing logons and workloads. Examples of such an operating system are MVS, VM, and VSE. VTAM, the access method, controls network resources and communication that occurs between resources. The term APPL refers to a number of application programs, of which Netview happens to be one.

Let me talk about another component, which is the channel responsible for connecting the host with a controller unit, such as the 3174 device. This channel is made up of a piece of hardware and some computer code, called *microcode*. It connects network resources directly to the host. The channel transmits data at a very high speed through short distances. Because of this, any directly attached resources must be in the same geographical location as the host.

In viewing Figure 18.1, note that the 3174 device is a cluster controller, which manages the communication. It directs the data that comes from the host to the resources attached to it. The cluster controller decides which resource or resources have access to which particular piece of data based on the destination. It also directs data that comes from resources up to the host. The cluster controller provides data from the resources with instructions that tell the host just what exactly needs to be done with the data.

Part of this network configuration is the workstation, shown in the bottom portion of Figure 18.1, which represents resources that allow the user to access the network. They are essentially the terminals from where users can send and receive information. Although they are not shown on the illustration, printers are also attached to the cluster controller even though they are not considered to be part of a given workstation.

18.2.2 Naming conventions

All resources in the network have two names. The first is the name you call the particular resource and the second is the name the resource is called by other resources. Naming conventions, by definition, are rules that specify what each resource in the network should be called. For example, it might be that each terminal name in your network begins with the four-letter designation TERM. By knowing and understanding the naming convention, you can quickly locate and interpret the data.

In this particular chapter, I have used the following conventions: all resources, except applications, begin with the character A to show they are in network NETA. The A is followed by 01 (which is a subarea number). More on this a bit later. The next character indicates the resource type:

Character	Designation
M	HOST
P	physical unit
A	logical unit

The last three or four characters left tell you about the resource. In light of this, let me modify the chart I initially introduced in Figure 18.1 to look like the one in Figure 18.2. NPM01, IMS01, CICS01, for example, are names for NPM, IMS, and CICS applications. A01MK is the name of the host. A01P4A0 is the cluster controller's name, while A01A4A02 and A01A4A03 are local terminal names.

When a user calls to report a problem, one of the first questions you ask is "what's your terminal's name?" If you were using the sample network described above, and the user's response were A01A4A03, you would know that the terminal was a local resource in network NETA, subarea 01. Then you could use a map of the network to find the terminal and its associated cluster controller.

18.2.3 Activity resources

The primary objective of a network is to allow users to communicate with one another. SNA provides the structure that enables this communication. SNA manages a network as if it were made up of two parts: a physical part and a logical part. Each resource must be physically and logically connected before it can communicate (exchange data) with any other resources.

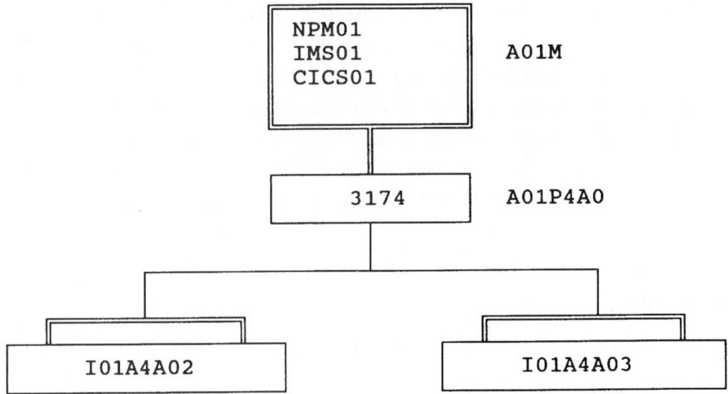

Figure 18.2 Network naming convention samples.

The physical connection in the network consists of hardware, such as the host computer, the cluster controller (3174), terminals, printers, and cables that connect the network resources. The physical connection is made when the terminal and control-unit power is switched on and the channel and cable connections are complete.

A logical connection, on the other hand, exists in a network when a resource has been defined to the network by systems programmers and is owned by an SSCP (System Service Control Point), which, for all practical purposes, is synonymous with VTAM.

These two things must happen before a resource can communicate in a network. The SSCP owns a resource when it knows about the resource and provides service for it.

The following is an example of the role a logical connection plays in your network. If someone came to your building and plugged a terminal into your network, it would not work unless your systems programmer had previously defined the terminal to the network. That would mean telling VTAM the name and the network location of that terminal.

When VTAM is started, after the terminal has been defined to the network it becomes the owner of the resources, and a logical connection is established. Then, if something goes wrong with any communication the terminal is having, VTAM is responsible for providing services to correct the problem.

After a resource is physically and logically connected, it is activated. Then it can communicate with other network services. The systems programmers define your resources, which then will be activated in the network. For example, a terminal could be defined as one of a group of terminals that should automatically be activated as soon as an associated cluster controller becomes active. The cluster controller could be part of a similar group of cluster controllers. These groups of resources, such as a group of cluster controllers, are called *major nodes*.

Resources are grouped into major nodes, and each individual resource within a major node is called a *minor node*. In the following, for example:

```
APPLSO1
IMS01
CICS01
NPM01
```

a collection of application-program definitions is an application major node. Here the major node is called APPLS01. Each application program (IMS01, CICS01, and NPM01) becomes a minor node. When you activate a major node, VTAM reads the definitions for the node and builds a table that lists all the minor nodes (individual resources) that make up the major node. This table is referred to as a *configuration list*.

If a minor node has been defined to become active, as soon as its major node becomes active, all of its minor nodes are also automatically activated. Otherwise, you must specifically activate the minor node. The major nodes must always be activated before any of the related minor nodes can become active. If the major nodes are not active, VTAM does not know about the minor nodes and, therefore, a logical connection does not exist.

In most cases, your systems programmer will define the major nodes to become active when VTAM starts. Then the major nodes will automatically activate the associated minor nodes (if the minor nodes were defined to become active when the major node was activated).

Consider Figure 18.3; the resources must be activated in a specific order:

1. SSCP in the host
2. PUs and LUs in the host
3. PUs in the cluster controller
4. LUs in the cluster controller

The resource between a given resource and the host are referred to as being upstream of that resource. Similarly, resources further from the host are referred to as being downstream of that resource. Resources upstream from an active resource must be activated first. For example, the cluster controller (3174) is upstream from the terminal, so it must be activated before either terminal (terminal 1 and 2 in Figure 18.3) can be activated. Note that the terminals are downstream from the cluster controller.

The activation hierarchy is particularly important for you to know. If a user calls to report that a terminal is not working, you must be able to trace back through the network to determine if the higher-level (upstream) resources are active.

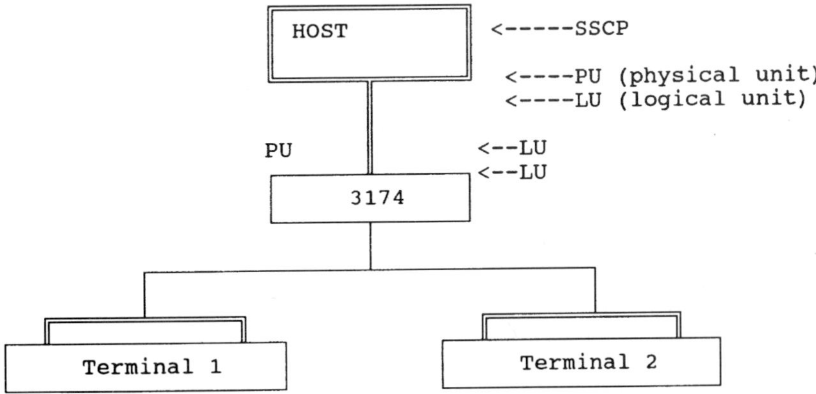

Figure 18.3 The sequence for activating a resource.

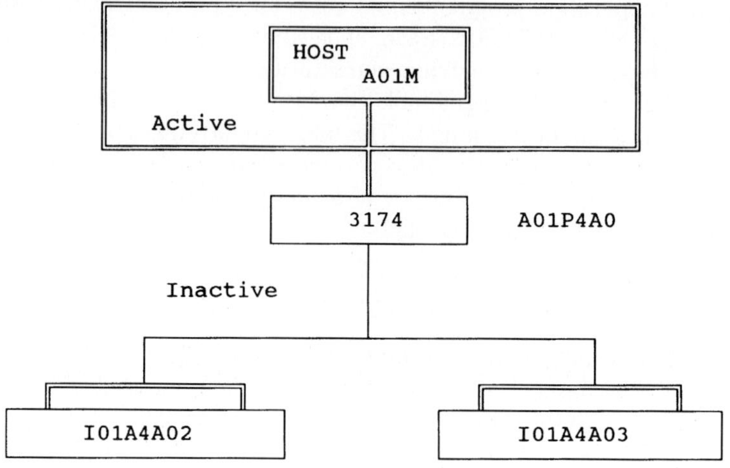

Figure 18.4 Activating a particular resource.

The Netview command you'll probably use to activate resources is ACT. Type ACT followed by the name of the resource, e.g., ACT A01P4A0, and then press the Enter key. You'll activate all three of the inactive resources shown in Figure 18.4. Go ahead and activate the first resource shown in Figure 18.4, ACT A01P4A0.

18.3 Logging On to Netview

As a network operator, one of your main tasks is to make sure that network resources are available when needed. To do that, you need to know how to activate and deactivate resources, monitor the network, and locate and fix a network problem.

The Netview program allows you to display the status of network resource and activate or deactivate resources. It provides a systematic way to determine the cause of network problems, and can be used with other problem-determination tools to resolve the problem.

Netview consists of a comprehensive set of tools to allow you to perform network management. These tools will help you to:

- Control the network
- Monitor the logical network
- Monitor the physical network
- Determine the status of network resources
- Automate the control and monitoring of the network

Netview's main components are:

- Netview
- Command facility

- Hardware monitor
- Session monitor
- Status monitor
- Help desk
- 4700 support
- Browse

The hardware monitor displays information about the physical network resources. The session monitor, on the other hand, displays information about the logical network resources. The status monitor displays the status of the network and its resources. The help desk guides you through a set of organized procedures in order to resolve certain network related problems. The 4700 support facility displays information about the 3600 and 4700 finance communication system. Last, the browse facility lets you look at the network log or Netview data sets. Not all of these functions will be expanded on in this chapter.

To use Netview programs, you must first log on the system. After you have logged on, you will see a list of things you can do. Figure 18.5 shows the initial Netview Panel. There are different ways you can get to this panel, depending on how it is installed in your organization. Once you have specified the operator I.D. and required password, a Netview Main Menu, shown in Figure 18.6, is displayed.

A Command Facility Panel, which provides you with a standardized screen layout, is presented in Figure 18.7. You can use this panel (also called NCCF) to control network resources and issue commands to the operating system. This facility provides the base service functions for network resources. To gain access to this facility, simply type NCCF next to the command line and press Enter.

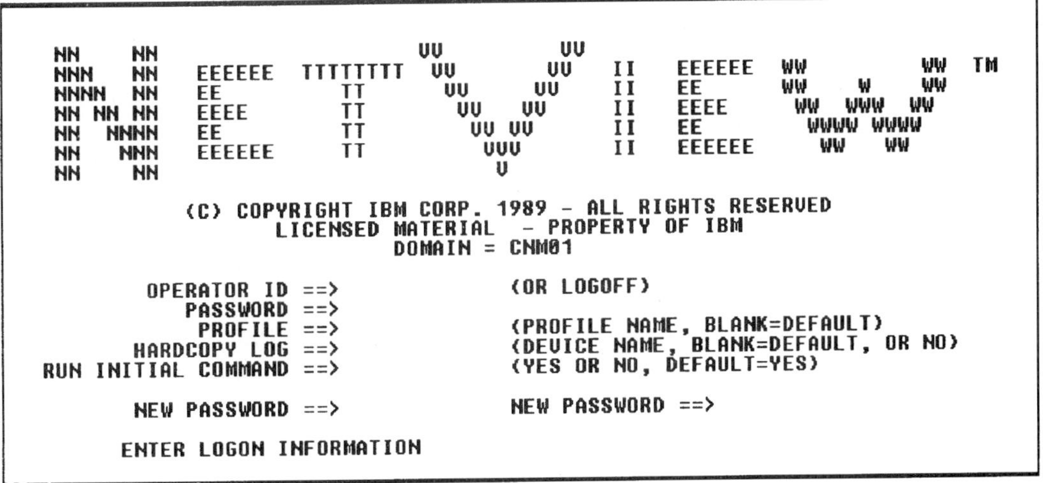

Figure 18.5 Initial Netview Panel.

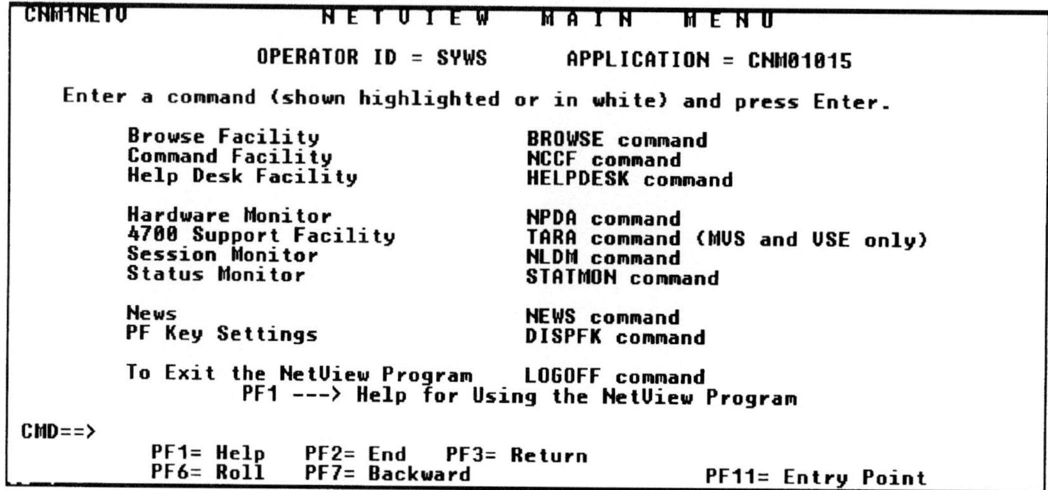

Figure 18.6 Netview Main System Menu.

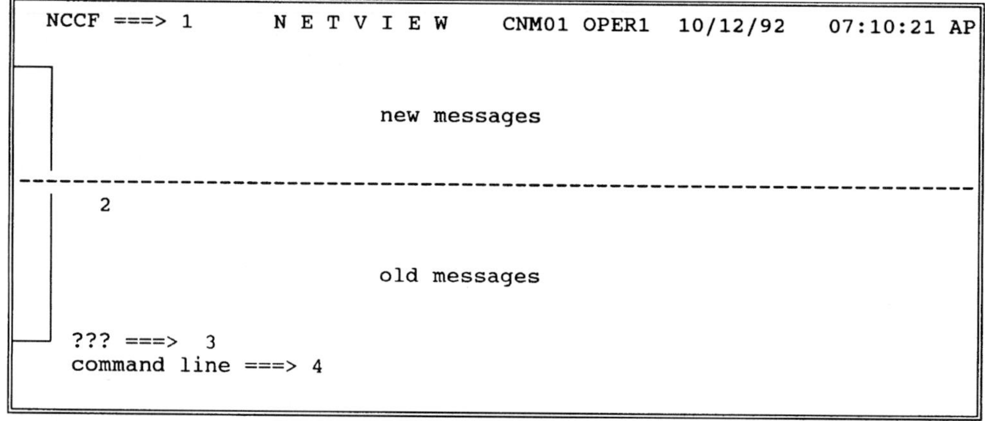

Figure 18.7 Standard Command Facility Panel in Netview.

Figure 18.7 contains an example of the Netview format. The panel is organized into four sections:

Session-identification line. The first line on the screen gives you the name of the panel that appears, and the name of the system (NETVIEW). The next field lists the session domain (CNM01) and your operator identifier (OPER1). Following those, the current date and time are listed. The last two fields, which contain a combination of either an A, H, or a blank, or a P, W, or a blank, indicate whether messages can be written to the screen.

Message area. The message area displays commands, responses, and messages from the system. The broken line separates the latest messages from the older ones.

These messages are continually updated. You can use this line to locate the most recent messages available in the system. They are the ones directly above the line.

Response area (???). Near the bottom of the screen is a line that begins with ???. This line is the response area. Look there for error messages.

Command line. The cursor is located in the command area. You communicate with the system by entering commands here, or you can invoke another Netview component. For example, type DISPFK and then press the Enter key. This will result in a panel showing PA and PF key settings. Review Figure 18.8 for more detail on this.

You can find the command that the PF or PA key sends to the system under the COMMAND column. In the case of PF1, help information about the command facility appears. Notice also that there might be some keys that cannot be set, such as PA1. You cannot change this key in any way. There might also be some keys that have not yet been set, such as PA3.

The chart in Figure 18.9 contains a cursory review of some of the commands I have talked about.

18.4 Remote Resource Concept

18.4.1 Remote resources

So far I have discussed only local resources and telecommunications in general. Suppose, however, that another cluster controller and its attached terminals are to be added to the network, but the cluster controller is not physically near the host computer. Assume it is in another building or across town, or perhaps even in another town.

A while back I mentioned that you could use a channel to attach a cluster controller to the host. But the new cluster controller cannot be attached using a chan-

```
NCCF          N E T V I E W                  CNM01 ALEX       01/24/92 14:39:30
 ' CNM01
DSI606I DISPLAY OF PF/PA KEY SETTINGS
DSI607I KEY    ----TYPE----    ----------COMMAND----------
DSI615I PA2    CANNOT BE SET   PREDEFINED FOR MOD = DSINDP
DSI616I PA3    NOT SET YET
DSI608I PF1    IMMED,APPEND    PFHELP
DSI608I PF2    IMMED,IGNORE    PFEND
DSI608I PF3    IMMED,IGNORE    RETURN
DSI608I PF4    IMMED,IGNORE    PFTOP
DSI608I PF5    IMMED,IGNORE    PFBOTTOM
DSI608I PF6    IMMED,IGNORE    ROLL
DSI608I PF7    IMMED,IGNORE    PFBACK
DSI608I PF8    IMMED,IGNORE    PFFORW
DSI608I PF9    IMMED,IGNORE    PFCOPY
DSI608I PF10   IMMED,IGNORE    DISPFK
DSI608I PF11   IMMED,IGNORE    HOLD
DSI608I PF12   IMMED,IGNORE    RETRIEVE
DSI608I PF13   IMMED,APPEND    PFHELP
DSI608I PF14   IMMED,IGNORE    PFEND
DSI608I PF15   IMMED,IGNORE    RETURN
DSI608I PF16   IMMED,IGNORE    PFTOP
 ??? ***
```

Figure 18.8 PA/PF key settings, displayed via the DISPFK command.

Command	To Do This
AUTOWRAP	Control how and when messages appear on the screen
DISPFK	Display your PF and PA keys
HELP NCFF	Display on-line help for the command facility
INACT	Deactivate a resource
LINES	Display the status of lines and channel links in the domain
LIST KEY = PFnn	Display the definition of a particular PF key
LOGOFF	End your Netview session
MAINMENU	Display the Netview main menu screen
NCCF	Enter the command facility
NEWS	Display information from the network control center
RETRIEVE	Place the last command you issued in the command area
SET PFnn	Change the setting of your PK keys

Figure 18.9 Some initial Netview commands.

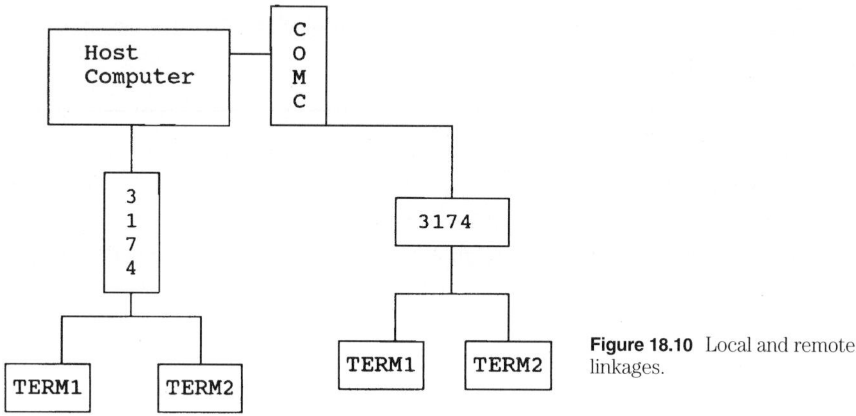

Figure 18.10 Local and remote linkages.

nel. A channel transmits data at a very high speed over short distances, and the distances between the new cluster controller and the host is far too great to use a channel. Because the second cluster controller cannot be attached by a channel to the host, it must be attached by a communication controller (COMC), which allows attachment of resources that cannot be attached locally to the host. Such resources are called *remote resources*.

The communication controller itself is a channel attached to the host computer. Besides routing data, the communication controller performs error recovery. Examples of such a controller are the IBM3720s and 3745s. It runs under the control of a network-control program such as IBM's ACF2/Network Control Program (NCP). The cluster controller is attached to the communication controller by a telecommunications link, such as a telephone wire, satellite, or microwave beam. At each end of this link there is a node for transmitting and receiving data. This diagram is depicted in Figure 18.10. Note that the modem close to the communication controller is referred to as a local modem. The one on the other end is the remote one.

18.4.2 Subareas

To help route data in a network, resources are divided into groups called *subareas*. A subarea can be a host computer and all the resources physically connected to it, except the communication controller. It can also be a communication controller and all the resources physically connected to it, except the host and other communication controllers.

In an example I used earlier, each subarea is assigned a unique number. The host is in subarea 1 (shown as SA01), and the communication controller is in subarea 3 (shown as SA03). An overview of this is presented in Figure 18.11.

The subarea address becomes part of the network address for each resource in the subarea, just as a zip-code number is part of the address for each person living in a particular zip-code area.

18.4.3 Domain

A *domain* consists of an SSCP (System Service Control Point), and the network resources it controls. (Earlier, I associated SSCP with VTAM.) If a network has only one SSCP, it has a single domain. This is referred to as a single-domain network. In this situation, all resources are defined and controlled by the same SSCP.

When a network has more than one SSCP, it is called a multiple-domain network. Consider the diagram shown in Figure 18.12. Note subarea SA02. If another host were added to the network, an additional subarea would also be added. In a network with multiple SSCPs (a multiple-domain network), resources can be defined to more than on SSCP. The domain the resource happens to be in depends on which resource gets activated.

18.4.4 Session

A *session* is a logical connection that lets two network-addressable units, or NADs, communicate with each other. The SSCP gets and keeps control over network re-

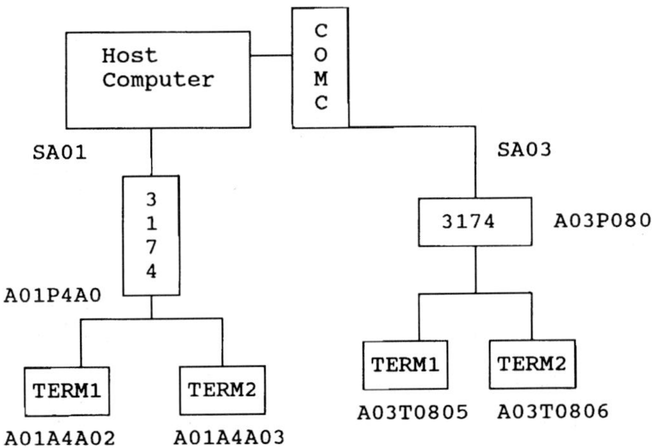

Figure 18.11 Subareas setup in a single domain.

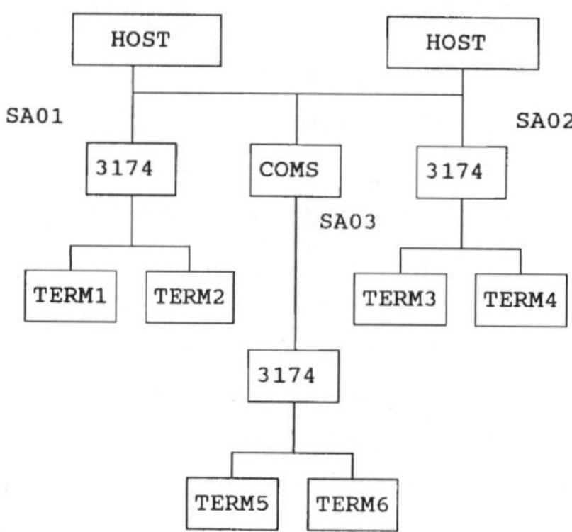

Figure 18.12 Multidomain environment.

sources by establishing sessions with the physical and logical units (PUs LUs), called SSCP-PU and SSCP-LU session respectively.

An SSCP-PU session controls a PU and its attached resources. The SSCP can ask the PU to activate or monitor the attached resources. The PU can also report errors about its resources to the SSCP. An SSCP-LU session is used to start or stop a kind of session called LU-LU (logical unit to logical unit). The primary purpose of a network is to allow end users to communicate. Two end users, such as a user at a terminal and an application at the host, can communicate with each other over an LU-LU session. An LU-LU session is a temporary connection between two end users and, to be established, a session can be started by either LU and must be accepted by the other.

Before an LU-LU session can be established, the SSCP must be in session with each of the LUs and with the PUs controlling the LUs. One of the LUs will ask the SSCP to establish the session. A BIND request establishes the session and sets up rules for the session, such as:

- Which LU transmits messages first
- How long the messages are
- What kind of responses are required

An LU-LU session is active until the end users finish exchanging data. Generally, a session lasts from logon to logoff. When the end users are through communicating, the logical unit that asked for the session in the first place will send an UNBIND request to the other logical terminal unit to terminate the session. The SSCP is notified that the session is being stopped. Then both LUs are available to start another session, either with each other or with other LUs.

18.5 Case Study 1: "Unable to Log On the System"

Suppose a user reports that he was unable to log on to application CICS11 from terminal T13012C1. You can first look at the terminal status on the command facility screen by typing D NET,ID=T13012C1,E. A panel similar to the one shown in Figure 18.13 will appear. Note that the terminal status is active. Because the terminal seems to be working, investigate the CICS11 application. To do this, type D NETID=CICS11,E and then press the Enter key. This will invoke the Application Status Panel shown in Figure 18.14.

Notice that the application is active and capable of supporting a session, if any is requested. (D tells Netview to display NET, which is simply the name of the VTAM currently running. ID refers to a terminal or application, whichever you happen to be looking at. E means everything.

So the next step is to find out just why the logon process has failed. To look at the session information for terminal T13012C1, do the following: type NLDM SESS T13012C1 and then press the Enter key one more time. (NLDM is the name of a product used by Netview. The result is shown in Figure 18.14.

The active SSCP-LU session is between the SSCP and terminal T13012C1. However, there is a BIND failure (BINDF) between the application CICS11 and terminal

```
NCCF       N E T V I E W              CN01   OPER1   07/12/92   10:32:40   A
* CNM01   D NET,ID=T13012C1,E
' CNM01
IST075I VTAM DISPLAY - NODE TYPE = LOGICAL UNIT
IST486I NAME=T13012CI(LU),STATUS=ACTIV,DESIRED STATE=ACTIV
IST597I CAPABILITY-PLU INHIBITED,SLU ENABLED ,SESSION LIMIT 00000001
IST598I NETID = NETC
IST081I LINE NAME = L12012 , LINE GROUP = G13S1 , MAJNOD = N139F4D
IST135I PHYSICAL UNIT = P13012C
IST082I DEVTYPE = LU , CONTROLLING PLU =
IST654I I/O TRACE = OFF, BUFFER TRACE = OFF
IST171I ACTIVE SESSIONS = 00000, SESSION REQUESTS = 00000
IST206I SESSIONS:
IST172I NO SESSIONS    EXIST
IST314I END
 ???
```

Figure 18.13 Terminal Status Panel.

```
NCCF       N E T V I E W              CN01   OPER1   07/12/92   10:32:40   A
* CNM01   D NET,ID=T13012C1,E
' CNM01
IST075I VTAM DISPLAY - NODE TYPE = LOGICAL UNIT
IST486I NAME=CICS11(APPLICATION) ,STATUS=ACTIV ,DESIRED STATE=ACTIV
IST597I CAPABILITY-PLU INHIBITED,SLU ENABLED ,SESSION LIMIT 00000001
IST598I NETID = NETC
IST654I I/O TRACE = OFF, BUFFER TRACE = OFF
IST081I JOB NAME = CICS11 , STEPNAME = CICS11
IST171I ACTIVE SESSION = 00000, SESSION REQUEST = 00003
IST206I SESSIONS:
IST634I NAME     STATUS     SESSION ID         SEND   RECV   VRN   TP   NETID
IST635I T13011A6 QUEUE-SEC 0080000846815915                              NETC
IST635I T13011A7 QUEUE-SEC 0080000846815916                              NETC
IST314I T13011A8 QUEUE-SEC 0080000846815917                              NETC
IST314I END
 ???
```

Figure 18.14 Application Status Panel.

```
NLDM.SESS                                                         PAGE    1
                              SESSION LIST
NAME:  T13012C1                                               DOMAIN: CNM01
---------------------------------------------------------------------------
   ***** PRIMARY ******          ***** SECONDARY ******
SEL#      NAME TYPE  DOM     NAME     TYPE     DOM      START TIME    END TIME
( 1)      M11  SSCP  CNM01   T13012C1 LU       CNM01    07/29 8:12:43 ***ACTIVE***
( 2)      CICS11 LU  CNM01   T13012C1 LU       CNM01    07/29 9:01:12 ***BINDF ***
                                                    REASON CODE 80 SENSE 08010000
( 3)      VNCA3  LU  N/A     T13012C1 LU       CNM01    07/29 9:50:12 08/12 9:59:07


END OF DATA
ENTER SELF# (CONFIG), SELF# AND CT (CONN.TEST), SELF# AND STR (TERM REASON)
CMD===>
```

Figure 18.15 Session List Panel.

```
NLDM.STER        SESSION TERMINATION REASON                      PAGE    1
-------- PRIMARY --------------------+ SECONDARY -------------------+-DOM -
NAME  CICS11 SA 00000008  EL 00AF  NAME T13012C1  SA  0000000D EL 00F9 CNM1
---------------------------------------------------------------------------

             TYPE:  BIND FAILURE
             REASON - (80) CINIT ERROR IN REACHING PLU

   SENSE DATA:
       CATEGORY - (08) RESOURCE NOT AVAILABLE: THE LU, PU, OR LINK SPECIFIED
       MODIFIER  - (01) IN AN RU IS NOT AVAILABLE
          BYTE 2 - (00)
          BYTE 3 - (00)

  ENTER 'R' TO RETURN TO PREVIOUS DISPLAY - OR COMMAND
  CMD===>
```

Figure 18.16 The Session Termination Reason Panel.

T13012C1. Consider the Session List Panel shown in Figure 18.15.

The next step is to look at the reason for the session termination. From the Session List Panel, display the reason for such termination. To do this, type 2 STR and then press Enter. This will invoke a Session Termination Reason Panel, highlighted in Figure 18.16. The message CINIT ERROR IN REACHING PLU indicates a failure at the primary LU because CICS11 has rejected the transaction. In this case, the user was using a terminal that was not known to the application CIVS11.

To correct this problem, you can open a problem report and tell whoever is handling CICS that a user on terminal T13012C1 is trying to log on.

18.6 Case Study 2: From TSO/ISPF to CICS without Logging Off

In this case study, I'd like to show you how to switch from an active ISPF session to CICS or vice versa via Netview without having to log off the current session. The average programmer needs to continually shift back and forth between sessions in testing and revising a program. The series of panels that appear in this section will show you how to save yourself time using some of the features available in the Netview system.

In Figure 18.17, I invoked the Netview logon screen as before. Here, I have entered the operator I.D. ALEX and a password that does not display. Then I pressed Enter and an interim Netview panel similar to the one in Figure 18.18 was displayed. This panel shows three question marks (???) in the lower left-hand corner of the screen, awaiting my logon to invoke ISPF/TSO. So following the question marks, I entered

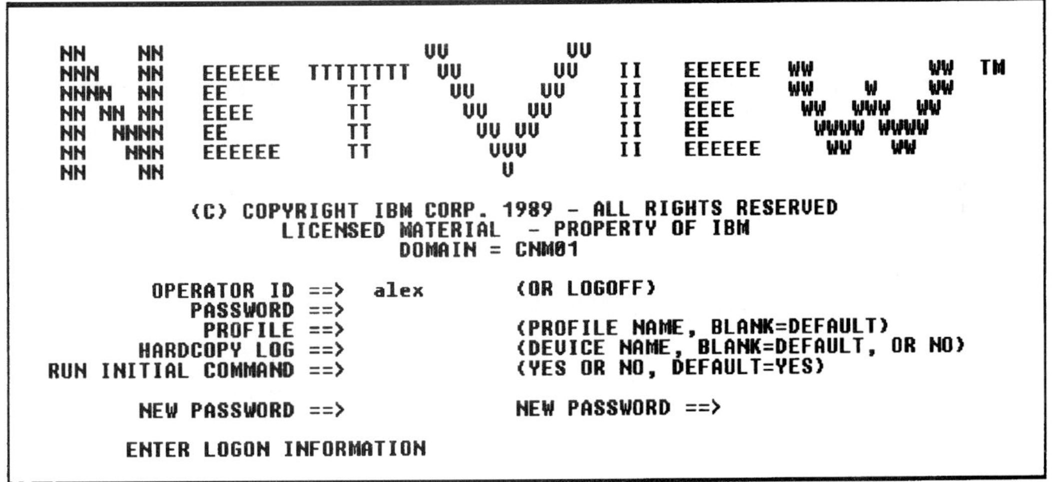

Figure 18.17 The Netview logon screen.

```
NCCF          N E T V I E W                CNM01 ALEX      01/27/92 15:45:34
- CNM01     DSI020I OPERATOR ALEX     LOGGED ON FROM TERMINAL LAN004A  USING
            PROFILE (DSIPROFE ), HCL (          )
- CNM01     DSI083I AUTOWRAP STOPPED
C CNM01     CNM357I PFKDEF  : PF KEY SETTINGS NOW ESTABLISHED.
            +               : "DISPFK" TO SEE YOUR PF KEY SETTINGS
C CNM01
                ENTER LOG|LOGOFF TO TERMINATE SESSION
                ENTER HELP, PFK1 OR PFK13 FOR HELP
                SYSTEM OPERATOR HAS BEEN NOTIFIED OF LOGON
                TO OBTAIN HELP FROM NETWORK CONTROL CENTER ENTER:
                   MSG PPT, TEXT
                       WHERE 'TEXT' IS THE QUESTION

C CNM01     **  NEWS FOR TODAY 01/27/92
C CNM01     **
C CNM01     **              NO NEW NEWS
C CNM01     **
C CNM01
C CNM01     DSI210I COMMAND LIST MAINMENU WARNING - COMMAND NOT IN OPERATOR
            SCOPE - COMMAND IGNORED
            VIEW 8 CNM1NETV
??? ***
```

Figure 18.18 An intermediate Netview Panel for an additional logon.

```
NCCF          N E T V I E W                  CNM01 ALEX       01/27/92 15:53:17
- CNM01     DSI020I OPERATOR ALEX     LOGGED ON FROM TERMINAL LAN004A  USING
            PROFILE (DSIPROFE ), HCL (          )
- CNM01     DSI083I AUTOWRAP STOPPED
C CNM01     CNM357I PFKDEF : PF KEY SETTINGS NOW ESTABLISHED.
            +              : "DISPFK" TO SEE YOUR PF KEY SETTINGS
C CNM01
                ENTER LOG|LOGOFF TO TERMINATE SESSION
                ENTER HELP, PFK1 OR PFK13 FOR HELP
                SYSTEM OPERATOR HAS BEEN NOTIFIED OF LOGON
                TO OBTAIN HELP FROM NETWORK CONTROL CENTER ENTER:
                   MSG PPT, TEXT
                       WHERE 'TEXT' IS THE QUESTION

C CNM01     **  NEWS FOR TODAY 01/27/92
C CNM01     **
C CNM01     **               NO NEW NEWS
C CNM01     **
C CNM01
C CNM01     DSI210I COMMAND LIST MAINMENU WARNING - COMMAND NOT IN OPERATOR
            SCOPE - COMMAND IGNORED
            VIEW 8 CNM1NETV
??? ***
LTSO15
```

Figure 18.19 TSO/ISPF prompt.

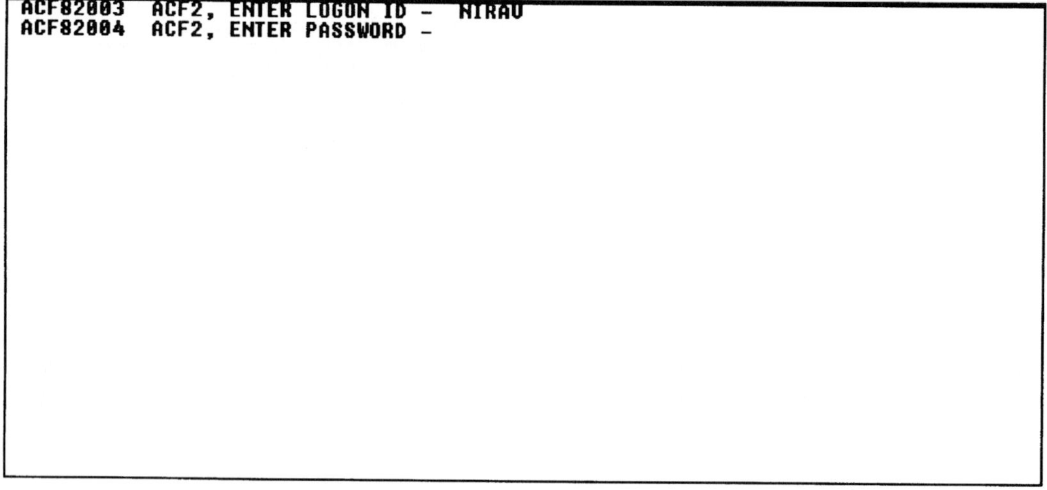

```
ACF82003  ACF2, ENTER LOGON ID -   NIRAV
ACF82004  ACF2, ENTER PASSWORD -
```

Figure 18.20 TSO/ISPF Sign-On Panel.

LTSO15 (see Figure 18.19) and pressed the Enter key, which put me directly into ISPF mode. The panel shown in Figure 18.20 requires the standard logon procedures to activate ISPF.

Figure 18.21 shows a typical ISPF Panel—the last procedure I was operating in before shifting back to CICS. At this point, I simply pressed the PA2 hotkey, which immediately took me out of the current routine while providing me with four terminal control options. This is depicted in Figure 18.22.

This screen is essentially a menu panel that I used to select option 1, thereby triggering the Interim Panel in Figure 18.23. Actually, Figures 18.23 and 18.24 represent a "before" and "after" snapshot of a desired target region, such as CICSDEVO. Having entered CICSDEVO underneath the question marks, I pressed the Enter key, which switched me to the requested CICS logon screen, shown in Figure 18.25. Note that, during the whole exercise, I did not have to logoff a particular session I was in to invoke the next. Likewise, to get back to ISPF, I simply pressed the PA2 hotkey to return to the previously displayed interim screen.

```
EDIT ---- NIRAU.STANDARD.CNTL(ARA91C) - 01.99 ---------------- COLUMNS 001 072
COMMAND ===>                                                   SCROLL ===> CSR
****** ***************************** TOP OF DATA ******************************
==MSG> -CAUTION- PROFILE CHANGED TO "NUMBER OFF" (FROM "NUMBER ON STD").
==MSG>        DATA DOES NOT HAVE VALID STANDARD NUMBERS.
000001        IDENTIFICATION DIVISION.
000002        PROGRAM-ID. ARA91C.
000003        DATE-COMPILED.
000004        ENVIRONMENT DIVISION.
000005        DATA DIVISION.
000006        WORKING-STORAGE SECTION.
. . . . . . . . . . . . . . . . . . . . . . . . . . . . . . . . . . . . . . .
OPTION ===>

                        ISPF PRIMARY OPTIONS MENU
.-----------------------------------------------------------------..
|.--------------------------------------------------------.----.  ..
|.      0  ISPF PARMS            J  DOC/TEXT JOB/SCAN  |    |----.---..
|.      1  BROWSE                P  PANVALET           |    |    |    ..
|.      2  EDIT                  I  INFO/MVS (OZ)      |    |    |     ..
|.      3  UTILITIES             F  FILE-AID           |....|    |   .....
|.      4  FOREGROUND            V  VPS60                   |....|........ ..
|.      5  BATCH                 S  SCREEN DEVELOPMENT FACILITY         ..|
|.      6  TSO                   T  TUTORIAL                            ..|
```

Figure 18.21 The last screen used in ISPF before shifting to a CICS session.

```
NETVIEW TERMINAL ACCESS FACILITY CONTROL OPTIONS:

1.   RETURN TO NETVIEW COMMAND FACILITY AND NOTIFY WHEN
     ADDITIONAL OUTPUT IS RECEIVED ON THIS SESSION.
     SESSION DOES NOT RUN WHILE DISCONNECTED.

2.   RETURN TO NETVIEW COMMAND FACILITY.
     SESSION RUNS WHILE DISCONNECTED.

3.   SEND PA02       TO TSO       (DISCONNECT KEY)

4.   RESUME THIS FULL SCREEN SESSION



DOMID = CNM01    OPID = ALEX

OPTION SELECTED:   1

NOTE: ANY OTHER VALUE WILL RESUME THIS SESSION
```

Figure 18.22 Terminal facility control option invoked via PA2.

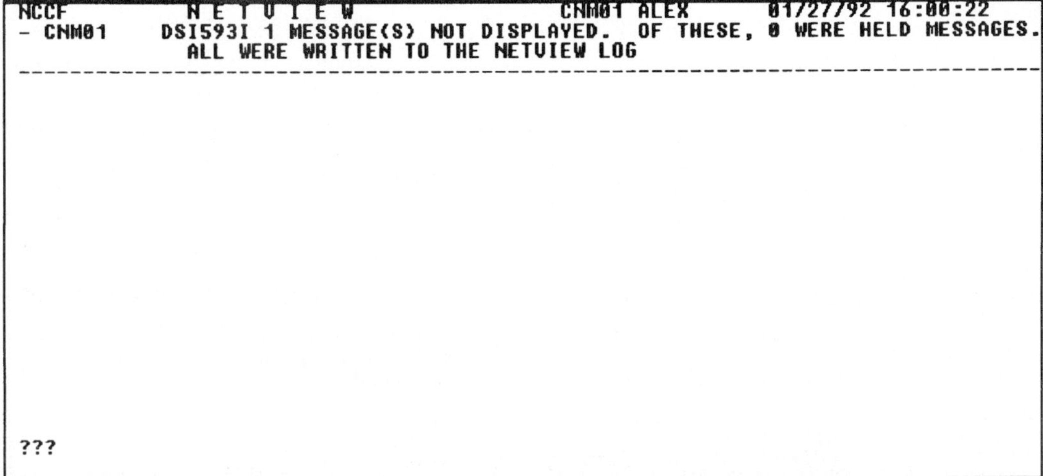
```
NCCF          N E T V I E W                CNM01 ALEX       01/27/92 16:00:22
- CNM01     DSI593I 1 MESSAGE(S) NOT DISPLAYED.  OF THESE, 0 WERE HELD MESSAGES.
              ALL WERE WRITTEN TO THE NETVIEW LOG
-----------------------------------------------------------------------------





???
```

Figure 18.23 An interim screen for defining your target region.

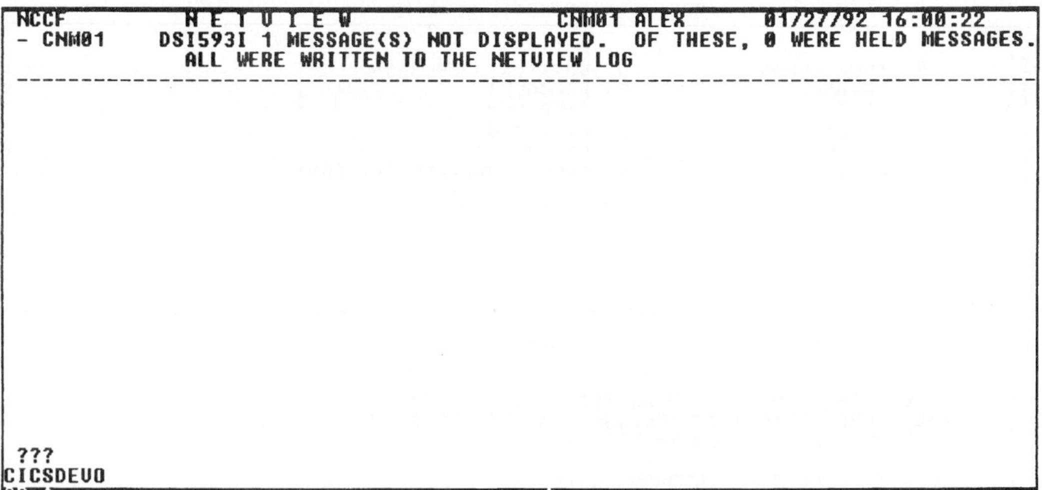
```
NCCF          N E T V I E W                CNM01 ALEX       01/27/92 16:00:22
- CNM01     DSI593I 1 MESSAGE(S) NOT DISPLAYED.  OF THESE, 0 WERE HELD MESSAGES.
              ALL WERE WRITTEN TO THE NETVIEW LOG
-----------------------------------------------------------------------------





???
CICSDEVO
```

Figure 18.24 Panel following the entry of a CICS region such as CICSDEVO.

Note that, in later release, if you were to use an IBM OS/2 microcomputer to emulate an IBM 3270 terminal, it is more practical to invoke a second 3270 session than using Netview.

One final comment on Netview. There are some features in this product that overlap Candle's Omegamon. However, the two products were engineered with different objectives in mind. A comprehensive overview of Omegamon is provided in one of my earlier publication *Mainframe Productivity Tools of the '90s* (John Wiley & Sons Inc.).

```
      SYSTEM: CICSDEV0 METRA CICS XA 2.1.1 ONLINE DEVELOPMENT SYSTEM
                       CICS SYSTEM SECURED BY ACF2/CICS 5.0
    TERMINAL: T015
        NODE: TAF0015

         DAY: MONDAY

 SYSTEM DATE: JANUARY 27, 1992
 SYSTEM TIME: 04:02 PM

    LOGON ID: ===>
    PASSWORD: ===>

NEW PASSWORD: ===>
(enter twice): ==>




CICS/VS - ACF2  (SYSTEM SIGN ON/OFF FACILITY)
```

Figure 18.25 A typical CICS logon screen.

Chapter

19

Coding CICS-Supplied Transactions

What prompted me to write a chapter on IBM-supplied transactions was simply that these transactions can be looked on simply as on-line utilities. However, unlike batch utilities, programmers in most CICS environments do not have access to an array of such transactions, most of which are controlled by a systems group, rather than by an application group.

Because of this inherent restriction in using these on-line utilities, I am going to talk about only a few, but certainly important, transaction types. Among these are:

CEDF. This transaction will be discussed in detail because it enables you to test your on-line program and resolve some of the problems that might be the result of incomplete data or faulty logic.

CECI. Enables you to browse a file or display a map before the program designed to handle it is completed.

CEMT. Allows you to issue a new copy, that is the latest version, of your application program.

CSSN and CSSF. Provides you with logon and logoff capabilities.

CICS-supported operations are usually initiated from a terminal, and they are referred to as *transactions*, each of which entails the use of tables, programs, and internal services. These transactions have identical codes (transid) that always start with the character C and are always four characters long. The table highlighted in Figure 19.1 is a list of IBM-supplied transactions that you might be able to use at your terminal.

In general, you start a CICS-supplied transaction by entering a transaction identification code. CICS-supplied transactions allow you to make inquiries about the con-

```
  CBRC   database-recovery control statement
  CBRC   DBRC on-line command transaction
  CEBR   temporary storage browse
* CECI   command-level interpreter
* CECS   command-level syntax checker
  CEDA   resource definition on-line
  CEDB   resource definition on-line (limited function)
  CEDC   resource definition on-line (limited function)
* CEDF   execute diagnostic facility
* CEMT   master terminal
  CESN   sign on (preferred to CSSN)
  CEST   supervisory call
  CMSG   message switching
  CRTE   routing
  CSFE   terminal test, trace, and storage
  CSMT   master terminal (superseded by CEMT)
  CSOT   treminal status (superseded by CEOT)
  CSPG   terminal paging
* CSSF   sign off
* CSSN   sign on
  CSST   supervisory terminal (superseded by CEST)
  CSTT   system statistics and monitoring
  CWTO   write to console operator
```

Figure 19.1 List of CICS-supplied transactions. Those marked by an asterisk will be covered in detail, starting with the CECI transactions.

tents of a database, update or add to the contents of such, or perform calculations, the result of which can be returned to you at your terminal.

If you use an IBM 3270 display terminal or similar (compatible) display device that has the appropriate features installed, you can also start a transaction by a PF key or other means. Simply invoke the CICS-supplied transaction by entering its transaction identifier, usually at the top of the screen. If you do not enter enough information, the transaction will prompt you for more. Once started, the transaction will processes the additional data. At the completion of this transaction, a message will inform you: STATUS: SESSION ENDED.

In general, CICS-supplied transactions accept any characters of a keyword that will uniquely identify it within the request. In this way, you can enter the keyword TASK as TA, TAS, or TASK, but you cannot use T because it can be confused with TIME, TERMINAL, TRANSACTION, and TRACE. In the syntax that displays on your screen, you will see the minimum permitted abbreviation in uppercase characters, with the reminder in lowercase.

Transactions in Figure 19.1 that are marked by an asterisk will be covered in detail, starting with the CECI transactions.

19.1 A Practical View of CICS-Supplied Transactions

19.1.1 CEDF-executed diagnostics facility

The purpose of this section is to show you how to use the Execute Diagnostics Facility transaction, referred to as CEDF, and explain how to modify any specific value during the execution of a transaction to temporarily prevent any undesirable results, such as not being able to find a particular record on file.

This presentation will show you the mechanics of CEDF in a frame-by-frame fashion, illustrated in a total of 19 screens (Figures 19.2 through 19.20). Although 19 screens to illustrate this cycle might seem plenty, in reality, I provided only those procedures that directly impact the system.

Start the Execute Diagnostics session by clearing the screen in front of you and entering the CEDF. CICS will respond by displaying a short message in the upper left-hand corner of the screen, informing you that you are now in EDF mode. To continue, clear the screen one more time and enter the transaction identifier of the program to be monitored. (Note that you might have to initiate a program through a menu, submenu, or seemingly distant (but hierarchically consistent) module, depending on the current program's path and dependencies.

In entering the transaction identifier AR90 (while omitting several screens of housekeeping procedures), the program ARC92C is invoked, and, more importantly, it is about to execute a HANDLE AID procedure. A snapshot of this is shown in Figure 19.2.

Note that there are a total of three keys defined in this frame: PF1 and PF4, as well as the Clear key. All other keys are inconsequential. When you press the Enter key for the second time, a new frame corresponding to the one shown in Figure 19.3 will be shown, containing a "normal" response.

The next set of frames, Figures 19.4 through 19.6, were triggered at the time the Enter key was pressed for the second time. Figure 19.4 shows the environment just prior to CICS issuing a SEND MAP command. This subsequently results in CICS displaying a map prototype in Figure 19.5 and the normal response to this statement, shown in Figure 19.6.

Following these screens, an EXEC CICS RETURN is issued (Figure 19.7), resulting in the termination of the AR90 task, following the reinvocation of the entire pro-

```
 TRANSACTION: AR90   PROGRAM: ARC92C      TASK NUMBER: 0000388   DISPLAY:  00
 STATUS:  ABOUT TO EXECUTE COMMAND
 EXEC CICS HANDLE AID
  ANYKEY
  CLEAR ()
  PF1 ()
  PF4









 OFFSET:X'000F60'    LINE:00263          EIBFN=X'0206'


ENTER:  CONTINUE
PF1 : UNDEFINED          PF2 : SWITCH HEX/CHAR      PF3 : UNDEFINED
PF4 : SUPPRESS DISPLAYS  PF5 : WORKING STORAGE      PF6 : USER DISPLAY
PF7 : SCROLL BACK        PF8 : SCROLL FORWARD       PF9 : STOP CONDITIONS
PF10: PREVIOUS DISPLAY   PF11: UNDEFINED            PF12: ABEND USER TASK
```

Figure 19.2 Handle AID command about to be executed.

```
TRANSACTION: AR90   PROGRAM: ARC92C      TASK NUMBER: 0000388    DISPLAY:  00
STATUS:  COMMAND EXECUTION COMPLETE
EXEC CICS HANDLE AID
 ANYKEY
 CLEAR ()
 PF1 ()
 PF4







OFFSET:X'000F60'    LINE:00263            EIBFN=X'0206'
RESPONSE: NORMAL                          EIBRESP=0

ENTER:  CONTINUE
PF1 : UNDEFINED             PF2 : SWITCH HEX/CHAR       PF3 : END EDF SESSION
PF4 : SUPPRESS DISPLAYS     PF5 : WORKING STORAGE       PF6 : USER DISPLAY
PF7 : SCROLL BACK           PF8 : SCROLL FORWARD        PF9 : STOP CONDITIONS
PF10: PREVIOUS DISPLAY      PF11: UNDEFINED             PF12: ABEND USER TASK
```

Figure 19.3 Completed HANDLE AID command and a normal return.

```
TRANSACTION: AR90   PROGRAM: ARC92C      TASK NUMBER: 0000388    DISPLAY:  00
STATUS:  ABOUT TO EXECUTE COMMAND
EXEC CICS SEND MAP
 MAP ('ARC92M7')
 FROM ('..............YAR92...0000    ...................................'...)
 MAPSET ('ARC92M ')
 CURSOR
 TERMINAL
 ERASE






OFFSET:X'0010BE'    LINE:00280            EIBFN=X'1804'


ENTER:  CONTINUE
PF1 : UNDEFINED             PF2 : SWITCH HEX/CHAR       PF3 : UNDEFINED
PF4 : SUPPRESS DISPLAYS     PF5 : WORKING STORAGE       PF6 : USER DISPLAY
PF7 : SCROLL BACK           PF8 : SCROLL FORWARD        PF9 : STOP CONDITIONS
PF10: PREVIOUS DISPLAY      PF11: UNDEFINED             PF12: ABEND USER TASK
```

Figure 19.4 SEND MAP command about to be issued.

gram, as highlighted in Figure 19.8. To indicate to CICS that you want to continually monitor the program through the EDF apparatus, reply YES.

As I stated before, this EDF session contains most but not all of the scenario in conjunction with the ARC92C change program; certain statements were omitted to accelerate the presentation. In Figure 19.9, a map appears with the cursor indicating the first position of the concatenated key. A customer number of 0100 was entered by the operator and, thus, the entire program was reinitiated, as shown in Figure 19.10. So the cycle continues on the receiving end of the map: Figures 19.11 and 19.12 represent the status before and after the successful completion of a HANDLE

AID, and Figures 19.13 and 19.14 provide you with a snapshot of the SEND command before and after execution.

You might have noticed the appearance of a map containing the customer master database between frames Figures 10.13 and 19.14 for perhaps a fraction of a second. This means that the panel was transmitted and read (response=normal), and that it will now continue uninterrupted. The record is about to be read, as displayed in Figure 19.15, based on the previously entered customer number.

```
 AR92                  CUSTOMER DATABASE MAINTENANCE                    0000


CUSTOMER NUMBER      :
CUSTOMER NAME        :
ADDRESS (1)          :
ADDRESS (2)          :
ADDRESS (3)          :
STATE                :
POSTAL CODE          :
TELEPHONE            :
CONTACT NAME         :
ABBREVIATED NAME     :
ATTENTION LINE1      :
ATTENTION LINE2      :




PF1: RETURN TO MENU     PF4: UPDATE RECORD
```

Figure 19.5 View of the physical map.

```
  TRANSACTION: AR90    PROGRAM: ARC92C       TASK NUMBER: 0000682   DISPLAY:  00
  STATUS:  COMMAND EXECUTION COMPLETE
  EXEC CICS SEND MAP
   MAP ('ARC92M7')
   FROM ('...............YAR92...0000      ................................'...)
   MAPSET ('ARC92M ')
   CURSOR
   TERMINAL
   ERASE






  OFFSET:X'0010BE'     LINE:00280           EIBFN=X'1804'
  RESPONSE: NORMAL                          EIBRESP=0

ENTER:  CONTINUE
PF1 : UNDEFINED           PF2 : SWITCH HEX/CHAR     PF3 : END EDF SESSION
PF4 : SUPPRESS DISPLAYS   PF5 : WORKING STORAGE     PF6 : USER DISPLAY
PF7 : SCROLL BACK         PF8 : SCROLL FORWARD      PF9 : STOP CONDITIONS
PF10: PREVIOUS DISPLAY    PF11: UNDEFINED           PF12: ABEND USER TASK
```

Figure 19.6 Completion of the SEND MAP command.

```
 TRANSACTION: AR90   PROGRAM: ARC92C       TASK NUMBER: 0000682   DISPLAY:  00
 STATUS:  ABOUT TO EXECUTE COMMAND
 EXEC CICS RETURN
  TRANSID ('AR92')
  COMMAREA ('R$$$$')
  LENGTH (5)









 OFFSET:X'001882'    LINE:00531           EIBFN=X'0E08'

ENTER:  CONTINUE
PF1 : UNDEFINED             PF2 : SWITCH HEX/CHAR      PF3 : UNDEFINED
PF4 : SUPPRESS DISPLAYS     PF5 : WORKING STORAGE      PF6 : USER DISPLAY
PF7 : SCROLL BACK           PF8 : SCROLL FORWARD       PF9 : STOP CONDITIONS
PF10: PREVIOUS DISPLAY      PF11: UNDEFINED            PF12: ABEND USER TASK
```

Figure 19.7 RETURN command about to be executed.

```
 TRANSACTION: AR90                         TASK NUMBER: 0000682   DISPLAY:  00
 STATUS:  TASK TERMINATION














TO CONTINUE EDF SESSION REPLY YES                                REPLY: YES_
ENTER:  CONTINUE
PF1 : UNDEFINED             PF2 : SWITCH HEX/CHAR      PF3 : END EDF SESSION
PF4 : SUPPRESS DISPLAYS     PF5 : WORKING STORAGE      PF6 : USER DISPLAY
PF7 : SCROLL BACK           PF8 : SCROLL FORWARD       PF9 : STOP CONDITIONS
PF10: PREVIOUS DISPLAY      PF11: UNDEFINED            PF12: UNDEFINED
```

Figure 19.8 Task was terminated, and a request to continue issued.

Figure 19.16 reveals that there is no such customer number on file. This is crucial, especially if the program being tested does not have a logically sound record-not-found routine, and thus comes to a sudden, abnormal termination.

Because EDF gives you the ability to change the contents of the RIDFLD, I have modified the key by replacing the current value of it (0100) with a new value, 0101. (Note that the same change was also made to the INTO field.) Once the Enter key is pressed (see Figure 19.17) and the file reread using the new key value, the completion of the operation (Figure 19.18) has a normal response code. Actually, think of a response code as a VSAM return code like the one used during the processing of a VSAM file in a batch run.

So now the map is sent one more time (see Figure 19.19), resulting in the display of the entire customer record, shown in Figure 19.20.

It is obvious from the way you have overridden a NOTFND condition that you can also prevent an ASRA or data exception from happening simply by changing a value or the contents of the WORKING-STORAGE SECTION prior to an execution. This enables you to complete a test unaffected and fix the program later on in the process, as time allows. As you can see, CEDF assisted you in finding the exact location of the problem and fixing or overriding the problem for a more permanent solution at some future point in time.

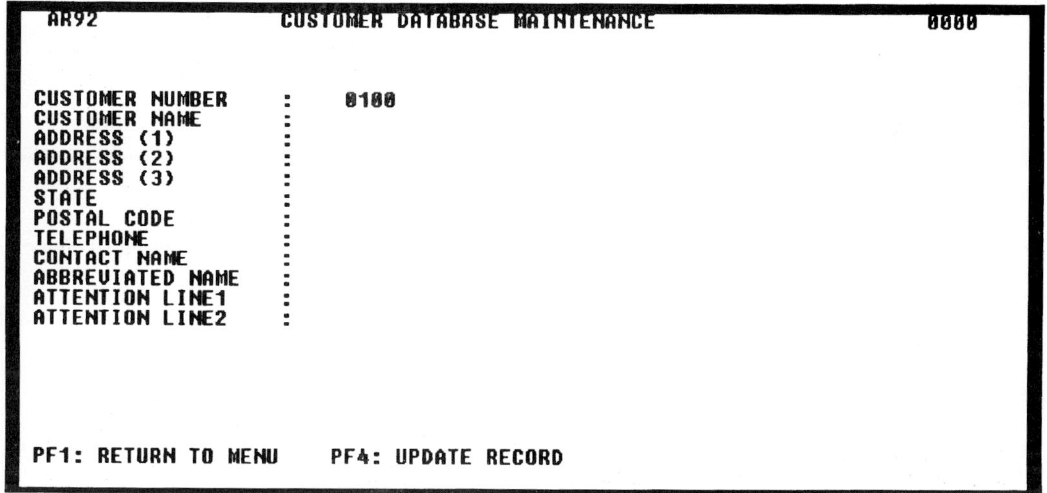

Figure 19.9 Display of the customer database map.

```
 TRANSACTION: AR92   PROGRAM: ARC92C      TASK NUMBER: 0000704   DISPLAY:  00
 STATUS:  PROGRAM INITIATION
    COMMAREA      = 'R$$$$'
    EIBTIME       = 160306
    EIBDATE       = 91269
    EIBTRNID      = 'AR92'
    EIBTASKN      = 704
    EIBTRMID      = '0000'

    EIBCPOSN      = 425
    EIBCALEN      = 5
    EIBAID        = X'7D'                                       AT X'00021642'
    EIBFN         = X'0000'                                     AT X'00021643'
    EIBRCODE      = X'000000000000'                             AT X'00021645'
    EIBDS         = '........'
+   EIBREQID      = '........'


ENTER:  CONTINUE
PF1 : UNDEFINED            PF2 : SWITCH HEX/CHAR     PF3 : END EDF SESSION
PF4 : SUPPRESS DISPLAYS    PF5 : WORKING STORAGE     PF6 : USER DISPLAY
PF7 : SCROLL BACK          PF8 : SCROLL FORWARD      PF9 : STOP CONDITIONS
PF10: PREVIOUS DISPLAY     PF11: UNDEFINED           PF12: UNDEFINED
```

Figure 19.10 Program reinitialization after a reinvoke.

```
TRANSACTION: AR92   PROGRAM: ARC92C      TASK NUMBER: 0000704    DISPLAY:  00
STATUS:  ABOUT TO EXECUTE COMMAND
EXEC CICS HANDLE AID
 ANYKEY
 CLEAR ()
 PF1 ()
 PF4










OFFSET:X'000F60'    LINE:00263          EIBFN=X'0206'


ENTER:  CONTINUE
PF1 : UNDEFINED           PF2 : SWITCH HEX/CHAR     PF3 : UNDEFINED
PF4 : SUPPRESS DISPLAYS   PF5 : WORKING STORAGE     PF6 : USER DISPLAY
PF7 : SCROLL BACK         PF8 : SCROLL FORWARD      PF9 : STOP CONDITIONS
PF10: PREVIOUS DISPLAY    PF11: UNDEFINED           PF12: ABEND USER TASK
```

Figure 19.11 HANDLE AID command about to be executed.

```
TRANSACTION: AR92   PROGRAM: ARC92C      TASK NUMBER: 0000704    DISPLAY:  00
STATUS:  COMMAND EXECUTION COMPLETE
EXEC CICS HANDLE AID
 ANYKEY
 CLEAR ()
 PF1 ()
 PF4










OFFSET:X'000F60'    LINE:00263          EIBFN=X'0206'
RESPONSE: NORMAL                        EIBRESP=0

ENTER:  CONTINUE
PF1 : UNDEFINED           PF2 : SWITCH HEX/CHAR     PF3 : END EDF SESSION
PF4 : SUPPRESS DISPLAYS   PF5 : WORKING STORAGE     PF6 : USER DISPLAY
PF7 : SCROLL BACK         PF8 : SCROLL FORWARD      PF9 : STOP CONDITIONS
PF10: PREVIOUS DISPLAY    PF11: UNDEFINED           PF12: ABEND USER TASK
```

Figure 19.12 HANDLE AID command executed with a normal response.

19.1.2 The CECI command

The CECI, or Command-Level Interpreter Transaction, enables you to enter a CICS command, check its syntax, and, if required, modify and in most cases execute it from your 3270 (or compatible) terminal.

A practical example of this will illustrate how you can display your BMS (Basic Mapping Support or map) prior to completing the actual CICS program that will send and receive the above transmission. This is useful in order to verify the proper layout and to catch any related problems, real or potential, that might exist relative to this map. Consider the following statement:

```
CECI SEND MAP(ARA21M2) MAPSET(ARA21M)
```

This is the first of three frames, shown in Figure 19.21. When you press the Enter key, a second panel will come up, shown in Figure 19.22, informing you that the CECI command (just like the CEDF transaction) is about to execute. Last, the actual screen display is presented in Figure 19.23.

Allow me to make the situation a bit more complicated. The objective is to physically browse through a file with insufficient information about most of the characteristics of the file to be processed. Suppose you are in the process of developing an inquiry program that requires you to know the full (rather than a generic) key. Once the program is completed, the only way you can test it if you know some of the val-

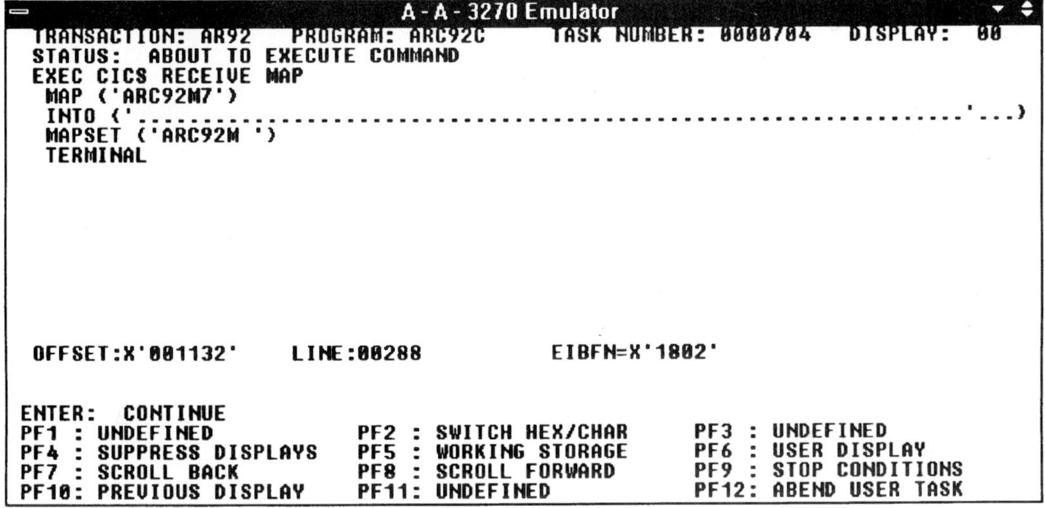

Figure 19.13 RECEIVE MAP command about to be executed.

```
TRANSACTION: AR92   PROGRAM: ARC92C      TASK NUMBER: 0000704   DISPLAY:  00
STATUS:  COMMAND EXECUTION COMPLETE
EXEC CICS RECEIVE MAP
 MAP ('ARC92M7')
 INTO ('.................................................0100...'...)
 MAPSET ('ARC92M ')
 TERMINAL




OFFSET:X'001132'    LINE:00288           EIBFN=X'1802'
RESPONSE: NORMAL                         EIBRESP=0

ENTER:  CONTINUE
PF1 : UNDEFINED            PF2 : SWITCH HEX/CHAR     PF3 : END EDF SESSION
PF4 : SUPPRESS DISPLAYS    PF5 : WORKING STORAGE     PF6 : USER DISPLAY
PF7 : SCROLL BACK          PF8 : SCROLL FORWARD      PF9 : STOP CONDITIONS
PF10: PREVIOUS DISPLAY     PF11: UNDEFINED           PF12: ABEND USER TASK
```

Figure 19.14 Status after the successful execution of a RECEIVE MAP.

```
TRANSACTION: AR92   PROGRAM: ARC92C      TASK NUMBER: 0000704   DISPLAY:  00
STATUS:  ABOUT TO EXECUTE COMMAND
EXEC CICS READ
 FILE ('RK501    ')
 INTO ('.0120000000000010001                    .........................'...)
 RIDFLD ('0120000000000010001                   ')
 UPDATE


OFFSET:X'0012A8'    LINE:00308           EIBFN=X'0602'

ENTER:  CONTINUE
PF1 : UNDEFINED           PF2 : SWITCH HEX/CHAR      PF3 : UNDEFINED
PF4 : SUPPRESS DISPLAYS   PF5 : WORKING STORAGE      PF6 : USER DISPLAY
PF7 : SCROLL BACK         PF8 : SCROLL FORWARD       PF9 : STOP CONDITIONS
PF10: PREVIOUS DISPLAY    PF11: UNDEFINED            PF12: ABEND USER TASK
```

Figure 19.15 READ command about to be executed.

```
TRANSACTION: AR92   PROGRAM: ARC92C      TASK NUMBER: 0000704   DISPLAY:  00
STATUS:  COMMAND EXECUTION COMPLETE
EXEC CICS READ
 FILE ('RK501    ')
 INTO ('.0120000000000010001                    .........................'...)
 RIDFLD ('0120000000000010001                   ')
 UPDATE


OFFSET:X'0012A8'    LINE:00308           EIBFN=X'0602'
RESPONSE: NOTFND                         EIBRESP=13

ENTER:  CONTINUE
PF1 : UNDEFINED           PF2 : SWITCH HEX/CHAR      PF3 : END EDF SESSION
PF4 : SUPPRESS DISPLAYS   PF5 : WORKING STORAGE      PF6 : USER DISPLAY
PF7 : SCROLL BACK         PF8 : SCROLL FORWARD       PF9 : STOP CONDITIONS
PF10: PREVIOUS DISPLAY    PF11: UNDEFINED            PF12: ABEND USER TASK
```

Figure 19.16 NOTFND condition displayed to record key 0100.

ues associated with the KSDS key, short of writing a browse program that would do it for you. Here is what to do:

Clear the screen and enter the transaction identifier, CECI, as before. This panel is shown in Figure 19.24. Once you have pressed the Enter key, a Dictionary Panel will appear on your screen, like the one in Figure 19.25.

Note that this panel simply lists all the commands associated with the CECI transaction. When using any of these commands, you need to use only the portion of the command that is displayed in uppercase, as explained earlier.

Rather than selecting a command off the list, I went ahead and pressed PF5 (VAR) in order to define to CICS an area in which the value of the key will be dumped once a STARTBR operation is initiated. This follow-up panel is displayed in Figure 19.26. Actually, Figures 19.26 and 19.27 go hand in hand. Figure 19.26 shows the panel prior to my definition of this key field, and Figure 19.27 gives you a subsequent snapshot. In Figure 19.27, I entered an area for the key called &KEY, and defined it as having a length of 15 bytes. If you don't know the actual key length of the field, make sure to enter some approximate length that'll be sufficient to hold the KSDS key.

```
  TRANSACTION: AR92   PROGRAM: ARC92C        TASK NUMBER: 0000746   DISPLAY:  00
  STATUS:  ABOUT TO EXECUTE COMMAND
  EXEC CICS READ
   FILE ('RK501    ')
   INTO ('.0120000000000010101                   ..........................'...)
   RIDFLD ('0120000000000010101                   ')
   UPDATE




  OFFSET:X'0012A8'    LINE:00308           EIBFN=X'0602'

 ENTER:  CONTINUE
 PF1 : UNDEFINED             PF2 : SWITCH HEX/CHAR     PF3 : UNDEFINED
 PF4 : SUPPRESS DISPLAYS     PF5 : WORKING STORAGE     PF6 : USER DISPLAY
 PF7 : SCROLL BACK           PF8 : SCROLL FORWARD      PF9 : STOP CONDITIONS
 PF10: PREVIOUS DISPLAY      PF11: UNDEFINED           PF12: ABEND USER TASK
```

Figure 19.17 Second READ command about to be executed.

```
  TRANSACTION: AR92   PROGRAM: ARC92C        TASK NUMBER: 0000746   DISPLAY:  00
  STATUS:  COMMAND EXECUTION COMPLETE
  EXEC CICS READ
   FILE ('RK501    ')
   INTO ('.0120000000000010101                   MR. EVERETT J. HAUCK        '...)
   RIDFLD ('0120000000000010101                   ')
   UPDATE




  OFFSET:X'0012A8'    LINE:00308           EIBFN=X'0602'
  RESPONSE: NORMAL                         EIBRESP=0

 ENTER:  CONTINUE
 PF1 : UNDEFINED             PF2 : SWITCH HEX/CHAR     PF3 : END EDF SESSION
 PF4 : SUPPRESS DISPLAYS     PF5 : WORKING STORAGE     PF6 : USER DISPLAY
 PF7 : SCROLL BACK           PF8 : SCROLL FORWARD      PF9 : STOP CONDITIONS
 PF10: PREVIOUS DISPLAY      PF11: UNDEFINED           PF12: ABEND USER TASK
```

Figure 19.18 Result of the READ—a normal response.

```
TRANSACTION: AR92   PROGRAM: ARC92C      TASK NUMBER: 0000746   DISPLAY:  00
STATUS:  ABOUT TO EXECUTE COMMAND
EXEC CICS SEND MAP
 MAP ('ARC92M7')
 FROM ('..............................................J0100...'...)
 DATAONLY
 MAPSET ('ARC92M ')
 CURSOR
 TERMINAL




 OFFSET:X'001998'    LINE:00543          EIBFN=X'1804'


ENTER:  CONTINUE
PF1 : UNDEFINED            PF2 : SWITCH HEX/CHAR     PF3 : UNDEFINED
PF4 : SUPPRESS DISPLAYS    PF5 : WORKING STORAGE     PF6 : USER DISPLAY
PF7 : SCROLL BACK          PF8 : SCROLL FORWARD      PF9 : STOP CONDITIONS
PF10: PREVIOUS DISPLAY     PF11: UNDEFINED           PF12: ABEND USER TASK
```

Figure 19.19 The “reissued”map.

```
 AR92                CUSTOMER DATABASE MAINTENANCE                    0000


CUSTOMER NUMBER     :     0100
CUSTOMER NAME       :     MR. EVERETT J. HAUCK
ADDRESS (1)         :     110 W. MAPLE
ADDRESS (2)         :
ADDRESS (3)         :     NEW LENOX
STATE               :     IL
POSTAL CODE         :     60451
TELEPHONE           :     000   000   0000
CONTACT NAME        :
ABBREVIATED NAME    :     HAUCK, EVERETT
ATTENTION LINE1     :     0000           00000   00
ATTENTION LINE2     :     <00<          0000000000 0



PF1: RETURN TO MENU    PF4: UPDATE RECORD
```

Figure 19.20 Display of record 0101.

When you press the Enter key, a previously displayed screen (shown in Figure 19.25) will appear where the following statement:

```
STARTBR  FILE(RK501) RIDFLD(&KEY)
```

was issued (see Figure 19.28). As you can see, the only thing you know about the file is the DD name; everything else is CICS-supplied or, more specifically, supplied by the CECI transaction. This step invokes the next two frames, shown in Figures 19.29 and 19.30, representing the "before" and "after" status of the executing command.

As in EDF, note that the response code at the completion of the command was normal. At this point, tab over to the upper left-hand corner of the screen (Figure 19.31), modify the previous STARTBR command to read READNEXT, and press Enter. The result of this is shown in two subsequent frames: Figures 19.32 and 19.33.

```
CECI SEND MAP(ARA21M2) MAPSET(ARA21M)
```

Figure 19.21 Issuing a CECI SEND MAP command.

```
  SEND MAP(ARA21M2) MAPSET(ARA21M)
  STATUS:  ABOUT TO EXECUTE COMMAND                                NAME=
   EXEC CICS  SENd Map( 'ARA21M2' )
    << FROm() > < Dataonly > | MAPOnly >
    < LEngth( +00007 ) >
    < MAPSet( 'ARA21M ' ) >
    < FMhparm() >
    < Reqid() >
    < LDc() | < ACTpartn() > < Outpartn() > >
    < MSr() >
    < Cursor() >
    < Set() | PAging | Terminal < Wait > < LAst > >
    < PRint >
    < FREekb >
    < ALarm >
    < L40 | L64 | L80 | Honeom >
    < NLeom >
    < ERASE | ERASEAup >
    < ACCum >
 +  < FRSet >


 PF 1 HELP 2 HEX 3 END 4 EIB 5 VAR 6 USER 7 SBH 8 SFH 9 MSG 10 SB 11 SF
```

Figure 19.22 CECI command about to be executed.

```
 AR28     INVOICE HEADER SCREEN FOR NON-RECURRING BILLINGS


  PROJECT NO :
  CREDIT MEMO.      (Y, N)      ORIGINAL INV# :
  CUSTOMER NO:                  CUSTOMER NAME :
  INVOICE NO :                  INVOICE AMOUNT:
  ACCOUNTING MM/YY:             BILLING DATE (MMDDYY)
  PERIOD DESCRIPT.:
  ____________________ SPECIAL INSTRUCTIONS ____________________



  ______________________________________________________________



    PF1: RETURN TO MENU
    PF3: HELP
```

Figure 19.23 Display of the physical map, the last frame.

```
 ceci

ACFAE139 ACF2/CICS: 0000     SIGNON COMPLETED:  LOGONID=NIRAV    NAME=ALEX VARSE
```

Figure 19.24 Entering the CICS-supplied transaction identifier CECI.

Note that you can scan the entire file without modifying the previously setup READ-NEXT instruction.

19.1.3 CEMT master terminal transaction

One of the most common operations in using the CEMT transaction is to update the Processing Program Table (PPT) to acquire a new version of your application program. Every time you need to recompile your program because of recent changes while CICS is up, you need to use either a CSMT- or a CEMT-supplied transaction. Consider that you have completed modifying your program and then successfully compiled it. Thus, switch over to CICS, clear the screen, and enter the instructions shown in Figure 19.34.

Now press the Enter key, and the next panel will verify that the latest copy of your ARC92C program is now available to CICS, and generally for the interactive processing cycle. This final panel is shown in Figure 19.35.

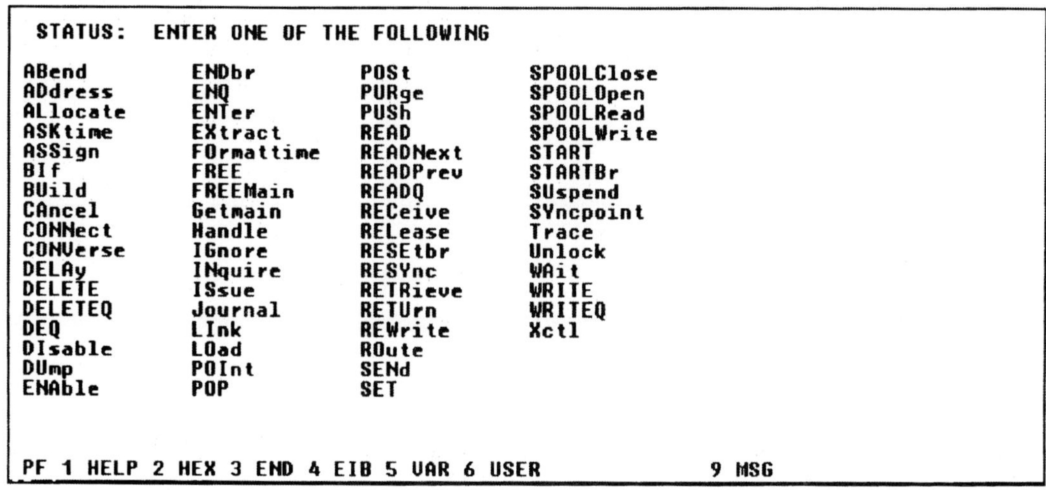

```
 STATUS:  ENTER ONE OF THE FOLLOWING

ABend         ENDbr         POSt          SPOOLClose
ADdress       ENQ           PURge         SPOOLOpen
ALlocate      ENTer         PUSh          SPOOLRead
ASKtime       EXtract       READ          SPOOLWrite
ASSign        FOrmattime    READNext      START
BIf           FREE          READPrev      STARTBr
BUild         FREEMain      READQ         SUspend
CAncel        Getmain       RECeive       SYncpoint
CONNect       Handle        RELease       Trace
CONVerse      IGnore        RESEtbr       Unlock
DELAy         INquire       RESYnc        WAit
DELETE        ISsue         RETRieve      WRITE
DELETEQ       Journal       RETUrn        WRITEQ
DEQ           LInk          REWrite       Xctl
DIsable       LOad          ROute
DUmp          POInt         SENd
ENAble        POP           SET

PF 1 HELP 2 HEX 3 END 4 EIB 5 VAR 6 USER              9 MSG
```

Figure 19.25 The result—a command selection, dictionary.

```
 VARIABLES
&DFHC         +00016    THIS IS A SAMPLE
&DFHW         +00046    EXEC CICS WRITEQ QUEUE('""CI0000') FROM(&DFHC)
&DFHR         +00045    EXEC CICS READQ QUEUE('""CI0000') INTO(&DFHC)

PF 1 HELP 2 HEX 3 END 4 EIB 5 VAR 6 USER              9 MSG
```

Figure 19.26 Variable storage to set up a record key.

```
 VARIABLES
&DFHC          +00016   THIS IS A SAMPLE
&DFHW          +00046   EXEC CICS WRITEQ QUEUE('""CI0000') FROM(&DFHC)
&DFHR          +00045   EXEC CICS READQ QUEUE('""CI0000') INTO(&DFHC)
&KEY           +00015









PF 1 HELP 2 HEX 3 END 4 EIB 5 VAR 6 USER              9 MSG
```

Figure 19.27 An area now set aside for the under &KEY.

```
 STARTBR FILE(RK501) RIDFLD(&KEY)
 STATUS:  ENTER ONE OF THE FOLLOWING

ABend          ENDbr          POSt           SPOOLClose
ADdress        ENQ            PURge          SPOOLOpen
ALlocate       ENTer          PUSh           SPOOLRead
ASKtime        EXtract        READ           SPOOLWrite
ASSign         FOrmattime     READNext       START
BIf            FREE           READPrev       STARTBr
BUild          FREEMain       READQ          SUspend
CAncel         Getmain        RECeive        SYncpoint
CONNect        Handle         RELease        Trace
CONVerse       IGnore         RESEtbr        Unlock
DELAy          INquire        RESYnc         WAit
DELETE         ISsue          RETRieve       WRITE
DELETEQ        Journal        RETUrn         WRITEQ
DEQ            LInk           REWrite        Xctl
DIsable        LOad           ROute
DUmp           POInt          SENd
ENAble         POP            SET

PF 1 HELP 2 HEX 3 END 4 EIB 5 VAR 6 USER              9 MSG
```

Figure 19.28 Entering the first command to start browsing.

19.1.4 CSSN and CSSF transactions

You must use CSSN to sign on to the CICS system before you can use the software's resources. Once you have requested to log on, a CICS Panel will prompt you for additional information, such as your logon I.D. and password. This transaction works in conjunction with a sign-on table, containing a list of all authorized CICS users.

Format for the CSSN transaction is either CSSN or CSSN NAME=....,PS=PASS-

WORD. An example of the latter is CSSN=ALEX,PS=BROWNLY. CSSF, on the other hand, is a sign-off transaction. There are two forms for the sign off. CSSF means you are signed off the system, but the terminal remains connected. CSSF LOGOFF means that you are logged off the system, while the terminal connection is discontinued.

```
STARTBR FILE(RK501) RIDFLD(&KEY)
STATUS:  ABOUT TO EXECUTE COMMAND                                    NAME=
 EXEC CICS  STARTBr
  File( 'RK501    ' )
  < Sysid() >
  RIdfld( '              ' )
  < Keylength() < GEneric > >
  < REqid( +00000 ) >
  < RBa | RRn | DEBRec | DEBKey >
  < GTeq | Equal >










PF 1 HELP 2 HEX 3 END 4 EIB 5 VAR 6 USER 7 SBH 8 SFH 9 MSG 10 SB 11 SF
```

Figure 19.29 BROWSE command about to be executed.

```
STARTBR FILE(RK501) RIDFLD(&KEY)
STATUS:  COMMAND EXECUTION COMPLETE                                  NAME=
 EXEC CICS  STARTBr
  File( 'RK501    ' )
  < Sysid() >
  RIdfld( '              ' )
  < Keylength() < GEneric > >
  < REqid( +00000 ) >
  < RBa | RRn | DEBRec | DEBKey >
  < GTeq | Equal >









 RESPONSE: NORMAL                              EIBRESP=+0000000000
PF 1 HELP 2 HEX 3 END 4 EIB 5 VAR 6 USER 7 SBH 8 SFH 9 MSG 10 SB 11 SF
```

Figure 19.30 The execution is complete and the return is normal.

```
READNEXT FILE(RK501) RIDFLD(&KEY)
STATUS:  COMMAND EXECUTION COMPLETE                              NAME=
 EXEC CICS  STARTBr
  File( 'RK501    ' )
  < Sysid() >
  RIdfld( '                ' )
  < Keylength() < GEneric > >
  < REqid( +00000 ) >
  < RBa | RRn | DEBRec | DEBKey >
  < GTeq | Equal >

 RESPONSE: NORMAL                              EIBRESP=+0000000000
PF 1 HELP 2 HEX 3 END 4 EIB 5 VAR 6 USER 7 SBH 8 SFH 9 MSG 10 SB 11 SF
```

Figure 19.31 Altering the command to read next.

```
READNEXT FILE(RK501) RIDFLD(&KEY)
STATUS:  ABOUT TO EXECUTE COMMAND                                NAME=
 EXEC CICS  READNext
  File( 'RK501    ' )
  < SYsid() >
  SEt() | Into()
  < Length() >
  RIdfld( '                ' )
  < Keylength() >
  < REqid( +00000 ) >
  < RBa | RRn >

PF 1 HELP 2 HEX 3 END 4 EIB 5 VAR 6 USER 7 SBH 8 SFH 9 MSG 10 SB 11 SF
```

Figure 19.32 READ NEXT about to be executed.

```
READNEXT FILE(RK501) RIDFLD(&KEY)
STATUS:  COMMAND EXECUTION COMPLETE                               NAME=
 EXEC CICS  READNext
  File( 'RK501    ' )
  < SYsid() >
  SEt() |
    Into( ' 011          00               00000000000010991273912' ... )
  < Length( +01100 ) >
  RIdfld( '011          ' )
  < Keylength() >
  < REqid( +00000 ) >
  < RBa | RRn >




 RESPONSE: NORMAL                          EIBRESP=+0000000000
PF 1 HELP 2 HEX 3 END 4 EIB 5 VAR 6 USER 7 SBH 8 SFH 9 MSG 10 SB 11 SF
```

Figure 19.33 The first record is displayed; you can now issue a READNEXT.

```
CEMT SET PROGRAM(ARC92C),NEWCOPY
 STATUS:  SESSION ENDED
```

Figure 19.34 Initiating a CEMT transaction for a new copy.

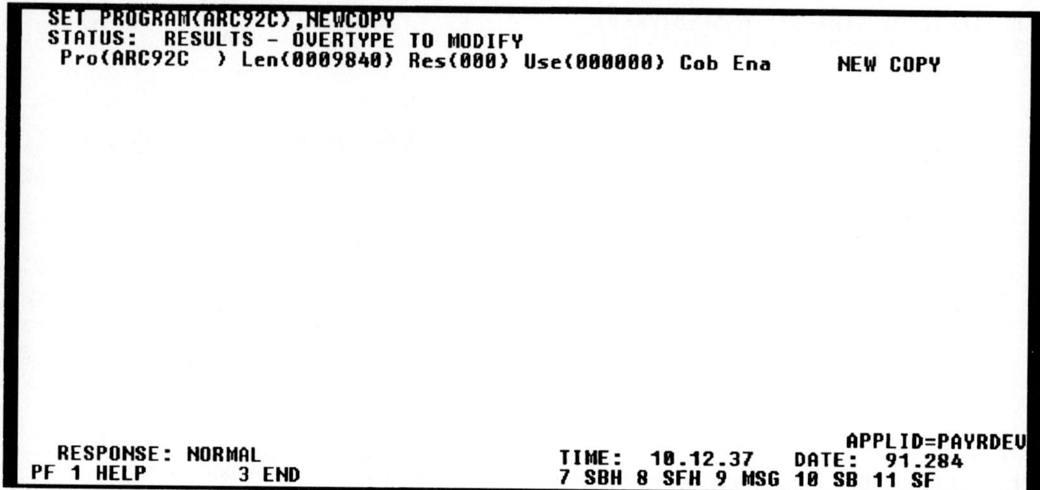

Figure 19.35 CICS response to the NEWCOPY request.

Appendix

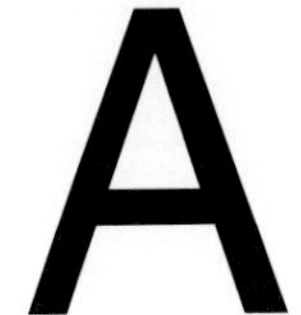

Mainline Program for Generating On-Line Reports

```
 IDENTIFICATION DIVISION.                                          11/22/91
 PROGRAM-ID.           RMP61C.                                     RMP61C
 AUTHOR.               JEFF MUELLER                                 LV098
 DATE-WRITTEN.         JULY 1991.                                   CL*81
 INSTALLATION.         METRA                                       RMP61C
 REMARKS.                                                          RMP61C
     THIS PROGRAM          :  RMP61C                                CL*81
          CICS TRANSACTION:  RP61                                   CL*81
          BMS MAPS USED    :  RMP61M                                CL*81
                                                                   RMP61C
*---------------------------------------------------------------    CL*54
*- THIS PROGRAM WILL PRINT A "MATERIAL RECOVERY" OR A "RECOVERY     CL*81
*- STOCKING LIST" REPORT. IT WRITES TO A TRANSIENT DATA QUEUE THAT  CL*81
*- INITIATES JOB ISS05C AND SENDS THE QUEUE TO THE PRINTER.         CL*81
*---------------------------------------------------------------- RMP61C
                                                                   RMP61C
 ENVIRONMENT DIVISION.                                             RMP61C
 DATA DIVISION.                                                    RMP61C
     EJECT                                                         RMP61C
 WORKING-STORAGE SECTION.                                          RMP61C
 77  PAN-VALET PICTURE X(24) VALUE '098RMP61C     11/22/91'.       RMP61C
 77  FILLER                       PIC X(24)       VALUE            RMP61C
                                  'RMP61C WORKING STORAGE'.         CL*81
*                                                                  RMP61C
*                                                                  RMP61C
 01  WS-PROG-NAME                 PIC X(08) VALUE 'RMP61C  '.       CL*81
 01  WS-TRNID                     PIC X(04) VALUE 'RP61'.           CL*81
 01  WS-MAP-NAME                  PIC X(08) VALUE 'RMP61M1  '.      CL*81
 01  WS-MAPSET-NAME               PIC X(08) VALUE 'RMP61M   '.      CL*81
 01  WS-PF9-SW                    PIC X(01) VALUE 'R'.              CL**2
 01  WS-QUEUE-NAME.                                                 CL**3
     05  WS-QUEUE-TERMID          PIC X(04) VALUE SPACES.           CL**3
     05  WS-QUEUE-TRANID          PIC X(04) VALUE SPACES.           CL**3
```

```
 01  WS-MAP-QUE-CNT             PIC S9(4) COMP VALUE +0.         RMP61C
 01  ITEM-NO                    PIC S9(04) COMP VALUE +0.            CL**3
 01  ITEM-PTR                   PIC S9(04) COMP VALUE +0.            CL*98
 01  WS-ITEM                    PIC S9(04) COMP VALUE +0.            CL**9
 01  MTIME-2                    PIC S9(16) COMP VALUE +0.            CL*53
 01  FDATE-2                    PIC S9(06) VALUE +0.                 CL*53
 01  WS-CONVERT-DATE            PIC S9(07) COMP-3 VALUE +0.          CL*53
 01  WS-EXTENDED-VALUE          PIC 9(6)V9(3) VALUE 0.               CL*55
 01  WS-TOTAL-EXTENDED-VALUE    PIC 9(6)V9(3) VALUE 0.               CL*55
 01  NEW-QTY-ON-HAND            PIC S9(7) COMP-3 VALUE +0.           CL*82
 01  OLD-QTY-ON-HAND            PIC S9(7) COMP-3 VALUE +0.           CL*98
*                                                                    CL**7
 01  WS-KEY-AREA.                                                    CL**7
     05  WS-GENERIC-KEY.                                             CL**7
         10  WS-DOCMT-TYPE      PIC X(03).                           CL**7
         10  WS-DOCMT-DEPT      PIC X(04).                           CL**7
         10  WS-DOCMT-NO        PIC X(07).                           CL*14
         10  FILLER             PIC X(26).                           CL*72
*                                                                RMP61C
 01  GL-FILE-KEY.                                                    CL*67
     05 WS-3                    PIC X(03).                           CL*67
     05 WS-4                    PIC X(04).                           CL*67
     05 WS-8                    PIC X(08).                           CL*67
     05 WS-9                    PIC X(09) VALUE SPACES.              CL*72
*                                                                    CL*67
 01  WS-ACCT-CODE.                                                   CL*70
     05  WS-ORG-DEPT.                                                CL*70
         10  WS-ORG-2           PIC X(02).                           CL*70
         10  WS-DEPT-4          PIC X(04).                           CL*70
     05  WS-FUNC-SRCE.                                               CL*70
         10  WS-FUN-4           PIC X(04).                           CL*70
         10  WS-SRCE-4          PIC X(04).                           CL*70
     05  WS-PROJECT             PIC X(06).                           CL*70
*                                                                    CL*70
 01  WK-RMI-DATE                PIC 9(6).                            CL*16
 01  WS-RMI-DATE REDEFINES WK-RMI-DATE.                              CL*16
     05  WK-RMI-MM              PIC XX.                              CL*16
     05  WK-RMI-DD              PIC XX.                              CL*16
     05  WK-RMI-YY              PIC XX.                              CL*16
*                                                                    CL*16
 01  WS-QUE-LENGTH              PIC S9(04) COMP VALUE +337.          CL**7
*                                                                    CL**7
 01  CICS-RESP                  PIC S9(08) COMP.                 RMP61C
 01  CA-LENGTH                  PIC S9(4)  COMP  VALUE +602.         CL*78
 01  CA-MAX-LENGTH              PIC S9(04) COMP  VALUE +376.     RMP61C
 01  CA-ERR-LENGTH              PIC S9(4)  COMP  VALUE +262.     RMP61C
 01  CA-ABEND-LENGTH            PIC S9(4)  COMP  VALUE +375.     RMP61C
 01  QUEUE-NUMBER               PIC S9(04) COMP  VALUE +0.           CL*67
*                                                                RMP61C
 01  WS-QUEUE-AREA.                                                  CL**5
     05  WS-RMK060-QUEUE        PIC X(336) VALUE SPACES.             CL**5
     05  WS-Q-LINE-COMMAND      PIC X(01)  VALUE SPACES.             CL**5
*                                                                    CL**5
 01  WS-QUEUE-LENGTH            PIC S9(04) COMP VALUE +337.          CL**5
*                                                                    CL**5
 01  WS-WORK-FIELDS.                                                 CL*16
     05  WS-PICK-PRNT-FLAG      PIC X(01) VALUE ' '.                 CL*96
     05  WS-VALID-DATA-SW       PIC X(01) VALUE 'Y'.                 CL**3
         88  VALID-DATA                   VALUE 'Y'.                 CL**3
         88  ERROR-DETECTED               VALUE 'N'.                 CL**3
     05  KEY-MATCH-SW           PIC X(01) VALUE 'Y'.                 CL**3
         88  KEY-MATCHED                  VALUE 'Y'.                 CL**3
         88  KEY-NOT-MATCHED              VALUE 'N'.                 CL**3
```

```
      05  END-OF-FILE-SW          PIC X(01) VALUE 'N'.             CL**3
          88  END-OF-FILE                   VALUE 'Y'.             CL**3
*                                                                 RMP61C
 01  WS-MQ-MIN                      PIC S9(04) COMP VALUE +0.     RMP61C
*                                                                 RMP61C
 01  WS-MQ-MAX                      PIC S9(04) COMP VALUE +16.    RMP61C
*                                                                 RMP61C
 ++INCLUDE ATTRLIST                                               RMP61C
*                                                                 RMP61C
*                                                                 RMP61C
 01  RECORD-AREA.                                                 RMP61C
*                                                                 RMP61C
      05  RECORD-DATA             PIC X(549).                      CL*73
*                                                                 RMP61C
 01  RMK000.                                                      06/06/90
*                                                                 RMK000
*   THIS IS THE COPYBOOK FOR THE CATALOG FILE                      LV001
*   IN METRA'S RAIL MATERIAL INVENTORY SYSTEM                     RMK000
*   THE RECORD IS 179 BYTES IN LENGTH                             RMK000
*                                                                 RMK000
       05  RMK000-PART-NUMBER.                                    RMK000
*                                                                 RMK000
           THIS IS THE KEY TO THE FILE                            RMK000
*                                                                 RMK000
           10   RMK000-CLASS-CODE                 PIC X(02).      RMK000
           10   RMK000-PART-ID                    PIC X(05).      RMK000
           10   RMK000-PART-CHECK-DIGIT           PIC X(01).      RMK000
       05  RMK000-FILLER                          PIC X(92).      RMK000
       05  FILLER REDEFINES RMK000-FILLER.                        RMK000
           10  RMK000-CLASS-CODE-2                PIC X(02).      RMK000
           10  RMK000-PART-DESCRIPTION.                           RMK000
               15  RMK000-PART-DESCRIPTION-30     PIC X(30).      RMK000
               15  RMK000-PART-DESCRIPTION-60     PIC X(30).      RMK000
               15  RMK000-PART-DESCRIPTION-90     PIC X(30).      RMK000
       05  FILLER REDEFINES RMK000-FILLER.                        RMK000
           10  RMK000-ALTERNATE-KEY-1.                            RMK000
               15  RMK000-CLASS-CODE-2-X          PIC X(02).      RMK000
               15  RMK000-PART-DESCRIPTION-30-X   PIC X(30).      RMK000
           10  FILLER                             PIC X(60).      RMK000
       05  FILLER REDEFINES RMK000-FILLER.                        RMK000
           10  FILLER                             PIC X(02).      RMK000
           10  RMK000-ALTERNATE-KEY-2.                            RMK000
               15  RMK000-PART-DESCRIPTION-30-XXX PIC X(30).      RMK000
           10  FILLER                             PIC X(60).      RMK000
*                                                                 RMK000
       05  RMK000-UOM.                                            RMK000
*                                                                 RMK000
           10  RMK000-UNIT-OF-MEASURE             PIC X(02).      RMK000
*                                                                 RMK000
       05  RMK000-USE-CODE                        PIC X(01).      RMK000
*                                                                 RMK000
           88  USE-CODE-VALID                VALUE 'A' 'D' 'P'.   RMK000
*                                                                 RMK000
           88  USE-CODE-ACTIVE               VALUE 'A'.           RMK000
*                                                                 RMK000
           88  USE-CODE-DELETE               VALUE 'D'.           RMK000
*                                                                 RMK000
           88  USE-CODE-PURCHASE-ONLY        VALUE 'P'.           RMK000
*                                                                 RMK000
       05  RMK000-COMMODITY-CODE                  PIC X(04).      RMK000
*                                                                 RMK000
       05  RMK000-SPECIFICATION                   PIC X(15).      RMK000
*                                                                 RMK000
```

```
       05  RMK000-SAFETY-DATA-SHEET              PIC X(01).        RMK000
      *                                                            RMK000
           88  SDS-VALID                 VALUE 'Y' 'N' 'P'.        RMK000
      *                                                            RMK000
           88  SAFETY-SHEET-EXISTS       VALUE 'Y'.                RMK000
      *                                                            RMK000
           88  SAFETY-SHEET-PENDING      VALUE 'P'.                RMK000
      *                                                            RMK000
           88  NO-SAFETY-SHEET           VALUE 'N'.                RMK000
      *                                                            RMK000
       05  RMK000-HAZARDOUS-MATERIAL-CODE        PIC X(06).        RMK000
      *                                                            RMK000
       05  RMK000-PART-SUPERCEDED-TO             PIC X(08).        RMK000
      *                                                            RMK000
       05  RMK000-SUPERCEDED-FLAG                PIC X(01).        RMK000
      *                                                            RMK000
           88  SUPERCEDED                VALUE 'Y'.                RMK000
      *                                                            RMK000
       05  RMK000-SUPERCESSION-DATE        PIC S9(07) COMP-3.      RMK000
      *                                                            RMK000
      *    FORMAT 0CCYYDDD                                         RMK000
      *                                                            RMK000
       05  RMK000-REFERENCE-PRICE    PIC S9(06)V9(03) COMP-3.      RMK000
      *                                                            RMK000
       05  RMK000-AVG-LEAD-TIME            PIC S9(03) COMP-3.      RMK000
      *                                                            RMK000
      * MAXIMUM AVERAGE LEAD TIME 999 DAYS                         RMK000
      *                                                            RMK000
       05  RMK000-UOM-CHANGE-FLAG          PIC X(01).              RMK000
      *                                                            RMK000
           88 UOM-CHANGE                 VALUE 'Y'.                RMK000
      *                                                            RMK000
       05  FILLER                          PIC X(29).              RMK000
      *                                                            RMP61C
       01  RMK020.                                                 06/18/92
      *                                                            RMK020
      * THIS IS THE COPY BOOK FOR THE ITEM FILE MASTER              LV004
      *                                                            RMK020
      * THE LENGTH OF THE RECORD IS                                RMK020
      *                                                            RMK020
      * THE KEY OF THE RECORD IS                                   RMK020
      *                                                            RMK020
       05  RMK020-ITEM-FILE-KEY.                                   RMK020
      *                                                            RMK020
           10  RMK020-PROJECT-NO.                                   CL**3
      *                                                             CL**3
               15  RMK020-GRANT-ID           PIC X(02).             CL**3
      *                                                             CL**3
               15  RMK020-PROJECT-ID         PIC X(04).             CL**3
      *                                                             CL**4
           10  RMK020-SITE-PART-NO-STATUS.                          CL**4
      *                                                             CL**4
               15  RMK020-SITE-ID              PIC X(05).           CL**4
      *                                                             CL**4
               15  RMK020-METRA-PART-NO.                            CL**4
      *                                                             CL**4
                   20  RMK020-METRA-CLASS-CODE PIC X(02).           CL**4
      *                                                             CL**4
                   20  RMK020-METRA-PART-ID    PIC X(05).           CL**4
      *                                                             CL**4
                   20  RMK020-METRA-CHECK-DIGIT PIC X(01).          CL**4
      *                                                             CL**4
               15  RMK020-STATUS               PIC X(01).           CL**4
```

```
      *                                                                 RMK020
           05  RMK020-QTY-ON-HAND                 PIC S9(07) COMP-3.    RMK020
      *                                                                 RMK020
           05  RMK020-QTY-ON-ORDER                PIC S9(07) COMP-3.    RMK020
      *                                                                 RMK020
           05  RMK020-QTY-RESERVED                PIC S9(07) COMP-3.    RMK020
      *                                                                 RMK020
           05  RMK020-AVG-UNIT-PRICE              PIC S9(06)V999 COMP-3.   CL**2
      *                                                                 RMK020
           05  RMK020-BIN-LOCATION                PIC X(10).            RMK020
      *                                                                 RMK020
           05  RMK020-ABC-CODE                    PIC X(01).            RMK020
      *                                                                 RMK020
           05  RMK020-SUPERCEDE-FLAG              PIC X(01).            RMK020
      *                                                                 RMK020
           05  RMK020-REPLENISHMENT-MTHD          PIC X(01).            RMK020
      *                                                                 RMK020
           05  RMK020-MIN-MAX-METHOD.                                   RMK020
      *                                                                 RMK020
               10  RMK020-MIN-STOCK-QTY           PIC S9(07) COMP-3.    RMK020
      *                                                                 RMK020
               10  RMK020-MAX-STOCK-QTY           PIC S9(07) COMP-3.    RMK020
      *                                                                 RMK020
           05  RMK020-FIXED-PERIOD-METHOD.                              RMK020
      *                                                                 RMK020
               10  RMK020-FIXED-PERIOD-DAYS       PIC S9(03) COMP-3.    RMK020
      *                                                                 RMK020
               10  RMK020-FIXED-PERIOD-QTY        PIC S9(07) COMP-3.    RMK020
      *                                                                 RMK020
           05  RMK020-FIXED-ORDER-QTY-METHOD.                           RMK020
      *                                                                 RMK020
               10  RMK020-FOQM-REORDER-POINT      PIC S9(07) COMP-3.    RMK020
      *                                                                 RMK020
               10  RMK020-FOQM-REORDER-QTY        PIC S9(07) COMP-3.    RMK020
      *                                                                 RMK020
           05  RMK020-SAFETY-STOCK-AMOUNT         PIC S9(07) COMP-3.    RMK020
      *                                                                 RMK020
           05  RMK020-USAGE-CURRENT-MONTH         PIC S9(07) COMP-3.    RMK020
      *                                                                 RMK020
           05  RMK020-USAGE-TABLE.                                      RMK020
      *                                                                 RMK020
               10  RMK020-USAGE-MNTH OCCURS 12 TIMES                    RMK020
                   INDEXED BY RMK020-USAG-INDEX.                        RMK020
                   15  RMK020-USAGE-QTY           PIC S9(07) COMP-3.    RMK020
      *                                                                 RMK020
           05  RMK020-USAGE-LAST-YEAR             PIC S9(09) COMP-3.    RMK020
      *                                                                 RMK020
           05  RMK020-LAST-ISSUE-DATE             PIC S9(07) COMP-3.    RMK020
      *                                                                 RMK020
           05  RMK020-REQUEST-CURRENT-MONTH       PIC S9(07) COMP-3.    RMK020
      *                                                                 RMK020
           05  RMK020-REQUESTED-TABLE.                                  RMK020
      *                                                                 RMK020
               10  RMK020-REQST-MNTH OCCURS 12 TIMES                    RMK020
                   INDEXED BY RMK020-REQST-INDEX.                       RMK020
                   15  RMK020-REQUEST-QTY         PIC S9(07) COMP-3.    RMK020
      *                                                                 RMK020
           05  RMK020-REQUEST-LAST-YEAR           PIC S9(09) COMP-3.    RMK020
      *                                                                 RMK020
           05  RMK020-LAST-CYCLE-COUNT-DATE       PIC S9(07) COMP-3.    RMK020
      *                                                                 RMK020
           05  RMK020-DAYS-BETWEEN-COUNTS         PIC S9(03) COMP-3.    RMK020
      *                                                                 RMK020
```

```
        05  RMK020-LAST-VENDOR                  PIC X(10).              RMK020
      *                                                                 RMK020
        05  RMK020-LAST-PO-PRICE                PIC S9(06)V999 COMP-3.   CL**2
      *                                                                 RMK020
        05  RMK020-LAST-ORDER-DATE              PIC S9(07) COMP-3.      RMK020
      *                                                                 RMK020
        05  RMK020-REORDER-IN-PROGRESS          PIC X(01).              RMK020
      *                                                                 RMK020
        05  RMK020-REORDER-IN-PROGRESS-QTY      PIC S9(07) COMP-3.      RMK020
      *                                                                 RMK020
        05  RMK020-ADJUSTMENT-CODE              PIC  X(02).              CL**3
      *                                                                  CL**3
        05  RMK020-CRITICAL-FLAG                PIC X(01).               CL**4
            88  RMK020-CRITICAL-PART                VALUE 'Y'.           CL**4
            88  RMK020-NON-CRITICAL-PART            VALUE ' '.           CL**4
      *                                                                  CL**4
        05  FILLER                              PIC X(45).               CL**4
      *                                                                 RMP61C
       ++INCLUDE RMK040                                                 RMP61C
      *                                                                  CL**3
       01  RMK050.                                                     01/24/92
      *---------------------------------------------------------*       RMK050
      *-  DOCUMENT HEADER RECORD - 175 BYTES  11/90             -*       LV005
      *---------------------------------------------------------*       RMK050
        05  RMK050-WIP-HDR-KEY.                                          CL**3
            10  RMK050-DOCMT-TYPE           PIC X(03).                   CL**2
                88  MTRL-REQUEST                VALUE '001'.            RMK050
                88  MTRL-REMOTE-USAGE           VALUE '002'.             CL**3
                88  MTRL-RE-STOCK               VALUE '003'.             CL**4
                88  MTRL-TRANSFER               VALUE '004'.             CL**3
                88  MTRL-BADORDER               VALUE '005'.             CL**3
                88  MTRL-REPAIR                 VALUE '006'.             CL**3
                88  MTRL-CYCLECNT               VALUE '007'.             CL**3
                88  MTRL-REALLOC                VALUE '008'.             CL**3
            10  RMK050-DOCMT-DEPT           PIC X(04).                   CL**3
            10  RMK050-DOCMT-NBR            PIC X(07).                   CL**3
            10 FILLER                       PIC X(26).                   CL**3
        05  RMK050-CREATION-DATA.                                       RMK050
            10  RMK050-CREATE-DATE          PIC S9(07) COMP-3.          RMK050
            10  RMK050-CREATE-SITE-ID       PIC X(05).                  RMK050
            10  RMK050-CREATE-USER-ID       PIC X(08).                  RMK050
            10  RMK050-CREATE-NAME          PIC X(25).                  RMK050
        05  FILLER REDEFINES RMK050-CREATION-DATA.                       CL**3
            10  RMK050-NEXT-DOCMT-NBR       PIC S9(07) COMP-3.           CL**3
            10  FILLER                      PIC X(38).                   CL**3
        05  RMK050-PROJECT                  PIC X(06).                  RMK050
        05  RMK050-DOCMT-STATUS             PIC X(01).                  RMK050
        05  RMK050-DOCMT-LINES              PIC 9(03).                   CL**3
        05  RMK050-REASON-DOCMT-OPEN        PIC X(01).                  RMK050
        05  RMK050-PRNT-FLAG                PIC X(01).                   CL**3
        05  RMK050-PICK-FLAG                PIC X(01).                   CL**3
        05  RMK050-UPDATE-DATA.                                         RMK050
            10  RMK050-UPDATE-DATE          PIC S9(07) COMP-3.          RMK050
            10  RMK050-UPDATE-USER-ID       PIC X(08).                  RMK050
            10  RMK050-UPDATE-USER-NAME     PIC X(25).                  RMK050
            10  RMK050-UPDATE-LINES         PIC 9(02).                  RMK050
        05  RMK050-RELATED-DOCMT-NBR        PIC X(12).                   CL**3
        05  RMK050-TRANSFER-FROM-SITE       PIC X(05).                  RMK050
        05  RMK050-REPAIR-SITE  REDEFINES  RMK050-TRANSFER-FROM-SITE     CL**4
                                            PIC X(05).                   CL**4
        05  RMK050-REMOTE-FLAGS.                                         CL**4
            10  REMOTE-PROJ-FLAG            PIC X(01).                   CL**4
```

```
                88  PROJ-NOTFND                VALUE '1'.            CL**4
        05  RMK050-PRNT-CNT                PIC 9(03).                CL**4
        05  RMK050-PICK-PRNT-CNT           PIC 9(03).                CL**4
        05  RMK050-SHIP-PRNT-FLAG          PIC X(01).                CL**4
        05  RMK050-SHIP-PRNT-CNT           PIC 9(03).                CL**4
        05  RMK050-STOCK-PRNT-FLAG         PIC X(01).                CL**4
        05  RMK050-STOCK-PRNT-CNT          PIC 9(03).                CL**4
        05  RMK050-REPAIR-TYPE             PIC X(01).                CL**4
            88 EXTERNAL-REPAIR                 VALUE 'E'.            CL**4
            88 INTERNAL-REPAIR                 VALUE 'I'.            CL**4
        05  RMK050-BADORDER-TYPE           PIC X(01).                CL**4
            88 UNIT-REPAIR-RETURN              VALUE 'R'.            CL**4
            88 UNIT-EXCHANGE                   VALUE 'E'.            CL**4
            88 COMPONET-TRACKING               VALUE 'C'.            CL**4
        05  RMK050-RELATED-DOCMT-DATE      PIC S9(07) COMP-3.        CL**5
        05  FILLER                         PIC X(03).                CL**5
      *                                                              CL**3
    01  RMK060.                                                   02/03/92
        05  RMK060-WIP-DETAIL-KEY.                                  RMK060
            10  RMK060-DOCMT-NBR           PIC X(07).                LV008
            10  RMK060-DOCMT-LINENO        PIC X(03).                CL**4
            10  RMK060-DOCMT-TYPE          PIC X(03).               RMK060
                88  MTRL-REQUEST               VALUE '001'.         RMK060
                88  MTRL-REMOTE-USAGE          VALUE '002'.          CL**4
                88  MTRL-RE-STOCK              VALUE '003'.          CL**5
                88  MTRL-TRANSFER              VALUE '004'.          CL**4
                88  MTRL-BADORDER              VALUE '005'.          CL**4
                88  MTRL-REPAIR                VALUE '006'.          CL**4
                88  MTRL-CYCLECNT              VALUE '007'.          CL**4
                88  MTRL-REALLOC               VALUE '008'.          CL**4
                88  PO-INTERFACE               VALUE '999'.          CL**5
            10  RMK060-PO-DOCMT-NBR        PIC X(10).                CL**5
            10  RMK060-PO-DOCMT-LINENO     PIC X(03).                CL**5
            10  RMK060-PO-DOCMT-SUPP       PIC X(02).                CL**5
            10  RMK060-PO-DOCMT-SITE       PIC X(05).                CL**5
            10 FILLER                      PIC X(07).                CL**5
        05  RMK060-DOCMT-LINE-STATUS       PIC X(01).               RMK060
        05  RMK060-DOCMT-DATE-REQUESTED    PIC S9(07) COMP-3.       RMK060
        05  RMK060-METRA-PART-NUMBER.                               RMK060
            10  RMK060-METRA-CLASS-CODE    PIC X(02).               RMK060
            10  RMK060-METRA-PART-ID       PIC X(05).               RMK060
            10  RMK060-METRA-CHECK-DIGIT   PIC X(01).                CL**4
        05  RMK060-METRA-PART-STATUS       PIC X(01).               RMK060
        05  RMK060-PART-DESCRIPTION.                                RMK060
            10  RMK060-PART-DESCRIPTION-45 PIC X(45).                CL**4
            10  RMK060-PART-DESCRIPTION-90 PIC X(45).                CL**4
        05  RMK060-FULL-MFG-PART-NO        PIC X(15).               RMK060
        05  RMK060-UNIT-OF-MEASURE         PIC X(02).               RMK060
        05  RMK060-QTY-REQUESTED           PIC S9(07) COMP-3.       RMK060
        05  RMK060-REFERENCE-PRICE         PIC S9(06)V9(03) COMP-3. RMK060
        05  RMK060-ACCT-CODE.                                        CL**4
            10 RMK060-ACCT-ORG             PIC X(02).                CL**4
            10 RMK060-ACCT-DEPT            PIC X(04).                CL**4
            10 RMK060-ACCT-FUNC            PIC X(04).                CL**4
            10 RMK060-ACCT-SRCE            PIC X(04).                CL**4
            10 RMK060-ACCT-PROJ            PIC X(06).                CL**4
        05  RMK060-DOCMT-LINE-COMMENTS.                             RMK060
            10  RMK060-LINE-COMMENT-20     PIC X(20).               RMK060
            10  RMK060-LINE-COMMENT-40     PIC X(20).               RMK060
        05  RMK060-BADORDER-TYPE           PIC X(01).                CL**6
        05  RMK060-REC-ORIGIN              PIC X(01).                CL**7
            88  RM-INVENTORY                   VALUE ' '.            CL**7
```

```
           88  PO-INTERFACE                     VALUE '9'.          CL**7
           88  PO-REPAIR                        VALUE 'E'.          CL**7
       05  RMK060-RESERVED-FLAG             PIC X(01).              CL**8
           88  RMK060-NOT-RESERVED              VALUE 'N'.          CL**8
           88  RMK060-RESERVED                  VALUE ' '.          CL**8
       05  FILLER                           PIC X(27).              CL**8
       05  RMK060-DATA                      PIC X(76).              CL**4
*--------------------------*                                        CL**3
*-  MATERIAL REQUEST DATA  -*                                       CL**3
*--------------------------*                                        CL**3
       05  RMK060-MTRL-REQST-DATA REDEFINES RMK060-DATA.          RMK060
           10  RMK060-MTRL-REQST-QTY-PICKED  PIC S9(07) COMP-3.   RMK060
           10  RMK060-MTRL-REQST-DATE-PICKED PIC S9(07) COMP-3.   RMK060
           10  RMK060-MTRL-REQST-QTY-FILLED  PIC S9(07) COMP-3.   RMK060
           10  RMK060-MTRL-REQST-EQUIP-NBR   PIC  X(10).            CL**4
           10  FILLER                        PIC  X(54).            CL**4
*--------------------------*                                        CL**5
*-  REMOTE SITE USAGE DATA -*                                       CL**5
*--------------------------*                                        CL**5
       05  RMK060-REMOTE-USAGE-DATA REDEFINES RMK060-DATA.          CL**5
           10  RMK060-REMOTE-SITE-QTY-PICKED  PIC S9(07) COMP-3.    CL**5
           10  RMK060-REMOTE-SITE-DATE-PICKED PIC S9(07) COMP-3.    CL**5
           10  RMK060-REMOTE-SITE-QTY-FILLED  PIC S9(07) COMP-3.    CL**5
           10  RMK060-REMOTE-SITE-EQUIP-NBR   PIC  X(10).           CL**5
           10  RMK060-REMOTE-FLAGS.                                 CL**5
               15  REMOTE-ACCT-FLAG           PIC  X(01).           CL**5
                   88 BAD-ACCT-CODE                VALUE '1'.       CL**5
               15  REMOTE-PART-FLAG           PIC  X(01).           CL**5
                   88 BAD-PART-NBR                 VALUE '1'.       CL**5
               15  REMOTE-QTY-FLAG            PIC  X(01).           CL**5
                   88 INSUFF-QTY                   VALUE '1'.       CL**5
           10  FILLER                         PIC  X(50).           CL**5
*---------------------------*                                       CL**3
*-  MATERIAL RECOVERY DATA  -*                                      CL**3
*---------------------------*                                       CL**3
       05  RMK060-MTRL-RECVY-DATA REDEFINES RMK060-DATA.          RMK060
           10  RMK060-MTRL-RECVY-EQUIP-NO     PIC  X(10).           CL**4
           10  RMK060-MTRL-RECVY-BIN-LOC      PIC  X(10).           CL**4
           10  RMK060-MTRL-RECVY-SCRAPPED-QTY PIC  S9(07) COMP-3.   CL**4
           10  FILLER                         PIC  X(52).           CL**4
*---------------------------*                                       CL**3
*-  MATERIAL TRANSFER DATA  -*                                      CL**3
*---------------------------*                                       CL**3
       05  RMK060-MTRL-TNSFR-DATA REDEFINES RMK060-DATA.          RMK060
           10  RMK060-MTRL-TNSFR-REQST-SITE  PIC   X(05).         RMK060
           10  RMK060-MTRL-TNSFR-QTY-RECVED  PIC  S9(07) COMP-3.  RMK060
           10  RMK060-MTRL-TNSFR-DATE-RECVED PIC  S9(07) COMP-3.  RMK060
           10  RMK060-MTRL-TNSFR-FROM-SITE   PIC   X(05).         RMK060
           10  RMK060-MTRL-TNSFR-FROM-PRICE  PIC  S9(06)V9(03)    RMK060
                                                  COMP-3.         RMK060
           10  RMK060-MTRL-TNSFR-QTY-PICKED  PIC  S9(07) COMP-3.  RMK060
           10  RMK060-MTRL-TNSFR-DATE-PICKED PIC  S9(07) COMP-3.  RMK060
           10  FILLER                        PIC  X(45).            CL**4
*---------------*                                                   CL**3
*-  REPAIR DATA -*                                                  CL**3
*---------------*                                                   CL**3
       05  RMK060-REPAIR-DATA REDEFINES RMK060-DATA.              RMK060
           10  RMK060-REPAIR-TAG-NO          PIC   X(07).           CL**4
           10  RMK060-REPAIR-SERIAL-NO       PIC   X(10).         RMK060
           10  RMK060-REPAIR-QTY             PIC  S9(07) COMP-3.  RMK060
           10  RMK060-REPAIR-SCRAPPED-QTY    PIC  S9(07) COMP-3.  RMK060
           10  RMK060-REPAIR-QTY-PICKED      PIC  S9(07) COMP-3.  RMK060
           10  RMK060-REPAIR-QTY-RECEVD      PIC  S9(07) COMP-3.  RMK060
```

```
           10  RMK060-REPAIR-EST-COMPL-DATE  PIC  S9(07) COMP-3.     RMK060
           10  RMK060-REPAIR-PO-NO           PIC   X(10).            RMK060
           10  RMK060-REPAIR-DATE-PICKED     PIC  S9(07) COMP-3.       CL**5
           10  RMK060-REPAIR-DATE-RECEVD     PIC  S9(07) COMP-3.       CL**5
           10  FILLER                        PIC   X(21).              CL**5
 *--------------------*                                                CL**3
 *-  BAD ORDER DATA  -*                                                CL**3
 *--------------------*                                                CL**3
       05  RMK060-BADORDER-DATA REDEFINES RMK060-DATA.               RMK060
           10  RMK060-BADORDER-EQUIP-NO      PIC  X(10).             RMK060
           10  RMK060-BADORDER-SERIAL-NO     PIC  X(10).             RMK060
           10  RMK060-BADORDER-BIN-LOC       PIC  X(10).             RMK060
           10  RMK060-BADORDER-SCRAPPED-QTY  PIC  S9(07) COMP-3.       CL**4
           10  RMK060-BADORDER-PREV-SCRAP    PIC  S9(07) COMP-3.       CL**5
           10  FILLER                        PIC  X(38).               CL**5
 *--------------------*                                                CL**3
 *-  CYCLE COUNT     -*                                                CL**3
 *--------------------*                                                CL**3
       05  RMK060-CYCLECNT-DATA REDEFINES RMK060-DATA.               RMK060
           10  RMK060-CYCLECNT-BIN-LOC       PIC  X(10).             RMK060
           10  FILLER                        PIC  X(66).               CL**4
 *---------------------------*                                         CL**3
 *-  MATERIAL-REALLOCATION  -*                                         CL**3
 *---------------------------*                                         CL**3
       05  RMK060-REALLOC-DATA REDEFINES RMK060-DATA.                RMK060
           10  RMK060-REALLOC-FROM-PROJ      PIC  X(06).             RMK060
           10  RMK060-REALLOC-FROM-SITE-ID   PIC  X(05).             RMK060
           10  RMK060-REALLOC-QTY-PICKED     PIC S9(07) COMP-3.      RMK060
           10  RMK060-REALLOC-TO-PROJ        PIC  X(06).             RMK060
           10  RMK060-REALLOC-TO-SITE-ID     PIC  X(05).             RMK060
           10  RMK060-REALLOC-QTY-RECEVD     PIC S9(07) COMP-3.      RMK060
           10  FILLER                        PIC  X(46).               CL**4
 *------------------------------*                                      CL**5
 *-  PURCHASE/ORDER/INTERFACE  -*                                      CL**5
 *------------------------------*                                      CL**5
       05  RMK060-PO-INTERFACE-DATA REDEFINES RMK060-DATA.             CL**5
 *-----------------------------------------------------------------*   CL**5
 *- RMK060-QTY-REQUESTED          ---> IS PO-QTY-ORDERED         -*   CL**5
 *- RMK060-DOCMT-DATE-REQUESTED   ---> IS PO-DATE-ORDERED        -*   CL**5
 *- RMK060-REFERENCE-PRICE        ---> IS PO-PRICE               -*   CL**5
 *-----------------------------------------------------------------*   CL**5
           10  RMK060-PO-VENDOR-ABBREV       PIC  X(08).               CL**5
           10  RMK060-PO-DELIVERY-DATE       PIC S9(07) COMP-3.        CL**5
           10  RMK060-PO-DATE-RECEIVED       PIC S9(07) COMP-3.        CL**5
           10  RMK060-PO-QTY-RECEIVED        PIC S9(07) COMP-3.        CL**5
           10  FILLER                        PIC  X(56).               CL**5
 *                                                                   RMP61C
  ++INCLUDE RMU8040W                                                   CL*15
 *                                                                     CL*15
  01  GLMASTR.                                                     08/26/92
 *----------------------------------------------------------*      GLK000C
 *- RMI GENL/LEDGER COPYBOOK - CREATED FROM PO (LDGRCD) -*          LV002
 *-                                              05/15/91 -*      GLK000C
 *----------------------------------------------------------*      GLK000C
      05  FILLER                     PIC X(01).                    GLK000C
      05  GL-VSAM-KEY.                                             GLK000C
          10  GL-COMPANY             PIC X(03).                    GLK000C
          10  GL-REC-TYPE            PIC X(04).                    GLK000C
          10  GL-ACCT-CODE           PIC X(08).                    GLK000C
          10  FILLER                 PIC X(09).                    GLK000C
      05  FILLER                     PIC X(07).                    GLK000C
      05  GL-LOC                     PIC X.                        GLK000C
      05  FILLER                     PIC X(449).                   GLK000C
```

```
       05  GL-ACCT-DESC            PIC X(19).               CL**2
       05  GL-ACCT-BOSS            PIC X(06).               CL**2
       05  FILLER                  PIC X(24).             GLK000C
       05  GL-TYPE                 PIC X.                 GLK000C
       05  FILLER                  PIC X(17).             GLK000C
      *                                                     CL*67
   ++INCLUDE BLK000C                                        CL*67
      *                                                     CL*67
   01  I-O-RET-HOLD              PIC S9(08) COMP.          RMP61C
      *                                                    RMP61C
      *                                                    RMP61C
   01  TS-JRNL.                                            RMP61C
      *                                                    RMP61C
       05  TS-FILENAME           PIC X(08).                RMP61C
      *                                                    RMP61C
       05  TS-KEY                PIC X(40).                RMP61C
      *                                                    RMP61C
       05  TS-JDATA.                                       RMP61C
           10  TS-JRNL-RECLEN          PIC S9(04) COMP.    RMP61C
           10  TS-JRNL-JFLEID          PIC S9(04) COMP.    RMP61C
           10  TS-JRNL-JTYPID          PIC  X(02).         RMP61C
      *                                                    RMP61C
   01  WS-JRNL-NAME.                                       RMP61C
      *                                                    RMP61C
       05  WS-JRNL-TERMID        PIC X(04).                RMP61C
      *                                                    RMP61C
       05  WS-JRNL-FILL          PIC X(04) VALUE 'JRNL'.   RMP61C
      *                                                    RMP61C
      *                                                    RMP61C
   01  MAP-STACK-QUEUE.                                    RMP61C
      *----------------------------*                       RMP61C
      *-      MAP QUEUE NAME      -*                       RMP61C
      *----------------------------*                       RMP61C
       05  MAP-TERMINAL           PIC  X(04).              RMP61C
       05  FILLER                 PIC  X(04) VALUE 'MAPS'. RMP61C
                                                           RMP61C
   01  MAP-DATA.                                           RMP61C
      *----------------------------*                       RMP61C
      *-  MAP QUEUE MAP RECORD    -*                       RMP61C
      *----------------------------*                       RMP61C
       05 MAP-CURSOR              PIC S9(04) COMP.         RMP61C
       05 MAP-RECORD              PIC  X(1920).            RMP61C
                                                           RMP61C
   01  MAP-REC-LENGTHS.                                    RMP61C
       05  MAP-DATA-LEN           PIC S9(04) COMP VALUE +1922. RMP61C
                                                           RMP61C
      *                                                    RMP61C
   ++INCLUDE RMCACOMM                                      RMP61C
   ++INCLUDE RMDOCOMM                                        CL**3
      *      05  RMCA-RMB1C-FILLER   PIC X(18).              CL**3
      *                                                    RMP61C
   01  WS-MSG-LINE               PIC X(79) VALUE SPACES.   RMP61C
      *                                                    RMP61C
   ++INCLUDE RMCAERR                                       RMP61C
      *                                                    RMP61C
      *-                           *- LENGTH: XXX BYTES -* 10/30/92
   01  I-O-REQUEST.                                        RMIOPARM
       05  I-O-RETCODE                PIC S9(08) COMP.       LV007
           88  I-O-NORMAL                 VALUE +0.        RMIOPARM
           88  I-O-ERROR                  VALUE +1.        RMIOPARM
           88  I-O-RDATT                  VALUE +2.        RMIOPARM
           88  I-O-WRBRK                  VALUE +3.        RMIOPARM
           88  I-O-EOF                    VALUE +4.        RMIOPARM
```

```
88  I-O-EODS               VALUE +5.          RMIOPARM
88  I-O-EOC                VALUE +6.          RMIOPARM
88  I-O-INBFMH             VALUE +7.          RMIOPARM
88  I-O-ENDINPT            VALUE +8.          RMIOPARM
88  I-O-NONVAL             VALUE +9.          RMIOPARM
88  I-O-NOSTART            VALUE +10.         RMIOPARM
88  I-O-TERMIDERR          VALUE +11.         RMIOPARM
88  I-O-DSIDERR            VALUE +12.         RMIOPARM
88  I-O-NOTFND             VALUE +13.         RMIOPARM
88  I-O-DUPREC             VALUE +14.         RMIOPARM
88  I-O-DUPKEY             VALUE +15.         RMIOPARM
88  I-O-INVREQ             VALUE +16.         RMIOPARM
88  I-O-IOERR              VALUE +17.         RMIOPARM
88  I-O-NOSPACE            VALUE +18.         RMIOPARM
88  I-O-NOTOPEN            VALUE +19.         RMIOPARM
88  I-O-ENDFILE            VALUE +20.         RMIOPARM
88  I-O-ILLOGIC            VALUE +21.         RMIOPARM
88  I-O-LENGERR            VALUE +22.         RMIOPARM
88  I-O-QZERO              VALUE +23.         RMIOPARM
88  I-O-SIGNAL             VALUE +24.         RMIOPARM
88  I-O-BUSY               VALUE +25.         RMIOPARM
88  I-O-ITEMERR            VALUE +26.         RMIOPARM
88  I-O-PGMIDERR           VALUE +27.         RMIOPARM
88  I-O-TRANSIDERR         VALUE +28.         RMIOPARM
88  I-O-ENDDATA            VALUE +29.         RMIOPARM
88  I-O-INVTSREQ           VALUE +30.         RMIOPARM
88  I-O-EXPIRED            VALUE +31.         RMIOPARM
88  I-O-RETPAGE            VALUE +32.         RMIOPARM
88  I-O-RTEFAIL            VALUE +33.         RMIOPARM
88  I-O-RTESOME            VALUE +34.         RMIOPARM
88  I-O-TSIOERR            VALUE +35.         RMIOPARM
88  I-O-MAPFAIL            VALUE +36.         RMIOPARM
88  I-O-INVERRTERM         VALUE +37.         RMIOPARM
88  I-O-INVMPSZ            VALUE +38.         RMIOPARM
88  I-O-IGREQID            VALUE +39.         RMIOPARM
88  I-O-OVERFLOW           VALUE +40.         RMIOPARM
88  I-O-INVLDC             VALUE +41.         RMIOPARM
88  I-O-NOSTG              VALUE +42.         RMIOPARM
88  I-O-JIDERR             VALUE +43.         RMIOPARM
88  I-O-QIDERR             VALUE +44.         RMIOPARM
88  I-O-NOJBUFSP           VALUE +45.         RMIOPARM
88  I-O-DSSTAT             VALUE +46.         RMIOPARM
88  I-O-SELNERR            VALUE +47.         RMIOPARM
88  I-O-FUNCERR            VALUE +48.         RMIOPARM
88  I-O-UNEXPIN            VALUE +49.         RMIOPARM
88  I-O-NOPASSBKRD         VALUE +50.         RMIOPARM
88  I-O-NOPASSBKWR         VALUE +51.         RMIOPARM
88  I-O-RESERVED-52        VALUE +52.         RMIOPARM
88  I-O-SYSIDERR           VALUE +53.         RMIOPARM
88  I-O-ISCINVREQ          VALUE +54.         RMIOPARM
88  I-O-ENQBUSY            VALUE +55.         RMIOPARM
88  I-O-ENVDEFERR          VALUE +56.         RMIOPARM
88  I-O-IGREQCD            VALUE +57.         RMIOPARM
88  I-O-SESSIONERR         VALUE +58.         RMIOPARM
88  I-O-SYSBUSY            VALUE +59.         RMIOPARM
88  I-O-SESSBUSY           VALUE +60.         RMIOPARM
88  I-O-NOTALLOC           VALUE +61.         RMIOPARM
88  I-O-CBIDERR            VALUE +62.         RMIOPARM
88  I-O-RESERVED-63        VALUE +63.         RMIOPARM
88  I-O-INVPARTNST         VALUE +64.         RMIOPARM
88  I-O-INVPARTN           VALUE +65.         RMIOPARM
88  I-O-PARTNFAIL          VALUE +66.         RMIOPARM
88  I-O-RESERVED-67        VALUE +67.         RMIOPARM
```

```
          88  I-O-RESERVED-68          VALUE +68.             RMIOPARM
          88  I-O-RESERVED-69          VALUE +69.             RMIOPARM
          88  I-O-NOTAUTH              VALUE +70.             RMIOPARM
          88  I-O-RESERVED-71          VALUE +71.             RMIOPARM
          88  I-O-RESERVED-72          VALUE +72.             RMIOPARM
          88  I-O-RESERVED-73          VALUE +73.             RMIOPARM
          88  I-O-RESERVED-74          VALUE +74.             RMIOPARM
          88  I-O-RESERVED-75          VALUE +75.             RMIOPARM
          88  I-O-RESERVED-76          VALUE +76.             RMIOPARM
          88  I-O-RESERVED-77          VALUE +77.             RMIOPARM
          88  I-O-RESERVED-78          VALUE +78.             RMIOPARM
          88  I-O-RESERVED-79          VALUE +79.             RMIOPARM
          88  I-O-NOSPOOL              VALUE +80.             RMIOPARM
          88  I-O-TERMERR              VALUE +81.             RMIOPARM
          88  I-O-ROLLEDBACK           VALUE +82.             RMIOPARM
          88  I-O-END                  VALUE +83.             RMIOPARM
          88  I-O-DISABLED             VALUE +84.             RMIOPARM
          88  I-O-ALLOCERR             VALUE +85.             RMIOPARM
          88  I-O-STRELERR             VALUE +86.             RMIOPARM
          88  I-O-OPENERR              VALUE +87.             RMIOPARM
          88  I-O-SPOLBUSY             VALUE +88.             RMIOPARM
          88  I-O-SPOLERR              VALUE +89.             RMIOPARM
          88  I-O-NODEIDER             VALUE +90.             RMIOPARM
          88  I-O-ERR-RECBUFF          VALUE +91.             RMIOPARM
          88  I-O-ERR-COMMAND          VALUE +92.             RMIOPARM
          88  I-O-ERR-TSQREAD          VALUE +93.             RMIOPARM
          88  I-O-ERR-EIB-MISSING      VALUE +94.             RMIOPARM
          88  I-O-ERR-NOTFND-ISS06A    VALUE +95.             RMIOPARM
          88  I-O-ERR-U1TYPE-MISSING   VALUE +96.             RMIOPARM
          88  I-O-ERR-TYPE-CONFLICT    VALUE +97.             RMIOPARM
          88  I-O-ERR-STK-OVERFL       VALUE +98.             RMIOPARM
          88  I-O-ERR-STK-UNDRFL       VALUE +99.             RMIOPARM
          88  I-O-ERR-VRECTYPE         VALUE +100.            RMIOPARM
          88  I-O-ERR-ACF2-DENIAL      VALUE +101.            RMIOPARM
          88  I-O-ERR-ACF2-MISSING     VALUE +102.            RMIOPARM
          88  I-O-ERR-NOTFND-ISS10A    VALUE +103.            RMIOPARM
          88  I-O-ERR-PATH-UPDATE      VALUE +104.            RMIOPARM
          88  I-O-GENKEY-LEN-MISSING   VALUE +105.               CL**7
      05  I-O-RETPGM-PTR         PIC S9(04)  COMP VALUE +0.   RMIOPARM
      05  I-O-RETPGM-STACK.                                   RMIOPARM
          10  I-O-RETPGM                                      RMIOPARM
              OCCURS 3 TIMES     PIC X(08).                   RMIOPARM
      05  I-O-FILENAME           PIC X(08).                   RMIOPARM
      05  I-O-FILEKEY            PIC X(40).                   RMIOPARM
      05  I-O-COMMAND            PIC X(08).                   RMIOPARM
      05  I-O-OPERATOR           PIC X(05).                   RMIOPARM
      05  I-O-GENERIC-KEYLEN     PIC S9(04) COMP.             RMIOPARM
*-->  05  FILLER                 PIC X(02).                      CL**7
      05  I-O-NUMREC-DELETED     PIC S9(04) COMP.                CL**7
      05  I-O-GENERIC            PIC X(08) VALUE SPACES.      RMIOPARM
      05  I-O-UPDATE             PIC X(08) VALUE SPACES.      RMIOPARM
      05  I-O-UPD-TYPE           PIC X(01).                   RMIOPARM
          88 I-O-ADD             VALUE 'A'.                   RMIOPARM
          88 I-O-CHNGE           VALUE 'C'.                   RMIOPARM
          88 I-O-DLETE           VALUE 'D'.                   RMIOPARM
          88 I-O-READONLY        VALUE 'R'.                   RMIOPARM
      05  I-O-ACF2-INTENT        PIC X(01).                   RMIOPARM
      05  FILLER                 PIC X(01).                   RMIOPARM
      05  I-O-VREC-TYPE          PIC S9(04) COMP VALUE -1.    RMIOPARM
      05  I-O-RETURNED-JDATA.                                 RMIOPARM
          10  I-O-RET-JLEN       PIC S9(04) COMP  VALUE +0.   RMIOPARM
          10  I-O-RET-JFILEID    PIC S9(04) COMP  VALUE +0.   RMIOPARM
          10  I-O-RET-JTYPEID    PIC  X(02) VALUE SPACES.     RMIOPARM
```

```
       05  I-O-COMMAND-VALUES.                                          RMIOPARM
           10  I-O-READ                PIC X(08) VALUE 'READ'.          RMIOPARM
           10  I-O-STARTBR             PIC X(08) VALUE 'STARTBR'.       RMIOPARM
           10  I-O-ENDBR               PIC X(08) VALUE 'ENDBR'.         RMIOPARM
           10  I-O-RESETBR             PIC X(08) VALUE 'RESETBR'.       RMIOPARM
           10  I-O-READNEXT            PIC X(08) VALUE 'READNEXT'.      RMIOPARM
           10  I-O-READPREV            PIC X(08) VALUE 'READPREV'.      RMIOPARM
           10  I-O-WRITE               PIC X(08) VALUE 'WRITE'.         RMIOPARM
           10  I-O-REWRITE             PIC X(08) VALUE 'REWRITE'.       RMIOPARM
           10  I-O-DELETE              PIC X(08) VALUE 'DELETE'.        RMIOPARM
       05  I-O-OPERATOR-VALUES.                                         RMIOPARM
           10  I-O-EQUAL               PIC X(05) VALUE 'EQUAL'.         RMIOPARM
           10  I-O-GTEQ                PIC X(05) VALUE 'GTEQ'.          RMIOPARM
       05  I-O-MODES-VALUES.                                            RMIOPARM
           10  I-O-GENERIC-MODE        PIC X(08) VALUE 'GENERIC'.       RMIOPARM
           10  I-O-UPDATE-MODE         PIC X(08) VALUE 'UPDATE'.        RMIOPARM
       05  I-O-ACF2-INTENT-VALUES.                                      RMIOPARM
           10 I-O-ACF2-ADD             PIC X(01) VALUE 'A'.             RMIOPARM
           10 I-O-ACF2-UPDATE          PIC X(01) VALUE 'U'.             RMIOPARM
           10 I-O-ACF2-DELETE          PIC X(01) VALUE 'D'.             RMIOPARM
           10 I-O-ACF2-READ            PIC X(01) VALUE 'R'.             RMIOPARM
       05  I-O-FILENAME-VALUE.                                          RMIOPARM
           10  RM-CATLG                PIC X(08) VALUE 'RMK000  '.      RMIOPARM
           10  RM-CATLG-PATH1          PIC X(08) VALUE 'RMK001  '.      RMIOPARM
           10  RM-CATLG-PATH2          PIC X(08) VALUE 'RMK002  '.      RMIOPARM
           10  RM-XREF                 PIC X(08) VALUE 'RMK010  '.      RMIOPARM
           10  RM-XREF-PATH1           PIC X(08) VALUE 'RMK011  '.      RMIOPARM
           10  RM-XREF-PATH2           PIC X(08) VALUE 'RMK012  '.      RMIOPARM
           10  RM-XREF-PATH3           PIC X(08) VALUE 'RMK013  '.      RMIOPARM
           10  RM-ITEM                 PIC X(08) VALUE 'RMK020  '.      RMIOPARM
           10  RM-ITEM-PATH1           PIC X(08) VALUE 'RMK021  '.      RMIOPARM
           10  RM-ITEM-PATH2           PIC X(08) VALUE 'RMK022  '.      RMIOPARM
           10  RM-REPLEN               PIC X(08) VALUE 'RMK030  '.      RMIOPARM
           10  RM-REPLEN-PATH1         PIC X(08) VALUE 'RMK031  '.      RMIOPARM
           10  RM-REPLEN-PATH2         PIC X(08) VALUE 'RMK032  '.      RMIOPARM
           10  RM-TABLE                PIC X(08) VALUE 'RMK040  '.      RMIOPARM
           10  RM-VENDOR               PIC X(08) VALUE 'VALIDM  '.      RMIOPARM
           10  RM-POMAST               PIC X(08) VALUE 'POMASTR '.      RMIOPARM
           10  RM-POCONV               PIC X(08) VALUE 'POCONV  '.      RMIOPARM
           10  RM-POBUYER              PIC X(08) VALUE 'POBUYER '.         CL**6
           10  RM-PROFILE              PIC X(08) VALUE 'ISK020  '.         CL**2
           10  RM-WIP-HEADER           PIC X(08) VALUE 'RMK050  '.         CL**2
           10  RM-WIP-DETAIL           PIC X(08) VALUE 'RMK060  '.         CL**2
           10  RM-WIP-DETAIL-PATH1     PIC X(08) VALUE 'RMK061  '.         CL**4
           10  RM-REORDER              PIC X(08) VALUE 'RMK070  '.         CL**4
           10  RM-REORDER-PATH1        PIC X(08) VALUE 'RMK071  '.         CL**4
           10  RM-BILMSTR              PIC X(08) VALUE 'ARA61C  '.         CL**3
           10  RM-GLMASTR              PIC X(08) VALUE 'GLMASTR '.         CL**3
           10  RM-CYCLE                PIC X(08) VALUE 'RMK080  '.         CL**5
           10  RM-CYCLE-PATH1          PIC X(08) VALUE 'RMK081  '.         CL**5
           10  RM-TRANS                PIC X(08) VALUE 'RMK090  '.         CL**5
           10  RM-TRANS-PATH1          PIC X(08) VALUE 'RMK091  '.         CL**5
       05  I-O-RAIL-SCHEDULE-FILES.                                        CL**6
           10  RS-KIT-HEADER           PIC X(08) VALUE 'RSK010  '.         CL**6
           10  RS-KIT-DETAIL           PIC X(08) VALUE 'RSK020  '.         CL**6
           10  RS-KIT-DETAIL-PATH1     PIC X(08) VALUE 'RSK021  '.         CL**6
           10  RS-SCH-MASTER           PIC X(08) VALUE 'RSK030  '.         CL**6
       05  I-O-JOURNAL-INFO.                                            RMIOPARM
           10  I-O-JRNL-RECNUM         PIC 9(01).                       RMIOPARM
           10  I-O-JRNL-WORKPGM        PIC X(08).                       RMIOPARM
       05  I-O-TOPS-FILES.                                                 CL**6
           10  TP-REPAIR-TBLE          PIC X(08) VALUE 'TEQREPAR'.         CL**6
           10  TP-EQUIP-PATH1          PIC X(08) VALUE 'TEQALT  '.         CL**6
```

```
           05  I-O-RAIL-SCHEDULE-FILE.                                  CL**6
               10  RS-SCH-MASTER-PATH1      PIC X(08) VALUE 'RSK031  '. CL**6
               10  RS-KIT-HEADER-PATH1      PIC X(08) VALUE 'RSK011  '. CL**6
           05  FILLER                       PIC X(08).                  CL**6
      ***                                                            RMIOPARM
      ***  END OF COPY MEMBER IOPARMS - 01/26/90, G.S.               RMIOPARM
      *                                                              RMP61C
       01  MTIME                        PIC S9(12) COMP.             RMP61C
       01  FDATE                        PIC X(08).                   RMP61C
       01  ADATE                        PIC X(08).                   RMP61C
       01  FTIME.                                                    RMP61C
           05  FHTIME                   PIC X(05).                   RMP61C
           05  FILLER                   PIC X(03).                   RMP61C
      *                                                              RMP61C
      *                                                              RMP61C
       ++INCLUDE RMP61M                                                 CL*81
      *                                                              RMP61C
       01  HOLD-DESCRIPTION.                                            CL*39
           05  HOLD-DESCRIPTION-1       PIC X(30)  VALUE SPACES.        CL*39
           05  HOLD-DESCRIPTION-2       PIC X(30)  VALUE SPACES.        CL*39
           05  HOLD-DESCRIPTION-3       PIC X(30)  VALUE SPACES.        CL*39
      *                                                                 CL*39
       01  LINE-CNTR                    PIC 9(02)  VALUE 99.            CL*38
       01  DESTINATION-ID               PIC X(04)  VALUE SPACES.        CL*37
       01  HOLD-DESTINATION-ID          PIC X(04)  VALUE SPACES.        CL*60
       01  LINE-LENGTH                  PIC S9(04) COMP VALUE +132.     CL*40
       01  PAGE-NUMBER                  PIC 9(03)  VALUE 0.             CL*38
      *                                                                 CL*37
       01  PRINT-QUEUE-RECORD.                                          CL*37
           05  CARRIAGE-CNTL            PIC X(01)  VALUE SPACES.        CL*37
           05  PRINT-DATA-LINE          PIC X(131) VALUE SPACES.        CL*37
      *                                                                 CL*37
       01  MR-HEADER-LINE-1.                                            CL*36
           05  FILLER                   PIC X(10)  VALUE 'R-RMP61C-1'.  CL*81
           05  FILLER                   PIC X(40)  VALUE SPACES.        CL*36
           05  FILLER                   PIC X(30)  VALUE                CL*36
               'RAIL MATERIAL INVENTORY SYSTEM'.                        CL*36
           05  FILLER                   PIC X(08)  VALUE SPACES.        CL*36
           05  FILLER                   PIC X(19)  VALUE                CL*36
               'DOCUMENT NUMBER  : '.                                   CL*36
           05  MR-HL-1-DOC-NUM          PIC X(07).                      CL*69
           05  FILLER                   PIC X(07)  VALUE SPACES.        CL*69
           05  FILLER                   PIC X(07)  VALUE 'PAGE : '.     CL*36
           05  MR-HL-1-PAGE-NUM         PIC 9(03).                      CL*36
      *                                                                 CL*36
       01  MR-HEADER-LINE-2.                                            CL*36
           05  FILLER                   PIC X(09)  VALUE 'SYSDATE: '.   CL*80
           05  MR-HL-2-SYSDATE          PIC X(08).                      CL*80
           05  FILLER                   PIC X(05)  VALUE SPACES.        CL*80
           05  FILLER                   PIC X(09)  VALUE 'SYSTIME: '.   CL*80
           05  MR-HL-2-SYSTIME          PIC X(05)  VALUE SPACES.        CL*80
           05  FILLER                   PIC X(21)  VALUE SPACES.        CL*80
           05  FILLER                   PIC X(17)  VALUE                CL*81
               'RESTOCK DOCUMENT '.                                     CL*94
           05  FILLER                   PIC X(14)  VALUE SPACES.        CL*81
           05  FILLER                   PIC X(19)  VALUE                CL*36
               'DOCUMENT DATE    : '.                                   CL*36
           05  MR-HL-2-MM               PIC X(02).                      CL*36
           05  FILLER                   PIC X(01)  VALUE '/'.           CL*36
           05  MR-HL-2-DD               PIC X(02).                      CL*36
           05  FILLER                   PIC X(01)  VALUE '/'.           CL*36
           05  MR-HL-2-YY               PIC X(02).                      CL*36
           05  FILLER                   PIC X(16)  VALUE SPACES.        CL*36
```

```
      *                                                                  CL*36
       01  MR-HEADER-LINE-3.                                             CL*36
           05  FILLER                  PIC X(88)  VALUE SPACES.          CL*36
           05  FILLER                  PIC X(19)  VALUE                  CL*36
               'DOCUMENT STATUS  : '.                                    CL*36
           05  MR-HL-3-DOC-STATUS      PIC X(01).                        CL*36
           05  FILLER                  PIC X(01)  VALUE SPACES.          CL*36
           05  FILLER                  PIC X(19)  VALUE                  CL*36
               'REASON OPEN      : '.                                    CL*36
           05  MR-HL-3-REASON-OPEN     PIC X(01).                        CL*36
           05  FILLER                  PIC X(02)  VALUE SPACES.          CL*36
      *                                                                  CL*36
       01  MR-HEADER-LINE-4.                                             CL*36
           05  FILLER                  PIC X(10)  VALUE 'USER ID : '.    CL*36
           05  MR-HL-4-USER-ID         PIC X(08).                        CL*36
           05  FILLER                  PIC X(13)  VALUE                  CL*36
               ' USER NAME : '.                                          CL*36
           05  MR-HL-4-USER-NAME       PIC X(20).                        CL*36
           05  FILLER                  PIC X(19)  VALUE                  CL*36
               '   DEPARTMENT    : '.                                    CL*36
           05  MR-HL-4-DEPT            PIC X(04).                        CL*36
           05  FILLER                  PIC X(14)  VALUE SPACES.          CL*36
           05  FILLER                  PIC X(19)  VALUE                  CL*36
               'DOCUMENT PRINTED : '.                                    CL*36
           05  MR-HL-4-DOC-PRINTED     PIC X(01).                        CL*36
           05  FILLER                  PIC X(01)  VALUE SPACES.          CL*36
           05  FILLER                  PIC X(19)  VALUE                  CL*36
               'STOCKLIST PRINTED: '.                                    CL*81
           05  MR-HL-4-PICKLIST-PRNTED PIC X(01).                        CL*36
           05  FILLER                  PIC X(02)  VALUE SPACES.          CL*36
      *                                                                  CL*36
       01  MR-HEADER-LINE-5.                                             CL*36
           05  FILLER                  PIC X(10)  VALUE 'SITE ID : '.    CL*36
           05  MR-HL-5-SITE-ID         PIC X(05).                        CL*36
           05  FILLER                  PIC X(16)  VALUE                  CL*36
               '     PROJECT   : '.                                      CL*36
           05  MR-HL-5-PROJECT         PIC X(06).                        CL*36
           05  FILLER                  PIC X(17)  VALUE SPACES.          CL*36
           05  FILLER                  PIC X(16)  VALUE                  CL*36
               'WORK ORDER NO : '.                                       CL*36
           05  MR-HL-5-WORK-ORDER-NO   PIC X(10).                        CL*36
           05  FILLER                  PIC X(51)  VALUE SPACES.          CL*36
      *                                                                  CL*36
       01  MR-HEADER-LINE-6.                                             CL*36
           05  FILLER                  PIC X(07)  VALUE SPACES.          CL*36
           05  FILLER                  PIC X(05)  VALUE 'METRA'.         CL*36
           05  FILLER                  PIC X(90)  VALUE SPACES.          CL*36
           05  FILLER                  PIC X(08)  VALUE 'QUANTITY'.      CL*81
           05  FILLER                  PIC X(21)  VALUE SPACES.          CL*81
      *                                                                  CL*36
       01  MR-HEADER-LINE-7.                                             CL*36
           05  FILLER                  PIC X(04)  VALUE 'ITEM'.          CL*36
           05  FILLER                  PIC X(03)  VALUE SPACES.          CL*36
           05  FILLER                  PIC X(04)  VALUE 'PART'.          CL*36
           05  FILLER                  PIC X(04)  VALUE SPACES.          CL*36
           05  FILLER                  PIC X(01)  VALUE 'S'.             CL*36
           05  FILLER                  PIC X(86)  VALUE SPACES.          CL*36
           05  FILLER                  PIC X(08)  VALUE 'RECOV. /'.      CL*81
           05  FILLER                  PIC X(02)  VALUE SPACES.          CL*81
           05  FILLER                  PIC X(07)  VALUE 'AVERAGE'.       CL*36
           05  FILLER                  PIC X(04)  VALUE SPACES.          CL*36
           05  FILLER                  PIC X(08)  VALUE 'EXTENDED'.      CL*36
      *                                                                  CL*36
```

```
       01  MR-HEADER-LINE-8.                                            CL*36
           05  FILLER                  PIC X(07)  VALUE ' NO     '.     CL*36
           05  FILLER                  PIC X(06)  VALUE 'NUMBER'.       CL*36
           05  FILLER                  PIC X(02)  VALUE SPACES.         CL*36
           05  FILLER                  PIC X(01)  VALUE 'T'.            CL*36
           05  FILLER                  PIC X(08)  VALUE SPACES.         CL*36
           05  FILLER                  PIC X(11)  VALUE 'DESCRIPTION'.  CL*36
           05  FILLER                  PIC X(13)  VALUE SPACES.         CL*36
           05  FILLER                  PIC X(12)  VALUE                 CL*36
               'ACCOUNT CODE'.                                          CL*36
           05  FILLER                  PIC X(12)  VALUE SPACES.         CL*36
           05  FILLER                  PIC X(22)  VALUE                 CL*36
               'DESCRIPTION OF ACCOUNT'.                                CL*36
           05  FILLER                  PIC X(08)  VALUE '    UM  '.     CL*36
           05  FILLER                  PIC X(08)  VALUE 'SCRAPPED'.     CL*81
           05  FILLER                  PIC X(03)  VALUE SPACES.         CL*81
           05  FILLER                  PIC X(05)  VALUE 'PRICE'.        CL*36
           05  FILLER                  PIC X(06)  VALUE SPACES.         CL*36
           05  FILLER                  PIC X(05)  VALUE 'VALUE'.        CL*36
           05  FILLER                  PIC X(02)  VALUE SPACES.         CL*36
      *                                                                 CL*36
       01  MR-DETAIL-LINE-1.                                            CL*36
           05  MR-DL-1-ITEM-NO         PIC X(03).                       CL*36
           05  FILLER                  PIC X(01)  VALUE SPACES.         CL*36
           05  MR-DL-1-METRA-CLASS-CD  PIC X(02).                       CL*39
           05  FILLER                  PIC X(01)  VALUE '-'.            CL*39
           05  MR-DL-1-METRA-PART-ID   PIC X(05).                       CL*39
           05  FILLER                  PIC X(01)  VALUE '-'.            CL*39
           05  MR-DL-1-METRA-CHECK-DGT PIC X(01).                       CL*39
           05  FILLER                  PIC X(01)  VALUE SPACES.         CL*36
           05  MR-DL-1-ST              PIC X(01).                       CL*36
           05  FILLER                  PIC X(01)  VALUE SPACES.         CL*36
           05  MR-DL-1-DESCRIPTION     PIC X(30).                       CL*36
           05  FILLER                  PIC X(01)  VALUE SPACES.         CL*36
           05  MR-DL-1-ACCT-ORG        PIC X(02).                       CL*39
           05  FILLER                  PIC X(01)  VALUE '-'.            CL*39
           05  MR-DL-1-ACCT-DEPT       PIC X(04).                       CL*39
           05  FILLER                  PIC X(01)  VALUE '-'.            CL*39
           05  MR-DL-1-ACCT-FUNC       PIC X(04).                       CL*39
           05  MR-DL-1-ACCT-SRCE       PIC X(04).                       CL*39
           05  FILLER                  PIC X(01)  VALUE '-'.            CL*39
           05  MR-DL-1-ACCT-PROJ       PIC X(06).                       CL*39
           05  FILLER                  PIC X(01)  VALUE SPACES.         CL*36
           05  MR-DL-1-ACCOUNT-DESC    PIC X(24).                       CL*36
           05  FILLER                  PIC X(02)  VALUE SPACES.         CL*87
           05  MR-DL-1-UM              PIC X(02).                       CL*87
           05  FILLER                  PIC X(02)  VALUE SPACES.         CL*87
           05  MR-DL-1-QTY-RECOVERED   PIC ZZZZZZ9.                     CL*81
           05  FILLER                  PIC X(01)  VALUE SPACES.         CL*57
           05  MR-DL-1-AVG-PRICE       PIC ZZZZZ9.999.                  CL*57
           05  FILLER                  PIC X(01)  VALUE SPACES.         CL*36
           05  MR-DL-1-EXTENDED-VALUE  PIC ZZZZZ9.999.                  CL*36
      *                                                                 CL*36
       01  MR-DETAIL-LINE-2.                                            CL*36
           05  FILLER                  PIC X(17)  VALUE SPACES.         CL*36
           05  MR-DL-2-DESCRIPTION     PIC X(30).                       CL*36
           05  FILLER                  PIC X(25)  VALUE SPACES.         CL*36
           05  MR-DL-2-ACCOUNT-DESC    PIC X(24).                       CL*36
           05  FILLER                  PIC X(06)  VALUE SPACES.         CL*36
           05  MR-DL-2-QTY-SCRAPPED    PIC ZZZZZZ9.                     CL*81
           05  FILLER                  PIC X(22)  VALUE SPACES.         CL*36
      *                                                                 CL*36
       01  MR-DETAIL-LINE-3.                                            CL*36
```

```
           05  FILLER                 PIC X(17)  VALUE SPACES.             CL*36
           05  MR-DL-3-DESCRIPTION    PIC X(30).                           CL*36
           05  FILLER                 PIC X(25)  VALUE SPACES.             CL*36
           05  MR-DL-3-ACCOUNT-DESC   PIC X(24).                           CL*36
           05  FILLER                 PIC X(35)  VALUE SPACES.             CL*36
      *                                                                    CL*36
       01  MR-DETAIL-LINE-4.                                               CL*36
           05  FILLER                 PIC X(08)  VALUE 'MFG-NO: '.         CL*80
           05  MR-DL-4-MFG-PART-NO    PIC X(15).                           CL*80
           05  FILLER                 PIC X(10)  VALUE SPACES.             CL*80
           05  FILLER                 PIC X(11)  VALUE                     CL*36
                'COMMENTS : '.                                             CL*36
           05  MR-DL-4-COMMENTS       PIC X(40).                           CL*36
           05  FILLER                 PIC X(04)  VALUE SPACES.             CL*36
           05  FILLER                 PIC X(11)  VALUE 'EQUIP. # : '.      CL*36
           05  MR-DL-4-EQUIP-NUMBER   PIC X(10).                           CL*36
           05  FILLER                 PIC X(22)  VALUE SPACES.             CL*80
      *                                                                    CL*36
       01  MR-TRAILER-LINE-1.                                              CL*36
           05  FILLER                 PIC X(97)  VALUE SPACES.             CL*36
           05  FILLER                 PIC X(24)  VALUE                     CL*36
                'TOTAL RECOVERED VALUE : '.                                CL*81
           05  MR-TL-1-TOTAL-REQ-VALUE PIC ZZZZZ9.999.                     CL*36
      *                                                                    CL*36
       01  MR-TRAILER-LINE-2.                                              CL*36
           05  FILLER                 PIC X(14)  VALUE                     CL*36
                'APPROVED BY : '.                                          CL*36
           05  FILLER                 PIC X(39)  VALUE                     CL*36
                '_______________________________________'.                 CL*36
           05  FILLER                 PIC X(11)  VALUE '   DATE  : '.      CL*36
           05  FILLER                 PIC X(21)  VALUE                     CL*36
                '_____ / _____ / _____'.                                   CL*36
           05  FILLER                 PIC X(46)  VALUE SPACES.             CL*36
      *                                                                    CL*36
       01  PL-HEADER-LINE-1.                                               CL*36
           05  FILLER                 PIC X(10)  VALUE 'R-RMP61C-2'.       CL*81
           05  FILLER                 PIC X(40)  VALUE SPACES.             CL*36
           05  FILLER                 PIC X(30)  VALUE                     CL*36
                'RAIL MATERIAL INVENTORY SYSTEM'.                          CL*36
           05  FILLER                 PIC X(08)  VALUE SPACES.             CL*36
           05  FILLER                 PIC X(19)  VALUE                     CL*36
                'DOCUMENT NUMBER  : '.                                     CL*36
           05  PL-HL-1-DOC-NUM        PIC X(07).                           CL*69
           05  FILLER                 PIC X(07)  VALUE SPACES.             CL*69
           05  FILLER                 PIC X(07)  VALUE 'PAGE : '.          CL*36
           05  PL-HL-1-PAGE-NUM       PIC 9(03).                           CL*36
      *                                                                    CL*36
       01  PL-HEADER-LINE-2.                                               CL*36
           05  FILLER                 PIC X(09)  VALUE 'SYSDATE: '.        CL*80
           05  PL-HL-2-SYSDATE        PIC X(08).                           CL*80
           05  FILLER                 PIC X(05)  VALUE SPACES.             CL*80
           05  FILLER                 PIC X(09)  VALUE 'SYSTIME: '.        CL*80
           05  PL-HL-2-SYSTIME        PIC X(05).                           CL*80
           05  FILLER                 PIC X(18)  VALUE SPACES.             CL*81
           05  FILLER                 PIC X(22)  VALUE                     CL*81
                'MTRL RESTOCKING TICKET'.                                  CL*94
           05  FILLER                 PIC X(12)  VALUE SPACES.             CL*81
           05  FILLER                 PIC X(19)  VALUE                     CL*36
                'DOCUMENT DATE    : '.                                     CL*36
           05  PL-HL-2-MM             PIC X(02).                           CL*36
           05  FILLER                 PIC X(01)  VALUE '/'.                CL*36
           05  PL-HL-2-DD             PIC X(02).                           CL*36
           05  FILLER                 PIC X(01)  VALUE '/'.                CL*36
```

```
        05  PL-HL-2-YY               PIC X(02).                        CL*36
        05  FILLER                   PIC X(16)  VALUE SPACES.          CL*36
      *                                                                CL*36
     01  PL-HEADER-LINE-3.                                             CL*36
        05  FILLER                   PIC X(88)  VALUE SPACES.          CL*36
        05  FILLER                   PIC X(19)  VALUE                  CL*36
             'DOCUMENT STATUS  : '.                                    CL*36
        05  PL-HL-3-DOC-STATUS       PIC X(01).                        CL*36
        05  FILLER                   PIC X(01)  VALUE SPACES.          CL*36
        05  FILLER                   PIC X(19)  VALUE                  CL*36
             'REASON OPEN      : '.                                    CL*36
        05  PL-HL-3-REASON-OPEN      PIC X(01).                        CL*36
        05  FILLER                   PIC X(02)  VALUE SPACES.          CL*36
      *                                                                CL*36
     01  PL-HEADER-LINE-4.                                             CL*36
        05  FILLER                   PIC X(10)  VALUE 'USER ID : '.    CL*36
        05  PL-HL-4-USER-ID          PIC X(08).                        CL*36
        05  FILLER                   PIC X(13)  VALUE                  CL*36
             ' USER NAME : '.                                          CL*36
        05  PL-HL-4-USER-NAME        PIC X(20).                        CL*36
        05  FILLER                   PIC X(19)  VALUE                  CL*36
             '   DEPARTMENT    : '.                                    CL*36
        05  PL-HL-4-DEPT             PIC X(04).                        CL*36
        05  FILLER                   PIC X(14)  VALUE SPACES.          CL*36
        05  FILLER                   PIC X(19)  VALUE                  CL*36
             'DOCUMENT PRINTED : '.                                    CL*36
        05  PL-HL-4-DOC-PRINTED      PIC X(01).                        CL*36
        05  FILLER                   PIC X(01)  VALUE SPACES.          CL*36
        05  FILLER                   PIC X(19)  VALUE                  CL*36
             'STOCKLIST PRINTED: '.                                    CL*81
        05  PL-HL-4-PICKLIST-PRNTED PIC X(01).                         CL*36
        05  FILLER                   PIC X(02)  VALUE SPACES.          CL*36
      *                                                                CL*36
     01  PL-HEADER-LINE-5.                                             CL*36
        05  FILLER                   PIC X(10)  VALUE 'SITE ID : '.    CL*36
        05  PL-HL-5-SITE-ID          PIC X(05).                        CL*36
        05  FILLER                   PIC X(16)  VALUE                  CL*36
             '     PROJECT   : '.                                      CL*36
        05  PL-HL-5-PROJECT          PIC X(06).                        CL*36
        05  FILLER                   PIC X(17)  VALUE SPACES.          CL*36
        05  FILLER                   PIC X(16)  VALUE                  CL*36
             'WORK ORDER NO : '.                                       CL*36
        05  PL-HL-5-WORK-ORDER-NO    PIC X(10).                        CL*36
        05  FILLER                   PIC X(51)  VALUE SPACES.          CL*36
      *                                                                CL*36
     01  PL-HEADER-LINE-6.                                             CL*36
        05  FILLER                   PIC X(19)  VALUE SPACES.          CL*36
        05  FILLER                   PIC X(05)  VALUE 'METRA'.         CL*36
        05  FILLER                   PIC X(75)  VALUE SPACES.          CL*81
        05  FILLER                   PIC X(03)  VALUE 'NEW'.           CL*81
        05  FILLER                   PIC X(29)  VALUE SPACES.          CL*81
      *                                                                CL*36
     01  PL-HEADER-LINE-7.                                             CL*36
        05  FILLER                   PIC X(04)  VALUE 'ITEM'.          CL*36
        05  FILLER                   PIC X(04)  VALUE SPACES.          CL*36
        05  FILLER                   PIC X(03)  VALUE 'BIN'.           CL*36
        05  FILLER                   PIC X(08)  VALUE SPACES.          CL*36
        05  FILLER                   PIC X(04)  VALUE 'PART'.          CL*36
        05  FILLER                   PIC X(06)  VALUE SPACES.          CL*36
        05  FILLER                   PIC X(01)  VALUE 'S'.             CL*36
        05  FILLER                   PIC X(44)  VALUE SPACES.          CL*81
        05  FILLER                   PIC X(04)  VALUE 'QTY.'.          CL*36
```

```
           05  FILLER                 PIC X(07)  VALUE SPACES.          CL*81
           05  FILLER                 PIC X(04)  VALUE 'QTY'.           CL*36
           05  FILLER                 PIC X(08)  VALUE SPACES.          CL*81
           05  FILLER                 PIC X(08)  VALUE 'QUANTITY'.      CL*81
           05  FILLER                 PIC X(08)  VALUE SPACES.          CL*81
           05  FILLER                 PIC X(04)  VALUE 'QTY'.           CL*36
           05  FILLER                 PIC X(09)  VALUE SPACES.          CL*81
           05  FILLER                 PIC X(04)  VALUE 'LINE'.          CL*81
           05  FILLER                 PIC X(01)  VALUE SPACES.          CL*36
      *                                                                 CL*36
       01  PL-HEADER-LINE-8.                                            CL*36
           05  FILLER                 PIC X(06)  VALUE ' NO   '.        CL*36
           05  FILLER                 PIC X(08)  VALUE 'LOCATION'.      CL*36
           05  FILLER                 PIC X(05)  VALUE SPACES.          CL*36
           05  FILLER                 PIC X(06)  VALUE 'NUMBER'.        CL*36
           05  FILLER                 PIC X(04)  VALUE SPACES.          CL*36
           05  FILLER                 PIC X(01)  VALUE 'T'.             CL*36
           05  FILLER                 PIC X(08)  VALUE SPACES.          CL*36
           05  FILLER                 PIC X(11)  VALUE                  CL*36
               'DESCRIPTION'.                                           CL*36
           05  FILLER                 PIC X(16)  VALUE SPACES.          CL*36
           05  FILLER                 PIC X(02)  VALUE 'UM'.            CL*36
           05  FILLER                 PIC X(05)  VALUE SPACES.          CL*81
           05  FILLER                 PIC X(07)  VALUE 'ON HAND'.       CL*36
           05  FILLER                 PIC X(04)  VALUE SPACES.          CL*81
           05  FILLER                 PIC X(09)  VALUE 'RECOVERED'.     CL*81
           05  FILLER                 PIC X(05)  VALUE SPACES.          CL*81
           05  FILLER                 PIC X(07)  VALUE 'ON HAND'.       CL*81
           05  FILLER                 PIC X(07)  VALUE SPACES.          CL*81
           05  FILLER                 PIC X(08)  VALUE 'SCRAPPED'.      CL*81
           05  FILLER                 PIC X(06)  VALUE SPACES.          CL*36
           05  FILLER                 PIC X(06)  VALUE 'STATUS'.        CL*36
      *                                                                 CL*36
       01  PL-DETAIL-LINE-1.                                            CL*36
           05  PL-DL-1-ITEM-NO        PIC X(03).                        CL*36
           05  FILLER                 PIC X(03)  VALUE SPACES.          CL*36
           05  PL-DL-1-BIN-LOCATION   PIC X(10).                        CL*36
           05  FILLER                 PIC X(02)  VALUE SPACES.          CL*36
           05  PL-DL-1-METRA-CLASS-CD PIC X(02).                        CL*50
           05  FILLER                 PIC X(01)  VALUE '-'.             CL*50
           05  PL-DL-1-METRA-PART-ID  PIC X(05).                        CL*50
           05  FILLER                 PIC X(01)  VALUE '-'.             CL*50
           05  PL-DL-1-METRA-CHECK-DGT PIC X(01).                       CL*50
           05  FILLER                 PIC X(01)  VALUE SPACES.          CL*36
           05  PL-DL-1-ST             PIC X(01).                        CL*36
           05  FILLER                 PIC X(02)  VALUE SPACES.          CL*36
           05  PL-DL-1-DESCRIPTION    PIC X(30).                        CL*36
           05  FILLER                 PIC X(03)  VALUE SPACES.          CL*36
           05  PL-DL-1-UM             PIC X(02).                        CL*36
           05  FILLER                 PIC X(05)  VALUE SPACES.          CL*81
           05  PL-DL-1-QTY-ON-HAND    PIC ZZZZZZ9.                      CL*36
           05  FILLER                 PIC X(05)  VALUE SPACES.          CL*81
           05  PL-DL-1-QTY-RECOVERED  PIC ZZZZZZ9.                      CL*81
           05  FILLER                 PIC X(06)  VALUE SPACES.          CL*81
           05  PL-DL-1-NEW-QTY-ON-HAND PIC ZZZZZZ9.                     CL*81
           05  FILLER                 PIC X(06)  VALUE SPACES.          CL*81
           05  FILLER                 PIC X(11)  VALUE                  CL*81
               '___________'.                                           CL*81
           05  FILLER                 PIC X(06)  VALUE SPACES.          CL*81
           05  PL-DL-1-LINE-STATUS    PIC X(01).                        CL*36
           05  FILLER                 PIC X(03)  VALUE SPACES.          CL*81
      *                                                                 CL*36
```

```
 01  PL-DETAIL-LINE-2.                                                  CL*36
     05  FILLER                   PIC X(32)  VALUE SPACES.              CL*36
     05  PL-DL-2-DESCRIPTION      PIC X(30).                            CL*36
     05  FILLER                   PIC X(69)  VALUE SPACES.              CL*36
*                                                                       CL*36
 01  PL-DETAIL-LINE-3.                                                  CL*36
     05  FILLER                   PIC X(32)  VALUE SPACES.              CL*36
     05  PL-DL-3-DESCRIPTION      PIC X(30).                            CL*36
     05  FILLER                   PIC X(69)  VALUE SPACES.              CL*36
*                                                                       CL*36
 01  PL-DETAIL-LINE-4.                                                  CL*36
     05  FILLER                   PIC X(08)  VALUE 'MFG-NO: '.          CL*80
     05  PL-DL-4-MFG-PART-NO      PIC X(15).                            CL*80
     05  FILLER                   PIC X(32)  VALUE SPACES.              CL*36
     05  FILLER                   PIC X(11)  VALUE 'COMMENTS : '.       CL*36
     05  PL-DL-4-COMMENTS         PIC X(40).                            CL*36
     05  FILLER                   PIC X(25)  VALUE SPACES.              CL*80
*                                                                       CL*36
 01  PL-TRAILER-LINE-1.                                                 CL*36
     05  FILLER                   PIC X(14)  VALUE                      CL*36
         'SHELVED BY  : '.                                              CL*81
     05  FILLER                   PIC X(39)  VALUE                      CL*36
         '_______________________________________'.                     CL*36
     05  FILLER                   PIC X(11)  VALUE '   DATE  : '.       CL*36
     05  FILLER                   PIC X(21)  VALUE                      CL*36
         '_____ / _____ / _____'.                                       CL*36
     05  FILLER                   PIC X(46)  VALUE SPACES.              CL*36
*                                                                     RMP61C
*                                                                     RMP61C
 01  DFHAID COPY DFHAID.                                              RMP61C
*                                                                     RMP61C
 01  DFHBMSCA COPY DFHBMSCA.                                          RMP61C
 LINKAGE SECTION.                                                     RMP61C
 01  DFHCOMMAREA.                                                     RMP61C
     05  FILLER                   PIC X(602).                           CL*78
    03  DFH-VAR-COMMAREA.                                             RMP61C
*                                                                     RMP61C
       05  FILLER               PIC X(18).                            RMP61C
*                                                                     RMP61C
*                                                                     RMP61C
*                                                                     RMP61C
     EJECT                                                            RMP61C
 PROCEDURE DIVISION.                                                  RMP61C
                                                                      RMP61C
*                                                                     RMP61C
 0000-MAINLINE-CONTROL.                                               RMP61C
*                                                                     RMP61C
     EXEC CICS HANDLE ABEND LABEL(9270-ABEND-ROUTINE)                 RMP61C
                       RESP(CICS-RESP)                                RMP61C
                       END-EXEC.                                      RMP61C
     IF  CICS-RESP = DFHRESP(NORMAL)                                  RMP61C
         NEXT SENTENCE                                                RMP61C
     ELSE                                                             RMP61C
         MOVE 'A'                        TO CA-ERR-TYPE               RMP61C
         MOVE 00050                      TO CA-ERR-NUM-PRG            RMP61C
         IF  EIBCALEN LESS THAN +375                                  RMP61C
             PERFORM 0100-INIT-COMM THRU 0100-EXIT                    RMP61C
             PERFORM 9000-ERR-RTNE THRU 9000-ERR-EXIT                 RMP61C
         ELSE                                                         RMP61C
             PERFORM 0200-INIT-COMM THRU 0200-EXIT                    RMP61C
             PERFORM 9000-ERR-RTNE THRU 9000-ERR-EXIT.                RMP61C
     IF  EIBCALEN LESS THAN +375                                      RMP61C
         PERFORM 0100-INIT-COMM THRU 0100-EXIT                        RMP61C
```

```
            MOVE 00012                      TO CA-ERR-NUM-PRG        RMP61C
            MOVE 'A'                        TO CA-ERR-TYPE           RMP61C
            PERFORM 9000-ERR-RTNE           THRU 9000-ERR-EXIT       RMP61C
        ELSE                                                         RMP61C
           PERFORM 0200-INIT-COMM THRU 0200-EXIT                     RMP61C
           MOVE WS-PROG-NAME                TO I-O-JRNL-WORKPGM      RMP61C
           IF  EIBCALEN EQUAL +375                                   RMP61C
               PERFORM 1000-FIRST-TIME-SEND THRU 1000-EXIT           RMP61C
           ELSE                                                      RMP61C
             MOVE EIBAID              TO  CA-ATTN-KEY                RMP61C
             IF CA-ATTN-KEY EQUAL DFHCLEAR                           RMP61C
                MOVE DFHPF3 TO CA-ATTN-KEY, EIBAID                     CL*74
                PERFORM 9030-PF3-RTNE THRU 9030-PF3-EXIT               CL*74
             ELSE                                                    RMP61C
               IF  CA-ATTN-KEY EQUAL DFHPF9                          RMP61C
                   PERFORM 9020-PF9-RTNE THRU 9020-PF9-EXIT          RMP61C
              ELSE                                                     CL*30
                IF CA-ATTN-KEY EQUAL DFHPF12                           CL*30
                      PERFORM 3000-PF12-RTNE THRU 3000-PF12-EXIT       CL*30
               ELSE                                                  RMP61C
                 IF  CA-ATTN-KEY EQUAL DFHPF3                        RMP61C
                     PERFORM 9030-PF3-RTNE THRU 9030-PF3-EXIT        RMP61C
                 ELSE                                                  CL*74
                   IF  CA-ATTN-KEY EQUAL DFHPF4                        CL*74
                       PERFORM 9025-PF4-RTNE THRU 9025-PF4-EXIT        CL*74
                   ELSE                                                CL*74
                     IF  CA-ATTN-KEY EQUAL DFHPF1                      CL*74
                         PERFORM 9040-PF1-RTNE THRU 9040-PF1-EXIT      CL*74
                     ELSE                                              CL*74
                       IF  CA-ATTN-KEY EQUAL DFHENTER                  CL*74
                           PERFORM 2000-ENTER-RTNE THRU 2000-EXIT      CL*74
                       ELSE                                            CL*74
 *                       INVALID KEY PRESSED                           CL*74
                         MOVE -1        TO SELL                        CL*74
                         MOVE 00001     TO CA-ERR-NUM-PRG              CL*74
                         MOVE 'P'       TO CA-ERR-TYPE                 CL*74
                         PERFORM 9000-ERR-RTNE                         CL*74
                            THRU 9000-ERR-EXIT                         CL*74
                         PERFORM 8000-SEND-ERR-MSG                     CL*74
                            THRU 8000-SEND-ERR-EXIT.                   CL*74
 *                                                                   RMP61C
        PERFORM 9200-CICS-RETURN THRU 9200-EXIT.                     RMP61C
        EJECT                                                        RMP61C
   0100-INIT-COMM.                                                   RMP61C
 *                                                                   RMP61C
        MOVE SPACES                     TO CA-COMMAREA.              RMP61C
        MOVE EIBTRNID                   TO CA-TRNID.                 RMP61C
        MOVE EIBTRMID                   TO CA-TRMID.                 RMP61C
        MOVE 1                          TO CA-SP                     RMP61C
                                           CA-PGM-PTR                RMP61C
                                           CA-MENU-PTR               RMP61C
                                           CA-TEMPQ-PTR.             RMP61C
        MOVE 0                          TO CA-MAP-PTR.               RMP61C
 *                                                                   RMP61C
   0100-EXIT.  EXIT.                                                 RMP61C
        SKIP3                                                        RMP61C
   0200-INIT-COMM.                                                   RMP61C
 *                                                                   RMP61C
        MOVE DFHCOMMAREA                 TO CA-COMMAREA.             RMP61C
        MOVE EIBCPOSN                    TO CA-CURSOR-POS.           RMP61C
        MOVE WS-MAP-NAME                 TO CA-MAPNAME.              RMP61C
        MOVE WS-MAPSET-NAME              TO CA-MAPSET.               RMP61C
        MOVE WS-TRNID                    TO CA-TRNID.                RMP61C
```

```
      *                                                                 RMP61C
       0200-EXIT.  EXIT.                                                RMP61C
           EJECT                                                        RMP61C
       0900-INITIALIZE-TAGALONG.                                           CL**6
           MOVE 'PRINT/REQUEST'           TO MODEII.                       CL*76
           MOVE 'P'                       TO CA-MODE-SW.                   CL**3
           MOVE SPACES TO                 CA-DOC-UPD-SW                    CL**3
                                          CA-PREV-ACCT                     CL**3
                                          CA-RMK050-WIP-HDR-KEY            CL**3
                                          CA-RMK050-CREATE-SITE-ID         CL**3
                                          CA-RMK050-CREATE-USER-ID         CL**3
                                          CA-RMK050-CREATE-NAME            CL**3
                                          CA-RMK050-PROJECT                CL**3
                                          CA-RMK050-DOCMT-STATUS           CL**3
                                          CA-RMK050-REASON-DOCMT-OPEN      CL**3
                                          CA-RMK050-PRNT-FLAG              CL**3
                                          CA-RMK050-PICK-FLAG              CL**3
                                          CA-RMK050-UPDATE-USER-ID         CL**3
                                          CA-RMK050-UPDATE-USER-NAME       CL**3
                                          CA-RMK050-RELATED-DOCMT-NBR      CL**3
                                          CA-RMK050-TRANSFER-FROM-SITE.    CL**3
           MOVE ZEROS TO                  CA-1ST-ITEM                      CL**3
                                          CA-LST-ITEM                      CL**3
                                          CA-LAST-ITEM                     CL**3
                                          CA-SCRN-TOP                      CL**3
                                          CA-SCRN-BOT                      CL**3
                                          CA-LINE-PTR                      CL**3
                                          CA-TOTL-LINES                    CL**3
                                          CA-TOTL-EXT                      CL**3
                                          CA-RMK050-DOCMT-LINES            CL**9
                                          CA-RMK050-CREATE-DATE            CL**3
                                          CA-RMK050-UPDATE-DATE            CL**3
                                          CA-RMK050-UPDATE-LINES.          CL**3
       0900-EXIT.  EXIT.                                                   CL**3
           EJECT                                                           CL**3
      *                                                                    CL**3
       1000-FIRST-TIME-SEND.                                            RMP61C
           MOVE +602                 TO CA-LENGTH.                         CL*78
      *                                                                    CL**3
           PERFORM 0900-INITIALIZE-TAGALONG THRU 0900-EXIT.                CL**3
      *                                                                    CL**3
           MOVE WS-QUEUE-NAME        TO   CA-QUEUE-NAME.                   CL*12
           MOVE WS-KEY-AREA          TO   RMK050-WIP-HDR-KEY.              CL*13
           MOVE RMK050-WIP-HDR-KEY   TO   CA-RMK050-WIP-HDR-KEY.           CL*13
           PERFORM 1100-READ-WIP-HDDR     THRU 1100-EXIT.                  CL**6
           IF I-O-NORMAL                                                   CL**3
              MOVE RECORD-AREA       TO   RMK050, CA-RMK050-REC            CL**3
              MOVE RMK050-DOCMT-NBR  TO   RMK060-DOCMT-NBR                 CL*13
              PERFORM 1200-STARTBR-WIP-DTL   THRU 1200-EXIT.               CL**3
      *                                                                    CL**3
           IF I-O-NORMAL                                                   CL**3
              MOVE 'Y'               TO   KEY-MATCH-SW                     CL**3
              PERFORM 1300-READ-NEXT-DTL  THRU 1300-EXIT VARYING           CL*46
                      WS-ITEM FROM 1 BY 1 UNTIL KEY-NOT-MATCHED            CL*46
              PERFORM 1350-ENDBR-WIP-DTL  THRU 1350-EXIT.                  CL**3
      *                                                                    CL**3
           PERFORM 1500-BUILD-MAP         THRU 1500-EXIT.                  CL**3
      *                                                                    CL**3
       1000-EXIT.  EXIT.                                                RMP61C
           EJECT                                                        RMP61C
      *                                                                    CL**4
       1100-READ-WIP-HDDR.                                                 CL**4
           MOVE RMK050-WIP-HDR-KEY TO I-O-FILEKEY.                         CL**4
```

```
           MOVE RMK050              TO RECORD-AREA.                     CL**4
           MOVE I-O-READ            TO I-O-COMMAND.                     CL**4
           MOVE I-O-EQUAL           TO I-O-OPERATOR.                    CL**4
           MOVE ZERO                TO I-O-GENERIC-KEYLEN.              CL**4
           MOVE SPACES              TO I-O-GENERIC.                     CL**4
           MOVE SPACES              TO I-O-UPDATE.                      CL**4
           MOVE 0                   TO I-O-VREC-TYPE.                   CL**4
           MOVE 'R'                 TO I-O-UPD-TYPE.                    CL**4
           MOVE I-O-ACF2-READ       TO I-O-ACF2-INTENT.                 CL**4
           MOVE RM-WIP-HEADER       TO I-O-FILENAME.                    CL**4
           MOVE WS-PROG-NAME        TO I-O-JRNL-WORKPGM.                CL**4
           PERFORM 9280-CALL-I-O-MODULE THRU 9280-I-O-EXIT.             CL**4
           IF  I-O-NORMAL                                               CL**4
               GO TO 1100-EXIT.                                         CL**4
      *                                                                 CL**4
           IF  I-O-NOTFND                                               CL**4
               MOVE 'A'     TO CA-ERR-TYPE                              CL**4
               MOVE 00313   TO CA-ERR-NUM-PRG                           CL**4
           ELSE                                                         CL**4
               MOVE 'A'           TO CA-ERR-TYPE                        CL**4
               MOVE I-O-RETCODE   TO CICS-RESP                          CL**4
               MOVE I-O-FILENAME  TO EIBRSRCE                           CL**4
               MOVE 000145        TO CA-ERR-NUM-PRG.                    CL**4
       1100-EXIT.  EXIT.                                                CL**4
           EJECT                                                        CL**4
      *                                                                 CL**4
      *                                                                 CL**4
       1200-STARTBR-WIP-DTL.                                            CL**4
           MOVE RMK060-WIP-DETAIL-KEY TO I-O-FILEKEY.                   CL*13
           MOVE RM-WIP-DETAIL         TO I-O-FILENAME.                  CL**4
           MOVE I-O-STARTBR           TO I-O-COMMAND.                   CL**4
           MOVE I-O-EQUAL             TO I-O-OPERATOR                   CL**4
           MOVE +7                    TO I-O-GENERIC-KEYLEN.            CL**4
           MOVE I-O-GENERIC-MODE      TO I-O-GENERIC.                   CL**4
           MOVE SPACES                TO I-O-UPDATE.                    CL**4
           MOVE 0                     TO I-O-VREC-TYPE.                 CL**4
           MOVE 'R'                   TO I-O-UPD-TYPE.                  CL**4
           MOVE I-O-ACF2-READ         TO I-O-ACF2-INTENT.               CL**4
           MOVE WS-PROG-NAME          TO I-O-JRNL-WORKPGM.              CL**4
           PERFORM 9280-CALL-I-O-MODULE THRU 9280-I-O-EXIT.             CL**4
           IF  I-O-NORMAL                                               CL**4
               GO TO 1200-EXIT.                                         CL**4
      *                                                                 CL**4
           IF  I-O-NOTFND                                               CL**4
               MOVE 'A'     TO CA-ERR-TYPE                              CL**4
               MOVE 00314   TO CA-ERR-NUM-PRG                           CL**4
           ELSE                                                         CL**4
               MOVE 'A'           TO CA-ERR-TYPE                        CL**4
               MOVE I-O-RETCODE   TO CICS-RESP                          CL**4
               MOVE I-O-FILENAME  TO EIBRSRCE                           CL**4
               MOVE 000145        TO CA-ERR-NUM-PRG.                    CL**4
       1200-EXIT.                                                       CL**4
      *                                                                 CL**4
       1300-READ-NEXT-DTL.                                              CL**4
           MOVE I-O-READNEXT          TO I-O-COMMAND.                   CL**4
           MOVE I-O-ACF2-READ         TO I-O-ACF2-INTENT.               CL**4
           MOVE RM-WIP-DETAIL         TO I-O-FILENAME.                  CL**4
           MOVE RMK060-WIP-DETAIL-KEY TO I-O-FILEKEY.                   CL**4
      *                                                                 CL**4
           PERFORM 9280-CALL-I-O-MODULE THRU 9280-I-O-EXIT.             CL**4
           IF  I-O-NORMAL                                               CL**4
               MOVE RECORD-AREA TO RMK060                               CL**4
               IF  RMK060-DOCMT-NBR = WS-DOCMT-NO                       CL**4
```

```
               MOVE WS-ITEM          TO ITEM-PTR                    CL*98
               ADD 1                 TO CA-1ST-ITEM                 CL*35
               MOVE RMK060           TO WS-QUEUE-AREA               CL**4
               MOVE '_'              TO WS-Q-LINE-COMMAND           CL**9
               PERFORM 1400-WRITE-TEMP-QUE THRU 1400-EXIT           CL**4
               GO TO 1300-EXIT                                      CL**4
           ELSE                                                     CL**4
               MOVE 'N' TO KEY-MATCH-SW                             CL**4
               GO TO 1300-EXIT.                                     CL**4
      *                                                             CL**4
           MOVE 'N' TO KEY-MATCH-SW.                                CL**4
           IF  I-O-ENDFILE                                          CL**4
               MOVE 'P'    TO CA-ERR-TYPE                           CL**4
               MOVE 'Y'    TO END-OF-FILE-SW                        CL**4
           ELSE                                                     CL**4
               MOVE 'A'          TO CA-ERR-TYPE                     CL**4
               MOVE I-O-RETCODE  TO CICS-RESP                       CL**4
               MOVE I-O-FILENAME TO EIBRSRCE                        CL**4
               MOVE 00145        TO CA-ERR-NUM-PRG.                 CL**4
       1300-EXIT.  EXIT.                                            CL**4
      *                                                             CL**4
       1350-ENDBR-WIP-DTL.                                          CL**4
           MOVE RM-WIP-DETAIL TO I-O-FILENAME.                      CL**4
           MOVE I-O-ENDBR     TO I-O-COMMAND.                       CL**4
           PERFORM 9280-CALL-I-O-MODULE THRU 9280-I-O-EXIT.         CL**4
           IF  NOT I-O-NORMAL                                       CL**4
               MOVE 'A'          TO CA-ERR-TYPE                     CL**4
               MOVE I-O-RETCODE  TO CICS-RESP                       CL**4
               MOVE I-O-FILENAME TO EIBRSRCE                        CL**4
               MOVE 000145       TO CA-ERR-NUM-PRG.                 CL**4
       1350-EXIT.  EXIT.                                            CL**4
      *                                                             CL**4
      *                                                             CL**4
       1400-WRITE-TEMP-QUE.                                         CL**4
           EXEC CICS                                                CL**4
               WRITEQ TS QUEUE (WS-QUEUE-NAME) FROM (WS-QUEUE-AREA) CL**4
                     LENGTH (WS-QUE-LENGTH)                         CL**4
                       ITEM (ITEM-PTR)                              CL*98
                       MAIN                                         CL**4
                       RESP (CICS-RESP)                             CL**4
           END-EXEC.                                                CL**4
           IF  CICS-RESP = DFHRESP (NORMAL)                         CL**4
               NEXT SENTENCE                                        CL**4
           ELSE                                                     CL**4
               MOVE 00315 TO CA-ERR-NUM-PRG                         CL**4
               MOVE 'A'   TO CA-ERR-TYPE.                           CL**4
       1400-EXIT.  EXIT.                                            CL**4
      *                                                             CL**4
       1500-BUILD-MAP.                                              CL**4
           MOVE CA-RMK050-DOCMT-NBR          TO REQNOI.             CL**4
           MOVE CA-RMK050-CREATE-SITE-ID     TO SITEI.              CL**4
           MOVE CA-RMK050-PROJECT            TO PROJECTI.           CL**5
           MOVE CA-RMK050-RELATED-DOCMT-NBR TO WRKORDI.             CL**5
           MOVE CA-RMK050-CREATE-USER-ID     TO REQBYI.             CL**4
           MOVE CA-RMK050-CREATE-NAME        TO NAMEI.              CL**4
           MOVE CA-RMK050-UPDATE-USER-ID     TO LSTUPBYI.           CL**4
           MOVE CA-RMK050-DOCMT-DEPT         TO DEPTI.              CL**4
           MOVE CA-RMK050-DOCMT-STATUS       TO DOCSTI.             CL**4
           MOVE CA-RMK050-REASON-DOCMT-OPEN TO RESOPENI.            CL**4
           MOVE CA-RMK050-PRNT-FLAG          TO DOCPRTI.            CL**4
           MOVE CA-RMK050-PICK-FLAG          TO PICPRTI.            CL**4
           MOVE 'PRINT/REQUEST'              TO MODEII.             CL**8
      *                                                             CL*15
```

```
      IF CA-RMK050-UPDATE-DATE > 0                                    CL*15
         MOVE CA-RMK050-UPDATE-DATE    TO RMDATE-CONVERT-DATE         CL*15
         MOVE +0                       TO RMDATE-DEFER                CL*15
         MOVE 5                        TO RMDATE-FORMAT               CL*15
         PERFORM 8040-CALL-DATE-RTNE THRU 8040-CALL-DATE-EXIT         CL*16
         MOVE RMDATE-MMDDYY            TO WK-RMI-DATE                 CL*16
         MOVE WK-RMI-MM                TO MONO                        CL*16
         MOVE WK-RMI-DD                TO DAO                         CL*16
         MOVE WK-RMI-YY                TO YRO                         CL*16
      ELSE                                                            CL*15
         MOVE ZEROS TO MONO                                           CL*15
                       DAO                                            CL*15
                       YRO.                                           CL*15
 *                                                                    CL*15
  1500-EXIT.  EXIT.                                                   CL**4
 *                                                                    CL**6
  2000-ENTER-RTNE.                                                   RMP61C
 *                                                                   RMP61C
      PERFORM 9050-RECEIVE-MAP  THRU 9050-RECEIVE-EXIT.              RMP61C
 *                                                                   RMP61C
      MOVE UNPROT-MDT                TO   SELA.                       CL*19
 *                                                                    CL*19
      IF SELI = SPACES OR LOW-VALUES OR  '_'                          CL*18
         MOVE UNPROT-BRT-MDT         TO   SELA                        CL*18
         MOVE 'P'                    TO   CA-ERR-TYPE                 CL*18
         MOVE -1                     TO   SELL                        CL*18
         MOVE 00002                  TO   CA-INST-NUM                 CL*20
         MOVE 00360                  TO   CA-ERR-NUM-PRG              CL*18
         MOVE 'N'                    TO   WS-VALID-DATA-SW            CL*18
         GO TO 2000-SEND-MAP.                                         CL*18
 *                                                                    CL*18
      IF SELI = '1' OR '2'                                            CL*81
         NEXT SENTENCE                                                CL*18
      ELSE                                                            CL*18
         MOVE UNPROT-BRT-MDT         TO   SELA                        CL*18
         MOVE 'P'                    TO   CA-ERR-TYPE                 CL*18
         MOVE 00002                  TO   CA-INST-NUM                 CL*20
         MOVE -1                     TO   SELL                        CL*18
         MOVE 00376                  TO   CA-ERR-NUM-PRG              CL*81
         MOVE 'N'                    TO   WS-VALID-DATA-SW            CL*21
         GO TO 2000-SEND-MAP.                                         CL*21
 *                                                                    CL*21
      IF (VALID-DATA)                                                 CL*81
         PERFORM 2010-READ-RMK040  THRU 2010-EXIT                     CL*56
         MOVE RMK040-SITE-PRINTER-DCT   TO  HOLD-DESTINATION-ID       CL*60
         MOVE RMK040-SITE-NAME       TO   PRTDESTI.                   CL*81
 *                                                                    CL*18
      IF VALID-DATA                                                   CL*18
         MOVE 'P'                    TO   CA-ERR-TYPE                 CL*18
         MOVE -1                     TO   SELL                        CL*19
         MOVE 00093                  TO   CA-INST-NUM.                CL*18
 *                                                                    CL*30
  2000-SEND-MAP.                                                      CL*18
 *                                                                    CL*18
      IF CA-ATTN-KEY = DFHPF12                                        CL*33
         GO TO 2000-EXIT.                                             CL*33
 *                                                                    CL*33
      PERFORM 9000-ERR-RTNE      THRU 9000-ERR-EXIT.                  CL*17
      PERFORM 8000-SEND-ERR-MSG THRU 8000-SEND-ERR-EXIT.              CL*17
 *                                                                   RMP61C
  2000-EXIT.  EXIT.                                                  RMP61C
      EJECT                                                          RMP61C
 *                                                                    CL*21
```

```
 2010-READ-RMK040.                                                        CL*21
     MOVE SPACES                      TO RMK040-TABLE-KEY.                CL*22
     MOVE 'SITE'                      TO RMK040-TABLE-NAME.               CL*22
     MOVE CA-RMK050-CREATE-SITE-ID    TO RMK040-ELEMT-KEY.                CL*22
     MOVE RMK040-TABLE-KEY            TO I-O-FILEKEY.                     CL*22
     MOVE RMK040                      TO RECORD-AREA.                     CL*22
     MOVE I-O-READ                    TO I-O-COMMAND.                     CL*22
     MOVE I-O-EQUAL                   TO I-O-OPERATOR                     CL*22
     MOVE ZERO                        TO I-O-GENERIC-KEYLEN               CL*22
                                         I-O-VREC-TYPE.                   CL*22
     MOVE SPACES                      TO I-O-GENERIC                      CL*22
                                         I-O-UPDATE.                      CL*22
     MOVE 'R'                         TO I-O-UPD-TYPE.                    CL*22
     MOVE I-O-ACF2-READ               TO I-O-ACF2-INTENT.                 CL*22
     MOVE RM-TABLE                    TO I-O-FILENAME.                    CL*22
     MOVE WS-PROG-NAME                TO I-O-JRNL-WORKPGM.                CL*22
     PERFORM 9280-CALL-I-O-MODULE THRU 9280-I-O-EXIT.                     CL*22
     IF  I-O-NORMAL                                                       CL*22
         MOVE RECORD-AREA             TO RMK040                           CL*24
         GO TO 2010-EXIT.                                                 CL*23
*                                                                         CL*22
     IF  I-O-NOTFND                                                       CL*22
         MOVE UNPROT-BRT-MDT TO SITEA                                     CL*22
         MOVE 'P'    TO CA-ERR-TYPE                                       CL*22
         MOVE 00002  TO   CA-INST-NUM                                     CL*26
         MOVE -1     TO SITEL                                             CL*26
         MOVE 00175  TO CA-ERR-NUM-PRG                                    CL*22
         MOVE 'N'    TO WS-VALID-DATA-SW                                  CL*26
     ELSE                                                                 CL*22
         MOVE 'P'            TO CA-ERR-TYPE                               CL*22
         MOVE 'N' TO WS-VALID-DATA-SW                                     CL*22
         MOVE I-O-RETCODE   TO CICS-RESP                                  CL*22
         MOVE I-O-FILENAME  TO EIBRSRCE                                   CL*22
         MOVE 000145        TO CA-ERR-NUM-PRG.                            CL*22
 2010-EXIT. EXIT.                                                         CL*22
*                                                                         CL*56
 3000-PF12-RTNE.                                                          CL*30
     PERFORM 2000-ENTER-RTNE   THRU 2000-EXIT.                            CL*31
     IF VALID-DATA                                                        CL*31
        NEXT SENTENCE                                                     CL*31
     ELSE                                                                 CL*31
        GO TO 3000-SEND-MAP.                                              CL*31
*                                                                         CL*84
*    IF (CA-RMK050-PICK-FLAG = 'Y') AND (SELI = '2')                      CL*92
*       MOVE 'P'                 TO    CA-ERR-TYPE                        CL*92
*       MOVE 00002               TO    CA-INST-NUM                        CL*92
*       MOVE -1                  TO    SELL                               CL*92
*       MOVE 00389               TO    CA-ERR-NUM-PRG                     CL*92
*       MOVE 'N'                 TO    WS-VALID-DATA-SW                   CL*92
*       GO TO 3000-SEND-MAP.                                              CL*92
*                                                                         CL*31
     MOVE HOLD-DESTINATION-ID  TO    DESTINATION-ID.                      CL*81
     MOVE CA-QUEUE-NAME        TO    WS-QUEUE-NAME.                       CL*47
*                                                                         CL*38
     MOVE 0 TO ITEM-PTR.                                                  CL*98
     EXEC CICS                                                            CL*38
          ENQ RESOURCE(DESTINATION-ID)                                    CL*38
              LENGTH(4)                                                   CL*38
     END-EXEC.                                                            CL*38
     IF SELI = '1'                                                        CL*81
        PERFORM 3100-PRINT-MATERIAL-LIST THRU 3100-EXIT                   CL*38
        CA-1ST-ITEM TIMES                                                 CL*48
        PERFORM 3150-PRINT-MATERIAL-LIST-TLR THRU 3150-EXIT.              CL*48
```

```
       EXEC CICS                                                    CL*38
          DEQ RESOURCE(DESTINATION-ID)                              CL*38
              LENGTH(4)                                             CL*38
       END-EXEC.                                                    CL*38
 *                                                                  CL*38
       MOVE HOLD-DESTINATION-ID        TO  DESTINATION-ID.          CL*60
       MOVE 0 TO ITEM-PTR, PAGE-NUMBER.                             CL*98
       MOVE 55 TO LINE-CNTR.                                        CL*48
       IF SELI = '2'                                                CL*81
          EXEC CICS                                                 CL*48
               ENQ RESOURCE(DESTINATION-ID)                         CL*48
                   LENGTH(4)                                        CL*48
          END-EXEC                                                  CL*48
          MOVE CA-RMK050-PICK-FLAG     TO   WS-PICK-PRNT-FLAG       CL*96
          PERFORM 3500-PRINT-PICK-LIST THRU 3500-EXIT               CL*38
          CA-1ST-ITEM TIMES                                         CL*48
          PERFORM 3550-PRINT-PICK-LIST-TLR THRU 3550-EXIT           CL*48
          EXEC CICS                                                 CL*48
               DEQ RESOURCE(DESTINATION-ID)                         CL*48
                   LENGTH(4)                                        CL*48
          END-EXEC.                                                 CL*48
 *                                                                  CL*31
       PERFORM 7150-UPDATE-WIP-HDDR-REC THRU 7150-EXIT.             CL*79
 *                                                                  CL*52
       IF SELI = '1'                                                CL*31
          MOVE 'P'               TO   CA-ERR-TYPE                   CL*34
          MOVE -1                TO   SELL                          CL*34
          MOVE 00363             TO   CA-ERR-NUM-PRG.               CL*34
 *                                                                  CL*31
       IF SELI = '2'                                                CL*31
          MOVE 'P'               TO   CA-ERR-TYPE                   CL*31
          MOVE -1                TO   SELL                          CL*31
          MOVE 00364             TO   CA-ERR-NUM-PRG.               CL*34
 *                                                                  CL*31
  3000-SEND-MAP.                                                    CL*31
 *                                                                  CL*31
       PERFORM 9000-ERR-RTNE     THRU 9000-ERR-EXIT.                CL*31
       PERFORM 8000-SEND-ERR-MSG THRU 8000-SEND-ERR-EXIT.           CL*31
 *                                                                  CL*31
  3000-PF12-EXIT.  EXIT.                                            CL*32
 *                                                                  CL*30
  3100-PRINT-MATERIAL-LIST.                                         CL*38
 *                                                                  CL*38
 *     READQ; CHECK LINE COUNT;  PRINT LINE (WRITE TD QUEUE)        CL*38
 *                                                                  CL*38
       ADD 1 TO ITEM-PTR.                                           CL*98
       EXEC CICS                                                    CL*38
            READQ TS QUEUE (WS-QUEUE-NAME)                          CL*38
                     INTO (WS-QUEUE-AREA)                           CL*38
                     LENGTH (WS-QUEUE-LENGTH)                       CL*38
                     ITEM (ITEM-PTR)                                CL*98
                     RESP (CICS-RESP)                               CL*38
       END-EXEC.                                                    CL*38
 *                                                                  CL*38
       MOVE WS-QUEUE-AREA TO RMK060.                                CL*38
 *                                                                  CL*38
       IF LINE-CNTR > 53                                            CL*38
          PERFORM 3130-MATERIAL-LIST-HEADINGS THRU 3130-EXIT.       CL*38
 *                                                                  CL*38
       MOVE RMK060-DOCMT-LINENO       TO  MR-DL-1-ITEM-NO.          CL*39
       MOVE RMK060-METRA-CLASS-CODE   TO  MR-DL-1-METRA-CLASS-CD.   CL*39
       MOVE RMK060-METRA-PART-ID      TO  MR-DL-1-METRA-PART-ID.    CL*39
       MOVE RMK060-METRA-CHECK-DIGIT  TO  MR-DL-1-METRA-CHECK-DGT.  CL*39
```

```
           MOVE RMK060-METRA-PART-STATUS TO  MR-DL-1-ST.                CL*39
           MOVE RMK060-PART-DESCRIPTION  TO  HOLD-DESCRIPTION.          CL*39
           MOVE HOLD-DESCRIPTION-1       TO  MR-DL-1-DESCRIPTION.       CL*39
           MOVE RMK060-ACCT-ORG          TO  MR-DL-1-ACCT-ORG.          CL*39
           MOVE RMK060-ACCT-DEPT         TO  MR-DL-1-ACCT-DEPT.         CL*39
           MOVE RMK060-ACCT-FUNC         TO  MR-DL-1-ACCT-FUNC.         CL*39
           MOVE RMK060-ACCT-SRCE         TO  MR-DL-1-ACCT-SRCE.         CL*39
           MOVE RMK060-ACCT-PROJ         TO  MR-DL-1-ACCT-PROJ.         CL*39
           MOVE RMK060-UNIT-OF-MEASURE   TO  MR-DL-1-UM.                CL*87
      *                                                                 CL*67
           MOVE RMK060-ACCT-CODE         TO  WS-ACCT-CODE.              CL*67
           MOVE '029'                    TO  WS-3.                      CL*67
           MOVE '0201'                   TO  WS-4.                      CL*67
           MOVE WS-ORG-DEPT              TO  WS-8.                      CL*67
           PERFORM 3160-ACCOUNT-DESC     THRU 3160-EXIT.                CL*58
      *                                                                 CL*67
           MOVE RMK060-QTY-REQUESTED     TO  MR-DL-1-QTY-RECOVERED.     CL*82
           MOVE RMK060-REFERENCE-PRICE   TO  MR-DL-1-AVG-PRICE.         CL*56
           MULTIPLY RMK060-QTY-REQUESTED BY RMK060-REFERENCE-PRICE      CL*56
                    GIVING WS-EXTENDED-VALUE.                           CL*56
           MOVE WS-EXTENDED-VALUE        TO  MR-DL-1-EXTENDED-VALUE.    CL*56
           IF RMK060-DOCMT-LINE-STATUS = 'C'                            CL*89
              NEXT SENTENCE                                             CL*89
           ELSE                                                         CL*89
              ADD WS-EXTENDED-VALUE      TO  WS-TOTAL-EXTENDED-VALUE.   CL*89
           MOVE '0'                      TO  CARRIAGE-CNTL.             CL*39
           MOVE MR-DETAIL-LINE-1         TO  PRINT-DATA-LINE.           CL*39
           PERFORM 3999-WRITE-TD-QUEUE   THRU 3999-EXIT.                CL*39
           MOVE HOLD-DESCRIPTION-2       TO  MR-DL-2-DESCRIPTION.       CL*68
      *                                                                 CL*68
           MOVE '029'                    TO  WS-3.                      CL*68
           MOVE '0203'                   TO  WS-4.                      CL*68
           MOVE WS-FUNC-SRCE             TO  WS-8.                      CL*68
           PERFORM 3161-ACCOUNT-DESC     THRU 3161-EXIT.                CL*68
      *                                                                 CL*68
           MOVE RMK060-MTRL-RECVY-SCRAPPED-QTY TO MR-DL-2-QTY-SCRAPPED. CL*82
           MOVE ' '                      TO  CARRIAGE-CNTL.             CL*39
           MOVE MR-DETAIL-LINE-2         TO  PRINT-DATA-LINE.           CL*39
           PERFORM 3999-WRITE-TD-QUEUE   THRU 3999-EXIT.                CL*39
      *                                                                 CL*39
           MOVE HOLD-DESCRIPTION-3         TO  MR-DL-3-DESCRIPTION.     CL*56
           IF WS-PROJECT NOT = LOW-VALUES AND SPACES AND '000000'       CL*68
              MOVE WS-PROJECT              TO  PROJ-NUM-KEY             CL*68
              PERFORM 3170-ACCT-BILLING-DESC  THRU 3170-EXIT.           CL*68
           MOVE ' '                        TO  CARRIAGE-CNTL.           CL*56
           MOVE MR-DETAIL-LINE-3           TO  PRINT-DATA-LINE.         CL*56
           PERFORM 3999-WRITE-TD-QUEUE     THRU 3999-EXIT.              CL*56
      *                                                                 CL*56
           MOVE RMK060-FULL-MFG-PART-NO     TO MR-DL-4-MFG-PART-NO.     CL*80
           MOVE RMK060-DOCMT-LINE-COMMENTS  TO MR-DL-4-COMMENTS.        CL*56
           MOVE RMK060-MTRL-REQST-EQUIP-NBR TO  MR-DL-4-EQUIP-NUMBER.   CL*56
           MOVE ' '                         TO  CARRIAGE-CNTL.          CL*56
           MOVE MR-DETAIL-LINE-4            TO  PRINT-DATA-LINE.        CL*56
           PERFORM 3999-WRITE-TD-QUEUE      THRU 3999-EXIT.             CL*56
      *                                                                 CL*39
           ADD 5                         TO  LINE-CNTR.                 CL*39
      *                                                                 CL*39
       3100-EXIT.  EXIT.                                                CL*38
      *                                                                 CL*38
       3130-MATERIAL-LIST-HEADINGS.                                     CL*38
      *                                                                 CL*38
           ADD 1 TO PAGE-NUMBER.                                        CL*38
           MOVE PAGE-NUMBER              TO  MR-HL-1-PAGE-NUM.          CL*38
```

```
       MOVE CA-RMK050-DOCMT-NBR       TO  MR-HL-1-DOC-NUM.          CL*38
       MOVE MR-HEADER-LINE-1          TO  PRINT-DATA-LINE.          CL*38
       MOVE '1'                       TO  CARRIAGE-CNTL.            CL*38
       PERFORM 3999-WRITE-TD-QUEUE    THRU 3999-EXIT.               CL*38
 *                                                                  CL*38
       MOVE MONI                      TO  MR-HL-2-MM.               CL*38
       MOVE DAI                       TO  MR-HL-2-DD.               CL*38
       MOVE YRI                       TO  MR-HL-2-YY.               CL*38
       PERFORM 8100-FORMAT-TIME       THRU   8100-FMT-TIM-EXIT.     CL*80
       MOVE MDATEO                    TO  MR-HL-2-SYSDATE.          CL*80
       MOVE MTIMEO                    TO  MR-HL-2-SYSTIME.          CL*80
       MOVE MR-HEADER-LINE-2          TO  PRINT-DATA-LINE.          CL*38
       MOVE ' '                       TO  CARRIAGE-CNTL.            CL*38
       PERFORM 3999-WRITE-TD-QUEUE    THRU 3999-EXIT.               CL*38
 *                                                                  CL*38
       MOVE CA-RMK050-DOCMT-STATUS    TO  MR-HL-3-DOC-STATUS.       CL*38
       MOVE CA-RMK050-REASON-DOCMT-OPEN  TO  MR-HL-3-REASON-OPEN.   CL*38
       MOVE MR-HEADER-LINE-3          TO  PRINT-DATA-LINE.          CL*38
       MOVE ' '                       TO  CARRIAGE-CNTL.            CL*38
       PERFORM 3999-WRITE-TD-QUEUE    THRU 3999-EXIT.               CL*38
 *                                                                  CL*38
       MOVE CA-RMK050-CREATE-USER-ID TO MR-HL-4-USER-ID.            CL*38
       MOVE CA-RMK050-CREATE-NAME     TO MR-HL-4-USER-NAME.         CL*38
       MOVE CA-RMK050-DOCMT-DEPT      TO MR-HL-4-DEPT.              CL*38
       IF (CA-RMK050-PRNT-FLAG = 'Y') OR (SELI = '1')               CL*87
          MOVE 'Y'                    TO MR-HL-4-DOC-PRINTED        CL*87
       ELSE                                                         CL*87
          MOVE 'N'                    TO MR-HL-4-DOC-PRINTED.       CL*87
       IF (CA-RMK050-PICK-FLAG = 'Y') OR (SELI = '2')               CL*88
          MOVE 'Y'                    TO MR-HL-4-PICKLIST-PRNTED    CL*87
       ELSE                                                         CL*87
          MOVE 'N'                    TO MR-HL-4-PICKLIST-PRNTED.   CL*87
       MOVE MR-HEADER-LINE-4          TO PRINT-DATA-LINE.           CL*38
       MOVE ' '                       TO CARRIAGE-CNTL.             CL*38
       PERFORM 3999-WRITE-TD-QUEUE    THRU 3999-EXIT.               CL*38
 *                                                                  CL*38
       MOVE CA-RMK050-CREATE-SITE-ID TO MR-HL-5-SITE-ID.            CL*38
       MOVE CA-RMK050-PROJECT         TO MR-HL-5-PROJECT.           CL*38
       MOVE CA-RMK050-RELATED-DOCMT-NBR TO MR-HL-5-WORK-ORDER-NO.   CL*38
       MOVE MR-HEADER-LINE-5          TO PRINT-DATA-LINE.           CL*38
       MOVE ' '                       TO CARRIAGE-CNTL.             CL*38
       PERFORM 3999-WRITE-TD-QUEUE    THRU 3999-EXIT.               CL*38
 *                                                                  CL*38
       MOVE MR-HEADER-LINE-6          TO PRINT-DATA-LINE.           CL*38
       MOVE '0'                       TO CARRIAGE-CNTL.             CL*38
       PERFORM 3999-WRITE-TD-QUEUE    THRU 3999-EXIT.               CL*38
 *                                                                  CL*38
       MOVE MR-HEADER-LINE-7          TO PRINT-DATA-LINE.           CL*38
       MOVE ' '                       TO CARRIAGE-CNTL.             CL*38
       PERFORM 3999-WRITE-TD-QUEUE    THRU 3999-EXIT.               CL*38
 *                                                                  CL*38
       MOVE MR-HEADER-LINE-8          TO PRINT-DATA-LINE.           CL*38
       MOVE ' '                       TO CARRIAGE-CNTL.             CL*38
       PERFORM 3999-WRITE-TD-QUEUE    THRU 3999-EXIT.               CL*38
 *                                                                  CL*38
       MOVE 9                         TO LINE-CNTR.                 CL*38
 *                                                                  CL*38
   3130-EXIT.    EXIT.                                              CL*38
 *                                                                  CL*38
   3150-PRINT-MATERIAL-LIST-TLR.                                    CL*40
 *   PRINT TRAILER LINES.                                           CL*38
 *                                                                  CL*39
       MOVE WS-TOTAL-EXTENDED-VALUE  TO MR-TL-1-TOTAL-REQ-VALUE.    CL*71
```

```
           MOVE MR-TRAILER-LINE-1          TO PRINT-DATA-LINE.          CL*40
           MOVE '0'                        TO CARRIAGE-CNTL.            CL*39
           PERFORM 3999-WRITE-TD-QUEUE     THRU 3999-EXIT.              CL*39
      *                                                                 CL*39
           MOVE MR-TRAILER-LINE-2          TO PRINT-DATA-LINE.          CL*40
           MOVE ' '                        TO CARRIAGE-CNTL.            CL*39
           PERFORM 3999-WRITE-TD-QUEUE     THRU 3999-EXIT.              CL*80
      *                                                                 CL*80
           MOVE '1'                        TO CARRIAGE-CNTL.            CL*80
           MOVE SPACES                     TO PRINT-DATA-LINE.          CL*80
           PERFORM 3999-WRITE-TD-QUEUE     THRU 3999-EXIT.              CL*39
      *                                                                 CL*39
       3150-EXIT.                                                       CL*38
      *                                                                 CL*38
       3160-ACCOUNT-DESC.                                               CL*56
           MOVE RM-GLMASTR             TO I-O-FILENAME.                 CL*68
           MOVE GL-FILE-KEY            TO I-O-FILEKEY.                  CL*68
           MOVE I-O-READ               TO I-O-COMMAND.                  CL*68
           MOVE I-O-EQUAL              TO I-O-OPERATOR.                 CL*68
           MOVE SPACES                 TO I-O-GENERIC.                  CL*68
           MOVE +0                     TO I-O-GENERIC-KEYLEN.           CL*68
           MOVE SPACES                 TO I-O-UPDATE.                   CL*68
           MOVE 'R'                    TO I-O-UPD-TYPE.                 CL*68
           MOVE 0                      TO I-O-VREC-TYPE.                CL*68
           MOVE I-O-ACF2-READ          TO I-O-ACF2-INTENT.              CL*68
           PERFORM 9280-CALL-I-O-MODULE THRU 9280-I-O-EXIT.             CL*68
           IF I-O-NORMAL                                                CL*68
              MOVE RECORD-AREA         TO GLMASTR                       CL*68
              MOVE GL-ACCT-DESC        TO MR-DL-1-ACCOUNT-DESC          CL*68
           ELSE                                                         CL*68
              MOVE SPACES              TO MR-DL-1-ACCOUNT-DESC.         CL*68
       3160-EXIT.                                                       CL*56
           EXIT.                                                        CL*56
      *                                                                 CL*68
       3161-ACCOUNT-DESC.                                               CL*68
           MOVE RM-GLMASTR             TO I-O-FILENAME.                 CL*68
           MOVE GL-FILE-KEY            TO I-O-FILEKEY.                  CL*68
           MOVE I-O-READ               TO I-O-COMMAND.                  CL*68
           MOVE I-O-EQUAL              TO I-O-OPERATOR.                 CL*68
           MOVE SPACES                 TO I-O-GENERIC.                  CL*68
           MOVE +0                     TO I-O-GENERIC-KEYLEN.           CL*68
           MOVE SPACES                 TO I-O-UPDATE.                   CL*68
           MOVE 'R'                    TO I-O-UPD-TYPE.                 CL*68
           MOVE 0                      TO I-O-VREC-TYPE.                CL*68
           MOVE I-O-ACF2-READ          TO I-O-ACF2-INTENT.              CL*68
           PERFORM 9280-CALL-I-O-MODULE THRU 9280-I-O-EXIT.             CL*68
           IF I-O-NORMAL                                                CL*68
              MOVE RECORD-AREA         TO GLMASTR                       CL*68
              MOVE GL-ACCT-DESC        TO MR-DL-2-ACCOUNT-DESC          CL*68
           ELSE                                                         CL*68
              MOVE SPACES              TO MR-DL-2-ACCOUNT-DESC.         CL*68
       3161-EXIT.                                                       CL*68
           EXIT.                                                        CL*68
      *                                                                 CL*56
       3170-ACCT-BILLING-DESC.                                          CL*56
           MOVE RM-BILMSTR             TO I-O-FILENAME.                 CL*68
           MOVE BILMSTR-VSAM-KEY       TO I-O-FILEKEY.                  CL*68
           MOVE I-O-READ               TO I-O-COMMAND.                  CL*68
           MOVE I-O-EQUAL              TO I-O-OPERATOR.                 CL*68
           MOVE SPACES                 TO I-O-GENERIC.                  CL*68
           MOVE +0                     TO I-O-GENERIC-KEYLEN.           CL*68
           MOVE SPACES                 TO I-O-UPDATE.                   CL*68
```

```
           MOVE 'R'                  TO I-O-UPD-TYPE.                  CL*68
           MOVE 0                    TO I-O-VREC-TYPE.                 CL*68
           MOVE I-O-ACF2-READ        TO I-O-ACF2-INTENT.               CL*68
           PERFORM 9280-CALL-I-O-MODULE THRU 9280-I-O-EXIT.            CL*68
           IF I-O-NORMAL                                               CL*68
              MOVE RECORD-AREA       TO BILMSTR                        CL*68
              MOVE INVLINE1(1)       TO MR-DL-3-ACCOUNT-DESC           CL*68
           ELSE                                                        CL*68
              MOVE SPACES            TO MR-DL-3-ACCOUNT-DESC.          CL*68
       3170-EXIT.                                                      CL*56
           EXIT.                                                       CL*56
      *                                                                CL*56
       3500-PRINT-PICK-LIST.                                           CL*41
      *                                                                CL*48
      *    READQ; CHECK LINE COUNT;  PRINT LINE (WRITE TD QUEUE)       CL*48
      *                                                                CL*48
           ADD 1 TO ITEM-PTR.                                          CL*98
           EXEC CICS                                                   CL*48
                READQ TS QUEUE (WS-QUEUE-NAME)                         CL*48
                         INTO (WS-QUEUE-AREA)                          CL*48
                         LENGTH (WS-QUEUE-LENGTH)                      CL*48
                         ITEM (ITEM-PTR)                               CL*98
                         RESP (CICS-RESP)                              CL*48
           END-EXEC.                                                   CL*48
      *                                                                CL*48
           IF LINE-CNTR > 53                                           CL*48
              PERFORM 3530-PICK-LIST-HEADINGS THRU 3530-EXIT.          CL*48
      *                                                                CL*98
           MOVE WS-QUEUE-AREA TO RMK060.                               CL*98
           IF (RMK060-DOCMT-LINE-STATUS = 'F') OR                      CL*98
              (RMK060-DOCMT-LINE-STATUS = 'C')                         CL*98
              GO TO 3500-EXIT.                                         CL*98
      *                                                                CL*48
           MOVE RMK060-DOCMT-LINENO       TO  PL-DL-1-ITEM-NO.         CL*50
      *                                                                CL*61
           MOVE CA-RMK050-PROJECT         TO  RMK020-PROJECT-NO.       CL*66
           MOVE CA-RMK050-CREATE-SITE-ID  TO  RMK020-SITE-ID.          CL*79
           MOVE RMK060-METRA-PART-STATUS  TO  RMK020-STATUS.           CL*61
           MOVE RMK060-METRA-PART-NUMBER  TO  RMK020-METRA-PART-NO.    CL*61
      *                                                                CL*61
           PERFORM 3560-FIND-BIN-LOCATION THRU 3560-EXIT.              CL*56
           MOVE RMK020-BIN-LOCATION       TO  PL-DL-1-BIN-LOCATION.    CL*61
           MOVE RMK060-METRA-CLASS-CODE   TO  PL-DL-1-METRA-CLASS-CD.  CL*50
           MOVE RMK060-METRA-PART-ID      TO  PL-DL-1-METRA-PART-ID.   CL*50
           MOVE RMK060-METRA-CHECK-DIGIT  TO  PL-DL-1-METRA-CHECK-DGT. CL*50
           MOVE RMK060-METRA-PART-STATUS  TO  PL-DL-1-ST.              CL*50
           MOVE RMK060-PART-DESCRIPTION   TO  HOLD-DESCRIPTION.        CL*50
           MOVE HOLD-DESCRIPTION-1        TO  PL-DL-1-DESCRIPTION.     CL*50
           MOVE RMK060-UNIT-OF-MEASURE    TO  PL-DL-1-UM.              CL*51
           MOVE RMK060-QTY-REQUESTED      TO  PL-DL-1-QTY-RECOVERED.   CL*82
      *                                                                CL*84
           IF (I-O-NORMAL) AND (WS-PICK-PRNT-FLAG = 'N')               CL*98
              MOVE RMK020-QTY-ON-HAND  TO  PL-DL-1-QTY-ON-HAND         CL*98
              ADD  RMK060-QTY-REQUESTED, RMK020-QTY-ON-HAND            CL*98
                   GIVING NEW-QTY-ON-HAND                              CL*98
              MOVE NEW-QTY-ON-HAND TO PL-DL-1-NEW-QTY-ON-HAND          CL*98
                                      RMK020-QTY-ON-HAND.              CL*98
      *                                                                CL*98
           IF (I-O-NORMAL) AND (WS-PICK-PRNT-FLAG = 'Y')               CL*98
              SUBTRACT RMK060-QTY-REQUESTED FROM RMK020-QTY-ON-HAND    CL*98
                       GIVING OLD-QTY-ON-HAND                          CL*98
              MOVE OLD-QTY-ON-HAND TO PL-DL-1-QTY-ON-HAND              CL*98
```

```
           MOVE RMK020-QTY-ON-HAND TO PL-DL-1-NEW-QTY-ON-HAND.            CL*98
                                                                          CL*98
      *                                                                   CL*98
        IF (I-O-NORMAL) AND (WS-PICK-PRNT-FLAG = 'N')                     CL*96
           PERFORM 3570-UPDATE-RMK020 THRU 3570-EXIT                      CL*92
        ELSE                                                              CL*92
           EXEC CICS UNLOCK DATASET('RMK020') END-EXEC.                   CL*93
      *                                                                   CL*84
        MOVE 'F'                       TO  PL-DL-1-LINE-STATUS.           CL*98
        MOVE '0'                       TO  CARRIAGE-CNTL.                 CL*50
        MOVE PL-DETAIL-LINE-1          TO  PRINT-DATA-LINE.               CL*50
        PERFORM 3999-WRITE-TD-QUEUE    THRU 3999-EXIT.                    CL*50
      *                                                                   CL*50
        MOVE HOLD-DESCRIPTION-2        TO  PL-DL-2-DESCRIPTION.           CL*50
        MOVE ' '                       TO  CARRIAGE-CNTL.                 CL*50
        MOVE PL-DETAIL-LINE-2          TO  PRINT-DATA-LINE.               CL*50
        PERFORM 3999-WRITE-TD-QUEUE    THRU 3999-EXIT.                    CL*50
      *                                                                   CL*50
        MOVE HOLD-DESCRIPTION-3        TO  PL-DL-3-DESCRIPTION.           CL*50
        MOVE ' '                       TO  CARRIAGE-CNTL.                 CL*50
        MOVE PL-DETAIL-LINE-3          TO  PRINT-DATA-LINE.               CL*50
        PERFORM 3999-WRITE-TD-QUEUE    THRU 3999-EXIT.                    CL*50
      *                                                                   CL*50
        MOVE RMK060-FULL-MFG-PART-NO      TO  PL-DL-4-MFG-PART-NO.        CL*80
        MOVE RMK060-DOCMT-LINE-COMMENTS   TO  PL-DL-4-COMMENTS.           CL*56
        MOVE ' '                          TO  CARRIAGE-CNTL.              CL*56
        MOVE PL-DETAIL-LINE-4             TO  PRINT-DATA-LINE.            CL*56
        PERFORM 3999-WRITE-TD-QUEUE       THRU 3999-EXIT.                 CL*56
      *                                                                   CL*50
        ADD 5                          TO  LINE-CNTR.                     CL*50
      *                                                                   CL*40
        PERFORM 7600-UPDATE-RMK060-RECORD THRU 7600-EXIT.                 CL*91
      *                                                                   CL*91
    3500-EXIT.  EXIT.                                                     CL*49
      *                                                                   CL*48
    3530-PICK-LIST-HEADINGS.                                              CL*48
      *                                                                   CL*48
        ADD 1 TO PAGE-NUMBER.                                             CL*48
        MOVE PAGE-NUMBER               TO  PL-HL-1-PAGE-NUM.              CL*48
        MOVE CA-RMK050-DOCMT-NBR       TO  PL-HL-1-DOC-NUM.               CL*48
        MOVE PL-HEADER-LINE-1          TO  PRINT-DATA-LINE.               CL*48
        MOVE '1'                       TO  CARRIAGE-CNTL.                 CL*48
        PERFORM 3999-WRITE-TD-QUEUE    THRU 3999-EXIT.                    CL*48
      *                                                                   CL*48
        MOVE MONI                      TO  PL-HL-2-MM.                    CL*48
        MOVE DAI                       TO  PL-HL-2-DD.                    CL*48
        MOVE YRI                       TO  PL-HL-2-YY.                    CL*48
        PERFORM 8100-FORMAT-TIME       THRU   8100-FMT-TIM-EXIT.          CL*80
        MOVE MDATEO                    TO  PL-HL-2-SYSDATE.               CL*80
        MOVE MTIMEO                    TO  PL-HL-2-SYSTIME.               CL*80
        MOVE PL-HEADER-LINE-2          TO  PRINT-DATA-LINE.               CL*48
        MOVE ' '                       TO  CARRIAGE-CNTL.                 CL*48
        PERFORM 3999-WRITE-TD-QUEUE    THRU 3999-EXIT.                    CL*48
      *                                                                   CL*48
        MOVE 'C'                       TO  PL-HL-3-DOC-STATUS.            CL*97
        MOVE ' '                       TO  PL-HL-3-REASON-OPEN.           CL*91
        MOVE PL-HEADER-LINE-3          TO  PRINT-DATA-LINE.               CL*48
        MOVE ' '                       TO  CARRIAGE-CNTL.                 CL*48
        PERFORM 3999-WRITE-TD-QUEUE    THRU 3999-EXIT.                    CL*48
      *                                                                   CL*48
        MOVE CA-RMK050-CREATE-USER-ID TO PL-HL-4-USER-ID.                 CL*48
        MOVE CA-RMK050-CREATE-NAME    TO PL-HL-4-USER-NAME.               CL*48
        MOVE CA-RMK050-DOCMT-DEPT     TO PL-HL-4-DEPT.                    CL*48
```

```
           IF (CA-RMK050-PRNT-FLAG = 'Y') OR (SELI = '1')                   CL*87
              MOVE 'Y'                     TO PL-HL-4-DOC-PRINTED           CL*87
           ELSE                                                             CL*87
              MOVE 'N'                     TO PL-HL-4-DOC-PRINTED.          CL*87
           IF (CA-RMK050-PICK-FLAG = 'Y') OR (SELI = '2')                   CL*96
              MOVE 'Y'                     TO PL-HL-4-PICKLIST-PRNTED       CL*87
           ELSE                                                             CL*87
              MOVE 'N'                     TO PL-HL-4-PICKLIST-PRNTED.      CL*87
           MOVE PL-HEADER-LINE-4           TO PRINT-DATA-LINE.              CL*48
           MOVE ' '                        TO CARRIAGE-CNTL.                CL*48
           PERFORM 3999-WRITE-TD-QUEUE     THRU 3999-EXIT.                  CL*48
      *                                                                     CL*48
           MOVE CA-RMK050-CREATE-SITE-ID TO PL-HL-5-SITE-ID.                CL*48
           MOVE CA-RMK050-PROJECT          TO PL-HL-5-PROJECT.              CL*48
           MOVE CA-RMK050-RELATED-DOCMT-NBR TO PL-HL-5-WORK-ORDER-NO.       CL*48
           MOVE PL-HEADER-LINE-5           TO PRINT-DATA-LINE.              CL*48
           MOVE ' '                        TO CARRIAGE-CNTL.                CL*48
           PERFORM 3999-WRITE-TD-QUEUE     THRU 3999-EXIT.                  CL*48
      *                                                                     CL*48
           MOVE PL-HEADER-LINE-6           TO PRINT-DATA-LINE.              CL*48
           MOVE '0'                        TO CARRIAGE-CNTL.                CL*48
           PERFORM 3999-WRITE-TD-QUEUE     THRU 3999-EXIT.                  CL*48
      *                                                                     CL*48
           MOVE PL-HEADER-LINE-7           TO PRINT-DATA-LINE.              CL*48
           MOVE ' '                        TO CARRIAGE-CNTL.                CL*48
           PERFORM 3999-WRITE-TD-QUEUE     THRU 3999-EXIT.                  CL*48
      *                                                                     CL*48
           MOVE PL-HEADER-LINE-8           TO PRINT-DATA-LINE.              CL*48
           MOVE ' '                        TO CARRIAGE-CNTL.                CL*48
           PERFORM 3999-WRITE-TD-QUEUE     THRU 3999-EXIT.                  CL*48
      *                                                                     CL*48
           MOVE 9                          TO LINE-CNTR.                    CL*48
      *                                                                     CL*48
       3530-EXIT.   EXIT.                                                   CL*48
      *                                                                     CL*48
       3550-PRINT-PICK-LIST-TLR.                                            CL*48
      *  PRINT TRAILER LINES.                                               CL*48
      *                                                                     CL*48
           MOVE PL-TRAILER-LINE-1          TO PRINT-DATA-LINE.              CL*48
           MOVE '0'                        TO CARRIAGE-CNTL.                CL*48
           PERFORM 3999-WRITE-TD-QUEUE     THRU 3999-EXIT.                  CL*80
      *                                                                     CL*80
           MOVE '1'                        TO CARRIAGE-CNTL.                CL*80
           MOVE SPACES                     TO PRINT-DATA-LINE.              CL*80
           PERFORM 3999-WRITE-TD-QUEUE     THRU 3999-EXIT.                  CL*48
      *                                                                     CL*48
       3550-EXIT.                                                           CL*48
      *                                                                     CL*40
       3560-FIND-BIN-LOCATION.                                              CL*56
           MOVE RM-ITEM                 TO I-O-FILENAME.                    CL*84
           MOVE RMK020-ITEM-FILE-KEY    TO I-O-FILEKEY.                     CL*84
           MOVE I-O-READ                TO I-O-COMMAND.                     CL*84
           MOVE I-O-EQUAL               TO I-O-OPERATOR.                    CL*84
           MOVE I-O-UPDATE-MODE         TO I-O-UPDATE.                      CL*84
           MOVE SPACES                  TO I-O-GENERIC.                     CL*84
           MOVE ZEROES                  TO I-O-GENERIC-KEYLEN.              CL*84
           MOVE 'C'                     TO I-O-UPD-TYPE.                    CL*84
           MOVE +0                      TO I-O-VREC-TYPE.                   CL*84
           MOVE I-O-ACF2-UPDATE         TO I-O-ACF2-INTENT.                 CL*84
                                                                            CL*61
           PERFORM 9280-CALL-I-O-MODULE THRU 9280-I-O-EXIT.                 CL*61
                                                                            CL*61
           IF I-O-NORMAL                                                    CL*61
```

```
           MOVE RECORD-AREA  TO  RMK020                               CL*61
        ELSE                                                          CL*61
           MOVE SPACES TO RMK020                                      CL*63
           MOVE ZEROES TO RMK020-QTY-ON-HAND.                         CL*63
    3560-EXIT.                                                        CL*56
        EXIT.                                                         CL*56
   *                                                                  CL*56
    3570-UPDATE-RMK020.                                               CL*85
        MOVE RMK020                TO RECORD-AREA.                    CL*85
        MOVE RMK020-ITEM-FILE-KEY  TO  I-O-FILEKEY.                   CL*85
        MOVE I-O-REWRITE           TO I-O-COMMAND.                    CL*85
        MOVE I-O-EQUAL             TO I-O-OPERATOR.                   CL*85
        MOVE ZEROES                TO I-O-GENERIC-KEYLEN              CL*85
                                      I-O-RETCODE.                    CL*85
        MOVE SPACES                TO I-O-GENERIC.                    CL*85
        MOVE I-O-UPDATE-MODE       TO I-O-UPDATE.                     CL*85
        MOVE 0                     TO I-O-VREC-TYPE.                  CL*85
        MOVE 'C'                   TO I-O-UPD-TYPE.                   CL*85
        MOVE I-O-ACF2-UPDATE       TO I-O-ACF2-INTENT.                CL*85
        MOVE RM-ITEM               TO I-O-FILENAME.                   CL*85
        MOVE WS-PROG-NAME          TO I-O-JRNL-WORKPGM.               CL*85
        PERFORM 9280-CALL-I-O-MODULE THRU 9280-I-O-EXIT.              CL*85
        IF  I-O-NORMAL                                                CL*85
            GO TO 3570-EXIT.                                          CL*85
   *                                                                  CL*85
        MOVE 'A'           TO CA-ERR-TYPE.                            CL*85
        MOVE I-O-RETCODE   TO CICS-RESP.                              CL*85
        MOVE I-O-FILENAME  TO EIBRSRCE.                               CL*85
        MOVE 000145        TO CA-ERR-NUM-PRG.                         CL*85
    3570-EXIT. EXIT.                                                  CL*85
   *                                                                  CL*85
    3999-WRITE-TD-QUEUE.                                              CL*38
        EXEC CICS                                                     CL*38
             WRITEQ TD QUEUE(DESTINATION-ID)                          CL*38
                       FROM(PRINT-QUEUE-RECORD)                       CL*38
                       LENGTH(LINE-LENGTH)                            CL*38
        END-EXEC.                                                     CL*38
    3999-EXIT.  EXIT.                                                 CL*38
   *                                                                  CL*52
    6900-CONVERT-UPDATE-DATE.                                         CL*52
        PERFORM 8200-FORMAT-TIME2 THRU 8200-EXIT.                     CL*52
        MOVE FDATE-2            TO WS-CONVERT-DATE.                   CL*52
        MOVE WS-CONVERT-DATE TO RMDATE-CONVERT-DATE.                  CL*52
        MOVE +0                 TO RMDATE-DEFER.                      CL*52
        MOVE 2                  TO RMDATE-FORMAT.                     CL*52
        PERFORM 8040-CALL-DATE-RTNE THRU 8040-CALL-DATE-EXIT.         CL*52
        IF  RMDATE-RETCODE = ZERO                                     CL*52
            NEXT SENTENCE                                             CL*52
        ELSE                                                          CL*52
            MOVE 'P'            TO CA-ERR-TYPE                        CL*52
            MOVE RMDATE-RETCODE TO CA-ERR-NUM-PRG                     CL*52
            GO TO 6900-EXIT.                                          CL*52
        MOVE RMDATE-CCYYDDD-PACKED TO RMK050-UPDATE-DATE.             CL*52
    6900-EXIT.  EXIT.                                                 CL*52
   *                                                                  CL*52
    7150-UPDATE-WIP-HDDR-REC.                                         CL*52
        IF SELI = '1'                                                 CL*52
           MOVE 'Y'    TO  CA-RMK050-PRNT-FLAG                        CL*80
                           DOCPRTI.                                   CL*80
        IF SELI = '2'                                                 CL*52
           MOVE 'Y'    TO  CA-RMK050-PICK-FLAG                        CL*96
                           PICPRTI                                    CL*81
           MOVE ' '    TO  CA-RMK050-REASON-DOCMT-OPEN                CL*91
```

```
                         RESOPENI                                  CL*98
           MOVE 'C'     TO   CA-RMK050-DOCMT-STATUS                CL*98
                             DOCSTI.                               CL*98
*                                                                  CL*52
        MOVE CA-RMK050-WIP-HDR-KEY TO RMK050-WIP-HDR-KEY.          CL*52
        PERFORM 7220-READ-HDDR-FOR-UPDATE THRU 7220-EXIT.          CL*52
        IF  I-O-NORMAL                                             CL*52
            MOVE CA-RMK050-REC TO RMK050                           CL*52
            PERFORM 6900-CONVERT-UPDATE-DATE THRU 6900-EXIT        CL*52
            PERFORM 7230-UPDATE-CNTL-REC THRU 7230-EXIT.           CL*52
 7150-EXIT. EXIT.                                                  CL*52
*                                                                  CL*52
 7220-READ-HDDR-FOR-UPDATE.                                        CL*52
        MOVE SPACES TO RECORD-AREA.                                CL*52
        MOVE RMK050-WIP-HDR-KEY TO I-O-FILEKEY.                    CL*52
        MOVE RMK050             TO RECORD-AREA.                    CL*52
        MOVE I-O-READ           TO I-O-COMMAND.                    CL*52
        MOVE I-O-EQUAL          TO I-O-OPERATOR.                   CL*52
        MOVE ZEROES             TO I-O-GENERIC-KEYLEN.             CL*52
        MOVE SPACES             TO I-O-GENERIC.                    CL*52
        MOVE I-O-UPDATE-MODE    TO I-O-UPDATE.                     CL*52
        MOVE 0                  TO I-O-VREC-TYPE.                  CL*52
        MOVE 'C'                TO I-O-UPD-TYPE.                   CL*52
        MOVE I-O-ACF2-UPDATE    TO I-O-ACF2-INTENT.                CL*52
        MOVE RM-WIP-HEADER      TO I-O-FILENAME.                   CL*52
        MOVE WS-PROG-NAME       TO I-O-JRNL-WORKPGM.               CL*52
        PERFORM 9280-CALL-I-O-MODULE THRU 9280-I-O-EXIT.           CL*52
        IF  CA-CREATE-MODE                                         CL*52
            IF  I-O-NOTFND                                         CL*52
                GO TO 7220-EXIT                                    CL*52
            ELSE                                                   CL*52
                IF  I-O-NORMAL                                     CL*52
                    IF  I-O-FILEKEY = ZEROS                        CL*52
                        GO TO 7220-EXIT                            CL*52
                    ELSE                                           CL*52
                        NEXT SENTENCE                              CL*52
                ELSE                                               CL*52
                    NEXT SENTENCE                                  CL*52
        ELSE                                                       CL*52
            IF  I-O-NORMAL                                         CL*52
                GO TO 7220-EXIT.                                   CL*52
*                                                                  CL*52
        MOVE 'A'           TO CA-ERR-TYPE.                         CL*52
        MOVE I-O-RETCODE   TO CICS-RESP.                           CL*52
        MOVE I-O-FILENAME  TO EIBRSRCE.                            CL*52
        MOVE 000145        TO CA-ERR-NUM-PRG.                      CL*52
 7220-EXIT. EXIT.                                                  CL*52
*                                                                  CL*52
 7230-UPDATE-CNTL-REC.                                             CL*52
        MOVE RMK050             TO RECORD-AREA.                    CL*52
        MOVE RMK050-WIP-HDR-KEY TO I-O-FILEKEY.                    CL*52
        MOVE I-O-REWRITE        TO I-O-COMMAND.                    CL*52
        MOVE I-O-EQUAL          TO I-O-OPERATOR.                   CL*52
        MOVE ZEROES             TO I-O-GENERIC-KEYLEN              CL*52
                                   I-O-RETCODE.                    CL*52
        MOVE SPACES             TO I-O-GENERIC.                    CL*52
        MOVE I-O-UPDATE-MODE    TO I-O-UPDATE.                     CL*52
        MOVE 0                  TO I-O-VREC-TYPE.                  CL*52
        MOVE 'C'                TO I-O-UPD-TYPE.                   CL*52
        MOVE I-O-ACF2-UPDATE    TO I-O-ACF2-INTENT.                CL*52
        MOVE RM-WIP-HEADER      TO I-O-FILENAME.                   CL*52
        MOVE WS-PROG-NAME       TO I-O-JRNL-WORKPGM.               CL*52
        PERFORM 9280-CALL-I-O-MODULE THRU 9280-I-O-EXIT.           CL*52
```

```
     IF  I-O-NORMAL                                              CL*52
         GO TO 7230-EXIT.                                        CL*52
*                                                                CL*52
     MOVE 'A'            TO CA-ERR-TYPE.                         CL*52
     MOVE I-O-RETCODE    TO CICS-RESP.                           CL*52
     MOVE I-O-FILENAME   TO EIBRSRCE.                            CL*52
     MOVE 000145         TO CA-ERR-NUM-PRG.                      CL*52
 7230-EXIT. EXIT.                                                CL*52
*                                                                CL*91
 7600-UPDATE-RMK060-RECORD.                                      CL*91
     PERFORM 7650-READ-RMK060-REC-UPDATE THRU 7650-EXIT.         CL*91
     PERFORM 7675-REWRITE-RMK060-REC THRU 7675-EXIT.             CL*91
 7600-EXIT. EXIT.                                                CL*91
*                                                                CL*91
 7650-READ-RMK060-REC-UPDATE.                                    CL*91
     MOVE RMK060-WIP-DETAIL-KEY  TO I-O-FILEKEY.                 CL*91
     MOVE RMK060                 TO RECORD-AREA.                 CL*91
     MOVE I-O-READ               TO I-O-COMMAND.                 CL*91
     MOVE I-O-EQUAL              TO I-O-OPERATOR.                CL*91
     MOVE ZERO                   TO I-O-GENERIC-KEYLEN.          CL*91
     MOVE SPACES                 TO I-O-GENERIC.                 CL*91
     MOVE I-O-UPDATE-MODE        TO I-O-UPDATE.                  CL*91
     MOVE 0                      TO I-O-VREC-TYPE.               CL*91
     MOVE 'C'                    TO I-O-UPD-TYPE.                CL*91
     MOVE I-O-ACF2-UPDATE        TO I-O-ACF2-INTENT.             CL*91
     MOVE RM-WIP-DETAIL          TO I-O-FILENAME.                CL*91
     MOVE WS-PROG-NAME           TO I-O-JRNL-WORKPGM.            CL*91
     PERFORM 9280-CALL-I-O-MODULE THRU 9280-I-O-EXIT.            CL*91
     IF  I-O-NORMAL                                              CL*91
         GO TO 7650-EXIT.                                        CL*91
*                                                                CL*91
     MOVE 'A'            TO CA-ERR-TYPE.                         CL*91
     MOVE I-O-RETCODE    TO CICS-RESP.                           CL*91
     MOVE I-O-FILENAME      TO EIBRSRCE.                         CL*91
     MOVE 000145         TO CA-ERR-NUM-PRG.                      CL*91
 7650-EXIT. EXIT.                                                CL*91
*                                                                CL*91
 7675-REWRITE-RMK060-REC.                                        CL*91
     MOVE RMK060-WIP-DETAIL-KEY TO I-O-FILEKEY.                  CL*91
     MOVE 'F'                   TO RMK060-DOCMT-LINE-STATUS.     CL*98
     MOVE RMK060                TO RECORD-AREA.                  CL*91
     MOVE I-O-REWRITE           TO I-O-COMMAND.                  CL*91
     MOVE I-O-EQUAL             TO I-O-OPERATOR.                 CL*91
     MOVE ZERO                  TO I-O-GENERIC-KEYLEN.           CL*91
     MOVE SPACES                TO I-O-GENERIC.                  CL*91
     MOVE I-O-UPDATE-MODE       TO I-O-UPDATE.                   CL*91
     MOVE 0                     TO I-O-VREC-TYPE.                CL*91
     MOVE 'C'                   TO I-O-UPD-TYPE.                 CL*91
     MOVE I-O-ACF2-UPDATE       TO I-O-ACF2-INTENT.              CL*91
     MOVE RM-WIP-DETAIL         TO I-O-FILENAME.                 CL*91
     MOVE WS-PROG-NAME          TO I-O-JRNL-WORKPGM.             CL*91
     PERFORM 9280-CALL-I-O-MODULE THRU 9280-I-O-EXIT.            CL*91
     IF  I-O-NORMAL                                              CL*91
         GO TO 7675-EXIT.                                        CL*91
*                                                                CL*91
     MOVE 'A'            TO CA-ERR-TYPE.                         CL*91
     MOVE I-O-RETCODE    TO CICS-RESP.                           CL*91
     MOVE I-O-FILENAME      TO EIBRSRCE.                         CL*91
     MOVE 000145         TO CA-ERR-NUM-PRG.                      CL*91
 7675-EXIT. EXIT.                                                CL*91
*                                                                CL*91
*                                                                CL*91
 8000-SEND-ERR-MSG.                                             RMP61C
```

```
 *                                                                 RMP61C
      MOVE CA-X-ERR-MSG              TO MSGO.                      RMP61C
      IF  CA-X-ERR-INST0 EQUAL SPACES                              RMP61C
          NEXT SENTENCE                                            RMP61C
      ELSE                                                         RMP61C
          MOVE CA-X-ERR-INST0       TO INSTO.                      RMP61C
      IF  CA-X-ERR-PFKEY0 EQUAL SPACES                             RMP61C
          NEXT SENTENCE                                            RMP61C
      ELSE                                                         RMP61C
          MOVE CA-X-ERR-PFKEY0      TO PFKEYO.                     RMP61C
      PERFORM 8500-SEND-DATA-ONLY  THRU 8500-EXIT.                 RMP61C
 *                                                                 RMP61C
  8000-SEND-ERR-EXIT.  EXIT.                                       RMP61C
      EJECT                                                        RMP61C
 *                                                                   CL*52
  ++INCLUDE RMU8040                                                  CL*52
 *                                                                   CL*52
  8100-FORMAT-TIME.                                                RMP61C
 *                                                                 RMP61C
      EXEC CICS ASKTIME ABSTIME(MTIME)                             RMP61C
                        RESP(CICS-RESP)                            RMP61C
      END-EXEC.                                                    RMP61C
      IF  CICS-RESP = DFHRESP(NORMAL)                              RMP61C
          NEXT SENTENCE                                            RMP61C
      ELSE                                                         RMP61C
          MOVE 00048    TO CA-ERR-NUM-PRG                          RMP61C
          MOVE 'A'      TO CA-ERR-TYPE                             RMP61C
          PERFORM 9000-ERR-RTNE                                    RMP61C
                  THRU 9000-ERR-EXIT                               RMP61C
          PERFORM 8000-SEND-ERR-MSG                                RMP61C
                  THRU 8000-SEND-ERR-EXIT.                         RMP61C
      EXEC CICS FORMATTIME ABSTIME(MTIME)                          RMP61C
                DATESEP    MMDDYY(FDATE)                           RMP61C
                TIME(FTIME) TIMESEP                                RMP61C
                RESP(CICS-RESP)                                    RMP61C
      END-EXEC.                                                    RMP61C
      IF  CICS-RESP = DFHRESP(NORMAL)                              RMP61C
          NEXT SENTENCE                                            RMP61C
      ELSE                                                         RMP61C
          MOVE 00049    TO CA-ERR-NUM-PRG                          RMP61C
          MOVE 'A'      TO CA-ERR-TYPE                             RMP61C
          PERFORM 9000-ERR-RTNE                                    RMP61C
                  THRU 9000-ERR-EXIT                               RMP61C
          PERFORM 8000-SEND-ERR-MSG                                RMP61C
                  THRU 8000-SEND-ERR-EXIT.                         RMP61C
      MOVE FDATE          TO MDATEO.                               RMP61C
      MOVE FHTIME         TO MTIMEO.                               RMP61C
 *                                                                 RMP61C
  8100-FMT-TIM-EXIT.  EXIT.                                        RMP61C
       EJECT                                                       RMP61C
  8200-FORMAT-TIME2.                                                 CL*52
      EXEC CICS ASKTIME ABSTIME(MTIME-2)                             CL*52
                        RESP(CICS-RESP)                              CL*52
      END-EXEC.                                                      CL*52
      IF  CICS-RESP = DFHRESP(NORMAL)                                CL*52
          NEXT SENTENCE                                              CL*52
      ELSE                                                           CL*52
          MOVE 00048    TO CA-ERR-NUM-PRG                            CL*52
          MOVE 'A'      TO CA-ERR-TYPE                               CL*52
          PERFORM 9000-ERR-RTNE                                      CL*52
                  THRU 9000-ERR-EXIT                                 CL*52
          PERFORM 8000-SEND-ERR-MSG                                  CL*52
                  THRU 8000-SEND-ERR-EXIT.                           CL*52
```

```
     EXEC CICS FORMATTIME ABSTIME(MTIME-2)                     CL*52
                          DATE(FDATE-2)                        CL*52
               RESP(CICS-RESP)                                 CL*52
     END-EXEC.                                                 CL*52
     IF  CICS-RESP = DFHRESP(NORMAL)                           CL*52
         GO TO 8200-EXIT                                       CL*52
     ELSE                                                      CL*52
         MOVE 00049    TO CA-ERR-NUM-PRG                       CL*52
         MOVE 'A'      TO CA-ERR-TYPE                          CL*52
         PERFORM 9000-ERR-RTNE                                 CL*52
                 THRU 9000-ERR-EXIT                            CL*52
         PERFORM 8000-SEND-ERR-MSG                             CL*52
                 THRU 8000-SEND-ERR-EXIT.                      CL*52
*                                                              CL*52
 8200-EXIT.  EXIT.                                             CL*52
*                                                              CL*52
 8500-SEND-DATA-ONLY.                                        RMP61C
*                                                            RMP61C
     PERFORM 8100-FORMAT-TIME THRU 8100-FMT-TIM-EXIT.        RMP61C
     EXEC CICS SEND MAP('RMP61M1')                             CL*81
                    MAPSET('RMP61M')                           CL*81
                    DATAONLY                                 RMP61C
                    RESP(CICS-RESP)                          RMP61C
                    FREEKB                                   RMP61C
                    CURSOR                                   RMP61C
     END-EXEC.                                               RMP61C
     IF  CICS-RESP NOT EQUAL DFHRESP(NORMAL)                 RMP61C
         MOVE 00016                TO CA-ERR-NUM-PRG         RMP61C
         MOVE 'A'                  TO CA-ERR-TYPE            RMP61C
         PERFORM 9000-ERR-RTNE THRU 9000-ERR-EXIT.           RMP61C
*                                                            RMP61C
 8500-EXIT.  EXIT.                                           RMP61C
     EJECT                                                   RMP61C
 9000-LINK-SEC.                                              RMP61C
*                                                            RMP61C
     MOVE SPACES TO       CA-DEST-PGM                        RMP61C
                          CA-USER-AUTH.                      RMP61C
*                                                            RMP61C
*                                                            RMP61C
*                                                            RMP61C
     EXEC CICS LINK PROGRAM('ISS04C')                        RMP61C
                    RESP(CICS-RESP)                          RMP61C
                    COMMAREA(CA-COMMAREA)                    RMP61C
                    LENGTH(CA-LENGTH)                        RMP61C
                    END-EXEC.                                RMP61C
*                                                            RMP61C
     IF  CICS-RESP = DFHRESP(NORMAL)                         RMP61C
         NEXT SENTENCE                                       RMP61C
     ELSE                                                    RMP61C
         MOVE 00008    TO CA-ERR-NUM-PRG                     RMP61C
         MOVE 'A'      TO CA-ERR-TYPE                        RMP61C
         PERFORM 9000-ERR-RTNE THRU 9000-ERR-EXIT.           RMP61C
*                                                            RMP61C
     IF CA-DEST-PGM  EQUAL SPACES                            RMP61C
        NEXT SENTENCE                                        RMP61C
     ELSE                                                    RMP61C
        MOVE 'Y'  TO      CA-USER-AUTH.                      RMP61C
*                                                            RMP61C
 9000-SEC-EXIT.  EXIT.                                       RMP61C
     EJECT                                                   RMP61C
 9010-CLEAR-RTNE.                                            RMP61C
*                                                            RMP61C
     PERFORM 9190-SET-CDEST     THRU 9190-CDEST-EXIT.        RMP61C
```

```
     MOVE CA-TEMPQ-PTR           TO CA-SP.                       RMP61C
     PERFORM 9220-POP-QSTACK     THRU 9220-POP-QSTCK-EXIT.       RMP61C
     MOVE 0                      TO CA-PGM-PTR.                  RMP61C
     PERFORM 9170-XCTL           THRU 9170-XCTL-EXIT.            RMP61C
*                                                                RMP61C
 9010-CLEAR-EXIT.  EXIT.                                         RMP61C
      EJECT                                                      RMP61C
 9020-PF9-RTNE.                                                  RMP61C
*                                                                RMP61C
     IF  WS-PF9-SW EQUAL  'A'                                    RMP61C
         MOVE 'Y'             TO CA-PF9-SW                       RMP61C
     ELSE                                                        RMP61C
         IF  WS-PF9-SW EQUAL 'R'                                 RMP61C
             IF EIBTRNID NOT EQUAL WS-TRNID                      RMP61C
                MOVE 'Y'      TO CA-PF9-SW                       RMP61C
             ELSE                                                RMP61C
                 MOVE 'N'     TO CA-PF9-SW                       RMP61C
         ELSE                                                    RMP61C
             MOVE 'N'         TO CA-PF9-SW.                      RMP61C
     IF  PF9-VALID                                               RMP61C
         IF  EIBTRNID EQUAL WS-TRNID                             RMP61C
             PERFORM 9050-RECEIVE-MAP                            RMP61C
                 THRU 9050-RECEIVE-EXIT                          RMP61C
             PERFORM 9060-PASS-DATA                              RMP61C
                 THRU 9060-PASS-DATA-EXIT                        RMP61C
             PERFORM 9070-SET-PF9-DEST                           RMP61C
                 THRU 9070-PF9-DEST-EXIT                         RMP61C
             PERFORM 9000-LINK-SEC                               RMP61C
                 THRU 9000-SEC-EXIT                              RMP61C
             IF  USER-AUTHORIZED                                 RMP61C
                 PERFORM 9130-SAVE-SCREEN                        RMP61C
                     THRU 9130-SAVE-SCREEN-EXIT                  RMP61C
                 PERFORM 9170-XCTL                               RMP61C
                     THRU  9170-XCTL-EXIT                        RMP61C
             ELSE                                                RMP61C
*                 MOVE 00003     TO CA-ERR-NUM-PRG               RMP61C
                  MOVE 'P'       TO CA-ERR-TYPE                  RMP61C
                  PERFORM 9000-ERR-RTNE                          RMP61C
                      THRU 9000-ERR-EXIT                         RMP61C
                  PERFORM 8000-SEND-ERR-MSG                      RMP61C
                      THRU 8000-SEND-ERR-EXIT                    RMP61C
          ELSE                                                   RMP61C
              MOVE CA-PGM-PTR    TO CA-SP                        RMP61C
              PERFORM 9100-PUSH-J-STACK                          RMP61C
                  THRU 9100-PUSH-JSTCK-EXIT                      RMP61C
              PERFORM 9120-RETRIEVE-DATA                         RMP61C
                  THRU 9120-RETRIEVE-DATA-EXIT                   RMP61C
              PERFORM 1000-FIRST-TIME-SEND                          CL*11
                  THRU 1000-EXIT                                    CL*11
              PERFORM 8000-FORMAT-MAP                            RMP61C
                  THRU 8000-FORMAT-EXIT                          RMP61C
              PERFORM 9080-SEND-MAP                              RMP61C
                  THRU 9080-SEND-EXIT                            RMP61C
     ELSE                                                        RMP61C
          MOVE 00001     TO CA-ERR-NUM-PRG                       RMP61C
          MOVE 'P'       TO CA-ERR-TYPE                          RMP61C
          PERFORM 9000-ERR-RTNE                                  RMP61C
              THRU 9000-ERR-EXIT                                 RMP61C
          PERFORM 8000-SEND-ERR-MSG                              RMP61C
              THRU 8000-SEND-ERR-EXIT.                           RMP61C
*                                                                RMP61C
 9020-PF9-EXIT.  EXIT.                                           RMP61C
     EJECT                                                       RMP61C
```

```
 9025-PF4-RTNE.                                                   CL*74
*                                                                 CL*74
     IF  EIBTRNID EQUAL WS-TRNID                                  CL*74
*        INVALID KEY PRESSED                                      CL*74
         MOVE -1        TO SELL                                   CL*74
         MOVE 00001     TO CA-ERR-NUM-PRG                         CL*74
         MOVE 'P'       TO CA-ERR-TYPE                            CL*74
         PERFORM 9000-ERR-RTNE THRU 9000-ERR-EXIT                 CL*74
         PERFORM 8000-SEND-ERR-MSG THRU 8000-SEND-ERR-EXIT        CL*74
     ELSE                                                         CL*74
         MOVE CA-PGM-PTR   TO CA-SP                               CL*74
         PERFORM 9100-PUSH-J-STACK                                CL*74
            THRU 9100-PUSH-JSTCK-EXIT                             CL*74
         PERFORM 9120-RETRIEVE-DATA                               CL*74
            THRU 9120-RETRIEVE-DATA-EXIT                          CL*74
         PERFORM 1000-FIRST-TIME-SEND                             CL*74
            THRU 1000-EXIT                                        CL*74
         PERFORM 8000-FORMAT-MAP                                  CL*74
            THRU 8000-FORMAT-EXIT                                 CL*74
         PERFORM 9080-SEND-MAP                                    CL*74
            THRU 9080-SEND-EXIT.                                  CL*75
*                                                                 CL*74
 9025-PF4-EXIT.  EXIT.                                            CL*74
     EJECT                                                        CL*74
 9030-PF3-RTNE.                                                 RMP61C
*                                                               RMP61C
     IF  EIBTRNID EQUAL WS-TRNID                                RMP61C
         MOVE CA-PGM-PTR       TO CA-SP                         RMP61C
         PERFORM 9110-POP-JSTACK                                RMP61C
             THRU 9110-POP-JSTCK-EXIT                           RMP61C
         MOVE CA-TEMPQ-PTR     TO CA-SP                         RMP61C
         PERFORM 9220-POP-QSTACK                                RMP61C
             THRU 9220-POP-QSTCK-EXIT                           RMP61C
         IF  CA-PGM-STACK EQUAL SPACES                          RMP61C
             PERFORM 9010-CLEAR-RTNE THRU 9010-CLEAR-EXIT       RMP61C
         ELSE                                                   RMP61C
*            PERFORM 9050-RECEIVE-MAP THRU 9050-RECEIVE-EXIT      CL*74
*            PERFORM 9060-PASS-DATA   THRU 9060-PASS-DATA-EXIT    CL*74
             PERFORM 9180-SET-DEST    THRU 9180-DEST-EXIT       RMP61C
             PERFORM 9170-XCTL        THRU 9170-XCTL-EXIT       RMP61C
     ELSE                                                       RMP61C
             PERFORM 9150-RETRIEVE-MAP                          RMP61C
                 THRU 9150-RETRIEVE-MAP-EXIT                    RMP61C
             PERFORM 9120-RETRIEVE-DATA                         RMP61C
                 THRU 9120-RETRIEVE-DATA-EXIT                   RMP61C
             PERFORM 1000-FIRST-TIME-SEND                         CL*10
                 THRU 1000-EXIT                                   CL*10
             PERFORM 8000-FORMAT-MAP                            RMP61C
                 THRU 8000-FORMAT-EXIT                          RMP61C
             PERFORM 9090-SEND-SAVE-MAP                         RMP61C
                 THRU 9090-SEND-SAVE-EXIT.                      RMP61C
                                                                RMP61C
*                                                               RMP61C
 9030-PF3-EXIT.  EXIT.                                          RMP61C
     EJECT                                                      RMP61C
 9040-PF1-RTNE.                                                 RMP61C
*                                                               RMP61C
      MOVE 00043     TO CA-ERR-NUM-PRG.                         RMP61C
      MOVE 'P'       TO CA-ERR-TYPE.                            RMP61C
      PERFORM 9000-ERR-RTNE                                     RMP61C
          THRU 9000-ERR-EXIT.                                   RMP61C
      PERFORM 8000-SEND-ERR-MSG                                 RMP61C
          THRU 8000-SEND-ERR-EXIT.                              RMP61C
```

```
 *                                                                      RMP61C
  9040-PF1-EXIT.  EXIT.                                                 RMP61C
  9050-RECEIVE-MAP.                                                     RMP61C
 *                                                                      RMP61C
 *                                                                      RMP61C
          EXEC CICS RECEIVE MAP('RMP61M1')                               CL*81
                            MAPSET('RMP61M')                             CL*81
                            INTO(RMP61M1I)                               CL*81
                            RESP(CICS-RESP)                             RMP61C
                            END-EXEC.                                   RMP61C
      IF  CICS-RESP = DFHRESP(NORMAL)                                   RMP61C
          NEXT SENTENCE                                                 RMP61C
      ELSE                                                              RMP61C
           MOVE 00022     TO CA-ERR-NUM-PRG                             RMP61C
           MOVE 'A'       TO CA-ERR-TYPE                                RMP61C
           PERFORM 9000-ERR-RTNE                                        RMP61C
               THRU 9000-ERR-EXIT.                                      RMP61C
 *                                                                      RMP61C
 *                                                                      RMP61C
  9050-RECEIVE-EXIT.  EXIT.                                             RMP61C
      EJECT                                                             RMP61C
      EJECT                                                             RMP61C
  9060-PASS-DATA.                                                       RMP61C
 *                                                                      RMP61C
 *                                                                      RMP61C
  9060-PASS-DATA-EXIT.  EXIT.                                           RMP61C
      EJECT                                                             RMP61C
  9070-SET-PF9-DEST.                                                    RMP61C
 *                                                                      RMP61C
      MOVE 09 TO CA-OPT.                                                RMP61C
 *                                                                      RMP61C
  9070-PF9-DEST-EXIT.  EXIT.                                            RMP61C
      EJECT                                                             RMP61C
  8000-FORMAT-MAP.                                                      RMP61C
 *                                                                      RMP61C
 *                                                                      RMP61C
      MOVE SKIP-BRT       TO MSGA.                                      RMP61C
      PERFORM 8100-FORMAT-TIME THRU 8100-FMT-TIM-EXIT.                  RMP61C
      MOVE CA-USERID      TO MOPIDO.                                    RMP61C
      MOVE CA-TRMID       TO MTRMIDO.                                   RMP61C
 *                                                                      RMP61C
 *                                                                      RMP61C
  8000-FORMAT-EXIT.  EXIT.                                              RMP61C
      EJECT                                                             RMP61C
  9080-SEND-MAP.                                                        RMP61C
 *                                                                      RMP61C
 *                                                                      RMP61C
          EXEC CICS SEND MAP('RMP61M1')                                  CL*81
                            MAPSET('RMP61M')                             CL*81
                            FROM(RMP61M1I)                               CL*81
                            ERASE                                       RMP61C
                            FREEKB                                      RMP61C
                            RESP(CICS-RESP)                             RMP61C
                            END-EXEC.                                   RMP61C
      IF  CICS-RESP = DFHRESP(NORMAL)                                   RMP61C
          NEXT SENTENCE                                                 RMP61C
      ELSE                                                              RMP61C
           MOVE 00016     TO CA-ERR-NUM-PRG                             RMP61C
           MOVE 'A'       TO CA-ERR-TYPE                                RMP61C
           PERFORM 9000-ERR-RTNE                                        RMP61C
               THRU 9000-ERR-EXIT.                                      RMP61C
 *                                                                      RMP61C
 *                                                                      RMP61C
```

```
 9080-SEND-EXIT.  EXIT.                                              RMP61C
     EJECT                                                           RMP61C
 9090-SEND-SAVE-MAP.                                                 RMP61C
*                                                                    RMP61C
*                                                                    RMP61C
           EXEC CICS SEND MAP('RMP61M1')                              CL*81
                          MAPSET('RMP61M')                            CL*81
                          FROM(RMP61M1I)                              CL*81
                          ERASE                                      RMP61C
                          FREEKB                                     RMP61C
                          CURSOR(MAP-CURSOR)                         RMP61C
                          RESP(CICS-RESP)                            RMP61C
                          END-EXEC.                                  RMP61C
     IF  CICS-RESP = DFHRESP(NORMAL)                                 RMP61C
         NEXT SENTENCE                                               RMP61C
     ELSE                                                            RMP61C
          MOVE 00016    TO CA-ERR-NUM-PRG                            RMP61C
          MOVE 'A'      TO CA-ERR-TYPE                               RMP61C
          PERFORM 9000-ERR-RTNE                                      RMP61C
              THRU 9000-ERR-EXIT.                                    RMP61C
*                                                                    RMP61C
*                                                                    RMP61C
 9090-SEND-SAVE-EXIT.  EXIT.                                         RMP61C
     EJECT                                                           RMP61C
 9100-PUSH-J-STACK.                                                  RMP61C
*                                                                    RMP61C
     IF CA-SP LESS THAN 8                                            RMP61C
        ADD +1       TO CA-SP                                        RMP61C
        MOVE WS-PROG-NAME TO CA-PGM-NAME (CA-SP)                     RMP61C
        MOVE CA-SP        TO CA-PGM-PTR                              RMP61C
     ELSE                                                            RMP61C
        MOVE 00006        TO CA-ERR-NUM-PRG                          RMP61C
        MOVE 'P'          TO CA-ERR-TYPE                             RMP61C
        PERFORM 9000-ERR-RTNE THRU 9000-ERR-EXIT                     RMP61C
        PERFORM 8000-SEND-ERR-MSG THRU 8000-SEND-ERR-EXIT.           RMP61C
*                                                                    RMP61C
 9100-PUSH-JSTCK-EXIT.  EXIT.                                        RMP61C
     EJECT                                                           RMP61C
 9110-POP-JSTACK.                                                    RMP61C
*                                                                    RMP61C
     IF  CA-SP  GREATER THAN 0                                       RMP61C
         MOVE SPACES TO CA-PGM-NAME (CA-SP)                          RMP61C
         SUBTRACT +1      FROM CA-SP                                 RMP61C
         MOVE CA-SP       TO CA-PGM-PTR                              RMP61C
     ELSE                                                            RMP61C
        MOVE 00006        TO CA-ERR-NUM-PRG                          RMP61C
        MOVE 'P'          TO CA-ERR-TYPE                             RMP61C
        PERFORM 9000-ERR-RTNE THRU 9000-ERR-EXIT                     RMP61C
        PERFORM 8000-SEND-ERR-MSG THRU 8000-SEND-ERR-EXIT.           RMP61C
*                                                                    RMP61C
 9110-POP-JSTCK-EXIT.  EXIT.                                         RMP61C
     EJECT                                                           RMP61C
 9120-RETRIEVE-DATA.                                                 RMP61C
*                                                                    RMP61C
     MOVE CA-KEY-AREA         TO WS-KEY-AREA.                         CL*10
     MOVE EIBTRMID            TO WS-QUEUE-TERMID.                     CL*10
     MOVE WS-TRNID            TO WS-QUEUE-TRANID.                     CL*65
     MOVE CA-TEMPQ-PTR        TO CA-SP.                               CL*80
     PERFORM 9210-PUSH-Q-STACK THRU 9210-PUSH-QSTCK-EXIT.             CL*10
*                                                                    RMP61C
 9120-RETRIEVE-DATA-EXIT.  EXIT.                                     RMP61C
      SKIP3                                                          RMP61C
 9130-SAVE-SCREEN.                                                   RMP61C
*----------------*                                                   RMP61C
```

```
           IF CA-MAP-PTR < WS-MQ-MAX                                    RMP61C
              PERFORM 9140-PUSH-MAP THRU 9140-PUSH-MAP-EXIT             RMP61C
           ELSE                                                         RMP61C
              MOVE 00044  TO CA-ERR-NUM-PRG                             RMP61C
              MOVE 'A'    TO CA-ERR-TYPE                                RMP61C
              PERFORM 9000-ERR-RTNE THRU 9000-ERR-EXIT.                 RMP61C
       9130-SAVE-SCREEN-EXIT.                                           RMP61C
           EXIT.                                                        RMP61C
                                                                        RMP61C
       9140-PUSH-MAP.                                                   RMP61C
      *--------------*                                                  RMP61C
           ADD +1 TO CA-MAP-PTR.                                        RMP61C
                                                                        RMP61C
           MOVE CA-TRMID TO MAP-TERMINAL.                               RMP61C
           MOVE RMP61M1I TO MAP-RECORD.                                    CL*81
           MOVE EIBCPOSN TO MAP-CURSOR.                                 RMP61C
                                                                        RMP61C
           IF CA-MAP-PTR > CA-MAP-QUE-CNT                               RMP61C
              ADD +1 TO CA-MAP-QUE-CNT                                  RMP61C
              EXEC CICS                                                 RMP61C
                   WRITEQ TS QUEUE (MAP-STACK-QUEUE)                    RMP61C
                     FROM (MAP-DATA)                                    RMP61C
                   LENGTH (MAP-DATA-LEN)                                RMP61C
                     ITEM (CA-MAP-PTR)                                  RMP61C
                     RESP (CICS-RESP)                                   RMP61C
                     NOSUSPEND                                          RMP61C
              END-EXEC                                                  RMP61C
           ELSE                                                         RMP61C
              EXEC CICS                                                 RMP61C
                   WRITEQ TS QUEUE (MAP-STACK-QUEUE)                    RMP61C
                     FROM (MAP-DATA)                                    RMP61C
                   LENGTH (MAP-DATA-LEN)                                RMP61C
                     ITEM (CA-MAP-PTR)                                  RMP61C
                     REWRITE                                            RMP61C
                     RESP (CICS-RESP)                                   RMP61C
                     NOSUSPEND                                          RMP61C
              END-EXEC.                                                 RMP61C
                                                                        RMP61C
           IF CICS-RESP = DFHRESP (NORMAL)                              RMP61C
              NEXT SENTENCE                                             RMP61C
           ELSE                                                         RMP61C
              MOVE 00045 TO CA-ERR-NUM-PRG                              RMP61C
              MOVE 'A'   TO CA-ERR-TYPE                                 RMP61C
              PERFORM 9000-ERR-RTNE THRU 9000-ERR-EXIT.                 RMP61C
                                                                        RMP61C
           ADD +1 TO CA-MAP-PTR.                                        RMP61C
                                                                        RMP61C
           IF CA-MAP-PTR > CA-MAP-QUE-CNT                               RMP61C
              ADD +1 TO CA-MAP-QUE-CNT                                  RMP61C
              EXEC CICS                                                 RMP61C
                WRITEQ TS QUEUE (MAP-STACK-QUEUE)                       RMP61C
                           FROM (STANDARD-COMMAREA)                     RMP61C
                         LENGTH (CA-MAX-LENGTH)                         RMP61C
                           ITEM (CA-MAP-PTR)                            RMP61C
                           RESP (CICS-RESP)                             RMP61C
                   NOSUSPEND                                            RMP61C
              END-EXEC                                                  RMP61C
           ELSE                                                         RMP61C
              EXEC CICS                                                 RMP61C
                WRITEQ TS QUEUE (MAP-STACK-QUEUE)                       RMP61C
                           FROM (STANDARD-COMMAREA)                     RMP61C
                         LENGTH (CA-MAX-LENGTH)                         RMP61C
                           ITEM (CA-MAP-PTR)                            RMP61C
```

```
                       REWRITE                                         RMP61C
                       RESP (CICS-RESP)                                RMP61C
                       NOSUSPEND                                       RMP61C
             END-EXEC.                                                 RMP61C
                                                                       RMP61C
           IF CICS-RESP = DFHRESP (NORMAL)                             RMP61C
              NEXT SENTENCE                                            RMP61C
           ELSE                                                        RMP61C
              MOVE 00045 TO CA-ERR-NUM-PRG                             RMP61C
              MOVE 'A'   TO CA-ERR-TYPE                                RMP61C
              PERFORM 9000-ERR-RTNE THRU 9000-ERR-EXIT.                RMP61C
                                                                       RMP61C
       9140-PUSH-MAP-EXIT.                                             RMP61C
      *------------------*                                             RMP61C
            EXIT.                                                      RMP61C
            SKIP3                                                      RMP61C
       9150-RETRIEVE-MAP.                                              RMP61C
      *------------------*                                             RMP61C
           IF CA-MAP-PTR > WS-MQ-MIN                                   RMP61C
              PERFORM 9160-POP-MAP THRU 9160-POP-MAP-EXIT              RMP61C
           ELSE                                                        RMP61C
              MOVE 00015  TO CA-ERR-NUM-PRG                            RMP61C
              MOVE 'A'    TO CA-ERR-TYPE                               RMP61C
              PERFORM 9000-ERR-RTNE THRU 9000-ERR-EXIT.                RMP61C
       9150-RETRIEVE-MAP-EXIT.                                         RMP61C
           EXIT.                                                       RMP61C
                                                                       RMP61C
       9160-POP-MAP.                                                   RMP61C
      *-------------*                                                  RMP61C
           MOVE CA-TRMID TO MAP-TERMINAL.                              RMP61C
           MOVE CA-MAP-QUE-CNT TO WS-MAP-QUE-CNT.                      RMP61C
                                                                       RMP61C
           EXEC CICS                                                   RMP61C
              READQ TS QUEUE (MAP-STACK-QUEUE) INTO (STANDARD-COMMAREA) RMP61C
                      LENGTH (CA-MAX-LENGTH)                           RMP61C
                        ITEM (CA-MAP-PTR)                              RMP61C
                        RESP (CICS-RESP)                               RMP61C
           END-EXEC.                                                   RMP61C
                                                                       RMP61C
           IF CICS-RESP = DFHRESP (NORMAL)                             RMP61C
              NEXT SENTENCE                                            RMP61C
           ELSE                                                        RMP61C
              MOVE 00046 TO CA-ERR-NUM-PRG                             RMP61C
              MOVE 'A'   TO CA-ERR-TYPE                                RMP61C
              PERFORM 9000-ERR-RTNE THRU 9000-ERR-EXIT.                RMP61C
                                                                       RMP61C
           MOVE WS-MAP-QUE-CNT TO CA-MAP-QUE-CNT.                      RMP61C
           ADD -1 TO CA-MAP-PTR.                                       RMP61C
                                                                       RMP61C
           EXEC CICS                                                   RMP61C
              READQ TS QUEUE (MAP-STACK-QUEUE) INTO (MAP-DATA)         RMP61C
                      LENGTH (MAP-DATA-LEN)                            RMP61C
                        ITEM (CA-MAP-PTR)                              RMP61C
                        RESP (CICS-RESP)                               RMP61C
           END-EXEC.                                                   RMP61C
                                                                       RMP61C
           IF CICS-RESP = DFHRESP (NORMAL)                             RMP61C
              NEXT SENTENCE                                            RMP61C
           ELSE                                                        RMP61C
              MOVE 00046 TO CA-ERR-NUM-PRG                             RMP61C
              MOVE 'A'   TO CA-ERR-TYPE                                RMP61C
              PERFORM 9000-ERR-RTNE THRU 9000-ERR-EXIT.                RMP61C
                                                                       RMP61C
```

```
           MOVE MAP-RECORD TO RMP61M1I.                                 CL*81
                                                                        RMP61C
           ADD -1 TO CA-MAP-PTR.                                        RMP61C
                                                                        RMP61C
           IF CA-MAP-PTR = WS-MQ-MIN                                    RMP61C
              EXEC CICS                                                 RMP61C
                   DELETEQ TS QUEUE (MAP-STACK-QUEUE)                   RMP61C
                   RESP(CICS-RESP)                                      RMP61C
              END-EXEC                                                  RMP61C
              IF CICS-RESP = DFHRESP(QIDERR)                            RMP61C
                 MOVE +0 TO CA-MAP-QUE-CNT                              RMP61C
              ELSE                                                      RMP61C
                  IF CICS-RESP = DFHRESP(NORMAL)                        RMP61C
                     MOVE +0 TO CA-MAP-QUE-CNT                          RMP61C
                  ELSE                                                  RMP61C
                     MOVE 00025 TO CA-ERR-NUM-PRG                       RMP61C
                     MOVE 'A'   TO CA-ERR-TYPE                          RMP61C
                     PERFORM 9000-ERR-RTNE THRU 9000-ERR-EXIT.          RMP61C
       9160-POP-MAP-EXIT.                                               RMP61C
      *------------------*                                              RMP61C
            EXIT.                                                       RMP61C
           EJECT                                                        RMP61C
       9170-XCTL.                                                       RMP61C
      *                                                                 RMP61C
           PERFORM 9300-DEL-JRNL THRU 9300-EXIT.                        RMP61C
      *                                                                 RMP61C
           EXEC CICS XCTL PROGRAM(CA-DEST-PGM)                          RMP61C
                          RESP(CICS-RESP)                               RMP61C
                          COMMAREA(CA-COMMAREA)                         RMP61C
                          LENGTH(CA-LENGTH)                             RMP61C
                          END-EXEC.                                     RMP61C
           IF  CICS-RESP = DFHRESP(NORMAL)                              RMP61C
               NEXT SENTENCE                                            RMP61C
           ELSE                                                         RMP61C
               MOVE 00010           TO CA-ERR-NUM-PRG                   RMP61C
               MOVE 'A'             TO CA-ERR-TYPE                      RMP61C
               PERFORM 9000-ERR-RTNE  THRU 9000-ERR-EXIT.               RMP61C
      *                                                                 RMP61C
       9170-XCTL-EXIT.  EXIT.                                           RMP61C
           EJECT                                                        RMP61C
       9180-SET-DEST.                                                   RMP61C
      *                                                                 RMP61C
           MOVE CA-PGM-NAME (CA-PGM-PTR) TO CA-DEST-PGM.                RMP61C
      *                                                                 RMP61C
       9180-DEST-EXIT.  EXIT.                                           RMP61C
           EJECT                                                        RMP61C
       9190-SET-CDEST.                                                  RMP61C
      *                                                                 RMP61C
           MOVE CA-MENU-PGM (CA-MENU-PTR) TO CA-DEST-PGM.               RMP61C
      *                                                                 RMP61C
       9190-CDEST-EXIT.  EXIT.                                          RMP61C
           EJECT                                                        RMP61C
       9200-CICS-RETURN.                                                RMP61C
      *                                                                 RMP61C
           PERFORM 9300-DEL-JRNL THRU 9300-EXIT.                        RMP61C
      *                                                                 RMP61C
           EXEC CICS RETURN                                             RMP61C
                            TRANSID(WS-TRNID)                           RMP61C
                            COMMAREA(CA-COMMAREA)                       RMP61C
                            LENGTH(CA-LENGTH)                           RMP61C
                            RESP(CICS-RESP)                             RMP61C
              END-EXEC.                                                 RMP61C
           IF  CICS-RESP = DFHRESP(NORMAL)                              RMP61C
```

```
            NEXT SENTENCE                                               RMP61C
        ELSE                                                            RMP61C
            MOVE 00013           TO CA-ERR-NUM-PRG                      RMP61C
            MOVE 'A'             TO CA-ERR-TYPE                         RMP61C
            PERFORM 9000-ERR-RTNE  THRU 9000-ERR-EXIT.                  RMP61C
      *                                                                 RMP61C
       9200-EXIT.  EXIT.                                                RMP61C
           EJECT                                                        RMP61C
      *                                                                 RMP61C
       9000-ERR-RTNE.                                                   RMP61C
      *                                                                 RMP61C
           IF  I-O-RETPGM-PTR GREATER THAN ZERO                         RMP61C
               MOVE I-O-RETPGM (I-O-RETPGM-PTR) TO                      RMP61C
                      CA-ERR-PROGRAM                                    RMP61C
           ELSE                                                         RMP61C
               MOVE WS-PROG-NAME TO CA-ERR-PROGRAM.                     RMP61C
           MOVE 'P'                    TO CA-ERR-PROG-TYPE.             RMP61C
           IF  CA-ERR-TYPE EQUAL 'P' OR 'D'                             RMP61C
               MOVE SPACES             TO CA-X-ERR-MSG                  RMP61C
                                          CA-X-ERR-INST0                RMP61C
                                          CA-X-ERR-PFKEY0               RMP61C
               MOVE CA-ERR-TYPE        TO CA-X-ERR-TYPE                 RMP61C
               MOVE CA-ERR-NUM-PRG     TO CA-X-ERR-NUM                  RMP61C
               MOVE CA-INST-NUM        TO CA-X-ERR-INST-NUM             RMP61C
               MOVE CA-PFKEY-NUM       TO CA-X-ERR-PFKEY-NUM            RMP61C
               MOVE CA-ERR-PROG-TYPE   TO CA-X-ERR-PROG-TYPE            RMP61C
               EXEC CICS LINK PROGRAM('ISS03C')                         RMP61C
                              RESP(CICS-RESP)                           RMP61C
                              COMMAREA(CA-X-ERR-COMMAREA)               RMP61C
                              LENGTH(CA-ERR-LENGTH)                     RMP61C
                              END-EXEC                                  RMP61C
               IF  CICS-RESP = DFHRESP(NORMAL)                          RMP61C
                   NEXT SENTENCE                                        RMP61C
               ELSE                                                     RMP61C
                   EXEC CICS ABEND ABCODE ('XERR')                      RMP61C
                                   NOHANDLE                             RMP61C
                                   CANCEL                               RMP61C
                                   END-EXEC                             RMP61C
           ELSE                                                         RMP61C
               IF  CA-ERR-TYPE EQUAL 'A'                                RMP61C
                   MOVE  CICS-RESP       TO CA-ERR-NUM-SYS              RMP61C
                   MOVE  EIBRSRCE        TO CA-ERR-RSRCE                RMP61C
                   EXEC CICS LINK PROGRAM('ISS03C')                     RMP61C
                                  RESP(CICS-RESP)                       RMP61C
                                  COMMAREA(CA-COMMAREA)                 RMP61C
                                  LENGTH(CA-ABEND-LENGTH)               RMP61C
                                  END-EXEC                              RMP61C
                   EXEC CICS ABEND ABCODE ('AERR')                      RMP61C
                                   NOHANDLE                             RMP61C
                                   CANCEL                               RMP61C
                                   END-EXEC.                            RMP61C
           MOVE 0                      TO CA-X-ERR-NUM                  RMP61C
                                          CA-X-ERR-INST-NUM             RMP61C
                                          CA-X-ERR-PFKEY-NUM            RMP61C
                                          CA-ERR-NUM-PRG                RMP61C
                                          CA-INST-NUM                   RMP61C
                                          CA-PFKEY-NUM.                 RMP61C
      *                                                                 RMP61C
       9000-ERR-EXIT.  EXIT.                                            RMP61C
           EJECT                                                        RMP61C
       9210-PUSH-Q-STACK.                                               RMP61C
      *                                                                 RMP61C
           IF   CA-SP LESS THAN 8                                       RMP61C
```

```
           ADD +1              TO CA-SP                                RMP61C
           MOVE WS-QUEUE-NAME  TO CA-TEMPQ-ID (CA-SP)                  RMP61C
           MOVE QUEUE-NUMBER   TO CA-TEMPQ-KEY (CA-SP)                 RMP61C
           MOVE CA-SP          TO CA-TEMPQ-PTR                         RMP61C
       ELSE                                                            RMP61C
           MOVE 00026           TO CA-ERR-NUM-PRG                      RMP61C
           MOVE 'A'             TO CA-ERR-TYPE                         RMP61C
           PERFORM 9000-ERR-RTNE  THRU 9000-ERR-EXIT                   RMP61C
           GO TO 9210-PUSH-QSTCK-EXIT.                                 RMP61C
 *                                                                     RMP61C
  9210-PUSH-QSTCK-EXIT.   EXIT.                                        RMP61C
       EJECT                                                           RMP61C
  9220-POP-QSTACK.                                                     RMP61C
 *                                                                     RMP61C
       IF  CA-TEMPQ-TRNID (CA-TEMPQ-PTR) EQUAL WS-TRNID                RMP61C
           PERFORM 9230-POP-QSTACK THRU 9230-POP-QSTACK-EXIT           RMP61C
           IF CA-SP GREATER THAN 0                                     RMP61C
              GO TO 9220-POP-QSTACK.                                   RMP61C
 *                                                                     RMP61C
  9220-POP-QSTCK-EXIT.   EXIT.                                         RMP61C
       EJECT                                                           RMP61C
  9230-POP-QSTACK.                                                     RMP61C
 *                                                                     RMP61C
       IF  CA-SP GREATER THAN 0                                        RMP61C
           PERFORM 9240-DEL-QUEUE THRU 9240-DEL-EXIT                   RMP61C
           MOVE SPACES TO CA-TEMPQ-NAME (CA-SP)                        RMP61C
           SUBTRACT 1     FROM CA-SP                                   RMP61C
           MOVE CA-SP  TO CA-TEMPQ-PTR                                 RMP61C
       ELSE                                                            RMP61C
           MOVE 00026           TO CA-ERR-NUM-PRG                      RMP61C
           MOVE 'A'             TO CA-ERR-TYPE                         RMP61C
           PERFORM 9000-ERR-RTNE  THRU 9000-ERR-EXIT.                  RMP61C
 *                                                                     RMP61C
  9230-POP-QSTACK-EXIT.  EXIT.                                         RMP61C
 *                                                                     RMP61C
  9240-DEL-QUEUE.                                                      RMP61C
 *                                                                     RMP61C
       MOVE CA-TEMPQ-ID (CA-SP) TO CA-QUEUE-ID.                        RMP61C
       IF  CA-TEMPQ-ALPHA-KEY (CA-SP) EQUAL HIGH-VALUES                RMP61C
           PERFORM 9250-DEL-TRAN THRU 9250-DEL-EXIT                    RMP61C
       ELSE                                                            RMP61C
           PERFORM 9260-DEL-TEMPSTR THRU 9260-DEL-EXIT.                RMP61C
 *                                                                     RMP61C
  9240-DEL-EXIT.  EXIT.                                                RMP61C
  9250-DEL-TRAN.                                                       RMP61C
 *                                                                     RMP61C
       EXEC CICS DELETEQ TD QUEUE(CA-QUEUE-ID)                         RMP61C
                            RESP(CICS-RESP)                            RMP61C
                            END-EXEC.                                  RMP61C
       IF  CICS-RESP = DFHRESP(NORMAL)                                 RMP61C
           NEXT SENTENCE                                               RMP61C
       ELSE                                                            RMP61C
           MOVE 00025           TO CA-ERR-NUM-PRG                      RMP61C
           MOVE 'A'             TO CA-ERR-TYPE                         RMP61C
           PERFORM 9000-ERR-RTNE  THRU 9000-ERR-EXIT.                  RMP61C
 *                                                                     RMP61C
 *                                                                     RMP61C
  9250-DEL-EXIT.  EXIT.                                                RMP61C
  9260-DEL-TEMPSTR.                                                    RMP61C
 *                                                                     RMP61C
       EXEC CICS DELETEQ TS QUEUE(CA-QUEUE-ID)                         RMP61C
                            RESP(CICS-RESP)                            RMP61C
                            END-EXEC.                                  RMP61C
```

```
           IF  CICS-RESP = DFHRESP(NORMAL)                                  RMP61C
               NEXT SENTENCE                                                RMP61C
           ELSE                                                             RMP61C
               MOVE 00025           TO CA-ERR-NUM-PRG                       RMP61C
               MOVE 'A'             TO CA-ERR-TYPE                          RMP61C
               PERFORM 9000-ERR-RTNE  THRU 9000-ERR-EXIT.                   RMP61C
      *                                                                     RMP61C
       9260-DEL-EXIT.  EXIT.                                                RMP61C
      *                                                                     RMP61C
           EJECT                                                            RMP61C
       9270-ABEND-ROUTINE.                                                  RMP61C
      *                                                                     RMP61C
           IF  I-O-RETPGM-PTR GREATER THAN ZERO                             RMP61C
               MOVE I-O-RETPGM (I-O-RETPGM-PTR) TO                          RMP61C
                      CA-ERR-PROGRAM                                        RMP61C
           ELSE                                                             RMP61C
               MOVE WS-PROG-NAME TO CA-ERR-PROGRAM.                         RMP61C
           MOVE 'P'                       TO CA-ERR-PROG-TYPE.              RMP61C
           MOVE 'A'              TO CA-ERR-TYPE.                            RMP61C
           MOVE  CICS-RESP       TO CA-ERR-NUM-SYS.                         RMP61C
           MOVE  EIBRSRCE        TO CA-ERR-RSRCE.                           RMP61C
           EXEC CICS LINK PROGRAM('ISS03C')                                 RMP61C
                          RESP(CICS-RESP)                                   RMP61C
                          COMMAREA(CA-COMMAREA)                             RMP61C
                          LENGTH(CA-ABEND-LENGTH)                           RMP61C
                          END-EXEC.                                         RMP61C
           EXEC CICS ABEND ABCODE ('AERR')                                  RMP61C
                           NOHANDLE                                         RMP61C
                           END-EXEC.                                        RMP61C
      *                                                                     RMP61C
       9270-EXIT.  EXIT.                                                    RMP61C
           EJECT                                                            RMP61C
      *                                                                     RMP61C
       9280-CALL-I-O-MODULE.                                                RMP61C
      *                                                                     RMP61C
      *                                                                     RMP61C
           CALL 'ISS06A' USING I-O-REQUEST, RECORD-AREA.                    RMP61C
      *                                                                     RMP61C
           PERFORM 9290-JOURNAL-CHECK THRU 9290-EXIT.                       RMP61C
      *                                                                     RMP61C
      *                                                                     RMP61C
       9280-I-O-EXIT.  EXIT.                                                RMP61C
           EJECT                                                            RMP61C
       9290-JOURNAL-CHECK.                                                  RMP61C
      *                                                                     RMP61C
           IF  I-O-NOTFND AND I-O-ADD                                       RMP61C
               NEXT SENTENCE                                                RMP61C
           ELSE                                                             RMP61C
               IF I-O-RETCODE NOT EQUAL ZERO                                RMP61C
                  GO TO 9290-EXIT.                                          RMP61C
           IF  I-O-READONLY                                                 RMP61C
              GO TO 9290-EXIT.                                              RMP61C
           MOVE I-O-RETCODE         TO      I-O-RET-HOLD.                   RMP61C
           MOVE I-O-FILENAME        TO      TS-FILENAME.                    RMP61C
           MOVE I-O-FILEKEY         TO      TS-KEY.                         RMP61C
           MOVE CA-TRMID            TO      WS-JRNL-TERMID.                 RMP61C
           MOVE I-O-RETURNED-JDATA  TO      TS-JDATA.                       RMP61C
           ADD 1                    TO      ITEM-NO.                        RMP61C
           EXEC CICS WRITEQ TS QUEUE(WS-JRNL-NAME)                          RMP61C
                               FROM (TS-JRNL)                               RMP61C
                               ITEM(ITEM-NO)                                RMP61C
                               LENGTH(54)                                   RMP61C
```

```
                          RESP(CICS-RESP)                                      RMP61C
                          END-EXEC.                                            RMP61C
      IF  CICS-RESP = DFHRESP(NORMAL)                                          RMP61C
          NEXT SENTENCE                                                        RMP61C
      ELSE                                                                     RMP61C
          MOVE 00000 TO CA-ERR-NUM-PRG                                         RMP61C
          MOVE 'A'   TO CA-ERR-TYPE                                            RMP61C
          PERFORM 9000-ERR-RTNE THRU 9000-ERR-EXIT.                            RMP61C
      MOVE I-O-RET-HOLD       TO      I-O-RETCODE.                             RMP61C
 *                                                                             RMP61C
  9290-EXIT.  EXIT.                                                            RMP61C
      EJECT                                                                    RMP61C
  9300-DEL-JRNL.                                                               RMP61C
 *                                                                             RMP61C
      MOVE CA-TRMID       TO WS-JRNL-TERMID.                                   RMP61C
      EXEC CICS DELETEQ TS                                                     RMP61C
                QUEUE(WS-JRNL-NAME)                                            RMP61C
                RESP(CICS-RESP)                                                RMP61C
                END-EXEC.                                                      RMP61C
      IF  CICS-RESP EQUAL DFHRESP(QIDERR)                                      RMP61C
          NEXT SENTENCE                                                        RMP61C
      ELSE                                                                     RMP61C
          IF  CICS-RESP EQUAL DFHRESP(NORMAL)                                  RMP61C
              NEXT SENTENCE                                                    RMP61C
          ELSE                                                                 RMP61C
              MOVE 00025 TO CA-ERR-NUM-PRG                                     RMP61C
              MOVE 'A'   TO CA-ERR-TYPE                                        RMP61C
              PERFORM 9000-ERR-RTNE THRU 9000-ERR-EXIT.                        RMP61C
 *                                                                             RMP61C
  9300-EXIT.   EXIT.                                                           RMP61C
 *                                                                               CL*15
```

Appendix

B

Error-Processing Program ISS03C

```
IDENTIFICATION DIVISION.                                                 10/13/92
PROGRAM-ID.          ISS03C.                                             ISS03C
AUTHOR.              JOHN J. J. LOUGHLIN - CGA.                            LV004
DATE-WRITTEN.        MAY 1989.                                           ISS03C
INSTALLATION.        METRA                                               ISS03C
REMARKS.                                                                 ISS03C
   THIS PROGRAM          :  ISS03C                                       ISS03C
        CICS TRANSACTION:  IS00                                          ISS03C
        BMS MAPS USED   :  ISM00M                                        ISS03C
ENVIRONMENT DIVISION.                                                    ISS03C
DATA DIVISION.                                                           ISS03C
    EJECT                                                                ISS03C
WORKING-STORAGE SECTION.                                                 ISS03C
77  PAN-VALET PICTURE X(24) VALUE '004ISS03C    10/13/92'.               ISS03C
01  WS-PROG-NAME                PIC X(08) VALUE 'ISS03C '.               ISS03C
01  WS-TRNID                    PIC X(04) VALUE 'IS00'.                  ISS03C
01  WS-MAP-NAME                 PIC X(08) VALUE '        '.              ISS03C
01  WS-MAPSET-NAME              PIC X(08) VALUE '        '.              ISS03C
01  WS-TABLE-NAME               PIC X(08) VALUE 'ISS03A  '.                CL**4
01  WS-MQ-MIN                   PIC S9(04) COMP  VALUE +0.               ISS03C
01  WS-ERR-NUM                  PIC S9(04) COMP.                         ISS03C
01  UNKNOWN-SW                  PIC X(01) VALUE '0'.                     ISS03C
    88  KNOWN                             VALUE '0'.                     ISS03C
01  WS-ZERO                     PIC S9(04) COMP VALUE +0.                ISS03C
*                                                                        ISS03C
01  TS-JRNL.                                                             ISS03C
*                                                                        ISS03C
     05  TS-JRNL-KEY.                                                    ISS03C
*                                                                        ISS03C
          10  TS-FILENAME             PIC X(08).                         ISS03C
*                                                                        ISS03C
          10  TS-KEY                  PIC X(40).                         ISS03C
*                                                                        ISS03C
     05  TS-JDATA.                                                       ISS03C
         10  TS-JRNL-RECLEN              PIC S9(04) COMP.                ISS03C
         10  TS-JRNL-JFLEID              PIC S9(04) COMP.                ISS03C
```

```
          10  TS-JRNL-JTYPID              PIC  X(02).            ISS03C
 *                                                               ISS03C
  01  EXIT-SW                    PIC 9(01) VALUE 0.              ISS03C
 *                                                               ISS03C
      88  NO-EXIT                          VALUE 0.              ISS03C
 *                                                               ISS03C
      88  EXIT-SW-ON                        VALUE 1 2.           ISS03C
 *                                                               ISS03C
  01  JRNL-LNGTH                PIC S9(04) COMP VALUE +54.       ISS03C
 *                                                               ISS03C
  01  WS-JRNL-NAME.                                              ISS03C
 *                                                               ISS03C
      05  WS-JRNL-TERMID         PIC X(04).                      ISS03C
 *                                                               ISS03C
      05  WS-JRNL-FILL           PIC X(04) VALUE 'JRNL'.         ISS03C
  01  WS-QUEUE-NAME.                                             ISS03C
      05  WS-QUEUE-TRMID         PIC X(04).                      ISS03C
      05  WS-QUEUE-FILLER        PIC X(04) VALUE 'JRNL'.         ISS03C
 *                                                                 CL**4
  01  ITEM-NO                    PIC S9(04) COMP VALUE +0.       ISS03C
 *                                                                 CL**4
  01  CHECK-WRITE-TABLE.                                         ISS03C
      05   CHECK-WRT-ENTRY OCCURS 100 TIMES                      ISS03C
           INDEXED BY WRT-TBL-INDX WRT-TBL-MAX.                  ISS03C
 *                                                               ISS03C
           10 CHK-WRT-KEY.                                       ISS03C
 *                                                               ISS03C
               15  CWK-FILENAME         PIC X(08).               ISS03C
 *                                                               ISS03C
               15  CWK-KEY              PIC X(40).               ISS03C
 *                                                               ISS03C
  01  CICS-RESP                  PIC S9(08) COMP.                ISS03C
  01  CA-LENGTH                  PIC S9(4)   COMP  VALUE +375.   ISS03C
  01  CA-JOURNAL-LENGTH          PIC S9(4)   COMP  VALUE +66.    ISS03C
  01  CA-ERR-LENGTH              PIC S9(4)   COMP  VALUE +262.   ISS03C
 *                                                               ISS03C
  01  MENU                       PIC X(01) VALUE 'M'.            ISS03C
 *                                                               ISS03C
 ++INCLUDE RMESSAGE                                                CL**2
 *                                                               ISS03C
  01  MSGA.                                                      ISS03C
      05  FILLER                 PIC X(28)                       ISS03C
               VALUE 'AN ERROR OCCURED IN PROGRAM '.             ISS03C
      05  PGRM-ID                PIC X(08).                      ISS03C
      05  FILLER                 PIC X(19)                       ISS03C
               VALUE 'THE EIBRSP CODE IS '.                      ISS03C
 *                                                               ISS03C
  01  WS-MSG-LINE                PIC X(79)    VALUE SPACES.      ISS03C
 *                                                               ISS03C
 ++INCLUDE RMCACOMM                                                CL**2
 *                                                               ISS03C
 ++INCLUDE RMCAERR                                                 CL**2
 *                                                               ISS03C
 ++INCLUDE ISERRM                                                  CL**2
 *                                                               ISS03C
 *                                                               ISS03C
 ++INCLUDE RMJRNCOM                                                CL**2
 *                                                               ISS03C
  01  MTIME                      PIC S9(12) COMP.                ISS03C
  01  FDATE                      PIC X(08).                      ISS03C
  01  ADATE                      PIC X(08).                      ISS03C
  01  FTIME.                                                     ISS03C
      05  FHTIME                 PIC X(05).                      ISS03C
      05  FILLER                 PIC X(03).                      ISS03C
```

```
*                                                                 ISS03C
*                                                                 ISS03C
*                                                                 ISS03C
 01  DFHAID COPY DFHAID.                                          ISS03C
*                                                                 ISS03C
 01  DFHBMSCA COPY DFHBMSCA.                                      ISS03C
 LINKAGE SECTION.                                                 ISS03C
 01  DFHCOMMAREA.                                                 ISS03C
*-----------------------------------------------------------*     ISS03C
*- RM STANDARD CICS/VS COMMAREA - LENGTH 375 BYTES.  11/89 -*     ISS03C
*-----------------------------------------------------------*     ISS03C
     02  DFH-FIX-COMMAREA.                                        ISS03C
         10  DFH-USERID                 PIC X(08).                ISS03C
         10  DFH-TRMID                  PIC X(04).                ISS03C
         10  DFH-ATTN-KEY               PIC X(01).                ISS03C
         10  DFH-TRNID                  PIC X(04).                ISS03C
         10  DFH-USER-AUTH              PIC X(01).                ISS03C
             88  USER-AUTHORIZED            VALUE 'Y'.            ISS03C
         10  DFH-MENU-PTR               PIC 9(01).                ISS03C
         10  DFH-MENU-STACK.                                      ISS03C
             15  DFH-MENU-PGM                                     ISS03C
                 OCCURS 8 TIMES         PIC X(08).                ISS03C
         10  DFH-PGM-PTR                PIC 9(01).                ISS03C
         10  DFH-PGM-STACK.                                       ISS03C
             15  DFH-PGM-NAME                                     ISS03C
                 OCCURS 8 TIMES         PIC X(08).                ISS03C
         10  DFH-TEMPQ-PTR              PIC 9(01).                ISS03C
         10  DFH-TEMPQ-STACK.                                     ISS03C
             15  DFH-TEMPQ-NAME                                   ISS03C
                 OCCURS 8 TIMES.                                  ISS03C
                 20  DFH-TEMPQ-ID.                                ISS03C
                     25  DFH-TEMPQ-TRMID PIC X(04).               ISS03C
                     25  DFH-TEMPQ-TRNID PIC X(04).               ISS03C
                 20  DFH-TEMPQ-KEY      PIC S9(04) COMP.          ISS03C
         10  DFH-KEY-AREA               PIC X(40).                ISS03C
         10  DFH-MAPSET                 PIC X(08).                ISS03C
         10  DFH-MAPNAME                PIC X(08).                ISS03C
         10  DFH-CURSOR-POS             PIC S9(04) COMP.          ISS03C
         10  DFH-OPT                    PIC 9(02).                ISS03C
         10  DFH-DEST-PGM               PIC X(08).                ISS03C
         10  DFH-PF9-SW                 PIC X(01).                ISS03C
             88  PF9-VALID                          VALUE 'Y'.    ISS03C
         10  DFH-ERROR-DATA.                                      ISS03C
             15  DFH-ERR-PROGRAM        PIC X(08).                ISS03C
             15  DFH-ERR-RSRCE          PIC X(08).                ISS03C
             15  DFH-ERR-TYPE           PIC X(01).                ISS03C
         10  DFH-ERROR-NUM.                                       ISS03C
             15  DFH-ERR-NUM-SYS        PIC S9(04) COMP.          ISS03C
             15  DFH-ERR-NUM-PRG        PIC 9(05).                ISS03C
         10  DFH-ERR-PROG-TYPE          PIC X(01).                ISS03C
         10  DFH-QUEUE-ID               PIC X(08).                ISS03C
         10  DFH-SP                     PIC 9(01).                ISS03C
         10  DFH-MAP-PTR                PIC S9(04) COMP.          ISS03C
         10  DFH-JUMP-IND               PIC X(01).                ISS03C
         10  DFH-INST-NUM               PIC S9(04) COMP.          ISS03C
         10  DFH-PFKEY-NUM              PIC S9(04) COMP.          ISS03C
         10  FILLER                     PIC X(35).                ISS03C
         10  DFH-VAR-COMMAREA.                                    ISS03C
             15  FILLER                 PIC X(01).                ISS03C
    02  DFH-VAR-COMMAREA REDEFINES DFH-FIX-COMMAREA.              ISS03C
     05  DFH-CA-X-ERR-TYPE         PIC X(01).                     ISS03C
     05  DFH-CA-X-ERR-NUM          PIC 9(05).                     ISS03C
     05  DFH-CA-X-ERR-INST-NUM     PIC S9(04) COMP.               ISS03C
     05  DFH-CA-X-ERR-PFKEY-NUM    PIC S9(04) COMP.               ISS03C
```

```
           05  DFH-CA-X-ERR-MSG          PIC X(79).                     ISS03C
           05  DFH-CA-X-ERR-INST0        PIC X(79).                     ISS03C
           05  DFH-CA-X-ERR-PFKEY0       PIC X(79).                     ISS03C
           05  DFH-CA-X-ERR-PROG-TYPE    PIC X(01).                     ISS03C
           05  DFH-CA-X-ERR-CURSOR-POS   PIC S9(04) COMP.               ISS03C
           05  DFH-CA-X-FILLER           PIC X(12).                     ISS03C
           05  DFH-FILLER               PIC X(103).                     ISS03C
      *-                                                                   CL**4
       01  PARMLIST.                                                       CL**4
           05  SET-BY-CICS                  PIC S9(08) COMP.               CL**4
           05  TABLE-PTR                    PIC S9(08) COMP.               CL**4
      *-                                                                   CL**4
       01  RM-MESSAGES.                                                    CL**4
           05  MSG-TABLE.                                                  CL**4
              10  MSG-ENTRY OCCURS 630 TIMES                               CL**4
                  ASCENDING KEY IS ME-MSG-NUM                              CL**4
                  INDEXED BY MSG-INDX.                                     CL**4
                   15  ME-MSG-NUM          PIC X(05).                      CL**4
                   15  ME-MSG              PIC X(77).                      CL**4
           05  MSG-ENTRY-X  REDEFINES MSG-TABLE OCCURS 630 TIMES.          CL**4
              10  ME-MSG-X                  PIC X(82).                     CL**4
      *                                                                 ISS03C
           EJECT                                                        ISS03C
       PROCEDURE DIVISION.                                              ISS03C
                                                                        ISS03C
       0000-MAINLINE-CONTROL.                                           ISS03C
           EXEC CICS LOAD PROGRAM (WS-TABLE-NAME)                          CL**4
                SET  (TABLE-PTR)                                           CL**4
                RESP (CICS-RESP)                                           CL**4
           END-EXEC.                                                       CL**4
                                                                           CL**4
           IF CICS-RESP = DFHRESP (NORMAL)                                 CL**4
              SERVICE RELOAD RM-MESSAGES                                   CL**4
           ELSE                                                            CL**4
              MOVE 00025 TO CA-ERR-NUM-PRG                                 CL**4
              MOVE 'A'   TO CA-ERR-TYPE                                    CL**4
              PERFORM 9000-ERR-RTNE THRU 9000-ERR-EXIT.                    CL**4
                                                                           CL**4
           IF  EIBCALEN EQUAL +262                                      ISS03C
               PERFORM 1200-INPF-LOOKUP          THRU 1200-EXIT         ISS03C
               IF  DFH-CA-X-ERR-TYPE EQUAL 'P'                          ISS03C
                   PERFORM 1000-LOOKUP           THRU 1000-EXIT         ISS03C
               ELSE                                                     ISS03C
                   PERFORM 1100-LOOKUP           THRU 1100-EXIT         ISS03C
           ELSE                                                         ISS03C
               IF  EIBCALEN EQUAL +375                                  ISS03C
                   PERFORM 2000-ABEND-RTNE   THRU 2000-EXIT             ISS03C
               ELSE                                                     ISS03C
                   PERFORM 3000-ABEND-RTNE   THRU 3000-EXIT.            ISS03C
           PERFORM 9000-CICS-RETURN.                                    ISS03C
                                                                        ISS03C
      *                                                                 ISS03C
           EJECT                                                        ISS03C
      *                                                                 ISS03C
       1000-LOOKUP.                                                     ISS03C
      *                                                                 ISS03C
           IF  DFH-CA-X-ERR-NUM EQUAL ZERO                              ISS03C
               MOVE SPACES               TO DFH-CA-X-ERR-MSG            ISS03C
               GO TO 1000-EXIT.                                         ISS03C
           MOVE 0 TO UNKNOWN-SW.                                        ISS03C
           SEARCH ALL MSG-ENTRY                                         ISS03C
                  AT END MOVE 1 TO UNKNOWN-SW                           ISS03C
                  WHEN ME-MSG-NUM (MSG-INDX) EQUAL DFH-CA-X-ERR-NUM.    ISS03C
           IF  KNOWN                                                    ISS03C
```

```
         MOVE ME-MSG-X (MSG-INDX) TO DFH-CA-X-ERR-MSG              ISS03C
     ELSE                                                          ISS03C
         MOVE 'UNKNOWN            ' TO DFH-CA-X-ERR-MSG.           ISS03C
     IF  DFH-CA-X-ERR-PROG-TYPE EQUAL MENU                         ISS03C
         EXEC CICS LINK PROGRAM('ISS01C')                          ISS03C
                        RESP(CICS-RESP)                            ISS03C
                        COMMAREA(DFHCOMMAREA)                      ISS03C
                        LENGTH(CA-ERR-LENGTH)                      ISS03C
                        END-EXEC                                   ISS03C
         IF  CICS-RESP = DFHRESP(NORMAL)                           ISS03C
             NEXT SENTENCE                                         ISS03C
         ELSE                                                      ISS03C
             PERFORM 9000-ERR-RTNE THRU 9000-ERR-EXIT.             ISS03C
*                                                                  ISS03C
 1000-EXIT.  EXIT.                                                 ISS03C
     EJECT                                                         ISS03C
 1100-LOOKUP.                                                      ISS03C
*                                                                  ISS03C
     IF  DFH-CA-X-ERR-NUM EQUAL ZERO                               ISS03C
         MOVE SPACES               TO DFH-CA-X-ERR-MSG             ISS03C
         GO TO 1100-EXIT.                                          ISS03C
     MOVE DFH-CA-X-ERR-NUM       TO WS-ERR-NUM.                    ISS03C
     MOVE 0                      TO UNKNOWN-SW.                    ISS03C
     SEARCH ALL ERR-MSG                                            ISS03C
            AT END MOVE 1         TO UNKNOWN-SW                    ISS03C
            WHEN ERR-KEY (ERR-INDEX)   EQUAL WS-ERR-NUM.           ISS03C
     IF  KNOWN                                                     ISS03C
         MOVE ERR-MSG0 (ERR-INDEX) TO DFH-CA-X-ERR-MSG             ISS03C
     ELSE                                                          ISS03C
         MOVE 'UNKNOWN'            TO DFH-CA-X-ERR-MSG.            ISS03C
*                                                                  ISS03C
 1100-EXIT.  EXIT.                                                 ISS03C
     EJECT                                                         ISS03C
 1200-INPF-LOOKUP.                                                 ISS03C
*                                                                  ISS03C
     IF  DFH-CA-X-ERR-INST-NUM EQUAL WS-ZERO                       ISS03C
         NEXT SENTENCE                                             ISS03C
     ELSE                                                          ISS03C
         PERFORM 1200-SEARCH-IN-PF-TBL      THRU 1200-SEARCH-EXIT  ISS03C
          VARYING INPF-INDX                                        ISS03C
          FROM 1 BY 1                                              ISS03C
          UNTIL INPF-INDX GREATER THAN INSTR-TBLE-SIZE             ISS03C
          OR IN-PF-NUMBER (INPF-INDX) EQUAL DFH-CA-X-ERR-INST-NUM  ISS03C
         IF  IN-PF-NUMBER (INPF-INDX) EQUAL DFH-CA-X-ERR-INST-NUM  ISS03C
             MOVE IN-PF-MESSAGE(INPF-INDX) TO DFH-CA-X-ERR-INST0   ISS03C
         ELSE                                                      ISS03C
             MOVE 'UNKNOWN'                TO DFH-CA-X-ERR-INST0.  ISS03C
     IF  DFH-CA-X-ERR-PFKEY-NUM EQUAL WS-ZERO                      ISS03C
         GO TO 1200-EXIT.                                          ISS03C
     PERFORM 1200-SEARCH-IN-PF-TBL      THRU 1200-SEARCH-EXIT      ISS03C
        VARYING INPF-INDX                                          ISS03C
        FROM 1 BY 1                                                ISS03C
        UNTIL INPF-INDX GREATER THAN INSTR-TBLE-SIZE               ISS03C
        OR IN-PF-NUMBER (INPF-INDX) EQUAL DFH-CA-X-ERR-PFKEY-NUM.  ISS03C
     IF  IN-PF-NUMBER (INPF-INDX) EQUAL DFH-CA-X-ERR-PFKEY-NUM     ISS03C
         MOVE IN-PF-MESSAGE(INPF-INDX) TO DFH-CA-X-ERR-PFKEY0      ISS03C
         ELSE                                                      ISS03C
             MOVE 'UNKNOWN'            TO DFH-CA-X-ERR-PFKEY0.     ISS03C
                                                                   ISS03C
 1200-EXIT.  EXIT.                                                 ISS03C
     EJECT                                                         ISS03C
 1200-SEARCH-IN-PF-TBL.                                            ISS03C
*                                                                  ISS03C
*                                                                  ISS03C
```

```
 1200-SEARCH-EXIT.  EXIT.                                           ISS03C
     EJECT                                                          ISS03C
 2000-ABEND-RTNE.                                                   ISS03C
*                                                                   ISS03C
     MOVE DFHCOMMAREA                  TO CA-COMMAREA.              ISS03C
     MOVE LOW-VALUES                   TO ISERRM1O.                 ISS03C
     MOVE 0 TO UNKNOWN-SW.                                          ISS03C
     SEARCH ALL MSG-ENTRY                                           ISS03C
            AT END MOVE 1 TO UNKNOWN-SW                             ISS03C
            WHEN ME-MSG-NUM (MSG-INDX) EQUAL CA-ERR-NUM-PRG.        ISS03C
     IF  KNOWN                                                      ISS03C
         MOVE ME-MSG (MSG-INDX) TO MSG0O                            ISS03C
     ELSE                                                           ISS03C
         MOVE 'UNKNOWN            ' TO MSG0O.                       ISS03C
     MOVE CA-ERR-NUM-SYS          TO WS-ERR-NUM.                    ISS03C
     MOVE 0                       TO UNKNOWN-SW.                    ISS03C
     SEARCH ALL ERR-MSG                                             ISS03C
            AT END MOVE 1           TO UNKNOWN-SW                   ISS03C
            WHEN ERR-KEY (ERR-INDEX)   EQUAL WS-ERR-NUM.            ISS03C
     IF  KNOWN                                                      ISS03C
         MOVE ERR-MSG0 (ERR-INDEX) TO EIBRSPO                       ISS03C
     ELSE                                                           ISS03C
         MOVE 'UNKNOWN'              TO EIBRSPO.                    ISS03C
     PERFORM 2020-FORMAT-MAP          THRU 2020-EXIT.               ISS03C
     PERFORM 2030-SEND-MAP            THRU 2030-EXIT.               ISS03C
     PERFORM 2040-ERASE-QSTACK        THRU 2040-ERAS-QSTCK-EXIT.    ISS03C
     PERFORM 2060-ERASE-MSTACK        THRU 2060-ERAS-MSTCK-EXIT.    ISS03C
     MOVE 0                         TO ITEM-NO.                     ISS03C
     SET WRT-TBL-MAX                TO 100.                         ISS03C
     MOVE 0                         TO EXIT-SW.                     ISS03C
     MOVE SPACES                    TO CHECK-WRITE-TABLE.           ISS03C
     PERFORM 2080-CREATE-JRNL-RCDS   THRU 2080-JRNL-EXIT            ISS03C
          UNTIL EXIT-SW-ON.                                         ISS03C
     PERFORM 2070-ERASE-JSTACK        THRU 2070-ERAS-JSTCK-EXIT.    ISS03C
     EXEC CICS SEND CONTROL FREEKB END-EXEC.                        ISS03C
*                                                                   ISS03C
 2000-EXIT.  EXIT.                                                  ISS03C
     SKIP3                                                          ISS03C
 2010-SEARCH-ERR-TBL.                                               ISS03C
*                                                                   ISS03C
*                                                                   ISS03C
 2010-EXIT.  EXIT.                                                  ISS03C
     SKIP3                                                          ISS03C
 2020-FORMAT-MAP.                                                   ISS03C
*                                                                   ISS03C
     EXEC CICS ASKTIME ABSTIME(MTIME) END-EXEC.                     ISS03C
     EXEC CICS FORMATTIME ABSTIME(MTIME)                            ISS03C
               DATESEP    MMDDYY(FDATE)                             ISS03C
               TIME(FTIME) TIMESEP                                  ISS03C
     END-EXEC.                                                      ISS03C
     MOVE FDATE                     TO MDATEO.                      ISS03C
     MOVE FHTIME                    TO MTIMEO.                      ISS03C
     MOVE CA-USERID                 TO MOPIDO.                      ISS03C
     MOVE CA-TRMID                  TO MTRMIDO.                     ISS03C
     MOVE CA-TRNID                  TO CTRNO.                       ISS03C
     MOVE CA-MENU-PGM (1)           TO CSTK1O.                      ISS03C
     MOVE CA-MENU-PGM (2)           TO CSTK2O.                      ISS03C
     MOVE CA-MENU-PGM (3)           TO CSTK3O.                      ISS03C
     MOVE CA-MENU-PGM (4)           TO CSTK4O.                      ISS03C
     MOVE CA-MENU-PGM (5)           TO CSTK5O.                      ISS03C
     MOVE CA-PGM-NAME (1)           TO JSTK1O.                      ISS03C
     MOVE CA-PGM-NAME (2)           TO JSTK2O.                      ISS03C
     MOVE CA-PGM-NAME (3)           TO JSTK3O.                      ISS03C
     MOVE CA-PGM-NAME (4)           TO JSTK4O.                      ISS03C
```

```
           MOVE CA-PGM-NAME (5)          TO JSTK5O.                     ISS03C
           MOVE CA-TEMPQ-ID (1)          TO QSTK1O.                     ISS03C
           MOVE CA-TEMPQ-ID (2)          TO QSTK2O.                     ISS03C
           MOVE CA-TEMPQ-ID (3)          TO QSTK3O.                     ISS03C
           MOVE CA-TEMPQ-ID (4)          TO QSTK4O.                     ISS03C
           MOVE CA-TEMPQ-ID (5)          TO QSTK5O                      ISS03C
           MOVE CA-KEY-AREA              TO KEYVO.                      ISS03C
           MOVE CA-MAP-PTR               TO MPTRO.                      ISS03C
           MOVE CA-MAP-QUE-CNT           TO MPCNTO.                       CL**4
           IF  CA-PGM-STACK EQUAL SPACES                                ISS03C
               MOVE CA-MENU-PGM (CA-MENU-PTR) TO CRPRGO                 ISS03C
           ELSE                                                         ISS03C
               MOVE CA-PGM-NAME (CA-PGM-PTR) TO CRPRGO.                 ISS03C
           MOVE CA-MAPNAME               TO CMAPO.                      ISS03C
           MOVE CA-MAPSET                TO CMAPSO.                     ISS03C
           MOVE CA-CURSOR-POS            TO CPOSO.                      ISS03C
           MOVE CA-OPT                   TO OPTO.                       ISS03C
           MOVE CA-DEST-PGM              TO DPRGO.                      ISS03C
           MOVE CA-PF9-SW                TO PF9O.                       ISS03C
           MOVE CA-ERR-RSRCE             TO EIBRSRCO.                   ISS03C
           IF CA-ATTN-KEY = DFHENTER                                      CL**9
              MOVE 'ENTER' TO  EIBAIDO                                    CL**9
           ELSE                                                           CL**9
           IF CA-ATTN-KEY = DFHCLEAR                                      CL**9
              MOVE 'CLEAR' TO  EIBAIDO                                    CL**9
           ELSE                                                           CL**9
           IF CA-ATTN-KEY = DFHPA1                                        CL**9
              MOVE 'PA1'   TO  EIBAIDO                                    CL**9
           ELSE                                                           CL**9
           IF CA-ATTN-KEY = DFHPA2                                        CL**9
              MOVE 'PA2'   TO  EIBAIDO                                    CL**9
           ELSE                                                           CL**9
           IF CA-ATTN-KEY = DFHPA3                                        CL**9
              MOVE 'PA3'   TO  EIBAIDO                                    CL**9
           ELSE                                                           CL**9
           IF CA-ATTN-KEY = DFHPF1                                        CL**9
              MOVE 'PF1'   TO  EIBAIDO                                    CL**9
           ELSE                                                           CL**9
           IF CA-ATTN-KEY = DFHPF2                                        CL**9
              MOVE 'PF2'   TO  EIBAIDO                                    CL**9
           ELSE                                                           CL**9
           IF CA-ATTN-KEY = DFHPF3                                        CL**9
              MOVE 'PF3'   TO  EIBAIDO                                    CL**9
           ELSE                                                           CL**9
           IF CA-ATTN-KEY = DFHPF4                                        CL**9
              MOVE 'PF4'   TO  EIBAIDO                                    CL**9
           ELSE                                                           CL**9
           IF CA-ATTN-KEY = DFHPF5                                        CL**9
              MOVE 'PF5'   TO  EIBAIDO                                    CL**9
           ELSE                                                           CL**9
           IF CA-ATTN-KEY = DFHPF6                                        CL**9
              MOVE 'PF6'   TO  EIBAIDO                                    CL**9
           ELSE                                                           CL**9
           IF CA-ATTN-KEY = DFHPF7                                        CL**9
              MOVE 'PF7'   TO  EIBAIDO                                    CL**9
           ELSE                                                           CL**9
           IF CA-ATTN-KEY = DFHPF8                                        CL**9
              MOVE 'PF8'   TO  EIBAIDO                                    CL**9
           ELSE                                                           CL**9
           IF CA-ATTN-KEY = DFHPF9                                        CL**9
              MOVE 'PF9'   TO  EIBAIDO                                    CL**9
           ELSE                                                           CL**9
           IF CA-ATTN-KEY = DFHPF10                                       CL**9
              MOVE 'PF10'  TO  EIBAIDO                                    CL**9
```

```
      ELSE                                                        CL**9
      IF CA-ATTN-KEY = DFHPF11                                    CL**9
         MOVE 'PF11'  TO  EIBAIDO                                 CL**9
      ELSE                                                        CL**9
      IF CA-ATTN-KEY = DFHPF12                                    CL**9
         MOVE 'PF12'  TO  EIBAIDO                                 CL**9
      ELSE                                                        CL**9
      IF CA-ATTN-KEY = DFHPF13                                    CL**9
         MOVE 'PF13'  TO  EIBAIDO                                 CL**9
      ELSE                                                        CL**9
      IF CA-ATTN-KEY = DFHPF14                                    CL**9
         MOVE 'PF14'  TO  EIBAIDO                                 CL**9
      ELSE                                                        CL**9
      IF CA-ATTN-KEY = DFHPF15                                    CL**9
         MOVE 'PF15'  TO  EIBAIDO                                 CL**9
      ELSE                                                        CL**9
      IF CA-ATTN-KEY = DFHPF16                                    CL**9
         MOVE 'PF16'  TO  EIBAIDO                                 CL**9
      ELSE                                                        CL**9
      IF CA-ATTN-KEY = DFHPF17                                    CL**9
         MOVE 'PF17'  TO  EIBAIDO                                 CL**9
      ELSE                                                        CL**9
      IF CA-ATTN-KEY = DFHPF18                                    CL**9
         MOVE 'PF18'  TO  EIBAIDO                                 CL**9
      ELSE                                                        CL**9
      IF CA-ATTN-KEY = DFHPF19                                    CL**9
         MOVE 'PF19'  TO  EIBAIDO                                 CL**9
      ELSE                                                        CL**9
      IF CA-ATTN-KEY = DFHPF20                                    CL**9
         MOVE 'PF20'  TO  EIBAIDO                                 CL**9
      ELSE                                                        CL**9
      IF CA-ATTN-KEY = DFHPF21                                    CL**9
         MOVE 'PF21'  TO  EIBAIDO                                 CL**9
      ELSE                                                        CL**9
      IF CA-ATTN-KEY = DFHPF22                                    CL**9
         MOVE 'PF22'  TO  EIBAIDO                                 CL**9
      ELSE                                                        CL**9
      IF CA-ATTN-KEY = DFHPF23                                    CL**9
         MOVE 'PF23'  TO  EIBAIDO                                 CL**9
      ELSE                                                        CL**9
      IF CA-ATTN-KEY = DFHPF24                                    CL**9
         MOVE 'PF24'  TO  EIBAIDO                                 CL*10
      ELSE                                                        CL*10
         MOVE CA-ATTN-KEY  TO  EIBAIDO.                           CL*10
 *                                                               ISS03C
  2020-EXIT.  EXIT.                                              ISS03C
      EJECT                                                      ISS03C
  2030-SEND-MAP.                                                 ISS03C
 *                                                               ISS03C
          EXEC CICS SEND MAP('ISERRM1')                          ISS03C
                         MAPSET('ISERRM')                        ISS03C
                         FROM(ISERRM1O)                          ISS03C
                         ERASE                                   ISS03C
                         FREEKB                                  ISS03C
                         RESP(CICS-RESP)                         ISS03C
                         END-EXEC.                               ISS03C
      IF  CICS-RESP = DFHRESP(NORMAL)                            ISS03C
          NEXT SENTENCE                                          ISS03C
      ELSE                                                       ISS03C
          PERFORM 9000-ERR-RTNE THRU 9000-ERR-EXIT.              ISS03C
 *                                                               ISS03C
  2030-EXIT.  EXIT.                                              ISS03C
      EJECT                                                      ISS03C
  2040-ERASE-QSTACK.                                             ISS03C
```

```
*                                                                 ISS03C
    IF  CA-TEMPQ-STACK EQUAL SPACES                               ISS03C
        GO TO 2040-ERAS-QSTCK-EXIT.                               ISS03C
    PERFORM 2050-DELETE-QUEUE THRU 2050-DEL-QUE-EXIT              ISS03C
            VARYING CA-TEMPQ-PTR FROM 1 BY 1                      ISS03C
            UNTIL CA-TEMPQ-PTR GREATER THAN 8 OR                    CL**2
            CA-TEMPQ-ID (CA-TEMPQ-PTR) EQUAL SPACES.              ISS03C
*                                                                 ISS03C
 2040-ERAS-QSTCK-EXIT.  EXIT.                                     ISS03C
    SKIP3                                                         ISS03C
 2050-DELETE-QUEUE.                                               ISS03C
*                                                                 ISS03C
    MOVE CA-TEMPQ-ID (CA-TEMPQ-PTR) TO CA-QUEUE-ID                ISS03C
    EXEC CICS DELETEQ TS                                          ISS03C
             QUEUE(CA-QUEUE-ID)                                   ISS03C
             RESP(CICS-RESP)                                      ISS03C
             END-EXEC.                                            ISS03C
    IF  CICS-RESP EQUAL DFHRESP(QIDERR)                           ISS03C
        NEXT SENTENCE                                             ISS03C
    ELSE                                                          ISS03C
        IF  CICS-RESP EQUAL DFHRESP(NORMAL)                       ISS03C
            NEXT SENTENCE                                         ISS03C
        ELSE                                                      ISS03C
            MOVE 00025 TO CA-ERR-NUM-PRG                          ISS03C
            MOVE 'A'   TO CA-ERR-TYPE                             ISS03C
            PERFORM 9000-ERR-RTNE THRU 9000-ERR-EXIT.             ISS03C
                                                                  ISS03C
*                                                                 ISS03C
 2050-DEL-QUE-EXIT.  EXIT.                                        ISS03C
     EJECT                                                        ISS03C
 2060-ERASE-MSTACK.                                               ISS03C
*                                                                 ISS03C
    IF  CA-MAP-PTR GREATER THAN WS-MQ-MIN                         ISS03C
        MOVE CA-TRMID TO CA-QUEUE-TRMID                           ISS03C
        MOVE 'MAPS'   TO CA-QUEUE-MAPID                           ISS03C
        EXEC CICS DELETEQ TS                                      ISS03C
                 QUEUE(CA-QUEUE-ID)                               ISS03C
                 RESP(CICS-RESP)                                  ISS03C
                 END-EXEC                                         ISS03C
        IF  CICS-RESP EQUAL DFHRESP(QIDERR)                       ISS03C
            NEXT SENTENCE                                         ISS03C
        ELSE                                                      ISS03C
            IF  CICS-RESP EQUAL DFHRESP(NORMAL)                   ISS03C
                NEXT SENTENCE                                     ISS03C
            ELSE                                                  ISS03C
                MOVE 00025 TO CA-ERR-NUM-PRG                      ISS03C
                MOVE 'A'   TO CA-ERR-TYPE                         ISS03C
                PERFORM 9000-ERR-RTNE  THRU 9000-ERR-EXIT.        ISS03C
                                                                  ISS03C
*                                                                 ISS03C
 2060-ERAS-MSTCK-EXIT.  EXIT.                                     ISS03C
    EJECT                                                         ISS03C
 2070-ERASE-JSTACK.                                               ISS03C
*                                                                 ISS03C
    MOVE SPACES TO CA-PGM-STACK.                                  ISS03C
*                                                                 ISS03C
 2070-ERAS-JSTCK-EXIT.  EXIT.                                     ISS03C
    EJECT                                                         ISS03C
 2080-CREATE-JRNL-RCDS.                                           ISS03C
*                                                                 ISS03C
    PERFORM 2090-OBTAIN-QUEUE THRU 2090-EXIT.                     ISS03C
    IF  NO-EXIT                                                   ISS03C
        PERFORM 2091-CHECK-WRT-TBL THRU 2091-EXIT                 ISS03C
                VARYING WRT-TBL-INDX                              ISS03C
```

```
                FROM 1 BY 1                                      ISS03C
                UNTIL CHK-WRT-KEY (WRT-TBL-INDX)                 ISS03C
                EQUAL TS-KEY                                     ISS03C
                OR  CHK-WRT-KEY (WRT-TBL-INDX)                   ISS03C
                    EQUAL SPACES                                 ISS03C
                OR  WRT-TBL-INDX GREATER WRT-TBL-MAX             ISS03C
       IF  CHK-WRT-KEY (WRT-TBL-INDX) EQUAL TS-JRNL-KEY          ISS03C
           GO TO 2080-JRNL-EXIT                                  ISS03C
       ELSE                                                      ISS03C
           IF  CHK-WRT-KEY (WRT-TBL-INDX) EQUAL SPACES           ISS03C
               IF  WRT-TBL-INDX NOT GREATER THAN WRT-TBL-MAX     ISS03C
                 MOVE TS-JRNL-KEY TO CHK-WRT-KEY (WRT-TBL-INDX)  ISS03C
                 PERFORM 2092-BUILD-JOURNAL-COMMAREA THRU        ISS03C
                       2092-EXIT                                 ISS03C
                 PERFORM 2093-LINK-JRNL-PGM THRU 2093-EXIT       ISS03C
                 GO TO 2080-JRNL-EXIT.                           ISS03C
    PERFORM 2094-DELETE-JOURNAL-QUEUE THRU 2094-EXIT.            ISS03C
*                                                                ISS03C
2080-JRNL-EXIT.  EXIT.                                           ISS03C
2090-OBTAIN-QUEUE.                                               ISS03C
*                                                                ISS03C
    MOVE CA-TRMID   TO WS-QUEUE-TRMID.                           ISS03C
    ADD 1           TO ITEM-NO.                                  ISS03C
    EXEC CICS READQ TS QUEUE(WS-QUEUE-NAME)                      ISS03C
                       INTO(TS-JRNL)                             ISS03C
                       ITEM(ITEM-NO)                             ISS03C
                       LENGTH(JRNL-LNGTH)                        ISS03C
                       RESP(CICS-RESP)                           ISS03C
                       END-EXEC.                                 ISS03C
    IF  CICS-RESP EQUAL DFHRESP(NORMAL)                          ISS03C
        NEXT SENTENCE                                            ISS03C
    ELSE                                                         ISS03C
        IF CICS-RESP EQUAL DFHRESP(QIDERR)                       ISS03C
           MOVE 1   TO EXIT-SW                                   ISS03C
        ELSE                                                     ISS03C
           IF  CICS-RESP EQUAL DFHRESP(ITEMERR)                  ISS03C
               MOVE 2 TO EXIT-SW                                 ISS03C
           ELSE                                                  ISS03C
               MOVE 1 TO EXIT-SW.                                ISS03C
*                                                                ISS03C
2090-EXIT.  EXIT.                                                ISS03C
2091-CHECK-WRT-TBL.                                              ISS03C
*                                                                ISS03C
*                                                                ISS03C
2091-EXIT.  EXIT.                                                ISS03C
2092-BUILD-JOURNAL-COMMAREA.                                     ISS03C
*                                                                ISS03C
     MOVE TS-JRNL-RECLEN            TO CA-JRNL-RECLEN.           ISS03C
     MOVE TS-JRNL-JFLEID            TO CA-JRNL-JFLEID.           ISS03C
     MOVE TS-JRNL-JTYPID            TO CA-JRNL-JTYPID.           ISS03C
     MOVE TS-FILENAME               TO CA-JRNL-RESOURCE.         ISS03C
     MOVE TS-KEY                    TO CA-JRNL-FKEY.             ISS03C
     IF  CA-PGM-PTR GREATER THAN ZERO                            ISS03C
     MOVE CA-PGM-NAME (CA-PGM-PTR)  TO CA-JRNL-WORKPGM.          ISS03C
*                                                                ISS03C
2092-EXIT.  EXIT.                                                ISS03C
2093-LINK-JRNL-PGM.                                              ISS03C
*                                                                ISS03C
    EXEC CICS LINK PROGRAM('ISS09C')                             ISS03C
              COMMAREA(JOURNAL-COMMAREA)                         ISS03C
              LENGTH(CA-JOURNAL-LENGTH)                          ISS03C
              RESP(CICS-RESP)                                    ISS03C
              END-EXEC.                                          ISS03C
    IF  CICS-RESP = DFHRESP(NORMAL)                              ISS03C
```

```
               NEXT SENTENCE                                            ISS03C
           ELSE                                                         ISS03C
               MOVE 'LINK TO JOURNAL PROGRAM FAILED' TO MSG2O.          ISS03C
           IF  CA-JRNL-OK                                               ISS03C
               NEXT SENTENCE                                            ISS03C
           ELSE                                                         ISS03C
               MOVE 'INTEGRITY OF JOURNAL COMPROMISED' TO MSG2O.        ISS03C
      *                                                                 ISS03C
       2093-EXIT.  EXIT.                                                ISS03C
      *                                                                 ISS03C
      *                                                                 ISS03C
       2094-DELETE-JOURNAL-QUEUE.                                       ISS03C
      *                                                                 ISS03C
           MOVE CA-TRMID       TO WS-JRNL-TERMID.                       ISS03C
           EXEC CICS DELETEQ TS                                         ISS03C
                     QUEUE(WS-JRNL-NAME)                                ISS03C
                     RESP(CICS-RESP)                                    ISS03C
                     END-EXEC.                                          ISS03C
           IF  CICS-RESP EQUAL DFHRESP(QIDERR)                          ISS03C
               NEXT SENTENCE                                            ISS03C
           ELSE                                                         ISS03C
               IF  CICS-RESP EQUAL DFHRESP(NORMAL)                      ISS03C
                   NEXT SENTENCE                                        ISS03C
               ELSE                                                     ISS03C
                   MOVE 00025 TO CA-ERR-NUM-PRG                         ISS03C
                   MOVE 'A'   TO CA-ERR-TYPE                            ISS03C
                   PERFORM 9000-ERR-RTNE THRU 9000-ERR-EXIT.            ISS03C
                                                                        ISS03C
      *                                                                 ISS03C
       2094-EXIT.  EXIT.                                                ISS03C
      *                                                                 ISS03C
       3000-ABEND-RTNE.                                                 ISS03C
      *                                                                 ISS03C
           MOVE 'AN UNAUTHORIZED ABEND HAS OCCURRED -                   ISS03C
      -    'NO CLEANUP PERFORMED' TO WS-MSG-LINE.                       ISS03C
           PERFORM 9300-SEND-MSG THRU 9300-EXIT.                        ISS03C
           PERFORM 9999-CICS-RETURN.                                    ISS03C
      *                                                                 ISS03C
       3000-EXIT.  EXIT.                                                ISS03C
       9000-CICS-RETURN.                                                ISS03C
      *                                                                 ISS03C
           EXEC CICS RETURN                                             ISS03C
              END-EXEC.                                                 ISS03C
      *                                                                 ISS03C
       9000-EXIT.  EXIT.                                                ISS03C
           EJECT                                                        ISS03C
       9000-ERR-RTNE.                                                   ISS03C
      *                                                                 ISS03C
           EXEC CICS ABEND ABCODE ('XERR')                              ISS03C
                           NOHANDLE                                     ISS03C
                           END-EXEC.                                    ISS03C
      *                                                                 ISS03C
       9000-ERR-EXIT.  EXIT.                                            ISS03C
      *                                                                 ISS03C
           EJECT                                                        ISS03C
       9300-SEND-MSG.                                                   ISS03C
      *                                                                 ISS03C
           EXEC CICS SEND TEXT FROM (WS-MSG-LINE)                       ISS03C
                     RESP(CICS-RESP)                                    ISS03C
                     LENGTH(79)                                         ISS03C
                     FREEKB                                             ISS03C
                     ERASE                                              ISS03C
                END-EXEC.                                               ISS03C
           IF  CICS-RESP = DFHRESP(NORMAL)                              ISS03C
```

```
              NEXT SENTENCE                                                 ISS03C
          ELSE                                                              ISS03C
              PERFORM 9000-ERR-RTNE THRU 9000-ERR-EXIT.                     ISS03C
      *                                                                     ISS03C
       9300-EXIT.  EXIT.                                                    ISS03C
      *                                                                     ISS03C
       9999-CICS-RETURN.                                                    ISS03C
          EXEC CICS RETURN                                                  ISS03C
             END-EXEC.                                                      ISS03C
```

Appendix

C

Sample Flowcharts

```
9. FLOWCHARTS                 METRA COMMUTER RAILS
-------------------------------------------------------------------------------------------------------------------------------------
|JOB - GLE70      GLE EDIT 10/91                      MSGCLASS - L                                                  AS OF: 11/19/91  |
|SYS - GLE70                                             CLASS - G                                                         12:32:45  |
|PROGRAMMER NAME -GLE EDIT 10/91                         ACCTG - (9000,AGLP)                                                         |
_____________________________________________________________________________________________________________________________________
JOB - GLE70

 GGGGGGGGGG   LL            EEEEEEEEEEEE  777777777777    00000000
GGGGGGGGGGGG  LL            EEEEEEEEEEEE  77777777777    0000000000
GG        GG  LL            EE            77       77   00        00
GG            LL            EE                   77     00        00
GG            LL            EE                  77      00        00
GG            LL            EEEEEEEE           77       00        00
GG     GGGGG  LL            EEEEEEEE           77       00        00
GG     GGGGG  LL            EE                 77       00        00
GG        GG  LL            EE                 77       00        00
GG        GG  LL            EE                 77       00        00
GGGGGGGGGGGG  LLLLLLLLLLLL  EEEEEEEEEEEE       77        0000000000
 GGGGGGGGGG   LLLLLLLLLLLL  EEEEEEEEEEEE       77         00000000
                          //*
                          //*
PROC - UCC11RMS

UU        UU   CCCCCCCCCC    CCCCCCCCCC        11            11        RRRRRRRRRRR   MM        MM   SSSSSSSSSS
UU        UU  CCCCCCCCCCCC  CCCCCCCCCCCC      111           111        RRRRRRRRRRRR  MMM      MMM  SSSSSSSSSSSS
UU        UU  CC        CC  CC        CC     1111          1111        RR        RR  MMMM    MMMM  SS        SS
UU        UU  CC            CC                 11            11        RR        RR  MM MM  MM MM  SS
UU        UU  CC            CC                 11            11        RR        RR  MM  MMMM  MM  SSS
UU        UU  CC            CC                 11            11        RRRRRRRRRRRR  MM   MM   MM   SSSSSSSSS
UU        UU  CC            CC                 11            11        RRRRRRRRRRR   MM        MM    SSSSSSSSS
UU        UU  CC            CC                 11            11        RR    RR      MM        MM           SSS
UU        UU  CC            CC                 11            11        RR     RR     MM        MM            SS
UU        UU  CC        CC  CC        CC       11            11        RR      RR    MM        MM  SS        SS
UUUUUUUUUUUU  CCCCCCCCCCCC  CCCCCCCCCCCC   1111111111    1111111111    RR       RR   MM        MM  SSSSSSSSSSSS
 UUUUUUUUUU    CCCCCCCCCC    CCCCCCCCCC    1111111111    1111111111    RR        RR  MM        MM   SSSSSSSSSS


$/*
                          $/*********USE FILE=70 FOR SOURCE IN "NIRXP.GLE70.DATA" 1-2
                          $/*********USE FILE=90 FOR SOURCE IN "NIRXP.GLE90.DATA" 1-2
                          $/*
                          //*
```

```
                         //*********************************************************************
                         //*        FORMERLY UCC11RMS
                         //*        CA-11 V2.0 RUN MANAGER (RMS) PROCEDURE
                         //*
                         //*        WARNING: IF YOU HAVE INSTALLED THE CA-DYNAM/TLMS INTERFACE
                         //*        TO CA-11, THEN THE CAIVMFI DD STATEMENT IS NEEDED
                         //*********************************************************************
                         //*
                                                                                                   INDEX NUMBER    1   1   1
  JOB -GLE70                GLE EDIT 10/91
  PROC-UCC11RMS  UCC11RMS  CA-11 RERUN/RESTART MANAGER
  PGM -U11RMS    RMS@20
  PARM-P
  COND-


                                                  +------------+              +-----------+  NAME-REPORT
                                                  |            |              |           |  DDN -RMSRPT     CLAS-L
                                 NO INPUT FILES+------>|  U11RMS    |-------------->|     1     |  COPY-   1
                                                  |            |              |      .___/
                                                  +------------+              +_____/

                                                  J-REGION = 8M
                                                  SYSUDUMP = L
PROC - GLE70

 GGGGGGGGGG   LL           EEEEEEEEEEEE  777777777777    00000000
GGGGGGGGGGGG  LL           EEEEEEEEEEEE  77777777777    0000000000
GG        GG  LL           EE            77       77   00        00
GG            LL           EE                    77    00        00
GG            LL           EE                   77     00        00
GG            LL           EEEEEEEE            77      00        00
GG      GGGGG LL           EEEEEEEE            77      00        00
GG      GGGGG LL           EE                  77      00        00
GG         GG LL           EE                  77      00        00
GG         GG LL           EE                  77      00        00
GGGGGGGGGGGG  LLLLLLLLLLLL EEEEEEEEEEEE        77       0000000000
 GGGGGGGGGG   LLLLLLLLLLLL EEEEEEEEEEEE        77        00000000
                         //*
                         //*********************************************************************
                         //*       I N P U T   P R O C E S S O R   P R O C E D U R E
                         //*********************************************************************
                         //*

                                                                                                   INDEX NUMBER    1   2   1
  JOB -GLE70                GLE EDIT 10/91
```

```
  PROC-GLE70     GLE70
  PGM -IDCAMS    INIT      IBM MVS UTILITY
  PARM-
  COND-
DSN -NIRXP.PROD.PARMLIB(GLEDEL)
                                -----------                                            3  -----------  DSN -NIRVP.GL70.NEWTRA1
DDN -SYSIN      DISP-S,*,*      (         (                                       PRE  3 (         (   DDN -SYSIN003   DISP-N,C,*
UNIT-3380       BLK - 6160     (     2   (---------+                            +------>(     4   (    UNIT-DISK       BLK -
FROM-           TO  -           (         (         |                            |NXT  7 (         (   FROM-GLE70      TO  -GLE70
                                -----------         |                            |     3  -----------
                                                    |                            |
                                                    |                            |
DSN -NIRVP.GL70.NEWTRA1.D       -----------         |                            |     3  -----------  DSN -NIRVP.GL70.NEWTRA1.D
DDN -SYSIN001   DISP-O,D,*      (         (         |                            |PRE  3 (         (   DDN -SYSIN004   DISP-N,C,*
UNIT-3380       BLK -22528     (     3   (---------+                            +------>(     4   (    UNIT-DISK       BLK -
FROM-           TO  -GLE70      (         ( NXT    3|                            |NXT  7 (         (   FROM-GLE70      TO  -GLE70
                                -----------        4|                            |     3  -----------
                                                    |                            |
                                                    |                            |
DSN -NIRVP.GL70.NEWTRA1         -----------         |      +------------+        |     5  -----------  DSN -NIRVP.GL70.NEWTRANS
DDN -SYSIN002   DISP-O,D,*      (         (         |      |            |        |PRE  3 (         (   DDN -SYSIN006   DISP-N,C,*
UNIT-3380       BLK -22528     (     3   (---------+------>|  IDCAMS    |-------+------>(     6   (    UNIT-DISK       BLK -
FROM-           TO  -GLE70      (         ( NXT    3|      |            |        |NXT  5 (         (   FROM-GLE70      TO  -GLE70
                                -----------        4|      +------------+        |     7  -----------
                                                    |                            |
                                                    |      J-REGION = 8M         |
DSN -NIRVP.GL70.NEWTRANS       +-----------+        |      SYSPRINT = L          |     5  -----------  DSN -NIRVP.GL70.NEWTRANS.D
DDN -SYSIN005   DISP-O,D,*     |           |        |                            |PRE  3 (         (   DDN -SYSIN007   DISP-N,C,*
UNIT-           BLK -          |     5     |-------+                            +------>(     6   (    UNIT-DISK       BLK -
FROM-           TO  -GLE70     |       UNK |NXT    3|                            |NXT  5 (         (   FROM-GLE70      TO  -GLE70
                               +-----------+       6|                            |     7  -----------
                                                    |                            |
                                                    |                            |
DSN -NIRVP.GL70.TRANS          +-----------+        |                            |     7  -----------  DSN -NIRVP.GL70.TRANS
DDN -SYSIN008   DISP-O,D,*     |           |        |                            |PRE  3 (         (   DDN -SYSIN009   DISP-N,C,*
UNIT-           BLK -          |     7     |-------+                            +------>(     8   (    UNIT-DISK       BLK -
FROM-           TO  -GLE70     |       UNK |NXT    3|                            |NXT 11 (         (   FROM-GLE70      TO  -GLE70
                               +-----------+       8|                            |     3  -----------
                                                    |                            |
                                                    |                            |
DSN -NIRVP.GL70.HLDVCHRS.NEW   +-----------+        |                            |     7  -----------  DSN -NIRVP.GL70.TRANS.D
DDN -SYSIN011   DISP-O,D,*     |           |        |                            |PRE  3 (         (   DDN -SYSIN010   DISP-N,C,*
UNIT-           BLK -          |     9     |-------+                            +------>(     8   (    UNIT-DISK       BLK -
FROM-           TO  -GLE70     |       UNK |NXT    3                             |NXT 11 (         (   FROM-GLE70      TO  -GLE70
                               +-----------+      10                             |     3  -----------
                                                                                 |
```

```
                                                            |
                                                            |      9  -----------  DSN -NIRVP.GL70.HLDVCHRS.NEW
                                                            |PRE   3 (          (  DDN -SYSIN012   DISP-N,C,*
                                                            +------>(    10    (   UNIT-DISK       BLK -
                                                            |NXT  13 (          (  FROM-GLE70      TO  -GLE70
                                                            |      8  -----------
                                                            |
                                                            |
                                                            |      9  -----------  DSN -NIRVP.GL70.HLDVCHRS.NEW.D
                                                            |PRE   3 (          (  DDN -SYSIN013   DISP-N,C,*
                                                            +------>(    10    (   UNIT-DISK       BLK -
                                                             NXT  13 (          (  FROM-GLE70      TO  -GLE70
                                                                   8  -----------
  THE CONTROL CARDS LISTED ARE FROM DDNAME - SYSIN     STEP - GLE70    INIT
----+----1----+----2----+----3----+----4----+----5----+----6----+----7----+----8
  DELETE -                                                                00041002
   NIRVP.GL70.NEWTRA1 -                                                   00042004
   PURGE -                                                                00043002
   CLUSTER                                                                00044002
  DEFINE CLUSTER (NAME (NIRVP.GL70.NEWTRA1) -                             00050004
         VOLUME (GL0002) -                                                00060009
         UNIQUE       -                                                   00070000
         NONINDEXED -                                                     00080000
         RECORDSIZE (80 80) TRACKS (5 1) ) -                              00100000
         DATA (NAME (NIRVP.GL70.NEWTRA1.D))                               00110004
  DELETE -                                                                00120000
   NIRVP.GL70.NEWTRANS -                                                  00130004
   PURGE -                                                                00140000
   CLUSTER                                                                00150000
  DEFINE CLUSTER (NAME (NIRVP.GL70.NEWTRANS) -                            00160004
         VOLUME (GL0001) -                                                00170012
         UNIQUE -                                                         00180005
         NONINDEXED -                                                     00190000
         RECORDSIZE (80 80) TRACKS (5 1) ) -                              00210000
         DATA (NAME (NIRVP.GL70.NEWTRANS.D))                              00220004
  DELETE -                                                                00230000
   NIRVP.GL70.TRANS -                                                     00240008
   PURGE -                                                                00250000
   CLUSTER                                                                00260000
  DEFINE CLUSTER (NAME (NIRVP.GL70.TRANS) -                               00270008
         VOLUME (GL0002) -                                                00280009
         UNIQUE -                                                         00290005
         NONINDEXED -                                                     00300000
         RECORDSIZE (150 150) CYLINDERS (8 1) ) -                         00310007
         DATA (NAME (NIRVP.GL70.TRANS.D))                                 00320008
```

```
                                  DELETE -                                                       00320108
                                   NIRVP.GL70.HLDVCHRS.NEW -                                     00320208
                                   PURGE -                                                       00320308
                                   CLUSTER                                                       00320408
                                  DEFINE CLUSTER (NAME (NIRVP.GL70.HLDVCHRS.NEW) -               00320508
                                         VOLUME (GL0002) -                                       00320609
                                         UNIQUE -                                                00320708
                                         NONINDEXED -                                            00320808
                                         RECORDSIZE (150 150) CYLINDERS (15 5) ) -               00320913
                                         DATA (NAME (NIRVP.GL70.HLDVCHRS.NEW.D))                 00321008
                                                                                                 00322006
                                  IF MAXCC LE 8 THEN DO                                          00330006
                                     SET MAXCC = 0                                               00340006
                                                                                                        INDEX NUMBER    1   2   2
  JOB -GLE70                 GLE EDIT 10/91
  PROC-GLE70      GLE70
  PGM -IEBGENER   PRNTDATA   IBM MVS UTILITY
  PARM-
  COND-

DSN -NIRXP.GLE70.DATA           -----------
DDN -SYSUT1     DISP-S,*,*     (          (
UNIT-3380       BLK -   80    (     2    (---------+
FROM-           TO  -GLE70     (          ( NXT   5|      +------------+                    +-----------+  NAME-REPORT
                                -----------      21|      |            |                    |           |  DDN -SYSUT2      CLAS-L
                                                   +----->|  IEBGENER  |------------------->|     3     |  COPY-   1
                                                   |      |            |                    |       .___/
DSN -NULLFILE                  +-----------+       |      +------------+                    +______/
DDN -SYSIN      DISP-*,*,*     |           |       |
UNIT-           BLK -          |     4     |-------+      J-REGION = 8M
FROM-           TO  -          |    DUMMY  |              SYSPRINT = L
                               +-----------+

                                                                                                        INDEX NUMBER    1   2   3
  JOB -GLE70                 GLE EDIT 10/91
  PROC-GLE70      GLE70
  PGM -IP110      IP110STP
  PARM-
  COND-
  REFERENCE FILE  STEPLIB    NIRXP.PROD.LOADLIB

                                                                                    +-----------+  NAME-REPORT
                                                                                    |           |  DDN -SYS006      CLAS-C
                                                                            +------>|     5     |  COPY-   1        FORM-2PTW
                                                                            |       |       .___/
                                                                            |       +______/
                                                                            |
```

```
                                                                               |
DSN -NIRVP.GL70.OLDTRANS        -----------                                    |         -----------  DSN -&&DATETP
DDN -SYS008     DISP-O,*,*     (         (                                     |        (         (   DDN -SYS013     DISP-N,D,D
UNIT-3380       BLK -22528    (     6    (---------+                           +------>(    8    (    UNIT-TEMP       BLK -   80
FROM-           TO  -          (         (         |                           |        (         (   FROM-           TO  -
                                -----------        |                           |         -----------
                                                   |                           |
                                                   |                           |
DSN -NIRVP.GL70.NEWTRANS        -----------       6|      +-------------+      |         -----------  DSN -&&DATEWK
DDN -SYS011     DISP-S,*,*     (         ( PRE   3|      |             |      |        (         (   DDN -SYS014     DISP-N,D,D
UNIT-DISK       BLK -         (     7    (---------+------>|  IP110      |------+------>(    9    (    UNIT-TEMP       BLK -   80
FROM-GLE70      TO  -GLE70     (         ( NXT   6|      |             |      |        (         (   FROM-           TO  -
                                -----------       6|      +-------------+      |         -----------
                                                   |                           |
                                                   |      J-REGION = 8M        |
DSN -NIRXP.GLE70.DATA           -----------       2|      SYSOUT   = L         |         -----------  DSN -&&CTLTP
DDN -SYS005     DISP-S,*,*     (         ( PRE   4|      SYSDBOUT = L         |        (         (   DDN -SYS015     DISP-N,D,D
UNIT-3380       BLK -   80    (    21    (---------+      SORTMSG  = L         +------>(   10    (    UNIT-TEMP       BLK - 1200
FROM-GLE70      TO  -          (         (                                     |        (         (   FROM-           TO  -
                                -----------                                    |         -----------
                                                                               |
                                                                               |
                                                                               |         -----------  DSN -&&CTLWK
                                                                               |        (         (   DDN -SYS016     DISP-N,D,D
                                                                               +------>(   11    (    UNIT-TEMP       BLK - 1200
                                                                               |        (         (   FROM-           TO  -
                                                                               |         -----------
                                                                               |
                                                                               |
                                                                               |         -----------  DSN -NIRXP.GL70.DATEFILE
                                                                               |        (         (   DDN -SYS018     DISP-N,C,*
                                                                               +------>(   12    (    UNIT-3380       BLK -   80
                                                                               |NXT   9 (         (   FROM-           TO  -GLE70
                                                                               |      8  -----------
                                                                               |
                                                                               |
                                                                               |         -----------  DSN -NIRXP.GL70.OPERCNTL
                                                                               |        (         (   DDN -SYS020     DISP-N,C,*
                                                                               +------>(   13    (    UNIT-3380       BLK -   80
                                                                               |NXT  18 (         (   FROM-           TO  -GLE70
                                                                               |      3  -----------
                                                                               |
                                                                               |
                                                                               |         -----------  DSN -NIRXP.GL70.CONTROL
                                                                               |        (         (   DDN -SYS021     DISP-N,C,*
                                                                               +------>(   14    (    UNIT-3380       BLK -   80
                                                                                NXT  18 (         (   FROM-           TO  -GLE70
                                                                                      4  -----------
```

```
                                                                                   INDEX NUMBER    1    2    4
  JOB -GLE70              GLE EDIT 10/91
  PROC-GLE70     GLE70
  PGM -EASYTREV  STEP03    PANSOPHIC UTILITY
  PARM-
  COND-

DSN -NIRVP.GL70.NEWTRANS         -----------      7
DDN -FILEA       DISP-S,*,*     (          ( PRE   5
UNIT-DISK        BLK -         (     6    (---------+
FROM-GLE70       TO  -          (          (         |
                                 -----------         |
                                                     |
                                                     |
DSN -NIRVP.GLE.VALIDM            -----------         |      +-------------+                -----------  DSN -NIRXP.GL70.NEWTRA1
DDN -FILISAM     DISP-S,*,*     (          (         |      |             |               (          (   DDN -NEWFILE     DISP-*,C,D
UNIT-3380        BLK - 4096    (     7    (---------+------>|  EASYTREV   |-------------->(     8    (   UNIT-SYSDA       BLK -  800
FROM-            TO  -          (          (         |      |             |       NXT   7 (          (   FROM-            TO  -GLE70
                                 -----------         |      +-------------+             2  -----------
                                                     |
                                                     |      J-REGION = 8M
DSN -NIRXP.PROD.PARMLIB(APGG)    -----------         |      SYSOUT   = L
DDN -SYSIN       DISP-S,*,*     (          (         |      SYSPRINT = C,,RTA1
UNIT-3380        BLK - 6160    (     9    (---------+
FROM-            TO  -          (          (
                                 -----------

  THE CONTROL CARDS LISTED ARE FROM DDNAME - SYSIN     STEP - GLE70    STEP03
----+----1----+----2----+----3----+----4----+----5----+----6----+----7----+----8
FILE FILEA VS
KEYINFO W-1 16 A COMP W-1 3 A REC W-4 1 A VEN W-5 10 A PAYIND W-15 1 A
RECTYPE W-16 1 A VENDNUM 21 10 A VENDNUM2 21 17 A ALLREC 1 80 A
CONUM 1 5 A MESSAGE W 25 A RECODE 20 1 A
VEND 21 17 A BATCH 16 4 A JOUN 10 6 A AMOUNT 62 11 N2 9999
FILE FILISAM IS
RECA 1 200 A RECODE 17 1 A SORTFLD 139 17 A NAME 18 35 A 9999
FILE PSTFILE FB-80-800
RECNUM 1 7 N 9999
FILE NEWFILE FB-80-800
9999
MESSAGE = *
IF RECODE NQ 1
   PUT NEWFILE FROM FILEA
   FLUNK
IF CONUM NQ G0290
   PUT NEWFILE FROM FILEA
   FLUNK
```

```
                        PUT NEWFILE FROM FILEA
                        FLUNK
                     IF 1 = 1
                        COMP = 029
                        VEN = VENDNUM
                        REC = 4
                        PAYIND = *
                        RECTYPE = A
                        READ FILISAM KEY KEYINFO
                     IF READSTAT = RNF
                        MESSAGE = (VEND.NUM.NOT ON FILE)
                        GO TO PRINT
                     IF READSTAT = *
                        VENDNUM2 = SORTFLD
                        PUT NEWFILE FROM FILEA
                        FLUNK
                     PRINT: IF FILE EQ FILE
                            PUT NEWFILE FROM FILEA
                            LIST CONUM 'COMPANY,NUMBER' VEND 'VENDOR,NUMBER' MORE
                                 JOUN 'JOURNAL,VOUCHER,NUMBER' BATCH 'PAGE,LINE,BATCH' MORE
                                 AMOUNT MESSAGE
                                                                        INDEX NUMBER   1   2   5
  JOB -GLE70               GLE EDIT 10/91
  PROC-GLE70     GLE70
  PGM -IDCAMS    STEP04    IBM MVS UTILITY
  PARM-
  COND-

DSN -NIRXP.GL70.NEWTRA1        -----------      8
DDN -DD1        DISP-S,*,*    (          ( PRE   6
UNIT-SYSDA      BLK -  800   (     2    (---------+
FROM-GLE70      TO  -GLE70    (          ( NXT  18|
                               -----------      6|
                                                 |
                                                 |
DSN -NIRVP.GL70.NEWTRA1        -----------      4|       +------------+
DDN -DD2        DISP-O,*,*    (          ( PRE   3|       |            |
UNIT-DISK       BLK -        (     3    (---------+------>|   IDCAMS   |-------+NO OUTPUT FILES
FROM-GLE70      TO  -GLE70    (          ( NXT   8|       |            |
                               -----------      6|       +------------+
                                                 |
DSN -NIRXP.PROD.PARMLIB(GLREPRO)                 |       J-REGION = 8M
                               -----------       |       SYSPRINT = L
DDN -SYSIN      DISP-S,*,*    (          (       |
UNIT-3380       BLK - 6160   (     4    (---------+
FROM-           TO  -GLE70    (          ( NXT  11
                               -----------      4
```

```
                            THE CONTROL CARDS LISTED ARE FROM DDNAME - SYSIN      STEP - GLE70    STEP04
                          ----+----1----+----2----+----3----+----4----+----5----+----6----+----7----+----8
                            REPRO INFILE(DD1) OUTFILE(DD2)                                         00010000
                                                                                                   00020002
                            IF MAXCC LE 12 THEN DO                                                 00030002
                               SET MAXCC = 0                                                       00040002
                                                                                                           INDEX NUMBER    1   2   6
  JOB -GLE70               GLE EDIT 10/91
  PROC-GLE70     GLE70
  PGM -GL100     GL100
  PARM-
  COND-
  REFERENCE FILE  STEPLIB   NIRXP.PROD.LOADLIB

                                                                                        +-----------+  NAME-REPORT
                                                                                        |           |  DDN -SYS006     CLAS-C
                                                                                +------>|     5     |  COPY-    1      FORM-2PTW
DSN -NIRVP.GL70.NEWTRA1         -----------       3        +------------+       |       |      .___/
DDN -SYS008     DISP-S,*,*      (         ( PRE   7        |            |       |       +_____/
UNIT-DISK       BLK -          (     6   (---------+------>| GL100      |-------+
FROM-GLE70      TO  -           (         (                |            |       |
                                -----------                +------------+       |         -----------  DSN -&&GL@VCHRS
                                                                                |        (         (   DDN -SYS014     DISP-N,P,*
                                                           J-REGION = 8M        +------>(     7    (   UNIT-TEMP       BLK -  800
                                                           SORTMSG   = L         NXT   9 (         (   FROM-           TO  -GLE70
                                                           SYSDBOUT  = L               5  -----------
                                                           SYSOUT    = L

                                                                                                           INDEX NUMBER    1   2   7
  JOB -GLE70               GLE EDIT 10/91
  PROC-GLE70     GLE70
  PGM -GL110     GL110
  PARM-
  COND-
  REFERENCE FILE  STEPLIB   NIRXP.PROD.LOADLIB

DSN -&&GL@VCHRS                 -----------       7                                     +-----------+  NAME-REPORT
DDN -SYS014     DISP-O,D,*      (         ( PRE   8                                     |           |  DDN -SYS006     CLAS-C
UNIT-TEMP       BLK -          (     5   (---------+                            +------>|     4     |  COPY-    1      FORM-2PTW
FROM-GLE70      TO  -           (         (         |                           |       |      .___/
                                -----------         |                           |       +_____/
                                                    |                           |
                                                    |                           |
DSN -NIRXP.GL70.DATEFILE        -----------      12|       +------------+       |         -----------  DSN -&&GL@BALCD
DDN -SYS018     DISP-S,*,*      (         ( PRE   5|       |            |       |        (         (   DDN -SYS015     DISP-N,P,*
UNIT-3380       BLK -   80     (     8   (---------+------>| GL110      |-------+------>(     6    (   UNIT-TEMP       BLK -  720
FROM-GLE70      TO  -GLE70      (         ( NXT  13|       |            |       |NXT  10 (         (   FROM-           TO  -GLE70
                                -----------       9|       +------------+       |      6  -----------
                                                   |                            |
```

```
                                                       |       J-REGION = 8M          |
DSN -NIRVP.GL70.COMPMAST        -----------            |       SYSDBOUT = L           |          -----------  DSN -&&GL@EDITD
DDN -SYS019      DISP-S,*,*   (          (             |       SYSOUT   = L           |        (           (  DDN -SYS016      DISP-N,P,*
UNIT-3380        BLK -22528  (     9    (---------+                                   +------>(     7     (  UNIT-TEMP        BLK - 2090
FROM-            TO  -GLE70   (          ( NXT  13                                     NXT  10 (           (  FROM-            TO  -GLE70
                                -----------      10                                          7  -----------

                                                                                                                 INDEX NUMBER    1   2   8
  JOB -GLE70               GLE EDIT 10/91
  PROC-GLE70      GLE70
  PGM -GL120      GL120
  PARM-
  COND-
  REFERENCE FILE  STEPLIB   NIRXP.PROD.LOADLIB

DSN -&&GL@BALCD                 -----------      6                                          +-----------+  NAME-REPORT
DDN -SYS015      DISP-O,D,*   (          ( PRE   9                                          |           |  DDN -SYS006      CLAS-C
UNIT-TEMP        BLK -       (     6    (---------+                                   +------>|     4     |  COPY-   1         FORM-2PTW
FROM-GLE70       TO  -        (          (         |       +------------+             |      |       .___/
                                -----------        |       |            |             |      +______/
                                                   +------>|   GL120    |-------+
                                                   |       |            |             |
DSN -&&GL@EDITD                 -----------      7|       +------------+             |          -----------  DSN -&&GL@TRANS
DDN -SYS016      DISP-O,D,*   (          ( PRE   9|                                   |        (           (  DDN -SYS013      DISP-N,P,*
UNIT-TEMP        BLK -       (     7    (---------+        J-REGION = 8M              +------>(     5     (  UNIT-TEMP        BLK - 1500
FROM-GLE70       TO  -        (          (                 SYSDBOUT = L                NXT  11 (           (  FROM-            TO  -GLE70
                                -----------                SYSOUT   = L                      2  -----------

                                                                                                                 INDEX NUMBER    1   2   9
  JOB -GLE70               GLE EDIT 10/91
  PROC-GLE70      GLE70
  PGM -IDCAMS     TRANSFLE  IBM MVS UTILITY
  PARM-
  COND-

DSN -&&GL@TRANS                 -----------      5
DDN -DD1         DISP-O,P,*   (          ( PRE  10
UNIT-TEMP        BLK - 1500  (     2    (---------+
FROM-GLE70       TO  -GLE70   (          ( NXT  13|
                                -----------      7|
                                                   |
                                                   |
DSN -NIRVP.GL70.TRANS           -----------      8|       +------------+
DDN -DD2         DISP-O,*,*   (          ( PRE   3|       |            |
UNIT-DISK        BLK -       (     3    (---------+------>|   IDCAMS   |-------+NO OUTPUT FILES
FROM-GLE70       TO  -GLE70   (          ( NXT  12|       |            |
                                -----------      8|       +------------+
```

```
                                                             |
DSN -NIRXP.PROD.PARMLIB(GLREPRO)                             |      J-REGION = 8M
                                 -----------            4|      SYSPRINT = L
DDN -SYSIN       DISP-S,*,*      (          ( PRE     7|
UNIT-3380        BLK - 6160     (     4    (---------+
FROM-GLE70       TO  -GLE70      (          ( NXT  15
                                 -----------            4

                              THE CONTROL CARDS LISTED ARE FROM DDNAME - SYSIN     STEF - GLE70    TRANSFLE
                            ----+----1----+----2----+----3----+----4----+----5----+----6----+----7----+----8
                              REPRO INFILE(DD1) OUTFILE(DD2)                                         00010000
                                                                                                     00020002
                              IF MAXCC LE 12 THEN DO                                                 00030002
                                 SET MAXCC = 0                                                       00040002
                                                                                                             INDEX NUMBER    1   2  10
  JOB -GLE70                 GLE EDIT 10/91
  PROC-GLE70      GLE70
  PGM -EASYTREV   GLLOAD     PANSOPHIC UTILITY
  PARM-
  COND-

DSN -NIRTL.TL.ARDOWN             -----------
DDN -FILEB       DISP-M,*,*      (          (
UNIT-3380        BLK - 6000     (     9    (---------+
FROM-            TO  -GLE70      (          ( NXT  12|
                                 -----------            9|
                                                         |
                                                         |
DSN -NIRVP.GL70.TRANS            -----------            3|      +------------+             9  -----------  DSN -NIRTL.TL.ARDOWN
DDN -FILEA       DISP-O,*,*      (          ( PRE  11|      |            |       PRE  12 (          (   DDN -FILEB       DISP-M,*,*
UNIT-DISK        BLK -          (     8    (---------+------>|  EASYTREV  |-------------->(     9    (   UNIT-3380        BLK - 6000
FROM-GLE70       TO  -GLE70      (          ( NXT  14|      |            |       NXT  17 (          (   FROM-            TO  -GLE70
                                 -----------            4|      +------------+             2  -----------
                                                         |
DSN -NIRXP.PROD.PARMLIB(GLEDOWN)                         |      J-REGION = 8M
                                 -----------             |      SYSOUT   = L
DDN -SYSIN       DISP-S,*,*      (          (            |      SYSPRINT = L
UNIT-3380        BLK - 6160     (    10    (---------+
FROM-            TO  -          (          (
                                 -----------

                              THE CONTROL CARDS LISTED ARE FROM DDNAME - SYSIN     STEP - GLE70    GLLOAD
                            ----+----1----+----2----+----3----+----4----+----5----+----6----+----7----+----8
                            FILE FILEA VS
```

```
SYS          5   1  N
ACCT         6   8  N
DIV         16   2  A
CLASS       18   2  N
JV          22   6  A
JVCK        22   2  A
JVCK1       25   3  A
FYY         28   4  N
BATCHNO     34   3  A
AMO         41   4  N
AMM         41   2  N
AYY         43   2  N
SCR         45   3  A
REF2        48   6  A
REF1        54   4  A
REF1CK      55   3  A
DEPT        58   4  A
AMT         62  11  N2-(ZZZ,ZZZ,ZZ9.99-)
DESC        73  20  A
BILLNO      84   6  A
ADESC       93  20  A
QTY        115   8  N1-(99999999-)
INVNO        1   6  A
ACCOUNT      7   8  N
INVAMT      15  11  N2
KEY         26   8  N1
IBATCH      34   3  A
IJV         37   6  A
IAMO        43   4  A
FILLER      47  33  A
WINVNO       W   6  A
WACCOUNT     W   8  N
WINVAMT      W  11  N2
WKEY         W   8  N1
WFILLER      W  37  A
WBATCH       W   3  A
WJV          W   6  A
WAMO         W   4  A
9999
FILE FILEB FB-80-6000
9999
JOB FILEA
IF SYS NQ  1
FLUNK
*
IF ACCT NQ 10200200-10201000
```

```
                         FLUNK
                         *
                         IF QTY = 0
                         FLUNK
                         *
                         IF QTY LS 0
                         QTY = QTY * -1
                         *
                         IF ACCT = 10200800
                         FLUNK
                         *
                         IF 1 = 1
                         WINVNO = BILLNO
                         WACCOUNT = ACCT
                         WINVAMT = AMT
                         WKEY = QTY
                         WFILLER = *
                         WBATCH = BATCHNO
                         WJV = JV
                         WAMO = AMO
                         INVNO = WINVNO
                         ACCOUNT = WACCOUNT
                         INVAMT = WINVAMT
                         KEY = WKEY
                         IBATCH = WBATCH
                         IJV = WJV
                         IAMO = WAMO
                         FILLER = WFILLER
                         *
                         WRITE
                                                                          INDEX NUMBER    1   2  11
  JOB -GLE70              GLE EDIT 10/91
  PROC-GLE70     GLE70
  PGM -GL130     GL130
  PARM-
  COND-
  REFERENCE FILE  STEPLIB   NIRXP.PROD.LOADLIB

DSN -NIRVP.GL70.HLDVCHRS.OLD    -----------
DDN -SYS008     DISP-S,*,*     (          (
UNIT-3380       BLK -22528    (     5    (---------+
FROM-           TO  -GLE70     (          ( NXT  14|
                                -----------        3|
                                                    |
```

```
                                                  |
DSN -&&GL@TRANS                 -----------      2|
DDN -SYS013     DISP-O,D,*     (         ( PRE  11|
UNIT-TEMP       BLK -         (     7   (---------+
FROM-GLE70      TO  -          (         (        |                                    +-----------+  NAME-REPORT
                                -----------       |                                    |           |  DDN -SYS006     CLAS-C
                                                  |                            +------>|     4     |  COPY-   1       FORM-2PTW
                                                  |                            |       |      .___/
DSN -NIRVP.GL70.HLDVCHRS.NEW    -----------     10|       +------------+       |       +_____/
DDN -SYS015     DISP-S,*,*     (         ( PRE   3|       |            |       |
UNIT-DISK       BLK -         (     8   (---------+------>|  GL130     |-------+
FROM-GLE70      TO  -GLE70     (         ( NXT  14|       |            |       |         -----------  DSN -&&GL@135I
                                -----------      5|       +------------+       |        (         (   DDN -SYS011     DISP-N,P,*
                                                  |                            +------>(     6   (    UNIT-TEMP       BLK - 1500
                                                  |       J-REGION = 8M                 (         (   FROM-           TO  -
DSN -NIRXP.GL70.DATEFILE        -----------      8|       SYSDBOUT = L                   -----------
DDN -SYS018     DISP-S,*,*     (         ( PRE   9|       SYSOUT   = L
UNIT-3380       BLK -   80    (     9   (---------+
FROM-GLE70      TO  -GLE70     (         ( NXT  18|
                                -----------      5|
                                                  |
                                                  |
DSN -NIRVP.GL70.COMPMAST        -----------      9|
DDN -SYS019     DISP-S,*,*     (         ( PRE   9|
UNIT-3380       BLK -22528    (    10   (---------+
FROM-GLE70      TO  -          (         (
                                -----------

                                                                                                          INDEX NUMBER    1   2  12
  JOB -GLE70               GLE EDIT 10/91
  PROC-GLE70     GLE70
  PGM -IDCAMS    ENDSTEP   IBM MVS UTILITY
  PARM-
  COND-
DSN -NIRXP.PROD.PARMLIB(GLEALDEL)
                                -----------
DDN -SYSIN      DISP-S,*,*     (         (
UNIT-3380       BLK - 6160    (     2   (---------+
FROM-           TO  -          (         (        |
                                -----------       |
                                                  |
                                                  |
```

```
DSN -NIRVP.GL70.HLDVCHRS.OLD.D  -----------      5|
DDN -SYSIN001    DISP-O,D,*      (          ( PRE  13|
UNIT-3380        BLK -22528     (     3    (---------+
FROM-GLE70       TO  -GLE70      (          ( NXT  14|                                   8  -----------  DSN -NIRVP.GL70.HLDVCHRS.OLD
                                  -----------      5|                             PRE  13 (          (  DDN -SYSIN005    DISP-N,C,*
                                                    |                           +------>(     5    (   UNIT-DISK        BLK -
                                                    |                           |        (          (  FROM-GLE70       TO  -
DSN -NIRVP.GL70.HLDVCHRS.OLD    -----------      5|      +-------------+       |         -----------
DDN -SYSIN002    DISP-O,D,*      (          ( PRE  13|      |             |       |
UNIT-3380        BLK -22528     (     3    (---------+------>|  IDCAMS     |-------+
FROM-GLE70       TO  -GLE70      (          ( NXT  14|      |             |       |     10  -----------  DSN -NIRVP.GL70.HLDVCHRS.OLD.D
                                  -----------      5|      +-------------+       |PRE   3 (          (  DDN -SYSIN007    DISP-N,C,*
                                                    |                           +------>(     6    (   UNIT-DISK        BLK -
                                                    |      J-REGION = 8M                 (          (  FROM-GLE70       TO  -
DSN -NIRVP.GL70.TRANS           -----------      8|      SYSPRINT = L                   -----------
DDN -SYSIN003    DISP-O,D,*      (          ( PRE  12|
UNIT-DISK        BLK -          (     4    (---------+
FROM-GLE70       TO  -           (          (        |
                                  -----------        |
                                                     |
                                                     |
DSN -NIRVP.GL70.HLDVCHRS.NEW    -----------      8|
DDN -SYSIN004    DISP-O,D,*      (          ( PRE  13|
UNIT-DISK        BLK -          (     5    (---------+
FROM-GLE70       TO  -           (          (        |
                                  -----------        |
                                                     |
                                                     |
DSN -NIRVP.GL70.HLDVCHRS.NEW.D  -----------     10|
DDN -SYSIN006    DISP-O,D,*      (          ( PRE   3|
UNIT-DISK        BLK -          (     6    (---------+
FROM-GLE70       TO  -           (          (
                                  -----------

  THE CONTROL CARDS LISTED ARE FROM DDNAME - SYSIN     STEP - GLE70    ENDSTEP
----+----1----+----2----+----3----+----4----+----5----+----6----+----7----+----8
  DELETE -                                                              02660000
   NIRVP.GL70.HLDVCHRS.OLD -                                            02670003
   PURGE -                                                              02680000
   CLUSTER                                                              02690000
  DELETE -                                                              02691004
   NIRVP.GL70.TRANS -                                                   02692004
   PURGE -                                                              02693004
   CLUSTER                                                              02694004
  ALTER -                                                               02700000
   NIRVP.GL70.HLDVCHRS.NEW -                                            02710003
   NEWNAME(NIRVP.GL70.HLDVCHRS.OLD)                                     02720003
```

```
                           ALTER -                                                                02730000
                            NIRVP.GL70.HLDVCHRS.NEW.D -                                           02740003
                            NEWNAME(NIRVP.GL70.HLDVCHRS.OLD.D)                                    02750003
                                                                                                          INDEX NUMBER    1   2  13
  JOB -GLE70                GLE EDIT 10/91
  PROC-GLE70      GLE70
  PGM -IDCAMS     USERCPY   IBM MVS UTILITY
  PARM-
  COND-

DSN -NIRVP.GL70.HLDVCHRS.OLD    -----------      5
DDN -DD1         DISP-S,*,*     (          ( PRE  14
UNIT-DISK        BLK -         (     2    (---------+
FROM-GLE70       TO  -GLE70     (          ( NXT  16|       +------------+                 -----------  DSN -NIRXT.GL70.HLDVCHRS
                                -----------      2|       |            |                (          (  DDN -DD2        DISP-*,C,D
                                                 +------>|  IDCAMS    |--------------->(     3    (   UNIT-3380       BLK - 1500
DSN -NIRXP.PROD.PARMLIB(GLREPRO)                 |       |            |                (          (  FROM-           TO  -
                                -----------      4|       +------------+                 -----------
DDN -SYSIN       DISP-S,*,*     (          ( PRE  11|
UNIT-3380        BLK - 6160    (     4    (---------+       J-REGION = 8M
FROM-GLE70       TO  -GLE70     (          ( NXT  16        SYSPRINT = L
                                -----------      4

                           THE CONTROL CARDS LISTED ARE FROM DDNAME - SYSIN     STEP - GLE70    USERCPY
                         ----+----1----+----2----+----3----+----4----+----5----+----6----+----7----+----8
                           REPRO INFILE(DD1) OUTFILE(DD2)                                         00010000
                                                                                                  00020002
                           IF MAXCC LE 12 THEN DO                                                 00030002
                              SET MAXCC = 0                                                       00040002
                                                                                                          INDEX NUMBER    1   2  14
  JOB -GLE70                GLE EDIT 10/91
  PROC-GLE70      GLE70
  PGM -IDCAMS     BKUPCPY   IBM MVS UTILITY
  PARM-
  COND-

DSN -NIRVP.GL70.HLDVCHRS.OLD    -----------      2
DDN -DD1         DISP-S,*,*     (          ( PRE  15
UNIT-DISK        BLK -         (     2    (---------+
FROM-GLE70       TO  -          (          (         |       +------------+                 -----------  DSN -NIRXP.GL70.HLD.BKUP(+1)
                                -----------       |       |            |                (          (  DDN -DD2        DISP-*,C,D
                                                 +------>|  IDCAMS    |--------------->(     3    (   UNIT-3380       BLK - 1500
DSN -NIRXP.PROD.PARMLIB(GLREPRO)                 |       |            |                (          (  FROM-           TO  -
                                -----------      4|       +------------+                 -----------
DDN -SYSIN       DISP-S,*,*     (          ( PRE  15|
UNIT-3380        BLK - 6160    (     4    (---------+       J-REGION = 8M
FROM-GLE70       TO  -GLE70     (          ( NXT  17        SYSPRINT = L
                                -----------      4
```

```
                          THE CONTROL CARDS LISTED ARE FROM DDNAME - SYSIN     STEP - GLE70    BKUPCPY
                         ----+----1----+----2----+----3----+----4----+----5----+----6----+----7----+----8
                          REPRO INFILE(DD1) OUTFILE(DD2)                                       00010000
                                                                                               00020002
                          IF MAXCC LE 12 THEN DO                                               00030002
                             SET MAXCC = 0                                                     00040002
                                                                                                       INDEX NUMBER    1   2  15
  JOB -GLE70                 GLE EDIT 10/91
  PROC-GLE70     GLE70
  PGM -IDCAMS    ARTLCPY     IBM MVS UTILITY
  PARM-
  COND-

DSN -NIRTL.TL.ARDOWN             -----------      9
DDN -DD1        DISP-S,*,*      (         ( PRE  12
UNIT-3380       BLK - 6000     (    2    (---------+
FROM-GLE70      TO  -           (         (        |      +------------+                      -----------  DSN -NIRXP.ARDOWN(+1)
                                 -----------       |      |            |                     (          (   DDN -DD2         DISP-*,C,D
                                                   +------>|   IDCAMS   |--------------->(     3    (   UNIT-3380        BLK - 6000
DSN -NIRXP.PROD.PARMLIB(GLREPRO)                   |      |            |                     (          (   FROM-            TO  -
                                 -----------      4|      +------------+                      -----------
DDN -SYSIN      DISP-S,*,*      (         ( PRE  16|
UNIT-3380       BLK - 6160     (    4    (---------+      J-REGION = 8M
FROM-GLE70      TO  -           (         (               SYSPRINT = L
                                 -----------

                          THE CONTROL CARDS LISTED ARE FROM DDNAME - SYSIN     STEP - GLE70    ARTLCPY
                         ----+----1----+----2----+----3----+----4----+----5----+----6----+----7----+----8
                          REPRO INFILE(DD1) OUTFILE(DD2)                                       00010000
                                                                                               00020002
                          IF MAXCC LE 12 THEN DO                                               00030002
                             SET MAXCC = 0                                                     00040002
                                                                                                       INDEX NUMBER    1   2  16
  JOB -GLE70                 GLE EDIT 10/91
  PROC-GLE70     GLE70
  PGM -IDCAMS    IP100SCR    IBM MVS UTILITY
  PARM-
  COND-
DSN -NIRXP.PROD.PARMLIB(GLE70SCR)
                                 -----------
DDN -SYSIN      DISP-S,*,*      (         (
UNIT-3380       BLK - 6160     (    2    (---------+
FROM-           TO  -           (         (        |
                                 -----------       |
                                                   |
```

```
                                                              |
DSN -NIRXP.GL70.OPERCNTL          -----------      13|
DDN -SYSIN001    DISP-O,D,*      (          ( PRE   5|
UNIT-3380        BLK -   80     (     3    (---------+
FROM-GLE70       TO  -           (          (        |
                                  -----------        |
                                                     |
                                                     |
DSN -NIRXP.GL70.CONTROL           -----------      14|       +------------+
DDN -SYSIN002    DISP-O,D,*      (          ( PRE   5|       |            |
UNIT-3380        BLK -   80     (     4    (---------+------>|  IDCAMS    |-------+NO OUTPUT FILES
FROM-GLE70       TO  -           (          (        |       |            |
                                  -----------        |       +------------+
                                                     |
                                                     |       J-REGION = 8M
DSN -NIRXP.GL70.DATEFILE          -----------       9|       SYSPRINT = L
DDN -SYSIN003    DISP-O,D,*      (          ( PRE  13|
UNIT-3380        BLK -   80     (     5    (---------+
FROM-GLE70       TO  -           (          (        |
                                  -----------        |
                                                     |
                                                     |
DSN -NIRXP.GL70.NEWTRA1           -----------       2|
DDN -SYSIN004    DISP-O,D,*      (          ( PRE   7|
UNIT-SYSDA       BLK -  800     (     6    (---------+
FROM-GLE70       TO  -           (          (
                                  -----------

                                     THE CONTROL CARDS LISTED ARE FROM DDNAME - SYSIN     STEP - GLE70     IP100SCR
                                   ----+----1----+----2----+----3----+----4----+----5----+----6----+----7----+----8
                                    DEL NIRXP.GL70.OPERCNTL                                                00010001
                                    DEL NIRXP.GL70.CONTROL                                                 00020001
                                    DEL NIRXP.GL70.DATEFILE                                                00030001
                                    DEL NIRXP.GL70.NEWTRA1                                                 00040001
                                    SET MAXCC = 0                                                          00050001
                                  DOCU/TEXT     5.5.1B (C) DIVERSIFIED SOFTWARE SYSTEMS
```

Appendix

D

The ISPF Line Commands

D.1 The Basic (Line) Commands

The ISPF line commands are called so because they maintain a member of a partitioned data set on a line-by-line basis. Line commands are part of the editing mechanism, and are entered by overtyping the sequence numbers at the beginning of the line. The purpose of this appendix is to get you acquainted with the so-called basic commands (INSERT, DELETE, and REPEAT), the MOVE/COPY commands, and the shift commands. These commands represent over 90% of the commands most frequently used by the ISPF user community. Others, such as the EXCLUDE/SHOW commands, the text-handling commands, and the miscellaneous commands, are used relatively infrequently.

The INSERT command allows you to insert one or a number of lines between a body of text. Consider the two frames shown in Figures D.1 and D.2. In the first frame, Figure D.1, I have inserted the line command I7 (insert 7 lines) in line 000600 prior to the /*, thereby overlaying the first three positions of the line-sequence number. When you press the Enter key, the response to the INSERT command will be displayed, as shown in Figure D.2. Note the extra lines inserted. If you were to press Enter a second time, all those lines without any additional entries would disappear. However, lines with nonblank entries would remain and their line number would be resequenced, according to the new entries.

The next line command, DELETE, is a bit more complicated. When deleting a line or lines, you can use either a simple delete or a block delete. When deleting a single line, all you have to do is position the cursor in the first digit of the line-sequence number, place the character D in that position (D00075), and press the Enter key. This will cause the erasure of line 000075 from the text editor. However, DELETE can also be used in block format, where you can mark the beginning and the ending of the block with DD ===> DD.

```
EDIT ---- NIRAV.STANDARD.CNTL(JCL120L) - 01.14 --------------- COLUMNS 001 072
COMMAND ===>                                                  SCROLL ===> PAGE
****** ***************************** TOP OF DATA ******************************
000100 //NIRAV JOB  (9000,AGLP),MSGLEVEL=(1,1),MSGCLASS=X,NOTIFY=NIRAV,
000200 //   REGION=8192K
000300 //*
000400 //CLOSFILE EXEC PGM=COMMAND,
000500 //             PARM='F PAYRDEVO,CEMT SET DAT(AR*) CLO ENA'
I70600 //*
000700 //PGMJCL   EXEC PGM=ARDP120C
000800 //STEPLIB  DD DSN=NIRXT.TEST.LOADLIB,DISP=SHR
000900 //SYSPRINT DD SYSOUT=*
001000 //SYSOUT   DD SYSOUT=*
001100 //SYSCOUNT DD SYSOUT=*
001200 //SYSDBOUT DD SYSOUT=*
001300 //PRTREP   DD SYSOUT=X
001400 //W12     DD DSN=NIRXT.AR.WK12,
001500 //         DISP=SHR
001600 //*
001700 //CLOSFILE EXEC PGM=COMMAND,
001800 //             PARM='F PAYRDEVO,CEMT SET DAT(AR*) CLO ENA'
****** **************************** BOTTOM OF DATA ****************************
```

Figure D.1 Panel prior to the Insert Line command.

```
EDIT ---- NIRAV.STANDARD.CNTL(JCL120L) - 01.14 --------------- COLUMNS 001 072
COMMAND ===>                                                  SCROLL ===> PAGE
****** ***************************** TOP OF DATA ******************************
000100 //NIRAV JOB  (9000,AGLP),MSGLEVEL=(1,1),MSGCLASS=X,NOTIFY=NIRAV,
000200 //   REGION=8192K
000300 //*
000400 //CLOSFILE EXEC PGM=COMMAND,
000500 //             PARM='F PAYRDEVO,CEMT SET DAT(AR*) CLO ENA'
000600 //*
''''''
''''''
''''''
''''''
''''''
''''''
''''''
000700 //PGMJCL   EXEC PGM=ARDP120C
000800 //STEPLIB  DD DSN=NIRXT.TEST.LOADLIB,DISP=SHR
000900 //SYSPRINT DD SYSOUT=*
001000 //SYSOUT   DD SYSOUT=*
001100 //SYSCOUNT DD SYSOUT=*
001200 //SYSDBOUT DD SYSOUT=*
001300 //PRTREP   DD SYSOUT=X
001400 //W12     DD DSN=NIRXT.AR.WK12,
```

Figure D.2 Panel following the insertion.

Look at the previous document example, in Figure D.3, and the same document after the delete operation, as highlighted in Figure D.4.

Note that, in Figure D.3, I placed a beginning block marker on line DD0008 and an ending block marker on line DD0012. Once I pressed the Enter key, the entire paragraph disappeared. Also note that block deletes can be accomplished through a line designator, such as D# #, where # # stands for the number of lines to be deleted from the beginning of the line that is being flagged. In the above situation, the line command D50008 would have produced the same result.

The third type of basic command is REPEAT. Think of this command as a multiple

COPY statement where the original line or lines can be repeated once or several times, as requested. Consider the examples shown in Figures D.5 and D.6.

Figure D.5 shows a simple SORTWORK statement. This was coded by the programmer into an ISPF member called DOCUMENT. Over in the left-hand corner of the line, I have issued a REPEAT command, R5. The result of this command is shown in Figure D.6, where a single line of JCL was repeated five additional times. In developing sort and utility JCLs, you can imagine the importance of such a command. All you have to do now is change the number corresponding to each SORTWORK area to read 01 through 06.

```
EDIT ---- NIRAV.STANDARD.CNTL(DOCUMENT) - 01.01 -------------- COLUMNS 001 072
COMMAND ===>                                                  SCROLL ===> PAGE
****** ****************************** TOP OF DATA ******************************
000001 The Pay History screen is invoked through PF6 on the Claims
000002 Entry/Update panel shown in Fig. 1.3. This panel allows you to
000003 enter any transaction associated with a payment. If you need to
000004 update the file through the screen, press PF12. If an entry was
000005 keyed in erroneously, you may overlay it with the correct data or
000006 you may use the space bar to erase a desired line.
000007
DD0008 If you need more than a single screen entry, you may scroll forward
000009 to continue the recording of additional transaction on subsequent
000010 screens. Page deletion is possible by entering the character "Y" next
000011 to the delete page header on the bottom of the screen shown if Fig.
DD0012 1.6.
****** ***************************** BOTTOM OF DATA ****************************
```

Figure D.3 The member document prior to deletion of the second paragraph.

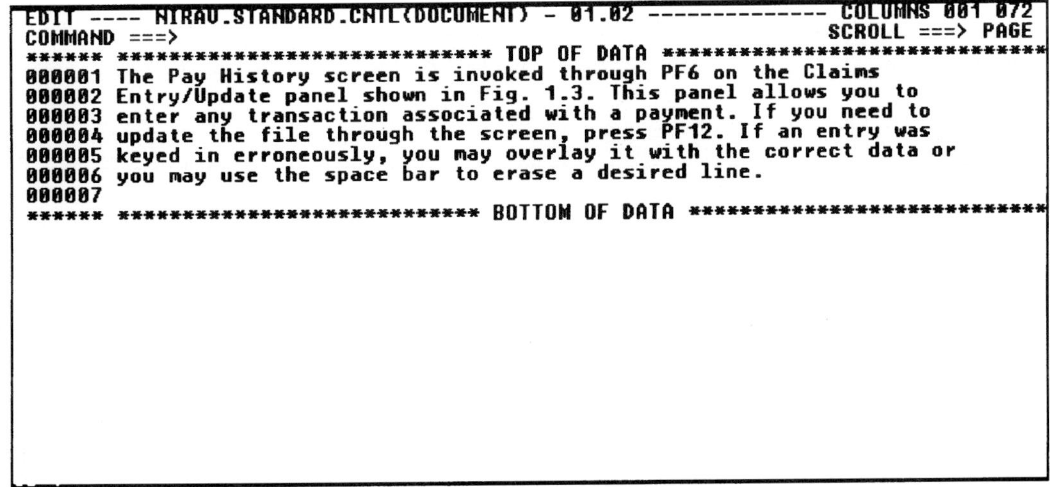

```
EDIT ---- NIRAV.STANDARD.CNTL(DOCUMENT) - 01.02 -------------- COLUMNS 001 072
COMMAND ===>                                                  SCROLL ===> PAGE
****** ****************************** TOP OF DATA ******************************
000001 The Pay History screen is invoked through PF6 on the Claims
000002 Entry/Update panel shown in Fig. 1.3. This panel allows you to
000003 enter any transaction associated with a payment. If you need to
000004 update the file through the screen, press PF12. If an entry was
000005 keyed in erroneously, you may overlay it with the correct data or
000006 you may use the space bar to erase a desired line.
000007
****** ***************************** BOTTOM OF DATA ****************************
```

Figure D.4 Following the block deletion, the second paragraph is gone.

```
EDIT ---- NIRAV.STANDARD.CNTL(DOCUMENT) - 01.04 --------------- COLUMNS 001 072
COMMAND ===>                                                  SCROLL ===> PAGE
****** ***************************** TOP OF DATA ******************************
R50001     //SORTWK01   DD   UNIT=SYSDA,SPACE=(CYL,(&SPC),,CONTIG)
****** **************************** BOTTOM OF DATA ****************************
```

Figure D.5 A single instruction prior to a Repeat Line command.

```
EDIT ---- NIRAV.STANDARD.CNTL(DOCUMENT) - 01.04 --------------- COLUMNS 001 072
COMMAND ===>                                                  SCROLL ===> PAGE
****** ***************************** TOP OF DATA ******************************
000001     //SORTWK01   DD   UNIT=SYSDA,SPACE=(CYL,(&SPC),,CONTIG)
000002     //SORTWK01   DD   UNIT=SYSDA,SPACE=(CYL,(&SPC),,CONTIG)
000003     //SORTWK01   DD   UNIT=SYSDA,SPACE=(CYL,(&SPC),,CONTIG)
```

Figure D.6 The instruction in Figure D.5 repeated five times.

There are two other formats of the REPEAT command. With the first one, a repeat block command, you can designate a start and end point for the block. Repeated lines begin right after the end block definition, but, unlike the COPY and the MOVE commands, you do not have to state a specific line location marking the command with a before (A) or an after (B) target status. Note that the beginning and the ending line of a repeat operation should be coded as RR and RR.

The second format of REPEAT is a single-line repetition that can be marked as R. The repeated line in this particular situation will be repeated immediately in the following line.

D.2 The MOVE, COPY and Shift Commands

The MOVE and COPY commands both have identical mechanics, even though they perform different functions. By identical mechanics, I mean that each command, unlike REPEAT, uses a marker to define the specific location in a document for a COPY or MOVE. As briefly mentioned in the previous section, these are A, meaning after, and B, meaning before, and they are indicators for moving or copying a single statement or block starting before or after a specified line. Consider the MOVE statement described in Figures D.7 and D.8.

```
EDIT ---- NIRAV.STANDARD.CNTL(DOCUMENT) - 01.05 -------------- COLUMNS 001 072
COMMAND ===>                                                  SCROLL ===> PAGE
****** ***************************** TOP OF DATA ******************************
000001 THIS IS THE FIRST LINE THAT WILL REMAIN IN LINE 000001.
000002
M00003 THIS LINE (000003) WILL BE MOVED BEFORE LINE 000008 OR IN LINE 000007
000004
000005 THIS LINE REMAINS IN LINE 000005.
000006
000007
B00008
000009
****** **************************** BOTTOM OF DATA ****************************
```

Figure D.7 Text before a Move statement marked with a B (for Before) flag.

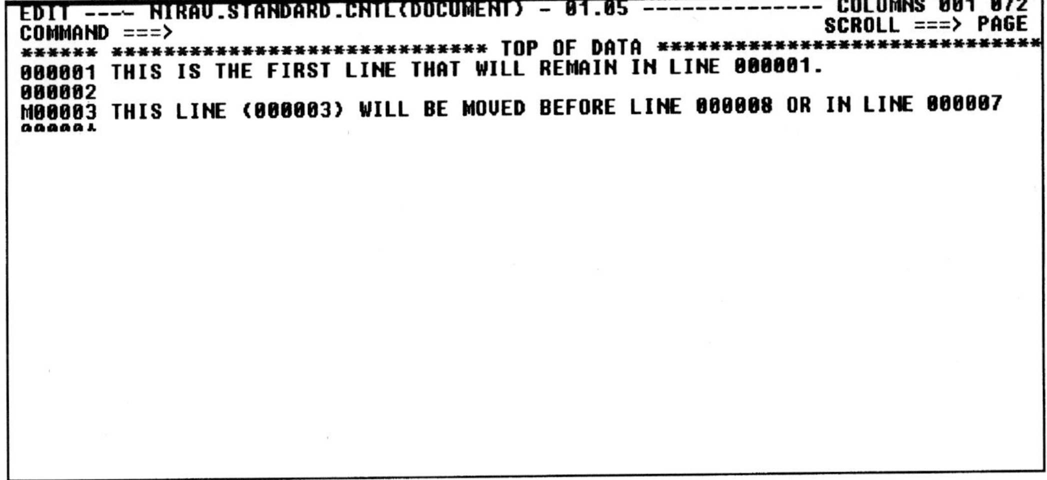

```
EDIT ---- NIRAV.STANDARD.CNTL(DOCUMENT) - 01.05 -------------- COLUMNS 001 072
COMMAND ===>                                                  SCROLL ===> PAGE
****** ***************************** TOP OF DATA ******************************
000001 THIS IS THE FIRST LINE THAT WILL REMAIN IN LINE 000001.
000002
M00003 THIS LINE (000003) WILL BE MOVED BEFORE LINE 000008 OR IN LINE 000007
```

Figure D.8 Text following the Move statement in Figure D.7

In these examples, line number 3 was moved before line number 8 to line number 7, leaving the other two lines on display unaffected. Another way this move could have been described to ISPF would have been an M in line 3, and an A in line 6.

Note that both the C, or COPY and M, or MOVE commands also use a block format (in conjunction with the A or B indicator). Just like using the REPEAT command in block mode, you need to describe the beginning line of the block as CC00020, and the end of the block as CC00050, including a target indicator like A000160.

A third component available under the ISPF line commands is a set of shift commands. There are two types of shift commands, those requiring either a right or left parenthesis, which triggers a shift in the columns in either direction, and those with greater-than or less-than signs, which is designed to shift the data itself. Both of these line delimiters are available in their basic formats, such as))5, for example, or as a block shift, indicated by a beginning and an ending block delimiter. A third form is a single)) delimiter in reference to a single line.

Let's look at some examples. Figure D.9 shows several lines out of alignment. All level-05 and level-10 statements (part of a COBOL program) should be moved back so that, instead of starting in column 1, they would start in line 12 or in line 17, respectively. To see the exact horizontal positions before and after the shift, I have included a COL line command.

Note that, in line 8, a single) is followed by the number 12. This tells ISPF that the statement in line 12 will be shifted by a total of 12 characters once the Enter key is pressed.

In lines 11 and 13 (affecting a total of three lines), I indicated a block shift. In the beginning (line 11),))12 tells ISPF to shift the entire block by as much as 12 char-

```
EDIT ---- NIRAU.STANDARD.CNTL(ARB49C) - 01.02 ---------------- COLUMNS 001 07
COMMAND ===>                                                    SCROLL ===> PAG
****** ***************************** TOP OF DATA ******************************
000001        IDENTIFICATION DIVISION.
000002        PROGRAM-ID. ARB49C.
000003        DATE-COMPILED.
000004        ENVIRONMENT DIVISION.
000005        DATA DIVISION.
000006        WORKING-STORAGE SECTION.
=COLS> ----+----1----+----2----+----3----+----4----+----5----+----6----+----7
000007        01  COMM-AREA.
)12008 05  SEND-REC-FLAG       PIC X(01).
000009        *
000010        01  STORE-KEY.
))1211 05  STORE-PREFIX        PIC X(01).
000012 05  STORE-INVNO         PIC 9(05).
))0013 05  STORE-FILL          PIC X(24) VALUE '   '.
000014        *
000015        01  INVOICE-RECORD.
))1216 05  INVOICE-KEY.
000017     10  INVOICE-PREFIX          PIC X.
000018     10  INVOICE-NUMBER          PIC 9(5).
000019     10  INVOICE-NUMBERX REDEFINES INVOICE-NUMBER
))0020                                 PIC X(5).
```

Figure D.9 A number of lines out of alignment.

```
EDIT ---- NIRAV.STANDARD.CNTL(ARB49C) - 01.02 ---------------- COLUMNS 001 072
COMMAND ===>                                                  SCROLL ===> PAGE
000001         IDENTIFICATION DIVISION.
000002         PROGRAM-ID. ARB49C.
000003         DATE-COMPILED.
000004         ENVIRONMENT DIVISION.
000005         DATA DIVISION.
000006         WORKING-STORAGE SECTION.
=COLS> ----+----1----+----2----+----3----+----4----+----5----+----6----+----7--
000007         01  COMM-AREA.
000008             05  SEND-REC-FLAG      PIC X(01).
000009        *
000010         01  STORE-KEY.
000011             05  STORE-PREFIX       PIC X(01).
000012             05  STORE-INVNO        PIC 9(05).
000013             05  STORE-FILL         PIC X(24) VALUE '  '.
000014        *
000015         01  INVOICE-RECORD.
000016             05  INVOICE-KEY.
000017                 10  INVOICE-PREFIX         PIC X.
000018                 10  INVOICE-NUMBER         PIC 9(5).
000019                 10  INVOICE-NUMBERX REDEFINES INVOICE-NUMBER
000020                                            PIC X(5).
000021       10  INVOICE-FILLER         PIC X(24) VALUE '  '.
```

Figure D.10 Requested lines aligned and highlighted.

acters. Note that the end-block delimiter does not require a number. Because none is indicated, the shift defaults to a 12-character shift. This is repeated in lines 16 through 20. Once you press the Enter key, the result of the above operation is shown in Figure D.10.

Index

D

E

ABOUT THE AUTHOR

Alex Varsegi, whose Command-Level CICS Programming was a CPBS main selection and whose earlier books with TAB/McGraw-Hill have enjoyed considerable success, is a senior manager for Metra Information Systems, the agency that establishes commuter standards in the Chicago area. In addition to Command-Level CICS Programming, he is the author of System Development Under CICS Command and VSAM and Mainframe High-Productivity Tools of the '90s.

ABOUT THE SERIES

The J. Ranade Series, with more than 75 published titles, are McGraw-Hill's primary vehicles for providing mini- and mainframe computing professionals with practical and timely concepts, solutions, and applications. The series cover DEC and IBM environments, communications, and networking.

Jay Ranade, Series Editor in Chief and best-selling computer author, is a Senior Systems Architect and Assistant V.P. at Merrill Lynch.